GOVERNING THE AMERICAN REPUBLIC

Economics, Law,
and Policies

ALAN STONE
University of Houston

RICHARD P. BARKE
University of Houston

St. Martin's Press   New York

GOVERNING THE AMERICAN REPUBLIC

Economics, Law, and Policies

To Frances Schnur
A. S.

To my mother, Lois Archer
R. P. B.

Library of Congress Catalog Number: 84-51074
Copyright © 1985 by St. Martin's Press, Inc.
All rights reserved.
Manufactured in the United States of America.
9876
fedc

For information, write:
St. Martin's Press, Inc.
175 Fifth Avenue
New York, NY 10010

cover design: Levavi & Levavi
text design: Levavi & Levavi/Jennie Nichols
photo research: June Lundborg
cover photo: Mark Antman/The Image Works

ISBN: 0-312-34108-3

ACKNOWLEDGMENTS

Page 1, Library of Congress, **60,** AP/Wide World Photos; **200,** UPI/The Bett-mann Archive, Inc.; **350,** Robert Capa/Magnum Photos, Inc.

PREFACE

Writing more than 2,300 years ago, Aristotle observed that the state came into existence to provide the bare *needs* of life, but its continuation is justified if it helps us to achieve the *good* life. Of course, not every state nor every policy undertaken necessarily moves in the direction of the "good life," no matter how that phrase is defined. Yet, the general observation that the good life is the justification of the state is as true today as it was when Aristotle lived. Nevertheless, many persons interested in the particulars of American government sometimes lose sight of Aristotle's observation. So concerned are they with describing processes, determining who will win particular elections, evaluating the implementation of particular public policies, and engaging in a host of other investigations that they lose sight of the fundamental task of government.

The Approach of This Book

While we make no claim to having solved the problem of achieving the good life—no one can—we hope that we have not lost sight of that goal. We have sought in this book to provide concepts that will allow students and their teachers to think about it in the context of American government. Concepts like cost, organization, incentives, constraints, benefits, allocation, and justice, introduced in Chapter 1, are intended to help students in this evaluation. In other chapters (particularly 2 and 13), we probe the various notions embraced within the term "rights." But as we try to make clear, these concepts and others employed in the book are not intended to provide ultimate answers but rather to frame in sharper focus the issues raised by American government. Our approach, then, is not one that may be labeled leftist, rightist, or centrist. Indeed, we ourselves differ sharply on some issues.

Our approach derives from a combined total of more than twenty years of teaching American-government courses at a variety of schools to a variety of students. More than any other factor, this breadth of experience has led us to produce the kind of book this is. Students, of course, vary in ability, energy, and interest. Yet, we have found that virtually all students become most interested in government when they can relate it to their own lives and practical concerns. Students have auto accidents, rent rooms, buy goods and services, watch television, and engage in a vast number of other activities that involve substantial government intervention. Thus, we have included a great deal of material on private law (a topic almost entirely ignored in most textbooks), economics, and social policy (including civil rights). In addition to three chapters devoted to these topics (6, 12, and 13), much additional material on them has been included in other chapters.

For the title of our book we selected, after much deliberation, *Governing the American Republic*. In contrast, most books on this topic use the word *democracy* or *government* in their titles. We rejected using the former term because it fails to capture the complex institutional structure devised by the American Founders and developed by succeeding generations of political actors. For example, there is nothing "democratic" about a judge rendering a decision in favor of a person espousing an unpopular view. Nor is there anything "democratic" about the Food and Drug Administration's rejection of a new drug because it has not been adequately tested. Certainly democracy, in the sense of majority preference, plays an important role in our system. But the structure devised by America's constitutional framers, and carried forward by others, is far more complex than "democracy."

We rejected the latter term—*government*—for different reasons. The institutions, processes, and policies of government in practice cannot be divorced from the social and economic arenas within which government must operate. The American Founders' conceptions of republicanism were, in no small part, devoted to defining the proper relationships between government and the other spheres of our lives. The idea of governing implies an active, creative process on the part of public officials. They continuously redefine the boundaries and interactions between government and the other spheres of our lives.

The interactions between government, the economy, and society have certainly grown more complex since the latter part of the eighteenth century as government has undertaken more and more tasks. From the birth of the republic to the present day, the task of achieving the good life has always involved a mixture of government, market mechanisms, and social institutions such as the family. The boundaries of each sphere have frequently shifted, and the proper role for each sphere will always be debated. But our view is that it is important to point out that there are many possible roads to the good life, and that as we study government we must simultaneously look at other social and economic possibilities. This we have tried to do.

The Structure and Content of This Book

In keeping with the approach of drawing connections between government and the wider aspects of American society, *Governing the American Republic* begins with an historical overview of the American people, their material lives, and their political culture. We attempt to draw connections between these subjects. As mentioned, the second half of Chapter 1 provides students with a set of concepts and organizing principles. In contrast to many texts, which present an array of discrete facts, these concepts allow the student to organize the material effectively. At the same time, they allow the student to evaluate policies, proposals, and institutions.

One of the most common problems that instructors face is placing historical events and documents in the context of their times. This is particularly germane in the case of a document like the Constitution, which still plays an important role in our daily lives. Accordingly, the study of the Constitution and federalism in Chapter 2 places the Constitution in the context of the ideological stream of which it was a part. Enlightenment thinkers such as Locke, Montesquieu, Newton, and Smith are examined to show what the Founders attempted to achieve in the Constitution. We then investigate how the Founders' views shaped the details of the governmental system that they devised.

Chapters 3 through 6 focus on the problem of participation. They discuss the various ways in which Americans participate in the political system to protect their rights, extend their benefits, or limit the costs that can be imposed upon them. Chapter 3 illuminates the diversity and complexity of the American participatory structure. Chapter 4 traces the history of the American party system, spells out the functions of political parties, and considers the reasons why the American system is a two-party, not multiparty one, and the implications of that system. Again, it allows the student to evaluate the merits and faults of the American party system instead of simply accepting it as the sole inevitable one. Chapter 5 examines voting, studying the implications of institutions and electoral procedures. It takes up the vital question of the effects of money and media upon elections.

Chapters 6 and 7 cover the topics of law and the system of justice. We point out in Chapter 6 that the legal system provides an important avenue for public participation. We examine there the functions of law, the categories of law, and the sources of law. These topics are usually either not considered at all in American government texts or treated perfunctorily. Yet, most students are apt to know government best through such activities as receiving a speeding ticket or signing a lease. The inclusion of this material can draw students into a better understanding of the role government plays in their lives. Chapter 7 describes in concrete detail the system of justice and the processes of the law. But instead of focusing almost exclusively on the rarefied atmosphere of the Supreme Court, our treatment covers processes from the lowest courts to the highest. Differences between civil and criminal process are emphasized. The chapter closes with an extended treatment of civil liberties, contrasting older approaches to modern ones.

The four institutional chapters (7 through 10) have a unique focus. The American Founders consciously designed the nation's institutions as they did because they expected that structures would dictate institutional behavior regardless of who occupied the leadership posts. As Madison observed in *The Federalist*, no. 10, "Enlightened statesmen will not always be at the helm." Accordingly, in each of these chapters we first look at the powers of the relevant institutional structures because the structures strongly influence institutional behavior. Concepts discussed in earlier chapters, such as incentives, costs, information and organization, are reintroduced in appropriate places to help the student understand the ways that institutions function. Thus, although we employ examples and discuss personalities where they illustrate principles, we do not expect such material to stand alone. Examples are used to provide students with a sense of how processes work. For instance, truth-in-packaging is used in Chapter 10 to illustrate the stages of the bureaucratic policymaking process. We have also attempted to cover important aspects of institutions that are sometimes given short shrift, such as the congressional budget process (Chapter 8).

Chapters 11 through 13 cover foreign, economic, and social policies. Frequently, we develop the historical context, so that students are better able to understand the reasons for the shapes of current policies and the debates about them. Can one, for example, understand current debates about American foreign policy without learning about the origins of the cold war and the theories to which it gave rise? Looking at policy issues historically helps students to evaluate them better, as well. For instance, in Chapter 13, we trace the development of the concept of rights and compare older conceptions with modern ones.

Throughout the book, we have endeavored to state fairly the various perspectives on important controversies and to supply as many pertinent facts as the length and the introductory nature of the text will allow. Even so, students will not have all their questions about the republic answered. But their questions about the role of government in achieving the good life should be better.

Special Features

As in most texts, there is a glossary of important terms at the back of the book. But we have gone a step further by putting key definitions in the margins of the page as the term or concept comes up in the text. We think this marginal glossary will aid students significantly in learning and reviewing the material.

Every chapter opens with an outline of its contents and concludes with an annotated bibliography. And in each chapter, we have placed "boxes" containing relevant documents or statistics, pertinent newspaper or journal excerpts, amusing anecdotes, and so on, which we hope will both interest students and shed additional light on important topics. These inserts are in addition to the more than one hundred photographs, charts, and tables.

Both an instructor's manual and a test file for this text are available. Finally, we wish to remind instructors that there is a separate *Study Guide* for this text, which students may find useful.

Acknowledgments

We are grateful to many people for their advice and aid in preparing this book. Diana Evans (University of California, Santa Barbara), Linda Fowler (Syracuse), Ted Harpham (University of Texas, Dallas), Joel Rogers (Rutgers), and Neil

Wintfeld generously read portions of the manuscript and aided in its improvement. We are delighted to thank our University of Houston colleagues—Jim Anderson, Tom Dumm, Joe Nogee, and Bruce Oppenheimer—for their thoughtful comments. Our wives, Celeste Stone and Nancy Barke, were our toughest critics; we learned much from them.

For St. Martin's Press, George C. Edwards III (Texas A&M University), Benjamin Ginsberg (Cornell University), Anne Hopkins (University of Tennessee), Stephen Mazurana (University of Northern Colorado), Michael Reagan (University of California, Riverside), Robert K. Toburen (Louisiana Tech University), and Martha K. Zebrowski (City University of New York) read the entire manuscript, providing considerable insight and information. Ralph Stone ably constructed many of the figures and tables. Finally, we deeply appreciate the efforts of Kenneth Nassau, Patricia Mansfield, Michael Weber, and many others at St. Martin's Press.

Alan Stone
Richard P. Barke

CONTENTS

GOVERNING THE AMERICAN REPUBLIC

Economics, Law,
and Policies

PART I

AMERICA: PRESENT AND PAST

The Basic Concepts of American Government

Your bedside clock radio clicks on at 7:00 A.M. and begins playing your favorite station. The time on the clock reflects an agreement—a standard—that was initially formed about 1880 by railroad companies, which needed a uniform set of time zones. It was later endorsed by the American government in the Standard Time Act of 1918, which gave the federal Interstate Commerce Commission the responsibility for setting time-zone boundaries. However, Congress retained the power to change the system of time, and thus it imposed daylight saving time, first during wars and then, over the complaints of many state governments, for six months of every year.

Your clock radio has been manufactured according to safety standards established by the Consumer Product Safety Commission (CPSC), and the Federal Communications Commission (FCC) has certified that the device will produce only minimal radio interference. The FCC has also issued a license to the broadcaster transmitting the music that awakens you, giving it the right to broadcast on a particular frequency, subject to certain requirements regarding technical specifications, program content, and employment practices. The Federal Trade Commission (FTC), which has the duty to protect the public from false and deceptive advertising, may have required an Advertisement Substantiation Report from any corporation that has bought airtime for its radio commercials.

With a commercial now playing on the radio, you decide that it's time to begin your day. Turning on a bedside light, you tap into a complex national system of electrical power generation and transmission, which involves private enterprise, government-owned enterprise, and both state and federal regulations. The electric current, which is sold to you at regulated rates, is generated in plants subject to environmental regulations. The plant is constructed of materials meeting government standards, and its employees' salaries and working conditions are subject to governmental control.

Walking into the bathroom, you turn on the water—another publicly controlled or, more likely, publicly owned utility—to take a shower; the contents of your bar of soap are regulated by the Food and Drug Administration. While you eat your breakfast of governmentally inspected, graded, and perhaps subsidized foodstuffs, you read the morning newspaper. The investigative reports about government waste or wrongdoing appear because of constitutional guarantees that protect writers and editors from censorship.

Later, you dress in clothes imported under international agreement from the other side of the world and then slip into shoes produced in the United States by workers who have organized into a labor union as guaranteed by public laws. The car in your driveway is subject to numerous safety and performance regulations that affect both its operation and its cost, and the gasoline that fuels it is the end result of a complicated process of private enterprise, governmental decisions, and international relations.

In this brief story of the beginning of a normal day, we have barely scratched

3

the surface of the complex system in which we live. In fact, it is doubtful that there is any area of modern American life that is entirely insulated from public influence. As social creatures, we depend on transportation and communication in order to interact with other people. Rules of conduct—both legal and unwritten—constrain our behavior in order to reduce violence and anarchy. Government and economics are the realms in which we exchange our ideals, our values, our labor, and our possessions. In this book, we will examine American politics, government, and policymaking, using concepts that reflect the pervasive interplay of policies, economics, law, and institutions.

Of course, our lives are not determined entirely by the public sphere; many of our decisions are private. For example, even though the FCC, the CPSC, the electric utilities, the United States Congress, and many private companies may have had some role in the start of your day, you are ultimately responsible for the time that your alarm sounds. (Your professor may require you to be in class at 8:00 A.M., but you can cut your class and bear the consequences.) Similarly, most consumer choices are made freely (although manufacturers and the government limit your choices through marketing decisions and public policies). The American political economy is a continually changing mixture of freedoms and constraints, privileges and duties, and private and public influences. It is a unique mix. Western Europe and other nations—including the Soviet Union—can also be characterized as mixed public-private political economies, ranging from near-totalitarianism to near-free markets, but none shows the same set of features as the American system.

In this brief chapter, we will provide an overview of the more easily described results of the complex interface of policies, economics, law, and institutions. The public and private decisions of Americans shape, and are shaped by, who we are, the quality of our lives, and how we learn, work, and consume. We stress here that we take no position on the "proper" mixture of private and public (i.e., "free market" versus governmental) roles in the American system, nor do we claim that the system has worked perfectly. It is clear that some of the most troublesome aspects of American life, such as discrimination, prejudice, and fear of violence, are more difficult to measure than the nation's achievements. Aggregate statistics such as those presented in this chapter can reveal overall success—for example, an increase in the total wealth of all individuals—while masking unjust allocations of that wealth. The various aspects of social justice will be discussed in Chapter 13. In the following section, we will focus on long-run changes in the American economy and their effects on American politics and government. In addition, we will present a rough statistical description of where Americans are now.

WHO AMERICANS ARE

It is appropriate to present here a profile of the American people—those who are affected by American national, state, and local governments.[1] On July 1, 1984, there were approximately 236 million Americans, most of whom were

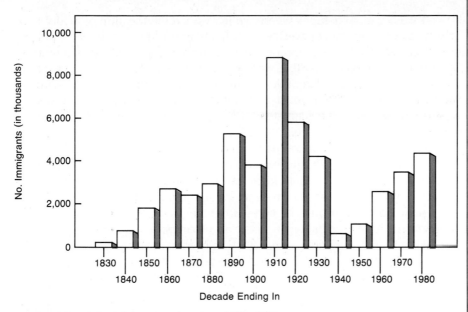

FIGURE 1-1 United States Immigration, 1820–1980

Sources: U.S. Bureau of the Census, *Historical Statistics of the United States, Colonial Times to Present*, Series C138–142 (Washington, D.C.. Government Printing Office, 1976); *Statistical Abstract of the United States, 1984* (Washington, D.C.: Government Printing Office, 1984), p. 88.

living within the nation's 3,618,770 square miles. Each year since 1940, the United States population has increased between 0.9 and 1.9 percent, so when you read these words, the population will be larger than the figure just cited. The birth rate, which has declined in recent years, is one factor that determines American population and its growth. Immigration is another; since 1965, between 297,000 and 601,000 people have been admitted annually to the United States (see Figure 1-1). And one of the most important factors in population and its growth is the general level of well-being. Due in large part to increased prosperity, improved sanitation facilities, and better health care, the American population is accelerating its historical trend of becoming older. In 1800, the median age of the population was 16 years; today it is over 31 years. The proportion of the population over age 65 has grown from 4.1 percent in 1900 to 11.3 percent, and by the year 2020, more than 15 percent of all Americans may be older than 65. (The effects are not uniformly distributed, however; in 1980, over 17 percent of Florida's population was at least 65 years old, while only 3 percent of Alaskans were 65 or older.[2]) Current estimates by the United States Census Bureau predict that the number of people 85 and older is likely to double in the next two decades.[3] Such changes have already affected the United States by increasing both the nation's medical costs and the drain on private and public retirement systems. The political and economic effects of an aging population will certainly proliferate within your lifetime.

Who we are also includes where we live, since the location of a person—urban, rural, easterner, or westerner—affects and reflects political and economic change. In 1790, the center of the American population was east of Baltimore, Maryland. By 1880, it was near Cincinnati, and during the 1970s, it crossed the Mississippi River into central Missouri (see Figure 1-2). The westward movement of the population initially resulted from the opening of the western frontier during the nineteenth century. However, today many people who are leaving the Snow Belt cities and states in favor of western and Sun Belt regions are following industrial and commercial jobs, not agricultural ones. From 1970 to 1980, the resident population of the western states increased 23.9 percent, and that of the South increased by 20.0 percent, but the resident populations of the north central states and northeastern states in that same period increased only 4.0 and 0.2 percent, respectively.

Americans have increasingly become an urban population (see Figure 1-3). In 1980, only 26.3 percent of the population lived in rural areas (that is, places with populations under 2,500), while the remainder lived in urban areas (places with populations above 2,500). Only 7.7 percent lived in the six largest

Year	Approximate Location of Population Center
1790 (Aug. 2)	23 miles east of Baltimore, Maryland
1850 (June 1)	23 miles southeast of Parkersburg, West Virginia
1900 (June 1)	6 miles southeast of Columbus, Indiana
1950 (Apr. 1)	8 miles north-northwest of Olney, Richland County, Illinois
1960 (Apr. 1)	In Clinton Co. about 6½ miles northwest of Centralia, Illinois
1970 (Apr. 1)	5.3 miles east-southeast of the Mascoutah City Hall in St. Clair County, Illinois
1980 (Apr. 1)	1 mile west of the Desoto City Hall in Jefferson County, Missouri

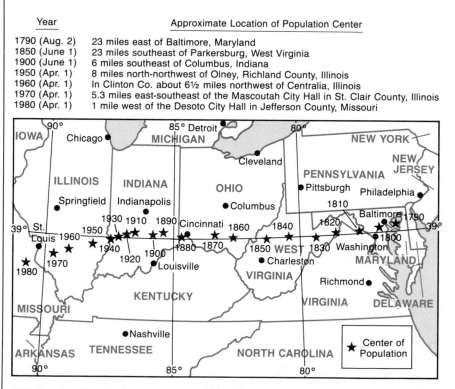

FIGURE 1-2   Center of Population, 1790–1980

Source: U.S. Bureau of the Census, *Census of Population: 1970*, vol. I.

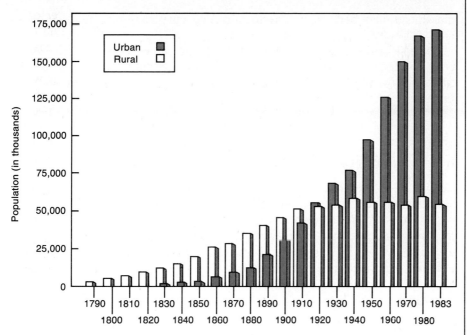

FIGURE 1-3   United States Population in Urban and Rural Territory, 1790–1983

Sources: U.S. Bureau of the Census, *Historical Statistics of the United States, Colonial Times to Present*, Series A57–72 (Washington, D.C.: Government Printing Office, 1976); *Statistical Abstract of the United States, 1984* (Washington, D.C.: Government Printing Office, 1984), pp. 18–19.

cities with populations above one million, while another 26.4 percent lived in cities with populations of 50,000 to one million. The largest proportion of Americans—39.6 percent—lived in suburbs, cities, and towns with populations ranging from 2,500 to 50,000. Thus, while the United States can be described as an urban nation, this does not mean that most Americans live in large cities. Rather, they live in a diversity of urban and rural settings.

In addition, Americans exhibit wide diversity in their ethnic, racial, and religious backgrounds. Of the approximately 226.5 million Americans living in 1980, a majority—more than 188.3 million—were white, but they came from a wide variety of ethnic and religious backgrounds. Minority groups included, among others, approximately 26.5 million blacks; 14.6 million persons of Spanish origin; 1.4 million Native Americans, Eskimos, and Aleuts; and 1.5 million Chinese- and Japanese-Americans. The reasons for these groups' special claim to minority status are readily understood. Their experiences in the United States constituted some of the most shameful episodes in American history. For example, blacks suffered slavery and the imposition of laws that discriminated against them, and many Japanese-Americans were detained in internment camps during World War II (1941–1945). Finally, all of the minorities mentioned have been treated as second-class citizens during much of American history.

Because of this history—and for other reasons as well—the distribution of goods and services in the United States has not benefited all groups equally. Nevertheless, as we will see, most Americans have fared better and better over time.

WHAT AMERICANS HAVE

As with other measures that summarize characteristics of millions of people, statistics on the income and wealth of Americans can be properly interpreted only if we pay careful attention to that which is being measured. For example, to cite the rise in total income for all Americans as proof of their improved well-being would be misleading, because not only do dollars buy less due to inflation, but the total population grows. Thus, the statistics must be adjusted for inflation (producing a measure called *real* or *constant dollars*) and for population growth, producing a *per capita* measure (see Table 1-1). In addi-

TABLE 1-1
PER-CAPITA GROSS NATIONAL PRODUCT FOR SELECTED NATIONS
(in United States Dollars)

Nation	GNP Per Capita[a]	Year
Brazil	$ 1,523	1978
Canada	$10,193	1982
France	$ 8,980	1980
East Germany	$ 5,340	1979
India	$ 150	1977
Israel	$ 3,332	1978
Japan	$ 8,460	1980
Mexico	$ 1,800	1980
Nigeria	$ 750	1980
Switzerland	$15,698	1981
United Kingdom	$ 7,216	1979
United States	$ 8,612	1978
USSR	$ 2,600	1976
West Germany	$11,142	1982

[a]GNP is the total national output of goods and services valued at market prices.

Source: *World Almanac, 1984* (New York: Newspaper Enterprise Association, 1984).

tion, income comes from many sources besides an employer—for example, rents, interest on investments, governmental transfer programs such as food stamps—and these must be included to get an accurate picture of personal economic growth. Finally, most Americans are painfully aware that not all income can be freely spent; some of it is earmarked for taxes. Taking all these factors into account, careful studies of changes in the real per-capita augmented disposable income of Americans have shown that they had about 77 percent more to spend in 1977 than in 1947.[4]

When we look at these data, we see that the distribution of wealth and income is very uneven. For example, in 1980 the per-capita income of Alaskans was $12,790, while for those living in Mississippi, it averaged only $6,580.[5] When we examine the median weekly earnings of various groups in 1982, we also find large variations. Men who were the sole support of their families earned $365 per week, while women who were the sole support of their families earned only $243. On the average, whites out-earned blacks and Hispanics, with each group's weekly earnings totaling $317, $247, and $242, respectively.

We can also examine the share of the total national income that different groups receive. In 1910, the top fifth of the population received about 46 percent of the national income, while the bottom fifth received only about 8 percent. In 1982, the top fifth still received about 42.7 percent, and the share of the bottom fifth had dropped to 4.7 percent. The richest 5 percent of the population has continued to receive about 16 percent of the total income. Such figures have prompted many social commentators to label the American political economy as corrupt and unjust, yet there has been a significant lack of popular support for the revolutionary changes that would be required to equalize incomes.

Income is only one part of what Americans have. We can also examine their wealth—that is, the value of the property and other assets that they own. We must remember that wealth and income are clearly related: wealth is commonly used to produce income. For those with incomes of at least one million dollars in 1978, over 90 percent of their income was generated by the wealth they held (e.g., saving accounts, bonds, real estate, corporate stock).[6] In 1972, an estimated thirteen million Americans held personal wealth worth sixty thousand dollars or more—about 30 percent of it in real estate and an equal amount in corporate stock; yet in 1977, over half the population had a total net worth of less than three thousand dollars. While the average American has continued to become more wealthy, the very rich have clearly maintained an advantage; about half of all corporate stocks and bonds are owned by the wealthiest 0.5 percent of Americans. Yet once again, there has been almost no demand for a change in the political and economic system that allows such disparities.

Instead, public attention has been focused on two particular factors about income. First, how many people live in poverty? Measures of poverty are commonly based on a *poverty line*—an average family income, usually based on triple the amount of an essential annual food budget—which changes as prices change. The official poverty line for a family of four in 1959 was $2,973; in 1982, the figure was $9,862. According to such measures, in 1936, during the Great Depression, 56 percent of American families lived in poverty, whereas in 1982 the proportion dropped to 12.2 percent. (This drop was due to many factors, such as social welfare programs, which will be discussed in Chapter 13, and economic growth.)

Second, to what degree are disparities in income and wealth based upon race and sex? In 1982, while about 9.6 percent of whites were living below the poverty line, 33 percent of blacks and 27.2 percent of Hispanics were so classified. Using a different measure, we see that in 1982, median family income for whites was $21,117, and for blacks it was $11,968. The average income of black men working full-time climbed from 63 percent of white male's pay in 1955 to 75 percent in 1982. Even so, the disparity between male and female average earnings has been largely unchanged for decades; women working full-time outside the home earn an average of 60 percent of the salaries of men.

The causes of such differences are sometimes subtle, making it difficult for government policymakers to decide how to—or whether to—institute programs to reduce income disparities. In general, most of the political spectrum in the United States is committed to redressing both the problems of poverty and of racial and sexual inequities, but vast differences exist regarding the best means to accomplish these goals. Conservatives are prone to rely more on free-market mechanisms (i.e., economic decisions made without coercion or government interference), while liberals are inclined to rely more heavily on government programs. In both cases, however, most of the American political spectrum prefers a mixed solution in which market mechanisms and public policies both play a part.

The problems of poverty and discrimination typify the American political consensus with respect to a wide range of other problems, such as the general state of the economy, social problems, consumer protection, the quality of telephone service, and pollution standards for automobiles. As we saw in the examples that began this chapter, the mixed free-market/government-intervention approach characterizes the most common and trivial as well as the most profound problems in the United States.

WHAT AMERICANS THINK: POLITICAL CULTURE

Just as the social and economic lives of Americans are far from identical, so also their personal beliefs and habits differ. We refer to this mixture of American ideas, customs, and behavior as *political culture.* But while we have a fairly clear sense of what is political (i.e., what government does, who does it, and how and why they do it), the word *culture* is shrouded in ambiguity. It can mean that which is excellent in the arts, literature, scholarship, and behavior (including political behavior), but it can also convey things that are far from excellent. *Culture* also refers to the way that a society does things that is transmitted from generation to generation and to the ideas that govern such conduct, no matter how lofty or how vulgar they may be.

Americans manifest culture—and political culture. For example, since the end of World War II, the United States has poured an enormous amount of money into primary, secondary, and college education. Measured by the number of years the average American spends in school, Americans are the most educated people in the world. Yet many have decried the declining educational attainments of Americans; some have gone so far as to proclaim a crisis in education.[7] One student of public opinion, for example, interviewed high-school and college students in Los Angeles and found a surprising degree of ignorance. Most of the students did not know where Toronto is, when the Civil War was fought, who Vladimir I. Lenin or Joseph Stalin was, what the Bill of Rights is, what NATO stands for, or what *anti-Semitism* means![8]

Many observers have also been disturbed by the attention that Americans pay to celebrity criteria in politics. In 1956, the sociologist C. Wright Mills observed that new forms of prestige were being created through the power of mass media.[9] Film stars and professional basketball players have been elected to high office in the United States. In recent presidential campaigns, actors and rock stars have made appearances on behalf of their favorite candidates.

Even when the worlds of show business and politics are not directly mixed, candidates for public office are often packaged like soap or cosmetics in order to appeal to the electorate (this will be discussed in Chapter 5). Students of modern mass advertising have commented upon the industry's reliance on symbols, subliminal messages, and appeals to emotional needs.[10] To an increasing extent, political candidates are being sold to the public, often successfully, by large staffs of public relations people, media representatives, and pollsters in ways that reveal little about their backgrounds or positions on public policy questions.

Although Americans are often content to view elections as popularity contests—even though there is no necessary connection between a candidate's ability to gather votes and his or her ability to judge policy alternatives or administer government bureaucracies—there is another side to the coin. Americans do have opinions on a large variety of topics, and as we will see in Chapter 3, they do prefer candidates whose ideas are similar to their own. Americans typically do not want long, comprehensive discussions about political issues from candidates, but they do search for key words, phrases, and cues that indicate agreement between the candidates' positions and their own.

As this brief discussion illustrates, our society consists of a complex mixture of beliefs, traditions, institutions, and perceptions. Rational judgment and irrationality, and information and ignorance are all components of the American political culture. Some views are held by virtually every citizen, while there are

MOST IMPORTANT PROBLEM TREND: PUBLIC'S TOP CONCERNS, 1935–1983

1983	Unemployment, high cost of living	*1959*	Keeping peace
1982	Unemployment, high cost of living	*1958*	Unemployment, keeping peace
1981	High cost of living, unemployment	*1957*	Race relations, keeping peace
1980	High cost of living, unemployment	*1956*	Keeping peace
1979	High cost of living, energy problems	*1955*	Keeping peace
1978	High cost of living, energy problems	*1954*	Keeping peace
1977	High cost of living, unemployment	*1953*	Keeping peace
1976	High cost of living, unemployment	*1952*	Korean war
1975	High cost of living, unemployment	*1951*	Korean war
1974	High cost of living, Watergate, energy crisis	*1950*	Labor unrest
1973	High cost of living, Watergate	*1949*	Labor unrest
1972	Vietnam	*1948*	Keeping peace
1971	Vietnam, high cost of living	*1947*	High cost of living, labor unrest
1970	Vietnam	*1946*	High cost of living
1969	Vietnam	*1945*	Winning war
1968	Vietnam	*1944*	Winning war
1967	Vietnam, high cost of living	*1943*	Winning war
1966	Vietnam	*1942*	Winning war
1965	Vietnam, race relations	*1941*	Keeping out of war, winning war
1964	Vietnam, race relations	*1940*	Keeping out of war
1963	Keeping peace, race relations	*1939*	Keeping out of war
1962	Keeping peace	*1938*	Keeping out of war
1961	Keeping peace	*1937*	Unemployment
1960	Keeping peace	*1936*	Unemployment
		1935	Unemployment

Source: *Gallup Report*, no. 213, June 1983, p. 50.

some important subjects about which Americans hold widely varying opinions. This is not surprising because Americans are a widely heterogeneous people. You would not expect members of San Francisco's gay community to hold the same sets of beliefs as the residents of a small, predominantly Baptist, Mississippi town. Yet both groups are part of the same American political culture. Thus, the United States has both a political culture (i.e., widely shared beliefs) and many political subcultures. These differences stem from such factors as the generation to which one belongs, the region of the country in which one lives, whether one lives in a rural or urban area, as well as social class, amount and quality of education, race, religion, and sex. Moreover, beliefs can change not only from generation to generation, but in a much shorter time as well.

One of the most striking paradoxes about American political culture is the simultaneous support and skepticism most Americans have for government and other institutions. For example, the University of Michigan's Institute for Social Research has been conducting public opinion surveys for many years.

One of the questions it asks is, "Would you say the government is pretty much run by a few big interests looking out for themselves or that it is run for the benefit of all people?" In 1964, only 29 percent of the public selected the "few big interests," and 64 percent responded "all people." The remainder either did not know or expressed no opinion. By 1980, however, public opinion on the question had reversed: 69 percent selected the "few big interests," while only 21 percent believed that government is run for "all people." And not only does the American public generally hold a low opinion of the motives of public officials, but it holds an even lower view of government efficiency. In 1964, when asked, "Do you think that people in the government waste a lot of money we pay in taxes, waste some of it, or don't waste very much of it?" 47 percent chose "a lot," 44 percent chose "some," and only 7 percent chose "don't waste very much." But by 1980, the figures for the three choices were 78, 17, and 2 percent, respectively.

If Americans have such a low degree of confidence in government, why have they not seriously challenged it? Why are they largely unresponsive to pleas for revolution, or at least for drastic change in government? Three reasons have been suggested. First, while many citizens are dissatisfied, they see other alternatives as even worse. Most Americans do not wish to support a government that will greatly expand its role, for example, by running business enterprises. Thus, dissatisfaction does not necessarily lead to a demand for change. Americans may want more or less government intervention in social and economic life, but the change they want is incremental, rather than a drastic revision of American government.

A second reason for the general acquiescence in government is that most Americans do not view government as the most important component of their lives. Rather, they see it as an inevitable component of something larger—the United States. In 1982, the National Opinion Research Center asked Americans to rank-order seven different aspects of life in terms of importance. Politics and public life came in last behind (1) family and children, (2) relatives, (3) friends and acquaintances, (4) career and work, (5) free time and relaxation, and (6) religion and church. And Americans are generally satisfied with the United States; in 1983, the Roper Organization surveyed American attitudes and found that many more Americans (66 percent) were optimistic about the quality of life than were pessimistic (16 percent).

By now, it should be obvious why many Americans disapprove of their government, but grant its legitimacy. That support is reinforced by a third characteristic of American political culture: the belief that if a game is played according to fair and consistently applied rules, then the outcome must be accepted, even if it is distasteful. (In Chapter 7, we will discuss this belief when we deal with the topic of due process.) Rules governing election to office, legislative voting, and courtroom procedure are largely—but not always—conceived as fair, providing an opportunity for all sides to win. And if one does not like particular candidates, policies, or procedures, one has a reasonable opportunity to change them.

As a result of the widely held view on fair procedure, the American political culture can accommodate a great variety of political subcultures and a diversity of opinions on different topics. As stated earlier, there are many bases for these differences, such as class, sex, education, and generation. One of the most important of these is the generational factor. It is obvious that the attitudes of today's students differ considerably from those of a comparable age group at the beginning of the twentieth century—and even more recently. In a 1982 survey conducted by the National Opinion Research Center, only 23 percent of 18-to-24-year-olds believed that distribution of pornography should be illegal, but 69 percent of those over 75 years of age would make such conduct unlawful; 55 percent of the 18-to-24-year-olds felt that an admitted Communist should be allowed to teach at a college, as opposed to 22 percent of those over 75. The young are less religious than their elders, and considerably more tolerant of other races and religions. It may be surprising to learn how much attitudes can change in only a few years; for example, high-school seniors in 1982 were significantly more likely to look favorably upon our system of doing things than were 1975 high-school seniors.

As we can see, American political culture in many ways parallels American material life. There are positive and negative elements in both. And neither is static. Like every other facet of American life, both material life and political culture are constantly changing.

LAW, ECONOMICS, POLICIES, AND INSTITUTIONS

Today, the problems viewed by Americans as most important are quite different from those considered important a hundred years ago. In the 1880s, many Americans were concerned about high and discriminatory railroad rates, the rate of immigration, the rapid growth of large firms and their restructuring into "trusts," frequent financial panics, declining cotton prices, and the miserable quality of much urban housing. Over the next few decades, laws were enacted and institutions created to deal with these problems (as we will discuss in Chapters 12 and 13).

The policies established in conjunction with the economic dynamics were sometimes successful in solving the problems. Immigrants, for example, have for the most part been successfully integrated into the United States, and financial panics, in which large numbers of people lost their savings, have mostly been overcome through bank-deposit insurance. Although some substandard urban housing remains, it has greatly improved since many states and municipalities enacted tenement housing laws. On the other hand, many American corporations are vastly larger than anything imagined during the 1880s, the antimonopoly laws notwithstanding. And, while the price of cotton, like that of many other agricultural commodities, has been stabilized through

The Statue of Liberty, shown here while being erected, was presented by France to the United States in 1885. (The Bettmann Archive, Inc.)

government programs, many people question whether the cost to taxpayers has been worth the benefits to cotton growers.

Most of today's problems differ greatly from those of a hundred years ago. Automobiles, aircraft, and a vast array of chemicals and synthetic materials not even dreamed of in the nineteenth century have led to great progress, but they have also created new concerns. Some of these have arisen, not because of technological or economic progress, but rather because of enhanced social awareness. Groups representing blacks, the handicapped, and women have achieved notable political gains in recent years, not because their problems are of recent origin, but because the groups organized, made demands, and raised the social awareness of those they represent (see Chapter 3). But today, just as in the 1880s, simply getting government to intervene does not mean that a problem will be solved or that it will be solved efficiently. Should Congress decree that the next hundred days will be sunny or that unemployment will disappear, it will make no difference. Similarly, problems may be solved in too costly a manner. For example, if Congress decreed that all automobiles must have nine-inch-thick armor plating, it would raise the average cost of an automobile to an unacceptable amount and would reduce fuel economy to near zero.

In order to understand what government does, as well as to evaluate the best mix of private-market behavior and public-sector intervention, we as citizens must understand the law, economics, policies, and institutions that shape and impel American government. To do so, however, we must first look at certain basic concepts that will be employed later in this book.

No device more radically transformed the American landscape than the automobile, an early example of which is seen here. (The Bettmann Archive, Inc.)

BASIC CONCEPTS

Cost

We usually think of *cost* in terms of money—for example, tomatoes cost seventy cents a pound. But the definition we will use herein shows that cost can be measured in terms other than money: *Cost is that which must be given up in order to buy, produce, accomplish, or maintain something.* From this definition, we see that tomato buyers and manufacturers who purchase raw materials incur costs. In addition, one who invests time or labor to produce or maintain something also gives up something valuable. Thus, time and labor are often expressed in terms of money and can measure cost. Even such things as pain or trouble, which are difficult to measure, may express cost.

From these obvious aspects of cost, which are largely relevant to economic activities, we will turn to less obvious ones that are important in the study of government. Suppose that you have ten dollars to spend in the supermarket. You may choose to buy fresh fruits and vegetables with the money, or you may spend it entirely on potato chips and pretzels. In any event, you cannot buy very many of the goods available in the supermarket. The concept of **opportunity cost** measures the cost of doing one thing rather than another. Similarly, a business firm incurs an opportunity cost when it produces one thing (e.g., small cars) rather than another (e.g., large trucks). Opportunity costs are very real. This fact was illustrated when the American automobile industry continued to produce large cars in the face of a growing demand for smaller ones.

opportunity cost: The economic cost of one activity measured by the sacrifice of not employing the same resources, such as time or money, in another activity.

In the realm of government, the concept of opportunity cost is also very real. Governments, like individuals and business firms, have limited resources at their command. It is possible that a given expenditure (say, $1 million) spent on one goal will benefit many more people than the same amount spent on another goal. For example, a sum of money allotted to regulate consumer fraud may be used to examine advertisements for yachts and luxury cars, or it may be directed toward regulating food, clothing, and other products that affect a much greater number of people. Furthermore, if government adopts the goal of preventing fraud directed at the poor, for example, a consumer education program may be less costly than—and achieve the same results as—prosecuting storekeepers. In short, the opportunity-cost concept requires us to think of both alternative government goals and means.

Another kind of cost—**information cost**—is also important for understanding government. We do not usually think of information in terms of cost because so much information seems to be free. Until the coming of cable television, the information that we received from television news appeared (falsely) to be free, although it was not. Similarly, when we purchase cough medicine, we do not think that the information supplied by the manufacturer is costly. Yet, these cases are not very different from paying for a newspaper or a lawyer's advice or a physician's diagnosis. For, although the costs of information may be concealed, they are always present. Sometimes a company manufacturing a drug spends tens of millions of dollars in order to develop information about the product's safety, effectiveness, and side effects. And this cost is passed on to the buyer as part of the purchase price.

Information is almost never free, and it is sometimes very costly; this is an important concern of government. Consider a long and costly trial; the underlying purpose of the trial is to obtain the information necessary to determine guilt or innocence. Consider the time and effort required to make an intelligent voting decision (see Chapter 3). Consider also an administrative agency like the FCC, which determines from among a large number of applicants which television stations should have the right to broadcast. The FCC must obtain information from each applicant, examine it, investigate on its own, evaluate all of the data, and make a decision. Congress, faced with a public problem such as air pollution, must schedule hearings, listen to many points of view, examine stacks of documents, evaluate it all, and draft a bill designed to meet the problem. Finally, consider the enormous sum the United States spends each year on intelligence activities in regard to the Soviet Union and other nations.

Another class of costs that we ordinarily do not think of when we consider government, but which is also very important, is **transaction costs.** Transaction costs result from negotiating, bargaining, and entering into agreements. The transaction costs that exist in many private activities are often easy to see. For example, when the owners of a large office building want to sell it, they must search for possible buyers, develop and present information about the

information cost: The cost incurred in obtaining information about the prospective use of resources.

transaction costs: The costs incurred in reaching and enforcing an agreement.

terms of sale, engage in a lengthy decisionmaking process about each offer and response, undertake a difficult and often time-consuming bargaining process, prepare and reach a final agreement, and finally, police the agreement to make sure that the other party abides by the terms reached. In many such instances, an expenditure of millions of dollars is involved.

Transaction costs are important in government too. For example, congressional representatives frequently hold different views on particular problems, such as air pollution. Precisely the same problems of negotiation, bargaining, and compromise that occur in the private sphere take place in Congress. The situation is compounded because legislators often represent important interest groups or firms located in their districts. It is not uncommon for Congress to reach no agreement on legislation. Indeed, proposed legislation can drag on for years before Congress ultimately acts. Similarly, in many matters, administrative agencies and courts are frequently involved in lengthy negotiations over appropriate settlements. The executive branch, too, must often bargain with Congress over major and minor matters, as well as negotiate with foreign governments over such diverse matters as trade agreements or arms-control arrangements. Transaction costs are high in American politics.

Costs are, of course, always to be measured against benefits. In many situations, there are attempts to lower costs. Before discussing benefits, however, we will look at one of the most important means used to reduce costs— organization.

Organization

Adam Smith began his famous work, *The Wealth of Nations*, with a discussion of the division of labor. Using pinmaking as an example, he pointed out that it is much less costly to make pins if different workers specialize in particular steps of the manufacturing process than if each person does all the required tasks. The modern factory or office in which each worker specializes in a small part of a much larger process shows that the principle Smith described has proceeded to a point far beyond anything he or his contemporaries could have dreamed of. Almost everyone, from the most unskilled laborer to the most highly skilled technician, has become a specialist in a small part of a total process. And the underlying reason in most enterprises is to reduce costs.

The division of labor requires two things in order to operate effectively. First, there must be a set of formal or informal rules so that each of us knows our proper function and does not duplicate the activities of others involved in the process. Second, there must be a group of persons whose function is to assign, coordinate, and supervise the activities of others involved in the process. A simple enterprise like a diner employs some people who prepare the food, some who sell it, others who order the supplies, still others who do the accounting, and so on. Above them stands management, which hires and fires employees, determines who does what in the total effort, and supervises the various parts of the process. Together, these rules, structures, and processes constitute **organization**—a set of interdependent parts coordinated into a whole.

In government, as in the private sector, the principal functions of organization are to reduce costs and efficiently coordinate effort. For this reason, executive-branch agencies are organized into offices, bureaus, divisions, sections, and task forces, each specializing in a particular part of the agency's work. The Environmental Protection Agency (EPA), for example, contains an Office of Radiation Programs that includes separate divisions of technology assessment and environmental analysis. Each division is headed by a director who, in turn, is supervised by a deputy assistant administrator. He or she reports to an assistant administrator for air, noise, and radiation. Similarly, Congress has developed into an organization consisting of specialized committees and subcommittees. For example, the House of Representatives contains an Education and Labor Committee consisting of subcommittees, one of which covers elementary, secondary, and vocational education. Each committee and subcommittee has a chairperson who engages in management activities in the same way those in the executive branch and its agencies do. The president may be viewed as the top manager of the national government enterprise. In this respect, government is no different from Jay's Diner or a giant firm like General Motors. And just as in the private sector, government frequently engages in reorganization in the quest to become more efficient and effective.

Incentives and Constraints

In any large organization, the persons filling the positions are apt to be motivated by a number of things. Some might seek, for example, to minimize their work efforts, while others might be motivated to work very hard. Some may be inherently dishonest, while others may be scrupulously honest. Given the variety of motivations that may exist within an individual, some means must be found to try to compel people to act pursuant to an organization's objectives. These means can be categorized as incentives and constraints.

An **incentive** is that which encourages or incites desired behavior—for example, the promise of a pay increase or a promotion. But incentives may be threatening as well as rewarding. The threat of dismissal or a pay cut for inferior effort or dishonesty constitutes a negative incentive, or *disincentive*. Incentives in organizations can be broken down into three categories. *Requirements* are incentives that tell members of an organization what their tasks are; assembly-line production workers must effectively operate the machines to which they are assigned, while FDA chemists must determine whether new drug products are safe for public consumption. *Demands* are incentives that request action. For example, interest groups with financial resources will often demand that Congress or administrative agencies take certain policy actions.

organization: A set of coordinated rules, structures, and processes established for a specific purpose.

incentive: That which encourages or incites desired behavior.

Finally, *opportunities* are incentives that promise rewards or reduce the threat of punishment for actions that can be taken. For example, as we will see in Chapter 11, certain legislators instituted efforts to enact a law requiring truthful labeling of the contents of unopened packages. They did so on their own, without significant public or interest-group pressure to enact such legislation. Many innovative administrative programs have come about because of opportunities incentives.

constraints: Rules or forces that limit or shape the conduct of members of a group or organization.

Constraints are rules or forces that limit or shape the conduct of members of an organization, such as relevant laws, internal rules and regulations, court decisions, and informal guidelines. For example, most factory workers are constrained by formal rules that dictate when they can take coffee breaks. In government organizations, a complex pattern of statutes, court decisions, and internal rules and regulations inform members about what they can and cannot do, as well as the proper procedures for doing them. FDA officials, for example, may not prevent the marketing of a drug simply because they do not like its taste; they must first follow statutes, rules, court decisions, and so on before they can take such action.

Constraints and incentives do not mean that members of an organization must act like robots. Rather, organizational personnel can exercise judgment, and so there can be considerable variation in how well people perform their tasks. Nevertheless, such judgment and its outcome take place within a structure of constraints and incentives.

Constraints and incentives are not self-executing. In any organization, there is a hierarchy of officials who mete out rewards and punishments. Automobile factory workers are overseen by supervisors, and government workers are directed by division chiefs, who in turn are supervised by bureau directors, and so on up the chain of command and control.

Benefit

benefit: Anything for the good of a person, organization, or thing.

A **benefit** is something that is for the good of a person, organization, or thing. When you go to a record store and purchase an album, you have benefited because to you the benefit of the transaction is greater than the cost; otherwise you would not have done it. The concept of a benefit should not, however, be confused with that of pleasure. Suppose you go to the dentist to have a cavity filled. Unless you are a masochist, you will probably not enjoy the experience. Nevertheless, you would not have your cavity filled unless you believed that you would be better off. To you, the benefit in this case exceeded the cost. As these illustrations show, benefit is a subjective concept; one person may prefer rock music, while another may enjoy only classical. If a higher authority ordered the classical-music lover to buy rock albums, there would be no benefit to the classical-music lover (although there might be to the higher authority).

This simple example helps to illustrate the major problem that government has in the realm of benefits. Obviously, when the government spends tax money to buy bombers, build highways, or conduct medical research, it is attempting to confer benefits. But, unlike the situation in which you go into a record store, a taxpayer has no personal choice. You must "consume" the bombers, highways, and medical research for which your taxes help pay. One of the most vexing problems of government, about which political philosophers have been concerned for centuries, is *when* government should act to confer benefits.

One of the least controversial situations involves **public goods**—that is, goods or services that cannot be withheld from any member of a community. Given the complexity of modern military technology, individuals or families cannot purchase personal missiles, bombers, or nuclear warheads to defend themselves against foreign nations. Such weapons purchased by the federal government provide public benefits. They protect you, your neighbors, your city, and your state. Although public goods are only one example of a situation calling for government intervention, they raise an important question that applies to every kind of government activity. Why should government, rather than markets or other private arrangements, provide particular kinds of benefits? And does government or some private arrangement provide the greatest **net benefit** (i.e., benefits minus costs)? These questions should be asked, not just in connection with a specific benefit, but with the concept of opportunity costs in mind. Governments, like individuals, must make choices; they cannot have everything at once.

These questions introduce still another important idea connected with costs and benefits: the **trade-off.** If a supercar were designed to last a hundred years and to completely prevent personal injury in collisions, it would resemble an enormous tank and cost more than half a million dollars. Few of us would be willing or able to spend such a sum for an automobile or to pay for the enormous amount of gasoline that it would require. Therefore, we are willing to trade off some degree of safety and durability for a reduction in selling price and operating cost. Almost every decision we make involves a trade-off. In the private sphere, the market mechanism arranges the trade-offs.

Governments are also faced with trade-off problems. It would be very nice if all pollutants were prohibited from entering the air. However, all automobile traffic would cease as a result and all factories would stop producing goods. Thus, governments must engage in making trade-offs. But this raises the important question, what mechanism should governments substitute for the market system that governs trade-offs in the private sphere? Government, then, is faced not only with the problem of what it should do and what activities should remain in the private sphere, but it is also faced with the question of how far to go once it undertakes an activity. To say simply that government should make policies regarding air pollution is not enough; what kind of policies it should make and what kind of trade-offs it should make are equally important.

public good: A benefit that is available to all members of a society, whether or not they are members of the group that was responsible for the production of the benefit; for example, military defense cannot be withheld from Americans who do not pay taxes.

net benefit: The result of subtracting the costs of a course of action from the benefits achieved.

trade-off: The incorporation and consideration of both costs and benefits in a course of action.

Still further complicating government's tasks is another important problem—allocation.

Allocation

Wealth, income, social status, tennis balls, and Picasso paintings are distributed unevenly in society. In part, this stems from personal choice. One person may want tennis balls, while another has no use for them. One person may enter a business with the hope of becoming a millionaire, while another may join a religious order that forgoes material wealth. But choice is only one aspect of the way in which things are distributed in a society. Many people may want to choose the same thing, but there is simply not enough of it to go around. The process of distributing and redistributing is called the *allocative process.* **Allocation,** the division of things into shares and portions, is used to describe both a process and a result. For example, wealth is divided very unevenly in this country. This is caused by certain factors and processes—choice is one of them. Market mechanisms, such as investment and profit, are important in leading to the resulting distribution of income and wealth. Market activity is also a major part of allocation as process. A business executive who started life very poor may use market mechanisms to become much richer than most Americans.

Some people think that choice and market mechanisms are the only proper way to distribute and redistribute wealth and assets. But this is just one point of view. An allocation system is not necessarily the same as a system of social justice. For example, the United States has a *graduated* income tax. Instead of everyone paying the same percentage of their income in taxes, the tax rate increases as one's income rises (see Chapter 13). Thus, some individuals may pay fifty percent of their income in taxes, while others pay no taxes at all. The social security system redistributes income from younger people to those who have retired, while inheritance taxes reallocate money from the estates of dead people to the living. Many public assistance programs, commonly called *welfare programs,* redistribute income from those above the poverty line to those below it. In all of these cases, government reallocates resources in conformity with concepts of social justice that do not accord with market allocations.

Because virtually every government program reallocates funds and because so many programs exist, no one has provided a general theory that explains every case. Some programs redistribute from the middle-income groups to the rich, while others do the opposite. Farmers are the beneficiaries of some programs; laborers benefit from others; and so on. To be complete in an evaluation of government programs, we should (1) first evaluate the probable costs and benefits of each program; (2) identify reasonable alternatives, which is usually not an easy task; and (3) understand clearly the values or ideas of justice that underlie choices, which is also difficult to do. Even if not perfect,

allocation: The division of things into shares and portions.

Bread line for a free meal at the Municipal Lodging House, New York, Christmas Day, 1931. (UPI/Bettmann Archive)

such an attempt can help us to exclude certain alternatives, although it may not point to a single most preferred, most efficient course. For example, your ideas on justice and fairness might lead you to support an income tax system in which rates rise as incomes rise. But if you also value investment for economic growth, you will not want to fix the minimum rate so high that no one has money to invest.

Justice

Almost every activity and process of government raises questions that must be answered by a combination of scientific principles and values. The most important value principle we hold is that government should be just. *Justice* is almost impossible to define. Nevertheless, we weigh every governmental action in terms of our ideas of justice. To take an extreme case, hardly anyone would consider it just to impose a prison sentence on a person simply because he or she has been accused of a crime. Most people would expect a fair trial, convincing evidence, and a jury verdict of "guilty" before they would consider such imprisonment to be just. And not many people would consider a society to be just if a few of its citizens lived in luxury while the rest of the people starved. Finally, most of us consider societies that suppress free speech to be unjust.

As these examples illustrate, the idea of justice begins with a set of fundamental principles about human existence. For example, most of us believe that people should be able to express their political ideas freely and without fear of punishment. All such values are concerned with the quality of human existence. But the idea of justice includes more than goals that people possess or are allowed to pursue; it also includes procedural fairness. Justice also includes the idea of truthfulness; we consider a public official who lies to be unjust. Finally, most of us believe that justice should include uniform standards, not arbitrariness. We would consider it unjust to throw one thief in jail because he or she is black and set another thief free because he or she is white.

POLITICS AND ECONOMICS

Politics and economics are hardly identical, especially in nations where the economic system is purportedly rooted in free markets (i.e., where economic decisions are made without coercion or government interference), but they do complement each other. We will see later in this book that some of the strongest opponents of public intrusion into economic affairs recognized that free markets are not self-enforcing; for example, when people refuse to pay their debts, only government can peaceably assure compliance with contracts. The institutions of government, the nature of its laws, and the economy and the policies it adopts all have an impact on each other. As we will see in Chapter 2, the American founders understood this very well.

In Chapter 1, we introduced such concepts as cost, organization, incentives, constraints, benefits, allocation, and justice to help you understand government. Although the American founders did not use the same terminology, they were keenly aware of the problems and limits of government as they fashioned the underlying principles of American government and its relation to the private sector.

NOTES

[1]Most of the statistics presented in this chapter are taken from either of two books published by the U.S. Department of Commerce, Bureau of the Census: *Historical Statistics of the United States, Colonial Times to 1970* (Washington, D.C.: Government Printing Office, 1975) and the annual editions of *Statistical Abstract of the United States.* Statistics from other sources are footnoted.

[2]William W. Lammers, *Public Policy and the Aging* (Washington, D.C.: Congressional Quarterly Press, 1983), p. 17.

[3]*Time,* September 19, 1983, p. 28.

[4]Alan S. Blinder, "The Level and Distribution of Economic Well-Being," in Martin Feldstein, ed., *The American Economy in Transition* (Chicago: University of Chicago Press, 1980), p. 423.

[5]*National Journal,* August 29, 1983, p. 1557.

[6]Internal Revenue Service, *Statistics of Income, 1978 Individual Income Tax Returns* (Washington, D.C.: Government Printing Office, 1978).

[7]National Commission on Excellence in Education, *A Nation at Risk: The Imperative for Educational Reform* (Washington, D.C.: Government Printing Office, 1983).

[8]Benjamin J. Stein, "Valley Girls View the World," *Public Opinion,* August/September 1983, pp. 18, 19.

[9]C. Wright Mills, *The Power Elite* (New York: Oxford University Press, 1956), chapter 4.

[10]Still the classic work is Vance Packard, *The Hidden Persuaders* (New York: David McKay, 1957). Also see Joe McGinniss, *The Selling of the President, 1968* (New York: Trident, 1969).

BIBLIOGRAPHY

Baumol, William. *Welfare Economics and a Theory of the State.* Cambridge: Harvard University Press, 1952. An excellent illustration of the use of economics to explain politics.

Buchanan, James, and Gordon Tullock. *The Calculus of Consent.* Ann Arbor: University of Michigan Press, 1962. A detailed introduction to the application of rational choice theory to political and economic phenomena.

Coase, Ronald H. "The Problem of Social Cost." *Journal of Law and Economics* (October 1960): pp. 1–44. A brilliant exploration of the problem of costs and benefits; especially useful for understanding government intervention in the economy.

Heilbroner, Robert. *The Worldly Philosophers.* 3rd ed. New York: Simon & Schuster, 1967. A clear exposition of the ideas of major economists; particularly attentive to their contributions to the relationship between economics and government.

Lebergott, Stanley. *Wealth and Want.* Princeton, N.J.: Princeton University Press, 1975. A succinct summary of changes in American life-styles and economic status.

Oliver, J. M. *Law and Economics.* London: Allen & Unwin, 1979. An excellent introduction to the relationships between law and the economic order.

Polanyi, Karl. *The Livelihood of Man.* New York: Academic Press, 1977. A brilliant study of the variations in political-economic arrangements that have been found throughout history.

Reagan, Michael. *The Managed Economy.* New York: Oxford University Press, 1963. A description of the interface between government and business.

Stein, Herbert A. *The Fiscal Revolution in America.* Chicago: University of Chicago Press, 1969. An exposition of how changing economic theories led to changes in American public policy.

Nation Building: Constitution and Commerce

M any people view politics as a game. In many ways, their observation is correct. Both politics and games—such as baseball, chess, and tennis—blend cooperation and competition; the participants agree to abide by certain rules and schedules, but they also compete within that framework. In both cases, a structure of authority, or a system of imposing costs, or both, exist to enforce the rules. Finally, in both systems, there are procedures by which existing rules can be changed: for example, professional baseball is played differently today than it was in 1900. And in the American system, the Constitution, the document containing the fundamental rules under which every aspect of the game of politics is played, can be changed too.

A constitution has certain characteristics that distinguish it from ordinary laws and regulations. First, it is paramount. Any conflict between a constitution and an ordinary law or regulation is resolved in favor of the former. Second, government is involved in virtually every activity of its citizens from birth to death or, as one person put it, from the womb to the tomb. Therefore, unless a constitution is to take up thousands of pages, it must be written in broad, general principles. Many of the phrases in the United States Constitution, such as "The President, Vice President, and all civil Officers of the United States shall be removed from Office on Impeachment for, and Conviction of, Treason, Bribery, or other High Crimes and Misdemeanors," have no obvious meaning. Instead, they require interpretation. What is a "high crime"? What is a "misdemeanor"? Furthermore, the Constitution was written in 1787, and words often change their meaning over time. For example, *misdemeanor* might have had a different ordinary meaning two hundred years ago than it has today.

Our first task, then, is to understand the historical context of the Constitution. What were the ideas of the American Founders? What principles guided them in preparing the Constitution? What problems were they trying to solve? Why did they think that the document they wrote would and should survive for numerous generations? We must, in short, get into the minds of the Founders in order to understand the Constitution that controls us today. First, we will look at the intellectual tradition of which they were part—the Enlightenment. Then, we will examine the practical and theoretical problems that they tried to solve in the Constitution. Finally, we will discuss why they constructed each of the three branches of the federal government as they did.

THE ROOTS OF THE CONSTITUTION

The Enlightenment

During the seventeenth and eighteenth centuries, the Enlightenment, a dramatic change in how thinking people viewed the world, took place.[1] The major figures in the Enlightenment shared a common way of looking at the world, and many of them addressed a common set of problems. Two important prin ciples guided them. The first was that through investigation and reason, people could discover useful knowledge; the second was that the application of such knowledge could promote humankind's well-being and happiness. Although these principles are taken for granted today, in the seventeenth century, they constituted a revolutionary break from Europe's medieval past. Until then, religious faith had been the accepted means of obtaining knowledge, and investigation largely consisted of interpreting the Bible, rather than investigating the world. Prior to the Enlightenment, progress—the idea that things could change for the better—was almost unthinkable. The fundamental approach to the human condition had been passive reliance on the will of God. Few believed that the application of knowledge through reason could lead to human betterment.

Although it is outside the scope of this book to analyze the development of the Enlightenment, several contributing factors should be noted. The first was the rise of science and the development of new mathematical tools. Isaac Newton, whose discoveries in physics and mathematics revolutionized these areas of learning, typified this factor. Next, the discovery of new lands, which, in turn, resulted in extensive foreign travel and greatly expanded trade opportunities, opened the eyes of many to different cultures and religious traditions. In addition, traditions older than Christianity, notably those of ancient Greece and Rome, were intensively reexamined. Finally, the spur of capitalism, notably in England, improved material life and changed the way people thought about the possibility of human advancement.

Adam Smith and the American Founders, in different but related ways, typify the Enlightenment. Smith sought to discover the causes of the differences in economic conditions between societies and in particular societies over time. In doing so, he used available evidence and reason. Religious faith played no role in his investigation. The conclusions that he drew led to a set of recommendations about the proper relationship between government and the economy. But Smith, like many other Enlightenment figures, was not an unreserved optimist. Although he advocated free markets as the best solution to the problem of material progress in most situations and, therefore, rejected most government intervention, his study of human psychology led him to conclude that businessmen would often try to use the state for their own selfish advantage, contrary to society's best interests.

Alexander Hamilton and James Madison were the most important figures in the development of the United States Constitution. They and their fellow Founders also took a skeptical view of human nature in looking at the preservation of individual liberty. They, too, examined the available evidence on the relationship of government and the liberty of individuals. By looking at the governments of classical Greece and Rome, as well as those of medieval and contemporary European governments, they reached an important conclusion about human psychology: many people, including rulers and those who are politically ambitious, will seek to benefit themselves at the expense of others. Some may seek power, others wealth, and still others, glory. Thus, there is a

Portraits of James Madison, left (The Bettmann Archive, Inc.), and Alexander Hamilton, right (from a painting by Trumbell/The Bettmann Archive, Inc.)

strong possibility of tyranny as long as it is advantageous for one person (or group) to exploit another person (or group).

Madison summarized the problem in one of his most famous writings, *The Federalist*, no. 51: "If men were angels, no government would be necessary. If angels were to govern men, neither external nor internal controls on government would be necessary." But men are not angels. Therefore, the task that Madison, Hamilton, and the other Founders set out to accomplish was to construct a government that would guard against tyranny and preserve individual liberty. In like manner, Adam Smith, in *The Wealth of Nations*, tried to construct an economy that would flourish, concluding that the political system that best preserved "natural liberty" corresponded to the best economic system—one that minimized state interference. For Smith, a complex view on what a government should and should not do was the solution (his view was often oversimplified by later commentators). For the American Founders, the solution—the Constitution—was more concrete. The Founders considered the Constitution to be the embodiment of a science of government. Unlike other ruling bodies, which grew in response to struggles and clashes over the years, the American government was deliberately constructed using the best knowledge of the Enlightenment. According to the historian J. R. Pole, the Constitution was commonly compared to the cosmic order discovered by Isaac Newton.[2] And interestingly, the concept of liberty, which was very important to the Founders, derives, in part, from Newton's physics.

Liberty and Rights

We owe much of our understanding of both the Declaration of Independence and the Constitution to historian Carl Becker, who demonstrated the important connections between eighteenth-century American thought and the work of

Isaac Newton.[3] This is not to say that all of the American Founders were scholars of physics, but rather that the style and substance of Newton's thought had become popularized and thus had influenced American leaders. Newton discovered that there is a natural order to the physical universe and that this order can be discovered by reason and investigation. In contrast to medieval thought, which focused upon God, nature became the focus of investigation in the Enlightenment; God was assumed to have created an order in nature, after which it became self-operating. This view influenced certain thinkers to try to discover the nature of the social world—that is, God's design for the world of people. For this reason, Enlightenment thinkers—most importantly the English philosopher John Locke (1632–1704)—tried to discover a *natural order* of humankind and the **natural rights** of individuals.[4] These ideas, which were derived from Newton, were important in both the Declaration of Independence and the Constitution.

Like other Enlightenment figures, Locke was unhappy with the unlimited power of kings, who frequently ruled badly or arbitrarily and oppressed their subjects. Such arbitrariness was the very opposite of the social order that paralleled the physical order Newton had discovered in the world. Order implied regular patterns and limits, not the unchecked ability of rulers to do anything that they wanted. Therefore, Locke reasoned that God could not have meant for people to live under such disorderly governments. And so he asked,

natural rights: The doctrine that individuals have certain rights by virtue of the laws of nature, including life, liberty, and the right to hold and dispose of property.

JAMES MADISON ON PROPERTY AND LIBERTY

This term [*property*] in its particular application means "that domination which one man claims and exercises over the external things of the world, in exclusion of every other individual."

In its larger and juster meaning, it embraces every thing to which a man may attach a value and have a right; and *which leaves to every one else the like advantage.*

In the former sense, a man's land, or merchandize, or money is called his property.

In the latter sense, a man has property in his opinions and the free communication of them.

He has a property of peculiar value in his religious opinions, and in the profession and practice dictated by them.

He has property very dear to him in the safety and liberty of his person.

He has an equal property in the free use of his faculties and free choice of the objects on which to employ them.

In a word, as a man is said to have a right to his property, he may be equally said to have a property in his rights.

Where an excess of power prevails, property of no sort is duly respected. No man is safe in his opinions, his person, his faculties or his possessions.

Where there is an excess of liberty, the effect is the same, tho' from an opposite cause.

Government is instituted to protect property of every sort; as well that which lies in the various rights of individuals, as that which the term particularly expresses. This being the end of government, that alone is a *just* government, which *impartially* secures to every man, whatever is his *own*. . . .

Conscience is the most sacred of all property; other property depending in part on positive law, the exercise of that, being a natural and inalienable right. To guard a man's house as his castle, to pay public and enforce private debts with the most exact faith, can give no title to invade a man's conscience which is more sacred than his castle. . . .

Source: *National Gazette*, March 29, 1792.

what kind of government *is* in keeping with the laws of human nature?

The style of reasoning that Locke used to reach his conclusions is unusual by modern standards; nevertheless, its influence upon the American Constitution and the ideas of liberty and rights was enormous. Locke was not interested in discovering a history of the human race, but in developing a theory of human nature and the relationship of government to it.

He began by observing that reason is the most important capacity that God gave to people; reason is an essential part of human nature. Next, he noted that people primarily want to be secure in their life, health, liberty, and possessions. But how is one to be secure? Individually, one cannot protect his or her security; for example, if government did not exist, a group of five people could forcefully deprive one person of his or her property. Therefore, Locke argued, reason leads us to surrender only as much power to government as will allow it to assure that our lives, health, liberty, and property are secure. This describes Americans' contract with their government. The United States government may make rules for the preceding purposes—and those purposes only. Americans, in turn, agree to abide by these rules as long as their rulers uphold their responsibilities under this agreement. If citizens disobey these rules, government can punish them. And if government violates this agreement, the citizens can reject it.

Of course, this argument is in many ways fiction. None of us ever explicitly entered into such an agreement. But to the eighteenth-century mind, the argument was a powerful one that was widely believed. More important, it provided the justification for American independence and contributed to the Constitution. From this argument, we can understand the ringing language of the Declaration of Independence that all men "are endowed by their Creator with certain unalienable rights, that among these are Life, Liberty and the pursuit of Happiness. That to secure these rights, Governments are instituted among Men, deriving their just powers from the consent of the governed." Further, we can see why it was important that the Declaration of Independence set forth a lengthy list of British acts that violated these fundamental rights. These violations were so serious that the American colonists had the right to declare their independence from the government of Great Britain. Thus, it can be seen that Newton's ideas on the physical universe ultimately contributed to the American Revolution of 1776.

Let us look more closely at the ideas of rights and liberty that underlie the Declaration of Independence, the United States Constitution, Adam Smith's *The Wealth of Nations,* and many other Enlightenment writings. To be sure, there were important differences among the abovementioned documents, as well as among both the many Enlightenment thinkers and the American Founders. Nevertheless, most of them shared the central ideas of rights and liberty. In their view, people were granted a large private sphere in which to individually pursue and enjoy their lives and their property—which included their thoughts—without government intervention. People had the liberty to pursue their rights, as long as they did not deprive others of their life, liberty, or property against their will. Government existed for the sole purpose of securing these rights, and so, for example, it could outlaw theft and murder. But it could not take an individual's life, liberty, or property unless that person interfered with another person's right to the same. This was the natural function of the laws of government.

liberty: Security under the rule of just laws.

Liberty, then, was seen as security under the rule of *just laws*—those laws that were impartially administered and designed to protect the natural rights of individuals. These central ideas are as consistent with limited monarchy, which was supported by Adam Smith, as they are with a republic, which was supported by Alexander Hamilton and James Madison. As we will discover in our examination of the Constitution, these ideas have nothing to do with majority rule (i.e., the theory that the main job of government is to carry out policies that the majority desire). The protection of private rights, not democ-

A page from Peter Zenger's newspaper, dated November 12, 1733, advocating freedom of the press. (New York Public Library Picture Collection)

racy, was uppermost in the minds of the American Founders as they prepared the Constitution. In fact, many of them looked upon majority rule with horror; they realized that tyranny could be instituted by majorities as well as by monarchies and aristocracies. To the Founders, a government was theoretically unjust if it deprived a single person of his or her rights without proper cause, even if the rest of the people supported that deprivation.

This illustrates what the Founders saw as the fundamental problem of government: it is one thing to decide upon general principles and a theory of what government ought to do and not do; it is quite another thing to design a government that can carry out those principles and that theory. This was the major task of those who shaped the American Constitution. In this task, they had a valuable tool—the doctrine of the separation of powers, advocated by another important Enlightenment thinker, the baron de Montesquieu (1689–1755).[5]

Separation of Powers

Montesquieu, born of French aristocratic parents, was typical of the major Enlightenment figures. He was learned in virtually every field, including the arts, natural sciences, history, and what we now call the social sciences. He wrote many important works; *On The Spirit of the Laws*, which took him fourteen years to write, is considered his masterpiece. The book brings together learning in politics, social life, economics, religion, and many other subjects. Translated into English in 1750, it influenced the American Founders almost immediately. Among Montesquieu's most important arguments was his advocacy of the separation-of-powers doctrine. His argument was accepted by most of the American Founders (Thomas Jefferson, who played no role in the preparation of the Constitution, was a major exception). They conceived the separation of powers as a major means of protecting natural rights. Accordingly, the Constitution as a whole was designed to carry out the doctrine, and each part of the original Constitution was expected to be consistent with the doctrine.

A central problem posed by government and those who occupy high positions in it is how to guard against abuse of the government's power. The American Founders held that while government should exist to secure rights, many governments had trampled the natural rights of individuals. Some system must therefore be instituted that controls leaders but at the same time allows them to protect the private sphere. The separation of powers was intended to be that system of control. Its underlying plan is to allocate power among the three branches of government—the executive, legislative, and judicial—in such a way that if one branch moves in the direction of tyranny, either of the other two will be able to check that movement. Thus, for example, in the American constitutional system, if Congress enacts tyrannical laws, the president has the power to veto them and the courts have the power to declare them unconstitutional.

The purpose of the separation-of-powers doctrine was concisely summed up by Louis Brandeis, one of our most famous Supreme Court justices: "The doctrine of the separation of powers was adopted by the convention of 1787 not to promote efficiency but to preclude the exercise of arbitrary power. The purpose was not to avoid friction, but by means of the inevitable friction incident to the distribution of governmental powers among three departments, to save the people from autocracy."[6]

One of the most dramatic examples of the separation-of-powers principle in action concerns President Richard Nixon, who was reelected in 1972 by an overwhelming majority to exercise the great powers of the presidency for a second term. Less than two years later, however, forced by the Supreme Court to surrender damaging evidence about illegal activities and charged by a committee of Congress with obstructing justice and abusing the powers of the presidency, Nixon was powerless to prevent his probable removal from office and was forced to resign. Of course, this episode is an extreme example of the clash of powers built into the American constitutional system; yet the principle operates, less dramatically, on a day-to-day basis. To the Founders, the institutions and fundamental laws embodying the separation-of-powers doctrine—not issues, personalities, or political strategies—would lay at the heart of American government and politics.

The framers of the American Constitution realized that other mechanisms exist to protect natural rights. However, they believed that without the support of the separation of powers, these mechanisms—for example, elections—would be insufficient. Throughout history, tyrants, such as Adolf Hitler, have used elections to reinforce their own tyranny and suppress the rights of others. Similarly, many tyrannical nations have constitutions defining the limits of what government may do and bills of rights that are intended to protect the individual. The Soviet Union, one of the most brutal tyrannies in the world, has both. The problem is, of course, that if it is left to government rulers to enforce limits against themselves, they will often either disregard them or interpret them to their own advantage. As the case of the Soviet Union shows, tyrants can no more be trusted to voluntarily restrain their power than foxes can be trusted to guard chicken coops. The American framers, then, did not reject elections, formal limits on power, or a bill of rights. They heartily endorsed each of these mechanisms, but knew that alone or even in combination they were insufficient to protect natural rights. To them, the separation of powers provided the most important protection of natural rights, integrity of elections, formal limits on powers, and a bill of rights.

According to the separation-of-powers doctrine, there are three distinct functions of government: the legislative, the executive, and the judicial. The *legislative function* consists of making laws as well as amending or revoking those already enacted. It also entails funding the administration of the laws. The *executive function* includes carrying out the laws, providing security to the public, defending the country against invasion, and conducting foreign policy. The *judicial function* consists of settling disputes that arise between individuals, punishing criminals, and protecting the rights of individuals from attacks upon them by government or other individuals. These definitions followed the historical development of the British system, which, as it grew increasingly more complex over the centuries, divided political labor in this way.

However, this particular division of government functions is not the critical aspect of the separation-of-powers doctrine. Political functions may be divided in other ways; for instance, nothing in the doctrine conflicts with dividing them into four, five, or more categories, each with its own institutions of government. The functional separation of government tasks, although sometimes confused with the separation-of-powers doctrine, is only the starting point.

Under the doctrine, the only way to check the abuse of power vested in one function is through the exercise of power vested in another. Since those whose rights are being violated are usually powerless to withstand the destruction of their rights, the separation-of-powers doctrine calls for the designing of government in such a way that power is checked by power. In the example of Richard Nixon's presidency, the power of the presidency was checked by the powers of Congress (i.e., the legislative power) and the courts (i.e., the judicial power).

The first solution, then, to the problem of using power as a check against power was to give each part of government a degree of authority over the other parts of government. The president's veto power illustrates this principle—and the intricacy of the Founders' design. Under the Constitution, Congress enacts the laws. This is the exercise of the legislative function. But the Constitution also gives the president power to veto bills passed by Congress. (The president must submit a statement of objections if he or she chooses to veto a bill.) Technically, the veto power constitutes the exercise of a legislative function because the president is participating in the making of laws. In the Founders' view, the president, by being given a degree of authority in the affairs of Congress, could thus check its power.

At this point, another problem under the separation-of-powers doctrine arises. If the president's veto power was absolute so that Congress could not overturn the veto under any circumstances, the president would have too much power and Congress would have too little. The president could use the veto power until Congress enacted what he or she wanted. In effect, Congress would be a rubber stamp. To the American Founders, this was an unacceptable tilt of power toward the executive branch. Consequently, they gave Congress the power to override a veto by a two-thirds vote in both the Senate and the House of Representatives. This solution is an example of how the Founders sought to attain the right balance of power against power throughout the Constitution. The Founders believed that the separation of powers was a natural law that would allow the system of government to come back into balance whenever one branch—the executive, legislative, or judicial—overreached itself and created an imbalance. In this respect, the separation-of-powers principle and its embodiment, the Constitution, reflected the Enlightenment. Both Isaac Newton's laws of mechanics and Adam Smith's laws of competition also contained ideas of imbalance coming back into equilibrium through natural laws.

Let us briefly summarize our discussion of the separation of powers so far. The purpose of government is to protect the people in the exercise of their natural rights. The separation-of-powers principle does this by: (1) limiting the powers that government may have, (2) dividing the powers among various departments or parts of government, and (3) creating an institutional structure that sets power against power in such a way that any imbalances will move back into equilibrium. But these good intentions could be defeated if the same group of people seized control of each part of government. If, for example, a group of big-business executives dominated the presidency, the Supreme Court, and both houses of Congress, the institutional structure could become a hollow shell. How can this be guarded against?

Mixed Government, Interests, and Commerce

Like most of the important Enlightenment figures, the American Founders were aware of the social forces outside government. Designing government in a particular way might go far in preserving the private sphere in which people could freely exercise rights. But the social setting outside government also had to contribute. The Founders knew that any government that ruled over an unhappy, poverty-stricken people, with little hope of improving their lives, would be unstable. Most of them believed that the commercial expansion and growing prosperity of the nation would guarantee that the government they designed would not fall into the hands of a small, tightly knit group of people. The Founders held that the commercial development of American society would help to assure that the separation-of-powers principle would work as they expected it to work. Like Adam Smith in the case of Great Britain, James Madison, Alexander Hamilton, and many others expected that the United States would flourish economically. For example, in *The Federalist,* no. 12, Hamilton wrote: "The prosperity of commerce is now perceived and acknowledged by all enlightened statesmen to be the most useful as well as the most productive source of national wealth, and has accordingly become a primary object of their political cares." Madison, in *The Federalist,* no. 14, confidently expected communications and transportation to greatly improve, and commerce to thereby flourish. Like Montesquieu, both men believed that liberty and commerce went hand in hand.

A few American statesmen disagreed with them.[7] Thomas Jefferson, who played no role in the preparation or adoption of the Constitution since he was serving in France as the American ambassador, rejected commerce and industry as the best economic path. In his judgment, people were best off in agricultural communities as self-sufficient, independent farmers. He believed that those who were close to the soil and who largely supported themselves were morally and intellectually superior to those whose labor was just a small part of a larger enterprise. Although Jefferson's America was not to be, his views are nevertheless still held by some Americans. Those who resent and dislike commerce in general or businesspeople in particular, those who look back wistfully to a rural, agricultural America, and those who resent large-scale institutions are Jefferson's heirs. But while these views were an important counterpoint to the development of American life, they did not provide its main theme, even during Jefferson's presidency.

Let us return to how the American Founders expected commerce and economic development to aid in maintaining the political system that the Constitution established. To do so, we must introduce the idea of *mixed government* and understand the difficulty of applying this idea to the United States. The idea is simple: government ought to be formed in such a way that the major groups in society can jointly participate in it. In this way, no single interest in society, no single group or social class can dominate the others. In the seventeenth century, the idea of mixed government was carried even further. Each large group or class in society was to be provided with a branch or part of government, and each would be given the power to check attempts by the others to dominate. At the same time, each would have an opportunity to protect its interests.

British government provided the model for the theorists of mixed government. As that government evolved over the centuries, the king or queen (who was considered to be a class as well as an individual) was represented in the institution of the monarchy, the aristocracy was represented in the House of Lords, and although few people could vote in the seventeenth or eighteenth centuries, the "common" people were represented in the House of Commons. Each of these institutions not only represented the interests of a large group or class, but also was able to check the tendencies of the others to dominate.

The Federalist No. 10 Principle

The major difficulty in applying the British mixed-government model to the United States was that neither the monarchy nor the aristocracy existed here. But clearly, it was necessary to arrange political competition so that no one group or class could dominate each part of government. The solution, developed by James Madison, has come to be called *The Federalist no. 10 principle* because it is contained in *The Federalist*, no. 10, which Madison wrote (see box on p. 38). Remember, the principle depends for its successful application on the development of a complex nation in which the division of labor and the number of occupations have proceeded far—in other words, a commercial nation rather than a simple agricultural one.

Madison believed that most people are primarily motivated by what they think is their self-interest. According to Adam Smith, most individuals are principally motivated by their "own gain." In business activities, people enter into arrangements that will increase their wealth. All other things being equal, a person will prefer a higher profit or wage to a lower one. A person in business will incur the cost of investing money in a company in order to reap the benefit

EXCERPTS FROM *THE FEDERALIST*, NO. 10, BY JAMES MADISON

Among the numerous advantages promised by a well-constructed Union, none deserves to be more accurately developed than its tendency to break and control the violence of faction. . . .

By a faction I understand a number of citizens, whether amounting to a majority or minority of the whole, who are united and actuated by some common impulse of passion, or of interest, adverse to the rights of other citizens, or to the permanent and aggregate interests of the community.

There are two methods of curing the mischiefs of faction: the one, by removing its causes; the other, by controlling its effects.

There are again two methods of removing the causes of faction: the one, by destroying the liberty which is essential to its existence; the other, by giving to every citizen the same opinions, the same passions, and the same interests.

It could never be more truly said than of the first remedy that it was worse than the disease. Liberty is to faction what air is to fire, an aliment without which it instantly expires. But it could not be a less folly to abolish liberty, which is essential to political life, because it nourishes faction than it would be to wish the annihilation of air, which is essential to animal life, because it imparts to fire its destructive agency.

The second expedient is as impracticable as the first would be unwise. As long as the reason of man continues fallible, and he is at liberty to exercise it, different opinions will be formed. As long as the connection subsists between his reason and his self-love, his opinions and his passions will have a reciprocal influence on each other; and the former will be objects to which the latter will attach themselves. The diversity in the faculties of men, from which the rights

of property originate, is not less an insuperable obstacle to a uniformity of interests. The protection of these faculties is the first object of government. From the protection of different and unequal faculties of acquiring property, the possession of different degrees and kinds of property immediately results; and from the influence of these on the sentiments and views of the respective proprietors ensues a division of the society into different interests and parties.

The latent causes of faction are thus sown in the nature of man. . . . So strong is this propensity of mankind to fall into mutual animosities that where no substantial occasion presents itself the most frivolous and fanciful distinctions have been sufficient to kindle their unfriendly passions and excite their most violent conflicts. But the most common and durable source of factions has been the various and unequal distribution of property. Those who hold and those who are without property have ever formed distinct interests in society. Those who are creditors, and those who are debtors, fall under a like discrimination. A landed interest, a manufacturing interest, a mercantile interest, a moneyed interest, with many lesser interests, grow up of necessity in civilized nations, and divide them into different classes, actuated by different sentiments and views. The regulation of these various and interfering interests forms the principal task of modern legislation and involves the spirit of party and faction in the necessary and ordinary operations of government. . . .

The inference to which we are brought is that the *causes* of faction cannot be removed and that relief is only to be sought in the means of controlling its *effects*.

If a faction consists of less than a majority, relief

interest group: An organization of people who share a common point of view and who attempt to influence government policies.

of eventually making more money. Just as business activities offer opportunities for gain, so do political activities. Government can be used to redistribute resources, just as the economic market can. A racial minority may use government to end racial discrimination. American steel producers may use government to make it more difficult for foreign competitors to sell steel in this country. When a number of people share the same goal—for instance, ending discrimination or limiting steel imports—they are known as an *interest*. When some of them band together into a formal organization that tries to use government to achieve these goals, they are known as an **interest group.**

is supplied by the republican principle, which enables the majority to defeat its sinister views by regular vote. It may clog the administration, it may convulse the society; but it will be unable to execute and mask its violence under the forms of the Constitution. When a majority is included in a faction, the form of popular government, on the other hand, enables it to sacrifice to its ruling passion or interest both the public good and the rights of other citizens. To secure the public good and private rights against the danger of such a faction, and at the same time to preserve the spirit and the form of popular government, is then the great object to which our inquiries are directed. . . .

From this view of the subject it may be concluded that a pure democracy, by which I mean a society consisting of a small number of citizens, who assemble and administer the government in person, can admit of no cure for the mischiefs of faction. A common passion or interest will, in almost every case, be felt by a majority of the whole; a communication and concert results from the form of government itself; and there is nothing to check the inducements to sacrifice the weaker party or an obnoxious individual. Hence it is that such democracies have ever been spectacles of turbulence and contention; have ever been found incompatible with personal security or the rights of property; and have in general been as short in their lives as they have been violent in their deaths. Theoretic politicians, who have patronized this species of government, have erroneously supposed that by reducing mankind to a perfect equality in their political rights, they would at the same time be perfectly equalized and assimilated in their possessions, their opinions, and their passions. . . .

The other point of difference is the greater number of citizens and extent of territory which may be brought within the compass of republican than of democratic government; and it is this circumstance principally which renders factious combinations less to be dreaded in the former than in the latter. The smaller the society, the fewer probably will be the distinct parties and interests composing it; the fewer the distinct parties and interests, the more frequently will a majority be found of the same party; and the smaller the number of individuals composing a majority, and the smaller the compass within which they are placed, the more easily will they concert and execute their plans of oppression. Extend the sphere and you take in a greater variety of parties and interests; you make it less probable that a majority of the whole will have a common motive to invade the rights of other citizens; or if such a common motive exists, it will be more difficult for all who feel it to discover their own strength and to act in unison with each other. Besides other impediments, it may be remarked that, where there is a consciousness of unjust or dishonorable purposes, communication is always checked by distrust in proportion to the number whose concurrence is necessary.

Hence, it clearly appears that the same advantage which a republic has over a democracy in controlling the effects of faction is enjoyed by a large over a small republic—is enjoyed by the Union over the States composing it. . . .

As a nation grows more complex, the number of interests and interest groups increases. According to Madison, in *The Federalist,* no. 10, "A landed interest, a manufacturing interest, a mercantile interest, a moneyed interest with many lesser interests grow up of necessity in civilized nations, and divide them into different classes, actuated by different sentiments and views." Consider the complexity and division of interests today compared to the time when Madison wrote these lines. What he called the "moneyed interest" is now divided into large and small commercial banks, savings-and-loan associations, mutual savings banks, credit unions, finance companies, money-market funds, and no

public interest: The interest of the entire population—or a majority of it—in contrast to a special interest.

on, each with its own organization that attempts to use government to achieve specific goals. This development has also occurred in social and other areas. Madison, as we will see, would have viewed this development favorably.

Interests and interest groups usually believe that their particular narrow concerns are in the **public interest.** But insofar as they use government to gain what they want, other interests lose. For example, if environmentalists prevent mining activities on public lands, mining interests lose—just as allowing mining on public lands means that environmentalists lose. Virtually every governmental decision involves winners and losers.

If one side in a controversy consistently lost, its rights could be violated. Worse, the loser might withdraw its support of governmental institutions. This, of course, would undermine the stability of the country. Madison called this outcome, as well as continuous disregard of minority rights and the public interest, the "mischiefs of faction." He then examined how the effects of the mischiefs of faction could be controlled.

He rejected, at the outset, majority rule as a solution because a majority interest controlling a majority of Congress would disregard the rights of minorities as well as the public interest. Madison's approach to the problem consisted of two parts: *refinement* and *enlargement*; the former was a matter of governmental structure, while the latter constituted his view of the direction in which the nation was, and should have been, moving. Refinement consisted of having select groups of people intermediate in the process between public choice and the selection of government officials. For example, when we vote for president, we are technically not voting for a president at all but for a select body known as electors, who in turn choose the president. We do not vote for judges, cabinet secretaries, or heads of administrative agencies in our national government. Finally, the Constitution originally provided for the choosing of

1789 SALARIES OF PUBLIC OFFICIALS IN THE STATE OF FRANKLIN

Before its admission to the Union in 1796, Tennessee was known as the state of Franklin. In 1789, the Franklin legislature enacted a statute setting up a pay scale for public officials. Their annual salaries were as follows:

Governor: 1,000 deer skins
Attorney general: 500 deer skins
Secretary of state: 500 raccoon skins
Secretary of treasury: 500 otter skins
County clerks: 300 beaver skins

In addition, justices of the peace received a fee of 1 muskrat skin for signing a warrant, and ministers of the gospel were paid 8 mink skins for performing a marriage.

Source: Ross M. Robertson, *History of the American Economy,* 3rd ed. (New York: Harcourt Brace Jovanovich, 1973), p. 73.

United States senators by state legislatures. However, this system was replaced by the direct public election of senators in 1913, when the Seventeenth Amendment was adopted.

In short, in the American national government, we only vote directly for senators and members of the House of Representatives. The underlying reason is that Madison and the other Founders intentionally built the theory of refinement into the Constitution. According to Madison, the persons in intermediate bodies such as the electoral college or state legislatures are more likely to select officials devoted to the public interest than are the relatively uninformed mass of voters who are more likely to consider only their narrow interests. (In contrast to the federal government, in all of the states, the people directly elect the governor, and in many states they choose state officials and judges. In Texas, for example, voters select the commissioner of agriculture and members of the Railroad Commission.)

Of course, Madison conceded that the process of refinement is not foolproof, because select intermediate groups might consist of corrupt or narrow-minded people. In any event, with the direct election of United States senators and the fact that, in practice, we do vote for president and not electors, American political institutions have tended to move away from refinement. Even so, it still plays some role in the national system.

Madison put much greater stock in *enlargement* than refinement as the answer to the mischiefs of faction. One way to introduce the idea of enlargement is to point to the fact that big cities, such as New York and Chicago, are more likely to be open to different viewpoints and unusual life-styles than are small towns, which are frequently intolerant to such viewpoints and life-styles. This general observation is as true of France or Japan, for example, as it is of the United States.

According to Madison's enlargement concept, the larger a unit, the greater the number of interests within it will probably be. Large American cities, for example, have many more economic interests, ethnic groups, religions, and so on, than do small towns. The same comparison applies (1) to complex societies based upon commerce in contrast to simpler, predominantly agricultural societies, and (2) to Congress versus state legislatures. As Madison stated, "The smaller the society, the fewer probably will be the distinct . . . interests composing it." As a result, the larger the society, the less likely it is that any single interest will be a majority. A simple set of examples will illustrate the principle. In a two-interest society, the composition of interests might look like this: $A = 75\%$ and $B = 25\%$. The possibility of interest A being able to suppress the rights of interest B is quite high. Now let us take a second example, that of a large society in which there are nine interests. The composition of interests might look like this: $A = 25\%$, $B = 20\%$, $C = 15\%$, $D = 10\%$, $E = 10\%$, $F = 5\%$, $G = 5\%$, $H = 5\%$, and $I = 5\%$. The possibility of any interest suppressing the rights of others in the second example is far lower than in the first example.

First, the transaction costs that would be required to form a majority in the second example would be high. For example, *A*, with 25 percent, would be the most likely interest to initiate such a coalition. *A* would have to offer something worthwhile to *B* and *C*—the most probable, but not the only possible, coalition—to join it. Second, smaller interests such as *C* have a strong incentive not to enter into such a coalition; it knows that if *D* through *I*'s rights are suppressed, its turn might be next. The same incentive applies to *B*.[8] For these reasons, Madison realized that a large, diverse society containing many interests tends to protect rights. Representation of interests through senators and members of the House of Representatives serves to protect the rights of minorities. The more interests that are represented in Congress, the better. And the larger and more complex the society—the more commercial the society is—the more likely it is that the natural rights of minorities will be protected.

The final step in the Founders' design, then, was to arrange Congress so that large numbers of interests would be represented. They accomplished this by creating the House of Representatives on the basis of territory *and* population. Each state has at least one congressional representative, and states with large populations have many more. Largely populated states are more likely to have many interests, with each of its congressional districts apt to have a different composition of interests than the others. New York State contains, for example, farm districts, ghetto districts, and suburban districts, while North Dakota, with a small population, is more homogeneous. New York City includes both the richest and the poorest congressional districts (in 1980, the Fifteenth Congressional District, on Manhattan's East Side, had a per-capita income of $15,687, while the Eighteenth, in the south Bronx, had a per-capita income of $3,567). Chicago's First Congressional District has a population that is 92 percent black, while that of western Minnesota, western Montana, and northern Wisconsin are each less than 0.1 percent black.

As the nation expanded and grew more complex, more and more interests would be included in the House of Representatives. The House established the enlargement concept, the Senate established the refinement concept, and the entire government structure outlined in the Constitution established the separation-of-powers doctrine. The whole scheme depended for its success upon the nation's growth and economic development. But the Founders were also faced with many practical problems that contributed to the shaping of the Constitution.

THE ROAD TO THE CONSTITUTION

Revolutions tend to follow a pattern, and the American Revolution was no exception. Revolutionaries frequently constitute an unstable coalition of many interests and views. From 1776 to 1789, the uneasy coalition that had successfully beaten the British formed a very weak central government.

Thirteen states with relatively independent governments, different religions, and different economies do not constitute a unified nation. When we add to these differences the sharp divisions over such major policy issues as (1) slavery and its spread and (2) whether the nation should take the road of commerce and economic development or the Jeffersonian path of small-scale agriculture, we can see that the task of nation-building was formidable indeed. Therefore, it is not surprising that at the outset, the states chose as less costly to their interests the path of *confederation*—a formal agreement among the states that surrendered few powers to a central authority.

The document that organized the states from shortly after the Revolution until the adoption of the Constitution was the **Articles of Confederation.** The Articles, which issued from the Continental Congress in 1777, had been ratified by each of the thirteen states by 1781. Perhaps the most important aspect of the Articles was that they implanted the germ of nationhood. The first Article stated, "The stile of this confederacy shall be the United States of America." The confederation was vested with relatively few national powers, including the power to wage war, establish a uniform currency, make treaties with foreign countries, and enter into debt for a few purposes. But it had no power to levy taxes to pay for any of these activities; only the states could do that. Nor could the confederation regulate commerce between states. Thus, each state could erect trade barriers between itself and other states in order to protect local interests. And while the confederation could coin money, each state could print whatever notes of currency it liked.

These and other defects hampered trade and commerce, and the economy was in terrible condition while the Articles were in force. Inflation was rampant, and creditors who loaned good money were repaid with virtually worthless paper notes. Prices rose rapidly until 1784, when a severe depression struck and prices declined sharply; producers, especially farmers, went further and further into debt. Under pressure from local producers, several states imposed severe taxes on imports from other states. The Congress, under the Articles, was powerless to reverse the trend that was eroding the development of the national system.

The path to the Constitutional Convention of 1787 had begun innocently enough two years earlier. In 1785, commissioners of Maryland and Virginia agreed upon navigation policies to ease trade moving in the waters shared by both states.[9] They also decided to call another navigation conference, which would include several other states. This proposal was submitted to the legislatures of Maryland and Virginia. James Madison, already seeing the opportunity to overhaul the shape of American government, persuaded the Virginia legislature to broaden the call to include all states in a general conference on commerce. Unfortunately, the conference, which was held in Annapolis, Maryland, during September 1786 was a disappointment. Delegates from only five states attended, and they decided that it would be futile to prepare a general commercial agreement that would cover all of the states.

Alexander Hamilton, the other major actor in the drama of the Constitution, attended the Annapolis conference as a delegate from New York. Under the

Articles of Confederation: The basic document, ratified March 1, 1781, that governed the relations among the states before the ratification of the Constitution.

leadership of Madison and Hamilton, the delegates requested the Congress to call a full-fledged convention that would thoroughly revise the Articles of Confederation in order to help solve the political-economic difficulties of the thirteen states. In February 1787, the Congress, after some hesitation and without mentioning the Annapolis request, endorsed the call for a convention to revise the Articles to begin in Philadelphia in May.

Certain uprisings, however, soon converted this call from one of simply revising the Articles to throwing them into the garbage dump of history and constructing a new government from scratch. In Massachusetts, Daniel Shays, a respected revolutionary war officer, led western Massachusetts farmers in an open rebellion against state authorities. *Shays' Rebellion* was the largest of several violent actions undertaken by poorer elements of society during the 1780s. Although each rebellion was beaten back, the men who assembled in Philadelphia knew that the worsening economic conditions would only lead to more instability. At the same time, they believed that attempts by some states to remedy these poor economic conditions would only worsen things. Rhode Island, for example, flooded itself with paper money and required creditors to accept it.

THE CONSTITUTIONAL CONVENTION

The Founders, the fifty-five delegates to the Constitutional Convention who assembled in Philadelphia during the late spring and early summer of 1787, represented twelve of the thirteen states (Rhode Island did not participate). They were relatively young men of substantial wealth and ability; only four of them were over sixty.

How do we know what the Founders intended? To answer this, we must first look at how the convention was conducted—its general rules and flavor—as well as the events that led to the ratification of the Constitution by state conventions (see Appendix B, the Constitution, Article VII). The rules of the convention, such as secrecy and frequent debate on the same point, were designed to promote careful and honest consideration, rather than quick action and the temptation to make speeches that would appeal to crowds. The Founders viewed it as their job to remain in session until they produced the best constitution possible. And so they sat from May 25 through September 17, 1787, meeting six days each week, drafting the Constitution of the United States. When the document had been completed, according to convention rules, it had to be ratified by nine states before it could be adopted as the law of the land.

Many of the delegates took personal notes of the proceedings, of which Madison's were the most comprehensive.[10] Two other sources of information about the Founders' underlying intentions are available from the period of ratification (1787–1790). The first is the debates of each of the state conventions called to ponder the question of ratification. The second and far more famous source is *The Federalist Papers*. These eighty-five papers, written by John Jay, James Madison, and Alexander Hamilton, were published in New York City newspapers under the name "Publius." The purpose of the papers was to explain and defend the Constitution to the people of New York so that the state convention would ratify it. While historians agree that *The Federalist Papers* had little impact upon the ratification vote in New York State, the papers' patient and full advocacy of each part of the Constitution has led to their acceptance as classics of American political thought. The convention debates, the state debates, and *The Federalist Papers* are not simply documents of historical interest. Rather, to this day, judges and other political actors use these sources to amplify and explain the intention of the Constitution. From these sources, we can learn much of what the Founders intended.

First, they undertook to create an effective government to replace the ineffective one created by the Articles of Confederation. The difficulty they encountered was to balance efficiency against the inefficiencies that always result from the necessary friction between interests and between the branches of government that are part of both *The Federalist* no. 10 idea and the separation-of-powers doctrine. Government would have to function well, but not so smoothly that it could lead to the oppression of natural rights. Therefore, the Founders were concerned with attracting capable and virtuous people to high government service. The concept of refinement, which we discussed earlier, was a solution to this problem. Since government bodies and not the public at large would select every high official except members of the House of Representatives, the Founders believed that better qualified persons would be selected. Today, those men would be shocked by the popularity-contest aspects of many modern elections.

The Founders' second intention was to create a strong, sound, and expanding national economy. (Of course, not everyone shared the Founders' views on how to do this.) Those parts of the Constitution that embody how the Founders wanted the economy to behave reflect their ideology. But do not infer that what they wanted would help only their own interests; rather, they believed that their views would help every class and group in the nation to prosper. For this reason, Article I, Sections 9 and 10, restricts the activities of states in various ways. States may not impose taxes on ships entering from other states. Nor may they coin money, issue paper notes or bills, or alter the terms of contracts already made between persons. Without the consent of Congress, no state can impose a tax on imports or exports, except as absolutely necessary to cover inspection expenses. Generally, powers over interstate and foreign commerce, previously vested in the states, were given to the national government under the Constitution. The purpose of all of these provisions was to reverse the tendency toward limiting markets that characterized the Articles of Confederation period.

The framers' third intention was to produce a document that would be supported by most of the interests in the country. For example, farmers would benefit because the increased power of the national government in foreign

View from City Point near Sea Street, Boston. As this drawing illustrates, commerce was flourishing in the early nineteenth century. (W. Bennett, circa 1810/Bettmann Archive, Inc.)

affairs promised to assist the enlargement of export markets for farm products. Furthermore, under the Constitution, the government's obligation to pay the nation's debts, coupled with the fact that only Congress could coin money, promised stabilized prices for farm products. *The Federalist,* no. 12, promised that the principal source of tax revenue to finance the government would be taxes upon trade, not land. We have already seen how the new Constitution would be advantageous to merchant and manufacturing interests. Creditors, too, would obviously benefit from provisions such as the one prohibiting states from changing the obligations of a contract. Finally, a prospering nation promised a better way for debtors to escape chronic indebtedness than had the schemes that some states devised under the Articles of Confederation.

There is one interest that must be singled out—the slaveholding interest. The records of the Constitutional Convention and numerous other documents showed that most of the Founders viewed slavery as the greatest affront to the rights of individuals. Nevertheless, they were willing to compromise on this issue in order to assure that the three states in which the slaveholding interest was strongest—North Carolina, South Carolina, and Georgia—entered the union. At the Virginia ratifying convention, after denouncing slavery as a great evil, Madison asserted that the southern states would not have entered into the Union of America, without the temporary permission of the slaveholders. In his view, it was important to make concessions to slaveholders in the Constitution—for example, slaves were counted as three-fifths of a person for purposes of representation—because slavery would have continued even if the southern states had not entered the Union. Accordingly, the original Constitution contains several concessions to the slaveholding states, but they have had no effect since the slaves were freed during the Civil War and the Thirteenth Amendment was ratified in 1865.

The fourth general intention of the framers was to produce a document that would be accepted by the states. We must remember that among the Founders' difficult tasks was getting the citizens to transfer their primary loyalty from their particular states to the nation. Not only did the slave states fear that they would be dominated by the free states, but the smaller states, such as New Jersey and Delaware, were equally concerned that they would be overpowered by the larger ones, such as Virginia and New York. At the outset of the convention, two plans—the New Jersey Plan and the Virginia Plan—were presented, which represented the preferences of the small and the large states, respectively. The Virginia Plan called for a two-house legislature, each elected on the basis of population, while the New Jersey Plan called for a one-house legislature in which each state would be equally represented. As with many of the other problems facing the convention, a compromise was reached. The cost of doing so was considered much smaller than the cost that would ensue if an acceptable Constitution was not produced. But these compromises had to fit within the basic separation-of-powers structure of the document.

Limited Government

The solution to transferring the loyalty of citizens from states to the national government lay in the ideas of **limited government** and **federalism.** Theoretically, a system of government can exist that is allowed to do anything, unless it is expressly forbidden to do so by a constitution or other laws. The United States Constitution, although it includes prohibitions on what government can do, goes further: the government cannot do anything that is not authorized under the Constitution. Therefore, a public official cannot lawfully act unless he or she can point to some language in the Constitution that authorizes the action. For example, Article I, Section 8, contains eighteen paragraphs listing the powers of Congress; unless it can point to some authorization in that list, Congress may not legislate on a matter. Thus, Congress could not pass a law requiring all Americans to dye their hair purple because it is not authorized to do so under Article I, Section 8. Yet, because of danger to health, it could ban the transportation of a hair dye from one state to others as it is allowed to "regulate Commerce . . . among the several States."

Federalism

Limited government not only aids people in the protection of their natural rights by imposing strict limits on national government action, but it also protects the states in the exercise of their powers for exactly the same reason. In this respect, limited government complements the principle of federalism,

limited government: A government that is limited, by a constitution or other means, in what it may do and how it may exercise its powers.

federalism: A system of government in which governing power is divided and shared among a central government and state governments.

a system of government that is a compromise between a unitary government, in which all power is located in a central authority, and a confederation, in which nearly all power is located in regional or local governments that surrender only a small portion of power to a central authority. From 1777 to 1787, Americans were organized under the Articles of Confederation. Article II stated, "Each state retains its sovereignty, freedom and independence," while Article III described the confederation as "a firm league of friendship."

Federalism, then, is a divison of governmental power between the national and the regional governments—in this case, the states. Since the national government is limited, a large amount of authority is located in the state governments. But Article VI of the Constitution says, in part, that the Constitution and the laws made under it "shall be the supreme Law of the Land." Any state laws, executive-branch actions, or judicial decisions that are in conflict with the Constitution or with a proper national law cannot be valid. This is the underlying meaning of the so-called **supremacy clause.** Thus, if the state of Nevada decided to coin money, its action would violate the Constitution and would accordingly be unlawful. On the other hand, there are instances in which both the national and the state governments have *concurrent powers*—that is, they may act in an area at the same time. Both the national and state governments may, for example, impose income taxes.

The Constitution says a lot about what state governments *cannot* do and very little about what they *can* do. State governments were already highly developed before the Constitutional Convention—and even before the Declaration of Independence. Colonial charters granted by the British had created a tradition of state government in the country. Beginning with New Hampshire, the states had gradually adopted constitutions in the period from 1776 to 1787. Many of these documents embraced the separation-of-powers doctrine, as well as the principle of limited government. The Virginia Constitution, which provided a bill of rights protecting individual liberties, became a model for other state constitutions, which, in turn, provided models for the United States Constitution. In addition, state governments were the heirs to a long tradition that embraced the practice of government and English legal experience. These traditions charted what the proper functions of state government are.

Thus, the Founders created a federal structure that was a compromise between a unitary government and a confederation. In doing so, they were able to meet the political objections of those who were unwilling to give up all state sovereignty, but who recognized the enormous cost of confederation or the even greater cost of each state going it alone. And in this compromise, the separation-of-powers principle was advanced by further fragmenting power. Not only was power divided between the branches of the national government, but in two other ways as well: it was divided (1) between the states and the national government, and (2) within state governments, which operated according to the separation of powers.

A major fear of the less populated states in accepting the Constitution was that the national government would be dominated by the states with greater

supremacy clause:
Clause in Article VI of the Constitution that asserts that the Constitution, treaties, and national laws are the supreme laws of the land.

populations. As a result, important compromises were reached that gave the smaller states more weight than that to which their populations would have entitled them. First, each state, regardless of population, has two members of the Senate. Second, although representation in the House of Representatives is based upon population, each state, regardless of how small it is, has at least one representative. Third, the composition of the electoral college that chooses the president is based, not upon population, but upon the total number of senators and representatives from each state.

To illustrate how this favors the less populated states, let us look at two states in the 1980 presidential election: Alaska and California. In that year, Alaska had three electors for about 403,000 persons (i.e., one elector for approximately every 134,333 persons), while California had 45 electors for approximately 22,294,000 people (i.e., one elector for every 495,422 persons). This was exactly the balance that the Founders sought to achieve so that the less populated states would ratify the Constitution. And once again, the compromise outcome aided the application of the separation-of-powers principle by further protecting these states and the interests they represent.

Popular Representation

The fifth general intention of the framers was to produce a document that the people would accept. It was, remember, the rumblings of popular discontent that had led to the drastic remedy of scrapping the Articles of Confederation and replacing it with a new form of government. Although the American Founders rejected popular democracy in the sense of majorities being able to dominate government and its policies, they strongly favored the idea of representation. The House of Representatives, the members of which would be elected by the people, was to be the part of government that represented the people's

Emigrants' resting place on road through western Pennsylvania, circa 1790. (New York Public Library Picture Collection)

direct preferences. But representation, they believed, should not be domination. Accordingly, the president, senators, and judges were not to be selected directly by the people. The Founders expected their limited and complex concept of representation to be accepted by the people in the ratification process.

However, the ratification process was not an easy one. In only eight of the thirteen state conventions did lopsided majorities favor ratification. Ratification carried in the greatly populated states of Massachusetts, Virginia, and New York by relatively narrow margins. Massachusetts ratified the Constitution only on the condition that a bill of rights would be added to it; this addition constitutes the first ten amendments to the document. Other opposition was based on local support for state paper-money schemes and for state tariffs on imports that the Constitution would have prohibited, as well as on the fear that state government would be crushed, fear that the president would eventually be a monarch, and fear of the drastic changes the Constitution would entail.

The most important division between the supporters of the Constitution and its opponents was between those persons who envisioned an extended commercial republic and those who sought an idyllic nation of small, self-sufficient agricultural producers. As the eminent historian Jackson T. Main concluded, "But after all these facts have been taken into account, we can return to the major generalization: that the struggle over the ratification of the Constitution was primarily a contest between the commercial and the non-commercial elements in the population."[11] Groups involved in commerce, including farmers and artisans, largely supported the Constitution, while opposition centered among persons isolated from the streams of commerce.

In any event, when Rhode Island became the last of the thirteen states to ratify on May 29, 1790, the issue was closed. The Constitution's basic structure was in place. Although it has been amended many times, most of that structure remains intact to this day.

THE POWERS OF AMERICAN GOVERNMENT

Legislative Power

The Founders' considerable fear of majority rule that could oppress minorities must be kept in mind as we look at the structure of the legislative branch that the Founders devised. Their fear of majority rule was reinforced by the nature of the legislative branch, because it alone has taxing power, controls spending decisions, and is the paymaster of the executive and judicial branches. In short, these two branches can easily become dependent upon the legislature, thereby upsetting the separation-of-powers doctrine. Accordingly, the Founders created several remedies to curtail legislative powers. First, they strengthened the other branches—for example, they created the executive veto. Later in this chapter, we will look at some other ways in which the executive and judicial branches were strengthened. In the following sections, we will look at some of the ways in which the Founders sought to curtail legislative power directly. These include (1) enumeration, (2) bicameralism and the different modes of election to each branch, and (3) the principles of representation.

Enumeration   Article I, Section 8, of the Constitution lists the things that Congress can do. The powers specified are known as **enumerated powers.** These include the power to "borrow Money on the credit of the United States" and "to regulate Commerce with foreign Nations, and among the several States." One of the enumerated powers stands out because of its elasticity: it allows Congress "to make all Laws which shall be necessary and proper for carrying into Execution the foregoing Powers." This broad clause leads to a great expansion of enumerated powers through the concept of **implied powers.**

This concept and its limits were spelled out in 1819 in the famous Supreme Court case of *McCulloch* v. *Maryland.* The case began when Congress passed a law in 1816 creating a national bank. Article I, Section 8, contains no language that specifically permits such legislation. Since such a bank would assist the commercial development of the country, those persons who still sought to create a nation of independent farmers objected to it. In 1818, Maryland imposed a tax on the Baltimore branch of the national bank, which the national government refused to pay. When the Maryland state courts convicted Mr. McCulloch, the cashier of the branch, for refusing to pay the tax, the federal government appealed to the Supreme Court.

John Marshall (1755–1835) was chief justice of the Court from 1801 to 1835. He was just as important in interpreting the Constitution during the republic's early years as were Madison and Hamilton in drafting the document. Marshall used what had been termed the *necessary-and-proper clause* in his decision in *McCulloch* v. *Maryland* to develop the concept of implied powers.

McCulloch v. *Maryland* raised many important questions, including the meaning of the necessary-and-proper clause. The Court unanimously held that the clause allowed Congress to charter a bank—even though that power was not enumerated in Article I, Section 8—because doing so was necessary and proper to the enumerated powers of collecting taxes, borrowing money, regulating commerce, and declaring and conducting war. This decision, then, was the foundation of the idea of implied powers. These powers allowed Congress to select methods, not otherwise forbidden by the Constitution, to carry out all of the other powers enumerated in Article I, Section 8. In the famous conclusion to the decision, Marshall wrote, "Let the end be legitimate, let it be within the scope of the Constitution, and all means which are appropriate, which are plainly adopted to that end, which are not prohibited, but consistent with the letter and spirit of the Constitution, are Constitutional."

As we can see, the bounds of Congress's enumerated powers were widened by the idea of implied powers. But it is wrong to think that they are almost unbounded. Not only do the Constitution's specific prohibitions restrict what Congress may do, but Congress must show that a reasonable relationship exists between its laws and the enumerated powers. To take an extreme ex-

enumerated powers: The powers of government explicitly granted by the Constitution.

implied powers: The constitutional provision in Article I, Section 8, that grants Congress the power to "make all Laws which shall be necessary and proper for carrying into Execution" the enumerated powers. Also called the *elastic clause.*

ample, Congress could not point to the enumerated power to levy taxes as a justification for a law requiring all dog owners to surrender their pets to local pounds. In addition, the enumerated powers are restricted by the Tenth Amendment, which states, "The powers not delegated to the United States by the Constitution, nor prohibited by it to the States, are reserved to the States respectively, or to the people." Much of our constitutional law since the founding has been devoted to determining, in case after case, how all of these restrictions limit Congress's exercise of its enumerated powers.

Bicameralism and the Principles of Representation   The American legislature consists of two parts: the Senate and the House of Representatives. This division (known as *bicameralism*), the different ways of selecting the individuals who would sit in each chamber, and the dissimilar terms of office (six years in the Senate and two in the House) were expected to lead to each chamber developing its own, and in part conflicting, set of interests.

Consider the many differences that exist today, even though senators are now directly elected by the people rather than selected by state legislatures. First of all, senators are elected for six-year terms, with approximately one-third of them being chosen every two years, whereas House members must run for office every other year. And because the Senate contains two members from each state, small-state interests are overrepresented relative to the House, in which state population is the major principle of representation.

Since any law must be passed by both chambers, Madison argued (in *The Federalist,* no. 62) that an infringement upon the rights of the people would become doubly difficult. Of course, he realized that this would also make it harder to enact legislation. But because of the Founders' values and their attitudes about the limited role of government, which emphasized the preservation of natural rights, they were willing to accept this situation. The natural rights of minorities would be even further protected because each chamber of Congress, in which a large number of interests would be represented, would be the embodiment of the *The Federalist* no. 10 principle. Compromise, bargaining, and tolerance of the views of others were the behaviors that the Founders expected from the legislature. And, of course, the powers given to the executive and judicial branches were expected to curb the potential for legislative abuse.

Executive Power

The branch of government that caused the most conceptual difficulty for the Founders was clearly the executive. The judicial and legislative branches could be modeled fairly closely on their British counterparts. But the executive? Copying the British monarchy was clearly out of the question; the abuse inherent in such excessive power was one of the causes of the Revolution. Even so, the Founders saw much that was admirable in the system, particularly the independence of the executive. Thus, the fear of creating too strong an executive and, as a result, a possible monarchy had to be weighed against the value of the president's independence and the need for a symbol of national unity.

These concerns notwithstanding, the Founders rejected the idea of an executive whose sole function is to carry out the will of the legislative branch. Their concern for the power of the legislative branch was greater than their fear of abuse of power by the executive branch. Accordingly, in addition to administering the laws and appointing administrative subordinates, the president was granted the following powers:

1. *legislative powers:* the power to make treaties with the advice and consent of the Senate and to veto legislation enacted by Congress
2. *advisory powers:* the power to recommend legislation to Congress and to call Congress into session
3. *prerogative powers:* the power to receive ambassadors and other foreign officials, to serve as commander-in-chief of the armed forces, and to grant pardons and reprieves

The final version of executive power is far more embracing than the narrow notion suggested by a few delegates early in the convention. The executive was provided with those necessary defenses required under the separation-of-powers principle. Moreover, some of the weight and symbolism attached to the British monarch, so desired by many delegates, was granted to the American president. Before doing so, however, the delegates carefully examined many aspects of the executive institution in order to assure that the executive was neither too powerful nor too weak with respect to the other branches.

The Founders even considered having three presidents who would share power equally. This view was, of course, rejected. To Madison, unifying the executive was a necessary counterweight to dividing the legislative branch: "As the weight of the legislative branch requires that it should be thus divided, the weakness of the executive may require, on the other hand, that it should be fortified." In order for the legislature to exercise a proper degree of control over the executive, the legislature must be able to fix specific responsibility and avoid the possibility of one person throwing such responsibility on the shoulders of another. Only with a single president could this be possible.

Far more deliberation revolved around the question of how the president should be elected. The final solution of election by electors was clearly a compromise, the result of serious dissatisfaction with other proposed alternatives. For example, selection of the executive by the legislature was unacceptable to many of the delegates because it would make the executive a mere puppet of the legislature. There was also considerable opposition to Madison's proposal of popular election due to the fear that "the people are uninformed, and would be misled by a few designing men."

Similarly, the length of the executive term and the question of re-eligibility were problems that were placed in the separation-of-powers context. The dominant view was that the longer the president's term, the more independent of the legislature he or she would be. Proposals to select a president for life, a very long time, or "during good behavior" were rejected on the ground that a long period in office might allow a president to consolidate power and establish a monarchy. A theory to balance these considerations was briefly stated by delegate Gouverneur Morris: "It is [the] most difficult of all rightly to balance the executive. Make him too weak: The Legislature will usurp his powers. Make him too strong: He will usurp on the Legislature." Morris preferred that the executive have a short period in office with the right to run again. A four-year term with the right to run again was the final choice; this system lasted until the Twenty-second Amendment, ratified in 1951, restricted a president to two terms.

As we can see, the Founders carefully considered the method of selecting the president and the term of office. The same can be said about the particulars of the powers that would supplement the traditional executive ones. The power of the president to make treaties with the advice and consent of the Senate illustrates this point. Placing this power in two branches, rather than one, stemmed from the Founders' views that a serious imbalance would occur if that important power was lodged in only one branch. The reason that the Senate, but not the House of Representatives, would be the legislative participant in treaty-making, was that matters relating to foreign policy often must be conducted in secrecy and the participation of so large a body as the House would make confidentiality impossible to maintain.

On the other hand, fear that executive power might expand in a war situation because of the president's position as commander-in-chief compelled the convention to vest in Congress the exclusive power to declare war. However, the Founders distinguished between making war and declaring war, with the former including the authority to repel sudden attacks and to act as commander-in-chief. These two functions, which had to be undertaken rapidly, could not be left in the hands of a slow, deliberative body like Congress.

It was on the problem of the executive veto (or *revisionary power,* as it was called) that the most comprehensive debate in the convention occurred. This executive power over legislation was, as we have seen, at the heart of Madison's development of the separation-of-powers doctrine. The overwhelming sense of the convention is summed up in Madison's statement: "Experience in all the States had evinced a powerful tendency in the Legislature to absorb all power into its vortex. This was the real source of danger to the American Constitution; and suggested the necessity of giving every defensive authority to the other departments that was consistent with republican principles."

The reason for the nearly universal support of a revisionary power stems, not simply from widespread acceptance of the separation-of-power doctrine, but also from a concrete appraisal of what might occur if the doctrine were not implemented. The delegates were aware that in the case of legislative dominance, popular majorities might compel legislatures to pass rash and oppressive laws. Some powers of restraint, such as the veto, were therefore necessary. In Hamilton's words: "The [veto] power . . . not only serves as a shield to the executive, but . . . establishes a salutory check upon the legislative body calculated to guard the community against the effects of faction, precipitancy, or of any impulse unfriendly to the public good, which may happen to influence a majority of that body."

But again the Founders were faced with the difficult problem of balance. An absolute veto—one that Congress could not override—was rejected because it would tilt the balance too far in the direction of executive dominance. Other proposals, including involving the judicial branch in the veto process, were rejected. The final compromise, intended to not vest too much power in either the executive or legislative branches, was an executive veto that could be overridden by a two-thirds vote of both the Senate and the House.

The problem of the grounds for removal of a president and the procedures that should be followed were also treated in terms of achieving just the right balance within a separation-of-powers context. Accordingly, the Founders rejected the extreme positions of Congress (1) being able to remove a president at will and (2) not being able to remove a president while in office. Therefore, the underlying theory was to make the president removable while ensuring that Congress could not do it easily or on frivolous grounds. The Founders came close to designating the Supreme Court as the forum in which an impeachment trial would take place once an impeachment indictment was voted by the House. But they changed the trial forum to the Senate because, after a president was convicted of an impeachment, the Supreme Court might have to hear the case again in a criminal case. This would violate an important principle of British law and the American law derived from it: that a court must hear a case with an open mind.

The final arrangement was to allow the House, by majority vote, to issue "articles of impeachment," which is similar to an indictment by a grand jury in a criminal case. The Senate, with the chief justice of the Supreme Court presiding, then acts like a court to determine whether the president should be convicted. A two-thirds vote of the senators present is required for conviction.

The balance problem is critical for understanding the grounds for impeachment. If the grounds are too broad or vague—for example, the word *maladministration* was considered and rejected—Congress would be able to rid itself of a president virtually at will. But if the grounds were too narrow—for instance, if they consisted of a short list of crimes—the president might be able to continue in office just because the framers had neglected to mention a particular crime. Accordingly, the Founders used the general phrase "High Crimes and Misdemeanors," which mixed the vague and the specific, to describe the type of conduct that should lead to a president's removal.

The Founders carefully considered the particulars of the executive branch, like the legislative, within the context of their guiding prinicples. But oddly, they did not exercise the same care in constructing the judicial branch.

Judicial Power

Of the three branches of government, the Founders gave the least attention to the judicial. Most of their discussions about the judicial branch concerned its possible association with the executive in the veto power, a nonjudicial function. The only other judicial topic seriously debated was how judges would be appointed. Clearly, the judiciary was viewed as a junior partner among the three branches. It was, in Hamilton's famous phrase, considered the "least dangerous" branch. Why? There are several reasons. First, the judicial branch, because it controls neither the sword nor the purse, is not directly involved in taxing or spending, or in war or peace—the major policy issues of society. According to Hamilton, on these issues it "can take no active resolution whatever." It seems not to have occurred to him that the judiciary could shape the direction of policy by forbidding certain conduct.

The Founders also attributed the judiciary's weakness to its lack of support, which resulted from the highly indirect manner of its selection; its permanence in office; and the specialized nature of what it does. Moreover, the judiciary is entirely dependent upon the executive branch to enforce its judgments. Finally, since the judiciary acts upon individual cases and not broad public policy covering classes of people, "individual oppression may now and then proceed from the courts of justice [but] the general liberty of the people can never be endangered from that quarter."

In view of what Hamilton termed the "natural feebleness" of the judiciary, what could be done to prevent it from being overpowered by the other branches? The Founders' principal reliance was on the permanency of the justices' office (i.e., "during good Behavior" rather than a stated number of years). Dependence by the judiciary on the legislature for reappointment could lead to the judges rendering decisions that they believed would please the legislature.

Nevertheless, there is a danger to permanent appointment—the danger of appointing judges with insufficient honesty, knowledge, or both. One means of guarding against this is permitting judges to hold office only during good behavior. Far more important, however, is preventing bad judges from taking office in the first place. This problem ultimately boils down to the question of who appoints the judges. It was feared that appointment by the executive alone would augment the power of the executive over the judiciary, making it a mere tool of the executive. On the other hand, if the power of appointing judges belonged entirely to the legislative branch, responsibility for bad appointments would not be fixed because so many people would be involved. As a result, a compromise was reached whereby the executive would appoint judges with the concurrence of the Senate. In this way, responsibility was fixed, yet a single executive would be prevented from appointing bad judges.

Judicial Review

Article III of the Constitution spells out many functions of the courts in the federal system. However, it says nothing about one of the judiciary's most important functions: **judicial review.**[12] This is the power of the courts to declare a statute or its administrative application in conflict with the Constitution to be null and void. In any conflict between a law and the Constitution, the latter prevails. And it is a function of the courts to make this determination in cases that come before them.

Support for the view that the judicial review function was implied in the Article III phrase "the judicial Power" can be found in the convention debates and *The Federalist Papers*.[13] In *The Federalist*, no. 78, Hamilton stated that a principal judicial function "must be to declare all acts contrary to the manifest tenor of the Constitution void" because "the interpretation of the laws is the proper and peculiar province of the courts." Furthermore, several of the states recognized judicial review in their constitutions or in practice. An early Supreme Court decision, *Hayburn's Case* (1792), implicitly recognized the doctrine. Yet it was not until Chief Justice Marshall's famous 1803 decision in *Marbury* v. *Madison* that the important principle of judicial review was explicitly set forth. According to Marshall, it is the duty of judges to decide what the law is in a particular case. In addition, if two laws conflict with each other, the judicial branch must decide which one applies. Thus, courts must decide if a law and the Constitution conflict; if they do, the courts must strike down the law because the Constitution prevails over ordinary laws. Moreover, he added, judges would violate their oath to support the Constitution if they failed to take the steps outlined.

Since the historic decision of *Marbury* v. *Madison*, judicial review has become an accepted part of our constitutional practice. And like the other parts of the Constitution, it is designed to protect natural rights, especially those of minorities. It has been used to protect all sorts of minorities—racial, economic, political, religious, and the like. Atheists, communists, blacks, Jehovah's Witnesses, business firms, and other minorities have protected their rights through judicial review.

judicial review: The power of the courts to declare legislative and executive actions to be unconstitutional and therefore prohibited.

THE CONSTITUTION IN PERSPECTIVE

We began this chapter by pointing out that the Constitution was intended to develop basic guidelines for the conduct of American life. We saw that the historical context and the basic values of the Founders led them to use a central framework, the separation-of-powers doctrine, which allocated power among branches of government in order to achieve their political and economic ends. They carefully designed the control mechanisms of the Constitution in order to achieve these ends. And in so doing, they were keenly aware of the costs and benefits of each institutional arrangement and alternative that they considered. A complex structure—the Constitution—emerged from their careful thinking. Never before in history had a government been so carefully designed.

The Founders also realized that changes and additions to the Constitution might be necessary from time to time, although they hoped these would be consistent with their vision of a great commercial republic. Constitutional changes should not be easy to make, nor should they be frivolous or the manifestation of some temporary trend. Thus, in Article V, the Founders designed a difficult but not impossible set of procedures to amend the Constitution. The First Congress proposed the Bill of Rights—the first ten amendments—in 1789; they were ratified in late 1791. Since then, many other amendments have been proposed, some of which have been ratified. With the solitary exception of the Eighteenth Amendment (1919), which banned the manufacture, sale, and transportation of liquor, the amendments have been well thought out and not subject to the passions of the moment. In this respect, the Founders' intentions have been largely fulfilled.

The expectation that the Constitution would aid the development of a great commercial republic has also been realized. Such a republic, as Madison pointed out, can protect the rights of minorities. But, as Thomas Jefferson argued, large institutions can submerge the individual. In much of the rest of this book, we will examine this tension and the attempts to resolve it.

NOTES

[1]An indispensable study of the Enlightenment is Peter Gay, *The Enlightenment: An Interpretation*, 2 vols. (New York: Norton, 1977). The bibliographic essay concluding the second volume is especially valuable.

[2]J. R. Pole, "Enlightenment and the Politics of Nature," in Roy Porter and Mikulas Teich, eds., *The Enlightenment in National Context* (Cambridge: Cambridge University Press, 1981), p. 195.

[3]Carl Becker, *The Declaration of Independence* (New York: Knopf, 1922).

[4]The argument is summarized from John Locke's *The Second Treatise of Civil Government*, which was first published in 1690. It is available in many modern editions.

[5]The theory of separation of powers is developed in baron de Montesquieu, *The Spirit of the Laws*, Book XI, which is available in many editions.

[6]Cited in Roscoe Pound, *The Development of Constitutional Guarantees of Liberty* (New Haven: Yale University Press, 1957), p. 94.

[7]See the commentary and documents collected in Michael B. Levy, ed., *Political Thought in America: An Anthology* (Homewood, Illinois: Dorsey, 1982), part III.

[8]See the discussions in Robert A. Dahl, *A Preface to Democratic Theory* (Chicago: University of Chicago Press, 1956), chapter 1, and in William H. Riker, *The Theory of Political Coalitions* (New Haven: Yale University Press, 1962).

[9]There is a vast and controversial literature interpreting the events leading to the Constitutional Convention. Probably the most neutral is the 1905 account of Andrew C. McLaughlin, *The Confederation and the Constitution* (New York: Collier, 1962).

[10]The most comprehensive collection of notes and documents on the Convention is Max Farrand, ed., *The Records of the Federal Convention of 1787*, 4 vols. (New Haven: Yale University Press, 1966).

[11]Jackson T. Main, *The Anti-Federalists* (Chapel Hill, North Carolina: University of North Carolina Press, 1961), p. 280.

[12]An important discussion of judicial review within the context of the separation-of-powers doctrine is M. J. C. Vile, *Constitutionalism and the Separation of Powers* (Oxford: Oxford University Press, 1967), pp. 157–171.

[13]Still the most persuasive argument that the founders intended judicial review to be included within the judicial power is Charles A. Beard, *The Supreme Court and the Constitution* (New York: Macmillan, 1912).

BIBLIOGRAPHY

Beard, Charles. *An Economic Interpretation of the Constitution of the United States.* New York: Macmillan, 1913. A pathbreaking study arguing that the Founders were motivated by economic self-interest in devising and promoting the Constitution. It has spawned a vast body of literature attacking this thesis.

———. *The Supreme Court and the Constitution.* New York: Macmillan, 1912. A history of the concept of judicial review through *Marbury* v. *Madison.*

Becker, Carl. *The Declaration of Independence.* New York: Knopf, 1922. A leading examination of the meaning and origin of the Declaration of Independence.

Corwin, Edwin S. *The "Higher Law" Background of American Constitutional Law.* Ithaca: Cornell University Press, 1955. The classic discussion of the idea of constitutionalism.

Farrand, Max. *The Framing of the Constitution of the United States.* New Haven: Yale University Press, 1913. A clear and detailed exposition of the Constitutional Convention of 1787.

———, ed. *The Records of the Federal Convention of 1787.* 4 vols. New Haven: Yale University Press, 1966. The most comprehensive collection of notes and documents pertaining to the Constitutional Convention.

Gay, Peter. *The Enlightenment: An Interpretation.* 2 vols. New York: Norton, 1977. An outstanding study of the Enlightenment and its influence on the founding of the United States.

Hamilton, Alexander, John Jay, and James Madison. *The Federalist Papers.* 1788. Historic articles explaining the provisions of the Constitution, prepared by three of its leading advocates. Available in many editions.

Levy, Michael B., ed. *Political Thought in America: An Anthology.* Homewood, Illinois: Dorsey, 1982. A carefully selected collection of documents on American political thought, with perceptive commentaries by the editor.

Main, Jackson T. *The Anti-Federalists.* Chapel Hill, North Carolina: University of North Carolina Press, 1961. A sympathetic study of the critics of the Constitution.

McLaughlin, Andrew C. *The Confederation and the Constitution.* New York: Collier, 1962. A lucid exposition of the events that led to the Constitution and the response of the Founders to them.

Vile, M. J. C. *Constitutionalism and the Separation of Powers.* Oxford: Oxford University Press, 1967. One of the best expositions of the doctrines underlying the Constitution.

PART II

LINKAGES: THE PEOPLE AND THE GOVERNMENT

CHAPTER 3

Participation and Interest Groups

In 1790, at the time of the first census, the American population numbered 3,929,214. Only 5 percent of the population lived in cities (defined then as areas with populations over 2,500). Fifty years later, the population had grown to 17,069,453, an increase that reflected the attraction that the new country held for people from many nations. By the end of the nineteenth century, an enormous number of immigrants was pouring into Ellis Island in New York Harbor for processing and acceptance into their new home; from 1841 through 1930, about 37 million Europeans moved to the United States. Industrialization, urbanization, improved medical care, and many other factors contributed to a steady increase in the size of the American population, and by 1980 it numbered 226,504,825.

As the number of people in the United States grew, the character of American society changed. Simply stated, life became more complicated. Today, the United States is a society in which information and organization have become fundamental parts of our personal and working lives. Most Americans face a vastly greater number of opportunities for spending their time and money than did their grandparents. As society has grown more complex, so has the task of managing our lives; at the same time that government has extended further into the daily affairs of Americans, the challenge of trying to influence it has simultaneously become greater. In this chapter, we will examine the ways in which that complexity shapes the behavior of citizens as they try to participate in political decisionmaking.

Americans are faced with an often bewildering array of political choices. While some of these are simplified by various rules, laws, and procedures (such as the primary election system, which reduces the number of candidates in the general election), many are so complicated that large numbers of citizens decide not to choose at all. For example, consider the variety of tasks that a thorough and conscientious voter must undertake in picking a candidate.

Mary Smith has a college education, a promising career, an interest in current events, and two children, about whose future she is very concerned. During a presidential election campaign, she focuses upon one of the many current political issues: the positions of the candidates on nuclear disarmament. To Mary, the topic is not only of crucial importance today; she believes it will haunt her children and their children if the correct policy is not found soon. Her search for information and her subsequent voting choice will depend on several factors.

First, Mary must have an idea of what her preferences are. Of course, she prefers peace to war, but does she believe that some forms of peace are less desirable than others—for example, the "peace" of Soviet domination of the United States? If she is to find the right candidate for her vote, Mary must know what she wants.

Second, Mary must know what her choices are. Although she may prefer total and unilateral disarmament, there may be no candidate who calls for the United States to lay down all of its arms, regardless of Soviet actions. In this case, it would be futile for Mary to insist on voting only for a candidate who supports such a policy.

Another consideration is Mary's understanding of, and confidence in, the possible outcome of her choice. For example, if she is extremely thorough, she will research whether the candidate with whom she agrees has kept promises made in the past. In addition, Mary should consider what will happen if her candidate wins. Many people believe that a well-intentioned president who calls for unilateral disarmament will, ironically, increase the chance for war, because the Soviets might take advantage of what they might see as American "softness." Mary might think about supporting a more moderate candidate than her first choice, which was based solely on a single policy stance.

Finally, this conscientious voter should contemplate the future. Could Mary's preferences change in ten years, after the policies she now supports have perhaps been implemented? For example, many citizens find that their attitudes about paycheck deductions for social security change as they approach retirement age. Even more difficult to assess is the future condition of the world. Perhaps technological advances in weapons research that now sound speculative will render Mary's current concerns moot. The Soviets or the Americans might develop a weapon that can destroy missiles in flight, making today's arsenal useless. In this case, Mary's basis for choosing a candidate in the current election would be meaningless.

Similar analogies can be developed for other forms of political participation. Although some choices are less ambiguous than the one just presented (e.g., a person's opposition to capital punishment is less likely to be changed by time or events), the implications for participation remain. In a complicated and changing world, a realistic citizen must recognize that the information needed to make a "correct" decision when participating in politics is often absent or ambiguous. Furthermore, accumulating information requires time that could be devoted to other activities, thereby creating an opportunity cost. Therefore, some people may choose to sit out an election rather than risk making a wrong political choice.

Even so, many people do become involved in politics in a variety of ways. After a brief discussion of the basis for participation—that is, what Americans think and know about politics—we will examine how and why they participate, both as individuals and in groups. We will pay particular attention to the costs and rewards of political participation, to the institutions and mechanisms that have been developed to facilitate or restrict the behavior of individuals and interest groups, and to the social costs raised by these issues.

PUBLIC OPINION

The example of Mary Smith illustrates how difficult it is to be well informed about political issues. Even the most public-minded, information-hungry citizen will run into obstacles. Just how strong is the Soviet Union compared to the United States? How many people who receive welfare could really work? How serious a problem is acid rain, and what is the "right" amount to spend to stop it? Even full-time political experts have trouble with such questions.

Knowledge and Ignorance

It would be unrealistic to expect most Americans to exert the effort necessary to remain fully informed about all major issues. Nevertheless, most American citizens have at least some knowledge about politics, economics, and social life, although the depth of that knowledge is rather shallow. For instance, Table 3-1 demonstrates that many Americans are ignorant of some of the most basic facts of political life. With these figures in mind, even the evening television news broadcast begins to seem overly sophisticated for a large portion of the public.

Of course, generalizations about citizens' knowledge and ignorance mask some crucial distinctions between groups. The most important factor affecting the level of one's political knowledge is education. Individuals with more years of schooling generally read more newspapers and magazines and talk more about politics, as do those who are active in public affairs or have higher incomes. Sex, race, and age make little difference in political knowledge once the education factor is taken into account.

Of course, lack of knowledge does not guarantee a lack of opinions. American citizens are very willing to express their ideas about most major policy issues, even though their level of understanding may be low. For example, in the 1980 National Election Study of the University of Michigan's Center for Political Studies, less than 10 percent of those polled had no opinion about

TABLE 3-1
LEVEL OF POLITICAL KNOWLEDGE AMONG AMERICANS, 1960–1979

Year Asked	Item	Percentage
1973	Can name governor of home state	89%
1978	Can name the vice president	79%
1969	Know the meaning of the term *wiretapping*	74%
1967	Can name their mayor	70%
1978	Know which party has majority in the U.S. House of Representatives	69%
1960	Have some understanding of the term *conservative*	63%
1978	Know how many U.S. senators represent their home state	52%
1973	Can name their congressional representative	46%
1973	Can name both U.S. senators from their state	39%
1978	Can name the current secretary of state	34%
1978	Know the length of term of members of the U.S. House of Representatives	30%
1977	Know the meaning of the term *no-fault insurance*	31%
1979	Know which two nations are involved in SALT	23%

Source: Robert S. Erikson, Norman R. Luttbeg, and Kent L. Tedin, *American Public Opinion: Its Origins, Content, and Impact*, 2nd ed. (New York: Wiley, 1980), p. 19.

abortion policy, women's rights, school busing, civil rights policy, or nuclear power plants. Although it is not wrong for people to have opinions on complex subjects about which they may have few facts, we need to ask from where their opinions come.

Ideology

Uninformed people could respond to pollsters' questions by randomly choosing from among the offered answers, and undoubtedly some of that goes on. However, researchers have looked closely at how people respond to polls and have found that many individuals view politics through a mental filter called **ideology:** a broad, coherent, and consistent set of beliefs and values. In modern America, the term is often equated with political positions such as **liberal** (which generally implies a willingness to have government take a more active role in business and social matters) and **conservative** (which usually implies a narrow role for government).

Of course, many people do not think of themselves as either liberal or conservative, while many of those who do cannot define the terms. Nevertheless, the responses of many Americans to survey questions suggest that their ideas are constrained by deeply held, perhaps even subconscious, beliefs. Ideology is a convenient way to bypass the problem of information cost; a detailed study of many complex issues can be replaced by blanket rejection simply because the issues are "too liberal" or "too conservative." However, we do not fully understand the sources of ideology, nor the factors that determine the intensity or stability of political values. In summary, while most Americans do not see themselves as ideologues, they tend to share some fundamental ideals (e.g., liberty, justice, equality) without giving much thought to the problems of achieving them.

Where Opinions Come From

Genetic researchers have not yet found a "liberal" gene, nor a "conservative" gene. Yet, in a sense, many of our political opinions are inherited, not biologically, but through a process called *political socialization.* Through continued exposure to various influences, we acquire values, beliefs, and attitudes. For example, by the age of ten, many children have learned enough about religion and politics to shape their perceptions for the rest of their lives.

The most important source of political values is the family. It is where most people first learn the basics of right and wrong, how to relate to other people, and so on. Parents make their political preferences known and provide political information to their children (e.g., through magazines and mealtime discussions). While none of this guarantees that Democratic parents will produce future Democratic voters, studies have found a strong relationship between parents' political beliefs and those of their children.

The schools may be as important as the family in producing political opinions. From an early age, children are exposed to the American flag, the pledge

ideology: A comprehensive and coherent set of basic beliefs about political, economic, and social values.

liberal: The ideological position that government has a proper and necessary role in intervening in social and economic affairs in order to improve people's lives.

conservative: An ideological position that is generally opposed to government interference in the lives of citizens or the affairs of business.

of allegiance, the story of George Washington ("I cannot tell a lie"), and the importance of democracy. Whether this emphasis on the legitimacy of our political system does more than reinforce the lessons taught at home is not clear; the children of middle-class parents usually go to middle-class schools with other middle-class children, so it is difficult to measure the impact of education alone on political values.

Other important effects on children's political opinions include peer groups, religion, social class, race, and the mass media. Once again, it is not easy to disentangle these from the influence of family. Studies have shown that when the opinions of a child's peers differ from those of his or her parents, the latter dominate. It has also been shown that, in general, Jewish children grow up more liberal than Catholic children, who, in turn, are more liberal than Protestant children. These tendencies and their causes are more difficult to understand than many physical, chemical, or biological phenomena, primarily because of social scientists' problems in observation and measurement.

Public Opinion Polling

Since the mid-1930s, *scientific polling* has become a major undertaking. First, a pollster must define the *population* or *universe* to be studied: for example, is the poll concerned with the opinions of all adult Americans, all students, or all residents of Omaha? Since few polls can ever interview all members of the relevant universe, the next task is to choose a *sample* of them. A representative sample of all Americans would have to include accurate percentages

President Harry Truman, gleeful after his reelection in 1948, holds an early edition of the Chicago Daily Tribune announcing that he had been defeated. The election polls were unanimously incorrect in their predictions. (UPI/Bettmann Archive)

of individuals of different sexes, races, social classes, regions, ages, ethnic backgrounds, and so on. A purely *random* sample could accidentally fail to include members of certain key groups, unless the sample was very large. Therefore, many pollsters today use *quota* or *stratified* samples, in which key groups are identified (e.g., by income level, race, and education), and then random samples are chosen from people in these categories. In this way, accurate national polls can be made with as few as 1,500 respondents. (See the accompanying box.)

How accurate is an opinion survey based on as little as 0.0012 percent of the population? Most professional polls today can produce *sampling errors* as small as 3 or 4 percent. For example, in three of the past four presidential elections, the Gallup and Harris polling organizations made correct predictions within 3 percent of the actual vote (the exception was 1976, when an unusually large segment of voters waited until the last day or two to make up their minds). However, the accuracy of the sample is only one factor in the exactness of a public opinion survey. Another is the measurement device: the questions asked.

Our fictitious voter, Mary Smith, might have a hard time answering the question, "Do you think the arms race should be continued, or do you favor unilateral disarmament by the United States?" Such "closed-ended" questions, to which only a few possible responses are allowed, can be difficult to write without introducing some bias or omitting some relevant nuance of the respondent's opinion. On the other hand, responses to "open-ended" questions such as, "What do you think our nuclear arms policy should be?" are difficult to categorize and compare. As a result, polling firms often pretest their surveys in order to discover ambiguities and "loaded" questions.

Another problem facing pollsters is the reliability of an apparently informed and sincere answer. Few people will admit to being bigots or Communist sympathizers and so they often lie to pollsters. People are also frequently reluctant to answer "don't know." In one study, when asked whether the "1975 Public Affairs Act" should be repealed, one-third of the respondents agreed or disagreed, even though no such law exists.[1]

Does Public Opinion Make a Difference?

In the remainder of this chapter, we will be looking at how political activity can translate citizens' wishes into public policies. We saw in Chapter 2 that the American Founders did not intend for public opinion to be directly translated into policy, but rather that the attitudes of the masses should be filtered through our political institutions.

Does public opinion ever affect policies? There is conflicting evidence. We can find examples in our history where the opinions of a large majority have not been translated into policy. For instance, in 1981, the Equal Rights Amendment was supported by 67 percent of the American public, about 70 percent of the public favored stronger gun-control legislation, and a majority of Americans believed that the Supreme Court had gone too far by banning prayer in

A TYPICAL PUBLIC OPINION SURVEY AND RESPONSE

Question: "I'd like your opinion of the chances of a world war breaking out in the next ten years. If 10 means it is absolutely certain that a world war will break out and 0 means that there is no chance of a world war breaking out, where on this scale of 10 to 0 would you rate the chances of world war breaking out in the next ten years?"

	More than 50% Chance	50%–50% Chance	Less than 50% Chance	No opinion
National	29%	20%	42%	9%
Sex				
Male	30	15	50	5
Female	28	24	35	13
Race				
White	27	20	44	9
Nonwhite	43	16	25	16
Education				
College	24	18	54	4
High school	28	26	40	6
Grade school	41	11	23	25
Region				
East	29	20	42	9
Midwest	28	23	40	9
South	30	23	38	9
West	29	12	50	9
Age				
18–24 years	40	24	35	1
25–34 years	32	20	44	4
35–49 years	25	26	41	8
50 & older	25	14	44	17
Income				
$30,000 and over	23	18	58	1
$20,000–$29,999	28	26	44	2
$10,000–$19,999	32	18	40	10
Under $10,000	36	18	28	18
Politics				
Republican	20	15	58	7
Democrat	35	24	32	9
Independent	30	19	44	7
Employed				
Full time	32	20	45	3
Part time	30	27	38	5
Not employed	26	19	37	18

Source: *Gallup Report*, no. 208, January 1983, p. 9. Question asked November 19–28, 1982.

public schools. Yet none of these preferences were on the verge of being enacted into law.

Some presidents have clearly opposed public opinion. Jimmy Carter pressed for a treaty returning the Panama Canal to Panama despite explicit opposition. Lyndon Johnson, who pushed for a tax increase during his administration even though pollsters determined that 79 percent of the American public opposed it, wrote in his memoirs that he "was aware that history's judgement would be based not on the Gallup Poll . . . but on what I did to steer the economy between the shoals of recession and the rocks of runaway inflation."[2] On the other hand, before the United States entered World War II, Franklin Roosevelt requested that pollsters ask certain questions about aid to England so that he could follow trends in public opinion. John Kennedy read one out of every fifty letters he received from the public, and presidents usually receive statistical summaries of all of their mail.

The only safe generalization about public opinion and public policy is that there is no inevitable connection between the two. Why? As we have seen, most of the public is not very aware of current events. For example, a March 1982 poll, conducted by NBC News and the Associated Press, found that 56 percent of the respondents had no opinion on whether Ronald Reagan was pursuing the correct policy on nuclear disarmament. In addition, the opinions of those who *are* informed usually serve as no more than general guides to those policymakers who want to adhere to public opinion. And those citizens who are knowledgeable are not representative of the entire population; they tend to have more years of schooling and higher incomes than the lesser informed, so following their opinion could create a bias in their favor.

The connection between public opinion and public policy, therefore, has to a large degree been weak. A person's political views are much more effective if he or she participates directly in politics, either individually or through interest groups. In the coming years, however, we may see a change. With the advent of two-way communication to individual homes through cable television, some see the birth of a "teledemocracy," in which public leaders can probe public opinion directly. Yet others worry that the problems that have plagued polling—identifying the universe (e.g., all cable subscribers?), choosing a sample (e.g., those who happen to be watching?), and carefully constructing accurate questions—could be made far worse by the new technology. The traditional forms of political participation to which we now turn may be more cumbersome, but they do have certain advantages.

PARTICIPATION IN AMERICA

A citizen participates in politics when he or she takes some kind of action, whether alone or together with others, to try to affect such political decisions as who will be president or what sort of policies will be made by legislators, judges, or bureaucrats (see Table 3-2). Clearly, this definition of political par-

TABLE 3-2
POLITICAL PARTICIPATION IN THE UNITED STATES

Type of Participation	*Percentage*
Report regularly voting in presidential elections[a]	72%
Report always voting in local elections	47%
Active in at least one organization involved in community problems	32%
Have worked with others to solve community problems	30%
Have attempted to persuade others to vote similarly	28%
Have actively worked for a party or candidate	26%
Have contacted a local government official about an issue or problem	20%
Have attended at least one political meeting in last three years	19%
Have contacted a state or national government official about an issue or problem	18%
Have formed a group or organization to solve some community problem	14%
Have contributed money to a party or candidate	13%
Currently a member of a political club or organization	8%

[a]Composite variable created from reports of voting in 1960 and 1964 presidential elections. Percentage is equal to those who report they voted in both elections.

Source: Sidney Verba and Norman H. Nie, *Participation in America* (New York: Harper & Row, 1972), p. 31.

ticipation includes a wide range of activities, from bomb-throwing to running for office. Among the most interesting aspects of participation are the costs and benefits of taking action, the legal and informal constraints against participation, and the implications of political action for the allocation of political and economic resources. These form the basis for our discussion of the major forms of political participation:

1. individual action, such as using the court system to bring a case
2. interest-group formation and activity
3. organized electoral activity (including party politics, which will be discussed in Chapters 4 and 5)

In this section, we will examine how Americans participate in government as individuals.

The ability and willingness of American citizens to make decisions for themselves is an important part of their culture. As we have seen, the roots of the American Revolution and of the republic that resulted from it, included issues of participation. Phrases such as "taxation without representation" and "the consent of the governed," as well as the guarantees found in the Bill of Rights, reflect the importance of citizen participation to the Founders of the nation. The American system of justice also includes elements of citizen participation:

for example, trial by a jury made up of the peers of the accused. Yet, we must remember that citizen participation in every election and policymaking activity was not wholly favored by the framers of the Constitution. When Alexander Hamilton referred to the American people as a "great beast," he was expressing a profound mistrust of the ability of the average citizen to make wise decisions. Another Founder, William Livingston, remarked that "the people have ever been and ever will be unfit to retain the exercize of power in their own hands."

These concerns about the ability of the people to contribute to American government were more than philosophical; the American political system reflected the distrust in the laws and practices that governed its elections for nearly two hundred years. For example, not until 1964 did the Supreme Court rule (in *Wesberry* v. *Sanders*) that the right to vote in the United States is fundamental to each person's political and civil rights. There was nothing in the Constitution that guaranteed the vote until the passage of the Fifteenth Amendment in 1870, and even then its provision of the right to vote regardless of "race, color, or previous condition of servitude" was easily avoided. In fact, it was not until about 1850 that most states had abolished requirements that only men owning personal property could vote (women were excluded).

INDIVIDUAL PARTICIPATION

Voting

If the framers of the Constitution had indeed attempted to reserve political power for the "gentlemen," they would surely have been disappointed at what they had wrought. For it soon became obvious that even with the denial of the

TABLE 3-3
VOTER TURNOUT IN AMERICAN PRESIDENTIAL ELECTIONS, 1932–1984

Year	Turnout Rate[a]	Year	Turnout Rate
1932	52.4%	1960	62.8%
1936	56.0%	1964	61.9%
1940	58.9%	1968	60.9%
1944	56.0%	1972	55.5%
1948	51.1%	1976	54.3%
1952	61.6%	1980	53.2%
1956	59.3%	1984	53.5%

[a]Turnout rate is based on residential population, including resident aliens, of voting age.

Source: U.S. Bureau of the Census, *Statistical Abstract of the United States, 1981* (Washington, D.C.: Government Printing Office, 1981), p. 496.

TABLE 3-4
VOTER TURNOUT IN SELECTED DEMOCRATIC NATIONS[a]

Nation	Voter Turnout	Nation	Voter Turnout
1. Belgium	94.6%	13. Denmark	83.2%
2. Australia	94.5%	14. Norway	82.0%
3. Austria	91.6%	15. Greece	78.6%
4. Sweden	90.7%	16. Israel	78.5%
5. Italy	90.4%	17. United Kingdom	76.3%
6. Iceland	89.3%	18. Japan	74.5%
7. New Zealand	89.0%	19. Canada	69.3%
8. Luxembourg	88.9%	20. Spain	68.1%
9. Germany	88.6%	21. Finland	64.3%
10. Netherlands	87.0%	22. Ireland	62.2%
11. France	85.9%	23. United States	52.6%
12. Portugal	84.2%	24. Switzerland	48.3%

[a]Data are for the most recent national election preceding 1981.

Source: David Glass, Peverill Squire, Raymond Wolfinger, "Voter Turnout: An International Comparison," *Public Opinion* (December/January 1984), p. 50.

vote to many Americans, the electorate could still reject the "aristocracy of intellect and culture." Historians refer to Andrew Jackson's election to the presidency in 1828 as a revolution partly because his appeal was primarily aimed at the masses:

> [W]hat seems to have enchanted people with General Jackson when he became a candidate for President was not any principles or policies he advocated but his breaches of decorum, real or alleged. Economically, the revolution signified that a nation of potential money-makers could not abide traditionary, conservative limitations on business enterprise, particularly by capitalists in Philadelphia. The Jacksonian revolution was a consequence of the Industrial Revolution and of a farm-born population's realization that now anyone in America could get rich and through his own efforts, if he had a fair chance.[3]

Thus, while participation in elections may be fundamental to the theory of democratic government, widespread participation was not viewed that way by the Founders—nor perhaps by a large number of Americans. Table 3-3 reveals the percentage of eligible voters who have cast ballots in presidential elections since 1932. Voter turnout, at least since World War I, has been low. If we compare American presidential election turnout figures with those in twenty-three other democracies, American participation ranks near the bottom (see Table 3-4). A strict comparison is difficult, of course, because some countries have weekend voting or impose fines for not voting. In addition, most political systems have different electoral rules, party systems, and traditions. (Another critical factor in voter turnout in the United States has been a history of institutional barriers to voting, such as poll taxes, literacy tests, and registration procedures that were intended to deny the vote to minorities. These will be examined in detail in Chapter 5.)

What causes people to vote or abstain? The most obvious reason for participation in elections is that people believe they have a direct personal stake in public policy. That is, they expect to receive a larger benefit from the decisions of one candidate than they would from those of another. This perceived difference in benefits (or "utility") provides an incentive to vote, although, as we shall see, an individual's personal share of a beneficial public decision may be very small. For example, a worker in the aerospace industry, who might generally identify with Democratic appeals to labor voters, would have a personal economic incentive to vote for a candidate who promised to buy more jets for the Pentagon. In 1972, Democratic candidate George McGovern, whom many saw as very liberal on social welfare issues, attracted 87 percent of the nonwhite vote, but only 32 percent of the white electorate—partly because many of the latter group believed that McGovern intended to redistribute wealth from middle-class whites to lower-class minorities.

Do people vote because they think they have a chance to change public policies? If so, very few citizens who contemplate voting would ever bother, because the likelihood that a single vote would determine the outcome of a national election is tiny. Even with only a 55.1 percent turnout in the 1980 presidential election, more than 84 million Americans cast ballots, and Ronald Reagan won by a margin of about 8.3 million votes. Each voter had a smaller chance of affecting the election result than of cashing in on a bet at the racetrack or holding a winning lottery ticket. For many voters, that chance was reduced even further by advances in the technology of television campaign coverage. With sophisticated "exit polling" (i.e., interviews with a carefully selected cross section of voters as they leave their voting places), the television networks are able to project the final national vote before the ballots are actually tallied. In 1980, the forecasts came long before the polls in the West had closed, since a complete sample of voters in eastern time zones was available soon after 7:00 P.M. (eastern standard time). Many California Democrats complained that the early projection of a Reagan landslide, coupled with Jimmy Carter's early concession speech, kept a good number of potential voters at home.

Finally, recall the example of Mary Smith, in which we saw some of the costs involved in casting a vote. While most voters do not go to the trouble of searching for all of the available information about candidates, even on a single issue, they do bear some costs. For example, even the most casual voter must acquire information about when, where, and how to cast a ballot. It takes time to travel to the polling place and to stand in line. Some voters will have transporation costs or may need to hire a babysitter. And voting imposes an opportunity cost, because the time required to vote could be spent in another activity, such as staying at work or going to a movie. All of these factors contribute to higher turnout rates among higher-income voters because they are more able to bear these costs than are low-income voters. This is one reason why only 34 percent of the unemployed voted in the November 1982 congressional election, as compared with 48.4 percent of those with jobs.

Why, then, do people vote? If the probability of being the "pivot" (casting the tie-breaking vote) is infinitesimal, if one citizen's share of the benefits created by a favored candidate's election is small, and if the information costs and opportunity costs are significant, why bother? As Anthony Downs has written, "When no one votes, democracy collapses. Yet if everyone who is not indifferent votes, in the next election each will abstain, since his ballot had so little effect previously (i.e., when everyone voted)."[4]

Psychological and Cultural Reasons for Voting   The dilemma is solved by what we could call psychological or cultural factors—for example, the feeling of personal satisfaction and loyal citizenship that comes from participating in an election. Peer pressure may also have an effect; while a citizen may not care about contributing to the legitimacy of government, friends and colleagues may, thereby providing an incentive to vote. Furthermore, political scientist Thomas Patterson found that during the 1976 presidential campaign, more than half the stories on network television news, in the major weekly news-magazines, and in the newspapers he examined focused on the "horse race" aspects of the campaign (e.g., strategy, who was winning), rather than on substantive policy issues or on the candidates' qualifications. As a result, for some people, voting for president may be similar to "voting" for the winner of the Super Bowl. Finally, it has been observed that some individuals may recognize the relative futility of such participation, but may vote anyway, just in case. John Ferejohn and Morris Fiorina have called this the "What if I didn't vote and my preferred candidate lost by one vote? I'd feel like killing myself" syndrome.[5]

In summary, voting, which some consider the most fundamental form of political participation for individuals in the United States or in any republic, is not widely practiced, and for some rather good reasons. A purely economic analysis of the information and opportunity costs associated with the act of voting, weighed against its direct personal benefits, would suggest that we should all ignore electoral campaigns. However, if everyone did, then at the next election each of us would see a great chance of being the crucial pivot, and turnout would increase. Because we do not observe total abstention, there must be other than economic factors (i.e., psychological and cultural notions of justice and legitimacy) that lead Americans to the polls.

Other Forms of Individual Participation

Although voting is by far the most common method by which individuals participate in American government, there are other types of individual participation as well.

Campaign Contributions   Contributors are frequently solicited by parties or other political organizations. For many citizens, the decision to donate money to a political cause or campaign is simply an exaggerated vote; the potential contributor needs the same general type of information that the potential voter needs. In one sense, giving money to a candidate or a political party is an organized, not an individual, act because it involves communication between at least two people (a contributor and a recipient).

Because of the secrecy historically accorded campaign contributors, it was difficult in the past to determine why people gave money to candidates or even who the contributors were. However, in 1972, new laws required candidates and parties to identify by name and address all individuals and groups who contributed or loaned more than a hundred dollars to presidential campaign committees. Political scientists Clifford Brown, Roman Hedges, and Lynda Powell, who studied a large sample of these contributors, found that those who give amounts over $100 to political campaigns differed from the general population in several ways.[6] The "large contributors" definitely had higher social and economic status: 27 percent reported a family income of over $100,000, and 76 percent had college degrees. In addition, contributors were more involved in other forms of participation, such as voting and writing letters to newspaper editors. This is not surprising. Once the costs of participation have been paid for one type of political activity (e.g., the accumulation of information about current events and the positions of candidates for the purpose of deciding to whom to contribute), the additional information cost of deciding for whom to vote is relatively small. This cost will also be discounted or ignored because a "large contributor" obviously sees a clear benefit (e.g., civic satisfaction or influencing votes) attached to gathering political information. In other words, once you know enough to contribute, you know enough to vote, write letters, and so on.

Running for Office   Once again, there are direct benefits from another type of individual political participation, running for office. If a citizen cares strongly about public affairs, then an attempt to personally shape government decisions will be gratifying, even if it is unsuccessful. James Q. Wilson distinguished between "amateurs" and "professionals" who participate in politics: "The principal reward of politics to the amateur is the sense of having satisfied a felt obligation to 'participate.' . . . The principal reward of the professional is to be found in the extrinsic satisfactions of participation—power, income, status, or the fun of the game."[7]

It is important to note that there are economic incentives in running for office, whatever the outcome. Political scientist Linda Fowler studied candidates for the U.S. House of Representatives from many districts in New York State: many of them, especially real-estate agents and lawyers, admitted that their campaigns were intended to make themselves well known in their communities. Jeane Kirkpatrick, a political scientist who went on to become the American ambassador to the United Nations, studied men and women who ran for state legislatures. She found that more men than women admitted they ran for office to help their careers; women were more likely to explain their candidacies in terms of serving their communities.[8]

Political Entrepreneurs   There are also individuals who attempt to affect politics from the outside, without running for elected office, accepting appointive posts, or entering coalitions with established political actors. We could call such people "political entrepreneurs," because, like their business counterparts, they typically take on entrenched and organized interests, sometimes with very few resources of their own. Often, these energetic people are crusaders for causes concerning the allocation of resources or the control of the behavior of others. For example, consumer advocate Ralph Nader began his public career in the 1960s when, as a young lawyer, he accused General Motors of knowingly selling dangerous cars. Nader not only reaped publicity; he also gained the financial wherewithal to organize a lobby after he successfully sued the automobile manufacturer for hiring a private investigator to spy on him (General Motors settled out of court in 1970 for $425,000). In 1978, Howard Jarvis, who directed an association of California apartment-owners, led a campaign in which the voters approved a proposition ordering the state to drastically cut their property taxes. Neither Jarvis nor Nader sought political office. Both men exhibited the kind of articulate dedication to their causes that attracts fervent followers. And although both stood to gain economically from their activities—lecture fees and book sales for Nader and tax relief for Jarvis—this was not their principal incentive for political entrepreneurship.

Of course, there are some disincentives to taking up controversial causes. For example, some scientists who feel strongly about questions of technological policy, such as nuclear power plant safety or the advisability of stricter health and safety regulations, worry about losing government research funds if they speak out. In 1968, A. Ernest Fitzgerald, a financial analyst in the Pentagon, revealed that it was costing $2 billion more to build an Air Force C-5A cargo plane than Congress had authorized and that Lockheed Corporation and the Air Force were trying to conceal the fact. Fitzgerald was fired. Although he was later rehired with back pay after it became known that President Richard Nixon had personally ordered his removal, he was not reinstated as a financial analyst.

The General Accounting Office has established a toll-free hotline (800-424-5454) for whistleblowing on fraud and waste in the government bureaucracy. However, there still remain subtle forms of retaliation against those who take it upon themselves to challenge how things are done. Nevertheless, we have seen frequent examples of political entrepreneurship in American political life. Perhaps no incentive is more effective in eliciting such participation than outrage; many political entrepreneurs throughout American history have believed that justice is much more than an abstract philosophical notion.

Litigation   In Chapter 6 we will discuss at length another form of citizen involvement in policymaking and governmental decisionmaking—judicial and administrative agency litigation. A brief mention is appropriate here, however, because when Americans use their right to take their cases to the courts, they are exercising a vital form of political participation. And when they defend themselves, they are doing the same: trying to shape policy through court decisions. Citizens can participate *indirectly* in the judicial process as well. Letters to legislators, the president, or administrators can lead to government litigation against lawbreakers. In addition, many government agencies maintain local offices or send employees into the field in order to encourage citizens to register their complaints. Such complaints often lead to litigation against alleged wrongdoers.

Direct Action   Finally, there is a variety of other means available to aroused citizens who wish to have their voices heard by public officials. These typically involve direct activity outside of the normal policymaking arenas of the electoral system, the courts, and personal lobbying. Some methods of action, of course, stretch the definition of the term *participation*. For example, a few individuals have employed hijacking, assassination, bribery, and terrorism as methods to change government policies. Other methods, although technically illegal, are less reprehensible—for example, nonviolent civil disobedience, such as refusal to pay taxes, draft evasion, and sit-ins. Still other forms of direct action are usually legal, although sometimes unconventional, such as politically motivated boycotts, marches, and demonstrations.

In some instances, individuals have been solicited by the government for their judgment and advice—or, some might argue, to lend legitimacy to governmental investigations or policies. For example, a homemaker from Middletown, Pennsylvania, a town located in the shadow of the nuclear power plant at Three Mile Island, was asked to serve on the president's commission that investigated the 1979 accident at the site. Most modern governmental task forces include one "ordinary" (i.e., nonexpert and unaffiliated) citizen to act

Antinuclear rally, New York City, June 12, 1982. (© Robert Houser/Photo Researchers, Inc.)

as a representative of the general public. However well-intentioned this type of participation may be, it may not contribute very much; evidence suggests that "public" representatives on panels and commissions, while not ignored when they speak or ask questions, are simply not prepared to contend with complex policy matters.

As we saw in Table 3-2, there are other ways for individuals to participate in politics besides the general categories just discussed. They may write letters to the president, to their representatives in Congress, to newspapers and magazines, and so on. They can individually lobby public officials or other voters. Regardless of the technique that they choose, most individuals in the United States who participate in government do so because they want to. The question that remains to be answered about individual participation is, Does it have any effect on government?

Effects of Individual Participation

The influence that individuals have on public policy is often difficult to detect and always hard to measure. The effect of citizens' participation depends greatly on the target of their actions. For one thing, there are enormous differences in momentum among public programs. A government regulation that provides significant benefits to an organized, large group will be difficult to deflect or stop, whereas a little-noticed program may be much easier to change.

We should also ask whether unorganized individuals can change government policy. Apparently, they can. While analysts may disagree on the fine details of whether votes matter, for example, ample evidence exists that elections, referenda, and initiatives do affect policy. (A **referendum** allows voters to endorse or reject their legislators' decisions; an **initiative** involves the judgment of the voters on legislation that some of the voters themselves have proposed.) For example, a detailed analysis of a 1972 ballot initiative in California that would have removed criminal penalties for the personal use of marijuana showed that in those counties where the initiative was soundly defeated, the courts soon became more severe in sentencing those convicted of possession; however, in the counties where the vote was more lenient, the courts also became more lenient.

A particularly important aspect of individual participation, with clear ramifications for public policy and the operation of American government, is that those who participate are those who choose to. This self-selection has two immediate effects. First, as the study of campaign contributors demonstrated, individual actors in politics are likely to be wealthier and more highly-educated than the general public. The uneducated don't write letters, the poor don't give money, and the unsuccessful don't harbor great political ambitions. For this reason, the effect of democratic participation on government is almost certainly biased in favor of certain groups in American society. Second, as we will see, the people who devote their time and energy to public affairs are those who care deeply about a certain issue or issues. Political activists are

referendum: An election in which citizens directly choose whether to approve a proposed public policy without the immediate intervention of their representatives.

initiative: A procedure by which citizens or groups can propose new laws or constitutional amendments by obtaining sufficient signatures on a petition, after which the general public votes on the proposal.

typically more liberal or more conservative (or more steadfastly dedicated to a single idea) than the general population. The "silent majority" to whom Richard Nixon appealed for support for his Vietnam policies were silent because they did not care enough to be vocal. Those who shouted were not ambivalent. We should not expect to find many neutral participants in American politics.

Finally, we should note the integrative function of individual participation. The German social theorist Werner Sombart may have been the first (in 1906) to point out how the extension of the voting franchise and the political rights promised by the Constitution have contributed to the moral contentment of American workers and their rejection of "bitter Socialist tendencies": "The last and poorest commoner has a part in the sacred sovereignty; at least formally, he is the People and the People are the State. In this way there grows up in every individual an unrestrained feeling of power, unrealistic though this may be. In his consciousness it is an undoubted reality. . . . For the most part the citizen does not lift a finger to remove the inconveniences of public life, but lives with the firm conviction that he only has to wish that they be brought to an end for that to happen."[9]

Why do so many Americans choose not to participate in politics as individuals? The most important reason, as we have seen, is the variety of costs associated with political actions—primarily information costs and opportunity costs—in contrast to the often minuscule individual share of the benefits. It is not surprising that people have found one way around that obstacle. Recall our discussion of political entrepreneurs: among their other functions, they reduce information costs for individuals in return for their votes or support. Remember what Ralph Nader did with his court settlement from General Motors: he established an organization of lobbyists.

Interest groups serve a number of functions in American political life. As we shall see as we examine organized political participation, some of the constraints and rewards that individuals face in politics also apply to groups. We will also explain some unique characteristics of groups (among other things, how information costs are distributed, and the transaction costs of doing this). Most important, we will look at why groups have played such a major role in American politics and what effect they have had.

POLITICAL PARTICIPATION IN GROUPS

We have seen that voting is at best only a blunt tool for trying to affect public policy and that none of the other major types of individual political action, such as running for office, litigation in the courts, and direct action, are practiced by many Americans. Yet most citizens believe that the United States has a legitimate government (i.e., one that is open to public influence), and most elected officials insist that they do respond to criticisms and suggestions from their constituents. Clearly, individual political action is not the only form of political participation. Given the benefits and costs of individual action, what form might we expect most political participation to take in the United States?

Many social theorists, such as Talcott Parsons, Gaetano Mosca, and Georg Simmel, have examined the phenomenon of human behavior in society, and some have found a universal joining tendency even in primitive people. As a society becomes more complex, institutions evolve that perform the newly required functions of the more complicated social system (e.g., economic and legal transactions, recordkeeping). Such institutions also take over some of the functions previously performed by families, such as care for children and the elderly. Sometimes these institutions are nonvoluntary: they may be governmental and therefore able to force people to participate. However, in democratic nations, participatory politics are generally voluntary. In fact, if we look at the history of American politics and at some of the greatest concerns of political philosophers, one concept of political participation constantly recurs: interest groups.[10]

Do Americans have a special tendency to form groups? Political scientists Sidney Verba, Norman Nie, and Jae-On Kim compared political participation in five countries (Table 3-5). Their data, gathered in the early 1960s, strongly indicates that United States citizens were more likely to participate in communal activities than were people in the other democratic systems surveyed. Similarly, based on his observations during a visit to the United States in 1831, the French nobleman Alexis de Tocqueville concluded:

> In no country in the world has the principle of association been more successfully used, or more unsparingly applied to a multitude of different objects, than in America. . . .
> In America, the citizens who form the minority associate, in order, in the first

TABLE 3-5
POLITICAL PARTICIPATION IN FIVE COUNTRIES

Area of Participation	Austria	India	Japan	Nigeria	United States
Vote in national elections	96%	59%	72%	66%	72%
Vote in local elections	93%	42%	–[a]	59%	47%
Have worked for a political party	10%	25%	25%	–	26%
Have attended political meetings	27%	14%	50%	–	19%
Belong to a political club	28%	6%	4%	–	8%
Belong to an organization engaged in solving community problems	9%	7%	11%	28%	32%
Have worked with a community group	–	18%	15%	32%	30%
Have helped form a local group	–	5%	5%	24%	14%

[a]Not available.

Source: Adapted from Sidney Verba, Norman H. Nie, and Jae-On Kim, *The Modes of Democratic Participation: A Cross-National Comparison* (Beverly Hills: Sage, 1971), p. 36.

place, to show their numerical strength, and so to diminish the moral authority of the majority; and in the second place, to stimulate competition, and to discover those arguments which are most fitted to act upon the majority. . . .[11]

Although many of these early associations were social, literary, or scientific societies, some of them also had political interests. For the most part, however, colonists and early citizens lacked both the city life and the leisure time necessary to form associations; the communication, organization, and opportunity costs were too high for widespread group politics. Not until after the Civil War did Americans form significant business and trade associations, agricultural organizations, or labor unions. Once such groups formed, however, they often had a devastating impact. A notable example is the Grange, or Patrons of Husbandry, a midwestern farm organization that began in 1867 and claimed a million members within eight years. Among its accomplishments, the Grange can be given some of the credit for the passage of the Interstate Commerce Act in 1887, which began governmental regulation of the railroads, and the Sherman Anti-Trust Act of 1890.

It is difficult to establish exactly when the first political organizations or clubs formed, because there have always been groups of citizens, bound by common interests in political issues, involved in American government. For example, historian Forrest McDonald identified at least twenty basic occupational groups, thirteen of them agrarian, that existed in 1787; each had differing interests and varying amounts and types of resources for affecting policy.[12] These groups included (1) poor and isolated subsistence farmers that public policy would probably never affect, (2) poor and nonisolated subsistence farmers with a potential interest in policy related to transportation facilities, and (3) at the other extreme, the great southern plantation aristocrats with their armies of slaves and near-monopolies on their crops. As we shall see, however, just because people have a common interest, it is not inevitable that they will form an organized interest group.

Since the beginning of the twentieth century and particularly in the last few decades, the political activity of organized interest groups has greatly expanded. Today, there are over six thousand trade and professional associations in the United States, and since more than one out of four have national headquarters in Washington, their concern with political matters is obvious. In *Lobbying for the People,* Jeffrey Berry estimated that there were eighty-three "public interest" groups in Washington in 1972–1973 and put the number of voluntary environmental organizations in the United States at around twenty thousand.[13] In 1980, the *Wall Street Journal* reported 14,019 associations, ranging from the American Producers of Italian-type Cheese Association to the Tapered Steel Transmission Pole Institute. The former group is interested in policies affecting the price of milk products and imported cheese, while the latter worries about whether government regulators will allow the costs of more expensive steel poles to be passed along to consumers by electric utility companies.

The concepts outlined in Chapter 1 are useful in understanding the role and behavior of organized interest groups, as are many of the aspects of individual political activity. And, as we shall see, some of the problems and assets unique to organized groups can help us to explain their occurrence, techniques, and effectiveness in the United States.

Why Do Groups Form?

The Advantages of Collective Action   There are many railroad companies in the United States, ranging in size from the Norfolk Southern Railway system, with operations in dozens of states, to numerous tiny railroads, each running one locomotive along a single stretch of track. The larger companies have a powerful national voice in their trade association, the Association of American Railroads. Because the smaller companies sometimes have interests that differ from their larger brethren, they have formed their own group, the American Short Line Railroad Association. Its slogan reveals its purpose: "Doing Collectively What Is Impossible for the Individual." What do these companies believe is impossible without collective action?

People generally will participate in activities and choose among alternatives in response to incentives and in such a way as to minimize costs and maximize benefits. Recall the discussion earlier in this chapter about the incentives, disincentives, costs, and benefits attached to individual political participation. The same reasoning can be applied to the formation of groups.

Mary Smith, our fictitious voter, confronted several obstacles in becoming a political participant. The first, discovering her own preferences, was a private matter in which no one else could help. Yet all of the other costs she faced could have been shared. Instead of searching by herself for information about all potential candidates and their positions, Mary could have shared the task with several other people. Each person could have investigated one candidate, and then they could have communicated their results to one another. Similarly, the other information costs involved in picking a candidate, such as predicting outcomes of choices and forecasting future events, could also have been reduced by dividing up the tasks. One of the great advantages of organizing is that information is usually cheaper to amass when that task is shared among members of a group.

Information is the most important commodity that interest groups produce. All groups accumulate and pass along information, but some groups do nothing else. Nearly all groups put out newsletters, journals, or press releases. For example, one such group is Consumers Union (CU), founded in 1936 to test consumer products, a task very few consumers are capable of doing, or can afford to do, by themselves. Today, CU has about 1.8 million members—that is, subscribers to its publication, *Consumer Reports.* Approximately ninety-nine percent of its budget is spent on product testing, publishing, and membership solicitations, while less than one percent is allocated for lobbying. When Ralph Nader resigned from the CU board in 1975, he complained about this distribution of resources: "While CU has stepped up its advocacy effort in the Washington and California offices and has included more investigative reporting in *Consumer Reports,* its overwhelming effort is in testing and communicating the results about products. Neither the majority of the Board, nor most of the upper management nor the employees' union leadership wants to urge or see the fundamental changes needed to make a truly Consumers Union of power, presence, and priority."[14]

Much more common in the political arena are groups who use their information for strategic purposes. Later in this chapter, we will see that many political interest groups, having taken advantage of the cost-saving division of labor in gathering information, apply that information as their primary weapon.

Another factor in the formation of groups is the symbolic function that they perform. There is often no expectation of individual economic benefit from participating in a symbolic group; the sense of belonging and the social ties that come from belonging to a group may be sufficient. For example, members of professional, ethnic, or religious groups identify themselves more closely with their colleagues when they belong to a symbolic organization. Moreover, associations such as the National Welfare Rights Organization generate a sense of cohesion and legitimacy among their members as they cooperate in expressing their beliefs and desires.

Interest-group formation can also serve ideological purposes. An ideological statement can usually be characterized as one in which objective facts are mixed with a broad schen.e of values, such as questions of justice or morality. But when we look at ideological interest groups, we need a more exact definition. The German sociologist Karl Mannheim made a distinction between types of ideology that is especially important in regard to interest groups.[15] Mannheim described "total ideology" in terms of fundamental and comprehensive concepts about humanity, society, and politics. From this, he distinguished "particular ideology," which is narrower in focus but no less intense and which may be applied to only a single issue.

We can observe the application of "total ideology" in groups such as Americans for Democratic Action, which acts as a self-appointed liberal watchdog on a wide range of issues, and its conservative counterpart, Americans for Constitutional Action. Other interest groups that show signs of total ideology are the John Birch Society, the United States Chamber of Commerce, and the American Civil Liberties Union. Because their principles are deep-rooted and their policy interests often vast, such groups tend to be long-lasting and stable. On the other hand, groups that pursue a "particular ideology" may come and go rather quickly as the issues that are important to them enter and exit the political agenda. Although it still exists, the Women's Christian Temperance Union faded when its absolute opposition to liquor consumption clashed unsuccessfully with the failure of Prohibition in the 1920s. The more radical civil-rights groups of the 1960s, such as the Student Nonviolent Coordinating Committee and the Black Panthers, were undercut by the failure of their tactics and the success of more moderate and more broadly-based civil-rights organizations (e.g., the National Association for the Advancement of Colored People, the Urban League). Of course, some single-issue groups, such as the National Rifle Association and its opposition to gun control, survive for long periods because they are concerned with issues that may never disappear.

It is important to recognize that the informational, symbolic, and ideological functions of interest groups are not mutually exclusive. Someone who joins a civil-rights organization because of an ideological commitment to racial justice may also receive symbolic benefits (e.g., a sense of racial unity) and information cost savings through group analysis of complex issues such as desegregation policy. In addition, many private benefits can be obtained by individuals who join groups; these **collective benefits** are shared by, and cannot be withheld from, all group members. For example, automobile manufacturers reaped collective benefits when they successfully organized their opposition to stringent air pollution regulations during the 1970s. When a physician joins the American Medical Association, he or she becomes eligible for reduced premiums on malpractice insurance. If you join Consumers Union, you receive monthly issues of *Consumer Reports.* Other groups offer low-rate group health and life insurance to their members. Because these collective benefits are unavailable to nonmembers, there is, for those who want such things, a real incentive to join these groups. Finally, collective benefits must be distinguished from **public benefits** that accrue to both group members and nonmembers (e.g., the benefits to all people when the Sierra Club successfully fights for tighter clean-air laws).

Sometimes, a positive benefit is really the absence of a negative benefit, or cost, or "disincentive." Some groups coerce people into joining. A significant example of such a disincentive is pressure by labor unions to maintain "closed shops"; technically illegal, closed shops are workplaces where every employee is required to belong to a union. Since nonunion, non–dues-paying workers in a unionized factory obtain many of the benefits secured by the union (thus earning them the label of **free riders**), organized labor tries very hard to persuade them to join the union. Occasionally, the disincentive is a threat of violence. More legal, but no more subtle, is social pressure; for example, the union at one factory in Houston prominently displays the names of all free riders on a large billboard over the entrance gate.

The Disadvantages of Collective Action Why do some groups form and sustain themselves, while other potential groups are never created? Why do automobile, steel, electrical power, and Italian-type cheese producers have organized interest groups, while the much more numerous consumers of these products remain largely unrepresented by groups?

Political economist Mancur Olson has explained a great deal not only about interest-group formation, but also about the operation and maintenance of political organizations: "Unless the number of individuals in a group is quite small, or unless there is coercion or some other special device to make individuals act in their common interest, *rational, self-interested individuals will*

collective benefit: A benefit that is distributed to all members of a group.

public benefit: A benefit that is available to all members of a society, whether or not they are members of the group that was responsible for the production of the benefit; for example, military defense cannot be withheld from Americans who do not pay taxes.

free rider: A person who receives the benefits of group (i.e., collective) action without contributing to the costs of obtaining those benefits.

not act to achieve their common or group interests."[16] The reasons are straightforward. First, if a large, organized interest group provides a *public* good in which an individual shares, there is not sufficient economic incentive for that person to join the group. He or she could argue with confidence that the group's efforts would hardly be aided by the addition of just one more member (i.e., the total pool of benefits that the group wins will not increase very much). Besides, why should one pay the cost of membership when the benefits can be received for free? This is the free-rider problem again, and it seems to characterize the political activity of large numbers of people with common interests, such as air-breathers or workers.

Second, if no group currently represents the political interests of a large class of people, why should anyone form one? We have already discussed the concept of *organization cost,* the resources necessary to communicate with and coordinate the activities of a group. In politics, the costs of organizing a large group can be enormous. Consider the postal fees involved in mailing membership applications to all cheese consumers, not to mention the cost of identifying and locating these people and printing the address labels and applications. The costs to the relatively few cheese producers of organizing their interests and the benefits to them from fixing their prices—a fictitious example!—clearly differ in magnitude from the costs and benefits to the more numerous cheese buyers, even if the consumers know that they are paying double the real cost of the product. No single individual has an economic incentive to act, and the costs of organizing are too high. So, the United States has no cheese-consumers association. Nevertheless, other political groups are being formed and surviving. Organizations such as the American Civil Liberties Union, the Fund for Animals, and Greenpeace represent causes from which members expect little or no personal material benefit. Although Mancur Olson was concerned only with economic incentives for collective action, he did not deny that some people will act based upon their sense of justice.[17]

Political groups sometimes begin as nonpolitical groups and then develop political concerns as the world around them changes. The Roman Catholic Church in the United States certainly was not begun as a political organization, but it has taken on some aspects of that role as questions such as federal aid to parochial schools, artificial birth control, and abortion have become public policy issues. Many trade associations that now lobby for changes in regulations or increases in import fees started out as organizations designed to set industry standards and to regulate themselves. Only after government began directly affecting their interests did these nonpolitical groups become involved in public affairs.

In addition, sometimes political interest groups form in direct response to the activities of other such organizations. The collective activity of men and women who advocate the Equal Rights Amendment spawned an anti-ERA movement. The National Rifle Association's success in opposing gun control has led to the formation of a group called Handgun Control, which has attracted 130,000 members and is imitating the NRA's recruitment and lobbying tactics.

Finally, occasionally events of no one's design provide an impetus for organized political action. For example, at the turn of the century, industry was growing faster than the technology of industrial safety. The result was a series of industrial accidents and a record of substandard working conditions. In 1907, the death of 361 coal miners at Monongah, West Virginia, coupled with a rash of similar disasters, stimulated an organized coal-mining safety movement. The iron-and-steel industry, in which workers faced a one-in-four chance of death or disability for every three hundred days on the job, found itself facing a new Association of Iron and Steel Electrical Engineers. This association prompted the formation of the National Safety Council.[18]

The Maintenance of Political Groups Just as many costs are involved in the creation of interest groups, there are similarly many costs in their operation. The same problems that deter groups from forming remain when a group does form. For example, we have seen that the equal division of collective benefits among all the individuals in a large group will usually produce such a small payoff to each prospective member that it is rational for the group not to form. For the same reason, there are situations in which those who join a group have an incentive to withhold benefits from those who do not join or are excluded.

To illustrate, let us consider a fictitious society of 100 people who have a total of $100. With a constitution that makes it legal for members of the winning coalition (i.e., the majority) to decide by majority rule to allocate benefits (i.e., the $100) to themselves and to deny benefits to those who do not make the political decisions (i.e., the minority), a strong incentive exists to reduce the size of that winning coalition. In other words, if members of the "government" were to divide the society's resources among its citizens, each person would receive exactly one dollar. Yet, if the decisionmakers were to form a winning group of fifty-one (the number necessary to win by majority rule), their share would be $100 divided by 51 or $1.96. (Remember that we are dealing here with groups that were formed to yield an economic benefit to their members, not with ideological groups for whom the individual payoff is irrelevant.) Thus, there is a tendency in groups to reduce their membership to the smallest possible number needed to continue winning. Political scientist William H. Riker has called this phenomenon a **minimum winning coalition**.[19]

This incentive to reduce the size of groups greatly affects their operation in the real world. Those who are excluded are usually minorities—not racial minorities, but those groups that lack enough votes to dominate. In fact, minorities and dissidents within a group face a double obstacle: not only are they ignored because their votes are usually not needed, but the dominant faction within the group will try to suppress or even remove dissidents and competitors. This may occur (1) for reasons of ideological purity and group cohesion, or (2) because granting membership in a group such as a professional association is equivalent to licensing a new competitor, or (3) because small groups sometimes possess tactical advantages and flexibility that large groups rarely have. In examining groups designed to help government officials

minimum winning coalition: The smallest number of members of a group needed for the group to continue winning.

make decisions about scientific issues, physicist Joel Primack has observed this last problem:

> An inherent problem with science advising is that scientists with strong views are automatically excluded from advisory committees. The rule is that a committee is supposed to achieve a consensus. A committee that does not reach consensus only confuses the policy maker whom the committee is supposed to be advising. The result is that some major concern may be raised by a provocative scientist or other spokesman, but when the committee investigates it nobody can understand what the problem is because that person was never asked to join the committee, since he might not be willing to compromise.[20]

It follows from this that the internal management of many interest groups and associations is not democratic. Grant McConnell examined the constitutions of American labor unions and other groups and found no analogues to the Bill of Rights. However, he did find detailed lists of membership duties, which he calls "bills of obligation," as well as sanctions against members who advertise their grievances against the associations.[21] The leadership in some interest groups is very independent of the rank and file who, after all, cannot compete with the opportunities available to a group's full-time staff and management. This is not new to the government of associations. In 1914, the German social theorist Robert Michels wrote about the **iron law of oligarchy.** Observing the behavior of many European associations and political parties, Michels found so many advantages for the leaders of organizations that oligarchy (i.e., rule by the few) was inevitable. The oligarchy makes the rules, controls public relations, determines what qualifies as "acceptable" opposition to the organization, and so on.

Finally, the phenomenon of organization costs that we observe in the formation of any group continues as long as a group exists. The great advantage of group formation—information cost-saving—spawns an inescapable disadvantage. The tasks of information-gathering and communication among the members of the group must be organized and administered, and the cost of doing so is often very large. For example, consider an association of industrial corporations that are confronted with a new workplace-safety regulation. By standardizing their equipment, factories, production practices, and products, these companies can lessen or remove certain types of risks to workers and thereby reduce the complexity of future safety management. But establishing standards is neither easy nor cheap: the different companies must share their production records, their plans for future expansion, and even their perceptions of what constitutes an unacceptable hazard. The bargaining that follows will consume time and personnel, as will the continuing overseeing of compliance with the standards that are produced.

All of the factors that affect the operation and survival of interest groups also affect the roles that they play in American politics. The need to suppress internal dissent has contributed to the increase in the number of political groups as dissatisfied members break away and form their own organizations.

iron law of oligarchy: A postulated characteristic of organizations that tend to become oligopolies (i.e., organizations ruled by the few).

Suppression of the demands of minorities within groups has caused some viewpoints to go unrepresented, yet it has also probably preserved some continuity in American politics because the more numerous moderates typically ignore or expel radical members. As we turn now to a survey of the different types of interest groups that affect American government, the general characteristics of group formation and operation should be kept in mind.

TYPES OF INTEREST GROUPS

Any list of political interest groups will be incomplete because many groups, although primarily nonpolitical, have some concern with public issues. It would be stretching the definition of *interest group* to include the established religions in the United States, yet many of them have been active in issues involving education, health, and even foreign policy. Although the following discussion briefly examines the major types of political organizations, remember that these categories are not inclusive. Rather, they serve as an indication of the vast number of interest groups with political concerns. (Political parties will be presented in Chapter 4.)

Individual Businesses

Apart from the many business associations that take an interest in public issues, there are many companies that independently pursue particular policies. They form offices to scrutinize, analyze, and influence public policy. More than five hundred corporations have full-time lobbyists in Washington. For example, Ford Motor Company has a staff of more than forty people in the capital, and even very small companies have found it useful to have Washington representatives. These people serve as two-way conduits of information: (1) they alert the home office about relevant events in Congress, the executive departments, and the agencies, and (2) they provide information to policymakers and bureaucrats about pending policy issues and how their companies view them. Of course, even if corporations did not hire their own lobbyists, they would still be political groups simply because of their crucial role in the United States. In fact, individual businesses do not always need to organize in order to be heard in Washington, because government officials who are responsible for policy affecting particular businesses commonly contact them for information and advice.

Washington Lawyers

Many corporations choose not to invest in their own full-time staffs in Washington, yet they still need someone to keep them informed and to represent their interests. Smaller companies, and even large corporations on especially important matters, will turn to people who have lengthy experience and many personal contacts in the corridors of the Capitol and governmental agencies.

Many of these individuals are former agency officials or retired politicians, so they know which questions to ask and who can answer them. Because they are not tied to particular interest groups, they can be flexible. These experts are generally referred to as "Washington lawyers," or even "superlawyers," but not all of them are attorneys.

Washington lawyers are sometimes accused of manipulating our democratic institutions, yet most of their activities are accepted by administrators, members of Congress, and other observers as routine and appropriate. For example, these representatives can advise their corporate clients in advance about whether the Federal Trade Commission or the Department of Justice is likely to object to a proposed corporate merger as monopolistic. In addition, they can skillfully represent a petitioner (such as a small company asking the FCC for a television broadcasting license) that might otherwise stumble in the complicated procedures of agencies. While the system that makes these Washington representatives necessary—and often wealthy—may be far from perfect, it would be unfair to label it as thoroughly corrupt.

Business Associations

There is an enormous variety of business and trade associations in the United States. In addition to some of the more obscure groups, there are also some very large business associations. In fact, some are so large that they represent not only individual businesses, but even other business groups. The largest "peak association" is the United States Chamber of Commerce. Formed in 1912, it has an annual budget of over $30 million and a membership of about seventy thousand business firms, twenty-five hundred local chambers of commerce, and thirteen hundred trade and professional associations. The National Association of Manufacturers, with a budget of about $10 million per year, is made up mainly of large corporations and includes about thirteen thousand members. The Business Roundtable is a much more exclusive group; composed of the chief executive officers of about two hundred of the country's largest corporations (e.g., General Motors, Du Pont, IBM, Sears Roebuck), the Roundtable takes advantage of its members' professional connections by having them, rather than a hired staff, do its lobbying.

There are also large but more specialized business groups that are often involved in governmental affairs. For example, the National Soft Drink Association and the American Meat Institute were important participants in the rewriting of national food-safety standard legislation in 1981. Other large business and trade groups include the American Petroleum Institute, which represents about 85 percent of all oil and gas interests in the United States, the American Bankers Association, and the Grocery Manufacturers of America.

Small businesses also have associations. More than half a million small companies belong to the National Federation of Independent Businesses or the National Small Business Association. These groups routinely inform the Small Business Committee of the House of Representatives and the Small

Business Administration, an independent government agency, about the wishes and concerns of their members. They also make sure that their members are aware of pending opportunities and threats in Washington—and of who is responsible for them.

A common misperception of the role of business groups in politics is that their interests are so similar that they comprise a massive and powerful lobby capable of getting nearly everything it wants. While it is true that the differences among business groups are usually fewer than the dissimilarities between business interests and outside groups, business simply cannot always win because there is no single business interest. Consider the National Association of Broadcasters (NAB), which represents more than 5,300 radio and television stations:

> Because the NAB's membership is so diverse, smaller, more specialized trade associations have sprung up over the years to protect the interests of television stations (Association of Maximum Service Telecasters), television translator stations (National Translator Association), UHF television stations (Council for UHF Broadcasting and the National Association of UHF Broadcasters), clear-channel AM radio stations (Clear Channel Broadcasting Service), daytime AM stations (Daytime Broadcasters Association), stations owned by blacks (National Association of Black-Owned Broadcasters), religious stations (National Religious Broadcasters), and AM and FM stations (National Radio Broadcasters Association). Moreover, a separate and perhaps more potent lobbying group is made up of the three national networks, whose Washington representatives work in a kind of loose alliance. Thus the broadcast lobby is not truly monolithic but comprises many associations supporting several different and sometimes conflicting specific interests. These associations have tended to weaken the NAB's lobbying power, since it sometimes cannot present a unified front on regulatory questions.[22]

The special nature of the business-government relationship in the United States is particularly clear when we examine business interest-group activity in other democratic systems. For example, political scientist Roy Macridis noted that in England more than 85 percent of all manufacturing concerns belong to the Federation of British Industries, whereas only 6 percent of their American counterparts belong to the National Association of Manufacturers. Asked Macridis, "Why is it that in England interest groups avoid large publicity campaigns and center their attention on the party and the cabinet, while in the United States interest groups perform important publicity and propaganda functions through the media of communications and center their efforts on the electorate and the legislature, primarily?"[23]

Macridis finds one answer in the fundamental precepts of American politics: "[T]he American political system *with multiple foci* of decision-making, for instance, makes the legislature and more particularly individual legislators more susceptible to pressure either directly or indirectly; *the diffusion of power in the political party in the United States makes any effort to control or influ-*

ence the party unrewarding for pressure groups."[24] Thus, while business groups sometimes flex their muscles and shape new legislation or regulations, their more common strategy is to lobby particularly well-placed government officials while waging a campaign to rally public opinion behind their cause.

Labor Unions

The organization of labor unions in the United States was marked by violence and political controversy. Before the Civil War, unions consisted primarily of mechanics and artisans in large cities. After the war, the beginning of large-scale organized labor movements was plagued by the one-sided dominance of politics by businessmen and by the suspicion with which many workers eyed unionization. Moreover, the courts saw such movements as a potential violation of the old common-law prohibition against "conspiracy in restraint of trade." In the 1860s and 1870s, coal miners terrorized the coalfields of Pennsylvania in an attempt to assert their rights. In 1886, in an effort to win an eight-hour workday, unions, along with some socialists and anarchists, sponsored a strike in Chicago that culminated in a riot in that city's Haymarket Square. When it was over, eight policemen were dead, and four strikers were eventually hanged based on questionable evidence.

By the 1930s, American labor groups had successfully organized into many labor unions. Although far from universal in agreement, together they formed a powerful political and economic force, particularly in the large mass-production industries and services such as automobile assembly and trucking. Then, in 1935, Congress passed the National Labor Relations Act, or Wagner Act. The act guaranteed workers the right to form and join unions, prohibited employers from discriminating between union and nonunion workers, and in effect, assured unions the right to sponsor many kinds of strikes (see Chapter 13). Along with other legislation passed in the 1930s, the Wagner Act brought labor unions into the normal political process.

Today, many question whether organized labor can compete with organized business. Part of the problem has been labor's chronic inability to unite. The nation's largest union, the AFL-CIO, was not formed until 1955, when the American Federation of Labor and Congress of Industrial Organizations were reunited (the CIO had seceded from the AFL in 1935 when militant groups led by John L. Lewis broke away). In 1982, of 235 unions in the United States, 101 belonged to the AFL-CIO, which had a total membership of about 14.7 million. The AFL-CIO has often found itself in competition with the nonmember unions, particularly the United Auto Workers (UAW) (1.3 million workers), the United Mine Workers (185,000 workers), and the Teamsters (1.9 million workers). The Teamsters and the UAW were created by their expulsion and withdrawal, respectively, from the AFL-CIO. If business groups are sometimes bothered by internal differences, labor groups are plagued by them.

The individual unions that comprise the AFL-CIO generally negotiate labor contracts with employers. Thus, the AFL-CIO's primary task, other than trying to resolve conflicts among its member unions, is to press for desirable gov-

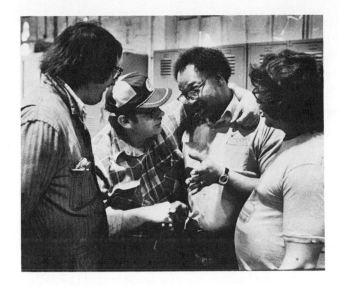

At a Buick torque converter plant in Flint, Michigan, an experimental worker-management relations is under way. Man, second from right, is the foreman-"adviser." Decisions are made by worker groups. (Michael Hayman/Photo Researchers, Inc.)

ernmental policies. In domestic matters, labor nearly always takes a liberal position, which generally is countered by the more conservative position of business groups. Through its political arm, the Committee on Political Education (COPE), the AFL-CIO lobbies for social programs such as unemployment insurance, medical care for the poor and elderly, and of course, workers' rights. Yet many of the issues on which labor takes a stand are irrelevant, or unknown, to its members. For example, the AFL-CIO strongly opposed the 1972 nomination to the Supreme Court of William Rehnquist, whom union leaders saw as potentially unfriendly on many social issues; most rank-and-file union members probably were unaware of the issue. On foreign policy matters, the position of labor groups is not always liberal; rather, it is often strongly anti-Communist. In the 1970s, many labor groups objected to American grain sales to the Soviet Union more than did American presidents, and some dockworkers went so far as to refuse to load or unload Soviet ships at American ports. Organized labor also opposed allowing the People's Republic of China to take a seat in the United Nations.

Labor unions face significant challenges in the 1980s. While the total number of organized workers has continued to climb, the percentage of American workers belonging to a union dropped from 28.0 percent in 1970 to 15 percent in 1983. As we will see when we examine political action committees, labor is being heavily outspent by business in campaign contributions. More important, many of the workers who join labor unions are ideologically opposed to some of labor's most fundamental political positions.

Public Interest Groups

Public Interest group is a general category into which we assign groups that seek a public good, rather than benefits for the members of a specific orga-

public interest group: An organization of individuals who claim to seek a public, not just a collective, good.

nization. Public interest groups usually claim that they counter the special interest groups by representing those who lack economic or political power. When we try to assign particular groups to this category, however, we run into some difficulty. Many public interest groups claim to be helping all members of society, often by attaching symbolic names to their organizations, such as "People's," "Freedom," and "Democratic." For example, a lobbying group was formed with the name "Emergency Committee for American Trade"; it consists of sixty-one large corporations that are trying to change parts of the 1977 Foreign Corrupt Practices Act, which prohibits bribes to officials of foreign governments in order to gain business.

Even groups that we might all agree are in the public interest are occasionally made up of individuals with self-interested, although sometimes subtle, motives for joining. It has been pointed out, primarily by the opponents of such groups, that environmental societies such as the Friends of the Earth, the Sierra Club, and the Wilderness Society are composed of an unrepresentative proportion of the young—that is, those who have the money, leisure time, and the physical ability to canoe, hike, and camp. The "public" good of unspoiled rivers and vistas is not likely to be shared by the inner-city poor, who will be disproportionately hurt by higher energy prices that will result from the failure to exploit oil and gas fields in remote, undeveloped areas. We cannot deny that while some goods are potentially available to all, there are few things that all can share equally. National defense is the most commonly cited public benefit, but the costs borne by a taxpayer who lives in the blast zone near a Strategic Air Command air base will be higher than for a citizen who resides far from a primary nuclear target.

The other major difficulty with public interest groups is that they can never actually represent the view of the entire public. We can all agree that poverty and disease are bad for everyone, so any action that improves the wealth and health of all in society, at no cost, is certainly in the public interest. Yet on the question of death, universal agreement does not exist. For example, groups have been formed to promote the legal acceptability of euthanasia, or "mercy killing," and the right of the terminally ill to die.

Some public interest groups have such broad goals that their primary objective seems to be to redefine "public interest" to fit their own perceptions. For instance, the American Civil Liberties Union (ACLU) is dedicated to protecting Americans' rights to free speech and assembly. Its vigilance has extended so far that in 1978 it obtained injunctions by which the courts ordered authorities not to interfere with an American Nazi parade in the predominantly Jewish city of Skokie, Illinois. It is no exaggeration to say that the scope of the First Amendment, which protects free speech, has been expanded largely because of the actions of the ACLU.

As already indicated, there is an enormous number of political groups that would claim the label *public interest.* In 1977, there were at least sixty "media reform groups" interested in television and radio broadcasting, including the United Church of Christ and the National Latino Media Coalition.[25] Like their business counterparts, these specialized interest groups are often in conflict with each other, even though each claims to represent the general public interest. As we observed previously, political interest groups sometimes form in response to the success of other political groups. Common Cause, a liberal, government "watchdog" group with hundreds of thousands of members, was soon challenged by the Conservative Caucus, and the conservative Heritage Foundation was established within a few years of Ralph Nader's consumer organizations, largely to counter the liberal leanings of Nader's research.

Single-Issue Groups

If, by **single-issue group,** we mean a group that is only interested in one policy question—for example, whether to return control of the Panama Canal to Panama—we will find in this category only groups that come and go too quickly to establish much of an organization or a mass membership. Such groups will usually disappear as soon as their one issue is resolved. If *single issue* is applied to one-issue areas such as workers' rights, resource conservation, or good government, then we could include most of the groups already described: labor, business, public interest, and so on. Single-issue groups are not used as forums for the expression of total ideologies, and their scope is narrower than that of entire economic sectors (e.g., business, labor). However, their long-range impact may be extensive. Political scientist E. E. Schattschneider referred to single-issue groups as organizations of private interests.[26]

In the last few decades, single-issue groups have proliferated and become much more active in politics. The 1960s saw a great increase in the number of civil-rights and antiwar groups. In the 1970s, the political activity of many religious groups grew, and conservative religious political groups were formed, including Moral Majority and The Religious Roundtable. The National Rifle Association, with its 1.8 million members, spent the 1970s successfully lob-

single-issue group: An interest group that tries to influence public policy in a single policy area.

The Gray Panthers, an interest group that claims to speak for the elderly, are seen here picketing. (© Bettye Lane/Photo Researchers, Inc.)

bying for the defeat of all attempts to strengthen the extremely weak Gun Control Act of 1968. Also formed during the 1970s were many groups to champion the interests of the elderly. Joining the National Council of Senior Citizens and the American Association of Retired Persons were groups representing elderly blacks and Hispanics; total membership of these groups exceeds 15 million. In the early 1980s, the arms-control movement coalesced into a "nuclear freeze" movement and organizations such as Ground Zero, which simply wants to alert people to the danger of nuclear arms.

Interest-group politics in recent years may one day be remembered as the time when special interest groups (which have been with us since the founding of the United States) came out of the closet. Not only did they grow in number, size, and activity, but they also grew in the sophistication of their tactics, as we will shortly see.

Governments as Interest Groups

In our discussion of the American federal system and the separation of powers, we showed that the American Founders intended for the different levels of government (national, state, and local) and the different functions of government (executive, legislative, and judicial) to check the power of each other. Because no government institution always dominates the others, the many agencies and departments at all levels of government frequently perform some of the same tasks as interest groups: that is, they organize interests, spread information, and advocate particular causes. In fact, some of the interest-group functions of government are inevitable, because bureaucrats, legislators, judges, and executives must influence the public agenda and often cannot escape limiting the scope of public debate.

There is a bit of hypocrisy in American governmental agencies being involved in advocacy politics. There are laws that forbid the use of public funds by agencies for the purpose of "public relations," yet most agencies have an office of public affairs or an office of information that produces press releases and publications, arranges speeches by agency officials, or sponsors traveling exhibits. Government offices also usually include "legislative liaisons," the function of which is the same as their interest-group counterparts: to lobby Congress.

When we examine the presidency, Congress, and the courts individually, we will see how they influence each other. Particularly bothersome to many observers are the instances in which government agencies attempt to influence policy by working through public opinion. The Department of Energy (DOE) and its predecessors have received the most criticism in this vein. A General Accounting Office report issued in 1978 documented how the Energy Research and Development Administration greatly increased its "nuclear power information" (i.e., pro-nuclear) activities in California shortly before a 1976 state referendum on nuclear energy. The Carter administration changed this emphasis; a 1980 congressional study criticized the DOE's public information programs for emphasizing solar energy and energy conservation and ignoring coal and nuclear energy. Later, under the Reagan administration, the DOE was forced to scuttle a $2-million pro-nuclear public information program that would have included "arranging public appearances and interviews with friendly journalists for DOE officials, hiring writers to prepare articles for popular magazines, arranging meetings with local government officials and private civic organizations, and holding seminars for the press."[27]

State and local governments are frequently involved in attempts to gain advantages from federal spending and taxing programs. Since the late 1960s, when Congress enacted hundreds of Lyndon Johnson's "categorical grant" programs giving federal revenues back to the states for specific purposes, state lobbyists have been trying to win favorable decisions from the bureaucrats who administer grant programs. To that end, public-sector organizations such as the National League of Cities, the National Conference of Mayors, the National Conference of State Legislatures, and the National Association of Counties have been active lobbyists. They also work on Congress to prevent unfavorable changes in the tax system; for example, in 1982, state governments actively opposed a congressional proposal to eliminate federal income tax deductions for state sales tax.

TECHNIQUES AND EFFECTIVENESS OF INTEREST-GROUP POLITICS

Interest groups possess three basic kinds of resources: money, information, and votes. The weapons in any interest group's resource arsenal will be an important factor in the goals and strategies that the group pursues, just as a nation's military strengths and weaknesses affect its foreign policy. It is useful to arrange the tactics of interest groups into three general categories: (1) direct communication with government officials, (2) lobbying through the groups' constituents, and (3) pressuring policymakers through elections and public opinion.[28] By examining how the resources of money, information, and votes are applied in each of these strategies, we can gain a general understanding of how groups operate.

Direct Communication with Government Officials

The representatives of the people are often unable to find out what the people want. Only a few Americans care enough about politics to contact their legislators. A larger number of citizens pay attention to public affairs but rarely become involved in them, while a larger percentage do not care about politics at all. One of the most productive strategies of interest-group politics is to fill that gap by providing lawmakers with information about public demands and support.

Political scientists have shown that for most interest groups, the most time consuming task is informing and listening to their own members, followed by doing the same with public officials. One reason that we have not used the term *pressure group* in this chapter is that groups rarely press. Instead, they are more likely to seek sympathetic legislators or agents in the executive branch and provide them with information that can be used to support their policy requests. In their contacts with officials, lobbyists most often seek to reinforce, not persuade. Only if a group is short of a winning majority and has sufficient resources will it attempt to expand its corps of supporters.

Three types of information are useful to a legislator in fighting a battle over a policy. The most important is usually technical information about current conditions, the operation of the proposed policy, and its likely effects. Members of Congress and their staffs rarely have the background, expertise, or spare time to investigate such matters themselves. As a result, they frequently depend upon—and even solicit—lobbyists from inside or outside the government to aid with information searches. Another useful type of information is a sort of strategic reconnaissance: interest-group representatives are often in a position to scout the legislative terrain, discover what enemies or obstacles may be faced, and suggest adjustments in the proposed law or possible coalitions with other legislators that will increase the chances of victory. Finally, interest groups, especially those active in a legislator's congressional district or state, can keep the legislator informed about the electoral climate at home, and how the official's actions may be received by his or her constituents.

amicus curiae ("friend of the court") brief: A written argument filed by interested individuals or groups to provide additional information or analysis of a case.

In addition, an interest group can become directly involved in the political process through the courts. Although an interest group can initiate a suit on its own, groups commonly band together to ask for relief through the judicial system. A group may also file an **amicus curiae** ("friend of the court") **brief,** recommending to the court new information or a particular decision. During the 1970s, direct action through the courts became very common, particularly in the area of environmental policy. The National Environmental Policy Act of 1969 made explicit provisions for group participation. The act allowed groups to assist in the preparation of environmental impact statements, which were required to justify any federal action with a potentially significant impact on the environment. In addition, it allowed groups to file lawsuits to block federal actions. However, in the early 1980s, several Supreme Court decisions narrowed the rights of environmental groups and private citizens to sue in environmental cases.

Because we are discussing only direct contact with public officials in this section, the group resource that some organizations are richest in—votes—is not relevant here. And the resource of money can only be indirectly used, because its direct transfer to judges or lawmakers, unless in the form of a campaign contribution, would constitute bribery. However, money is a necessary asset for the accumulation and spread of information. For example, it is very costly to perform the research necessary to obtain information on the public health impacts of a change in regulations on leaded gasoline, and public interest groups are usually much poorer than their business or trade association counterparts. In fact, public interest groups have a problem. One of the most effective ways for them to raise money is to offer tax deductibility to donors, and an effective way for the groups to keep most of the donations is to be exempt from income tax. However, tax-exempt status is narrowly defined by the Internal Revenue Code, so if an interest group makes a "substantial" lobbying effort, it can lose this status.

Lobbying Through Constituents

Interest groups often try to influence legislators by agitating or recruiting the electorate. When we examine Congress, we will see that the susceptibility of its members to constituency influence varies according to policy areas. For example, a senator from a farm state will be particularly sensitive to the demands of farm groups on agricultural issues, and even a liberal legislator from Massachusetts may support construction of a new fighter aircraft if some of his or her constituents manufacture aircraft engines. Interest-group influence through constituents is often very strong. The National Rifle Association uses a telephone network to warn its members of impending gun-control measures and can arrange for many thousands of telegrams to be sent to Capitol Hill within hours.

Some groups send their members newsletters that include postcards or form letters ready to be signed and mailed to Congress. During the 1982 attempt to deregulate the telecommunications industry, the American Telephone & Telegraph Company (AT&T) mailed letters to its stockholders asking them to contact their representatives and senators and request that they oppose a bill that would have restricted AT&T's ability to compete in the telecommunications market after its breakup. The accompanying box was included in each letter. And yet, AT&T complained that a deceptive letter was sent by the National Coalition for Fair Rates and Competition—AT&T's competitors—to constituents of members of an important congressional committee; that letter included a sample letter favoring the legislation in question, with the constituent's name and the congressional representative's address already printed on it.

Do these tactics work? Some members of Congress insist that mass mailings, especially form letters, are commonly disregarded, while others admit that huge sacks of mail piling up in their offices are certainly noticed. An estimated tens of millions of letters and telegrams were sent to Congress at the instigation of the commercial banking and savings-and-loan industry in opposition to a proposed withholding tax on interest and dividends in 1983. Even though legislators acknowledged that the letter writers were generally wrong about what the bill would have done, it was soundly defeated.

One constraint on overzealous lobbying by interest groups is the feeling of many Americans that intensive group participation, especially by businesses, is wrong. In his 1976 presidential campaign, Jimmy Carter often complained about the influence of special interests in Washington. During the congressional debate over the Natural Gas Policy Act of 1978, the large oil and gas corporations in the United States refrained from putting huge resources directly

Who to write and who to call to protest

Who should you contact to express your views on H.R. 5158?

First, your own Congressman and Senators. You can write a letter, place a telephone call, or even visit their local offices.

Your letter should be addressed to:

**The Honorable (name)
U.S. House of Representatives
Washington, D.C. 20515**

(or)

**The Honorable (name)
U.S. Senate
Washington, D.C. 20510**

If you're not sure who represents your district in the House, you can call this toll-free AT&T number for assistance: 800 257-5050. If you live in New Jersey, call 800 452-0200. These numbers will be in operation from 9 a.m. to 6 p.m., Eastern time, Monday through Friday.

Your local board of elections, the League of Women Voters and other groups in your community will also gladly assist you with information and guidance.

In addition, here is a list of the members of the U.S. House Committee on Energy and Commerce, which is expected to consider the bill after Congress' Easter recess. Certain members, as indicated, also belong to the Subcommittee on Telecommunications, Consumer Protection and Finance, which originated the bill. You may want to contact some member of this committee, particularly if he or she is from your state. And if your own Congressman appears on the list, your letter or call can be all the more effective.

*Chairman, John D. Dingell (Mich.)
*Ranking Minority Leader, James T. Broyhill (N.C.)
*Subcommittee Chairman, Timothy E. Wirth (Colo.)

Cleve Benedict (W. Va.)
*Thomas J. Bliley, Jr. (Va.)
Clarence J. Brown (Ohio)
Dan R. Coats (Ind.)
Tom Corcoran (Ill.)
*Cardiss Collins (Ill.)
*James M. Collins (Texas)
W. E. Dannemeyer (Cal.)
James J. Florio (NJ)
Albert Gore, Jr. (Tenn.)
Phil Gramm (Texas)
Ralph M. Hall (Texas)
Gary A. Lee (NY)
Mickey Leland (Texas)
Norman F. Lent (NY)
*Thomas A. Luken (Ohio)
Edward R. Madigan (Ill.)
*Edward J. Markey (Mass.)
*Marc L. Marks (Pa.)
Barbara A. Mikulski (Md.)
A. Toby Moffett (Conn.)

*Carlos J. Moorhead (Cal.)
*Ronald M. Mottl (Ohio)
Richard L. Ottinger (NY)
*Matthew J. Rinaldo (NJ)
Don Ritter (Pa.)
Harold Rogers (Ky.)
Jim Santini (Nev.)
*James H. Scheuer (NY)
Philip R. Sharp (Ind.)
Richard C. Shelby (Ala.)
*"Al" B. Swift (Wash.)
Mike Synar (Okla.)
*Thomas J. Tauke (Iowa)
*W. J. (Billy) Tauzin (La.)
Doug Walgren (Pa.)
*Henry A. Waxman (Cal.)
Bob Whittaker (Kan.)
Ron Wyden (Ore.)

*Subcommittee on Telecommunications, Consumer Protection and Finance.

Members of the House Committee on the Judiciary also may be called upon to consider the bill following the Easter recess. You may want to contact some member of this committee as well.

Peter Rodino (NJ) Chairman
Robert McClory (Ill.)
   Ranking Minority Member
John M. Ashbrook (Ohio)
Jack Brooks (Tex.)
M. Caldwell Butler (Va.)
John Conyers, Jr. (Mich.)
George E. Danielson (Cal.)
Don Edwards (Cal.)
Billy Lee Evans (Ga.)
Hamilton Fish, Jr. (NY)
Barney Frank (Mass.)
Dan Glickman (Kan.)
Sam B. Hall, Jr. (Tex.)
William J. Hughes (NJ)

Henry J. Hyde (Ill.)
Robert W. Kastenmeier (Wis.)
Thomas N. Kindness (Ohio)
Dan Lungren (Cal.)
Romano L. Mazzoli (Ky.)
Bill McCollum (Fla.)
Carlos J. Moorhead (Cal.)
Tom Railsback (Ill.)
Harold S. Sawyer (Mich.)
Patricia Schroeder (Colo.)
John F. Seiberling (Ohio)
F. J. Sensenbrenner, Jr. (Wis.)
Mike Synar (Okla.)
Harold Washington (Ill.)

into their support of price deregulation. Pietro S. Nivola described the role of the energy industry.

> There were important limitations on the style and extent of the lobbying effort led by the large oil and gas corporations. One constraint was their concern lest the cause of deregulation suffer from a conspicuous campaign waged directly for it by "big oil." With public suspicion of the oil-gas lobby still running deep, zealous intervention by the industry's leading firms could backfire, provoking another round of legislative recriminations and investigations. . . .
>
> Further counseling caution and restraint were recollections of the setbacks that had resulted from excessive industry pressure during previous gas deregulation battles. In 1956 both houses of Congress had actually adopted legislation gutting [a proregulation Supreme Court] decision by exempting most producers from [Federal Power Commission] jurisdiction. But with the disclosure that a senator had been the object of an attempted bribe by the Superior Oil Company of California, President Eisenhower felt compelled to veto the bill, citing the bribery incident as an "arrogant" affront to "the integrity of governmental processes". . . .
>
> Consequently, as the larger firms renewed their drive to obtain more favorable natural gas legislation in 1977–78, they resorted increasingly to other tactics—specifically, "grass-roots" mobilization of allied interests through a coordinating organization named the Natural Gas Supply Committee (NGSC). Instead of just approaching members of Congress directly, the committee urged a variety of third parties at the state or district level to exert influence.[29]

Many small interest groups have no such options. They cannot recruit other like-minded associations and they need not worry about overdoing their lobbying activities, because such groups often promote isolated issues and cannot afford extravagant lobbying campaigns. In other words, great size and large budgets are mixed blessings.

Lobbying Through Elections and Public Opinion

Attempts by interest groups to influence election campaigns or public opinion are not new in American politics. What is new, and of great concern, is the increasing likelihood that in an age when election campaigns, including advertising through the mass media, are becoming more dependent on expensive technologies, only the wealthy will be able to be heard and only those with wealthy supporters will be elected.

Of course, money is not the only way for interest groups to lobby. They may issue press releases that expose wrongdoing or "wrong" policymaking; for example, Ralph Nader's consumer and political groups have been particularly successful at attracting media attention. Interest groups also frequently mobilize volunteers to work on election campaigns; in 1982, environmental groups organized about fifteen thousand volunteers to help about seventy carefully chosen congressional candidates facing tough races. Endorsements by interest groups can also be important to candidates. Two years before the 1984 presidential election, nearly every contender for the Democratic nomination attended an assembly of the 160,000-member Sheet Metal Workers' International Association in search of the union's endorsement.

In Chapter 5, as we discuss politics and the American electoral system, the role of Political Action Committees (PACs) will be examined in detail. Here, it will suffice to mention that contributions from interest-group PACs to candidates are raising the cost of elections and thus may be redistributing the basis of political power from votes to financial support. In fact, PACs are becoming so important that some interest groups may be forsaking the use of information and votes and relying on monetary contributions alone.

The importance of wealth in affecting elections and public opinion is not confined to the PAC phenomenon. Interest groups, particularly business associations, have turned increasingly to the use of initiatives and referenda as a means for changing public policy. Earlier in this chapter, we discussed Proposition 13 and antinuclear and pro-marijuana decriminalization issues on the ballot in California. There have also been nuclear energy issues voted upon in Montana, Oregon, and Washington; tax policy battles in Massachusetts (Proposition 2½) and in North Dakota; and an initiative in California to ban smoking in public places. A public interest group, the Council on Economic Priorities, found that Standard Oil Company of California, R. J. Reynolds Tobacco, Philip Morris, and Union Electric of St. Louis each spent over $1 million in 1980 on such initiatives. In campaigns where these business groups outspent their rivals, they won eleven out of fourteen. Although it is difficult to prove that these expenditures caused the defeat of antibusiness measures, corporations certainly expected them to have an impact.

Perhaps the best evidence of the increasing significance of the PAC as an interest-group resource is its adoption by groups that traditionally have relied on information and vote mobilization in order to influence politics. Although PACs have been formed primarily by labor unions and trade associations, by the 1980s, environmental and public interest groups were beginning to rely more heavily on their own campaign contribution committees. To some, this makes the PAC phenomenon less ominous: if only one type of interest group can use what may be an important type of access to public officials, an imbalance of political influence could result. Yet even if other types of groups use PACs, the shift to greater reliance on funds is an advantage for those who have, or can raise, more money.

Once again, it is difficult to answer whether money is better spent on a political party, candidate, or ballot initiative. Many factors can affect the transmission of political demands from individual voters or interest groups through the electoral system, into the White House, courts, or Congress, and finally into public policy. In fact, many have wondered whether elections really matter at all. Much of the remainder of this book will be concerned with how the various institutions and processes of American government translate public values into public actions. Therefore, we will end this chapter with a discussion of how interest groups, as institutions, fit into the larger scheme of government.

REGULATION OF INTEREST GROUPS

Interest groups play a peculiar role in American politics. On the one hand, they are crucial mechanisms for communications between citizens and public officials. As we have seen, individuals are unlikely to participate in politics by themselves, because their single voices are not easily heard and they can expect few worthwhile individual benefits from participation. Therefore, they form groups. At the same time, interest groups have generally been treated as aberrations in the American political system, with public figures commonly suggesting that the participation of these groups is inherently corrupting and undemocratic. The greatest fear about interest-group activity is that unequal opportunities to influence public offficials will result from the unequal distribution of money among such groups. Yet, the greatest virtue of interest-group participation is the realization of First Amendment rights of free speech and assembly. Thus, efforts to regulate groups have been justified on the basis of reducing the relative power of big money while carefully protecting political rights.

The first such attempt took place in Wisconsin in 1905, when that state required lobbyists to register as such, banned them from the floor of legislatures, and required them to publicly account for their lobbying expenditures. The first attempt at federal control was the Federal Corrupt Practices Act of 1925, which had practically no effect. It was later supplanted by the Federal Regulation of Lobbying Act of 1946. This law, which was intended to control lobbying by requiring public disclosure of expenditures rather than by limiting group activity, was also generally ignored, because the Supreme Court interpreted it to apply only to groups whose principal purpose was to affect legislation. This decision thus excluded General Motors, the American Medical Association, and so on, because lobbying is not their principal purpose for existing.

By the late 1960s, electoral reform was once again on the public agenda. The costs of presidential and congressional election campaigns were skyrocketing, and in response Congress passed the Federal Election Campaign Act of 1971. While the act was intended to make interest-group participation in elections more honest and open, it may have had the opposite effect. First of all, campaign contributions from individual business firms, which had been prohibited since 1907, were made legal. Then, amendments to the act in 1974 and 1976 led to a proliferation of PACs established by corporations and other groups. The number of PACs grew from 516 in 1974 to 3,479 in 1982, and their campaign contributions increased from $12 million in the 1974 congressional races to $135 million in 1980 (including $60 million for congressional candidates).

INTEREST GROUPS IN AMERICAN POLITICS

According to Karl Marx, the ideas that control a society are the ideas of its dominant class. It is not clear whether the United States has had a dominant class, because different groups have found a variety of access points to the policymaking institutions of government. Numerous examples can be found in American history of public decisions that recognize the demands and rights of various groups. Even among groups that could be designated as elite, there is often profound disagreement about public policies. There are wealthy liberals and wealthy conservatives. Some corporate leaders oppose any warming of relations with Communist countries, while other business executives see improved trade relations as a means for assuring international cooperation—and larger markets. Yet, one of the most important characteristics of American society is the general agreement among nearly all participants in politics, whatever their ideological viewpoint, that the system of American government is basically legitimate. Many improvements may be demanded, but the fundamental American political structure is not in danger of radical attack. This consensus has important consequences for the influence exerted by different types of interest groups.

According to political economist Charles E. Lindblom, in a mixed political economy such as the American system, business and political leaders share common goals: producing goods and services, employing people, and paying out income shares to workers. Business firms will produce only if they are offered the proper incentives (i.e., profits for their investors). Therefore, democratic governments in mixed political economies have a special incentive to cooperate with the corporate sector; as President Eisenhower's secretary of defense, Charles Wilson, who had previously been president of General Motors, once said, "What's good for General Motors is good for the country." Another analysis of interest-group politics makes much the same point. Robert Holsworth has written that by joining in the basic consensus about the American sytem, liberal interest groups assured the failure of their proposed reforms. According to Holsworth, Ralph Nader has never questioned the underlying structure of the American political economy, but has only sniped at a few of its most obvious failings. Without getting at the root causes of social and economic problems, consumer groups and other liberal organizations have not only defeated themselves; they have also dealt a sharp blow to the cause of American liberalism, because liberals ultimately cannot advance policies that fundamentally undermine the vitality of American business. Thus, while significant costs can be, and have been, imposed upon business by government, a point is reached when this can go no further.[30]

There can be no doubt that producer groups—corporations—have many advantages over consumer groups in political action. They have greater financial and organizational resources, they can avoid the problems inherent to group formation by large collectivities (as Mancur Olson described), and they can exploit the belief of many Americans that the promotion of the private sector of the economy is fundamental to the public interest. Yet, although the automobile industry actively opposed clean-air regulations in the 1960s and 1970s and the airline industry was nearly unanimous in opposing airline deregulation in the late 1970s, they lost because they were outside of the consensus on what the "public interest" was. As we turn now to an examination of American political parties, we will see further evidence that the blending of a complex set of economic incentives and political values has created a political system in the United States that is much too complicated to be crudely characterized as one controlled by the privileged.

NOTES

[1]George F. Bishop, Robert W. Oldendick, Alfred J. Tuchfarber, and Stephen E. Bennett, "Pseudo-Opinions on Public Affairs," *Public Opinion Quarterly* 44 (Summer 1980): 201.

[2]Lyndon B. Johnson, *The Vantage Point* (New York: Holt, Rinehart, and Winston, 1971).

[3]Bray Hammond, *Banks and Politics in America* (Princeton: Princeton University Press, 1957), p. 328.

[4]Anthony Downs, *An Economic Theory of Democracy* (New York: Harper & Row, 1957), p. 267.

[5]Thomas E. Patterson, *The Mass Media Election: How Americans Choose Their President* (New York: Praeger, 1980); and John A. Ferejohn and Morris P. Fiorina, "The Paradox of Not Voting: A Decision Theoretic Analysis," *American Political Science Review* 67 (1974): 525–536.

[6]Clifford W. Brown, Jr., Roman B. Hedges, and Lynda W. Powell, "Modes of Elite Political Participation: Contributors to the 1972 Presidential Candidates," *American Journal of Political Science* 24 (May 1980): 261–262.

[7]James Q. Wilson, *The Amateur Democrat* (Chicago: University of Chicago Press, 1966), p. 4.

[8]Jeane Kirkpatrick, *Political Woman* (New York: Basic Books, 1974).

[9]Werner Sombart, *Why Is There No Socialism in the United States?*, trans. Patricia M. Hocking and C. T. Husbands (London: Macmillan, 1976), p. 56.

[10]See David B. Truman, *The Governmental Process: Political Interests and Public Opinion*, 2nd ed. (New York: Knopf, 1951).

[11]Alexis de Tocqueville, *Democracy in America*, vol. I (New York: Schocken, 1961), pp. 216, 222–223.

[12]Forrest McDonald, *We the People: The Economic Origins of the Constitution* (Chicago: University of Chicago Press, 1958).

[13]Jeffrey Berry, *Lobbying for the People* (Princeton: Princeton University Press, 1977).

[14]Cited and discussed in Andrew S. McFarland, *Public Interest Lobbies: Decision Making on Energy* (Washington, D.C.: American Enterprise Institute, 1976), p. 90.

[15]Karl Mannheim, *Ideology and Utopia* (New York: Harcourt Brace & World, 1936), chapter 2.

[16]Mancur Olson, Jr., *The Logic of Collective Action: Public Goods and the Theory of Groups* (Cambridge: Harvard University Press, 1965), p. 2. Emphasis in the original.

[17]For a discussion of the importance of political goals as inducements for people to form or join groups, see Terry M. Moe, *The Organization of Interests* (Chicago: University of Chicago Press, 1980).

[18]William Graebner, *Coal-Mining Safety in the Progressive Period* (Lexington: University of Kentucky Press, 1976).

[19]William H. Riker, *The Theory of Political Coalitions* (New Haven: Yale University Press, 1962).

[20]Joel Primack, "Scientists and Political Activity: Insiders, Outsiders, and the Need for a New Ideology," in Sanford A. Lakoff, ed., *Science and Ethical Responsibility* (Reading, Massachusetts: Addison-Wesley, 1980), p. 228.

[21]Grant McConnell, *Private Power and American Democracy* (New York: Knopf, 1966), chapter 5.

[22]Erwin G. Krasnow, Lawrence D. Longley, and Herbert A. Terry, *The Politics of Broadcast Regulation*, 3rd ed. (New York: St. Martin's, 1982), p. 53.

[23]Roy Macridis, "Interest Groups in Comparative Analysis," *Journal of Politics* 23 (1961): 35.

[24]Ibid.

[25]Krasnow et al., *The Politics of Broadcast Regulation*, p. 57.

[26]E. E. Schattschneider, *The Semisovereign People* (New York: Holt, Rinehart & Winston, 1960).

[27]*Science*, October 30, 1981, p. 527.

[28]Berry, *Lobbying for the People*, chapter 8.

[29]Pietro S. Nivola, "Energy Policy and the Congress: The Politics of the Natural Gas Policy Act of 1978," *Public Policy* 28 (Fall 1980): 502–504.

[30]Charles E. Lindblom, *Politics and Markets* (New York: Basic, 1977); and Robert Holsworth, "Why Liberalism Failed," in Alan Stone and Edward Harpham, eds., *The Political Economy of Public Policy* (Beverly Hills: Sage, 1982).

BIBLIOGRAPHY

Berry, Jeffrey M. *Lobbying for the People.* Princeton: Princeton University Press, 1977. An in-depth study of the behavior of public interest groups.

Erickson, Robert S., Norman G. Luttbeg, and Kent L. Tedin. *American Public Opinion: Its Origins, Content, and Impact.* 2nd ed. New York: Wiley, 1980. A comprehensive collection of much of the scientific analysis of public opinion.

Gormley, William T., Jr. *The Politics of Public Utility Regulation.* Pittsburgh: University of Pittsburgh Press, 1983. A description of the regulatory process at the state level, with particular emphasis on the patterns and effectiveness of participation by utility companies, consumer advocates, and others.

Lowi, Theodore J. *The End of Liberalism.* 2nd ed. New York: Norton, 1979. A provocative study of the implications of the increased importance of interest groups.

McConnell, Grant. *Private Power and American Democracy.* New York: Knopf, 1966. A critique of the pluralist theory of groups in American politics.

Olson, Mancur, Jr. *The Logic of Collective Action: Public Goods and the Theory of Groups.* Cambridge: Harvard University Press, 1965. A landmark study of the problems facing the formation and maintenance of groups.

Ornstein, Norman J., and Shirley Elder. *Interest Groups, Lobbying, and Policymaking.* Washington: Congressional Quarterly Press, 1978. A useful analysis of the techniques and effectiveness of lobbies, with three illuminating case studies.

Truman, David B. *The Governmental Process: Political Interests and Public Opinion, 2nd ed.* New York: Knopf, 1951. A timeless study of the importance of groups in American politics.

Verba, Sidney, and Norman H. Nie. *Participation in America: Political Democracy and Social Equality.* New York: Harper & Row, 1972. An analysis, based on thorough survey data, of the reasons that Americans participate in politics and of the effects of this participation on their leaders.

Wolfinger, Raymond E., and Steven J. Rosenstone. *Who Votes?* New Haven: Yale University Press, 1980. A detailed examination of the incentives for and obstacles to voting.

Political Parties: Organized Participation and Control

American political parties are not mentioned in the Constitution, nor were they considered in the debates at the Constitutional Convention. When the Founders thought about the agents of political conflict, they focused on the impact of interests, not parties. Almost immediately after the organization of the new government, groups became divided over such issues as American fiscal policy and the resumption of trade with England. Gradually, these temporary interests entered into coalitions with other interests, leading to the development of political parties by 1796. The framers of the Constitution did not see this as a favorable development. For example, George Washington, in his farewell address to the nation, warned of "the baneful effects of the spirit of party."

In view of Washington's great influence and the absence of parties from the Constitution, how did they begin and grow? For the answer, we must look first to the Constitution. While it contains nothing about the role of parties in elections or in Congress nor anything specific about the electorate's constitutional right to form and operate parties, it does guarantee a number of political rights that might not ensure the growth of parties, but that certainly allow them to exist. The congressional privileges in Article I provided factions within the legislature with the freedom to organize and speak without outside interference. Effective parties would have been impossible without the First Amendment's guarantee of free speech. And the promise of religious liberty ensured by the same amendment indicated a rejection of the historical European intolerance of religious factions. Even the procedural protections in the Bill of Rights—such as the protection from self-incrimination, arbitrary imprisonment, and unreasonable search and seizure—grew from a tradition of the suppression of minorities and were designed, at least in part, to allow both individual and organized dissent.

One obstacle to the acceptance of parties as a legitimate part of government may have been the fuzzy distinction between *party* and *faction.* The two words were often used interchangeably in the late 1700s, and a faction was generally viewed as a narrow, self-interested group. Over the last two centuries, some American political parties may have fit this description, but the term *party* has been applied more frequently to organizations with a more positive role. Today, a political party, in its ideal form, is an organization that performs six basic functions.

THE IDEAL FUNCTIONS OF POLITICAL PARTIES

First, the primary purpose of political parties is to win elections and thereby acquire power. In the same way that Adam Smith saw us all as self-interested, economic actors, parties can be viewed as self-interested, political actors. There is nothing inherently unjust or detrimental to society in this; just as Smith saw an "invisible hand" guiding our competitive private economic actions to produce increased welfare for all, the behavior of parties as they

109

compete for votes produces the socially desirable effects that they achieve. Democracy in America depends on the opportunities and constraints on power seekers as they compete for the people's vote, and parties are a fundamental part of that competition.

In pursuit of electoral victories, parties serve a second function: they perform useful political and electoral services, although at a cost, for the public. For example, while we will examine arguments that parties provide only sparse, self-serving, and mainly symbolic information to the public, it is possible that without such simplified information as party labels for candidates, many voters would know absolutely nothing about political questions and choices. This is due to the high costs to unorganized voters of becoming knowledgeable about many possible public actions. We will also see that parties serve important electoral functions in American politics by organizing and administering elections at all levels of government. The Constitution is vague about who or what should carry out its provisions for the selection by the public of the nation's leaders. Once again, the parties have been able to make this activity clearly advantageous to themselves, yet the electorate as a whole benefits. Similarly, parties simplify and organize the public agenda, discovering the issues about which the public is particularly concerned, and condensing a mass of potential problems into a relatively manageable electoral or legislative package. Although a price is paid by segments of the public because some important issues are removed from the public agenda, the alternative would be chaos on the ballot and in our political institutions.

Third, in an indirect way, party politics preserves social order. Because the American electorate is not homogeneous, it could be divided into a large number of ethnic, racial, religious, economic, and regional minorities, each with possibly strident and unyielding views. But the political system may effectively exclude minorities that do not participate in the large coalitions of the Democratic and Republican parties, who are usually the only winners. Thus, there is a powerful incentive for small groups to cooperate so that they may join those coalitions. At the same time, the parties, in order to build coalitions, must promise to distribute at least some benefits to those who support it.

Fourth, the American party system reflects and extends the fundamental principles of separation of power and federalism throughout the political system. The party system is often fragmented and decentralized among the local, state, congressional, and presidential levels. Although a few parties have simultaneously shown great strength in Congress and the White House, for example, it is unlikely that any party could ever monopolize control of political offices across the entire federal system.

Fifth, parties link citizens to their government by making it possible for them to know who is responsible for the success or failure of a policy.[1] Although few voters could identify the senators or representatives who sponsored a policy failure, they are likely to know which party to blame. This function is not as straightforward as it may seem. Remember, the United States was not formed as a democracy, in which citizens directly participate in government; the Founders openly distrusted such a system. Instead, the nation was formed as a republic, in which citizen influence would be exerted indirectly through representative institutions. This indirectness is partly responsible for the blurring of accountability that has weakened the link between citizens and the government.

American parties began when members of Congress with similar interests banded together in their legislative activities. Thus, *parties in the legislature coordinate the choices of elected officials, facilitate communication among members, and organize like-minded colleagues.* As in the electorate, the party in Congress reduces information and transaction costs.

Of course, not all of the ideal functions of political parties have always been performed by the parties that have existed in the United States. For example, particular parties have at times monopolized political power in some state and local governments, thereby denying the electorate the useful electoral services provided by competition between parties. As we will see, the American party system has developed in such a way that legitimate dissent has sometimes been squelched. And it can be argued that the citizen-government link has been a less important feature of parties than their desire to attain positions of power.

Furthermore, within this definition of a political party, there is considerable room for variation. For example, many European parties are tightly knit, with well-bounded, rather stable coalitions of interests. Unlike the French Communists, the Dutch Catholic People's Party, and the Swedish Center Party, to name only a few, American political parties have heterogeneous constituencies. They therefore perform their ideal functions somewhat irresponsibly, according to some critics. (Responsible parties take unambiguous positions on issues so that the voters can hold them accountable for the failures and successes of public policy.) Nevertheless, the effective performance of the six electoral and legislative tasks is important for the success of a political party. The calls for party reform are loudest when a party fails to properly carry out one or more of these functions.

One of the six ideal functions of parties is of paramount importance. It might be possible to devise some agency, private or public, that could be trusted to handle the mechanics of elections (e.g., registering voters and arranging candidate lists) without the assistance of political parties. It might also be possible that some other type of group could inform the voters about current issues and suggest which are of the most immediate importance; in fact, that is precisely what many interest groups do. But what separates parties from interest groups is the basic task of offering candidates to the public who will stake their political future on a set of policies for which the party stands. The League of Women Voters, the AFL-CIO, and the United States Chamber of Commerce may help voters save information costs, but no one campaigns for election on their tickets. What often appears to be an unseemly scramble for votes is one price that we pay for the peculiarly American version of democracy.

In the remainder of this chapter, we will discuss the evolution of the current American two-party system, its operations at the various levels of government, and the reasons that people become involved with parties. The six ideal functions of political parties should be kept in mind, because they provide a useful framework for organizing and understanding the behavior of American parties.

THE RISE OF THE TWO-PARTY SYSTEM

The first two American presidential elections, held in 1789 and 1792, were hardly what we would today consider typical.[2] First of all, there were no political parties. And, with George Washington's heroic leadership available for the presidency, there was little opposition. In addition, the Constitution provided that the presidential candidate with the second highest number of votes would become the vice president. A change in this provision was necessitated, however, because in 1800 there was a tie between Thomas Jefferson and Aaron Burr. The final outcome of this election, the selection of Jefferson as president, was decided by the House of Representatives, as required by the Constitution. In 1804, the Twelfth Amendment, which provided that the offices of president and vice president be filled separately, was adopted.

While in office, President Washington saw the movement toward the division of legislators into voting blocs as a disturbing trend. The most pressing crisis facing the new nation was the huge debts it had inherited from the revolutionary war and from the confederation years. Large amounts were owed to Americans, the French government, and Dutch bankers, all of whom were demanding payment. Alexander Hamilton proposed a two-part solution: (1) the national government would issue new bonds for the full amount of indebtedness to whomever presented evidence that money was owed, and (2) the federal government would assume the debts of all the states. It was largely over this financial program that the first serious division in Congress occurred. Hamilton's plan would have required the federal government to develop new sources of revenue to pay off the states' debts through taxes on imported goods and an excise tax on American liquor. This would have caused the states to lose a great deal of power as the national government took over more of the country's pool of possible taxes. Those who opposed Hamilton called themselves "republicans" (later they became "Democrat-Republicans" and eventually "Democrats") and began to organize in Congress to plan their strategy. In response, Hamilton's supporters, the "federalists," also began to organize a bloc in Congress. Thus, by the 1796 election, the new nation had two fledgling parties: the Federalists and the Democrat-Republicans (or "anti-Federalists").

The Federalists successfully elected John Adams as president in 1796. During the next four years, they were accused of trying to begin a war with France. By 1800, the Democrat-Republicans were able to exploit both their effective congressional caucus (by which party members in Congress met to designate a nominee for president) and dissension among their Federalist rivals to capture the presidency. Thus began more than two decades of one-party dominance of American politics. However, in 1824, the Democrat-Republican party broke apart. The congressional caucus system collapsed, because, with everyone claiming to be Democrat-Republicans, the usefulness of the party label for the electorate and the importance of party as an organizing principle disappeared. Simultaneously, political participation was increasing, and many saw the caucus as undemocratic. In 1824, the Democrat-Republican congressional-caucus candidate received the *fewest* electoral votes, thus effectively killing the traditional nominating system. No candidate won a majority, once again forcing the election into the House of Representatives; John Quincy Adams of Massachusetts, who had fifteen fewer electoral votes than Andrew Jackson, was chosen.

The election of 1828 was a turning point in American politics. First, the one-party system that ended in 1824 gave birth to the modern two-party system. Second, the 1828 election was marked by extreme regionalism: voters in New England gave John Quincy Adams more than 75 percent of the vote, while more than 86 percent of all southerners voted for Tennessean Andrew Jackson. Although such extreme regional differences have abated somewhat, American parties have continued to draw their strength from various parts of the country. Finally, the election of 1828 stands out because Jackson was elected by the electorate without the help of Congress. Even though the Founders had written a Constitution that rejected a parliamentary system (i.e., one in which the legislature would choose the chief executive), not until 1828 was a president elected who had not first formed a solid core of support in Congress.

Andrew Jackson maintained his strength in 1832, but the effects of regionalism continued to be felt. Many southerners were violently opposed to Jackson's running mate, Martin van Buren of New York. By 1836, these disen-

Andrew Jackson, president of the United States, 1828–1836. Jackson's election marked the end of the congressional caucus system for choosing presidential candidates and began the era of the two-party system. (New York Public Library Picture Collection)

chanted Democrats and others formed the Whig party, thereby continuing the new two-party system. The Whigs successfully competed with the Democrats for the next twenty years.

In 1836, there were two parties competing in every state, and only in a few was one party clearly dominant. By 1840, the Whigs were fully organized and were similar to the Democrats in structure, function, and campaign techniques such as the use of symbols and slogans. Nominations were made by conventions of party members, not by caucuses of legislators. The size of the electorate had grown as property qualifications for voting were eliminated and all white males became eligible to vote. And presidential electors, who under the Constitution directly select the president, were beginning to be elected by the people rather than by state legislators.

The two-party system that came out of the turmoil of the "Jacksonian revolution" has remained fairly stable since 1840. However, there have been changes in the parties themselves. The 1850s were racked with conflicts over (1) religion (giving rise to the American, or Know-Nothing, party, which demanded that Catholics and immigrants be excluded from public office) and (2) slavery. Demands were being made by new territories as they became states, and the great westward expansion spawned redistributions of wealth that government was either being asked to prohibit or encourage--depending on each state's position. In short, in a time of social change, the political system naturally reflected the turmoil.

As we have seen, the framers of the Constitution wrestled with the problem of slavery and produced the "Three-Fifths Compromise," in which, for electoral purposes, each slave was counted as equal to only 60 percent of a free white person. However, by the late 1840s, the morality of slavery and the proper national policy toward it had become an immediate and divisive political question. The controversy gave birth to a temporary third party, the Free Soil party, which helped to destroy the Whigs by the early 1850s. The resulting electoral void was filled by another new party which claimed the Jeffersonian, and therefore respected, name of Republican. The new Republican party was formed largely from opponents of the 1854 Kansas-Nebraska Act, which had allowed slavery to be extended into the western territories. As the Civil War began, American politics was characterized by:

1. a Democratic party that was split into northern and southern camps
2. another third party, the Constitutional Union, which by simply supporting the Constitution and the Union garnered nearly as many electoral votes as the two democratic groups
3. a new Republican party that was riding the wave of mounting outrage over slavery

The Democrats not only suffered defeat in 1860, but they also acquired the stigma of having supported slavery. The result was a division within the Democratic party between urban liberals in the North and rural conservatives in the South, a split that lasted for more than a century. The Republicans, on the other hand, exploiting the postwar popularity of Abraham Lincoln, stayed in the White House for two dozen years. The major issues of the last part of the nineteenth century included the tariff (to protect American industry from foreign imports), sound money, strong banks, and aid for western expansion—issues on which most Republicans took stances favoring the development of business and industry.

Because of the string of Republican successes, the Democrats gradually began to realize where their hopes lay. By the mid-1880s, they were nominating candidates who proclaimed probusiness-development policies similar to those of the Republicans. Accordingly, some people who rejected this philosophy, particularly in the West and the South, formed alternative third parties, of which the Populist, or People's, party was the most important. Largely because of the success of industrialism, from 1860 until the beginning of the Great Depression in 1929, the Republican party dominated American elections and political institutions, losing only four of eighteen presidential campaigns.

During the bleakest days of the Great Depression, one out of every four workers in America was unemployed, personal income dropped by 25 percent between 1928 and 1933, and as much as one-third of the population was undernourished. Many older voters quickly forgot that they had previously credited business (and the Republican party) for the nearly continuous success of the economic system since the Civil War. Thus, in 1932, by proclaiming confidence and competence, Democrat Franklin Roosevelt was able to put together a coalition of farm, labor, minority, southern, and unemployed middle-class voters that swept him to a landslide victory.[3] This "grand coalition" not only gave the Democratic party a mandate to enact the sweeping changes in economic and social policies embodied in Roosevelt's "New Deal" legislation, but, except for Republican Dwight Eisenhower's two terms in the White House (1953–1961), it continued until the late 1960s. (The New Deal will be discussed in Chapters 12 and 13.)

Within a half-dozen years of the stock-market crash of 1929, there were clear signs that the economy was recovering (however, there was a short-lived but sharp economic decline in 1937–1938). The Republican party was much slower to recover from the effects of the Depression than was the American economy. The party's role in Congress was to be the minority opposition for all but four of the forty-eight years following the start of the New Deal. A large proportion of those who became eligible to vote during and after the New Deal would never seriously consider electing a Republican.

After the 1936 election, there were seventy-five Democrats in the Senate, in contrast to only seventeen Republicans, and the Democrats dominated the House with 333 seats. Yet, while they were riding high on Roosevelt's success, all was not perfect for the Democrats. The old North-South split that had divided the party since the Civil War continued to cause problems. For example, in 1928, the Democrats had nominated Al Smith, the Roman Catholic governor of New York, as their presidential candidate; however, to many south-

Al Smith, the Roman Catholic governor of New York, was the Democratic nominee for president in 1928. Many southerners could not bring themselves to vote for the "Happy Warrior," and as a result, the Republican party won electoral votes in the South for the first time in fifty years. (The Bettmann Archive, Inc.)

conservative coalition: A coalition of ideologically compatible Republican and Democratic members of Congress.

critical election: An election in which large numbers of voters make long-term changes in their party preference.

realignment: An election in which enough voters switch their party allegiance to cause a reversal in the majority-minority status of the parties.

erners, a northern, urban, non-Protestant was out of the question. As a result, the Republican party won southern electoral votes for the first time since Reconstruction, and its candidate, Herbert Hoover, won the presidency. At first, the Democrats in Congress were united in support of Roosevelt's New Deal, but by the late 1930s, many southern Democrats were frequently voting with most of the Republicans. Today, the **conservative coalition,** which consists of most Republicans and conservative southern Democrats in Congress, continues to oppose expansion of New Deal programs and new social-welfare legislation. Nevertheless, since the 1930s, the Democrats have maintained a significant lead over the Republicans in voter allegiance.

From this rather brief survey of American political history, several aspects of parties in the American electoral system stand out. First, it is clear that as times and issues change, the fortunes of political parties rise and fall. Voter interests and preferences are altered by such events as a war or an economic slump; during these **critical elections,** the party system undergoes a **realignment** as large numbers of voters make lasting changes in their party preference.[4] And because no party has dominated the political system for the entire history of the republic, we can infer that no party has been able to react perfectly to these changes. Second, this fallibility has led to periodic *internal reforms* as party leaders try to adjust their procedures and strategies to attract more voters.[5] Because the legitimacy of parties has never been seriously questioned since the early days of the nation, these self-adjustments have probably contributed to the acceptance of the party system by most Americans. Finally, we note again the striking tendency for Americans to support a two-party system.

THE TWO-PARTY SYSTEM AND THE FATE OF MINOR PARTIES

As we have seen, American society is characterized by a multitude of various interests, such as labor, business, farmers, urban workers, developers, and conservationists, each of which makes demands upon government. One way that these demands are expressed is through interest groups. Why, if there is such a diversity of interests in the United States, have there almost always been only two major political parties? Based on an examination of this question by political scientist V. O. Key, we will describe several factors that have contributed to this phenomenon.[6]

Beliefs and Attitudes

Unlike many European societies, the social structure of the United States is characterized by a general faith in upward mobility (i.e., the ability to get ahead if one tries hard enough) and by a lack of class consciousness. When asked, few Americans will place themselves into "upper" or "lower" classes; workers do not identify with a "labor" class or a "labor" party. It is much more common for Americans to claim to be "middle class" or "middle-of-the-road" and to agree on issues of justice and equality, at least in the abstract. Their "moderate" class position translates into "moderate" politics.

Figure 4-1 illustrates the results of public opinion surveys, conducted by the

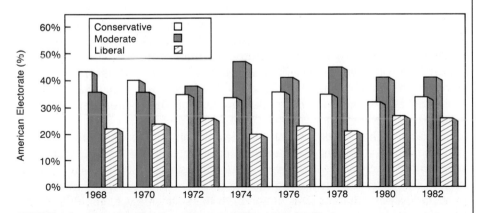

FIGURE 4-1 How the American Electorate Perceives Itself

Source: Surveys by Louis Harris and Associates, reported in *Public Opinion* (September/October 1978), p. 23; data for 1980 and 1982 from National Opinion Research Center, University of Connecticut.

Center for Political Studies at the University of Michigan, in which Americans were asked whether they considered themselves to be "liberal" or "conservative." It is obvious that most of them claimed to be in the middle of the scale. Whether they agree on the meanings of *liberal* and *conservative* is a separate question; it is safe to assume that the two-thirds of the population who think of themselves as relatively "moderate" will be suspicious of candidates or parties who campaign on very liberal or conservative platforms. Anthony Downs observed that in such an electorate, not only will the major parties move toward the center of the ideological spectrum, where most voters are, but third parties will be strongly disadvantaged because they will be blocked away from the center by the established major parties.[7] Many of the third-party movements that occurred over the last century have demonstrated Downs's point by unsuccessfully promoting causes at the extremes of various policy positions. For such a socially heterogeneous nation, the United States has a paradoxically homogeneous set of political attitudes and therefore "acceptable" party platforms.

Institutional Factors

As in many areas of everyday life, the rules of a game can have a great, if not determining, effect on an outcome. In American politics and government, the basic rules are in the Constitution and are difficult to change for personal advantage, but some of the specific procedures that have been established to carry out the Constitution's provisions have been manipulable. The rules of the electoral system have a powerful effect on who succeeds in the game of elections. The Constitution was not specific about how elections are to be managed. For example, in Article I, Section 2, the Founders made it clear that representatives were to be apportioned to the states on the basis of population. Until the middle of the nineteenth century, many states elected at-large members; that is, a state entitled to three representatives would allow each voter to select three names from a ballot, and the top three candidates would go to Congress, where each would represent the entire state. But, consistent with James Madison's recognition (in *The Federalist,* No. 10) of the necessity to have "interests" represented in Congress, that body began in 1842 to pass a series of laws that led to the modern system of **single-member districts (SMDs).**

single-member district (SMD): An electoral district in which voters may choose only one candidate for an office, with the common result that minority parties often win no seats despite significant electoral support.

The difference between an SMD electoral system and its alternatives is crucial for the development of a party system. For example, in a *proportional representation system,* which many democracies use, each party receives a seat in the legislature in rough proportion to its vote. Therefore, in a three-seat state, a party that receives one-third of the statewide vote should get one seat. But the same party in an SMD electoral system could find itself with no seats; if the vote distribution is 51 percent for party A and 49 percent for party B in each of the state's three districts, and only one representative can be chosen from each district, then party B will always lose. Thus, an SMD system is sometimes called a "winner-take-all" system. In a nation with such a system, it is much more difficult for a third party to win elections. (Although there are many multimember electoral districts at the state and local level, many of them involve nonpartisan contests, and they have had little effect on easing the path for third parties.)

This argument has been used to explain the lack of third parties in the United States. Just as the two-party system in the House of Representatives is favored by the SMD, so is the two-party system in the Senate (because only senators can be chosen from each state) and in presidential elections (because there the winner clearly takes all). Yet, with a few exceptions, parliamentary elections in England have also been based on SMDs, and third parties have not only survived there, but one, the Labour Party, even replaced the majority Liberal Party. Another factor is thus needed to explain the American party system: the method by which the president is chosen.

In England, the executive, or prime minister, is chosen from among the members of the House of Commons by virtue of being the leader of the majority party. A third party's support can be crucial for the selection of the national executive, because if neither party holds a clear majority (i.e., if neither party wins 50 percent plus one of the seats in the House of Commons), it must enter into a coalition with another party in order to form a government. Thus, third parties often play pivotal roles in the selection and maintenance of the British executive. In contrast, the American president is chosen in 50 SMDs—that is, the fifty states. With a winner-take-all system in each state, third parties in the United States rarely win any electoral votes; not since 1824, when John Quincy Adams was appointed president by Congress, has a presidential candidate failed to receive a majority of electoral votes.

There is yet another set of institutional factors that serve to maintain the American two-party system and discourage third parties. To be placed on an election ballot (i.e., to be a possible alternative to voters), a third party must overcome some very large obstacles. Perhaps you have been stopped on the street by someone asking you to sign a petition to get the Libertarian party or the United States Labor party on your state's ballot. In most states, minor parties must collect a number of valid signatures on such petitions in proportion to the number of voters participating in the previous election—a proportion that can be manipulated to make qualification more difficult. In 1980, independent presidential candidate John Anderson was forced to devote a large amount of effort simply to qualify on each state's ballot. Similarly, the 1974 federal-election-campaign reforms made it possible for presidential candidates to collect federal funds to subsidize their campaigns. However, to qualify for such funds, Anderson first had to sue for a share, then he had to qualify for the ballot in ten states, and then he had to obtain at least 5 percent of the national vote in early primaries. He qualified in every state and won 7 percent of the vote, yet he collected only $4 million. In contrast, Ronald Reagan and Jimmy Carter received over $60 million each in direct and indirect subsidies.

Yet, despite all of these obstacles, minor parties and independent candidates do form. Some, like the Prohibition party and the Socialist Labor party, have had long lives, whereas others have burst upon the electoral scene and just as suddenly disappeared. Some have formed because particular ethnic, social, or regional factions within a major party became too intense to be accommodated through compromise; for example, the Know-Nothing party of the 1850s could not have fit within any broad-based party. Other minor parties, such as the Free Soil and Abolitionist, were created to promote specific issues; when their causes were adopted by major parties, these minor parties dropped from the public eye or were absorbed into major parties. In general, then, the United States has had a two-party political system since the 1820s.

The Effects of the Two-Party System

Among the many features of the American political system that can be associated with the dominance of two major parties, several stand out as especially important. On the positive side, the two-party system is a valuable link between the people and the government. The bargaining among party leaders that is needed to form party coalitions is not necessary, so the popular vote is decisive

IS THERE A DIFFERENCE BETWEEN THE DEMOCRATIC AND REPUBLICAN PARTIES?

Question: Do you feel that the Democratic party or the Republican party can do a better job of handling . . . or don't you think there is any real difference between them?

Party Best Able to Handle:	No Difference/ No Opinion	Democratic Party	Republican Party
Reducing crime	58%	23%	19%
Stopping spread of communism	52%	19%	29%
Dealing effectively with USSR	48%	24%	28%
Providing quality education	47%	36%	17%
Reducing risk of nuclear war	46%	34%	20%
Providing health care	46%	43%	11%
Reducing waste and inefficiency in government	45%	23%	32%
Protecting environment	45%	43%	12%
Providing jobs	39%	46%	15%
Keeping defense strong	37%	21%	42%
Controlling inflation	36%	27%	37%
Helping the poor	34%	54%	12%

Source: Survey by Yankelovich, Skelly, and White, September 20–22, 1983.

in determining which political group runs the country. The two-party system also implies party responsibility, because a party in office cannot blame its mistakes on a coalition partner. In addition, the constitutional system of fixed terms for the president and Congress would be incompatible with a multiparty system. If a coalition government breaks up during the middle of a term—that is, if enough coalition members spurn the old majority, thereby reducing it to a minority—new elections must be held within a short time of the government's collapse.

As we have seen, however, certain drawbacks result from the dominance of two parties. Our electoral system, based on SMDs, exaggerates the size of a majority; for example, although the Democrats never won more than 60 percent of the popular vote for the House of Representatives from 1930 through 1980, there were ten elections in which they won more than 60 percent of the seats in the House. And once, in 1936, they captured almost 80 percent of the nation's congressional districts. Just as serious, to some observers, is the tendency for the major parties to cluster around the middle of every issue or to avoid a firm stand on potentially divisive issues, thereby reducing meaningful political debate and depriving voters of the greatest benefit that parties should provide to individuals: a reduction in information costs.

THE FEDERAL STRUCTURE OF AMERICAN PARTIES

In our discussion of the two-party system, we have treated the parties as national organizations—as if there were continuous, single, but not always unanimous, groups to which we could point and say, "There is the party." But political parties in the United States are highly decentralized. We can identify:

1. state and local parties, which operate largely under their own rules and under state and local laws
2. national parties, which seem to exist only during presidential election campaigns
3. congressional parties, which reshape every two years as members of Congress come and go
4. presidential parties, which often bear little resemblance to any of the other levels of parties
5. the parties as they exist in the electorate (i.e., mostly in the form of tenuous and fluctuating psychological attachments)

This complicated scheme for organizing political parties is unique to the United States. In parliamentary systems, such as that in Great Britain, there is a necessary link between the party in the legislature and the party in the executive branch. In other multiparty systems, such as those in the Netherlands or Sweden, parties survive primarily by attracting a cadre of voters who can rely on a party's consistency at all levels of government. Why has fragmentation occurred in the American party system? How have parties survived, and occasionally flourished, under it? After all, if parties are organizations and if organizational success depends on commonality of purpose and centrality of authority, the Democratic and Republican parties should have collapsed long ago. As our brief history of the two-party system revealed, neither the Democrats nor the Republicans have been blessed with total unanimity or cohesion over the last century.

Before we begin our discussion of why American parties are so fragmented, we must note several broad effects of the federal party structure. First, while most Americans would claim to be politically moderate or ideologically middle-of-the-road, they certainly do not agree on every public issue. Through the division of the major parties into state, local, congressional, and presidential levels, each party can appeal to disparate groups within American society. The Democrats exploit the loose ties within the party in order to encompass both northern liberals and southern conservatives. Likewise, the Republicans can appeal to voters from different regions and with different viewpoints because, for example, New York State Republicans are not identical to Rocky Mountain Republicans.

In addition, the complexity of the American parties tends to diminish somewhat one of the greatest advantages of political group formation: the reduction of costs, especially information costs, for individuals. Ideally, if a voter knows only that candidate Smith is a Democrat, then the voter should nevertheless know where Smith stands on many issues. But if the Democratic party is fragmented so that Smith could be a northern urban liberal or a southern rural

Slaves seated around a stove awaiting auction, circa 1840. The issue of slavery divided the Democratic party in the nineteenth century into northern and southern factions. The Democrats survived because party decentralization allowed strong disputes within the party. (The Bettmann Archive, Inc.)

conservative, the voter might know nothing. Yet fragmentation and decentralization are not the same as chaos; because the parties are loosely organized according to a federal structure, much of the information-cost–saving function of parties is preserved. In other words, a voter in Alabama knows that the Democrat on the state ballot is not a part of the "other" more liberal Democratic party in the north, but rather is a southern Democrat and therefore likely to be relatively conservative. Similarly, a voter who is knowledgeable and enthusiastic about a Republican presidential candidate, but uninformed about the local Republican congressional candidate, can assume that the party tie will encourage the member of Congress to cooperate with the president's policies. There is more uncertainty for the voter in such a system, because the parties can take advantage of ambiguity and appeal to many different groups simultaneously. However, as we shall see now as we turn to the nature of the federal party system, voters nevertheless receive an information-cost saving because of the links among the different levels of party organization.

State and Local Parties

Because of the great variety of ways in which state and local parties have been organized, it is difficult to generalize about them (see Table 4-1). There have been states, mostly in the South, in which one party, usually the Democrats, has held a virtual monopoly over electoral power; these states have become more competitive since the 1960s. Other states have a history of competitive, two-party systems. In many states, the party organization is tightly organized and controlled, with a core of professional supporters who promote the party first and individual candidates second; in other states, the party organizations

---

TABLE 4-1
ELECTED STATE AND LOCAL OFFICIALS, 1977

Type of Government	No. Governments	Total Elected Officials	Average No. Elected Officials per Government
State	50	15,294	305.9
All local	79,862	474,971[a]	5.9
Counties	3,042	62,922	20.7
Municipalities	18,862	134,017	7.1
Townships	16,822	118,966	7.1
School districts	15,174	87,062	5.7
Special districts	25,962	72,377	2.8

[a]Adjusted to exclude officials serving both county and township or city governments.

Source: U.S. Bureau of the Census, *Statistical Abstract of the United States, 1981* (Washington, D.C.: Government Printing Office, 1981), p. 493.

are much looser. Furthermore, each state party is controlled by the state's electoral laws, which vary widely from one state to another. (Remember, there is virtually no national regulation of political parties in the United States.)

Nevertheless, there are some similarities between state and local parties. It is helpful to picture a party as a pyramid, with precinct organizations, consisting of only a few thousand voters, at the bottom; then, ascending the pyramid, ward or township organizations and county committees; and finally, the state central committee. (Do not forget that factions often exist within state and local parties.) Local-party organization is important, because the efforts of precinct and county party committees will have a significant effect on elections at all levels of government and on the distribution of benefits that result from backing the correct candidates. The presidential delegate-selection process begins at the local level, where many patronage jobs are available to be filled by local party leaders.

Because of the permanence and significance of state and local party politics, it is at these levels that government imposes the greatest restraints on parties. Most states now regulate various aspects of party membership, party organization, caucuses, primaries, conventions, and even procedures by which parties choose their officers. This involvement became widespread in the 1890s, after most states adopted the **Australian ballot** system, which:

Australian ballot: A secret ballot for voting, begun in the United States in 1888.

1. employs nonpartisan election officials to print ballots at public expense
2. lists all candidates nominated by the parties
3. allows voters to obtain ballots only on election day at a polling place
4. guarantees the voter secrecy in making choices
5. erects safeguards so that only official ballots are cast[8]

Because party rules are not uniform across states, they are often the cause of bitter disputes within parties. For example, although Mississippi's 1968 Democratic party delegates were chosen in accordance with Mississippi law, the all-white delegation was excluded from the national convention because of a conflict with national party rules requiring equal opportunity for all in each state's delegate-selection procedures.

National Parties

The national Democratic and Republican parties each consist of four major parts: (1) a national committee, (2) a national convention, (3) a national chairman or chairwoman, and (4) the congressional campaign committees. Although the national committee is a conspicuous organization and an appointment to it is considered an honor for state party officials, it has relatively few important functions. It arranges locations and agendas for the national convention, coordinates the party campaigns during presidential elections, and attempts to take care of money matters. Overseeing financial matters is not a simple task, because the national party must compete with individual candidates and state and local parties for contributions. These efforts are supervised by the national chairman, who is picked by the party's presidential candidate soon after the national convention. The national chairman whose party loses in the general election is usually soon replaced by the choice of the national committee.

The national convention is the supreme authority of a national party. Meeting in the summer of a presidential election year, the convention:

1. nominates the party's presidential and vice-presidential candidates
2. adopts a party platform (which was shaped by a subcommittee of the national committee before the convention began)
3. accepts or rejects proposed changes in party rules
4. decides disputes about the credentials of state party delegates

In Chapter 5, we will describe these functions in greater detail.

Each party also has a congressional campaign committee for each chamber of Congress. Because the national committee is primarily dedicated to electing a president, members of Congress form their own committees to coordinate strategies and provide financial assistance to congressional candidates, especially to newcomers who are challenging incumbents of the other party. Like the national committee, congressional campaign committees are not the core of the federal party system, but during midterm elections when no presidential race occurs, they may be the only vestige of a national party organization. Nevertheless, such committees are rarely able to contribute significant amounts of money to candidates. The real power is at the state and local level and in the campaigns of individual congressional and presidential candidates.

Congressional Parties

As we have seen, American political parties began during the first decade of the nation's history when like-minded members of Congress recognized their common interests and formed divisions within the legislature in order to promote or oppose proposed policies. However, party politics was not exclusively congressional for very long. Even before 1800, some members of Congress attempted to sway votes by appealing to the constituents of their colleagues. Thus, to accurately characterize congressional parties, we must consider two aspects of them: (1) parties within Congress and (2) congressional parties in the electorate.

Few candidates for Congress are originally recruited by local political parties; rather, they usually make their own decisions to run for office. Thus, the relationship between members of Congress and local party organizations remains distant after an election. This should not be surprising if we recall several of the major features of the American political system. First, as the Founders intended, the separation of powers into three branches, the bisection of the legislative branch, and the principle of federalism have resulted in many different constituencies in the American electorate. Each level of government and each constitutional branch of government has its own set of opportunities and problems. Members of the House of Representatives campaign for office on a different set of issues than do candidates for state assemblies or governorships. In addition, because the powers and terms of office in the two chambers of Congress differ, senators and representatives also appeal to different constituencies. And, of course, only the president has the entire nation as an electorate. Therefore, no single party organization at any level could bridge so many interests.

Nevertheless, there is a congressional party in the electorate. Successful candidates almost always campaign with a party label (see Table 4-2). Even though members of Congress generally eschew strong ties with local and national parties after their election, they still must see some benefit in calling themselves "Democrats" or "Republicans." Political scientists have found such an advantage: party voting (i.e., the tendency for voters who identify with a party to vote for its candidates) seems to be especially important in races for the House of Representatives. Such candidates' names are likely to be relatively unknown to voters, and a party label thus becomes a useful informational tool.

To fully explain the importance of political parties in Congress after an election is over, we need to examine the procedures and structures within Congress, a task that we defer until Chapter 8. Yet, we must distinguish the peripheral roles of parties in the congressional electorate from the central role of parties in congressional organization, because the party system within Congress, together with the congressional committee system, is a key organizing principle in both the Senate and the House. Nearly all of the structural features of Congress, such as committee assignments and chairmanships, committee staff assignments, seniority, and leadership positions, are shaped by the relative strengths of the two parties in Congress.

There are several reasons why parties play such an important role in Congress. One explanation—that because there are presidential parties and parties in the electorate, then there must be parties in Congress—is not very scientific; however, it does remind us of the tendency at all levels of American politics for sides (usually two) to form. Other explanations are internal to Congress. First, political parties in Congress act as organizational devices. With parties in the legislature working to promote cohesion among groups of representatives, the promoters of each bill being considered do not need to start from scratch to form a supporting coalition. A Republican sponsor of new legislation can appeal for the endorsement of the party leaders and know that much bargaining, negotiation, and compromise, with the attendant transaction costs and delays of that process, will be avoided.

Second, congressional parties act as information-cost–saving devices. For example, House Democrats have formed a Steering and Policy Committee to coordinate, recommend, and schedule legislative efforts, and to inform Democratic members about party positions. Each party's leaders in the House and Senate perform similar functions. In addition, party becomes an important

TABLE 4-2
COMPOSITION OF CONGRESS, BY POLITICAL PARTY, 1939–1981

Year	Party[a]	President	Congress	House of Representatives			Senate		
				Majority	Minority	Other	Majority	Minority	Other
1939	D	F. Roosevelt	76	D-261	R-164	4	D-69	R-23	4
1941	D	F. Roosevelt	77	D-268	R-162	5	D-66	R-28	2
1943	D	F. Roosevelt	78	D-218	R-208	4	D-58	R-37	1
1945	D	F. Roosevelt	79	D-242	R-190	2	D-56	R-38	1
1947	D	Truman	80	R-245	D-188	1	R-51	D-45	–
1949	D	Truman	81	D-263	R-171	1	D-54	R-42	–
1951	D	Truman	82	D-234	R-199	1	D-49	R-47	–
1953	R	Eisenhower	83	R-221	D-211	1	R-48	D-47	1
1955	R	Eisenhower	84	D-232	R-203	–	D-48	R-47	1
1957	R	Eisenhower	85	D-233	R-200	–	D-49	R-47	–
1959	R	Eisenhower	86	D-284	R-153	–	D-65	R-35	–
1961	D	Kennedy	87	D-263	R-174	–	D-65	R-35	–
1963	D	Kennedy	88	D-258	R-177	–	D-67	R-33	–
1965	D	Johnson	89	D-295	R-140	–	D-68	R-32	–
1967	D	Johnson	90	D-247	R-187	–	D-64	R-36	–
1969	R	Nixon	91	D-243	R-192	–	D-57	R-43	–
1971	R	Nixon	92	D-254	R-180	–	D-55	R-45	–
1973	R	Nixon	93	D-240	R-192	–	D-57	R-43	–
1975	R	Ford	94	D 291	R-144	–	D-61	R-38	–
1977	D	Carter	95	D-292	R 143	–	D-62	R-38	–
1979	D	Carter	96	D-276	R-157	–	D-59	R-41	–
1981	R	Reagan	97	D-243	R-192	–	R-54	D-46	–
1983	R	Reagan	98	D-269	R-166	–	R-54	D-46	–

[a]D = Democrat; R = Republican. Independent-Democrats and Independents who caucused with Democrats are included with Democrat totals. Conservative-Republicans are included with Republican totals.

Sources: U.S. Bureau of the Census, *Statistical Abstract of the United States, 1981* (Washington: Government Printing Office, 1981), p. 490; *Spring 1983 Guide to American Government* (Washington: Congressional Quarterly Press, 1982).

"cue" for members of Congress who are pressed for time and lack expertise on most policy matters.

A third function of the Democratic and Republican parties in Congress is to impose some control over the activities of individual members of Congress. Because party leaders have some power to grant or withhold favors, such as desired committee assignments or endorsements of pet bills, they can discipline many congressional representatives. Disruptive and extreme legislative behavior is thereby discouraged.

These functions of parties within Congress should not be taken as a suggestion that the congressional party system always works smoothly. Senate Democrats and Republicans have different interests and incentives than do their House counterparts. Thus, we could characterize Congress as having four parties, not two. Each member of Congress owes his or her primary loyalty to his or her constituency, not to a national, state, local, or congressional party. Thus, members of Congress will defer to their colleagues or to their party leaders only when contrary signals from their constituents are weak.

The congressional party system is constantly in flux. The party organizations in each chamber must be re-formed every two years as incumbents are defeated and challengers take their seats. Major changes are required when an election reverses the majority and minority statuses of congressional parties, because the leaders of the House and the Senate are chosen from the majority party of each. Committee chairmen may have been defeated, and because the partisan makeup of each committee is determined by the relative strength of the parties in the relevant chamber, committee assignments must be adjusted. And each party's behavior will change in view of the mandate that the electorate is believed to have expressed at the polls. Finally, despite their fragmented and inconstant nature, there has still been some continuity over the years in the House and Senate Democratic and Republican parties.

As we turn now to presidential parties, the final category in the federal party system, we will see that, unlike any of the other types of parties, the presidential party is an independent organization that is almost completely reborn every four years.

Presidential Parties

Watergate: General term encompassing a variety of misdeeds and crimes associated with the 1972 reelection campaign of President Richard Nixon, which led to his resignation in 1974.

The period of the **Watergate** scandal (1972–1974) was of great concern to many Republicans, because a Republican president, Richard Nixon, was accused of an assortment of illegal and improper activities. As a result, Nixon became the first president ever to resign from office. Many observers expected the Republican party to be devastated in future elections as voters associated congressional, state, and local Republicans with the dishonored president. That catastrophe never occurred, however. It is true that the Republican party lost many seats in Congress in 1974, but (1) the party in the White House usually loses congressional seats in midterm elections, (2) there was an economic recession at the time, which further damaged the president's party, and (3) the Republicans nearly won the presidential election in 1976. The party did not emerge unscathed, however; many "good" Republicans chose not to run, fewer voters who identified with the Republican party turned out at the polls, and Republican candidates received smaller contributions than in previous years. Nevertheless, little permanent damage was done to the party as a result of Watergate.

Why were Republicans not punished for the sins of Richard Nixon? The answer lies in the independent nature of the party in a presidential campaign and in the White House. Consider the 1972 campaign: Nixon himself deliberately disassociated himself from the national Republican party by establishing his own reelection committee, the Committee to Re-Elect the President. Nixon was not the first candidate to put distance between himself and the national party; for example, in 1952, Dwight Eisenhower fought against being identified with the minority-party label attached to the Republicans. In Nixon's case, the segregation from the national party was not merely cosmetic. Even though he had been reelected by an overwhelming margin, his success rate in Congress in 1973, based on measures on which he took a position, was the lowest of any president in twenty years.

Clearly, to be a Republican in the White House in 1973 was not the same as being a Republican in Congress. Nevertheless, the party of the president is far from meaningless. It provides information to many voters, especially to party identifiers. In 1976, for example, 89 percent of those who considered themselves Republicans voted for Gerald Ford, while 80 percent of Democrats voted for Jimmy Carter. A particularly popular presidential candidate can carry along congressional, state, or local candidates of the same party on his coattails, as some voters simplify their decisions and vote a **straight ticket;** however, so many factors affect election results that attributing a precise percentage of the vote to something as vague as a **coattail effect** is dangerous. An unpopular candidate can, of course, have a detrimental effect on other campaigns. Party affiliations are also valuable in the formation of alliances between members of Congress and the president as the legislature considers new policies, treaties, and appointments. But as every president has discovered, party ties are useful only in the absence of stronger incentives, and there are often more powerful influences on a member of Congress's vote than the president's party label.

The importance of the president's partisan affiliation is also reduced by the nature of the job. While we expect the president to be the head of his or her party and to set the party's course for the term of office, we also demand that the president be "above politics" in the roles of commander-in-chief, head of state, and chief diplomat. Thus, we can summarize by pointing out that, during an election campaign, presidential candidates, in effect, form their own party, loosely constrained by tradition and the demands of the congressional parties. The presidential party continues to follow an independent course because the separation of powers exists among the branches of government and because different incentives are available to elected officials at the various levels of government.

PARTY PERSONNEL

Until now, we have been primarily concerned with the parties as organizations. In this section, we will look at the people who, after all, constitute a political party: that is, the voters and activists.

straight ticket: Voting for candidates of only one party in an election.

coattail effect: The phenomenon of candidates for less prestigious offices benefiting from being on the same ballot as a more popular candidate (usually a presidential candidate).

Party Identifiers

Partisan identification is impossible to observe directly, because it exists only in the minds of voters. Therefore, partisanship is hard to measure and difficult to define. Being a *party identifier* means more than saying "I am a Democrat" and carrying a registration card to that effect. Does it also mean that the individual votes only for the candidates of his or her party in all elections? No, it does not. As we have seen, there is often little continuity among the different levels of each party. Rather, a *party identifier* has a psychological inclination, not a formal membership or predictable behavior.[9] He or she views politics through the filter of a general predisposition in favor of one party, but does not necessarily support the party in all elections.

To understand party identification, we must consider where it comes from and what effect it has on votes. As we saw in our discussion of political socialization in Chapter 3, the roots of party identification are not simple. Although researchers have discovered that the most important sources of the political orientation of Americans are parents, schools, peers, and such influences as television and magazines, the political learning process does not end after adolescence.

Party identification is important because it can affect political behavior, especially voting. Since 1952, the Survey Research Center of the University of Michigan has asked a nationwide sample of voters the same question every two years: "Generally speaking, do you think of yourself as a Republican, a Democrat, an independent, or what?" Further questions probe the strength of the identification and the leanings of self-identified, independent voters. Table 4-3 indicates that the proportion of independent voters has been increasing; some observers fear that the lack of voter stability seemingly implied by strong partisan identification will result in increasing instability in national politics.[10] But in the same table, it is clear that Democratic partisans have consistently outnumbered Republican partisans by about three to two, so why have the Democrats lost so many elections? And what does *partisan attachment* mean?

TABLE 4-3
PARTY IDENTIFICATION IN THE UNITED STATES, 1952–1980

Party Identification	1952	1956	1960	1964	1968	1972	1976	1980
Strong Democrat	22%	21%	21%	26%	20%	15%	15%	18%
Weak Democrat	25%	23%	25%	25%	25%	25%	25%	23%
Independent, leaning Democrat	10%	7%	8%	9%	10%	11%	12%	11%
Independent	5%	9%	8%	8%	11%	13%	14%	13%
Independent, leaning Republican	7%	8%	7%	6%	9%	10%	10%	10%
Weak Republican	14%	14%	13%	13%	14%	13%	14%	14%
Strong Republican	13%	15%	14%	11%	10%	10%	9%	8%

Source: Survey Research Center, Center for Political Studies, University of Michigan.

Other questions in the survey—about actual behavior, not partisan attachments—have allowed researchers to evaluate the importance of party identification over the years. Of course, there are problems with such a study, because a person can claim to be a lifelong Republican one year and profess an eternal attachment to the Democrats in the next election. Nevertheless, party identification is a useful, but not foolproof, predictor of political behavior. For example, surveys have shown that from 1952 through 1976, an average of 87 percent of "strong Democrats" voted for Democratic presidential candidates, while only 66 percent of "weak Democrats" voted with the party. Republicans have been more loyal; over the same period, an average of only about 3 percent of "strong Republicans" and 16 percent of "weak Republicans" defected. The numbers vary, of course; greater defection from party loyalty occurred, for example, when the Republicans nominated a very conservative candidate, Barry Goldwater, in 1964, and when the Democrats endorsed a very liberal candidate, George McGovern, in 1972. In addition, over the last twenty years, there has been a marked general increase in the defection rate, at least among Democrats.

Party identification has also been observed to reduce the likelihood of **split-ticket** voting (i.e., voting in one election for *both* Democrats and Republicans). From 1952 through 1968, only about 15 percent of all voters cast ballots for different parties in presidential and congressional elections. (The level of split-ticket voting in state and local elections was much higher—about one in three—reflecting again the effects of the federal party system.) Like defections, however, split-ticket voting has increased greatly. In the 1970s, the proportion of all voters casting presidential-congressional split-ticket votes grew to nearly 30 percent, and the state-local rate increased to nearly 60 percent. Even among self-identified partisans, the number of split-ticket voters has increased.

split ticket: A vote for candidates of different parties in the same election.

Clearly, party identification has been a powerful predictor of various types of voting behavior, but it has declined significantly since the 1950s. Several reasons can be suggested. First of all, voters have become better educated and more knowledgeable about issues, thereby making the information-cost–saving function of parties less relevant.[11] Moreover, perhaps the parties have changed, not the voters; in their scramble for the votes at the center of the political spectrum, the Democrats and Republicans may have converged to the point that many voters now see little difference between them. Whatever the reason, it is clear that there has been a gradual downward trend in party identification.

This is not the first time that the partisan makeup of the American electorate has changed. As we saw earlier, there have been critical elections in United States history—for example, during Andrew Jackson's administration (1829–1837), in 1860, around 1896, and during the New Deal. At these times, party coalitions underwent major and lasting changes, the general thrust of public policies was redirected, and large numbers of voters permanently shifted their party allegiance. Recent partisan and electoral changes have been compared to these realignments, but only history can determine whether the increasing independence of voters and the Republican surge in the 1980 election constitute turning points in American politics. If the disenchanted partisans who have fled the Democratic and Republican parties are an indication that either the two-party system or the two parties currently in the system are unresponsive to the voters' demands, then a significant realignment may have occurred.

Party Activists

Many voters are retrospective; that is, they choose more in reaction to the past performance of the party in power than on the basis of future expectations. Other partisans are more future-oriented. They find candidates or aspects of a party platform that they wish to promote, attend local political caucuses and committee meetings, distribute bumper stickers, write letters, contribute money, and so on. These *party activists* differ in some important ways from most party identifiers.

Because their behavior entails the same kinds of costs as interest-group participants (see Chapter 3), activists must be more highly motivated to participate than identifiers are. Activists see a higher value attached to the public and private benefits that they promote, and many are motivated by a sense of knowing what the "correct" public policies are. Some activists seek office within a party or a patronage job after a successful campaign. Party activists also differ in social and economic characteristics from those who merely vote; they are more likely to be white, highly-educated, and earning above-average incomes.

Delegates on the floor of the Republican National Convention, Detroit, Michigan, July 1980. (Steve Kagan/Photo Researchers, Inc.)

TABLE 4-4
POLITICAL ATTITUDES OF PARTY DELEGATES AND VOTERS, 1980

	Liberal	Moderate	Conservative
Democratic delegates	46%	42%	6%
Democratic party members	21%	52%	21%
Adult Americans	17%	49%	28%
Republican party members	8%	46%	41%
Republican delegates	2%	36%	58%

Samples of delegates to 1980 national conventions, rank-and-file party members, and adult Americans were asked to characterize their political leanings.

Sources: *New York Times/CBS News* poll, August 2–7, 1981, and *CBS News* polls of delegates.

One of the most significant characteristics of party activists is the difference between their political demands and those of the average voter, even the average voter within the same party. Since the 1950s, when surveys first asked such questions, Democratic-party activists have been more liberal than the average Democratic voter, and much more liberal than the average American voter; their Republican counterparts are similarly more conservative. Table 4-4 compares the political leanings of convention delegates, who include the most active activists, with the ideological identifications of other groups of voters. Because 1980 was a particularly good year for conservative Republicans, the differences in political attitudes shown in the table may be unusually large. Even so, they clearly indicate the general variance in ideology between party activists and the public.[12]

The tendency of party activists to be less moderate than the general electorate has shaped several aspects of American politics. Most important, when more than one person is vying for a party nomination at any level of government, the mechanism by which the candidate is chosen is generally internal to the party. When nominees are chosen by party caucuses, the active members of the party (e.g., those who attend precinct and county committee meetings) have the greatest influence in choosing the nominee. When nominees are selected through state primaries, the influence of the more extreme activists is less. Thus, while a candidate may want to appeal to the mass of voters in the middle of the ideological spectrum in the general election, there is very real pressure from activists early in the campaign to take positions to liberal or conservative extremes. Financial supporters are also likely to pull candidates to the edges of the ideological spectrum. Finally, because activists are highly motivated, they are much more likely than party identifiers to vote in general elections, thus extending their disproportionate influence. According to some analysts, these features of party politics have prevented the two major parties from proposing exactly the same cautious and moderate policies.

PARTY POLITICS IN AMERICA

In this chapter, we have examined the ideal functions prescribed for political parties, the development of the two-party system in the United States, the relationships among the various parties at the many levels of our federal system, and the actors who form and support the parties. Before turning to the characteristics and operation of the American electoral system, we should pause to consider the most important conclusions to be drawn from the discussion so far.

Political parties are important to voters and to public officials. They can ease the translation of public attitudes and demands into policy by acting as a communications link between individuals and political leaders, and by organizing the behavior of leaders in a way comprehendible to voters. Thus, parties should advance the aims of representative government by making participation easier and by allowing voters to hold elected officials accountable for their actions.

The party system does not work perfectly, however. It has been plagued by inefficiencies, errors, and abuses of trust; a cynic could observe that in its failings, the party system reflects American life. Sometimes, parties cannot keep up with rapidly changing times and suffer agonizing punishments at the hands of jaded voters. At other times, voters may slowly drift away from the parties, causing a gradual shift in political attachments that no one quite understands. It is ironic that the party system, which the Founders distrusted and which many Americans disdain because of its apparently selfish dedication to the accumulation of political influence, can best serve the public by responding to its wishes through the competitive struggle for votes and power.

NOTES

[1]The basic argument in favor of responsible parties was made in *Toward a More Responsible Two-Party System,* a special supplement to the *American Political Science Review* (September 1950).

[2]For useful histories of the American party system, see Richard Hofstadter, *The Idea of a Party System* (Berkeley: University of California Press, 1969), and Everett C. Ladd, Jr., *American Political Parties* (New York: Norton, 1970).

[3]On Roosevelt's "grand coalition," see Everett C. Ladd, Jr., and Charles D. Hadley, *Transformations of the American Party System,* 2nd ed. (New York: Norton, 1978), chapter 1, and Angus Campbell, Phillip E. Converse, Donald E. Miller, and Donald E. Stokes, *The American Voter* (New York: Wiley, 1960), pp. 146–155.

[4]Walter Dean Burnham, *Critical Elections and the Mainsprings of American Politics* (New York: Norton, 1970).

[5]Austin Ranney, *Curing the Mischiefs of Faction: Party Reform in America* (Berkeley: University of California Press, 1975), chapter 1.

[6]V. O. Key, Jr., *Politics, Parties, and Pressure Groups*, 5th ed. (New York: Crowell, 1964), chapter 10.

[7]Anthony Downs, *An Economic Theory of Democracy* (New York: Harper & Row, 1957), chapter 8.

[8]Jerrold G. Rusk, "The Effect of the Australian Ballot Reform on Split-Ticket Voting: 1876–1908," *American Political Science Review* 64 (1970): 1220–1238.

[9]For discussions of the fundamentals of party identification, see Campbell et al., *The American Voter,* and Ian Budge, Ivor Crewe, and Dennis Farlie, *Party Identification and Beyond* (New York: Wiley, 1976).

[10]Norman H. Nie, Sidney Verba, and John R. Petrocik, *The Changing American Voter,* enlarged ed. (Cambridge: Harvard University Press, 1979), chapter 19.

[11]See David E. RePass, "Issue Salience and Party Choice," *American Political Science Review* 65 (June 1971): 389–400.

[12]Michael J. Malbin, "The Conventions, Platforms, and Issue Activists," in Austin Ranney, ed., *The American Elections of 1980* (Washington: American Enterprise Institute, 1981), pp. 99–141; and Herbert McCloskey, Paul J. Hoffman, and Rosemary O'Hara, "Issue Conflict and Consensus among Party Leaders and Followers," *American Political Science Review* 54 (June 1960): 406–429.

BIBLIOGRAPHY

Chambers, William, and Walter Dean Burnham, eds. *The American Party System.* 2nd ed. New York: Oxford University Press, 1975. A collection of essays on the formation, development, and behavior of American parties.

Key, V. O., Jr. *Politics, Parties, and Pressure Groups.* 5th ed. New York: Crowell, 1964. Out of date, but still a classic, this text may be the most impressive work ever written on the American electoral system.

Ladd, Everett C., Jr., and Charles D. Hadley. *Transformations of the American Party System,* 2nd ed. New York: Norton, 1978. An analysis of party coalitions over the past fifty years, with particular emphasis on the Democratic New Deal coalition.

Nie, Norman H., Sidney Verba, and John R. Petrocik. *The Changing American Voter.* Cambridge: Harvard University Press, 1976. An exhaustive use of survey data to examine the changes in partisanship, issue voting, and so on during the past few decades.

Pomper, Gerald M., ed. *Party Renewal in America.* New York: Praeger, 1980. A collection of studies of the purported decline in American parties.

Ranney, Austin. *Curing the Mischiefs of Faction: Party Reform in America.* Berkeley: University of California Press, 1975. A detailed but clear study of several attempts to reform the national parties, particularly the post-1968 reforms.

Sartori, Giovanni. *Parties and Party System.* New York: Cambridge University Press, 1976. A broad, cross-national examination of the functions and operations of party systems.

Sorauf, Frank J. *Party Politics in America.* 3rd ed. Boston: Little, Brown, 1976. A complete and comprehensive text on the structure and behavior of American parties.

The Democratic Control: Elections in America

A large proportion of the Constitution of the United States concerns the electoral system. Articles I and II include the procedures by which representatives, senators, and the president are to be selected, with detailed instructions regarding timetables and qualifications of candidates. Although the American Founders carefully considered how elections should work, many of their original provisions have been changed or abolished. Ten amendments to the Constitution, many of which show a relationship between the civil rights of citizens and the American electoral system, are evidence of a gradual evolution of ideas, which continues today, about the connections between citizens and public officials. In this chapter, we will describe the electoral process as it currently exists. In order to understand why the rules for choosing leaders are as they are, we will also examine the factors that have shaped the procedures over two centuries.

THE IDEA OF ELECTIONS

Neither representative government nor the election of leaders began in North America. During the thirteenth century, English kings realized that the increasing complexity and cost of government required the cooperation of men of wealth, especially great landowners. As a result, the monarchy began to consult with representatives of the landowners, thereby gaining their acceptance, if not their support. In the fourteenth century, knights and citizens were sent to London with the authority to represent their communities in Parliament. Although participation in the selection of these representatives was severely limited, a form of elections had begun.

Today, many countries in the world have "representative assemblies," "democratic elections," and so on. Many such nations have electoral systems similar to our own, with parties, campaigns, secret ballots, and the like. Yet other nations hold "elections" that are, in fact, charades. For example, the constitution of the Soviet Union boasts of universal suffrage, popular participation, and legitimacy of the power of the government, yet it offers its citizens only one choice at the polls.

The principles of representation and elections in the United States are based on centuries of traditions and beliefs. When we speak of the "American electoral system," we are not referring to a unified and constant set of rules and procedures. In fact, there is no set of rules governing the entire array of electoral practices in the United States. The system consists of constitutional requirements, federal and state laws, party rules, judicial decisions, and customs. The Census Bureau listed 82,341 "governments" in the United States in 1982, including one national government, fifty states, and many counties, municipalities, townships, school districts, and special districts, such as independent public housing authorities and local power districts, most of which have offices filled through elections. Yet the basic principles to which all electoral systems in the United States must adhere are in the national Constitution, so we will focus herein on national elections.

ELECTIONS UNDER THE CONSTITUTION

Political parties, like sellers of consumer products, must compete with each other. The "buyers" of parties—the voters—can exercise their preferences, just as buyers of competing brands of automobiles can. Shoppers can choose which car to buy or they can decide not to buy one, and eligible voters can choose candidates or abstain from voting. Thus, like business firms, political parties design strategies and policies that will maximize their chances of winning. In doing so, they seek both to expand their "sales" to the uncommitted and to draw votes away from the opposition.

While significant similarities exist between economic and political markets, there are also major differences. First, political parties are often constrained by a set of ideas or an ideology that limits their appeal. Left-wing parties based upon trade-union support do not try to attract business leaders; in contrast, a business firm can usually be indifferent about who buys its products. Second, in the business arena, individual preference is usually more easily realized than in the political arena. For example, ten people in a supermarket may choose ten different brands of mouthwash, but in politics, 50.1 percent of the people in a congressional district can realize their preference, while the 49.9 percent who choose the losing candidate do not. Because of the importance of electoral rules, the men who wrote the Constitution were very attentive to them. In the following section, we will examine these basic rules and how many of them have changed.

Terms of Office

The terms of office of the president, vice president, senators, and members of Congress are outlined in the Constitution. Article I, Section II, states, "The House of Representatives shall be composed of Members chosen every second Year by the People of the several States . . . ." The Seventeenth Amendment, ratified in 1913, states, "The Senate of the United States shall be composed of two Senators from each State, elected by the people thereof, for six years . . . ."

According to Article I, Section 3, "Immediately after they shall be assembled in Consequence of the first Election, they shall be divided as equally as may be into three Classes. The Seats of the Senators of the first Class shall be vacated at the Expiration of the second Year, of the second Class at the Expiration of the fourth Year, and of the third Class at the Expiration of the sixth Year, so that one third may be chosen every second Year . . . ."

And Article II, Section 1, states, "The executive Power shall be vested in a President of the United States of America. He shall hold his Office during the Term of four Years, and, together with the Vice President, chosen for the same term . . . ."

We have already discussed the reasons for the different lengths of terms of office for representatives, senators, and the president, and described some of the effects of staggered terms on the fragmentation of the parties among the branches of government. A few members of the Constitutional Convention advocated life terms for senators. Moreover, there was strong pressure for one-year terms for representatives, against which the authors of *The Federalist,* no. 53, successfully argued. Since then, the six-year and two-year terms for senators and representatives, respectively, have not been seriously challenged.

There has been extended debate over the length of the presidential term, however. While a few delegates to the Constitutional Convention proposed that a president hold office "during good behavior," with no fixed term, the major controversy was over whether the chief executive should hold a single seven-year term or a four-year term with eligibility for reelection. Once it was decided that Congress would not choose the president, the latter position was adopted. However, the issue did not die. Since 1828, the suggestion has been made that the Constitution be amended to provide for a single six-year term, and this proposal continues to be made today. So far, the only change in the length of the presidential term occurred in 1951 when the Twenty-second Amendment was ratified, limiting a president to two full elected terms, plus up to two years "of a term to which some other person was elected." This amendment, favored primarily by Republicans and southern Democrats, was a reaction to Franklin Roosevelt's unprecedented four terms in office.

Qualifications of Candidates

According to Article I, Section 2, "No Person shall be a Representative who shall not have attained to the age of twenty-five Years, and been seven Years a Citizen of the United States, and who shall not, when elected, be an Inhabitant of that State in which he shall be chosen." Article I, Section 3, states, "No Person shall be a Senator who shall not have attained to the Age of thirty Years, and been nine Years a Citizen of the United States, and who shall not, when elected, be an Inhabitant of that State for which he shall be chosen."

Eligibility for the presidency is discussed in Article II, Section 1: "No Person except a natural born Citizen, or a Citizen of the United States, at the time of the Adoption of this Constitution, shall be eligible to the Office of President; neither shall any Person be eligible to that Office who shall not have attained to the Age of thirty-five Years, and been fourteen Years a Resident within the United States."

For the most part, these provisions of the Constitution have not been very controversial. Questions about the qualifications for the office of the presidency have included whether Henry Kissinger, secretary of state in the Nixon and Ford administrations, could have occupied the White House under presidential succession procedures, because he was not born in the United States.

Only two significant questions have been raised about congressional qualifications. First, Article I, Section 6, forbids senators and representatives from concurrently "holding any Office under the United States," thus maintaining

PROGRESS FOR BLACK ELECTED OFFICIALS, 1970–1980		
	No. Black Elected Officials	
Level	1970	1980
Federal	10	18
State	169	336
Local	715	2,977
Judicial and law enforcement	213	563
Schools	362	1,266
Total	1,469	5,160

the separation of powers (1) by excluding executive-branch personnel from congressional membership and (2) by prohibiting military officers on active duty from serving in Congress. When Ronald Reagan, after his election in 1980, proposed appointing Nevada senator Paul Laxalt to be a special congressional liaison with the White House, Article 1, Section 6, was invoked to object to the move. Laxalt did not get the job.

The second question is whether Congress itself can add to the constitutional list of qualifications. Changes have been made based on Article I, Section 5: "Each House shall be the Judge of the Elections, Returns and Qualifications of its own Members," and "Each House may . . . with the Concurrence of two thirds, expel a Member." By tradition, but not by the Constitution, members of the House are required to be residents of the districts they represent. In addition, Congress has occasionally excluded or expelled members on other grounds not mentioned in the Constitution. For example, a representative from Utah was denied his seat in 1900 because he was a polygamist; two others were refused their seats in 1928 because too much money had been spent on their campaigns. Expulsions are more difficult and therefore more rare. Members who may face removal from Congress are likely to resign, with protestations of innocence, before the House or Senate can act. In 1982, for instance, Senator Harrison Williams of New Jersey resigned while being investigated for acceptance of bribes.

Number of Elected Officials

The apportionment of members of Congress is outlined in Article I, Section 2, of the Constitution: "Representatives . . . shall be apportioned among the several States which may be included within this Union, according to their respective Numbers. . . . The actual Enumeration shall be made within three Years after the first Meeting of the Congress of the United States, and within every subsequent Term of ten Years, in such Manner as they shall by Law direct. The Number of Representatives shall not exceed one for every thirty Thousand, but each State shall have at Least one Representative."

According to Article I, Section 3, "The Senate of the United States shall be composed of two Senators from each State." Article II, Section 1, states: "The executive Power shall be vested in a President of the United States of America."

Each state, regardless of its size or population, has two senators. In Chapter 2, we discussed the dispute between large and small states at the Constitutional Convention over the shape of the new Congress; the *Connecticut compromise* called for membership of the House of Representatives to be apportioned by population, and, to compensate the smaller states, for the Senate to have equal representation of all states. The Founders decided against three senators per state because the poorer and more distant states from the capital complained of transportation costs. A single senator, on the other hand, would have had far too much influence. Thus, today we have the mathematically convenient number of one hundred senators.

Article I, Section 2, of the Constitution includes the basic formula by which the size of the House of Representatives is determined:

1. the Three-Fifths Compromise by which five slaves equaled three voters for apportionment purposes
2. the minimum ratio of representatives to citizens (i.e., no more than one member per thirty thousand inhabitants)
3. the assigning of sixty-five seats, pending the first census

The three-fifths provision was eliminated by the Fourteenth Amendment. Other changes have been more complicated.

As the American population increased, so did the size of the House of Representatives. If the ratio of members of Congress to voters was the same today as the minimum stated in the Constitution, the House would consist of more than seventy-five hundred representatives! In its early years, the House tried to keep the apportionment low, yet it did allow a slow increase in the number of members (see Table 5-1). By 1920, however, the House had grown so large that it decided to limit the number of seats to 435 (the total climbed to 437 after Hawaii and Alaska were admitted to the Union in 1959, but dropped back to 435 after the next census). When one state gains sufficient population and another loses enough people, the first state gains seats in the House at the expense of the other. For example, after the 1980 census, the Frost Belt lost seventeen seats and the Sun Belt gained seventeen (see Table 5-2). As a result, major political implications followed.

Unit of Representation

The president, of course, was intended to be the national executive, so the unit represented in the White House is the population of the entire United States. Although different presidents draw varying amounts of support from certain sections of the nation, few candidates for the office have been willing to write off any regions.

TABLE 5-1
APPORTIONMENT OF MEMBERS OF THE HOUSE OF
REPRESENTATIVES FROM ADOPTION OF THE CONSTITUTION
TO 1980

Year	Total Representatives	Apportionment Ratio (× 1,000)
1788	65	30
1790	106	33
1800	142	33
1810	186	35
1820	213	40
1830	242	48
1840	232	71
1850	237	93
1860	243	127
1870	293	131
1880	332	152
1890	357	174
1900	391	194
1910	435	211
1920[a]	435	243
1930	435	281
1940	435	301
1950	435	345
1960	437	410
1970	435	469
1980	435	521

[a]No reapportionment.

Source: U.S. Bureau of the Census, *Historical Statistics of the United States,* Part 2 (Washington, D.C.: Government Printing Office, 1975), p. 1085.

Similarly, senators were to be elected on a statewide basis by the state legislatures and thus would represent their entire states. Because each state elects only one senator in a given year, senatorial elections have been analogous to single-member district (SMD) elections, which, as we discussed in Chapter 4, reduce the chances that a third party will form in the Senate. The other major effect of the Senate's unit of representation is that, as the Founders intended, citizens of low-population states have a great advantage: a senator from California represents about ten million people, while a senator from Alaska represents only about 150,000 people.

The unit of representation in the House of Representatives is much more complicated, partly because of ambiguities in the Constitution and other laws, and partly because the determination of who can vote for whom will greatly

TABLE 5-2
THE SUN-BELT SHIFT, 1970–1980

State	Seats 1980	Seats 1982	Change[a]
Gaining Seats			
Arizona	4	5	+1
California	43	45	+2
Colorado	5	6	+1
Florida	15	19	+4
Nevada	1	2	+1
New Mexico	2	3	+1
Oregon	4	5	+1
Tennessee	8	9	+1
Texas	24	27	+3
Utah	2	3	+1
Washington	7	8	+1
Losing Seats			
Illinois	24	22	−2
Indiana	11	10	−1
Massachusetts	12	11	−1
Michigan	19	18	−1
Missouri	10	9	−1
New Jersey	15	14	−1
New York	39	34	−5
Ohio	23	21	−2
Pennsylvania	25	23	−2
South Dakota	2	1	−1

[a]Changes in the allocation of seats in the House of Representatives based on the 1980 census.
Sources: *Congressional Quarterly Weekly Report,* January 10, 1981, p. 1981; November 15, 1980, p. 3375.

affect the outcome of elections. Until 1842, some states selected all of their representatives on an at-large basis; then Congress required state legislatures to divide congressional districts along geographical lines. Since then, most states have been divided into SMDs. Oddly, a 1929 law dropped the districting requirement, so today a state can, if it wishes, choose its representatives on a statewide basis; however, none does.

If a state chooses to divide itself into congressional districts, it faces a major task. In the early 1960s, the Supreme Court upheld federal jurisdiction, first over state reapportionment plans in *Baker* v. *Carr* and then over congressional reapportionment in *Wesberry* v. *Sanders,* and required that representation reflect equal population as precisely as possible. Both of these cases grew out of questions about the composition of electoral units (see next section) and the Fourteenth Amendment's "equal protection" guarantee.[1] The Supreme Court ruled that no variance, no matter how small, is permitted from the *one-person, one-vote* formula without justification (e.g., solid evidence of expected shifts in population). The Court has allowed deviations between district populations as large as 9.9 percent, but it generally rejects any redistricting plan, whatever the justification, if a purposeful bias against a particular racial or political group can be shown.

The one-person, one-vote requirement poses some enormous difficulties for states. After each census, redistricting plans must be devised quickly, yet practical and political problems and possible judicial objections must be anticipated. In the 1973 case of *White* v. *Weiser,* the Supreme Court required Texas to devise a plan with population differences between districts of less than 0.2 percent—or 696 people out of a district of 466,000.[2] And since the populations of some districts change radically over a few years—a 30-percent increase in five years is not impossible—the task can be very complicated. Yet, the biggest problem is not simply counting people and drawing lines on a map; each redistricting plan has the potential of drastically revising the partisan and minority composition of each congressional district, which is the source of great controversy.

Composition of Electoral Units

There is no flexibility in the composition of the electoral units of the president and senators. The nation and the states are what they are. But because the states are not homogeneous—because there are Democratic cities, Republican suburbs, black neighborhoods, white neighborhoods, and so on—the shape and location of a congressional district can determine which candidate, which party, and which interests are elected to the House of Representatives. The political aspect of districting has been an issue at least since 1812, when Governor Elbridge Gerry of Massachusetts supervised a redrawing of district lines in that state. To benefit Gerry's party, one district was shaped somewhat like a salamander; hence, the term **gerrymander.** A more recent example of a gerrymandered district was proposed in 1982 by Democratic representative Phillip Burton of California. Figure 5-1 illustrates his unsuccessful plan to reshape California's Sixth Congressional District, which was represented by his brother John, in order to include as many Democratic voters as possible.

The Supreme Court resisted becoming involved in such "political" questions as the composition of electoral units until the 1960s and 1970s when civil-rights activists successfully challenged state-redistricting plans. In effect, the Supreme Court created new laws in areas where Congress had failed to act; it struck down districting plans that placed some voters "in a position of constitutionally unjustifiable inequality" by diluting the vote of any citizen. The Court also ruled against apportionment plans that create numerically equal

gerrymander: To divide a territorial area into voting districts in such a way as to give an unfair advantage to one political party.

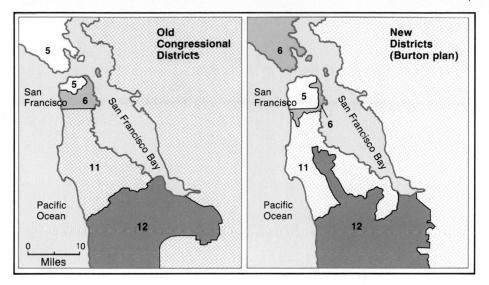

FIGURE 5–1 Phillip Burton's 1982 plan to reshape California's Sixth Congressional District

Source: *Time*, March 15, 1982, p. 15.

districts, but with either "purposeful" or "inherent" bias against racial or political groups.

These equal-protection rulings apply not only to presidential and congressional elections, but have been extended by the courts to cover the elections of any officials who are to perform governmental functions, such as the trustees of a junior-college district. Thus, although the delegates to the Constitutional Convention decided not to put precise electoral instructions in the Constitution (e.g., a guarantee of the right to vote), we now have in modern America a doctrine that was proclaimed by the Supreme Court in *Wesberry* v. *Sanders*: "Other rights . . . are illusionary . . . if the right to vote is undermined." While the Senate has a constitutional exception to the one-person, one-vote requirement, all other electoral districts at the national, state, and local level must adhere to it.

Suffrage

The United States has never been a nation of voters. The Constitution was not subjected to the electorate for its approval, nor were any of its amendments. And it provided for only one-half of one of three branches of government to be directly chosen by citizens. Therefore, at the start of the republic, only 3 percent of the population were allowed to cast ballots.

Adjustments in the Constitution since the eighteenth century and a large

Carrying paper lanterns, suffragettes pause before a huge voting-rights parade in New York City in 1912, eight years before ratification of the Nineteenth Amendment. (Library of Congress)

quantity of legislative and judicial decisions prove that the right to vote is now considered to be fundamental. Originally, only males who owned certain types and amounts of property were allowed to vote; this requirement was dropped by nearly all states by 1850. However, for elections to certain offices with only limited governmental powers, such as supervisor of a water-storage district, property ownership may be a valid qualification for voting.[3] Women were not enfranchised anywhere until 1869, when the territory of Wyoming allowed them to vote; their right to participate in national elections was not assured until 1920 when the Nineteenth Amendment was ratified. American Indians were admitted into the national electorate in 1924, although residents of reservations are still often excluded from state elections. Residents of the District of Columbia were given the right to vote for presidential candidates in 1961 by the Twenty-third Amendment, and in 1971, eighteen-year-old citizens, who had been denied the vote in most states, where the voting age was usually twenty-one, were enfranchised by the Twenty-sixth Amendment.

The entry of most of these groups into the electorate was relatively straightforward once constitutional and statutory guarantees of their voting rights were enacted. However, the opposite was true for the enfranchisement of blacks. Although the passage of the Fifteenth Amendment in 1870 required that "[t]he right of citizens of the United States to vote shall not be denied or abridged by the United States or by any State on account of race, color, or previous condition of servitude," enforcement of this principle proved extremely difficult. After seven years of federal supervision of the participation of black voters in the South, first violent, then more "respectable" methods of excluding blacks and poor whites were developed.[4]

Beginning in 1890, Mississippi's state constitution required (1) payment of a two-dollar *poll tax* a year before an election; (2) lengthy *residence requirements* designed to exclude many blacks who were, in effect, migrant workers; and (3) a *literacy test* by which voters had to be able to read a portion of the state constitution or "reasonably" interpret a portion when it was read to them. Because these restrictions did not specifically deny a particular group the vote, the Supreme Court ruled that they did not violate the Fifteenth Amendment, and many other southern states adopted them. Nonsouthern states also used literacy tests; in New England, they were used to exclude ethnic immigrants, and in the West to exclude Orientals. As it turned out, many poor and illiterate white Americans were affected by the new restrictions, so grandfather clauses were added to state constitutions; if a citizen could show that a direct ancestor was registered to vote on January 1, 1867 (shortly before Congress prohibited the denial of the vote to freed slaves), then he would be qualified to vote. Some of these provisions were barred during the next half-century by Supreme Court decisions, yet even in 1940, for example, only 0.19 percent of Louisiana's blacks were registered to vote.

Further restrictions on black voting were created in the late nineteenth century by a new electoral system by which a party's nominees were chosen. For many years, the Democratic party in ten southern states was so dominant that a general election was usually just an endorsement of the Democratic nominee chosen in a **white primary.** Therefore, the only meaningful political choice occurred during the Democratic primary, and southern states allowed the political parties to impose their own qualifications for voting in their primaries. Until 1944, when the Supreme Court ruled against the white primary in *Smith* v. *Allwright,* few blacks could participate in southern Democratic primaries.[5] Yet even with an increasingly sympathetic Supreme Court, the participation of blacks in the electoral process made slow progress; by 1956, the percentage of the black voting-age population registered to vote in the South was still generally under 30 percent.

One of the most significant and effective pieces of civil-rights legislation in American history was the Voting Rights Act of 1965. This act forbade the use of any test or device to deny or abridge voting rights in any state or political subdivision in which more than 50 percent of the eligible voters had not voted in the 1964 presidential election or had not been registered. A panel of federal judges would be set up to review any new voting test for its potential to deny voting rights. The act allowed federal registrars to be sent to any county where the United States attorney general found voter registration to be unduly restrictive. The effect of the Voting Rights Act is clear: six southern states eliminated literacy tests, federal registrars were dispatched to about sixty southern counties, and by 1970, black registration in the eleven affected southern states had risen to 66 percent (compared to 83 percent for white voters).

In 1970, 1975, and 1982, the Voting Rights Act was renewed and revised to cover not only the six-and-one-half southern states originally included, but an additional eighteen states, including parts of New York and California, as well.

white primary: A primary election in which black citizens were forbidden or strongly discouraged from participating.

Moreover, the Voting Rights Act has been used to block gerrymandering and at-large elections when the effect could be shown to be the dilution of minority votes.

The major form of voting restriction that remains today was addressed by the 1970 Voting Rights Act when Congress set a nationwide requirement for length of residence as a prerequisite for voter registration. Although the Supreme Court later ruled that only federal elections were affected by the congressional action, most states voluntarily reduced their residency requirements. Other court decisions have ruled that residency requirements of more than thirty to fifty days divide voters into two classes (i.e., old and new residents) for which there is no justification and that it restricts the right to interstate travel. The controversies over voter registration by mail or on the day of an election have not been treated as constitutional questions, and remain intense. It is generally believed that a liberalization of voting requirements would disproportionately benefit the Democratic party, because those who are not registered to vote tend to be poorer and black, and therefore more Democratic than most registered voters.

The Electoral College

According to the Constitution, Americans vote only for presidential electors, not directly for the president. Electors in each of the fifty states are selected by a method designated by the state legislature and are equal in number to the sum of the state's United States senators and representatives; in addition, the District of Columbia was granted three electoral votes by the Twenty-third Amendment. Thus, there are 538 electoral-college votes, of which a candidate needs at least 270 in order to win. The victorious electors in each state meet on the first Monday after the second Wednesday in December, when they cast their ballots and send them to Congress. Early in January, congressional leaders formally count the ballots and announce the winner of the presidential campaign.

The electoral-college system has been criticized almost since the beginning of the republic. Many believe that it is undemocratic and that the voters should have the right to choose the president directly. In addition, the electoral college can produce some odd results. In case of a tie—or if no candidate wins a majority due to a third-party candidate's winning electoral votes—the Constitution requires the House of Representatives to choose the president. As mentioned previously, this happened in 1800, when Thomas Jefferson and Aaron Burr each polled 73 electoral votes. On two occasions, in 1876 and 1888, a president who had won fewer popular votes than his opponent was elected by the electoral college. Recently, there have been several close calls: a shift of 9,000 votes in Illinois and Missouri would have cost John Kennedy the 1960 election, and Jimmy Carter would have lost in 1976 if about 9,000 voters in Hawaii and Ohio had supported Gerald Ford.

There are also statistical biases built into the electoral-college system. The electoral college exaggerates the size of the winning candidate's mandate. For example, Ronald Reagan won 51 percent of the popular vote in 1980, but 91 percent of the electoral vote. Furthermore, the less populated states, which are guaranteed a minimum of three electors, have a disproportionate share of the electoral vote, whereas the densely populated states benefit from the extra attention—and, most likely, the extra promises—that their large blocs of electoral votes attract. Not surprisingly, there have been hundreds of proposals for reforming or abolishing the electoral college.

The idea of electing the president directly so that the victorious candidate would be the one with the largest number of popular votes is the simplest alternative to the electoral college. However, most such proposals would require a candidate to win a minimum percentage of the total vote—usually 40 to 50 percent; otherwise, a runoff election would be necessary. Therefore, the consequences of such a system must be considered. First, the party system would be weakened because coalitions would be formed and deals negotiated in order to give one candidate the necessary 40 to 50 percent in a multicandidate race. In addition, a runoff election would extend both the campaign and its costs. And, of course, the groups which currently find the electoral-college system to their advantage would strenuously object to any changes.

The alternative to the electoral college that has drawn the most support from politicians and academics is the *national bonus plan.* A compromise between the electoral college and a direct election, the plan would award a bonus of 102 electoral votes (two per state, plus two for the District of Columbia) to the winner of the most popular votes. Under this system, the chances of a "perverse" outcome such as those that resulted in 1876 and 1888 would be practically nonexistent. Once again, there are consequences that must be considered. As with a direct election system, the bonus plan would deprive some states of their current advantages. More serious under the bonus plan is the potential for a candidate who is very popular in only one region of the country to win the popular vote, and therefore the bonus, and thus possibly fragment the nation. In summary, any constitutional amendment proposing to either reform or do away with the electoral college would face a tough challenge in surviving the two parties in Congress and the state legislatures that would have to ratify it.

From the preceding discussion, we can see that the modern American electoral system is a complex set of institutions and procedures that have developed under both constitutional and political constraints. The methods by which party convention delegates are chosen, those by which state party primaries are held, and even the procedures within the national conventions are never neutral. Parties have had to make trade-offs in their electoral strategies, because one group's gain is usually seen by another group as a loss, and they have been subject to the controls of law and to the American conception of political justice.

AMERICAN ELECTORAL INSTITUTIONS

Except in small communities, nearly all American elections consist of two phases: nomination and general election. In the nomination phase, candidates from the same party compete for the party's endorsement and the opportunity to run in the general election on their party's ticket. Because (1) the battle for nomination is often fought among many men and women within a party and (2) factors outside a candidate's control, such as the competitiveness of a state party or the overall economic situation, can determine which party wins the general election, winning the nomination is usually not only necessary for a candidate's election, but is often also sufficient.

The general-election phase, which usually involves a two-person race between a Republican and a Democrat, revolves around issues and strategies that differ from those in the primary campaigns. In the following sections, we will discuss both nominating procedures and the general-election campaign.

Caucuses and Primaries

As soon as parties arose in the United States, a system was needed to pick their candidates. Nominations for state offices were made by legislative party caucuses, in which members of the state legislature picked their party's candidates. As we saw in our discussion of the rise of the two-party system in Chapter 4, the congressional caucus was used to select presidential candidates until 1824. It was then replaced by the party convention, which consisted of delegates chosen by party members at precinct, township, and county committee meetings. The convention method, which was the most common technique for choosing almost all party candidates from 1835 until the end of the nineteenth century, came under increasing attack because it was subject to dominance and manipulation by party bosses. After 1900, except for presidential nominations, the party convention was discarded by all but a few states.

Opposition to the control of nominations by a few party leaders was related to the Progressive movement, an upper- and middle-class movement of social and political reform in the late nineteenth and early twentieth centuries. Among other objectives, Progressives wanted to erode the strength of party organizations, and one way to accomplish this was to "democratize" candidate-selection procedures. Thus, the Progressives were attracted to the primary election system, in which voters would first choose their party's candidates and then later select from among the nominees of all parties in the general election. The first primary was held in 1842, and there was some experimentation with primaries from 1860 to 1900. Between 1900 and 1917, all but four states adopted primaries for at least some state and local nominations, and many also indicated their choices for presidential nominations by direct primaries.

While primaries continued to be used for state and local elections, the presidential primary-election system gradually lost appeal over the next five decades, and by 1968 only about sixteen states still used presidential primaries. After their national convention that year, however, the Democrats instituted

THE ACTIVITIES OF STATE AND LOCAL PARTIES: MAJOR EVENTS IN THE TEXAS DEMOCRATIC PARTY'S 1984 ELECTION CAMPAIGN

Feb. 13	County Executive Committees elect Temporary Chairs for Senatorial District Conventions in counties which hold Senatorial District Conventions.
March 19	County Executive Committees set times and places for Precinct and County Conventions, allocate one State Convention Delegate and Alternate to each precinct for every 300 votes it cast for the 1982 Democratic Gubernatorial Nominee, and group precincts casting fewer than 300 votes on the basis of geographic proximity and demographic similarity.
April 5	Deadline for registering to vote for May 5 primary.
April 25	County Chairs post at County Courthouses the times and places of Precinct and County Conventions.
May 5	Primary Election, 7 A.M.–7 P.M. Precinct Conventions convene at 7:15 P.M., usually at the same polling places.
May 7–June 7	National Delegate Candidates file in writing with the State Party Chair. Forms are available from State Party Office, from County Chairs, and at County and Senatorial District Conventions.
May 8	County Executive Committees elect 8–15 County Convention or Senatorial District Delegates to Convention Committees on Credentials, Nominations, Platform and Resolutions, and Rules and Procedures.
May 19	County and Senatorial District Conventions.
June 15–16	State Convention in Houston.
June 16–23	National Delegates meet to elect members of Standing Committees on Credentials, Platform, and Rules of the National Convention.
July 15–19	National Convention in San Francisco.
Sept. 7–8	State Convention in Dallas.
Nov. 6	General Election.

reforms that greatly increased the number of presidential primaries in order to encourage popular participation in delegate selection. The Republicans followed their rival's lead, and by 1984 there were Democratic presidential primaries in twenty-six states and Republican ones in twenty-nine.

There are several basic types of primaries used in the United States today, and each affects the final choice of a candidate in the general election. The most common is the **closed primary,** used in about twenty states, in which a voter can select only candidates in the party in which the voter is registered.[6] Thus, a Democratic voter cannot vote for a Republican primary candidate; otherwise, the Democrat could vote for the Republican least likely to win the general election! Fourteen primary states use an **open primary,** in which party registration is not required. While crossover voting is a possibility in open primaries, advocates of the system consider it more democratic and more

closed primary: A primary election in which only registered party members can vote.

open primary: A primary election in which voters can vote for members of any party regardless of their own party membership.

nonpartisan primary: A primary in which candidates do not run as members of political parties.

runoff primary: An election following a primary, in which the two candidates winning the largest shares of the vote face each other in a two-person race, thereby guaranteeing that one will win a majority, as opposed to a mere plurality.

plurality: The number of votes received in an election by the leading candidate or proposal, but not necessarily the majority.

majority: More than fifty percent of the votes cast.

secret than the closed primary. And three states—Alaska, Washington, and Louisiana—use variations of **nonpartisan primaries,** or "blanket" primaries, in which voters can split their tickets, choosing Democrats for some offices and Republicans for others. Such nonpartisan primaries are more common at the local level, where they are used for the selection of judges and school-board officials, who often claim to be above party politics.

Finally, some states hold **runoff primaries.** If no candidate for a party's nomination receives more than a certain percentage—usually 50 percent—of the vote, another primary is held in which voters choose between the top two candidates in the first race. Runoffs were particularly common in the South, where the Democratic party dominated politics to the extent that many candidates would run as Democrats and few would run as Republicans. With a dozen people running for the same nomination, the candidate with the most votes (i.e., the winner of a **plurality**) usually had far less than a **majority** (i.e., 50 percent plus one) of the votes. Therefore, the party would "unite" behind a single candidate with a "clear" mandate, which was often the result of bargains made by the leading candidates between the first primary and the runoff primary.

As direct primaries have become more common, so has criticism of them. Primaries, which were intended to weaken the control of party bosses on the nomination process, have apparently weakened the party system as a whole. Because primaries are expensive, candidates must go outside their party to find funding. In addition, because no clearance by party leaders is required, anyone, of any background or ideology, can claim to represent a party. The result may be both confusion for voters and a loss of identity for the party. Benjamin Ginsberg has observed that primaries inhibit the formation of third parties by allowing ambitious outsiders the opportunity to run for office within a major party rather than against it.[7] Primaries also reflect a particular bias in the electoral system. Voter turnout is usually much lower in primary elections than in general elections, and those who are motivated to participate in primaries tend to be more ideologically rigid and extreme, more highly educated, and wealthier than the average voter.

Of course, some of these criticisms can apply to other methods of choosing party candidates; for example, those who participate in state party conventions are no more representative of the public than are voters in primaries. Nevertheless, the current primary system bears a special responsibility for a very real problem in today's elections. In 1980, for example, the first presidential primary was held on February 26 in New Hampshire. Ronald Reagan, first among the Republicans with 49.6 percent of the votes, was declared the front-runner. By March 19, after the Illinois primary, the Republican nomination was, according to many, sewn up. Reagan had accumulated 51.3 percent of the Republican votes. Although there were twenty-six more primaries to go and more than 75 percent of all Republican voters still awaiting their turn at the polls, four Republican candidates dropped out of the race, and Gerald Ford decided not to try to regain his former job. The same situation existed in the Democratic primaries. By the end of March, Jimmy Carter had already won one-third of the delegates needed for the Democratic nomination. Although voters in states such as New York, Pennsylvania, and California would cast the majority of their ballots for Senator Edward Kennedy, Carter was proclaimed the winner by the news media.

Such a system is unjust, some say, because media attention and financial support flow to the winners of small but early primaries, thereby giving these races a disproportionate influence on party nominations. (Even so, New Hampshire officials consider the income produced by the extensive media coverage of its primary so important that they have exacted promises from both parties to allow it to remain first.) Furthermore, the drawn-out primary season is costly in terms of time and money and in wear and tear on candidates and the public.

Two solutions have been proposed. First, surveys have shown that about three-fourths of the American public support a single national primary, with all state primaries and conventions taking place on the same day. Problems with such a system include the advantage to well known candidates, the added importance of the national news media, and the absolute elimination of a role for party leaders in picking candidates. The second alternative is a set of regional primaries—four or five, perhaps one a month, in regions roughly matching the time zones—which would reduce the costs of primaries while allowing the voters a longer opportunity to see the candidates in action. The regional primary system may be the more popular alternative, but those who benefit from the current system are likely to oppose any change at all.

Delegates and the Conventions

In most presidential primaries, the voters only participate indirectly in the nomination of presidential candidates, because what they are actually doing is selecting delegates to the Republican or Democratic conventions. It is these delegates who will select the presidential nominee. How delegates are chosen affects the outcome of the nomination process, because some candidates adopt campaign strategies that emphasize the mass media and thereby reach more primary voters, while others focus on persuading local and state party officials who will dominate caucuses and conventions. As we have seen, the most common system for delegate selection today is the primary; caucuses or state conventions are used to select delegates in fourteen states.

How delegates vote is a major concern because it is only through these votes that the electorate can influence the nomination outcome. Until their 1972 convention, the Democrats allowed state parties to enforce a **unit rule,** by which a majority of a state's delegation could force the entire delegation to vote as a bloc during the first polling of delegates at the convention. The "winner-take-all" primary, in which all delegates would be pledged to the winner of a state's primary, was abolished by the Democrats before their 1976 convention. The Republicans, largely because of their homogeneity, have allowed each state to choose its own method of selecting delegates.

unit rule: A now-obsolete requirement of political parties that delegations at a party convention must vote as a bloc.

Another controversial form of regulating delegate voting has been the "pledged" delegate. Since most delegates are chosen on the basis of their professed support of a particular candidate, many have believed that delegates should be compelled to vote for that candidate on the first ballot at the national convention. However, if no candidate received a majority of delegate votes on the first try, the delegates would then be free to vote as they wished on subsequent ballots. Of course, candidates who enter the convention with a compelling lead support the pledged-delegate concept, while those with a shortage of pledged delegates call for an "open" convention of free-thinking men and women. This was a major controversy at the 1980 Democratic convention; because Jimmy Carter's popularity had dropped by about thirty percent in the three months preceding the convention, Edward Kennedy's supporters argued that the pledged-delegate system would assure the nomination of a sure loser. Carter's forces defeated the insurgents because, as the incumbent president and the front-runner, Carter had a major say in convention rules.

It should be emphasized that the majority of Democratic and Republican delegates to the parties' conventions (in 1980, a total of 3,331 Democratic and 1,994 Republican delegates, along with 2,053 Democratic and 1,994 Republican alternates, and in 1984, a total of 3,915 Democratic and 2,187 Republican delegates) were not chosen as individuals by voters in state primaries. The ballots that voters mark usually offer "delegates for" the various candidates, and then state party officials select the individuals who will attend the convention. This task has become much more complex since the Democratic party's McGovern-Fraser Commission (1969–1972) produced new criteria for delegate selection. The commission not only abolished the unit rule, but more significantly, it imposed quotas to guarantee certain percentages of females, racial minorities, and delegates under the age of thirty. As a result, the dominance of the convention by public officials and state and local party leaders decreased, and the proportion of women and black delegates increased from 13 and 5.5 percent in 1968 to 40 and 15 percent, respectively, in 1972. In contrast, only 15 percent of all Democratic members of the House of Representatives and 18 percent of Democratic senators were delegates in 1976. In 1978, the Democrats' Winograd Commission increased the size of each state's delegation by 10 percent to allow more participation by elected and party officials. However, because the 1980 convention saw little increase in their influence and in recognition of the party's need for the organizational skills and support of its professionals, the Hunt Commission issued yet another change in 1982: a given percentage of Democratic delegates should henceforth be elected party officials. The Republicans, on the other hand, are more decentralized. Although they have encouraged state parties to bring more women, minority, and young voters into party procedures, the states retain the freedom to choose whomever they desire.

The ostensible purpose of the national party convention is to nominate candidates for the presidency and vice presidency, but not since 1952 has a party needed more than one ballot to choose a candidate. However, there have been several close calls. For example, in 1960, with the states voting in alphabetical order, not until Wisconsin, the forty-ninth state polled, cast its fifteen votes, was John Kennedy's nomination assured. In addition, Gerald Ford went to the 1976 Republican convention with only thirty-nine more delegates than Ronald Reagan.

In reality, the major functions of the four-day party conventions are publicity and party unification. Publicity, which is of obvious value, is fulfilled by the massive media attention accorded the gathering. Not only do the parties get free network airtime in which to make speeches, show films, and demonstrate their enthusiasm for their candidates, but under the federal election campaign reforms of the 1970s, millions of federal tax dollars are also allocated to help pay for the party conventions and to help pay the security costs incurred by the cities that host the conventions.

The second major function of conventions, party unification, is much less easily achieved than publicity. As we have seen, a national party organization is a fragile phantom with few powers and even fewer resources. Yet, to achieve its goal—the election of a president—a party needs organizational unity. The often bitter disputes among contenders for the nomination must be resolved; the support of all party leaders, including defeated candidates for the nomination, must be secured; and the nation must be shown that the successful nominee stands on a substantive and correct platform of electoral pledges.

Some conventions have been described as love feasts in which the nominee was chosen by acclamation or with little opposition, and in which the content of the platform was beyond dispute. Much more common, however, are conventions that losing factions see as a last opportunity to influence party matters. Sometimes disputes occur over the credentials of various state delegations; for example, the Democratic delegation from Mississippi was excluded in 1964 for reasons involving civil rights, and the 1972 Democratic delegates from Illinois were not seated partly because they failed to comply with the McGovern-Fraser Commission quotas for women, minorities, and delegates under thirty years of age. Other convention battles involve the adoption of party rules for the next four years, a period for which the losing factions are certain to be already planning. Platform disputes are also common; these often involve ideological minorities within a party that are unable to convince the party's platform committee of the justness of their cause and are willing to take their battle to the convention floor.

Despite such internal quarrels, most national party conventions are not very suspenseful. By the third day of the convention, during which presidential candidates are nominated and the delegates polled, the outcome is usually known. The great mystery and glamour of the convention are reserved for the fourth and final day, when the nominee's choice for a running mate is announced (the vice-presidential nominee is usually an unsuccessful presidential candidate who will balance the ticket by appealing to a different region or party faction than the presidential nominee); voted upon (without much suspense); and presented to the delegates and the television cameras, arm in arm with the candidate, amid great celebration and rejoicing. Thus ends the first phase of the national electoral process. Although the second phase is no less important or spectacular, it is usually simpler.

The General Election Campaign

The folk drama of an American presidential campaign begins to be reshaped even before the convention delegates return to their home states. The candidates assess the damage caused by intraparty battles for the nomination and begin the arduous task of healing wounds and creating allies. The pace of the campaign quickens. Now, instead of being able to concentrate on a few states at a time, the candidates are likely to begin the day in Texas, attend a luncheon in Tennessee, and appear at an evening rally in Chicago. Their campaign organizations shift their focus from fellow party members to the real enemy.

THE 1984 ELECTIONS

On November 6, 1984, Ronald Reagan was elected to a second term in the White House. During the presidential campaign, the most important issues were the arms race, the federal deficit, and presidential leadership. The Democratic nominee, Walter Mondale of Minnesota, hit hard at the nuclear arms buildup and the incumbent's failure to meet personally with Soviet leaders. Mondale's attempt to focus attention on the fairness of Reagan programs was undermined by his controversial pledge to seek tax increases, which he claimed would be necessary regardless of who won the election. However, these issues were overshadowed by Reagan's personal popularity, his image as a strong leader, and the widespread belief that his economic policies had worked. Religion was also raised as an important issue during the campaign, but its impact on voter choices was ambiguous.

The significance of Mondale's historic choice of Representative Geraldine Ferraro of New York, the first woman ever to be nominated by a major political party in the United States for the office of vice president, was obscured by questions about her family's finances. Surveys showed that the selection of Ferraro caused nearly equal numbers of voters to either support or spurn the Democratic ticket. Nevertheless, Ferraro's nomination broke new ground, and American women can now reasonably aspire to the highest office in the nation.

During the first of two televised debates with Mondale, Reagan's reputation as "the Great Communicator" was temporarily undermined by a shaky performance; most viewers surveyed found the president to be uninformed and confused. However, Reagan was reelected by one of the largest electoral vote margins (525 to 13) in American history and received 59.1 percent of the popular vote.

Intense voter registration drives by both parties resulted in only a slight increase in voter turnout. The Republican party retained its majority in the Senate with a margin of 53 to 47 seats, having lost two seats to the Democrats. In the House of Representatives, the Republicans gained more than a dozen seats, but the Democrats nevertheless maintained their sizable majority. Thus, President Reagan began his second term still faced with a divided Congress, which weakened his claim of having received a clear mandate from the people.

Democrats Walter Mondale and Geraldine Ferraro (AP/Wide World Photos)

And, now that the preliminary rounds are over, many voters finally begin to pay attention to national politics.

During a general election campaign, the Republican and Democratic nominees must appeal to a national audience, so their campaign organizations become even more important than they were during the primaries. Certain states will be seen as "sure wins," while others will be picked as crucial and deserving of special effort. The eleven most populous states—including Michigan, Pennsylvania, Ohio, and Texas—have enough electoral votes to determine the result of the general election, so would-be presidents tend to spend a lot of time in them. Public appearances must be scheduled across the country, requiring advance workers to organize and coordinate meetings, speeches, television appearances, and media coverage. In consultation with their advisers, candidates will prepare position papers in order to advertise their views—these statements are often long on slogans and short on details. Volunteers will be recruited to canvass voters on the street or door-to-door. An enormous

Republicans Ronald Reagan and George Bush (UPI/Bettmann Archive)

number of public opinion polls will appear, commissioned by television networks, newspapers, and candidates for offices at all levels. Finally, each candidate—especially an incumbent president who must appear to be applying himself fully to his job—will enlist prominent party members to help with the campaign.

Many people, including political scientists, journalists, and practicing politicians, have tried to isolate the factors that determine the outcome of a general election. Not surprisingly, this has turned out to be a difficult task. Every general election has its own idiosyncrasies. Although the condition of the economy is always an issue, no one has yet proven an exact relationship between, for example, the rate of inflation or unemployment and support for the incumbent candidate; many voters are likely to be aware not only of the current rate of inflation or unemployment, but also of whether the trend is toward an improvement or worsening of the economy. In addition, different parts of the electorate will rank the importance of economic issues higher or lower than that of defense, welfare, or other issues. There are unique features to each election that can drastically shape the course of the campaign. Such factors in the 1980 presidential campaign included the American hostages in Iran, the independent candidacy of John Anderson, and voter perceptions of the personalities and capabilities of Ronald Reagan and Jimmy Carter.

It is also during the general-election campaign that candidates are likely to moderate their views. No longer dependent on the more extreme activists who aided them in their nomination bids, presidential contenders now shape their appeal to the entire electorate. Thus, in 1980, Ronald Reagan surprised some of his supporters, who disapproved of increased government spending or involvement in business affairs, by backing federal aid to New York City and government-guaranteed loans for the Chrysler Corporation. Every candidate wants to appear strong but temperate on defense issues, frugal yet fair on social welfare issues, and a humble but proud servant of the public, so the public inevitably is presented with contradictions, reversals, and hedgings. Rather than admit that any public policy that benefits some group will hurt another, candidates avoid discussions of trade-offs and offer benefits to all instead.

Finally, on the first Tuesday after the first Monday in November, after all of the television commercials, personal appearances, strategy sessions, and voter surveys, about half of the eligible voters in the United States will go to their local firehouses, schools, or town halls to vote (see the discussion of voter turnout in Chapter 3). In most locations, the voter will enter a booth, draw a curtain, and either mark a paper ballot or select the appropriate levers on a voting machine. Some voters will cast absentee ballots; for example, armed forces personnel and college students away from home will mark their ballots, have them notarized, and mail them to their hometowns. After the polls are closed, officials will tabulate the ballots and report the results to the city or county clerk or the board of elections. Although the results will be quickly announced to the press and party leaders, the count will not be official until it is certified and registered with local and state authorities. Unless there is a dispute about the vote count, the electoral process will have ended—except for the presidential race. As we saw earlier, the presidential election process involves more than the casting of votes; not until the electoral votes are formally counted about two months after the general election will the nation officially have a president-elect.

DISTORTIONS IN AMERICAN ELECTIONS?

In this and the preceding chapter, we have seen how the Constitution has constrained the evolution of American party and electoral systems as they have been affected by social and economic forces. However, we have also seen that there has been plenty of room for the American electoral process to change. We close this chapter by examining the allegedly increasing influence of money and the mass media in American politics. To some, the combination of financial and technological manipulation of the electoral process threatens many of its best characteristics, while to others the financial and technological changes are simply the result of new concepts of freedom of speech and a mass electronic society.

Democracy for the Wealthy?

The fears about political money generally reflect several phenomena:

1. the escalating expenditures by campaign committees
2. the rapidly increasing number of political action committees (PACs)
3. growing concerns about the impact of expenditures and PACs on the behavior of elected officials

The Cost of Campaigns Total expenditures for presidential and congressional campaigns have greatly increased over the last three decades. Table 5-3 indicates both a rise in presidential campaign costs from 1960 through 1968 and the slower rate of growth in these costs after passage of the 1971 Federal Election Campaign Act and its 1974 and 1976 amendments. Since 1976, expenditures by presidential candidates and the sources and sizes of campaign contributions have been controlled by the Federal Election Campaign Act (see Table 5-4). Candidates for the presidency could accept federal subsidies for their campaigns and conventions, but they also had to accept limits on spending.

The costs of campaigns for the House of Representatives and the Senate have continued to rise, however, because Congress did not include itself in many of the campaign-finance reform measures imposed on the presidency

TABLE 5-3
**PRESIDENTIAL CAMPAIGN EXPENDITURES, MAJOR PARTY
CANDIDATES, 1960–1980**

Year	Primary Elections	General Election
1960	$ 2,600,000[a]	$19,925,000
1964	$ 10,500,000[a]	$24,783,000
1968	$ 45,000,000	$36,996,000
1972	$ 53,664,000	$91,400,000
1976	$ 72,321,923	$43,947,713
1980	$110,435,270	$73,000,000

[a]Estimates.

Sources: Herbert E. Alexander, *Financing the 1960 Election* (Princeton, New Jersey: Citizen's Research Foundation, 1962), pp. 16–20; *Financing the 1964 Election* (Princeton, New Jersey: Citizen's Research Foundation, 1966), p. 30; *Financing the 1972 Election* (Lexington, Massachusetts: Lexington, 1976), pp. 98, 223; *Financing the 1976 Election* (Lexington, Massachusetts: Lexington, 1980), p. 211; *Financing Politics* (Washington, D.C.: Congressional Quarterly Press, 1976), p. 20; and Federal Election Commission data.

during the 1970s. Although it did attempt to control itself by limiting the amount of money that candidates or their families could spend on their own campaigns, that provision was overturned by the Supreme Court in *Buckley* v. *Valeo* in 1976 as an infringement of free speech.[8] Thus, in 1982, Governor John D. Rockefeller IV of West Virginia was able to spend about $11 million of his own money to successfully campaign to retain his position, while Senate-hopeful Mark Dayton of Minnesota and New York gubernatorial candidate Lewis Lehrman each spent over $6 million of their own money, but lost. In Table 5-5, we can see that the 1982 midterm congressional elections cost nearly five times what they cost only ten years earlier. In the early 1980s, a typical campaign for a seat in the House cost nearly $300,000, while an average Senate campaign cost about $2 million.

There is nothing inherently evil about high levels of campaign expenditures. If more citizens are supporting their favorite candidates by contributing to their campaigns, then the recent trend could indicate increased political participation. We could hope that part of the result of increased campaign spending is an increase in information available to voters. As mentioned, the Supreme Court ruled in *Buckley* v. *Valeo* that spending one's own money in a political campaign is a form of political expression protected by the First Amendment. Yet, at the same time, the Supreme Court also found that Congress may limit the amount of money that an individual or group may give to a candidate, because it is a valid function of government to stop the fact or appearance of corruption that can result from large contributions.

TABLE 5-4
REGULATION OF CAMPAIGN CONTRIBUTIONS AND EXPENDITURES

Source of Contributions	*Limitations*
Individuals	• $1,000 per candidate per primary, runoff, and general election. • Except for presidential candidates receiving public funds, candidates can give unlimited amounts to their own campaigns. • $5,000 per PAC per year. • $20,000 per year to a national party committee. • No limit on individual expenditures for "independent advertising." • Maximum of $25,000 per year.
Political action committees	• $5,000 per candidate per election. • $5,000 per PAC per year. • $15,000 per year to a national party committee. • No total limit.
Party committees	• $17,500 per senatorial candidate per year. • $5,000 per congressional candidate per year. • No limit on contributions to party committees. • No total limit.
Corporations, unions	• No contributions to individual candidates. • May pay administrative and fund-raising costs of PACs. • No contributions to party committees.

Spending	*Limitations*
Presidential primary election	$10 million per candidate for all primaries
Presidential general election	$20 million per candidate
Presidential nominating convention	$2 million for each major party
Senate primary election	$100,000 or $0.08 per voter, whichever is greater
Senate general election	$150,000 or $0.12 per voter, whichever is greater
House primary election	$70,000 per candidate
House general election	$70,000 per candidate

Sources of Money   Like taxes, political contributions ultimately come from individuals, although they may be channeled to candidates in many imaginative ways. The most direct route is for people to donate money to candidates by mailing checks or making donations at political gatherings. However, even this method has become complicated. During the 1970s, many businesses

TABLE 5-5
CONGRESSIONAL CAMPAIGN EXPENDITURES, 1972–1982

Year	Senate	House of Representatives
1972	$ 26,443,964	$ 39,959,376
1974	$ 27,904,495	$ 46,700,000
1976	$ 38,100,000	$ 60,907,960
1978	$ 87,000,000	$111,000,000
1980	$105,000,000	$137,000,000
1982[a]	$139,000,000	$204,000,000

[a]1982 figures are estimates.

Sources: William J. Crotty and Gary C. Jacobson, *American Parties in Decline* (Boston: Little, Brown, 1980), p. 103; Richard E. Cohen, "Costly Campaigns: Candidates Learn that Reach the Voters Is Expensive," *National Journal,* April 16, 1983, p. 785; R. A. Diamond, ed., *Dollar Politics,* vol. II (Washington: Congressional Quarterly Press, 1973), p. 73; *Congressional Quarterly,* June 14, 1975, p. 1240; Roland D. McDevitt, "The Changing Dynamics of Fund Raising in House Campaigns," in Herbert E. Alexander, ed., *Political Finance* (Beverly Hills: Sage, 1979), p. 137.

were formed for the purpose of compiling, selling, and using lists of names and addresses to which appeals for money could be sent. In the 1982 midterm congressional elections, computerized direct-mail solicitations involved 500 million pieces of mail, which produced about 5.5 million responses.

Another traditional source of campaign funds is the political party. National party organizations, especially the Republicans, have become adept large-scale fund-raisers (see Table 5-6). However, their efforts on behalf of individual candidates are restricted by federal election laws that limit the national party

TABLE 5-6
SOURCES OF CAMPAIGN FUNDS, 1982 CONGRESSIONAL ELECTIONS[a]

Committee	Republicans	Democrats
National committees	$79,000,000	$15,500,000
Senatorial campaign committees	$47,000,000	$ 2,200,000
Congressional campaign committees	$57,300,000	$ 6,300,000
Political action committees	$38,000,000	$45,100,000
Business	$18,000,000	$ 9,400,000
Labor	$ 1,100,000	$19,100,000
Associations (trade, professional, etc.)	$12,400,000	$ 9,300,000
Ideological	$ 5,200,000	$ 5,400,000
Other	$ 1,300,000	$ 1,900,000

[a]Includes funds received from January 1, 1981, through November 22, 1982.

Source: Federal Election Commission data.

groups to (1) donations of $10,000 each in cash and (2) an additional amount, adjusted to keep up with inflation (e.g., in 1982, it was $36,880), for services, such as paying advertising bills. The bulk of each party's money is spent on activities not connected to individual candidates, such as commercials shown on national network television.

Much of the "new" money in political campaigns originates in political action committees (PACs), which were briefly discussed in Chapter 3. As we saw, PACs are becoming more common across the political spectrum. Not only do we have business and labor PACs, but PACs for trade and professional associations, public interest groups, and ideological groups as well. Before 1971, labor unions and corporations were forbidden from giving to campaigns, although many did anyway; labor unions, for example, provided funds through the AFL-CIO Committee on Political Education. Then, the Federal Election Campaign Act (FECA) of 1971 allowed such groups to donate up to $5,000 to each candidate. In 1976, amendments to the act authorized these groups to form PACs, which would collect voluntary contributions from at least fifty members or employees and distribute them to at least five candidates. PAC contributions were limited to a maximum of $5,000 per candidate in primaries and $5,000 in general elections.

Today, there are thousands of PACs, and their campaign contributions are likely to continue growing at an enormous rate in future years (see Table 5-7). It would require an act of Congress to restrict their activity, and even though members of Congress commonly lament the growth of PACs on the grounds that they escalate the cost of campaigns and give the false impression that Congress can be "bought," it is these officeholders who disproportionately benefit from PAC largess. In 1982, for example, congressional incumbents received $54.8 million from PACs, while their opponents got only $16.1 million.

TABLE 5-7
TOTAL POLITICAL ACTION COMMITTEE CONTRIBUTIONS TO CONGRESSIONAL CANDIDATES

Political Action Committees	Contributions ($ million)				
	1974	1976	1978	1980	1982
Corporate	2.5	7.1	9.8	19.2	27.4
Labor	6.3	8.2	10.3	13.1	20.2
Associations (trade, professional, etc.)	2.3	4.5	11.5	16.1	21.7
Other	1.4	2.8	3.5	6.9	13.9
Total	12.5	22.6	35.1	55.3	83.1[a]

[a]Numbers do not add up to totals due to rounding.

Source: Federal Election Commission data.

The Impact of Money   Most fears about the role of PACs and increasing campaign costs focus on two questions: (1) can money buy an election? and (2) can money buy a legislator's vote? The evidence on the first question is mixed. Contributors seek to distribute their money wisely; thus, candidates who are expected to lose by wide margins usually find it difficult to raise funds. For many reasons, incumbent officeholders have a distinct advantage in fund-raising. But political scientist Gary Jacobson found that the effect of campaign spending by challengers is generally much greater than that of spending by incumbents:

> Defeating an incumbent is expensive, and relatively few challengers have been able to raise enough funds to be serious threats. But those who do acquire sufficient resources can make incumbents feel anything but safe. For incumbents, spending a great deal of money on the campaign is a sign of weakness rather than strength. In fact, the more money they spend on the campaign, the worse they do on election day. Spending money does not cost them votes, to be sure; rather, incumbents raise and spend more money the more strongly they feel themselves challenged. . . . Therefore, the more spent by both the challenger and the incumbent, the greater the challenger's share of the vote.[9]

According to Jacobson, incumbents have many tools at their disposal, including free mailing privileges, mass-media publicity, casework, and personal contacts. They can exploit these advantages "so thoroughly that the additional increment of information about their virtues put forth in the campaign adds little or nothing to what is already known and felt about them."[10] In contrast, money spent by challengers has the effect of overcoming these advantages. Thus, we can find many elections in which money clearly did not dictate the outcome; for example, in 1982, Texas Governor William Clements, Jr., put about $12 million into his campaign, outspending his Democratic challenger Mark White by about two to one, yet lost by a sizable margin.

Many Americans worry that increasing campaign costs may make it necessary for public officials to accept or even solicit contributions from groups that may expect a *quid pro quo* for their investment. Many members of Congress share this concern, and some admit to feeling the pressure of obligation; for example, in 1983, Representative Richard Ottinger of New York commented, "I take money from labor, and I have to think twice in voting against their interests. I shouldn't have to do that."[11] There is much evidence to suggest that large contributors try to direct their money to legislators who are in the best position to help them. Committee chairpersons or legislators on committees with jurisdiction over a PAC's issues are especially likely to receive contributions; in 1982, the forty-two members of the House Energy and Commerce Committee received $4,984,310 in PAC contributions, or about $118,674 each. Sometimes lobbyists even brag about the influence of their money. For instance, The Associated Milk Producers, Inc., a dairy-farmer cooperative with only 33,000 members, contributed $1.1 million to the 1982 congressional elections and then issued a claim that 92 percent of its candidates had been elected.[12]

Congressional scholars have been plagued by the difficulty of ascribing a particular vote by a congressman or senator to a single factor. As important as campaign contributions may be, legislators still must worry about the interests of their constituents, negative publicity, the effects of cross-pressures (i.e., when two conflicting interest groups both donate to a campaign), and, we hope, personal conscience. Attempts to measure the impact of PAC contributions have revealed this complexity. One study of the influence of the dairy lobby found that reciprocity exists between legislators and contributors, but "the influence of contributions on voting is found to be substantially smaller than that of constituency, ideology, and party. Part of the explanation is that the dairy PACs in 1976 'rewarded' congressmen who voted for price supports even when a congressman was [already] compelled by his constituency to do so."[13]

Nevertheless, concern about the implications of large-scale contributions has continued. In the words of a moderately conservative Republican senator, Robert Dole of Kansas, "When these political action committees give money, they expect something in return other than good government." And, as Dole pointed out, PAC money does not flow from all political interests equally: "Poor people don't make campaign contributions. You might get a different result if there were a Poor-PAC up here."[14] Even so, both the Democratic and Republican parties claim to represent the interests of the poor, and important legislation has been enacted on behalf of the poor. In the final analysis, it may not be as important whether the increasing cost of campaigns affects votes as it is whether most people think it does.

Mass Media in American Elections

Controlled Media? Two of the most frequent complaints about the mass media, which include television, radio, newspapers, and magazines, are that (1) they are mostly liberal and (2) they are controlled by a few large corporations that allow us to hear only what they want us to hear. The charge that the media are too liberal was pressed by Richard Nixon and his first vice president, Spiro Agnew, in response to the growing disenchantment with the Vietnam war. In fact, surveys have shown that reporters and news executives do tend to be more liberal and more Democratic than the general public. In part, however, the "liberalness" of the press may also result from the public being more interested in news of social problems and political scandals than in news of the smooth operation of the political system.

The charge that control of the national press is held by relatively few corporations also has some merit. Although there are over seven hundred television stations in the United States, the three commercial networks account for about 90 percent of the programming and nearly all of the national news stories. There are over eighteen hundred daily newspapers, but most of their national news comes from the wire services of the Associated Press and United Press International, and many of these newspapers are owned by large chains such as Knight-Ridder and Gannett. And while there are thousands of American magazines, the major newsmagazines, *Time* and *Newsweek,* are owned by large media conglomerates. Yet, it is ironic, when one thinks of their big-business ownership, that the mass media are commonly accused of being too liberal.

The Media and Electoral Persuasion   The most important reason for the escalation of political expenditures is the growing reliance on mass media, especially television, by candidates. Of course, the press has always been important in American politics, but in a different way. For much of the first century of the republic, the nation was saturated with partisan newspapers; even small cities had more than one daily newspaper, and they generally carried much more political news than do today's newspapers. By 1916, however, the modern age of mass-media campaigns began in full force when the Republicans used newspaper advertisements and direct mailings to criticize Woodrow Wilson.

In the 1950s, television became increasingly important to political campaigns. The impact of the visual image, the speed with which information could be spread to millions of viewers, and the relatively low cost per viewer made the new medium a major factor in American politics. Analyses of the Kennedy-Nixon debates during the 1960 presidential race have suggested that many voters cast their ballots for Kennedy largely on the basis of his better performance. By 1968, candidates were hiring media consultants to design their campaigns around the use of television, leading one writer to call his

President Woodrow Wilson's campaign truck proclaims the major issues of the 1916 presidential campaign and demonstrates one form of political advertising in the era before radio and television. (UPI/Bettmann Archive)

book about the Nixon campaign, *The Selling of the President*.[15] In 1980, Ronald Reagan and Jimmy Carter each devoted about 60 percent of their federal campaign subsidies to the purchase of political advertising, most of it on television. Senate candidates commonly spend 60 to 80 percent of their funds on advertising, with as much as 95 percent of the advertising budget going to television commercials. Most House candidates spend about half their advertising money on television. Yet, in 1982, a congressman from northern New Jersey spent only about 10 percent of his advertising budget on television, because his district was located within New York City's television market, where millions of voters were not eligible to vote for him.

Incumbent officeholders, especially presidents, have a special advantage with regard to the media. They can be indirect, by leaking carefully chosen information, beneficial to their cause, to the press. Members of Congress can use the congressional videotaping studio to prepare statements to be distributed to television stations at home. They can also send press releases to news organizations, which may print the information as news. The president can summon network television cameras into the White House for prime-time messages or news conferences. While the Federal Communications Commission administers the *equal-time doctrine*, which requires networks to give the opposition party a chance to rebut the president's messages, the president always draws more attention. The networks may try to be careful during election campaigns to distinguish between presidential messages and political messages, but presidents are usually adept at finding ways to appear on the evening news.

The Role of Media   As we find so often in the study of politics, it is difficult to ascribe a precise amount of influence to a single factor such as television. However, television is the major source of news and political information for most Americans. About 97 percent of American homes have at least one television set, and it is the prime source of news for at least 60 percent of the electorate (20 percent cite newspapers as their major source of information). The pervasiveness of the medium has led some political analysts to describe television reporters as the "new kingmakers," replacing party leaders as the link between the electorate and the candidates. For example, in 1980, CBS's Walter Cronkite played an active role in the consideration of Gerald Ford as Ronald Reagan's vice president by getting Ford to suggest his willingness to run during an on-the-air interview. Announcements by television newscasters of the front-runners or likely winners in elections are widely believed to have a significant impact on voter choices, turnout, and contributions.

However, there may be a tendency to exaggerate the role of newscasters simply because of their visibility. Attempts to measure the effectiveness of television advertising and news coverage have indicated the need for caution in attributing too much influence to it. Although widespread name recognition is necessary for a candidate's victory and the electronic media are effective disseminators of advertising, television commercials do not guarantee success. Similarly, news coverage often focuses more on the campaign contest than on the issues, and often provides only superficial reporting about complex policy questions. Televised news stories usually last less than ninety seconds, so the emphasis is more on enthralling visuals and entertaining slogans than on historical background or factual analysis. Despite news programs on public television and innovations such as C-SPAN, a cable television network that carries live proceedings from Capitol Hill, commercial television remains the primary source of political information for most Americans. The content and style of its news concern many observers.

In summary, several things are certain about the role of the media in modern elections. First, television costs account for an increasing percentage of campaign expenditures, and thus are a major factor in the escalating costs of campaigns. Second, marketing experts have not yet discovered a foolproof method for making their television advertising dollars produce the desired results. And finally, regardless of the findings of those who study the media and elections, candidates are certain to continue devoting more of their campaign resources to the electronic media, including cable television.

In this chapter, we have examined the many institutional features of the American system of elections and related their development to the Constitution and its changes over the last two hundred years. The major events in elections—caucuses, primaries, delegate selection, and conventions—were analyzed, and the virtues and flaws in the electoral college system were examined. Finally, the major current issues in the American electoral system—money and media—were discussed.

We turn now to the third major path for participation in government. Whereas political activism, whether in the form of voting or campaigning, is primarily voluntary, participation in the legal system has a very different complexion, because it is often involuntary or inspired by unhappy events. The legal system is also characterized by a more complex set of formal rules than the electoral system. However, as we shall see, they both derive their fundamental principles from the same set of basic beliefs about the proper relationship among people, and between individuals and the state.

NOTES

[1] Baker v. Carr, 369 U.S. 186 (1962); Wesberry v. Sanders, 376 U.S. 1 (1964).

[2] White v. Weiser, 412 U.S. 783 (1973).

[3] Salyer Land Co. v. Tulare Water District, 410 U.S. 719 (1973).

[4] See C. Vann Woodward, *The Origins of the New South, 1877–1913* (Baton Rouge: Louisiana State University Press, 1971), chapter 12.

[5] Smith v. Allwright, 321 U.S. 649 (1944).

[6] Austin Ranney, ed., *The American Elections of 1980* (Washington, D.C.: American Enterprise Institute, 1981), appendix D, pp. 366–367.

[7]Benjamin Ginsberg, *The Consequences of Consent: Elections, Citizen Control and Popular Acquiescence* (Reading, Mass.: Addison-Wesley, 1982), chapter 4.

[8]Buckley v. Valeo, 424 U.S. 1 (1976).

[9]Gary C. Jacobson, *The Politics of Congressional Elections* (Boston: Little, Brown, 1983), p. 42.

[10]Ibid.

[11]*Congressional Quarterly* (March 12, 1983): pp. 504–505.

[12]Brooks Jackson, "The Problem with PACs," *Wall Street Journal* (November 15, 1982), p. 28.

[13]W. P. Welch, "Campaign Contributions and Legislative Voting: Milk Money and Dairy Price Supports," *Western Political Quarterly* 35 (December 1982): 478–495.

[14]Albert R. Hunt, "Special-Interest Money Increasingly Influences What Congress Enacts," *Wall Street Journal,* September 26, 1982, p. 1.

[15]Joe McGinniss, *The Selling of the President 1968* (New York: Trident, 1969).

BIBLIOGRAPHY

Alexander, Herbert E. *Financing Politics: Money, Elections, and Political Reform.* 2nd ed. Washington, D.C.: Congressional Quarterly Press, 1980. A review of campaign finance reform.

Burnham, Walter Dean. *Critical Elections and the Mainsprings of American Politics.* New York: Norton, 1970. An examination of realigning elections and changes in the electorate, from 1896 through the 1960s.

Campbell, Angus, Phillip E. Converse, Donald E. Miller, and Donald E. Stokes. *The American Voter.* New York: Wiley, 1960. The seminal voting study that introduced many of the concepts still used by political scientists in the study of American elections.

Crotty, William J. *Political Reform and the American Experiment.* New York: Crowell, 1977. An examination of restrictions on voting, campaign finance, and electoral reform.

Downs, Anthony. *An Economic Theory of Democracy.* New York: Harper & Row, 1957. A largely abstract but very enlightening book about a different perspective on parties, voters, and elections.

Jacobson, Gary C. *The Politics of Congressional Elections.* Boston: Little, Brown, 1983. An up-to-date analysis of congressional election campaigns and their implications, and particularly useful on the effects of campaign spending.

Page, Benjamin I. *Choices and Echoes in Presidential Elections.* Chicago: University of Chicago Press, 1978. A thorough discussion of modern election campaigns and the effects of the role of modern media in elections.

Patterson, Thomas W. *The Mass Media Election.* New York: Praeger, 1980. Analyzes the performance of the media and the use of mass communications during presidential election campaigns.

Wayne, Stephen J. *The Road to the White House.* rev. ed. New York: St. Martin's, 1981. A good summary of presidential election campaigns, with a "nuts and bolts" approach to the electoral system.

CHAPTER

6

The Nature of American Law

WHAT IS LAW?
The Functions of Law
The Elements of Law

AN OVERVIEW OF AMERICAN LAW

SOURCES AND CATEGORIES OF LAW
Common Law
Statutory Law
Administrative Law
Constitutional Law
Public Law and Private Law

Most of us do not ordinarily think of law in terms of participating in our political system. Nor do we usually consider that such ordinary activities as buying groceries, renting an apartment, working for an employer, or walking on a sidewalk rather than on someone's lawn are intimately connected with government. Yet we participate in the legal system when we do such ordinary things as buy food or drive an automobile. We may participate actively—for example, when we vote in an election or use the courts to sue another person—or we may participate passively—for example, when we obey the law or decide not to vote.

Every nation has a legal system. In this chapter, we will examine the substance and process of American law. What is its quality? Are its procedures fair? Are different persons and groups treated equally under the law? Does the legal system allow society to function effectively, yet at the same time permit individuals and groups to redress wrongs that they have suffered at the hands of others? To ask such questions is to realize that the provision of a legal system is one of the most important functions that a government can undertake. In this chapter, we will examine what law is expected to do, as well as the major categories of American law. In Chapter 7, we will consider how the legal system is expected to work through the courts and other governmental institutions.

WHAT IS LAW?

Law is a collection of rules that government establishes to supervise the relations among individuals, groups, and governments.[1] An act as simple as buying a loaf of bread in a supermarket is covered by a large number of legal principles. Not only are bakers and retailers governed by federal, state, and local laws covering the bread's safety and wholesomeness, but the mere act of purchasing it is governed by state laws and judicial decisions covering sales. If the store failed to give you the bread after you paid for it, you could sue the store, usually in small claims court. When we think of law, we usually think about such great matters as school integration or whether women can be excluded from the military draft. But virtually every interaction between people and organizations is controlled by a set of legal rules. Most of the law is concerned with the practical problems of everyday life: buying and selling, owning and leasing, how we operate cars, and so on. Law constrains our behavior while promising us the benefits of a just society. It is no exaggeration to say that it is in the legal rules covering ordinary events that government has the greatest impact upon citizens.

Law covers more than the relations among individuals and organizations, however. It also covers the relationships between governments and persons or organizations. A police officer—an agent of the government—may arrest

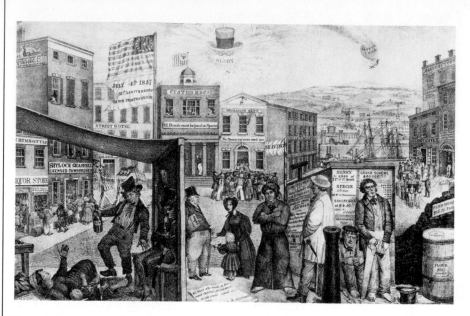

Financial panics, such as the one in 1837 illustrated here, are less likely to occur today because of modern banking laws. (H. R. Robinson/The Bettmann Archive)

you if you are driving while drunk. The officer may request that you take a chemical test to determine the amount of alcohol in your bloodstream, warning you that if you refuse, your driver's license will be suspended. But he or she may not break your arm if you decline to take the test. Law, then, imposes duties (e.g., arrest drunk drivers), as well as restrictions on how these duties may be carried out. In the American system of law, *procedure*—how something is done—is just as important as *substance*. And unless some activity in the private sphere is prohibited by law, a public official may not legally act against it. Thus, American government is called "a government of laws and not a government of men."

Of course, government officials, from police officers to presidents, do not always act impartially or pursuant to the law. In fact, there have been many cases in which persons wronged by public officials have used the legal system to vindicate themselves and to show that public officials acted unlawfully. A system of law, in short, does not guarantee that the persons under it will always obey it. Nor does it guarantee that the results will always be in accord with everyone's idea of justice; Americans, for instance, are far from unanimous in what they believe to be just. Nevertheless, a legal system serves several important functions that guarantee a better society than one run by rulers who simply do what they want or one in which no one is constrained by the control of law.

The Functions of Law

A system of law serves several important functions.[2] *First, in American society, law is the principal mechanism for maintaining social control.* Some societies exert control principally through a show of force. More primitive societies sometimes maintain social control through beliefs about the supernatural qualities and powers of leaders or through the uniform, unquestioned acceptance of religious beliefs by all members of the society. But in American society, there are many different religions and belief systems. We recognize that many leaders have faults, and we do not look to them for divine guidance. Force is, of course, present in American society, but it is intended to be used only as a last resort. Law, then, is the most important means for maintaining social control in our society. The American public considers other institutions, such as elections, to be legitimate because they are governed by legal rules.

Second, law promotes and supports ethical standards in society. Sometimes, ethics comes first; at other times, law does. For example, it is wrong to take another person's life under most circumstances, partly because it is unlawful. Most of us, however, would not consider killing another person to be unethical if our own lives were directly threatened by that person. The law makes such ethical distinctions for us. Even when individuals engage in acts of civil disobedience, they do so, usually not because they reject the law, but because they are appealing to a higher law. In 1956, when Martin Luther King, Jr., triggered the civil-rights movement with the Montgomery, Alabama, bus boycott, he did so, not to break the law, but because Alabama's racial segregation laws conflicted with a higher law—the Constitution—which demanded racial integration.

Martin Luther King, Jr., leading a march in 1965 in Selma, Alabama, which dramatized the need for a federal voting-rights law. (Bruce Davidson © 1967 Magnum Photos)

Third, law provides rules of conduct. Let us take a common example. Two small children are fighting over a toy truck. A parent intervenes, saying, "That's Lee's truck, not Pat's. Pat, give the truck to Lee." This simple statement introduces the complex notion of property to the youngsters and tells them how to behave with respect to property. The parent did not, of course, give the children a lengthy lecture about rules governing ownership. Nor was the parent an expert on the subject of personal property. Yet, an important principle was transmitted to the youngsters: one who owns property has a right to it that is superior to the claims of others. Many similar messages concerning legal rules and principles are taught beginning in early childhood. Few Americans read scholarly treatises on the law of personal property, or contract, or crime. Yet, most of them have a pretty good sense of the country's basic legal rules and of the appropriate conduct that is expected of them.

Fourth, law serves functional needs for the economy and the society. For example, the rules of property and the rules governing contracts are expected to aid the processes of exchange and production in American society. When the X Steel Corporation hires an employee to work in its steel mill, it has done several things. First, it has entered into a labor contract that is enforceable in the courts. Second, it has made decisions about the use of its property—the steel mill and the machines in it. Many have observed that the great freedom the law gives to people and organizations in making contracts or using property is an important factor in the working of the United States economy. Law serves the functional needs, then, of the economic system. But laws such as those covering child abuse or divorce are also intended to serve the functional needs of the social system. Every law does not serve such needs effectively; in fact, many laws may conflict with more effective functioning of the economic or social system. But, in principle at least, law is intended to serve these needs. However, as with so many other things, the trade-off problem frequently arises. The law, too, is involved in the difficult problem of measuring the costs and benefits of alternative actions.

Finally, the law provides a peaceable mechanism for settling disputes. Disputes and differences have arisen among people ever since they came to live together in groups. During most of human history, violence has been the principal way of settling disputes, and even today, violence through war is the way in which many international disagreements are solved.

In the United States, the fact that an individual can settle a dispute with the government is more important than the use of the law to solve differences between individuals or organizations. Many take for granted this remarkable feature of the American political system: individuals can fight the government, and they can win! Americans do not have to rebel if they believe that a law is unconstitutional or that its application to them is legally wrong. They can contest anything from a traffic offense to the weightiest constitutional question. In all kinds of matters, it is common for the courts to decide in favor of the private individual and against the government.

WHERE DO CASES COME FROM?

In the late 1920s, a passenger carrying a package of fireworks was assisted onto a Long Island Rail Road (LIRR) train by one of the railroad's conductors. In the process, the conductor knocked the parcel to the ground. The package exploded, causing a set of scales many feet away to fall upon and injure one Mrs. Palsgraf, who was waiting on the railroad platform for another train.

This incident led to one of the most famous cases in American legal history: could Mrs. Palsgraf recover damages from the LIRR? New York State's highest court held that she could not, because the railroad's duty of care did not extend to such an unforeseeable event. Factual situations such as this one constitute the raw material upon which judges act in developing the common law.

Source: *Palsgraf* v. *Long Island Rail Road Co.,* 248 N.Y. 339 (1928).

The law is thus one of the major devices in contemporary American society for achieving social control and unity. It helps to supply and maintain ethics and values, guides conduct, aids social and economic relationships, and settles disputes. Its success in any one of these functions, of course, helps it to succeed in the others. Laws pervade almost every human activity from the moment of conception until after death: there are laws governing abortion and laws governing the disposition of a deceased person's property. The law covers areas ranging from the speed limit on highways to the rights of individuals who purchase goods in a store. In short, the law structures how we may and may not participate in social and political life.

The Elements of Law

Rules of Conduct   *Shoplifters Will Be Prosecuted!* is a sign posted in many stores. Such a sign conveys many of the important elements of law. Of course, all laws are different, but most of them share certain characteristics, or *elements.* The most obvious element of law is that, as mentioned previously, it provides rules of conduct. Although one may behave in many ways when in a department store, one may not take articles for sale without paying for them.

Sometimes rules are very restrictive, limiting conduct in narrow ways and not permitting any deviation. For example, a pharmaceutical company that wants to market a new drug is lawfully bound to perform a rigid set of testing procedures from which it may not stray. On the other hand, some rules of conduct ban only one course of conduct from among many that may be chosen. For instance, a person can go into a store intending to purchase something, find nothing that he or she likes, and walk out. Or a person can enter a store simply to browse. These behaviors are entirely lawful; only a few, such as shoplifting or intentionally destroying the articles for sale, are prohibited.

private bill: A bill submitted to Congress or a state legislature to aid one individual rather than a class of citizens or all citizens.

Jurisdiction over Persons   Laws also cover different categories of people or organizations. Sometimes, these categories are quite broad; for example, every person is a potential shoplifter, so the law against shoplifting applies to all of us. But other laws cover much narrower categories, such as railroads, electric utilities, private charities, and accountants. Sometimes, a category may consist of only one person. In fact, Congress passes many laws, known as **private bills,** which cover just a single person. There have also been tax laws that have intentionally affected just one person or company. Although laws may cover categories ranging from one person to everyone, the categories must be reasonable. For example, a law stating that only green-eyed people could be prosecuted for shoplifting would be unreasonable, because no sensible reason for such a law could be provided. People whose eyes are not green are just as capable of shoplifting as green-eyed people are, and it is just as wrong for them to do it.

Relief   Whether one is included in a category voluntarily or comes within it automatically, once an organization or person is included, the third fundamental element of law comes into play. Laws distribute and redistribute costs and benefits. In a word, law is used in the process of allocation.[3] Laws distribute costs and benefits in several ways. First, a law may grant relief to a party. Assume that your friend promises to pay you $200 if you complete the Boston Marathon and that you do finish the race, but your friend fails to pay up. You can sue your friend. If you can prove the breach of promise, the court will order your friend to pay you $200. In this way, the law is used to redistribute resources through the allocation process.

Of course, not every legal redistribution involves money. Sometimes, the relief granted to one of the parties may involve other benefits. For example, suppose a firm opened a glue factory in a residential neighborhood. The terrible stench resulting from gluemaking would make it impossible for the residents to enjoy their homes. Under these circumstances, the residents are not interested in money, but rather in ending the gluemaking. The relief they seek by going to court, is an injunction against future gluemaking in their area. If the residents are successful, the benefit that they will have obtained—the ending of gluemaking in their vicinity—has a value, but it is not directly measured in monetary terms. On the other hand, the owners of the glue factory will have incurred costs that are easily measured in monetary terms: they must stop production until they relocate, and they must pay the costs of relocation. In the glue-factory case, just as in the Boston Marathon case, the law has been used to redistribute costs and benefits.

There are also laws that allocate by apparently only imposing costs or ordering benefits. The former case can be illustrated by several examples. If *A* murders *B*, *A* may be punished by imprisonment or execution. These are clear costs! But, unfortunately, it is too late for *B* to be granted a benefit. Yet when we examine this situation more closely, we see that here, too, there are people who benefit. Those who might otherwise commit murder may be deterred from doing so when they consider the severe penalties. In this way, society benefits because the law prevents some people from being murdered. Similarly, when the Federal Trade Commission, which is charged with preventing false advertising, orders a company to stop claiming that its patent medicine will cure cancer, this benefits all those who might have bought the product instead of seeking effective treatment.

Just as there are situations in which the law apparently imposes costs without conferring benefits (because the benefits, while real, are not immediate and obvious), so also there are situations in which benefits are obvious, but costs are not. For instance, among the duties of the Federal Communications Commission is the allocation of licenses to broadcast radio and television over certain frequencies in particular areas. The successful applicants for such a license obviously benefit. On the other hand, the unsuccessful applicants incur transaction costs, for example, in making presentations to the agency. More important, many people have argued that, because of restrictive licensing, the viewing and listening public incurs significant opportunity costs in the form of limited programming. In short, virtually every law involves the allocation of costs and benefits.

Procedure   The fourth major element of law is procedure. Often, politicians contrast American and Soviet societies by saying that the former is governed by "the rule of law" and not "the rule of men." The distinction pertains to procedure. In the Soviet Union, the whim or decision of a government official may affect a citizen without the application of a fixed law or without following an orderly, regular procedure. For example, it has been common in the Soviet Union for the government to imprison dissidents or place them in insane asylums. In contrast, the United States requires that anyone who will be affected by some legal action must first be afforded a reasonable opportunity to challenge the action. Second, the steps that an affected person or organization must take to assert or defend a claim must be spelled out in written rules as far as possible. Third, these rules must be made and published in advance of any action to which they will apply. Fourth, these rules must be consistently applied to every person or organization who may be affected by similar government actions. Together, these steps constitute the heart of procedure—the basic rules of the game in law.

Every law passed by Congress, state legislatures, or local legislative bodies such as city councils contains procedural provisions or refers, implicitly or explicitly, to procedures that already exist. Each governmental body has internal rules of procedure. Courts, legislatures, and administrative bodies all have such rules. And government institutions are as bound by such rules as individuals and organizations are. There are even procedural rules for determining the meaning of obscure or unclear procedural rules! All government bodies, especially courts, are called upon to interpret the underlying meanings of procedural rules.

To illustrate, let us look at the way in which, for example, a man is imprisoned under the American system. A man charged with a crime must be served with some notice to that effect. He must be afforded an opportunity to defend himself in an impartial court where strict rules of evidence and procedure apply. He has the right to obtain a lawyer and to be tried by a jury selected according to certain rules. The jury is bound by certain rules in determining whether the defendant is guilty. There are procedures for appealing a jury's decision as well as procedures for sentencing a person who has been convicted of a crime. A significant failure to follow these procedural rules can reverse a conviction. This process is controlled by still another set of procedural rules. Precisely the same structure of highly formal rules applies to any other kind of proceeding.

Many people complain about procedural rules and the "red tape" of government, viewing it as a waste of time. Others have used and abused procedure for no other purpose than to stall for time. Still, it is the heart of our legal system. Without strict rules of procedure such as those that characterize our political system, our legal system could degenerate into one that resembles the Soviet Union's, in which government can simply pick up ordinary people and make them disappear. The greatest benefit of strict procedure, even with its potential for abuse, is that rigid rules deter tyranny.

We have seen in this section that all laws have four characteristics:

1. They provide rules for conduct.
2. They cover some categories of organizations and people, and exempt others.
3. They allocate costs and benefits.
4. Their application is governed by regular and orderly procedures.

There are, of course, great differences in the ways that each of these characteristics is applied to the vast number of laws, institutions, and proceedings in our complex governmental system.

AN OVERVIEW OF AMERICAN LAW

Virtually every institution at every level of government—federal, state, and local—is involved in the process of making and/or enforcing the law, or rules and regulations based on laws.[4] Sometimes, the law is called something else besides "the law": for example, laws are often called "ordinances" by local governments, "rules, regulations, and administrative decisions" by administrative agencies, and "statutes and acts" by legislatures.

Different governmental institutions can become involved in the same law at different times. For example, in 1914, Congress passed the Federal Trade Commission Act, which created an administrative agency, the Federal Trade Commission (FTC), to classify and prohibit "unfair methods of competition." This phrase was deliberately left vague so that the FTC, subject to certain guidelines, could spell out which business methods would be "unfair." The FTC's job is to make specific rules about business practices.

Early in its history, the FTC decided that false and misleading advertising was an unfair method of competition. As time went on, it fleshed out the meaning of false and misleading advertising in a large number of cases. In one case, the FTC held to be false and misleading the claims of an encyclopedia company that told its subscribers that an encyclopedia set would be theirs free if they agreed to buy a series of loose-leaf supplements over the years. After the encyclopedia company protested the FTC ruling, the court of appeals held that only the dullest, most naive people would believe that a company in business for profit would give away expensive encyclopedia sets. Therefore, it ruled, no one interested in such a product would be misled. But then the Supreme Court reversed the court of appeals decision, holding that even the most stupid person is entitled to protection against false, misleading claims.

As this example shows, law must be considered an ongoing process that involves various parts of government and different levels. Congress, the executive branch, and the courts have all been involved in this narrow area of the law. In addition, as we have seen, different levels of the government may consider a matter. In the encyclopedia case, the FTC, the court of appeals, and the Supreme Court all took part. Finally, we should remember that encyclopedia companies, other firms that might use "free" claims in their advertising, and large numbers of consumers were affected by the decisions in just this one case. Not every legal principle involves the same group of actors as the encyclopedia decision. Rather, there are many different combinations, depending on the specific legal principles and type of law under consideration. All legal principles and all types of law must be viewed, not in static terms, but as ongoing processes. After the Supreme Court's 1937 *Federal Trade Commission* v. *Standard Education Society* decision, many other questions on the meaning of "free" offers arose, and they continue to arise today.[5]

Now let us see how widespread the law is in our society and examine the enormous opportunities for active participation that it provides. No one has bothered to count the number of legal matters considered by federal, state, and local administrative bodies, which is much greater than the number of cases considered by the courts. Fortunately, the *Statistical Abstract of the United States* provides data about cases at the federal and state but not local court levels. Table 6-1 shows the number of new cases brought in the federal district courts in selected years from 1960 through 1980. The most important thing to note, other than volume, is the rising trend. Table 6-2 shows the number of cases brought in selected state (but not local) courts during 1977. (Note that these figures do not include ordinary traffic violations, which are handled in local courts, along with many other matters.)

We need go no further to illustrate the vast scope of the law in action. The number of cases and administrative actions each year is in the millions. How is one to categorize this vast body of material? One of the traditional methods of classification is according to the sources of the law. Courts and administrators cannot simply do what they want; they must point to a source of law.

TABLE 6-1
CIVIL AND CRIMINAL CASES BEGUN IN FEDERAL DISTRICT COURTS IN SELECTED YEARS

Year	No. Cases
1960	87,400
1965	99,300
1970	126,400
1975	158,400
1980	196,800

Source: U.S. Bureau of the Census, *Statistical Abstract of the United States, 1982–83* (Washington, D.C.: Government Printing Office, 1982), p. 188.

SOURCES AND CATEGORIES OF LAW

common law:
Customary, judge-made law that relies on precedents and prevailing customs rather than on explicit statutes or constitutional authority.

statutory law: Law created by legislatures.

administrative law:
The general procedural guidelines developed by courts and legislative bodies concerning how administrative agencies should conduct themselves.

Common law is a body of law, made entirely by judges, that can be traced back to twelfth-century England. The common law grows out of the decisions made in actual controversies between people, organizations, or both.

Statutory law is the law made by legislatures, including Congress, state legislatures, and city councils. When common law and statutory law conflict, the latter always prevails. Both common law and statutory law develop through cases decided by judges, who interpret any language in statutes that might be unclear.

Administrative law consists of the decisions, rules, and regulations that administrative agencies are constantly called upon to make. For example, your local public utility commission decides whether the electric company is entitled to a rate increase, and it develops rules and regulations regarding the

TABLE 6-2
NEW CASES BROUGHT IN 1977 IN SELECTED STATES

State	New Cases
California	713,900
Florida	418,900
Maryland	136,300
Massachusetts	66,600
New York	147,400
Ohio	483,200
Virginia	117,400

Source: U.S. Bureau of the Census, *Statistical Abstract of the United States, 1982–83* (Washington, D.C.: Government Printing Office, 1982) p. 189.

accounting practices of electric utilities. Administrative law consists of the general procedural guidelines developed by courts and legislative bodies concerning how administrative agencies should decide cases. In addition, all substantive administrative-agency decisions, rules, and regulations must be based upon statutes authorizing the agency to act.

Constitutional law is law based upon the Constitution, including all of its amendments. Whenever any common law, statutory law, or administrative decision, rule, or regulation conflicts with the Constitution, the Constitution prevails. States also have constitutions, and therefore they have state constitutional law.

Law may be categorized not only by source, but also on the basis of the distribution of benefits. When a society benefits, the state brings the action, and the category is called **public law.** When benefits accrue to a specific person or group, the category is called **private law.** A person or group, not government, must bring a case in private law. Sometimes, the same event may give rise to both public and private law. For example, if a person sets fire to a house, the homeowner may sue the arsonist for the damages to the home. This is private law. But arson is also a crime—and all crimes belong under the category of public law. If arsonists go unpunished, society in general would be endangered. Consequently, the state will prosecute arsonists. All criminal law is public law, and as we shall see, there are many other kinds of public law.[6]

Common Law

As mentioned previously, the principles that the courts use in deciding matters can often be traced back to twelfth-century England. For example, let us assume that a homeowner is fed up with a factory that dumps nontoxic chemical wastes into a lake that they both share. The homeowner could sue the company under the theory of "nuisance," which originated as early as the twelfth century. The judge deciding the case would apply the thought of judges that began accumulating more than eight hundred years ago.[7] In a matter of this kind, it is probable that neither Congress nor the homeowner's state legislature has enacted a statute covering this particular situation. The judge will therefore

constitutional law: Law based upon an interpretation of the Constitution.

public law: Legal action, usually brought by a government agency, intended to benefit the public.

private law: Legal action, brought by an individual or private association, which is intended to remedy a wrong against the individual or association.

THE WAYS OF THE LAW ARE SOMETIMES MYSTERIOUS

A man attempted to commit suicide in 1983 by jumping in front of a New York City subway train. He survived and later sued the transit authority for his injuries on the grounds that the train operator was negligent. A settlement was reached in which the transit authority agreed to pay the man $650,000. Under the theory of the settlement, the train operator's negligence was comparatively greater than that of the man who tried to kill himself.

use the common law in making a decision. While legislatures make many laws regulating conduct—i.e., statutory law—there is also a vast body of law that is made exclusively by judges without any legislative participation. This is common law.[8]

Before the Norman conquest of England in 1066, feudal courts settled disputes between people on the basis of local customs that had endured over many generations. After the conquest, England gradually developed a central court system in which the king's courts, coexisting with local courts, sought to discover and apply customs that were widespread throughout the country. By the middle of the thirteenth century, the king's courts had created a uniform law based on these customs. In this undertaking, the king's courts used a concept called **stare decisis,** which is still a fundamental principle in the legal systems of the United States, England, and other nations with a common-law tradition. *Stare decisis,* which in Latin means "to stand by things that have been decided," is the principle that the prior decision of a court becomes a precedent for future guidance in similar cases. Using the doctrine of *stare decisis,* the English court system gradually created a legal system that was common to the entire country—the common law.

It is impossible to understand American law without understanding *stare decisis.* Benjamin Cardozo, one of the country's great judges, stated, "The first thing . . . [a judge] does is to compare the case before him with the precedents, whether stored in his mind or hidden in the books."[9] If the judge finds a prior case in his or her court or in a higher court and that case is identical to the one before the judge, he or she is bound by the earlier decision, unless he or she can show that the earlier court ignored some very important fact that might change the result of the present case.

For example, suppose you paid a company to supply you with a chair in six weeks and the company failed to deliver it. A court deciding a case brought on these facts would establish the principle that one who breaches a contract by failing to deliver the goods within the time specified in the contract must pay the other party damages. In a second case, involving the purchase of a painting not delivered within the ten weeks agreed upon, another court would be bound by the doctrine of *stare decisis* to follow the rule in the first case. However, if, in a third case, a contract called for the delivery of an exotic, rare fabric within a "reasonable time," the judge could decide that the principle of the first case does not apply and could reach a different conclusion, thereby setting a new precedent. Over the centuries, courts have used this case-by-case system to build up an enormous and complex body of common-law principles.

During the course of the common law's development, judges have devised many substantive concepts to deal with the practical controversies that come before them. These concepts are important, not only to those who come before courts, but also to legislators, administrators, and ordinary people in the daily conduct of their lives. The most fundamental of these concepts are so deeply ingrained in our social and economic lives that we should examine them closely.

stare decisis: Legal doctrine under which a court's decision constitutes a precedent that should be followed by that court, and courts inferior to it, when resolving future disputes; literally, "let the decision stand."

Property   At first, the idea of **property** covered concrete, useful items—for example, houses and jewelry. Gradually, however, it came to include things that were representational. For instance, a stock certificate of a hundred shares in a corporation is not valuable in and of itself. You cannot consume or use a stock certificate. Nevertheless, it is valuable because it gives you certain rights, such as the right to sell it. On the other hand, certain "things" once considered property no longer are. Little more than a hundred years ago, some human beings were categorized as property in the United States. The Thirteenth Amendment removed them from that category. Today, many analysts concerned with environmental problems want to make "rights to pollute" a kind of property. As the world changes, so does the legal meaning of the term. For example, do computer software or television programs qualify as "property"?

The fundamental concept of property, then, is more concerned with a collection of rights than with physical objects.[10] Our basic task is thus to set forth the most important of these rights. In doing so, it is important to note that the physical possession of a thing is not the same as a property right. If X steals your car, X has possession, but the car remains your property. In general, there are four principal rights connected with the concept of property: (1) possession, (2) exclusion, (3) use, and (4) alienability.

The central idea of *possession* is simply that you have a right to possess your property: for example, the automobile that was stolen from you, or the stock certificate in your bank vault, or the dollar bills now in your wallet. Possession of a thing gives you a certain set of rights, but they are not unlimited. For instance, you may own stock in General Motors, but you do not have the right to sell the company's automobiles.

The second right associated with property is *exclusion*. A person who owns a house has the exclusive and sole right to it—unless the house is rented to someone else. And only you have the exclusive right to the money in your wallet.

Exclusion implies the third characteristic of property: *use*. One may use property in any way consistent with the superior rights of exclusion. If you own a watch, you may use it to tell time or you may smash it to bits. However, if you lease a watch from another person, your right to use it will be limited by the superior rights of the owner, who will probably forbid you to smash it.

The final right associated with property is *alienation,* which is simply the right to dispose of property rights. If you own a parcel of land, you can alienate it by selling it, leasing it, giving it away, or willing it to an heir. However, like other property rights, alienation is not an absolute right. Not only is it limited by the property interest that you have, but it may be limited to some extent by contract and government regulation as well.

Contract   It is obvious that the concept of property is fundamental to an economic system, such as capitalism, which allows private ownership. It thus follows that the concept of **contract,** a mechanism for transferring property from one person to another, is necessary if the legal system is to mesh closely with the operating needs of a capitalist society. During the Middle Ages, the

property: A collection of rights over things that are guaranteed and protected by government.

contract: A formal agreement between people, business firms, or the government to do something.

concept of a free contract was incomprehensible and even sinful to certain persons—principally theologians—who thought about economic affairs. They looked for a just price and did not necessarily consider the market prices at which goods ordinarily were traded to be just. They also rejected the lending of money at interest, or usury, as being un-Christian. When we consider how widely held these ideas were, we can appreciate how revolutionary a breakthrough capitalism and the closely associated concept of free contract were. For, except insofar as state intervention prevents it, the parties to a contract can arrange terms in any way they see fit. If you want to sell your used automobile to another person, the negotiating process and not a just price, will determine the price and other terms of the contract. On the other hand, you may freely decide not to enter into an agreement if its terms are not acceptable to you. Freedom of choice is central to the concept of contract that developed in England as it became a capitalist society.

When we consider the close connection between business practices and contract, we can readily understand its basic elements. First, there must be an *offer*. Second, there must be an *acceptance* of the exact terms of the offer. A deviation from the terms of the offer is a rejection of the offer, or a *counteroffer*. Only after both parties complete their negotiations and are in complete accord on the terms is there an offer and acceptance. In addition, a third element must be present: *consideration*. Since the concept of contract was fashioned for the needs of a capitalist society, it does not cover gifts. Rather, the element of consideration requires that each side give up or promise to give up something of value. For example, you give a man $500, and he gives you a used car; you have both given up something valuable.

These elements of contract formation—offer, acceptance, and consideration—only begin to embrace the whole law of contracts. They determine whether a contract has been formed, and they are important because an enormous number of activities involves contracts. Other rules cover breach of contract, excuses for performing the contract, illegal bargains, and so on. Buying and selling goods and services, owning and leasing dwellings, working for someone, and even marriage and divorce are covered by the law of contracts (or some subcategory of it). Contract, too, is obviously linked closely with property, because it is the mechanism through which we transfer property.

tort: A private or civil wrong or injury, other than a breach of contract, for which a court will provide a remedy in the form of an action for damages.

Tort   In French, *tort* means "wrong." A third basic common-law idea, **tort,** defies a comprehensive definition.[11] Rather, the concept must be viewed as a catalog of civil wrongs that are not covered by contractual obligations. Slandering someone is a tort; driving negligently is a tort; falsely misrepresenting something to another person in order to induce that person into entering a contract is a tort. None of these activities, including misrepresentation before entering a contract, involves an obligation into which one enters voluntarily. The law of torts imposes rules of conduct upon us in order that we might live in a civil society. We cannot disregard such rules; for example, we cannot renounce our obligation not to drive 100 miles per hour in a 30-mile-per-hour

A head-on collision near Anchorage, Alaska, which killed one person and injured many. Such accidents lead to more legal cases than does any other kind of event. (UPI/ Bettmann Archive)

zone. Like the other basic legal concepts, tort generally helps maintain both social and economic order.

Conversion, the unauthorized exercise of the rights of ownership over another person's property, illustrates this dual purpose. For example, buying stolen goods and refusing to return them to the rightful owner is a conversion. In this situation, the law protects the social order. Instead of using violence to reassume control over their stolen property, people can resort to the courts. And once again, the tort of conversion protects the economic order, because it implicitly recognizes the concepts and distribution of property discussed earlier.

While there are many kinds of torts, the legal actions brought under them have one common purpose: the granting of *relief* to the person upon whom harm has been inflicted. Sometimes this is done by making the defendant compensate the plaintiff for harm done. Thus, if *A*'s negligent driving causes *B*'s car to be wrecked, *A* must pay to *B* as damages the value of the wrecked car. But, at other times, compensation will not grant adequate relief to the person injured. To use our earlier example, suppose a glue factory emitting noxious odors is located unlawfully in a residential neighborhood. Simply paying the residents damages while continuing the manufacture of glue does not provide adequate relief. In such cases, courts provide *equitable relief,* which requires the defendant not to do something (i.e., not to operate a glue factory in a residential neighborhood) or to actively do something (i.e., to move the factory to another location).

Common Law and Statute Law   The basic concepts of *stare decisis,* property, contract, and tort and the many ideas derived from them were already part of the basic fabric of the law when the American colonists declared their independence from England in 1776. When independence came, the thirteen states passed laws declaring that the common law of England was the law of the state. (Except for Louisiana, all states subsequently admitted to the Union did the same.) These laws are called *reception statutes.* Some states provided for the common law in their constitutions. Because the common law is concerned with new, practical questions that arise as social changes occur, the common law of each state gradually began to diverge from English common law, and under the American federal system of government, each state began to develop rules that differed from those of other states.[12] This presented no problem when business transactions were local. However, with the development of a national economy in which persons and companies from different parts of the country could participate, variations among state laws led to uncertainty about which rules should apply. The solution was the enactment by legislatures of uniform state laws. This process, which began in the 1890s, continues to the present day.

Statutory Law

Common law is essentially judge-made law. But almost as old as common law is statutory law—that is, law made by legislatures. Both systems grew up together, and today they constitute important components of the vast body of state law. There are two important differences between common law and statutory law. First, there is no federal common law; there is only the common law of each state, which became part of state law through reception statutes and state constitutional provisions. Second, as the uniform-law example illustrates, statutory law prevails over common law. When a legislature enacts a law on a subject, any common-law rules that are in conflict with the statute are void.

Statutory laws have come more and more to modify common law during the twentieth century.[13] First, as we have seen, there is frequently a need for state-to-state uniformity. Second, changes in public philosophy—the growth of the positive state—have sometimes led to modifications in the common law. For example, under the common law, workers and employers would be free to enter into any wage agreement that they decided upon. However, certain statutes require employers to pay employees a minimum wage, because it is believed that wages below certain levels are unjust or otherwise socially undesirable. Third, some subjects are considered too complex for judges to handle well without considerable statutory guidance. After all, judges are trained in the law. They are not experts in such policy areas as air-pollution abatement or the safety features of automobiles. In addition, in most cases, judges must rely for their fact-finding upon juries consisting of ordinary people from many walks of life. Statutory law, in contrast, can considerably reduce information costs by vesting authority over a subject in an expert administrative agency that will deal with that subject on a day-to-day basis.

Statutory law can also be more comprehensive than common law. The common-law system proceeds on a case-by-case basis, and these cases must involve real disputes between parties. A person cannot ask a court to answer a question about the legality of an action before the action is taken. Under the common-law system, a court can only decide an issue after an action has been taken and someone objects to it. Of course, once such an issue is settled, other people and organizations will be guided by the decision. But the continual onward march of the common law shows how many issues remain to be settled and how extensive the area is for which no guidance is provided. In contrast, statutory law can be comprehensive and provide guidance before a real controversy occurs. For example, a series of environmental laws Congress has enacted since the mid-1960s has provided a much more comprehensive list of the duties of persons and organizations than has the eight-hundred-year common law of nuisance, which covers the same general area. Statutory law, too, may quickly change the direction of policy; a new statute may change overnight five hundred years of common-law precedent. In contrast, although common law may change the direction of policy, the powerful doctrine of *stare decisis* acts as a brake upon such change.

Critics of statutory law argue that legislation is subject to the electoral and interest-group pressures and compromises described in earlier chapters. The inevitable result is not law that reflects the best policy, but a hodgepodge that may reflect politics at its worst. The public interest, these critics say, is not the same thing as the reconciliation of interest-group demands that statutory law represents. Furthermore, they say, statutory law is often enacted under the influence of strong emotions. Many issues, such as abortion on demand or gun control, raise emotions to such a level that legislators do not use their judgment in preparing laws. In contrast, these critics say that judges are not subject to such pressures and can weigh opposing views dispassionately and outside the realm of electoral and interest-group politics.

Critics of statutory law have made still another complaint. They claim that legislators often act upon a problem before they have gathered a sufficient amount of concrete information. Of course, legislators hold hearings, but, according to the critics, these hearings often consist of (1) prepared statements that discuss a problem in the abstract and (2) superficial questioning of witnesses by badly prepared legislators. In contrast to statutory law, the common law is made only after two sides expend the costs necessary to provide concrete information about the actual effects of contested activities. Each side in a common-law matter vigorously, sometimes viciously, attempts to show a judge that the other side's witnesses and arguments are wrong. Thus, these critics conclude, the benefits that result from the information costs expended are much greater in the common-law system than in the statutory-law system. To this, the advocates of statutory law reply that a system in which each side is only interested in advancing its cause and will conceal or distort information to do so is not a good way to make public policy in complex matters.

It is obvious that costs and benefits exist under both systems, and it would be foolhardy to try to settle here a debate that continues to rage. One point, however, is apparent. Those who draft statutes can rarely consider every kind of situation that will arise under them; nor can they be sure that the meaning of every word that they put into a statute is crystal clear. As a result, many people and organizations raise questions about the application of a statutory law to them, and these issues are settled in courts in much the same way that courts decide common-law issues. For example, suppose a law says, "It shall be unlawful for an individual to practice medicine in this state unless he or she has attended a certified medical school." Does this law include chiropractors and faith healers? Do they "practice medicine?" In such a case, the courts must examine the meaning of the disputed words, as well as the intention of the legislators who drafted the statute.

At other times, the complexity of a subject leads Congress or state legislatures to create an administrative agency charged with promulgating specific rules, subject to general guidelines that the legislature includes in a statute. For example, because Congress could not enact a statute covering every type of unfair business competition, it created the Federal Trade Commission. Similarly, the number of hazards presented by various consumer products is so great that Congress could not keep track of them all. Accordingly, in 1972, it created the Consumer Product Safety Commission to deal with the particulars of the subject. The large number of such agencies and their many rules, decisions, and procedures will be discussed in the following section.

Administrative Law

An administrative agency is a governmental body created by a legislature to administer certain statutes. For example, the Food and Drug Administration oversees a set of laws pertaining to the safety and effectiveness of drugs and the wholesomeness of food, and the Federal Communications Commission administers laws relating to telephone communication and to radio and television broadcasting. While the rules, regulations, and decisions of an administrative agency must be authorized by the statute giving the agency its power, the statutes are often vague, thus allowing the agency great breadth. Accordingly, one of the most important questions in this area is, how can administrative agencies be controlled?

As we shall see in Chapters 9 and 11, many control mechanisms exist within the executive and legislative branches as well as within each agency. But one of the most important control mechanisms is administrative law, which is enforced by the courts.[14] Administrative law is the body of law that places limits on the powers and actions of administrative agencies. In the national system, these limits are based upon the Constitution and acts of Congress. The Administrative Procedure Act (APA) imposes many requirements on regulatory agencies. They must, for example, include findings and conclusions of fact and law in their decisions, as well as the reasons for them. Failure to uphold the requirements imposed by the APA can result in a reversal of the agency's decision by the courts.

Administrative agencies do many things, but two of their activities are particularly important. Agencies make general rules and regulations, which is similar to legislative activity, and they make specific decisions, which is similar to judicial activity. Some of their other duties, such as enforcing their decisions, are patterned on executive functions. Because they undertake a mixture of executive, legislative, and judicial activities, administrative agencies are not easily classified within the framework developed by the American Founders. Therefore, some commentators have classified these agencies as the "fourth branch" of government. Now let us look at rulemaking and decisionmaking to see how administrative law attempts to control this fourth branch.

Rulemaking is the process of establishing a general rule that will control the behavior of members of a particular group. (For example, the Federal Trade Commission [FTC] once proposed a rule that would forbid food-processing firms from advertising a product as "natural" if it contained any synthetic or artificial ingredients.) Rulemaking involves several steps. First, the agency drafts a proposed rule on a subject. Second, the agency publishes the proposed rule in a daily government publication, *The Federal Register,* giving a date scheduled for hearings on the matter and information about how to participate in these hearings. Third, the agency asks individuals and organizations that might have an interest in the matter to supply information at the hearing. Fourth, the hearing consists of (1) the submission of documents and prepared statements by interested individuals, organizations, and agency staff and (2) an opportunity for the agency's officials and sometimes others to question the witnesses. Finally, the agency's officials consider all of this information and prepare a rule, together with the reasons for it, and publish it in *The Federal Register.* Unless one of the parties appeals to the courts, the rule becomes binding, just like a statute, upon the group to which the rule is directed.

In contrast to a rule or regulation, a *decision* applies to a particular individual or organization, not to a large group. If the FTC orders the Zilch Food Processing Company to stop advertising its yogurt as "natural" when, in fact, the yogurt contains thirty synthetic chemicals, the agency is engaging in decisionmaking, not rulemaking.

Let us look at the steps in one kind of decisionmaking. First, the agency staff investigates whether an individual or organization may be violating either a statute, a rule or regulation, or a prior decision (agencies also use the *stare decisis* principle). If the staff decides that a probable violation exists, it issues a complaint, which the accused person or organization must answer within a certain period (often 60 days). After several other steps, known as "pretrial procedure," a trial on the issues takes place in a manner similar to that which takes place in a court. And paralleling court practice, the presiding judge (usually called an "administrative law judge") writes an opinion setting forth findings of fact, conclusions of law, and an order either dismissing the matter or directing the defendant or respondent to alter its behavior in a way that will bring it into conformance with laws and regulations.

There are many other types of rulemaking and decisionmaking, including decisions that award damages, rather than forbid unlawful conduct. This discussion will allow us to see the role of administrative law in American government. For once an administrative agency has acted, courts may review the agency's actions. The most important aspect of this review is that the administrative agency's actions must conform to the requirements of the Constitution. In the case of a state or local administrative agency, its actions must conform to the state constitution. Second, the action of the administrative agency must be authorized by a statute that justifies it. Just as Congress may only do those things authorized by Article I, Section 8, of the Constitution, so also administrative agencies may only do those things that can be justified under the laws passed by Congress pertaining to the agency. For example, the FTC, which is charged with administering laws about methods of business competition, could not act against foreign spies because it is not authorized to do so.

As we observed earlier, the most important source of administrative law at the federal level is the Administrative Procedure Act (APA), which was enacted in 1946 and amended several times since. The APA is a lengthy law covering in great detail every aspect of what administrative agencies do. For example, it tells agencies how to conduct hearings and trials, outlining the rights that must be given to private persons and organizations in such hearings, the rules of evidence in hearings, the burden of proof, and the contents of decisions. Courts, on appeal, can review an agency's entire undertaking from the period before formal proceedings began through the agency's final decision to see whether the agency has followed the APA's requirements. If it has not, its decision can be reversed by the courts. This accounts for a large proportion of what is commonly called "red tape."

The APA's requirements are not so formal that it is difficult for well-intentioned administrative agencies to follow them. In fact, the APA allows agencies considerable flexibility in procedure and wide discretion in applying the laws that they are charged with enforcing. The APA seeks to balance two competing considerations. First, it recognizes the need for agencies to make decisions without incurring (1) excessive information costs in obtaining the information necessary to make decisions and (2) excessive transaction costs in the procedures required to make decisions. Agencies are largely free to make choices that will reduce such costs. And second, the APA balances these concerns with protecting the rights of persons and organizations that an agency action may affect. It is often not easy for an agency to balance ease of administration with fairness. Nevertheless, a large body of administrative law has developed over the years that tries to balance the need for administrative efficiency with the protection of individuals and organizations.

Administrative law is based partially upon statutes, most importantly the APA, and upon the Constitution. In the hierarchy of American law, constitutional law sits at the peak. Just as any administrative action in conflict with a statute must fall, so any administrative action or statute in conflict with the Constitution must fall. We turn now to that most important branch of law—constitutional law.

Constitutional Law

Constitutional law is the body of law that has interpreted and applied the original Constitution and its twenty-six amendments.[15] As you might expect, the volume of cases and doctrines that are included under the heading of constitutional law is enormous. Upon assuming office, every judge, administrator, and other public official in the United States takes an oath to uphold the Constitution. Therefore, each of these people is frequently called upon to measure his or her actions against the Constitution. Of course, public officials sometimes act contrary to the Constitution, and many of them, from low-level bureaucrats, such as prison guards, to the highest official, the president, have had their actions challenged on constitutional grounds. Many of these objections are considered in the courts, and a substantial number of them have been heard by the Supreme Court, the ultimate authority in interpreting the Constitution under the doctrine of judicial review.

How can we categorize the vast body of constitutional law? One way to get an overview is to divide the original Constitution and its amendments into four large categories: structure, the Bill of Rights, civil rights, and all other rights.

The first category, structure, comes from the original Constitution, which was largely concerned with defining duties, relationships, and limitations of the legislative, executive, and judicial branches. Under his commander-in-chief authority, can the president order troops to seize and operate a steel mill during a national emergency? Does Congress have the power to tax illegal bookmaking activities? Can the federal courts render advisory opinions before a real case or controversy has evolved? Such questions are typical of the structural category, the source of which is largely the original Constitution.

The **Bill of Rights,** which consists of the first ten amendments to the Constitution, is the second category.[16] As their name implies, these amendments are largely concerned with the protection of citizen's rights. They were not part of the original Constitution, because, although most of the Founders did not object to the amendments, they thought that they were unnecessary for several reasons. First, as we saw in Chapter 3, the separation-of-powers doctrine was expected to protect natural rights. Second, *The Federalist* no. 10 principle, coupled with the development of a great commercial republic, was believed to be an additional protection of these rights. Third, because the Constitution provided for a limited government and because an invasion of natural rights could not be construed as a proper exercise of these limited powers, such an attack on rights would obviously be unconstitutional. Fourth, the states guaranteed these rights in their constitutions.

Bill of Rights: The first ten amendments to the Constitution.

While the states were considering ratification, it became apparent that certain people, such as Thomas Jefferson, whose support was considered crucial, would not give their support unless a bill of rights was appended to the Constitution. In particular, the support of Massachusetts for ratification was contingent upon such an addition. The Founders readily agreed, and in his first inaugural address, George Washington urged the adoption of what we now call the Bill of Rights. James Madison took the lead in drafting them in a coherent form. After debate over such matters as whether conscientious objectors should be exempted from compulsory military service, an idea that was rejected, Congress sent the amendments to the states on September 25, 1789. The last of the necessary eleven states ratified them on December 15, 1791.

The Bill of Rights is intended to assure that the national government cannot diminish natural rights. The Ninth Amendment, in particular, makes this clear. With the exception of the Tenth Amendment, the Bill of Rights applies only to the activities of the federal government, and not to those of the states. The Tenth Amendment reserves to the states and the people all powers not granted to the federal government.

The Bill of Rights can be divided into four major categories. First, freedom of speech, religion, assembly, and press are protected. Second, the right of the states to maintain a militia and to arm it, but not the right of individuals to bear arms otherwise, is guaranteed by the Second Amendment.[17] Third, the Third Amendment restricts the quartering of soldiers in private homes. Fourth, procedural protections for those engaged in criminal trials and other governmental proceedings are spelled out in the Fourth through Eighth Amendments. In short, the general thrust of the Bill of Rights is to protect the private sphere from government intrusion in a variety of areas.

The third category of constitutional law—*civil rights*—is embodied in the Thirteenth through Fifteenth Amendments, which were adopted between 1865 and 1870. As the dates indicate, these amendments were adopted in the aftermath of the Civil War and can only be understood in the context of this war. Essentially, the three amendments sought to extend civil rights to the newly freed slaves and to make sure that the former slave states would not be able to reestablish slavery or deprive those freed of their natural rights. Accordingly, the Thirteenth Amendment banned slavery, and the Fourteenth Amendment made citizens of the former slaves and forbade states to abridge or limit the natural rights of citizens. In this way, the rights set forth in the Bill of Rights gradually came to be applicable to states and their relations to people. Finally, the Fifteenth Amendment prohibits the United States and the individual states from denying or abridging the right to vote on the basis of "race, color, or previous condition of servitude." In short, in order to protect rights, this third category of constitutional law granted the national government considerable power to intervene in matters that were previously of sole concern to the states.

The fourth category of constitutional law is the "all other." It includes all of the remaining amendments, such as the Nineteenth, which granted women the right to vote in 1920. This category also encompasses portions of the original Constitution that do not define the duties, relationships, and limitations of the three branches—for example, the provision that forbids a state to impair the obligations of contract; these miscellaneous matters are largely contained in Article I, Sections 9 and 10, and Articles IV and VI. Just because these provisions and amendments cannot be tied together in a neat little bundle like the Bill of Rights, we should not think of them as unimportant. Although some of them are of little or no consequence today, others still engender considerable controversy.

Constitutional law is deeply affected by one of the Constitution's original provisions—the amending process. We saw in Chapter 3 that the Founders sought to impose high transaction costs upon the process of enacting a statute, a process that is much easier than that of amending the Constitution. An amendment can be proposed either (1) by Congress, which must approve the proposal by a two-thirds majority in both houses, or (2) by a national constitutional convention called by Congress after two-thirds of the state legislatures have requested one. Although a national convention has never been successfully requested, in 1967, a call for one fell only one state short of the thirty-four necessary.

An amendment can be ratified by two methods. The usual procedure is for legislatures in three-fourths of the states to approve a proposed amendment. The other process, state ratifying conventions, has been used only once, in order to pass the Twenty-first Amendment, which repealed prohibition. Thus, a simple majority in one quarter plus one of the state legislatures, or one-third plus one of the United States senators or representatives, can block an amendment. The Founders required a large consensus because they distrusted the masses, which therefore only have a direct voice in amending the Constitution if state ratifying conventions are elected. Moreover, they believed that the Constitution was a comprehensive, sufficiently general document that would embrace many novel situations and great changes in the nation's political economy.

From these considerations, an important characteristic of constitutional law follows: the Constitution must be interpreted more flexibly than statutes. Given the scope of the Constitution, the high transaction costs incurred in amending it, and conversely, the relatively low transaction costs required to block an amendment, the courts should avoid interpreting the Constitution in a manner that thwarts the legislative and executive branches unless they have invaded natural rights or clearly violated the Constitution. This approach to *judicial review* has been called the "Marshall principle," after Chief Justice John Marshall, who helped to establish it in 1803. In order to declare a statute unconstitutional, there must be "a clear and unequivocal breach of the Constitution, not a doubtful and argumentative implication." Accordingly, the proper role of the courts in judicial review is much narrower than is popularly thought. Only when a law is unconstitutional beyond any doubt should it be declared void; any other principle for interpreting the Constitution could eventually erode support for it.

A famous example will illustrate this. In 1857, the Supreme Court, in the famous *Dred Scott* v. *Sandford* case, declared unconstitutional the 1820 Missouri Compromise law, a statute Congress enacted to limit the spread of slavery, on the grounds that slaves were property and not persons. Consequently, any statute that deprived masters of their "slave property" when the slaves were brought into free territory violated the due process clause of the Constitution. In a bitterly split decision, the Court decided that blacks could not have the rights of citizens because they were not "persons" as the Court interpreted that word in the Constitution. Of course, Congress, and a minority of the Court, had reached the opposite conclusion, and under the Marshall principle, the congressional view should have been accepted. Congress, not the courts, should have the prevailing say in policy based upon the Constitution when its view is plausible, as it was in the Dred Scott case.

The result of this overturning of the will of the legislature by a few judges was to bring the Civil War ever closer. Other instances of such activism in judicial review, such as declaring the income tax unconstitutional on questionable grounds in 1895, did not lead to a civil war. However, they did erode support for the judicial branch. Moreover, such activism interferes with the carefully designed system of the Founders—spelled out in *The Federalist*, no. 10, and elsewhere—on how public policy should be made in the American system.

Public Law and Private Law

Earlier in this chapter, we saw that the distinction between public law and private law is primarily concerned with the distribution of benefits. At first glance, the distinction is simple. If two homeowners sue a builder for faulty construction that led to the collapse of their house, they are seeking to recover damages by redistributing income from the builder to themselves. The homeowners are not trying to redistribute resources to society, the public, or any other person. This is a clear example of private law. On the other hand, when the state convicts a person for arson or murder, it will benefit all of society by helping to preserve public order. All criminal law is designed to preserve the public order and is therefore within the category of public law. At the same time, as we saw earlier, a family whose home is burned down may sue the arsonist for personal damage to its property. The same event, in a word, may lead to both public *and* private law.

In other instances, the distinction between public and private law is somewhat fuzzy. Let us take *Shelley* v. *Kraemer* (1948), a famous civil-rights case, to illustrate the difficulty. This case concerned blacks in St. Louis, Missouri, who purchased houses in violation of deed restrictions prohibiting the sale of certain property to blacks. Other property owners, who were subject to the same deed restrictions, sued in a local court to prevent the black buyers from taking possession of the property. At first, this case appeared to be a private controversy. But it went all the way to the Supreme Court, and when it did, the Court decided that racially restrictive covenants were unconstitutional. This ruling had general applicability to every home in the nation. Thus, *Shelley* v. *Kraemer* did not completely fall into either the category of public or private law. On the one hand, the narrow issue concerned specific home-buyers, and the decision of the Court allowed them to lawfully occupy their homes. These people received the benefits of the decision—an example of private law. But on the other hand, the case resulted in an important policy principle about residential racial segregation that would affect a large number of people and help to alter residential patterns in the future. Thus, rather than being mutually exclusive, public law and private law are at opposite ends of a continuum, with many cases falling at various points in between.

The public law–private law distinction leads us to ask, Who receives the benefits and who pays the costs? There is no doubt that the twentieth century has witnessed a remarkable growth—some would say an explosion—in the direction of public law. Private law, based on the number of cases brought, has also increased sharply. But more and more, areas that were once exclusively resolved in cases between individuals or private organizations, or both, now involve government bringing action against an individual or organization on the public's behalf. Furthermore, the conduct demanded of those subject to such government action is often much higher than that demanded in the nineteenth century. To understand these developments and some of the reasons for them, let us look at the example of consumer fraud.

During the 1800s, the problem of consumer deception was largely controlled by the common law of contract and fraud. The common-law standards were relatively clear-cut. Let us assume that in 1880 you purchased a horse and the

Extravagant claims for cures, such as the one portrayed here, were partly responsible for the enactment of consumer-protection laws. (The Bettmann Archive)

seller failed to tell you that the animal was sick. Two weeks later, after only moderate exertion, the horse died, and you then learned that the horse had been ill before you bought it. You sued the seller.

Who would have won? The seller would have won because, under the common law in 1880, the seller had done nothing wrong. The seller was under no obligation to reveal that the animal was not well. If the seller had knowingly lied or evaded answering your questions about the state of the horse's health and you had relied upon those statements, you could have recovered damages. But if the seller said nothing and you did not inquire about the horse's health, you would have been out of luck. And there was no government agency to which you could have complained.

Now let us move the clock forward to the 1980s. You have the flu, so you go to a drugstore to buy a medication that promises to reduce your aches and pains. You take the medicine, but an hour later your symptoms are worse. The remedy has not worked. At this point, you might write to the Federal Trade Commission (FTC) about any advertising concerning the product, and the FTC can bring a public action, against the manufacturer, with no expense to you other than the cost of mailing the letter. Even if the manufacturer honestly believes that the medicine will work as directed, the FTC can enter an order against it if the claim is misleading. In addition, before the drug could have been marketed, the Food and Drug Administration (FDA) would have required an extensive testing program. Indeed, it is unlikely that the FDA would have allowed the drug to be marketed unless the substance could, in fact, do what it is supposed to do. Furthermore, the FDA regulates the labeling of claims, requiring information to be provided about side effects, and so on. Although drug products are closely regulated, a similar transition from private law to the higher standards of public law could be shown with respect to a large number of products, especially consumer products.

Some of the major reasons for the increasingly greater role of public law in what were once matters of dispute between private parties are not hard to discover. First, the goods and services that we now buy are far more complex than those of a century ago. The costs that an individual would incur to determine whether a flu remedy is safe and effective would be extremely high relative to the cost of the product. Without government intervention, how many of us could spend $100,000 to test a drug product that sells for $5? Furthermore, if one finds that a product is dangerous or ineffective, the costs of bringing a lawsuit and developing the evidence would be high. Many people cannot afford such expenses in the hope of ultimately recovering damages. And in this age of mass merchandising, any problem that affects one person as a result of using a product will probably affect thousands, perhaps millions, of other people. As a result, government has, in effect, displaced a large portion of costs upon the business firms that make, distribute, and sell products, and upon itself as it brings public actions against those who might have violated the law.

Of course, not every twentieth-century public-law development can be ex-

THE BIGGEST CASE IN HISTORY

How big can a law case become? The biggest case in American history was *United States* v. *A.T.&T.*, in which the Department of Justice, under the Sherman Anti-Trust Act, sought to break up American Telephone & Telegraph, the world's largest telephone company. In January 1982, more than seven years after the complaint was filed, an agreement was finally reached. Under the settlement, AT&T agreed to divest itself of its local operating companies and to assist them in becoming independent. If a settlement had not been reached, the case could have dragged on for many more years. As it was, the records of the case included more than 25,000 transcript pages and 144,000 pages of exhibits. If the trial had continued, the two sides were prepared to submit an additional 631,000 pages of exhibits!

plained in this way. But a great many of them can be explained by combining an interventionist public philosophy with considerations of costs and benefits and where they fall. Furthermore, we should remember that the old private-law remedies have not been replaced; rather, as we have observed, they have often been expanded as public law has supplemented them. And even when government is not directly involved in bringing public-law actions, other mechanisms have been developed to reduce private costs and distribute benefits more widely. These include "public-interest" law firms, government-financed lawsuits, and private organizations that help to finance lawsuits brought by individuals. For example, civil-rights organizations traditionally finance and supply lawyers for individual members of minority groups who believe that they have been deprived of their civil rights. Similarly, civil liberties organizations have incurred the same costs for individuals whose rights to freedom of speech, press, religion, or assembly have been challenged. Labor unions and trade associations have done the same for individuals seeking to establish principles in which these organizations are interested. Again, individuals and organizations have intervened in actions brought by others, or have brought class actions—that is, actions brought by a few members of a group on behalf of the entire group. However, the complex rules covering intervention and class actions tend to discourage these legal techniques.

In short, public law, and mechanisms that seek to attain the benefits of public law, have come to cover more and more of our activities in the twentieth century. From the simplest to the most complex and unusual activities, we find that laws enacted by national, state, and local legislative bodies, as well as administrative rules, regulations, and decisions, play a significant role in what were once largely private activities. But we should not forget that the private law that once largely guided conduct has not been eliminated; it still coexists with public law. In both cases, however, law is not self-enforcing. The legal system requires an institutional structure to make it work. In the next chapter, we will examine that structure.

NOTES

[1]One of the best analyses of law is by Max Weber, *Economy and Society* (New York: Bedminster Press, 1968), chapter VIII.

[2]An excellent description of the functions of law is contained in Robert S. Summers, *Law: Its Nature, Functions and Limits*, 2d ed. (Englewood Cliffs, New Jersey: Prentice-Hall, 1972).

[3]An excellent discussion of this function is contained in Richard A. Posner, *Economic Analysis of Law*, 2d ed. (Boston: Little, Brown, 1977), chapter 19.

[4]The best overview of law in America is Lawrence M. Friedman, *A History of American Law* (New York: Simon & Schuster, 1973).

[5]Federal Trade Commission v. Standard Education Society 302 U.S. 112 (1937).

[6]One of the best political-science–oriented studies of public law is Walter B. Murphy and Joseph Tanenhaus, *The Study of Public Law* (New York: Random House, 1972).

[7]An excellent, concise history of the common law is Frederick G. Kempin, Jr., *Historical Introduction to Anglo-American Law* (St. Paul: West, 1973).

[8]The classic study of the common law, first published in 1881, is Oliver Wendell Holmes, *The Common Law* (Cambridge: Harvard University Press, 1963).

[9]Benjamin Cardozo, *The Nature of the Judicial Process* (New Haven: Yale University Press, 1970), p. 34.

[10]A detailed examination of property law is A. James Casner and W. Barton Leach, *Cases and Texts on Property* (Boston: Little, Brown, 1969).

[11]The standard text on torts is William Prosser, *The Law of Torts* (St. Paul: West, 1971).

[12]Friedman, *A History of American Law*, pp. 95–99.

[13]An excellent short introduction to the subject is Jack Davies, *Legislative Law and Process* (St. Paul: West, 1975).

[14]The standard treatise is Kenneth Davis, *Administrative Law Text*, 3d ed. (St. Paul: West, 1972).

[15]Of the many fine studies of American constitutional law, the most comprehensive is Congressional Research Service, Library of Congress, *The Constitution of the United States of America: Analysis and Interpretation* (Washington, D.C.: Government Printing Office, 1973) and its appendices.

[16]A detailed account of the history of the Bill of Rights is Robert A. Rutland, *The Birth of the Bill of Rights* (Chapel Hill, North Carolina: University of North Carolina Press, 1962).

[17]U.S. v. Warin, 530 F.2d 103 (1976).

BIBLIOGRAPHY

Brody, David E. *The American Legal System.* Lexington, Massachusetts: D.C. Heath, 1978. An excellent survey of many areas of public and private law, including excerpts of cases.

Davis, Kenneth. *Administrative Law Text.* 3d ed. St. Paul: West, 1972. A comprehensive treatment of this important topic.

Friedman, Lawrence M. *A History of American Law.* New York: Simon & Schuster, 1973. The best short history of American law from colonial times to the early 1970s.

Hirsch, Werner Z. *Law and Economics: An Introductory Analysis.* New York: Academic Press, 1979. An outstanding effort by an economist to apply political economy concepts to public and private law.

Holmes, Oliver Wendell. *The Common Law.* Cambridge: Harvard University Press, 1963. An excellent brief history, originally published in 1881, by one of America's greatest jurists.

Hurst, James Willard. *Law and Social Process in United States History.* New York: Da Capo, 1972. Four remarkable essays showing the social impact of legal action.

Murphy, Walter B., and Joseph Tanenhaus. *The Study of Public Law.* New York: Random House, 1972. One of the best behavioral studies by political scientists of public law.

Posner, Richard A. *Economic Analysis of Law.* Boston: Little, Brown, 1977. An outstanding analysis of many legal areas employing economic analysis.

Pound, Roscoe. *An Introduction to the Philosophy of Law.* New Haven: Yale University Press, 1968. A probing sociological analysis of law by a leading philosopher of law.

Summers, Robert S. *Law: Its Nature, Functions and Limits.* 2d ed. Englewood Cliffs, New Jersey: Prentice-Hall, 1972. An outstanding introduction to the nature and functions of law.

Weber, Max. *Economy and Society.* vol. 2. New York: Bedminister Press, 1968. A classic sociological study of law, outstanding in its coverage of many legal systems.

PART III

INSTITUTIONS: POWER AND STRUCTURE

The Structure of Justice

I n August 1935, Lloyd Gaines, a young black man, graduated with a bachelor of arts degree from Lincoln University, a university maintained by the state of Missouri for blacks. Missouri, like many other states at the time, had an educational system segregated at every level by race. Gaines's ambition was to become a lawyer, and thus he applied for admission to the University of Missouri School of Law. In doing so, Lloyd Gaines would be in the forefront of one of the most dramatic policy changes in American history.

The University of Missouri School of Law refused Lloyd Gaines entrance because it was an all-white school. Instead, he was informed that the state would pay his tuition and fees if he attended a law school that admitted blacks in one of four adjacent states, for Missouri did not have a law school for blacks. But Lloyd Gaines did not want to attend law school in a neighboring state. He wanted to enroll in the University of Missouri School of Law, which conceded that he was qualified for admission in every respect but one—his race. Gaines brought suit in the state courts against the university registrar and lost. However, in an appeal to the United States Supreme Court, Gaines was finally vindicated. The Court ruled in 1938 that by operating only a white law school, Missouri was granting privileges to white students and denying them to blacks.[1] Although the Court was not yet ready to declare segregated schools inherently discriminatory, it had begun to reverse the trend for state and federal courts to approve racially segregated school systems.[2] Never again would the Court approve a system of segregated education.

In 1950, the Court invalidated practices that segregated graduate students at the University of Oklahoma. It also required the University of Texas Law School to admit qualified black students, even though the state operated a separate law school for blacks. The Court found that the latter school was inferior to the University of Texas Law School, which had a larger library, a more distinguished faculty, and so on. These cases, which involved relatively few students, were a prelude to the Court's 1954 *Brown* v. *Board of Education of Topeka, Kansas* decision in which segregated public schools were held to be inherently discriminatory. No public-school arrangements in which the students were segregated according to race could be constitutional because "to separate [schoolchildren] from others of similar age and qualifications solely because of their race generates a feeling of inferiority as to their status in the community that may affect their hearts and minds in a way unlikely ever to be undone."[3]

This line of cases involving school segregation is in many ways dramatic and unique, but it typifies what courts do. Above all else, courts are involved in the process of rendering decisions in individual cases in which persons (including such entities as corporations, which are legally considered "persons") claim that they have been wronged. Lloyd Gaines believed that the state of Missouri had wronged him, and accordingly, he instituted a lawsuit. Yet, as Gaines's case and others involving school segregation show, courts, like legislatures and members of the executive branch, can make public policy that

203

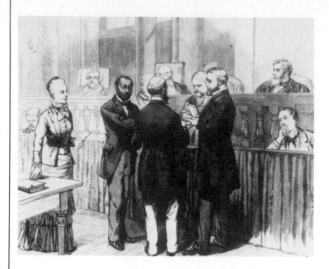

Admission to the United States Supreme Court of the first black lawyer, circa 1880. (The Bettmann Archive)

affects many people who are not parties to the lawsuit. The same principle that required that Gaines be admitted to the University of Missouri Law School also required the admission of other qualified black students to previously all-white law schools. In addition, the principle applied not only to law schools, but to other professional and graduate schools as well. Thus, the criticism that some individuals have made that courts should not make public policy is misplaced. Courts sometimes form new public policy when they decide individual claims of justice, just as they sometimes apply settled public policy in other cases. But they are always involved in public policy.

Courts operate within a context of highly technical rules. They employ concepts, theories, decisionmaking processes, and a vocabulary that only trained lawyers can readily understand. But ultimately, as public policymakers, courts are just as involved in the process of allocation as legislators and executive-branch officials are. For example, they redistribute costs and benefits by awarding monetary damages, assigning penalties, and establishing rights. Like legislators and executive-branch officials, they too must consider trade-offs, but they do so in an entirely different manner. Typically, one side wins and the other loses in a contested court case that reaches the judgment stage. But most cases never reach that stage; rather, they are settled by a compromise between the two parties.

In many ways, the judicial system differs sharply from conventional politics. It is often possible for small and weak groups and individuals to win. Criminals, atheists challenging public-school prayer, and even spies have successfully used the judicial process. In this chapter, we will first examine the constitutional role of the courts, then the organization of the judicial system, and finally the judicial process.

THE CONSTITUTIONAL ROLE OF THE COURTS

We saw in Chapter 3 that the Founders said little about the structure of the federal court system. Not even judicial review, the power of the federal courts to review the constitutionality of legislation, was mentioned in the Constitution. Many of the most important federal judicial powers had to be implied from the document, a task that was accomplished while John Marshall was chief justice of the Supreme Court (1801–1835).

Article III, Sections 1 and 2, are the principal constitutional provisions concerning the federal courts. Section 1 establishes a Supreme Court and permits Congress to create, restructure, or terminate "inferior Courts." As early as 1789, Congress responded by creating the district courts, the lowest level of courts in the federal system. It is in these courts that most federal trials take place. Although Congress has enacted many statutes pertaining to the district courts, their basic structure has remained approximately the same since 1789. Each state has at least one district court, and some larger ones have as many as four. In 1983, there were eighty-nine district courts in the fifty states, plus one in the District of Columbia. Depending on its volume of business, each of these courts had from one to twenty-seven judges, including one chief judge. While only one judge is required to sit in most cases, there are some types of cases in which Congress has decreed that three judges must sit.

Congress also used its constitutional power to create an intermediate level of courts. The present system, which is known as the United States courts of appeals, was created in 1891. Under the system, the country is divided geographically into twelve circuits, each of which has a court of appeals. These courts have two principal functions: (1) they hear appeals from federal district courts located within the circuit and (2) they hear appeals from federal administrative bodies, such as the Federal Trade Commission or the National Labor Relations Board. In 1983, each court of appeals had from four to twenty-three judges, again depending upon its volume of business. Appeals are ordinarily heard and decided by a group of three judges.

At the highest level in the federal system is the only court explicitly created by the Constitution—the United States Supreme Court. Although the Court is both a trial and appeals court, its appellate work is far more important. Under Article III, Section 2, its original (i.e., trial) jurisdiction extends to "all Cases affecting Ambassadors, other public Ministers and Consuls, and those in which a State shall be party." Its appellate jurisdiction includes all cases (1) arising under the Constitution, federal laws, and treaties; (2) in which the national government is a party; and (3) between citizens of different states (i.e., *diversity of citizenship cases*). While the Constitution does not specify how many justices should sit in the Supreme Court, the number has remained at nine since 1869. This figure has become so deeply ingrained that all attempts to contract or enlarge it, such as an attempt by Franklin Roosevelt in 1937 to increase the number of justices, have been handily beaten back.

The United States Supreme Court, 1982. From left, seated are Thurgood Marshall, William Brennan, Jr., Warren Burger, Byron White, Harry Blackmun; standing, from left, are John Paul Stevens, Lewis Powell, William Rehnquist, and Sandra Day O'Connor. (© Supreme Court Historical Society)

As mentioned previously, judicial review, the most important duty of the Supreme Court—as well as one of the most important duties of the district courts and courts of appeals—was not explicitly set forth in the Constitution. Nevertheless, since *Marbury* v. *Madison* (1803), the power of the Court to declare unconstitutional those state laws, executive-branch actions, state constitutions, and laws of Congress that conflict with the Constitution has been widely accepted. The Supreme Court has used this power to strike down many more state actions than federal actions. A major reason for this is that federal officials are more likely to consider the impact of the fundamental document under which they operate than are state officials, who tend to focus upon state constitutions and local concerns. For example, in the past, police officers who were deciding whether to search a car for narcotics were much more likely to consider local laws than the Constitution; yet the Supreme Court ultimately had to decide in many such cases whether the search violated constitutional provisions.

FEDERALISM AND THE COURTS

Public officials—and all other Americans—must be aware of law at the federal, state, and local levels. A system in which authority is divided between strong national level and state or regional ones is a *federal* system. But this definition fails to convey the complexity of the American federal system, especially as it applies to the courts. Several principles will help to unravel this complexity. First, and most important, as the Lloyd Gaines case illustrated, when federal laws or rules or the Constitution conflict with state or local laws, rules, or constitutions, the former prevail. Second, in order to be valid, federal laws and rules must be authorized by, and not be in conflict with, the Constitution. Third, states may legitimately control all conduct not prohibited by the Constitution. For example, states may impose a blood test before a marriage can be contracted; this is not prohibited by the Constitution. But states may not, for example, forbid blacks and whites from marrying because such a law is in conflict with constitutional requirements.

The federal system is further complicated by the full-faith-and-credit clause of the Constitution (Article IV, Section 1), which states that "Full Faith and Credit shall be given in each State to the public Acts, Records, and judicial Proceedings of every other State." Thus, for example, contracts entered into in Texas may be enforced in California, and corporations chartered in New Jersey may do business in Michigan. And, although Supreme Court decisions on the subject were unclear for a while, in most situations divorces granted in one state must be recognized in another. But even though state courts must take into account the laws and rules of the national government and the other states, a substantial sphere exists in which states operate independently of other authorities. Most activities that affect the ordinary citizen—for example, domestic relations, automobile safety, the sale of goods and homes, and the forming of a business, as well as the disputes arising under them—are governed by the laws and rules of the states in which the activities take place. The administration of law in the United States is thus a complex labyrinth of fifty state court systems, each independent of and yet interrelated with, the federal court system.

AMERICAN COURT SYSTEMS

In 1972, the fifty states and the District of Columbia contained 17,057 courts. In addition, each state organized its system differently, so that there were wide variations in the number of courts that could not be accounted for on the basis of population. For example, Missouri had 531 courts, while the more largely populated state of California had only 370 courts. In addition, each court may have a different number of judges assigned to it. The *National Survey of Court Organization,* undertaken by the United States Department of Justice, found that on July 1, 1971, there were 23,073 authorized judgeships in the fifty states and Washington, D.C. Of this total, California had 1,068, while Missouri had 547. These figures suggest that great differences exist in court organization from state to state. Court systems constantly change, so if a comparable census were taken today, it would show figures considerably different from those disclosed in 1972.

Just as substantial differences exist in court systems, so also are there significant differences in the way judges are selected. In state systems, most judges are elected by the voters on either a partisan or nonpartisan basis. Because voters often have scanty information about the qualifications of judicial candidates and little inclination to expend the resources necessary to learn about them—especially when judges are selected in the same election as the president or a governor—local bar associations often provide a summary of information. To do this, they investigate the qualifications and integrity of persons interested in becoming judges and publicize the findings. Even so, these findings do not necessarily carry great weight with voters.

A second method, used in a few states, is selection of judges by the legislature alone. Although the information available to legislators about judicial candidates is usually greater than that available to voters, there is no evidence that judges selected by legislators are more honest or competent than those chosen by voters.

The third method of choosing judges, which is employed in the federal and some state systems, is selection by the chief executive, followed by confirmation by one or both houses of the legislature. In the federal system, only the Senate's approval is required.

The federal selection system has been thoroughly studied. Hamilton pointed out in *The Federalist,* no. 76, that the Founders required the Senate's concurrence in order to prevent the appointment of unfit candidates. According to Hamilton, the president, knowing of the Senate's ability to reject a nominee, would have a strong incentive to appoint fit people. Approximately 20 percent of presidential nominations to the Supreme Court have failed, some on grounds of fitness and others on political grounds. Thus, the confirmation process can act to influence the views of courts if judges are appointed whose views are in accord with those of the legislature—or at least not widely at variance with legislative views on questions that are apt to reach the courts.

Certain informal mores under this system tend to further both executive and legislative influence, but not necessarily control, over judicial outcomes in specific cases. First, appointees to the federal courts are overwhelmingly of the same political party as the president. For example, 92.2 percent of President Richard Nixon's appointees to the United States district courts were Republicans, whereas 94.8 percent of Lyndon Johnson's appointees were Democrats. In most administrations, officials within the Justice Department initiate the search for candidates who reflect the president's general judicial views. At the district-court level, the United States senators from the state in which a vacancy exists can play an important role in initiating a nomination by investigating and clearing the potential nominee. The Federal Bureau of Investigation (FBI) checks out the person's character, while the American Bar Association's Committee on the Federal Judiciary conducts an inquiry into his or her character and intellectual fitness. Usually, the president will not place a candidate's name in nomination until he or she has satisfactorily passed these "tests." In recent times, considerable attention has been devoted to selecting candidates from groups previously underrepresented in the judiciary, such as blacks, Hispanics, and women.

JURISDICTION

The central concept that divides the labor between courts in each system is **jurisdiction**—that is, the range of authority of a court. For example, some courts in a system may only hear criminal cases while others may only rule on domestic-relations matters. Some courts may only hear trials, while others may only consider appeals. Little consistency in structure is to be found from state to state or between the federal system and any state system. Each state's constitution and legislative acts (and similarly, the Constitution and acts of Congress in the federal system) define the jurisdiction of each court in a system. Unless a court can show that it has jurisdiction over a matter brought before it, the court may not decide the case.[4]

There are many types of jurisdiction, among which the most important are:

1. *subject-matter jurisdiction:* the kind of case a court may consider (i.e., civil, criminal, or both).
2. *original jurisdiction:* the right to try and pass judgment upon the law and facts of a case.
3. *appellate jurisdiction:* the right to hear an appeal from the courts of original jurisdiction and to review the records of their decisions.
4. *jurisdiction over a person:* the right of a court to order a person or organization to comply with the court's judgment. Usually, the person or organization is served with a summons or other document within the borders of the state having jurisdiction. In the federal system, the summons is generally served within the nation's boundaries.

As we have seen, the basic contour of jurisdiction in the federal court system is set by Article III of the Constitution.[5] Several statutes have delineated the structure of the federal system, consistent with the outlines provided by the Constitution. The general route of a federal case is presented in Figure 7-1. Of course, there are exceptions and qualifications to this route. The most important is the three-judge district court, which is convened in cases in which a state statute is being challenged as unconstitutional. For example, if Wyoming enacted a statute forbidding redheads to drink in taverns, such a statute could be challenged under the Fourteenth Amendment. The proper place to bring the case would be a three-judge district court. An appeal to its decisions would go directly to the Supreme Court, bypassing the courts of appeals. In order to keep down the number of cases before three-judge district courts, they only hear cases that challenge a statute; they do not consider cases

jurisdiction: The authority of a court or court system to consider or decide a case.

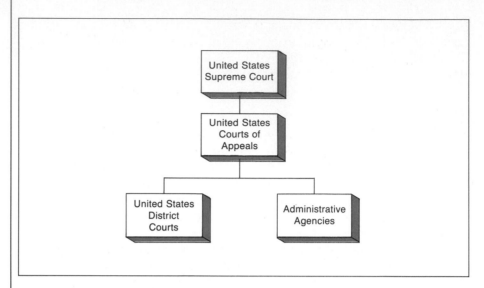

FIGURE 7–1   The Structure of Appeal

involving improper, state executive-branch action under a valid statute. In addition to the three-judge district court, there are other federal courts of limited jurisdiction, each with its own particular route of appeal.

Jurisdiction, then, is the first important matter with which a person using the judicial system must be concerned. When jurisdiction is asserted, the legal process begins to operate. Before examining this process in three types of cases—civil, criminal, and those involving a civil-liberties question—let us examine what courts do.

PRIVATE RIGHTS AND PUBLIC POLICY

Every case in the American legal system, whether it be major or minor, civil or criminal, public or private, shares one characteristic. Each asserts that a wrong has occurred for which the law provides a remedy. If A murders B (a wrong), the law provides the remedy of imprisonment. If C refuses to pay a debt owed to D (a wrong), the law provides the remedy of monetary damages to D. From this fundamental principle, an important corollary follows: that is, courts are inherently concerned with the allocation of costs and benefits.

The machinery of the judicial system does not begin to operate until after a wrong has taken place. C must have refused to pay D; A must have murdered B. If you want to challenge a military-draft law, you must refuse to register. Unlike legislative acts or executive orders, which can take effect before a wrong occurs or before anyone is affected by them, the judicial system cannot begin to operate until an alleged wrong takes place. In other words, the courts will only decide cases or controversies; they will not decide hypothetical questions, nor will they consider questions presented by someone who may initiate a lawsuit unless that person has already been wronged.

Wrongs may stem from many sources. The most important of these are federal and state constitutions and statutes, municipal ordinances, treaties to which the United States is a party, administrative rules and regulations, the precedent that can be found in case law based on statutes, the common law, and the terms of private agreements between parties. These sources also establish the remedies, the three most important of which are (1) criminal, (2) legal, and (3) equitable. Criminal remedies are intended to punish, usually through fine or imprisonment. Both legal and equitable remedies are used in civil cases; legal remedies are intended to compensate, usually in money, for harm sustained, whereas equitable remedies attempt to correct a situation by restructuring the relations between the parties. Thus, if *A* negligently wrecks *B*'s automobile, *B* may sue *A* for damages actually sustained. In contrast, however, if *C* is pouring garbage into a lake shared with *D,* a monetary award would be an insufficient remedy; an equitable remedy would be to compel *C* to stop polluting the lake.

Courts, then, focus on individual actions. But do not conclude from this that courts do not make public policy; on the contrary, they often do. For example, the famous civil rights case of *Loving* v. *Virginia* (1967) involved a man and woman of different races who were refused the right to wed in Virginia because a state statute forbade interracial marriage.[6] The couple sued to compel state officials to let them marry. When the case reached the Supreme Court, the Court held at one level (i.e., individual rights and remedies) that Virginia officials had to allow the plaintiffs to marry. But at a second level, the Court established an important public-policy principle: state statutes that impose restrictions based upon race are unconstitutional. Thus, simply by performing their proper function of deciding specific cases, courts sometimes make public policies that will affect large numbers of people who are not parties to a lawsuit. Often, courts do not establish public policies because they are bound by a clear statute or a common-law principle, but sometimes they must do so. Indeed, courts sometimes make sweeping public-policy changes in areas, such as civil rights, in which legislatures are reluctant to act.

Whether a case is brought under an established principle or is intended to establish a new one, the major problems that affect judicial activity are the same. Judicial processes are expensive to conduct, and of course, the more expensive they are, the more likely they are to favor the side with superior financial resources and to disfavor, or deny access to, persons or firms with weak financial resources. Thus, in the interest of fairness, there is an incentive to minimize the costs necessary to obtain information and to engage in the transactions the legal process requires. But, on the other hand, the overriding goal of the Anglo-American legal system is to produce justice. Excessively limiting the amount of information that may be presented and unduly restricting the opportunity to present legal arguments could impede the attainment of that goal. The legal processes at which we will look are intended to balance these conflicting impulses, and they should be evaluated accordingly.

THE CIVIL CASE

An action in a civil case is begun by preparing and filing a *summons* and a *complaint.* The summons is a form requiring a defendant to appear in court to answer a complaint within a certain period of time (usually twenty or thirty days) after the documents are served. The complaint is a brief statement of facts on which the plaintiff's claim is based. The defendant may request a postponement, which is usually granted if the matter is sufficiently complex. But if the defendant fails to answer, the judgment will be granted to the plaintiff. The defendant's answer may dispute the facts in the case; it may claim that the particular court in which the case has been brought lacks jurisdiction; or it may make a motion to dismiss the claim because no legal violation has been shown in the complaint. The differences between the complaint and the answer give rise to the issues of the case, some of which may be issues of law, while others are issues of fact.

We have observed previously that information is costly to gather and to present. There are few arenas in which information is more costly than in the formal surroundings of a courtroom trial; the plaintiff and defendant both might bring a hundred witnesses to the courtroom and present three hundred documents to prove their cases. As a result, every court system has developed an elaborate system of pretrial procedure (also called *discovery*) in order to narrow the issues and reduce the trial costs. At the same time, discovery requires each side to indicate before the trial what it will prove. In this way, surprise is greatly reduced, and each side is able to carefully consider the information it will introduce at the trial to rebut the other side's presentation.

Although the purpose of discovery is to reduce costs, surprises, and issues, there have been instances in which skillful lawyers have thwarted these intentions and used pretrial procedure to delay the trial itself. But the widespread adoption of discovery in all the states' civil court systems, as well as the fact that a large number of cases are settled during this phase, indicates that overall the system has worked well. At the end of the pretrial process, parties are usually ready to go to trial over a smaller number of issues, and thus they incur lower costs than would be the case without discovery. Before beginning the presentation of evidence, however, each side must engage in one more important activity—the selection of a jury.

The Jury

The Sixth Amendment requires that a person tried in a federal court shall have the right of trial by jury in criminal cases in "the State and district wherein the crime shall have been committed." The Seventh Amendment provides that in all civil trials "where the value in controversy shall exceed twenty dollars, the right of trial by jury shall be preserved." The language in the Sixth Amendment differs greatly from that in the Seventh Amendment.[7] This has led to different requirements being imposed upon the states. Under the Fourteenth Amendment, no state shall deprive anyone of "life, liberty or property" without due process of law. In general, the right of jury trial is much more fundamental in criminal matters than it is in civil matters.

In a criminal case, it is usual, but not necessary, that a jury consist of twelve persons. All that the Constitution requires is that the number of jurors be sufficient to provide wide deliberation on the factual issues, and that most of the jury agree on a verdict. A major difference between federal and state criminal jury systems, however, is that a unanimous verdict is constitutionally required in the former, but convictions by a substantial majority (i.e., nine to three) are permissible in the latter. However, when a state criminal jury is small, the verdict must be unanimous.

The Seventh Amendment's civil-trial requirements are less demanding, yet more complex. First, it requires jury trials only in common-law cases for which jury trials were customary when the amendment was ratified in 1791 and for similar cases that arise under statute. Some types of common-law cases did not require a jury trial at the time of the amendment's ratification, and therefore they continue to be excluded from the amendment's coverage.

Under most circumstances, the Fourteenth Amendment does not require the states to adopt a jury system in civil trials. Accordingly, there is considerable variation among states concerning the right to a jury trial in civil matters. The amount of money in controversy and the type of action usually determine whether a jury trial is available.

One important requirement is applicable in both civil and criminal cases: the jury must be impartial. Therefore, the method of selecting the jurors must be impartial. The method used today is random selection from registered voter rolls. Even though this system cannot assure that jurors will be unbiased, it is probably the best that can be employed.

The Trial

After the pretrial proceedings have been concluded and the jury has been selected, the civil trial begins. At this point, another body of law—the *law of evidence*—determines what the jury may hear, the documents and other exhibits that will be received into evidence, and the exhibits that will be excluded. Like the law in so many areas, the law of evidence is a composite of constitutional, statutory, and common-law requirements. Its major purpose is to strike a balance between the quality and the quantity of information.

Suppose two people—*A,* a person untrained in astronomy who has consumed a quart of gin, and *B,* a trained astronomer—claim to have seen an unidentified flying object (UFO). Because the information that we receive about an event is rarely experienced directly but most often comes to our attention after the event takes place, we must consider the circumstances surrounding the event in evaluating its quality. Thus, in evaluating the quality of information, we note that *A* was drunk and *B* is a professional astronomer.

Suppose a court could only convict a person of murder if a police officer actually witnessed the crime being committed. Under such circumstances, few murderers would ever be convicted. Accordingly, the law of evidence is designed to exclude low-quality information without imposing standards so high that they exclude from consideration the vast quantity of moderately reliable information about an event.

A trial ordinarily begins with the plaintiff's attorney describing the case to the jury (or to the judge if there is no jury) and setting forth the principal facts that the attorney expects to prove. The attorney then calls witnesses, examining them in order and allowing them to introduce relevant documents. For example, in a case involving the ownership of land, an official of a title company might be asked to describe the company's report, which the plaintiff's attorney will then introduce. After all the witnesses have been examined, the defendant's attorney is permitted to cross-examine them. Periodically, one attorney will object to the other's line of questioning or to the introduction of a document, on the basis of the rules of evidence or some other ground. The judge's rulings on such objections may later constitute grounds for appeal for the side losing the case.

After the plaintiff's attorney has completed his or her presentation of the case, the defendant's attorney usually makes a *motion for a directed verdict.* This motion is based upon the view that the evidence entered in the plaintiff's behalf has failed to prove the allegations of the complaint. Unless a case is very weak, however, the trial judge usually refuses to grant the motion, preferring instead to hear both sides fully. The defendant's case is then presented in the same manner as the plaintiff's: the defense attorney makes a statement to the jury and examines witnesses, whom the plaintiff's attorney has the right to cross-examine. After the defense rests, the plaintiff's attorney may rebut any new evidence that has been raised by the defendant's attorney. The defense may then bring forth additional evidence in surrebuttal under the same ground rules as the rebuttal. Finally, the attorneys for both sides make closing statements in an attempt to persuade the jury to accept their respective version of the facts.

In most cases, the judge then instructs the jury on the law and charges it with the duty of reaching a decision on the evidence and finding a verdict for the plaintiff or the defendant. If it finds for the plaintiff, it must also determine the amount of the damages. If the jury cannot agree on a verdict (i.e., if it is a "hung jury"), the judge declares a mistrial, and a new trial can take place. As we will discuss in a later section, the side that loses in a trial can appeal to a higher court.

CRIME AND DUE PROCESS

What Is Due Process?

Criminal procedure is far more complex than civil procedure. It covers every step in a crime from the investigation before arrest through appeal. In contrast to civil procedure, criminal procedure is far more rigidly bound by the Constitution, and the lawyers must constantly consider the constitutional implications of each action they take. If we recall the fundamental purpose of the Constitution, it is easy to understand this preoccupation. John Locke and the Founders were particularly concerned with government's capacity for arbitrariness versus the natural rights of individuals. One of the principal ways in which a government can erode these rights is by arbitrarily treating people as criminals and depriving them of liberty. One's life cannot be one's own, one's liberty cannot be one's own, and one's property (including one's ideas) cannot be one's own if government can arbitrarily search a person's home, arrest him or her, and throw the individual into prison without being required to use reasonable procedures first. The Bill of Rights was in large part designed to provide protection against such a government.

If we look at the Bill of Rights, many of the guarantees that we do not think of as being related to criminal law turn out to be so upon further reflection. For example, the First Amendment is concerned with the freedoms of speech, press, religion, and assembly. But when an executive-branch official or Congress abridges one of these freedoms, it usually does so by making an act criminal or by imposing some penalty for exercising such rights. Thus, the branch of constitutional law that deals with such freedoms, known as **civil liberties,** is intimately concerned with criminal law. Similarly, the Fourth Amendment's prohibition of unreasonable search and seizure is concerned with criminal procedure and law, as are the Sixth and Eighth Amendments. But the heart of the Bill of Rights is the Fifth Amendment's statement that "No person shall . . . be deprived of life, liberty, or property, without due process of law."

The concept of **due process** has a long history in English law, and its particulars reflect many deep, bitter struggles in both English and American history.[8] These struggles usually pitted a group of people—such as religious and political dissenters, and persons objecting to an arbitrary tax or fee—against the monarchy in England and against some governmental authority in the United States.

Powell v. *Alabama* (1932), an important Supreme Court decision, will illuminate some of the underlying ideas behind due process.[9] Seven young black men, known as the "Scottsboro Boys," were convicted of raping two white women aboard a freight train on its way through Alabama. Their legal representatives had been afforded virtually no opportunity to prepare their defense. The case reached the Supreme Court on the issue of whether the trial court's

civil liberties: The rights of citizens to fair trials, as well as the rights to speak, write, read, meet, and worship without government interference.

due process: Protection, mandated by the Fifth and Fourteenth Amendments, from arbitrary or unfair deprivation by the states of an individual's "life, liberty, or property."

failure to assure the defendants adequate legal representation was a denial of due process. The Court held that it was, and the Scottsboro Boys were entitled to a new trial. The defendants had obviously been at a serious disadvantage relative to the state, which had substantial resources and skilled lawyers. The Court was principally concerned with the question of fairness. A trial should be arranged in such a way that the government does not enjoy an unreasonable advantage over those it acts against. Words like *fairness* are invariably present in due process decisions. Just as we would consider a boxing match between two men to be unfair if one of the fighters had his hands tied behind his back, so we should also think that a legal contest is unfair if one of the parties is effectively deprived of one of the most important resources—an attorney.

While due process includes procedural fairness, it embraces other principles as well. Government enjoys advantages over individuals because of its monopoly of lawful force and authority. However, government's potential for abusing its power requires that individuals be afforded added protections. In an age when notorious criminals often assert such protections, it is difficult for some people to understand their importance to the weak and helpless. Suppose that government could smash down your door without a warrant or throw you in jail for refusing to incriminate yourself? Simply because a few individuals abuse these protections does not justify granting government the power to trample upon due process. One is entitled to the use of an attorney in a capital criminal trial, not only because it is fair, but also because it guards against government's power.

The third basic thread in the concept of due process is that government must not be arbitrary. *Arbitrary* has two meanings. The first concerns treating certain individuals or groups differently than others without justifiable reason. Treating blacks differently than whites, an example of such arbitrariness, is usually dealt with under the Fourteenth Amendment's equal-protection-of-the-law provision. But *arbitrary* also refers to an action taken in which no reasonable connection can be shown between the law (or actions taken under it) and the reasons government has advanced for it. This second meaning raises due process, not equal-protection-of-the-law, questions.

The Supreme Court decision in *Tot* v. *United States* (1943) illustrates this second, due-process kind of arbitrariness.[10] The Federal Firearms Act, which outlawed the interstate shipment of firearms, included a provision that a convicted felon who was in possession of firearms would be assumed to have received them from another state. The Supreme Court held that this assumption was arbitrary and violated due process. There was no logical reason to conclude (1) that a convicted felon in possession of firearms obtained them from out of state, but (2) that a person who was not convicted of a crime and possessed firearms did *not* obtain them from out of state.

In summary, due process is not a single idea. Rather, it is a set of ideas connected by the overriding principle that restraints must be placed on the ability of government to deprive individuals of their life, liberty, or property in the name of the law. Due process, therefore, includes the ideas of (1) a fair opportunity to defend oneself, (2) the protection of the private sphere, and (3) the prevention of arbitrary government action. Determining how to trade off these principles against government's legitimate concern in protecting the social order is not simple. Costs and benefits are not easily assessed when important values are in conflict. As a result, it is not unusual for judges to take different viewpoints in close cases. The problem is compounded when we remember that the due process language of the Fifth Amendment, which applies only to the national government, is identical to the due process language of the Fourteenth Amendment, which applies only to the states. The Supreme Court, then, has been faced with the problem of which rights enumerated in the Bill of Rights—applicable only to the national government—are incorporated by implication into the Fourteenth Amendment's due process language. For example, is the right to counsel in a major criminal case implied in the Fourteenth Amendment? As we saw, it is. What guiding theory did the Court use in making this determination?

Although the Court has not been totally consistent, since the early 1960s it has largely been guided by the theory of **selective incorporation.** Once it has been decided that a right is "of the very essence of ordered liberty," that right is included by implication within the Fourteenth Amendment.[11] As a result, the standards applicable to the federal and state governments will be the same once a right is determined to be fundamental. For example, the right to a trial by jury in a criminal case is considered fundamental. Most of the rights included within the Bill of Rights have been incorporated into the Fourteenth Amendment, and therefore made applicable to the states. Thus, in the next sections, as we follow a criminal proceeding from its beginning to its conclusion, assume that, in general, the same principles apply at the federal and state levels.

selective incorporation: The theory that guides the Supreme Court in determining which of the protections of the Bill of Rights are applicable to the states through the Fourteenth Amendment.

The Investigation

An investigation to determine whether a person has committed a crime may begin in one of three ways:

1. A law-enforcement officer may actually witness the commission of the crime.
2. Someone may tell law-enforcement officers that the crime has been committed.
3. A law-enforcement organization may undertake an investigation on its own to determine whether the crime has been committed.

The second of these categories is by far the most prevalent way of discovering crime. One can appreciate why when one realizes that in 1980, approximately 9,684,000 persons were arrested in the United States for crimes other than traffic offenses. Of that total, approximately 2,196,000 people were arrested for "serious crimes," such as murder, manslaughter, rape, arson, and theft. Yet the number of federal, state, and local police employees, including clerks and other support employees, was less than seven hundred thousand (see Table 7-1).

As Table 7-2 indicates, law enforcement in this country is primarily a local activity. Police officers must be aware that any evidence obtained in violation of the Fourth Amendment's prohibition of "unreasonable searches and seizures" usually will not be admitted in court.[12] This protection extends not only to physical evidence such as guns, drugs, and documents, but also to the interception of messages through wiretapping or by eavesdropping through a listening device not connected into a telephone network. Thus, for example, recordings of a defendant's telephone conversations, which were obtained by attaching an eavesdropping device to the outside of a public telephone booth, have been ruled inadmissible. In addition, under a doctrine called "the fruit of the poisonous tree," evidence obtained as a result of information secured through illegal wiretapping or eavesdropping may also not be admissible in court. Therefore, if the police learn through illegal wiretapping where guns used in a robbery are hidden, the guns are not admissible in court.

How then can police officers lawfully obtain evidence? The Fourth Amendment provides that "no Warrants shall issue, but upon probable cause." Thus, if the police wish to obtain a *search warrant,* they must file with a judge an affidavit, or statement, indicating that (1) the information sought is connected with criminal activity and (2) the things sought will probably be found in the place to be searched. When the police, acting upon a lawful search warrant,

TABLE 7-1
CRIMES BY TYPE, 1957–1982 (number of offenses in thousands)

| Year | Total | Murder[a] | Violent Crime | | | Property Crimes[b] |
			Rape	Robbery	Assault	
1982	12,857	21.0	77.8	537	650	11,572
1981	13,290	22.5	81.5	574	644	11,968
1978	11,141	19.6	67.1	417	558	10,080
1975	11,257	20.5	56.1	465	485	10,230
1972	8,249	18.7	46.9	376	393	7,414
1969	5,013	15.0	37.0	297	308	4,357
1966	3,272	11.0	26.0	157	233	2,846
1963	2,442	9.0	17.0	116	172	2,128
1960	2,020	9.0	17.0	107	153	1,734
1957	1,422	8.0	13.0	67	111	1,224

[a]Includes nonnegligent manslaughter.
[b]Includes burglary, larceny theft, and motor vehicle theft.

Sources: U.S. Bureau of the Census, *Historical Statistics of the United States, Colonial Times to Present,* Series H 952–961 (Washington, D.C.: Government Printing Office, 1982); U.S. Bureau of the Census, *Statistical Abstract of the United States, 1982–83,* (Washington, D.C.: Government Printing Office, 1982), p. 174.

**TABLE 7-2
FULL-TIME EQUIVALENT POLICE EMPLOYEES**

Year	Local	State	Federal
1970	394,000	56,000	40,000
1975	463,000	92,000	69,000
1979	489,000	92,000	73,000

Source: U.S. Bureau of the Census, *Statistical Abstract of the United States, 1982–83* (Washington, D.C.: Government Printing Office, 1982), p. 183.

examine the premises for the items named and discover other evidence of crime as well, they may seize the latter and use it in court. In the case of wiretapping or eavesdropping, a judge must issue an *interception order* for a limited period of time. The police must show that normal methods of obtaining information are not possible or are too dangerous.

Under certain circumstances, the police can lawfully dispense with a search warrant or interception order. For instance, a search warrant is not necessary if a police officer is in the process of making a lawful arrest, but the search must be limited to the arrested person and the surrounding area. Second, a warrantless search or an electronic interception is justified under emergency situations when evidence may be moved (e.g., as in a car), may disappear, or be easily destroyed. For this reason, a blood test to determine whether a driver is drunk may be conducted without a warrant. Third, under the "hot pursuit" doctrine, the police may follow a suspect onto any premises and search the suspect there. Fourth, if a suspect voluntarily consents to a search, no warrant is necessary. Fifth, a search warrant is unnecessary if a police officer seeks to

Police officer searching a suspect. (©1979 Ken Love/Black Star)

briefly stop and frisk a suspect under circumstances reasonably arousing the officer's suspicion.

We will assume that our police officers have finished their investigation and have concluded that an arrest is in order. Their constitutional obligations, as we will see, have just begun.

From Arrest to Trial

Unlike the investigation phase, an arrest warrant is usually not required in a serious criminal matter. The arresting officers need only show that they have "reasonable grounds to believe" that a felony has been committed and that the person arrested committed it. This is true even if the officers have ample time to obtain a warrant. In the case of misdemeanors, however, officers may usually arrest without a warrant only when the crime occurred in their presence.

Now let us assume that the police have received reports from several storeowners that their stores have been robbed. The storeowners have each provided the same description of the thief, so the police know that they are looking for a single suspect. From their sources in the criminal underground, the police are told that the suspect is probably Joe Doe, who, though unemployed, has been spending a lot of money recently. The police are ready to arrest Joe Doe.

At this point, the procedures outlined by the Supreme Court in the *Miranda* decision (1966) must be carefully followed.[13] As soon as any questioning of the suspect begins, he must be told that he has the right to remain silent, that any statement he makes may be used against him, that he has the right to an attorney at all stages of the proceeding, and that, if he cannot afford an attorney, one will be appointed. Joe Doe may waive any of these rights, but the waiver must be done intelligently and without coercion. If, on the other hand, Doe indicates that he wishes an attorney present before continuing, the questioning must stop until he has had a reasonable opportunity to obtain and consult an attorney. Finally, even if he has already answered some questions, Joe Doe may decide to remain silent until "he has consulted with an attorney and thereafter consents to be questioned." If the police fail to abide by any of these standards, any statements Doe makes will be inadmissible in court.

Many persons in the law-enforcement field have complained bitterly about the Miranda standards. They claim that the procedure thwarts effective investigation. Law-enforcement officials accept that coerced confessions should not be admitted into evidence; however, under the Miranda standard, even a voluntary confession is not admissible if the police do not rigidly adhere to the Miranda requirements. For example, statements voluntarily made by a suspect in his own home after being placed under arrest were ruled inadmissible when the Miranda warnings were not given. Similarly, a failure to warn an arrested person that he or she was entitled to an attorney at every stage from questioning onward, not just at the trial, has resulted in the exclusion of evidence. Many law-enforcement officials argue that these complex, rigid rules place an intolerable burden upon police officers, convert criminal procedure into a technical game, and encourage certain criminals to believe that a shrewd lawyer will always find some technical failing on the part of the police that will lead to acquittal.

But those who support the Miranda rule—principally criminal lawyers and civil libertarians—argue that the police have often coerced confessions and obtained fraudulent information from persons accused of a crime. The coercion is often not physical, but psychological. In the *Miranda* decision, the Supreme Court quoted police manuals that instructed officers in the use of psychological techniques on fearful suspects who are isolated in interrogation rooms. Supporters of the Miranda rule have also pointed out that accused persons have sometimes confessed to crimes, spelling out in detail how the act was done, while later evidence has shown that their confessions were false.

The supporters of the Miranda rule believe that it clearly follows from the constitutional standard known as the **privilege against self-incrimination.** The Fifth Amendment states that "no person . . . shall be compelled in any criminal case to be a witness against himself." (This requirement has been applied to the states through the Fourteenth Amendment.) In England, the privilege against self-incrimination was the focal point of the late-sixteenth and early-seventeenth-century struggle over whether the nation was to be an absolute monarchy in which the king's power would be unchecked or an ordered nation bounded by laws and rights. The privilege was closely associated with the principles that one is innocent until proven guilty, that one's home should not be unlawfully broken into, and that the use of torture to extract confessions is unjust. For these reasons, the privilege against self-incrimination was viewed as one of the most important victories in the struggle for the establishment and preservation of natural rights.

Regardless of its pros and cons, police in the United States must uphold the Miranda standard. We will assume that the police have informed Joe Doe of his rights in questioning him about the robbery described earlier, that they have arrested him, and that Doe has hired Rae Roe as his attorney. In most states, within a reasonable time after his arrest, Joe Doe must be brought before a judge or magistrate who will inform him of the charges brought against him and the future course of the proceeding. The most important part of this appearance concerns *bail,* which is a pledge of property or money by the accused to assure his appearance for trial. In general, the more serious the crime is, the higher the bail.

The Eighth Amendment provides that "excessive bail shall not be required." Even though this standard has not been incorporated into the Fourteenth Amendment, except in capital cases, most state constitutions have similar guarantees. In general, a judge or magistrate is expected to set a bail amount that will assure that the accused person will stand trial and not flee. Any amount greater than that is "excessive."

The next stage in the criminal process in felony cases is the *preliminary examination.* The purpose of the preliminary examination is to examine the

privilege against self-incrimination: A rule contained in the Fifth Amendment (and by incorporation to the states through the Fourteenth Amendment) that a person may not be compelled to give testimony that might lead to his or her indictment or conviction for a crime.

prosecution's case and to determine whether there is probable cause that a felony has been committed and that the person charged was responsible for it. Thus, the preliminary examination will prevent someone from coming to trial if the charges are groundless or the evidence is very weak. The preliminary examination is not required when a grand jury has returned an indictment, which led to the arrest.

If the judge or magistrate in charge of the preliminary hearing does not find probable cause, the accused is discharged; otherwise, the accused must next face a criminal prosecution. This begins when the government prosecutor files either an *indictment* or an *information.* An indictment, which is the end product of a grand-jury proceeding against the accused, is required in all federal felony cases. But in most states, the prosecutor has the choice of indictment or information.

In state systems, prosecutors generally prefer the information option when it is available. An *information* is a written accusation of the crime prepared by the prosecuting attorney. It sets forth the date, time, and place the crime allegedly took place and the specific crime (or crimes) with which the defendant is charged. The charges may include any crimes supported by the evidence taken at the preliminary hearing (which does not usually occur in the grand-jury option).

A grand jury, which usually consists of sixteen members of the community, is selected in the same way that a civil jury is. The grand jury does not determine guilt or innocence, but simply whether the accused person should be indicted. The prosecutor presents to the grand jury a *bill of indictment,* which is a written summary of the crime. In the secret hearings that follow, the prosecutor offers evidence and witnesses, which members of the grand jury may examine. Because neither the accused person nor his or her lawyer is present at the grand-jury proceedings, the prosecutor often dominates the proceedings. Rules of evidence are extremely flexible, so the prosecutor may introduce some evidence that would not be admissible at the trial. If the evidence satisfies the required proportion of grand jurors (i.e., usually twelve of sixteen) that the accused person will be convicted of the crime, they endorse the bill of indictment.

arraignment: A criminal proceeding in which a prisoner is informed of the charges against him or her and is required to plead an answer to the charges.

One last step occurs before the trial stage—the **arraignment.** The defendant is called into the court in which he will be tried. There, the accused is informed in a public hearing of the charges pending, and asked how he will plead. At this point, the defendant's attorney has several options. First, the attorney may make one or more of several motions that question the procedures used, the lack of evidence, or the legal charge. The court may deny the motions and require the defendant to plead, or it may grant one of the motions, discharging the defendant or requiring the filing of a new indictment or information. If the defendant is required to plead, he has three choices:

1. He may plead *not guilty.* The case will then go to trial.
2. He may plead *nolo contendere* (i.e., "no contest"), which is a plea of guilty

with an important qualification—it cannot later be used against the defendant in any civil proceeding as an admission of guilt. Thus, if Joe Doe makes this plea, the storeowners cannot use it as evidence in a civil proceeding to recover damages.

3. The third plea that may be entered is *guilty;* it may be used as evidence in a civil proceeding.

In addition, some states recognize a fourth plea of *not guilty by reason of insanity.* In other states, this issue is raised at the trial.

More than eighty percent of criminal charges end in guilty pleas. In 1980, for example, in the United States district courts, a total of 23,111 guilty pleas were entered, whereas 5,487 convictions by judge or jury were recorded. The process by which these guilty pleas are entered is known as *plea bargaining.* From the perspective of prosecutors, the transaction costs in negotiating a plea are considerably less than those that the state will incur in a full-scale criminal trial. The greater the number of pending matters, the greater is a prosecutor's incentive to arrange a bargained plea. The defendant is moved not only by the incentive arising from lower transaction costs but, more important, by the fact that the penalty will be lower than it would be if he or she were convicted after a full trial. Since both sides have strong incentives to enter into such an arrangement, it is not surprising that such a large percentage of crimes are disposed of in this way.

Many observers object to plea bargaining, claiming that defendants are often not punished severely enough, considering the crimes they have committed. While there is something to be said for their claim, these observers forget that each side at the outset of a trial faces serious risks and substantial costs. Justice is a costly process. Accordingly, both sides are often willing to engage in the trade-off that plea bargaining entails. In this respect, the American system of justice is no different than economic transactions that involve bargaining.

The Trial and Sentencing

Trials in criminal cases do not vary much from those in civil cases; the same orderly procedure that we described in civil cases applies to criminal ones as well. One significant difference, however, is that discovery plays a much smaller role in criminal cases, mainly because defendants in criminal cases do not have to disclose anything about their defense under the privilege against self-incrimination. Why, then, should prosecuting attorneys be required to reveal their evidence? After all, it would give defendants an undue advantage. However, the federal rules and those of certain states have liberalized discovery somewhat, most notably by allowing the defense attorney to inspect any pretrial statement made by a government witness (except those made to the grand jury) *after* the witness has testified at the trial. This aids the defense in cross-examining these witnesses.

Other than discovery, the major differences between civil and criminal trials stem from constitutional requirements applicable to the latter. Under the Sixth Amendment, an individual is entitled to a speedy criminal trial. In contrast, in civil cases, when a court's calendar is lengthy, many years may elapse between the time a complaint is issued and the time of trial. In a criminal case, the defendant is not compelled to testify because of the privilege against self-incrimination. In civil cases, however, defendants may be required to testify. Finally, the prosecution in a criminal case must prove its case "beyond a reasonable doubt." In most civil proceedings, the plaintiff must prove its case by a "preponderance of the evidence"; that is, most of the evidence must be in the plaintiff's favor.

After a criminal trial, the judge, as in a civil case, must instruct the jury on the law. The jury may find the defendant not guilty. If that is the finding, the defendant, under the **double jeopardy** provision of the Fifth Amendment, may not be tried again on the same charge or a lesser one related to it. For example, if the defendant is acquitted of murder, he or she may not be indicted under a manslaughter or assault charge arising from the same event. But if the defendant was tried in a federal court, he or she may be tried in a state court on the same charge (and vice versa).

If the jury finds the defendant guilty of the crime, the next step is sentencing. Some states permit juries to recommend or determine a sentence. But in most states and the federal system, it is the judge's job to impose a sentence within the range allowed by the statute covering the crime.

If the defendant has been convicted, all is not lost. Under Article I, Section 9, at any stage of the proceeding or afterward, the defendant may file a **habeas corpus writ,** which challenges the government's right to detain or imprison him or her. Or, the defendant may appeal on the basis of procedural or substantive errors of law. Later, we will look at the nature of appeal, but now we will look at a particular set of cases that raises special questions. These cases involve the civil liberties guaranteed in the First Amendment—that is, freedom of speech, press, religion, and assembly.

CIVIL LIBERTIES

Where Do We Draw the Line?

The meanings of words often change over time. And the difficulty of determining the original meanings is compounded when words are used in a limited context such as in the Bill of Rights. Nowhere is the difficulty of understanding the intended meaning of words more difficult than in the First Amendment, which states in part, "Congress shall make no law respecting an establishment of religion, or prohibiting the free exercise thereof; of abridging the freedom of speech, or of the press." While a rich documentation exists to help us to understand the intention of the original Constitution, the historical record on the First Amendment is meager.

double jeopardy: A constitutional requirement that a person acquitted of a crime may not be tried again on the same charge or a lesser one related to it.

writ of habeas corpus: A writ directed to a person (e.g., a government official) who is detaining another individual, requiring a justification for the confinement.

Fortunately, one scholar, Leonard W. Levy, has collected a great deal of the available information on the First Amendment and placed it in the context of the times.[14] Levy points to the work of the English jurist, Sir William Blackstone (1732–1780), as providing the basic understanding of civil liberties that most of the leading early-nineteenth-century figures had.[15] James Madison, it should be noted, was an exception. His views of civil liberties were more liberal and modern than those of most of his contemporaries. Even so, Madison favored the prosecution of Loyalist speakers and the burning of their pamphlets during the revolutionary period.

The Nineteenth-Century View of Civil Liberties

Not long before the eighteenth century, people had been treated with unusual cruelty for simply *thinking* "false doctrines." Particularly in the realm of religion, Catholics tortured Protestants, Protestants tortured Catholics, and both groups tortured members of smaller Christian sects, members of other religions, and nonbelievers.

In understanding the early-nineteenth-century, or the "Blackstone," view of civil liberties, one must examine three separate components: the thought, the speech, and the action that follows from the speech. For example, if you are at the head of an unruly mob poised to charge at a police station, you first think of what you are about to say, you shout "charge," and the mob charges the police station. Sir William Blackstone and the American Founders were proud of the progress in civility that the Enlightenment had brought, because no longer were persons treated as criminals merely for their thoughts.

In England and the United States, then, great strides in the history of tolerance of ideas had taken place. The critical question for Blackstone and the supporters of the First Amendment was where to draw the line between speech and the action that followed from it. Clearly, in the example just given, the cry of "charge" is closely linked with the action taken against the police station. Then and now, such an exercise of speech would be treated criminally because it incited a riot. The exercise of free speech, press, assembly and religion is not absolute, and the supporters of the First Amendment never intended it to be. Just as property was not an absolute collection of rights but rather was restrained by tort and crime, the First Amendment rights were conceived the same way.

The Modern View

Although the underlying nineteenth-century principle remains, modern courts are usually far more tolerant of speech than were their nineteenth-century counterparts. Our society is far more diverse than it was then. And yet, even though many dissident voices have been raised over the years, we have remained a stable society. In contrast, civil disobedience was common in both England and America in the 1600s through the early 1800s. Furthermore, the first professional police department in this country, New York City's, was not established until 1844. Given the costs incurred through a breach of the peace and the ease with which these spread, it is not surprising that the rules regarding permissible speech were much stricter than they are today. Moreover, we now have considerably greater knowledge about the connection between speech and action. For example, most studies have shown that a person's exposure to pornography does not increase the likelihood that he or she will commit a crime, contrary to the view of many people in earlier eras.

Ultimately, however, courts, legislators, and administrators must wrestle with the same problem that confronted their eighteenth- and nineteenth-century predecessors: Where do we draw the line?[16] Generally, the form of a statement makes no constitutional difference; the same principles usually apply to speech, the printed word, or a sign carried by a demonstrator.

Freedom of Speech, Press, and Association

As in the case of the due-process criminal provisions, the First Amendment guarantees apply to the states through the Fourteenth Amendment. But, as indicated, these rights are not absolute. Thus, statutes punishing the publication of obscene literature or incitement to riot have been upheld as constitutional. When government imposes restrictions on free speech, courts must try to balance the policy favoring that right against the legitimate interest of government to make lawful policies. Courts must ask whether the restriction on speech is a narrow one that can accomplish its legitimate purpose or whether it restricts freedom of speech, press, or assembly too broadly (see accompanying box). For example, if a city forbade political parades on all public streets on the grounds that the flow of traffic would be impeded, that would be unconstitutional. On the other hand, if the city required a political organization to parade in such a way that a traffic jam was not created on a main street, that restriction would be permissible.

First-Amendment protections have been traditionally claimed—and violated—in cases involving unpopular causes and groups. Sometimes this un-

---

FREEDOM OF SPEECH?

Because of a large number of notes written and passed by seventh- and eighth-graders, administrators at Prairie Junior High School in Des Moines, Iowa, imposed a rule banning note-passing among students. Penalties for breaking the rule included suspension from school. One seventh-grader, suspended for receiving a note in the school lunchroom, appealed to the State Department of Instruction. After considering the matter, a panel of the department declared in May 1983 that the note-passing rule was unconstitutional because it violated the students' right to freedom of speech.

Source: *Fortune*, October 17, 1983, p. 31.

American Nazis demonstrating at San Francisco State University. (©1980 Janet Fries/Black Star)

popularity can readily be understood—for example, when the rights of those, such as Nazis, who would deprive others of their rights, are protected. Nevertheless, like the separation-of-powers doctrine, the First Amendment was intended to preserve the rights of minority viewpoints, even when the overwhelming majority of people find them loathsome. If a group does no more than advocate its views in a peaceful manner, the protection of the First Amendment is absolute. Problems with the freedoms of speech, press, and assembly arise when these rights are connected with some unlawful or foreseeable action. We will look at three types of problems for which the Supreme Court has developed rules on where to draw the line.

The first of these concerns groups that, instead of using voting, interest-group activity, or litigation to attain political ends, have allegedly used speech to promote the use of violence in achieving their political goals. Many of these cases have involved the Communist party or the Ku Klux Klan. The second type of problem concerns freedom of assembly in which people gather to picket, march, sit in, or listen to speeches to publicize their grievances. Here, the problem is not the underlying purpose of the individuals or organization, but rather whether the activity may interfere with one of government's legitimate functions, such as preserving peace or assuring the orderly flow of traffic. Finally, we will look at a problem that the First Amendment's framers never considered: what is speech?

Speech and Prohibited Means   Whether political speech is constitutional when it is so revolutionary that it could lead to the violent overthrow of the government is a question that has been carefully considered by the Supreme Court.[17] Most of the cases have involved members of the Communist party or related groups. Many public officials and legislatures have claimed that the Communists seek ultimately to violently overthrow the American government. Accordingly, the federal and state governments have at times imposed restrictions on the Communist party and its members and subjected them to criminal penalties. In the most important of these cases, Communists were convicted for violating statutes that outlaw Communist doctrines that teach the violent overthrow of government.

To determine whether such political speech is protected by the First Amendment, the Supreme Court has devised the *clear-and-present-danger test*.[18] The Court looks at (1) the extent of the danger and (2) the closeness, or imminence, of the unlawful action. First, the Court examines whether the defendant is capable of undertaking the unlawful action. For example, a political party consisting of five people would hardly be able to overthrow the government, but if its membership were two thousand, the capability for takeover could be present.

Second, the Court asks whether the unlawful action is imminent. If a group or individual advocates unlawful conduct that will take place in the distant future, that speech is protected by the First Amendment. If the government fails to show either the substantial extent of the danger or its imminence, the speech in question is protected. Even then, the government's action may be unconstitutional if the statute upon which it is based is too broad. For example, in 1931, the Court held that a California law that made it a felony to display a red flag as a symbol of opposition to the federal government was too vague to be constitutional.[19]

Even when an organization is found under the clear-and-present-danger test to be engaging in criminal conduct, an individual can be punished for belonging to the group only under certain circumstances. First, the government must prove that the person knew of the organization's illegal aims. If the individual did not, he or she is protected under the First Amendment. Second, the person must have joined the organization with the intention of furthering its illegal goals.

A state or national law requiring an organization that has engaged in criminal activity to disclose its membership list is constitutional. Thus, New York State was able to obtain the membership list of the Ku Klux Klan, because it had engaged in violent, criminal activity.[20] Finally, the national and state governments can require employees to swear to uphold the Constitution and to oppose the overthrow of the government through illegal means.

Freedom of Assembly   There can be a conflict between a city or town's interest in maintaining public order and a group's desire to use the streets peaceably to assemble. Local governments have an interest in keeping streets and sidewalks open, free of trash, and relatively noise-free. Clearly, no group has the right to assemble in a residential neighborhood at 4:00 A.M. The Supreme Court has upheld municipal regulations that:

1. permit a reasonable opportunity for a group to assemble
2. do not discriminate in favor of some groups and against others
3. attempt to balance the city or town's interests with the group's

Under the rules developed by the Supreme Court, a city or town may require an organization seeking to parade, assemble, or picket to apply for a license specifying the date, time, and location of the activity. The city or town must have developed clearly defined, reasonable standards before the application. The local officials must have no voice in determining which groups will be permitted to demonstrate and which will not. Nor can the standards regarding assembly be written in vague terms; for example, an ordinance allowing public officials to inquire into the morals of persons seeking to parade would not be specific enough. Finally, a city cannot ban a parade because opponents of the group seeking the permit might commit acts of violence in retaliation. Under such circumstances, it is the municipality's responsibility to protect the group exercising its right to assemble.

Once a demonstration has begun, the clear-and-present-danger test is applied. Interference by the demonstrators with the flow of traffic (other than that allowed under the permit), fighting, rioting, or any other breach of the peace are grounds for ending the assembly and arresting violators. But when no breach of the peace or other public disorder is imminent, the police may not end the demonstration. Nor may they end it simply because passersby object to the sentiments expressed, for example, by making hostile gestures. In brief, assembly is a highly protected right, and the burden of showing that it should be restricted clearly rests upon the government.

Obscenity and Free Speech   The Supreme Court has made it clear that *symbolic speech*—any means of communicating literary, social, political, or other serious ideas—will be afforded the same protection as verbal speech and will be subject to the same restrictions. Thus, books, pamphlets, handbills, signs, cartoons, drawings, and any other means by which groups or individuals make their views known are protected. The message conveyed need not be comprehensive or persuasive to be protected. In fact, it may even be provocative. A peace demonstrator charged with breaching the peace in 1968 for wearing a jacket bearing the words, "Fuck the Draft," was constitutionally vindicated in 1971 because the phrase expressed his sentiments on a public issue.[21]

The most difficult free-speech issue has concerned material pertaining to sex.[22] Sexually oriented literature has been condemned because of widespread beliefs that reading it leads to antisocial or immoral sexual conduct and that it generally loosens the restraints that cause individuals to behave civilly toward one another. Indeed, recent sociological research disputes the claim that reading sexually oriented literature has ill effects. But the Court instead has excluded certain sexually oriented literature on the theory that the First Amendment's protection does not extend to it.

Not all sexually oriented literature has been held to be obscene. The Court has defined obscene material as that which describes or pictures sexual conduct that (1) appeals to the prurient (i.e., erotic) interest in sex, (2) portrays sex in a patently offensive way, and (3) does not have serious literary, artistic, political, or scientific value. All three criteria must be met if the material is to be unprotected. Since the first two criteria are personal and not objective, the Supreme Court, in *Miller* v. *California* (1973), required that sexually oriented literature should be judged by the average person applying his or her contemporary community standards and considering the subject material as a whole. Given the wide range of preferences with respect to every part of this test, it is not surprising that the determination of obscenity has become extremely complex. More important, the law fails to provide any reasonable guidelines to conduct except in one area: sexually oriented material involving or aimed at children is not protected by the First Amendment.

Religion

The First Amendment protects the free exercise of religion, just as it does the freedom of speech, press, and assembly. In addition, the amendment prohibits Congress from passing any law establishing a religion. The establishment clause was inserted in response to the fear that factions could develop along religious lines and one religion could thus come to dominate the rest, making itself an established church. In a nation inhabited by many different religions, some of which were persecuted in Europe, it was important to remove this source of potential dissension. Thus, under the establishment principle, which applies to the states under the Fourteenth Amendment, every statute that affects religion must have (1) a secular (i.e., nonreligious) purpose, (2) a principal effect that does not help or hinder religion, and (3) a minor amount of government entanglement with religion.

These criteria are not always easy to apply. Nevertheless, the Court has ruled that a substantial amount of public aid to church-supported schools is constitutional. For example, states may lend secular textbooks to parochial schools because their purpose is to instruct students in secular subjects. Similarly, the public provision of health services in and transportation to and from church-supported schools has been upheld as constitutional. However, government payment of transportation for a parochial-school field trip was ruled to be unconstitutional because the teachers could have used the experience to advance religion. In brief, unless government funds or services for religious groups are used only for public purposes, they are not likely to be constitutional.

Just as the establishment clause forbids government aid to a religion or a set of religious institutions, such as schools, so also it prohibits aiding religion in general. Even though Madison may not have been typical of those who supported the clause, he did state that it was intended not to compel men to worship God in any manner contrary to their conscience. Based on this, the Supreme Court has invalidated prayer and Bible reading in public schools, the teaching of religious views on creation, release time in public-school class-rooms for religious instruction, and the posting of the Ten Commandments in a public school. However, the Court has permitted release time for pupils to study religion away from public schools and has allowed student absences from public schools for religious participation; to hold otherwise would have prevented the free exercise of religion.

The clause allowing the free exercise of religion is subject to the same principles that freedom of speech, press, and assembly are. For instance, one may not engage in unlawful conduct under the guise of practicing religion. To take an extreme case, which arose in Canada, one may not make human sacrifices because of religious beliefs. Similarly, religion cannot be used as a constitutional justification to evade military training or service, although there are statutes that may permit this.

As in civil or criminal matters, courts in civil-liberties cases perform a par-adoxical function: they both protect rights and restrict them. This task involves a difficult trade-off of a complex of benefits and costs interlaced with values. As we have seen, courts are not free to exercise their particular whims while engaging in this process. Rather, they are bound by many strict rules and procedures. For example, as discussed previously, the Constitution always prevails over a statute with which it is in conflict. Similarly, courts must abide by rules of evidence that have been developed over the centuries and that have been designed to trade off the quality and reliability of information with each side's opportunity to present its views.

APPEAL

In subsequent chapters, we will see that important checks exist with respect to executive and legislative power; so also are trial courts checked. The process of appeal, in which the actions of lower courts are reviewed by an independent, higher court, is an important part of our legal system that acts as a check upon judicial conduct. As we saw at the beginning of this chapter, Lloyd Gaines unsuccessfully sought admission to the University of Missouri School of Law in state courts, but was vindicated by the Supreme Court. Appeal is an integral part of the court system.

The federal courts and most states have a three-level system in which (1) trials are conducted at the lowest level, (2) appeals are made to the courts at the intermediate levels, and (3) reviews of the intermediate-court decisions are made by the highest-level court. In the federal system, the courts at the three levels for most kinds of cases are the district courts, the courts of appeals, and the Supreme Court. In most systems, the appeal from the trial court to the intermediate-level court is a matter of right; the intermediate court *must* review the decision of the trial court. But an appeal from the intermediate level to the highest court is generally not a matter of right. Rather, the highest court can usually exercise discretion to determine which appeals it will decide.

Appeal to an intermediate court from a trial court is a matter of right, but few cases are actually appealed in the federal and state court systems. First of all, a party losing in a trial court often sees little hope of reversing the court's decision. Moreover, appeals are extremely expensive. Although special provisions allow states to pay for the appeals of the very poor, most people must pay high filing fees, the costs of printing a large number of briefs, and, of course, attorney's fees. For the same reasons, few intermediate-court decisions are appealed to the highest courts in the federal and state systems. Thus, appeals are largely used by organizations, the rich, the poor, and those whose claims attract the financial support of interest groups. Middle-class persons and small firms are less likely to use appellate procedure.

Intermediate courts review three types of issues raised in trial-court proceedings. The largest number of these concerns procedural matters in the trial court. As we saw earlier, trial judges must decide questions of evidence and procedure, and motions and objections are constantly made by both sides during a trial. Therefore, it is not surprising that even the wisest judge makes a few errors. However, the costs of litigation would rise astronomically if *any* error made by a trial judge could lead to a new trial. Accordingly, appellate courts will not reverse an error of procedure in the trial court if it is a "harmless error." Rather, the error must have either violated the losing party's constitutional rights or perhaps affected the outcome of the trial. Most of the minor skirmishes that occur during trials do not meet these criteria.

Intermediate courts also consider whether the evidence in the trial court was sufficient to support the verdict. A jury is expected to decide which version of the facts presented in a trial is correct. Sometimes, there may be sufficient evidence to support both versions, but the jury will select only one. However, situations may also exist in which the evidence, looked at from the perspective of the side that *won,* cannot support the verdict. In this case, an intermediate appellate court can, as a matter of law, find that the verdict was contrary to the evidence.

Finally, an appeals court can examine the conclusions of law decided by the trial court. The appeals court may independently review the discussion and conclusion of substantive law undertaken by the trial court, and it is not bound to follow the legal conclusion of the trial court. In contrast, a trial court is limited by the findings of the appeals court that decides its case, but not by other appeals courts. Thus, a trial court in North Dakota is not bound by an appeals court in Louisiana, while a United States district court in Mississippi is not limited by the decisions of the United States court of appeals in Boston, because the latter does not have jurisdiction in Mississippi.

An appeals court can do three things. *First, it can affirm the judgment of the lower court.* It is not unusual for an appeals court to affirm the lower court's judgment on different grounds than those provided by the lower court.

Its legal reasons may differ from those of the trial court, but lead to the same verdict. *Second, it may reverse the judgment of the lower court* because it finds that the lower court's view of the law is wrong and that the correct view compels judgment for the party that lost in the lower court. *Finally, the appeals court may remand the case to the trial court,* either for (1) a full-scale, new trial or (2) the taking of evidence on something that the appeals court considers important for the disposition of the case, but that was not considered in the trial court. These actions are not necessarily inconsistent; an appeals court may remand in part and reverse in part, for example, on different issues and counts of a complaint.

Whereas appeals to the intermediate courts are usually a matter of right under statutes and state constitutions (but not under the Constitution), appeals to the highest courts are usually discretionary. For example, while appeals to the Supreme Court from a state-court judgment, upholding a state law challenged on the ground that it violated the Constitution, are matters of right, most appeals to the Court are not. Rather, in most instances, a party seeking a decision from the Court must submit a document called a *writ of certiorari* to the Court.[23] The Court's rule governs the granting of such a writ, but the rule is so broad that it is virtually meaningless. In general, the Court will review a case only if four justices think that it should. Many cases of great policy importance are reviewed, but some are not. On the other hand, the Court will review cases of concern to a relatively small number of persons. When it does review a case, the Court writes a decision that binds every court, legislature, and executive-branch administrator in the land.

NOTES

[1]Missouri ex. rel. Gaines v. Canada, 305 U.S. 337 (1938).

[2]See Roberts v. Boston, 5 Cush. 198 (Mass. 1849); King v. Gallagher, 93 N.Y. 438 (1883); Cumming v. Richmond County Board of Education, 175 U.S. 528 (1899); Berea College v. Kentucky, 211 U.S. 45 (1908); and Gong Lum v. Rice, 275 U.S. 78 (1927).

[3]Brown v. Board of Education of Topeka, Kansas, 347 U.S. 483 (1954).

[4]A comprehensive discussion of the concepts of jurisdiction are contained in International Shoe Co. v. Washington, 326 U.S. 310 (1945).

[5]An excellent discussion of the structure of the federal court system is Howard Ball, *Courts and Politics: The Federal Judicial System* (Englewood Cliffs, New Jersey: Prentice-Hall, 1980), chapter 3.

[6]Loving vs. Virginia, 388 U.S. 1 (1967).

[7]A superb evaluation of the jury system is M. Bloomstein, *Verdict: The Jury System* (New York: Dodd-Mead, 1968).

[8]A comprehensive history is Leonard W. Levy, *Origins of the Fifth Amendment* (New York: Oxford University Press, 1968).

[9]Powell v. Alabama, 287 U.S. 45 (1932). See also Gideon v. Wainwright, 372 U.S. 335 (1963).

[10]Tot v. United States, 319 U.S. 463 (1943).

[11]The leading cases are Palko v. Connecticut, 302 U.S. 319 (1937) and Rochin v. California, 342 U.S. 165 (1952).

[12]Some of the leading principles are discussed in Katz v. United States, 389 U.S. 347 (1967), a case involving FBI eavesdropping on conversations held by an alleged gambler in a public telephone booth.

[13]Miranda v. Arizona, 384 U.S. 436 (1966).

[14]Leonard W. Levy, *Legacy of Suppression: Freedom of Speech and Press in Early American History* (Cambridge: Howard University Press, 1960).

[15]J. W. Ehrlich, *Ehrlich's Blackstone,* vol. 2 (New York: Capricorn Books, 1959), pp. 281–429.

[16]An excellent analytical discussion of the various positions taken on the issues is Martin Shapiro, *Freedom of Speech: The Supreme Court and Judicial Review* (Englewood Cliffs, New Jersey: Prentice-Hall, 1966).

[17]A comprehensive review of the cases decided until 1969 is Thomas I. Emerson, *The System of Freedom of Expression* (New York: Random House Vintage, 1970).

[18]The leading case, considerably modified by subsequent Supreme Court decisions, is Dennis v. the United States, 341 U.S. 494 (1951).

[19]Stromberg v. California, 283 U.S. 359 (1931).

[20]Bryant v. Zimmerman, 278 U.S. 63 (1928).

[21]Cohen v. California, 403 U.S. 15 (1971).

[22]A good analytical discussion of the issues is contained in Harry Kalven, "The Metaphysics of the Law of Obscenity," in Philip B. Kurland, ed., *The Supreme Court and The Constitution* (Chicago: University of Chicago Press, 1965), pp. 1–45.

[23]On the Supreme Court, see Robert G. McCloskey, *The American Supreme Court* (Chicago: University of Chicago Press, 1960).

BIBLIOGRAPHY

Ball, Howard. *Courts and Politics: The Federal Judicial System.* Englewood Cliffs, New Jersey: Prentice-Hall, 1980. An excellent, nontechnical examination of the federal judicial system.

Cohen, William, and John Kaplan. *Bill of Rights: Constitutional Law for Undergraduates.* Mineola, New York: Foundation Press, 1976. A comprehensive casebook designed for undergraduates.

Ehrlich, J. W. *Ehrlich's Blackstone.* 2 vols. New York: Capricorn Books, 1959. An edited collection taken from the great English legal theorist's major work. Indispensable to an understanding of the underlying reasons for many legal rules.

Emerson, Thomas I. *The System of Freedom of Expression.* New York: Random House Vintage, 1970. A passionate, detailed examination of many of the problems that have arisen under the First Amendment.

Faulkner, Robert K. *The Jurisprudence of John Marshall.* Princeton: Princeton University Press, 1968. A major insight into the legal thinking of the great chief justice.

Goebel, Julius. *History of the Supreme Court of the United States: Antecedents and Beginnings to 1801.* New York: Macmillan, 1971. A detailed study of the origin and early history of the Supreme Court.

Kurland, Philip B. ed. *The Supreme Court and the Constitution.* Chicago: University of Chicago Press, 1965. A probing collection of seven essays into constitutional topics.

Levi, Edward H. *An Introduction to Legal Reasoning.* Chicago: University of Chicago Press, 1949. Still the best study of how lawyers and jurists reason.

Levy, Leonard W. *Origins of the Fifth Amendment.* New York: Oxford University Press, 1968. The outstanding exposition of the subject.

McCloskey, Robert G. *The American Supreme Court.* Chicago: University of Chicago Press, 1960. An excellent brief history of the Court.

Reynolds, William L. *Judicial Process in a Nutshell.* St. Paul: West, 1980. A concise introduction to how the legal system works.

Shapiro, Martin. *Freedom of Speech: The Supreme Court and Judicial Review.* Englewood Cliffs, New Jersey: Prentice-Hall, 1966. A work that usefully categorizes the various conceptual approaches taken on free-speech problems.

CHAPTER 8

Congress and the Legislative Function

The United States may be described as a nation in which citizens are linked to the state by voluntary political participation and by a system of laws. As we have seen, direct involvement by Americans in the affairs of the government is rare because of the high costs of individual action and the disincentives for people to directly participate through group formation. Americans generally participate through the republican methods of representative government: citizens select individuals to represent their interests in matters of state. We have also stressed the importance of the American legal system as a complex set of controls and guarantees that originate in the Constitution and that are usually put into practice by legislative statutes.

Congress is referred to as the "first branch of government" because it is described in Article I of the Constitution, and the label is appropriate. Congress—the representative legislature—is the center of republican political participation, and the source of governing statutes, in the United States. Although Congress is endowed by the Constitution with certain explicit functions, privileges, and limitations, the realities of political life have reshaped its role in ways that the Founders never foresaw, and therefore did not write into the Constitution.

In this chapter, we will examine the ideal functions of Congress, as expressed in the Constitution, as well as the other duties and constraints that Congress has acquired over the past two centuries. In particular, we will see that many fundamental concepts (e.g., costs, constraints, organization, incentives, control, and allocation) are useful in understanding the structure and processes of the legislative branch.

There are, of course, a variety of useful approaches to the study of Congress. As Woodrow Wilson wrote in 1885, in the first detailed study of Congress, "Like a vast picture thronged with figures of equal prominence and crowded with elaborate and obtrusive details, Congress is hard to see satisfactorily and appreciatively at a single view and from a single standpoint."[1] Scholars have contributed to our knowledge by examining the psychology of congressional representatives, the sociology of groups in the Senate and the House of Representatives, and the effects of electoral pressures on the voting behavior of legislators.

THE ORIGINS OF THE LEGISLATURE

Although the Constitution established a Congress that was, and still is, unique, the legislature was not an American invention. Its roots extend back for seven centuries, and several other nations had developed legislatures of their own that served as models for the American Founders. In England, during the reign of Edward I (1272–1307), the "Great Council" was convened to advise the king; it consisted of lay and ecclesiastical magnates. In roughly the same era, the French *parlement* (*parler* means "to speak") was providing the foundation for a second major function of legislatures: the French assembly was one in which principal vassals could speak on public affairs. Gradually, in both France and England, the legislating function emerged. At first, legislatures merely examined laws made by the executive to see whether they conformed to principles of law and justice; soon, however, they began to take over the function of preparing and enacting laws. During the fourteenth century, the legislative *caucus,* or *committee,* was developed; groups of legislators were charged with managing a bill or controlling a subject matter, a device that we today call "division of labor." Finally, the early assemblies became places where members could express discontent with the monarch's powers in an orderly way.

In the century before the American Revolution, each of the American colonies developed a political system consisting of a governor and an elected assembly. Tensions grew between governors and legislatures, but neither clearly dominated because the colonists feared both an absolute majority in the legislature and the governor's potential as an agent of tyrants. During the Revolution and in the years before ratification of the Constitution, nearly all of the colonies replaced their provincial governments with state governments. While the constitutions of the new states varied, they all provided for the division of power between executives and legislatures. The challenge to the framers of the Constitution was to devise a national system that would unite the states yet preserve their independent identity. Congress was in large part a response to that challenge.

THE CONSTITUTIONAL POWERS OF CONGRESS

In Chapter 2, we discussed the concerns of the Founders at the Constitutional Convention and their solutions to the problems of concentrated power versus the absence of power. Their experience under the Articles of Confederation had demonstrated the need for a political system based not only on the separation of functions but also on the granting of sufficient power to the institutions of government to allow them to operate effectively. For the principle of separation of powers to work, several assumptions had to be fulfilled. These assumptions tell us a great deal about how the Founders thought Congress would behave.

First, as in the economic system, political actors were assumed to be self-interested individuals; in politics, however, these individuals would be motivated by a basic desire for power that would be constrained by constitutional checks and balances. Second, each branch of government would cooperate with the others but would resist yielding any of its powers. Third, the legislature would operate cohesively despite its division into two chambers, each marked by internal divisions and disputes. Each branch of government would be controlled by the incentives available to its members, the restraints imposed by law, and the costs of disorganization. We should keep these concepts in mind as we examine the actual functioning of Congress.

The system of elections and the conditions of office for senators and representatives were intended to shape their incentives. The necessity of responding to the public's interests would be conditioned by the control that the voters would have over their representatives' careers. The Constitution provided only the foundation of an organizational scheme for Congress, however; the structures and processes of the legislative branch have developed largely as a function of pressures and constraints outside the Constitution.

In the next section, we will discuss the organization of Congress. The proper starting point for an explanation of Congress is the set of constitutional powers and limitations provided by the Founders—in effect, the laws that Congress must obey.

Enumerated Powers

The Constitution specifies many of the powers of Congress. The most important of these enumerated powers fall into three general categories: finance, regulation of commerce, and military and war powers. There are also a number of miscellaneous enumerated powers (see Appendix B, The Constitution, Article I, Section 8).

Finance Powers   The writers of the Constitution quickly eliminated one of the greatest flaws in the Articles of Confederation: "The Congress shall have power to lay and collect Taxes, Duties, Imposts and Excises, to pay the Debts and provide for the common Defence and general Welfare of the United States . . . . To borrow Money on the credit of the United States; . . . To coin Money, regulate the Value thereof. . . ." Thus, Congress was given the power to tax. And the particular language that was used ("to . . . provide for the common Defence and general Welfare") was especially significant. Congress soon reasoned that if it could tax for the general welfare, it could spend for the same purpose, and "general Welfare" has since been applied to many aspects of government (e.g., spending for education, highway construction, and social security).

Another vague term is related to the power of Congress to tax. When Article I, Section 9, was written, the sentence "No Capitation, or other direct, Tax shall be laid, unless in Proportion to the Census or Enumeration herein before directed to be taken," was intended to prohibit a special tax on slaves; it had other consequences, however. The first federal income tax was overturned by the Supreme Court in 1895 because it was not apportioned among the states according to their populations. Actually, the first income tax was imposed during the Civil War, but it was labeled an "excise" tax, and so was not revoked by the courts. Not until passage of the Sixteenth Amendment in 1913 did the present method of income taxation become permissible.

The Power to Regulate Commerce   The following phrase, often referred to as the **commerce clause,** has become one of the most important governmental powers enumerated in the Constitution: "To regulate Commerce with foreign Nations, and among the several States, and with the Indian Tribes." Its purpose

commerce clause: The constitutional provision giving Congress authority to regulate commerce with foreign nations and among the states.

was clear: that the federal government, not the states, should regulate foreign commerce; that cooperation among the states should be encouraged by allowing the national legislature to impose uniform duties and commercial regulations on trade among the states; and that no state would be allowed to discriminate or retaliate against the trade of another. In practice, the commerce clause has been more problematic.

With regard to foreign commerce, there has been little dispute that the states should be prohibited from imposing their own rules on trade with other nations. If each state had such a right, the transaction costs for businesses would be greatly increased as they tried to sort out the complex sets of state regulations applying to each foreign contract.

Until around the turn of the twentieth century, the Supreme Court generally interpreted "commerce" to mean transportation (although the Court did include the transmission of electricity, gas, and information across state lines as "commerce"). Thus, the manufacturing, production, and sale of a product were not seen to be within the scope of Congress's power to regulate commerce. Similarly, the Court usually held that "interstate" commerce did not include activities that took place entirely within one state, unless those activities had a "direct and immediate" effect on interstate transactions. Thus, it ruled in favor of federal regulation of railroad rates on purely intrastate shipments, because those rates would affect the prices of goods that would compete in the market with goods produced in other states.

Black man entering the "colored" entrance of a movie theater in Belzoni, Mississippi, in October 1939. The commerce clause was invoked by Congress in the 1964 Civil Rights Act as constitutional authority for the prohibition of segregation in theaters, restaurants, and hotels. (Library of Congress)

A less confusing, but to some a more questionable, interpretation of the commerce clause has dominated since the 1930s. This more liberal doctrine has had an enormous impact on the size of government and the scope of federal involvement in the marketplace. In 1918, the Supreme Court overturned a law regulating child labor because the commerce clause did not give Congress the power to "regulate matters entrusted to local authority [child labor] by prohibition of the movement of commodities in interstate commerce." Yet, in 1937, the Court ruled that Congress could require collective bargaining in all industries "affecting" interstate commerce, regardless of geographic location.[2] Since that decision, the Constitution has been interpreted as giving Congress the power to pass legislation affecting many areas of economic and social life. For example, in the Civil Rights Act of 1964, Congress was able to ban racial discrimination in places of public accommodation (e.g., theaters, hotels, and restaurants) because those businesses might serve out-of-state customers or buy supplies from interstate distributors. Thus, today "commerce" includes not only the exchange of commodities but also the transportation of goods, people, animals, gas, and oil; the transmission of information by wire, radio, and satellite; the writing of insurance policies; and many aspects of manufacturing, mining, and fishing.

In addition, the definition of "regulation" has been expanded to now include the congressional power to promote interstate commerce by such means as building interstate highways or chartering a private corporation (i.e., Amtrak) to operate American passenger trains. The courts have even interpreted Congress's power over commerce as being similar to a federal police power that allows the legislature to regulate interstate activity it considers harmful to the public health, welfare, or morality. Small wonder, then, that the commerce clause has been called the "cornerstone" of much of the federal law that has expanded the role of the government in the United States.

Military and War Powers   The most dramatic of the congressional powers in foreign affairs is the power to declare war. According to Article I, Section 8, Congress has the power, "To declare war . . . To raise and support Armies . . . To provide and maintain a Navy; To make Rules for the Government and Regulation of the land and naval Forces; To provide for organizing, arming, and disciplining the Militia . . . ." Article II, Section 3, states that the president "shall have Power, by and with the Advice and Consent of the Senate, to make Treaties, provided two thirds of the Senators present concur; and he shall nominate, and by and with the Advice and Consent of the Senate, shall appoint Ambassadors."

Congress has declared war only five times in American history—in 1812, 1846, 1898, 1917, and 1941—but the United States has been involved in many more than five armed conflicts. Opponents of the Vietnam war were disappointed to discover that according to the Constitution, to *make* war is an executive power, while the congressional role is often only a declaration that a state of war exists. As we will see in the discussion of the War Powers Resolution in Chapter 11, one of the effects of the Vietnam war was to upset the implicit constitutional balance between the Congress and the executive in making war.

The Constitution also provided for cooperation between the executive and Congress in the making of treaties. The Founders viewed treaties with foreign nations as a peculiar form of governmental action. Hamilton wrote in *The Federalist,* no. 75, that treaty-making "relates neither to the execution of subsisting laws, nor the enaction of new ones," and therefore was neither a purely legislative function nor an exclusively executive one. According to Hamilton, the reason for allowing the Senate a role in treaty-making, while excluding the House of Representatives, was that the Senate would exhibit "accurate and comprehensive knowledge of foreign politics; a steady and systematic adherence to the same views; a nice and uniform sensibility to national character; decision, *secrecy,* and despatch." Whether Hamilton's trust in the Senate has been justified is a question that has frequently been raised. Nevertheless, the supremacy clause (Article VI) establishes that treaties are "the supreme Law of the Land" on an equal footing with the Constitution, although subject to alteration by subsequent congressional statute.

Congress has other military and war powers. The conscription of men into the military by the draft has been judged to be a part of the congressional power to "raise and support Armies." Although the draft was rejected by Congress when it was first proposed during the War of 1812, it was invoked during the Civil War and has often been used since. Congress also has the power to mobilize the militia (now called the National Guard). In addition, because Congress was given the power to "make Rules for the Government and Regulation of the land and naval Forces," it is Congress that provides the procedures for military justice, in the Uniform Code of Military Justice. Article III, concerning the federal judiciary, does not apply to military courts, and many of the rights provided by the Bill of Rights do not apply to courts-martial. For example, military personnel are not guaranteed jury trials or grand-jury indictments.

There are many other ways in which Congress can affect military and foreign policy. In connection with its war powers, Congress can control prices, wages, and rents or take over the telephone, telegraph, and railroad systems. It can refuse to appropriate the funds necessary for the waging of war, or it can stipulate in its appropriations bills that money cannot be spent for particular purposes (e.g., the provision of arms or foreign aid to another nation). And through debates, resolutions, legislative hearings, and other public and private means, Congress can inform the executive of its wishes and demands. Nevertheless, as we will see in Chapter 9, there are areas in which the Constitution has been unclear about the extent of congressional powers in military and foreign affairs.

Miscellaneous Enumerated Powers of Congress   There are many other enumerated congressional powers in Article I, Section 8, and elsewhere in the Constitution. Some of these powers—such as the power to admit new states into the Union, impeachment, and amendment of the Constitution—are rarely used.

Other powers are more commonly exercised but rarely publicized; for example, Congress has the power to "establish an uniform Rule of Naturalization" of new citizens, it authorizes patents and copyrights, it legislates on maritime matters, and is responsible for "Post Offices and post Roads." However, there is always a potential for controversy; in the early nineteenth century, the construction of post roads, the routes over which mail was carried, was intensely and successfully opposed by those who questioned the role of government in providing such public goods. The constitutional duty of Congress to govern the District of Columbia has been a task that most members of Congress would gladly relinquish. And finally, under Article III, Section 2, Congress has the power to establish and oversee federal courts below the level of the Supreme Court and to fix the appellate jurisdiction of the Court.

Implied Powers

The last clause in Article I, Section 8, states that the Congress has the power "to make all Laws which shall be necessary and proper for carrying into Execution the foregoing Powers, and all other Powers vested by this Constitution in the Government of the United States, or in any Department or Officer thereof." This has been called the "sweeping clause" because it suggested that Congress has powers under the Constitution that are not clearly enumerated. As we saw in Chapter 2, the Supreme Court ruled in *McCulloch* v. *Maryland* (1819) that a liberal interpretation was to be given to the phrase "necessary and proper."[3] In other cases, the Court has ruled that the Constitution does not intend all employees of the executive branch to be under the exclusive control of the president, and that as Congress pursues the legislative function—passing laws— it must have the power to investigate and interrogate public officials and private citizens in order to acquire needed information. It is also necessary and proper that Congress be able to evaluate the effects of its actions.

Thus, Congress has implied powers to investigate and oversee the actions of government and citizens on all matters within the jurisdiction of the legislative branch. Congress can force individuals to appear before the House or the Senate or any congressional committee to answer questions. The courts have no power to prevent Congress from requiring attendance, and will rarely become involved in disputes between Congress and the president on matters of executive privilege—the protection of presidential communications made in the exercise of executive power. In *U.S.* v. *Nixon* (1974), the Supreme Court required President Richard Nixon to surrender tapes of his conversations with White House aides regarding the Watergate break-in, but also ruled that executive-privilege claims were legitimate if secrecy was in the national interest (e.g., as in matters regarding diplomacy or military matters).[4]

Another implied congressional power is that of *eminent domain*. Governments must have the power to take private property from individuals or corporations, whether for taxes, as a fine, or for necessary public purposes (e.g., a military post). The Constitution does not explicitly allow Congress to exercise the power of eminent domain, but the Fifth Amendment declares that no person shall be "deprived of life, liberty, or property, without due process of law; nor shall private property be taken for public use, without just compensation." Thus, the power of eminent domain is recognized through the limitations imposed upon it.

Enabling Powers

By its amendments, the Constitution has conferred powers on Congress. Several constitutional amendments include such phrases as "Congress shall have power to enforce this article by appropriate legislation." This phrase gave Congress the power to pass laws regarding the abolition of slavery, the guarantee of due process by the states, and the right to vote. The **enabling powers** have been of particular significance in the passage of civil-rights legislation during the last two decades.

Concurrent Powers

Finally, there are certain powers that Congress can exercise concurrently with the executive or the states. For example, the regulation of interstate commerce by the federal legislature overlaps with the regulation of commerce within state boundaries by the states. And although the "supremacy clause" of the Constitution declares that "This Constitution, and the Laws of the United States which shall be made in Pursuance thereof . . . shall be the supreme Law of the Land," there are nevertheless areas in which both the federal and state governments have legitimate responsibilities. It is therefore not surprising that the exercise of **concurrent powers** by any branch or level of government occasionally sparks a conflict over constitutional boundaries.

Restrictions on Congressional Power

If American society were simple and unchanging, we might be able to describe the behavior of Congress merely by listing the legislative powers set forth in the Constitution, although it might also be necessary to mention the constitutional limitations on Congress (e.g., in certain matters relating to slave trade, taxation, appropriations, and, of course, civil rights and liberties). However, there are always incentives for going beyond a strict, narrow interpretation of the Constitution, and new situations arise that are not clearly covered by the basic rules. In the final analysis, the expansion of congressional power is constrained only by the safeguards of limited government, the separation of powers, judicial review, and electoral responsibility—the same principles that maintain the powers of Congress by endowing it with legitimacy.

THE TASKS OF CONGRESS

Some organizations are blessed with simple goals. For example, a corporation is an organization with the straightforward, though not always easy, goal of making a profit. A business must perform other tasks, of course, such as

enabling powers: Governmental powers conferred by constitutional phrases such as "Congress shall have power to enforce this article by appropriate legislation."

concurrent powers: Powers shared by the states and the national government.

advertising, planning, and maintaining friendly labor-management relations, but these are incidental to the primary objective of producing wealth for stockholders and employees.

In contrast, Congress has a complex set of institutional goals. In this section, we will examine what Congress is expected to do, both under the Constitution and by the demands of the political system. In Chapters 4 and 5, we discussed some of the *electoral* tasks of Congress—both formal (to receive the votes of the electoral college, to resolve ties in presidential votes) and informal (to educate the public, to inform the president about the mood of the electorate, and so on). Most of the *judicial* tasks of Congress are listed in the Constitution: senatorial consent for judicial appointments, impeachment, determination of qualifications of its own members, and so on. The other major tasks of Congress can be categorized into three general groups: legislation, oversight, and representation.

Legislative Tasks

The Constitution provides that "all legislative Powers herein granted" are assigned to Congress. The precise language of this phrase is important; the last two words remind us that Congress does not have an unrestricted or exclusive claim to legislative power, but can exercise only those powers that are based on some constitutional provision. Some legislative power also resides in the executive as he proposes or vetoes legislation, and in the courts as they interpret, apply, and sometimes expand the Constitution and legislative statutes. Furthermore, Congress may delegate its legislative power to the executive or to an agency, although it must make clear the policy that should be pursued; in 1935, in two important decisions (*Panama Refining Co.* v. *Ryan, Schechter Poultry Corp.* v. *United States*), the Supreme Court insisted that Congress could share its legislative power only if it provided clear standards to guide the president or the agency.[5]

Although the location of the legislative function is occasionally blurry, there can be no question that its major characteristic, lawmaking, is inherently political; that is, laws are not neutral. Various interests win, lose, or do both in part. The legislative task of Congress, therefore, involves far more than establishing the facts and the merits of problems, projecting the objectively appropriate answers, and discovering the proper policies to achieve solutions. It involves the push and pull of many groups and individuals, both within and outside of the government (e.g., voters, interest groups, and the president), at many different stages of the legislative process.

For example, the ideas that can become laws may originate in many different sources. Constituents, interest groups, lobbyists, congressional staff, executive-branch personnel, and, of course, the congressional representatives themselves can all suggest legislation. Considering the high information costs to members of Congress of learning enough to propose needed legislation on all possible topics, the expertise and concern of outsiders is very useful, particularly if those outsiders understand the fine points of writing laws in suitable

CONGRESS'S LESS SERIOUS WORK

Members of both houses introduced approximately seven hundred resolutions in 1981. For example, the House of Representatives voted on a resolution by Representative John Ashbrook (R-Ohio) to declare the fourth Sunday in October as "National Mother-in-Law Day." The vote was 305 ayes and 66 nays, with 28 voting "present." It was estimated that the printing and distribution of this one resolution alone cost nearly $1,300.

legislative language. And political actors outside of Congress can influence legislation not only at its initial stage, but also during the continuing legislative process. As a bill works its way through Congress, there are many access points at which political forces can affect its content and chances for passage. At each stage, the success of the legislative task depends on a variety of factors; these include the openness of a bill's sponsors to changes, the amount of information available, questions of jurisdiction, the communication to congressional representatives of the benefits and costs to each of them in the bill's passage or defeat, the mobilization of political support, and so on.

Finally, we should draw special attention to the scope of Congress's legislative task. Table 8-1 presents one measure of the workload of Congress. A Congress lasts for two years, beginning in January of the year following an election of a House of Representatives, and is divided into two sessions. The number of legislative measures introduced and passed in various years suggests that, with considerable fluctuation, the burden on members of Congress as they consider new legislation has not changed much since the beginning of this century. A "private" bill is one that affects a named individual, usually for relief from immigration and naturalization laws, as contrasted with a "public" bill of general application. The sharp decline in the number of bills introduced in the 1970s was due largely to a change in the rules. This change allowed many members of the Congress to cosponsor legislation in order to avoid the submission of identical bills. The drop in the number of bills passed reflected an increase in **omnibus bills** that combined many legislative proposals into large single packages. In fact, the other tasks of Congress have grown so much in recent years that many observers wonder whether Congress will be able to legislate effectively in the future.

omnibus bill: Piece of legislation to which many amendments on various subjects are attached.

Oversight Tasks

The Legislative Reorganization Act of 1946, Section 136, states: "To assist the Congress in appraising the administration of the laws and in developing such amendments or related legislation as it may deem necessary, each standing committee of the Senate and the House of Representatives shall exercise continuous watchfulness of the execution by the administrative agencies concerned of any laws." Congress cannot administer its own laws. After a bill is passed by Congress and signed into law by the president, the senators and representatives responsible for creating the law are given no clear constitutional powers to interfere with its execution. Congress can only follow the progress of the law to see whether it has been implemented in the way it was intended to be. If members of Congress are unhappy with the administration of the law, they can reduce appropriations to those responsible for the error, pass new legislation to correct the fault, or delay the appointment of new personnel to the agency or department charged with carrying out the legislative policy. Since effective *congressional oversight* often results in new legislation, it is sometimes difficult to distinguish the legislative task from the oversight task.

There are several mechanisms by which Congress oversees the administration of laws.[6] Perhaps the most dramatic is a committee hearing. In the United States, the separation of powers creates an institutional, and geographical, gulf between administrators and legislators. Congress must invite or compel executive-branch personnel to explain their actions before a committee or subcommittee. Other interested parties (e.g., those affected, interest-group representatives, private citizens, and academics) can also be invited to offer their comments. Although the grilling of an administrative spokesman before tele-

TABLE 8-1
NUMBER OF BILLS SUBMITTED IN SELECTED CONGRESSES

Congress	Dates	Bills Introduced	Passed Public	Passed Private	Total
97th	1981–1982	11,490	473	56	529
96th	1979–1980	12,583	613	123	736
91st	1969–1970	26,303	695	246	941
86th	1959–1960	18,261	800	492	1,292
81st	1949–1950	14,988	921	1,103	2,024
76th	1939–1940	16,105	1,005	657	1,662
71st	1929–1930	24,453	1,009	513	1,522
66th	1919–1920	21,967	470	124	594
61st	1909–1910	44,363	595	289	884
56th	1899–1900	20,893	443	1,499	1,942
51st	1889–1890	19,630	611	1,640	2,251
46th	1879–1880	10,067	372	278	650
41st	1869–1870	5,314	470	299	769
21st	1829–1830	856	152	217	369
1st	1789–1790	144	108	10	118

Sources: U.S. Bureau of the Census, *Historical Statistics of the United States, Colonial Times to 1970*, Series Y 189–198 (Washington, D.C.: Government Printing Office, 1976); U.S. Bureau of the Census, *Statistical Abstract of the United States, 1984* (Washington, D.C.: Government Printing Office, 1984), p. 256.

vision cameras is often intense, such hearings are not always used for grandstanding or publicity-seeking. Actually, at many committee hearings a large amount of information is presented. Congressional staff usually research the topic being overseen, informing legislators of their findings, and the exchanges between legislators and witnesses simultaneously inform Congress and warn administrators about the concerns of the legislature.

Another important by-product of the oversight task is to inform the public. The House Select Committee on Assassinations was created to investigate the assassinations of John Kennedy and Martin Luther King, Jr., but its most important function may have been to educate the public about the weakness in popular conspiracy theories relating to the deaths of the two leaders. Of course, it is possible to carry the investigatory function of Congress too far under the pretense of oversight. Senator Joseph McCarthy's well-publicized hearings in the 1950s on the presence of Communists in government often did little more than provide embarrassing details about personal lives.

Another congressional tool for overseeing the administration of laws is the appropriations process. This "power of the purse" was bestowed on Congress by the Constitution, which forbade the use of Treasury funds unless appropriated by law; it has become one of the most important tools of the legislature. Since 1946, congressional permission to spend public money has consisted of (1) the various committees of Congress authorizing the creation of new policies and setting ceilings on expenditures for those policies, and (2) the appropriations committees and subcommittees actually appropriating funds from the United States Treasury. Thus, for most programs, there are at least four oversight points in the legislative structure: the authorizing and appropriating committees of both the House and the Senate. (Of course, the actual process, as we shall see, is much more convoluted, and many programs, once begun, do not need to be reauthorized.)

Once again, the time and information demands upon Congress often result in only sporadic oversight of the bureaucracy through the appropriations process. A threatened cut in funding can be an effective stick to wave over the heads of wayward administrators, but with shorter budget authorization periods and an increased number of subcommittees whose sole task is to oversee the bureaucracy, congressional oversight is probably becoming a larger source of anxiety for bureaucrats.

Congress has considered adopting a legislating technique that would require only occasional oversight of the bureaucracy. **Sunset laws**, begun in Colorado in 1976, authorize government programs for limited terms (usually from five to ten years), after which they must be specifically and deliberately reauthorized by the legislature. While the idea of having bureaucrats justify the continuation of their programs is attractive, some members of Congress are concerned about the additional burden that sunset laws would place on their ability to consider new policies.

Still another device for institutionalizing legislative oversight was the **legislative veto,** which was declared unconstitutional by the Supreme Court in

sunset laws:
Legislation requiring government agencies to be periodically reviewed and reauthorized or face automatic abolition.

legislative veto: A provision in a bill that allowed one or both chambers of Congress to overturn an action by an executive or independent agency; it was ruled unconstitutional in 1983.

1983. Under the legislative veto, by provision in a bill, either congressional chamber, or even a committee of the House or Senate, was allowed to veto a proposal by the president or an agency within sixty or ninety days. The legislative veto was especially attractive to those who were concerned with the growing power of the executive or the bureaucracy. However, it was held to violate the constitutional principle of separation of powers because it circumvented the constitutional scheme required for legislative enactment, which includes passage by both houses and an opportunity for presidential veto. As a result of the Supreme Court's action, legislative veto provisions in more than two hundred statutes (but not the remainder of the laws of which they were a part) became unconstitutional.

The control that Congress can exercise over executive or agency actions in carrying out its will is limited by the high costs involved in oversight. Since the members of Congress are pressed for time in carrying out their legislative tasks, they have relatively few remaining resources (primarily time) with which to review administrative actions. The opportunity for effective oversight is reduced even further by the demands of the third major task of members of Congress: representing their constituents.

Representation Tasks

If legislating and oversight are the primary tasks of members of Congress, then representation is their primary responsibility. Members of Congress are elected to be the voice of the people in government, serving their interests and reflecting their wishes. Thus, representation can be viewed as a principle that guides all of the other tasks of Congress. But one of the most enduring questions about representative government is how to apply that principle to the day-to-day activities of legislating, investigating, overseeing, and so on.

In the eighteenth century, the English philosopher Edmund Burke proposed that elected representatives follow their own judgment on policy questions. Presumably, legislators would be more knowledgeable about public issues, and perhaps even wiser, than people in other occupations, so the nation would benefit by allowing members of a legislature to vote according to their understanding of problems. At each election, voters would have the opportunity to remove those legislators who had violated their trust; thus, the Burkean representatives were called *trustees*.

Another way to view representation is to think of elected officials as *agents* of the people, voting according to their demands and responding to their preferences. A congressional representative from a rural district with a strong stake in agricultural policy would vote in favor of the interests of farmers, even if he or she suspected that a policy might not be in the best interest of the entire nation. According to this point of view, the political system properly rewards representatives who respond to electoral incentives to allocate resources to particular groups.

Of course, there are problems with applying both of these ideal roles. Given the threat of electoral removal, few legislators will always vote according to their own conscience and ignore the demands of constituents. Yet, no legislator can hope to exactly know the views of his or her constituents on all pending legislation. In practice, members of Congress generally apply the representative principle both as trustees of the people *and* as agents of their electoral constituencies.

The role a legislator assumes depends heavily on the perceived costs, benefits, and incentives of different forms of behavior. A legislator with a "safe" seat (i.e., a legislator who is confident about reelection) will worry less about electoral punishment for a "wrong" vote than will a legislator from a competitive district or state. (Of course, the seat may be safe partly because the legislator was a careful agent of his or her constituents in the past.) A legislator who receives a large amount of constituent mail about a policy has a strong incentive to vote in accordance with the constituents' preference, because those voters have paid the cost of a relatively unusual action (i.e., writing to a representative) and will therefore watch the legislator's vote and impose sanctions against him or her (i.e., by supporting another candidate) if the wrong vote is cast.

It is difficult to generalize about how the representative task is carried out because of the complexity of Congress and the variety of links between legislators and their constituents. For one thing, many districts and states are heterogeneous, with mixtures of farm interests and urban interests, labor and management, liberals and conservatives. We cannot always say that a legislator who takes a prolabor stance on an issue has "been responsive" to his or her constituents, since another group (in this case, management) has *not* been gratified. Therefore, when we ask whether a legislator is being "representative," we must ask "Representative of whom?" Richard Fenno has described a congressional representative's constituency as a set of concentric circles consisting of:

1. the geographical constituency (i.e., the district)
2. the reelection constituency (i.e., the voters)
3. the primary constituency (i.e., the loyal supporters)
4. the personal constituency (i.e., the representative's intimate advisers and friends)[7]

Because each of these groups provides different amounts of information and incentives to legislators, and because there are high transaction costs in finding compromise solutions to the demands of various constituents, the task of representation can be very complicated.

In recent years, the job of legislators has become even more complex as they have assumed an additional representative role. In Scandinavian countries, citizens can complain about mistreatment or bureaucratic intransigence to an official ombudsman, who investigates problems and negotiates solutions between the people and their government. In the United States, Congress to a large degree has accepted this task. As the only institutional link between citizens and the federal bureaucracy, members of Congress are in a position to inquire about missing social security checks, contemplated agency actions, and many other problems that develop in their districts or states. These tasks are described by the term **casework.**

Because Congress creates and sustains the bureaucracy, some people have suggested that it has deliberately allowed the bureaucracy to become too large and inaccessible to individual citizens, and that it reaps rewards when grateful voters remember the legislator who interceded with the bureaucracy.[8] Surveys of voters show that most people expect their representative or senator to intercede for them. Congress has responded by drastically increasing its staff and the number of offices across the nation at which citizens can appeal for help. Constituency service has become a major part of the legislator's job.

Finally, the representative principle is often invoked by legislators to explain why they try so diligently to maximize the amount of federal funds spent in their districts and states. **Pork-barrel** projects are a common phenomenon in Congress as members propose public-works projects (e.g., dams, highways, and federal buildings) that will benefit their constituents. In order to distribute appropriations to the voters at home, each legislator has an incentive to support the attempts by other legislators to do the same; pork-barrel projects therefore usually have a good chance of passing Congress. It is not an accident that a side effect of assuring that the district or state gets at least one dollar in expenditures for each dollar sent to Washington is that the member of Congress also obtains the gratitude of many voters.

casework: Services that members of Congress perform for individual constituents, such as assisting them with bureaucratic procedures.

pork barrel: Legislation that selectively provides benefits to the constituency of a particular member of Congress.

Norris Dam, on the Clinch River in east Tennessee, was built during the 1930s by the Tennessee Valley Authority. Although such projects control floods and generate electric power, they also serve pork-barrel purposes. (Tennessee Valley Authority)

Congressional Incentives

Given the variety of tasks that members of Congress are expected to perform, we can identify many incentives that explain congressional behavior. It is difficult to attribute a legislator's vote to a particular incentive because motives are often obscure or mixed. For example, unless both a member of Congress and his or her constituents have clearly declared their positions on a policy matter, it is a major challenge to ascribe a legislator's vote to either personal conscience or electoral pressure. Many critics of American politics forget that a vote for a bill that aids a large campaign contributor is not necessarily a "bought vote." Similarly, a pork-barrel project might be objectively justifiable if a legislator's district has high unemployment or has the appropriate natural resources for a needed dam, canal, and so on.

Congressional scholars have described several major incentives that can explain various aspects of congressional behavior.[9] The first, *reelection*, is the most pervasive, because it is the prerequisite for continuing to pursue all other goals. According to David Mayhew, the simple assumption that "Congressmen are single-minded seekers of re-election" explains a large percentage of what legislators do.[10] Many aspects of congressional voting patterns, behavior in committee hearings, and contact with constituents and lobbyists are related to this goal. For example, the wide use of the **franking privilege,** by which senators and representatives mail newsletters and other "official" materials at taxpayers' expense, clearly serves the reelection goal. (The 1982 cost to taxpayers for mailings by senators was $48 million for 234 million pieces of mail—or an average of three pieces for every household in the United States.) And, as mentioned in Chapter 5, the high cost of modern congressional elections means that some members of Congress have spent more than half of their spare time simply trying to retire their campaign debts, which in 1982 sometimes exceeded $500,000. Many members of Congress also desire to campaign for the presidency, and this goal can affect both their votes and their attendance records. Yet, we have seen that the continual struggle for electoral success is not a pathological accident in American politics; it is a means by which the people can control their government.

Another incentive follows directly from the legislative task: members of Congress often have an interest in particular policy problems; thus, *policymaking* is also one of their major goals. There are many interest groups and other sources of pressure to encourage those legislators who might not be personally motivated to do anything but run for reelection to take their policymaking duties seriously. Policymaking contributes to a third incentive: the benefit from maintaining the prestige of Congress. Many of the advantages and rewards that cause individuals to become candidates for congressional office depend on the vitality and strength of Congress within the American political system. Within the congressional system, a fourth incentive—status within the House or Senate—also operates. A position of leadership or the respect of colleagues is helpful in obtaining electoral victories and the passage of pet legislation.

Finally, it must be recognized that very few people hope to become rich as

franking privilege: Privilege that allows members of Congress to send material through the mail without paying postage costs.

representatives or senators. Many candidates for Congress must forsake the opportunity to make far more than their congressional salaries: in mid-1984, members of the House and Senate were paid $72,200. Most members make additional money through speaking fees; although these sums are restricted in the House and Senate to 30 percent of a member's salary, they have grown from a total of about $2.3 million in 1980 to $4.4 million in 1982. In 1983, there were twenty-two millionaires in the Senate, twenty-five in the House of Representatives, two in the Supreme Court, and one in the White House, but most were wealthy before taking office. Thus, in general, campaigns for Congress cannot be attributed to the incentive of windfall wealth. In the next section, as we discuss the structure and organization of the congressional process, the importance of institutional maintenance and internal prestige incentives will become clearer.

All of these tasks and incentives involve congressional decisions that allocate resources or rights among citizens and groups. In Chapter 3, we discussed the functions of interest groups as they attempt to affect these decisions. Because most members of Congress respond to more than one type of incentive (i.e., they generally want to do more than simply be reelected), lobbyists often find it difficult to sway congressional votes, despite large campaign contributions. The most important point to draw from this discussion of congressional tasks and incentives is that we should not oversimplify the behavior of legislators as they make decisions.

THE MANAGEMENT OF THE CONGRESSIONAL PROCESS

Like other organizations, Congress has developed a structure with formal rules, fixed roles for its members, and a hierarchy of tasks and responsibilities. Also like many other organizations, however, Congress cannot be described solely in terms of the formal rules and processes it uses. Prodded by certain problems (e.g., the high cost of organization, transactions, and information) and incentives (e.g., avoiding responsibility for unpleasant but necessary decisions), members of Congress have developed many informal rules and modes of behavior. In this section, we will consider the control of Congress by its parties and leaders and by the other groups that congressional representatives have formed to aid the legislative process.

The fundamental aim of an organization is to arrange human behavior in constructive ways. Congressional organization requires a reduction in information and transaction costs, control of the hierarchy of roles and tasks, the provision of incentives for members to fulfill their responsibilities to the legislature, and the allocation of resources (e.g., pork-barrel projects and the perquisites of office). Only a large, permanent, and reasonably fair mechanism could survive the challenge of this set of duties, and the leadership of the congressional parties has managed to do so almost since the beginning of the nation.

Party is a pervasive factor in the structure and processes of Congress. Members are elected as partisans (although, as we have seen in Chapter 4, there are many different applications of that term), and this is an important basis for committee assignment, seniority, staff allocations, and voting. The role of party and leadership is especially critical in the House of Representatives, where the large number of members makes some form of structured cooperation essential. We will see that the committee system has the effect of decentralizing power and authority in the House and the Senate; the party system holds all of the pieces together.

However, we should point out an important general characteristic of congressional parties and leadership. For an organizing principle to be effective, there must be a reason for the individual members of the organization to cooperate, especially if it means occasionally yielding a personal gain to the collective purpose. Congressional parties and their leaders cannot deny a member his or her seat except in the extreme cases of criminal or blatantly unethical behavior. They can, however, remove members from desired committee assignments; Texas Democrat Phil Gramm switched to the Republican party in 1983 after being removed from the important House Budget Committee for allegedly sharing Democratic strategies with the Republican White House—or "quarterbacking in both huddles." The main tool of congressional leaders is not force or threats. In both chambers, the role of leaders is to facilitate bargains, form coalitions, and "keep the peace within the family." Because the emphasis is on cooperation and bargaining, no congressional leader has ever had absolute power over either the House or the Senate, although several have been extremely powerful (e.g., Speaker Joseph Cannon from 1903 to 1911 in the House, and Senate majority leader Lyndon Johnson from 1955 to 1961).

Executive-Branch Leadership

One potentially strong leader of Congress is the president. As one of only two nationally elected public officials, the president is the most visible and influential person in Washington, and much of Congress's information about national problems and policies is provided by, and filtered through, the executive branch. In addition, the Constitution gives the president several responsibilities that relate to the legislative process. The president can propose or veto legislation. Although Congress was outraged when Abraham Lincoln submitted drafts of bills during the Civil War, it has been generally receptive to presidential legislative initiatives since Franklin Roosevelt introduced emergency anti-Depression policies in 1933. The threat of a presidential veto often causes members of Congress to bend to the president's will.

There are severe constraints on the power of the president as a leader of Congress, however. The legislature jealously guards most of its constitutional prerogatives under the flag of separation of powers, and presidents find that even congressional representatives who belong to their party often go their own way. Nevertheless, presidents do exercise significant leadership of Congress by structuring its agenda and by mobilizing public and interest-group pressure. When the president claims prime television time for a press conference or a speech, he is exerting influence that members of Congress cannot match.

The vice president is the only other nationally elected public official to whom the Constitution also gives some legislative leadership powers. Although the vice president is the presiding officer (i.e., president) of the Senate, most vice presidents are rarely present in the chamber, and they usually play a minor role in Senate affairs; for example, the vice president votes only in the case of a tie. The Senate elects a **president pro tempore** (usually the most senior member of the majority party) to preside in the vice president's absence. Occasionally, vice presidents do exercise some leadership powers. For example, in 1975, Nelson Rockefeller actively participated in a trimming of the Senate filibuster rule by refusing to allow a proponent of the filibuster to delay a vote. Yet, without many formal responsibilities, the vice president is something of an alien in Congress. In addition, the vice president may be a member of the minority party, which further reduces his or her influence.

Leadership Within Congress

For effective and continuous leadership, we must look to the members of each chamber. Republicans and Democrats have designated individuals to organize and lead the House and Senate, and they have formed groups to facilitate the communications between leaders and the rank and file. Other than the vice president and the president pro tempore of the Senate, only one officer of Congress—the **Speaker of the House** of Representatives—is mentioned in the Constitution. All other leadership positions and groups in Congress have evolved in response to the needs of the institution.

The House votes at the beginning of each two-year Congress for a Speaker of the House. Both parties nominate candidates, but since the members vote on a strict party-line basis, the Speaker is the choice of the majority party, and he or she will remain in that position as long as the party balance in the House allows. Although in the past, the process of selecting a Speaker was often difficult (in 1849, for example, the chore required three weeks), in recent years it has been relatively straightforward.

During the late nineteenth century, the minority party in the House found numerous ways to obstruct the legislative process, and largely in response, the majority party expanded the powers of House Speakers. By the turn of the century, the majority party controlled the House, and the Speaker controlled the majority party. As "czar" of the House, the Speaker appointed committee members, chaired the Rules Committee (which could limit debate and amendments to bills), and controlled the floor agenda. The seniority system was weak, so those representatives who opposed the Speaker risked losing their privileges (e.g., chairmanship of a committee), and the rules of the House allowed Speakers to bypass uncooperative members. Between 1909 and 1911,

president pro tempore: The presiding officer of the Senate when the vice president is absent.

Speaker of the House: The presiding officer and usually the most powerful member of the House of Representatives.

the House membership revolted against the power of Speaker Joe Cannon, replacing his privileges with more decentralized rule and a focus on bargaining rather than coercion. To effectively lead the House of Representatives today, a Speaker must be a communications center, a strategist, a partisan, and, when the prestige of the entire House is at stake, a nonpartisan; in the words of a former representative, Richard Bolling, "the Speaker is both coach and quarterback."

The formal function of the Speaker is to preside over the House of Representatives by organizing its agenda, by supervising floor debate (e.g., putting questions to a vote, ruling on points of order, and recognizing members who wish to speak), and by managing committee action (e.g., referring bills to committees and appointing members to select and conference committees). The informal powers of the Speaker are also crucial to his success in office. Using his personal influence, the Speaker attempts to shape his party's policy by controlling information and by arranging coalitions of members. For example, Speaker Thomas P. ("Tip") O'Neill responded to the movement toward increased participation of all members by making use of "task forces" and often appointing junior members to chair them; these ad hoc groups oversee the passage of particular bills.

majority leader: The leader and chief strategist of the majority party in a legislature; for example, the Senate and the House of Representatives each have a majority leader.

minority leader: The leader of the minority party in a legislature.

The Speaker is expected, at least on critical matters, to put the interest of the House above that of his party. While he remains the principal representative of the majority party, much of the party organizing, and most organizing for the minority party, is performed by the *floor leaders*. The **majority** and **minority leaders** marshal their troops, plot strategy, arrange bargains and partisan coalitions, and generally act as clearinghouses for information. Because the floor leaders do not have many formal powers, they rely primarily on their organizational and persuasive skills to broker support for their parties' programs.

Floor leaders are particularly important in the Senate. Because the vice president and president pro tem do not have much influence in the Senate, that chamber has no formal counterpart to the Speaker of the House. The majority leader of the Senate therefore assumes many of the roles of the House Speaker and the House majority leader in forging coalitions and plotting strategy. Furthermore, because the formal procedures of the Senate are more lax than those of the House, there is usually more room for the Senate majority leader to maneuver. The Senate majority leader has no formal powers other than the referral of bills to committees. Therefore, he must rely heavily on his persuasive abilities and his parliamentary skills.

whip: An assistant floor leader of the majority or minority party in the House or Senate who serves as a communications link between party leaders and party members.

The majority and minority leaders in each chamber are assisted by the party **whips.** Except for the House Democratic whips, who are picked by their floor leader, whips are chosen by the party caucuses; their primary function is to provide two-way communication between the party leadership and members. The whips and their assistants are adept at polling their colleagues on upcoming votes so that the floor leaders will know the chances of success and the best strategies for shaping winning coalitions. They also mobilize the rank and file on important questions by explaining the party's position and assuring that they cast their votes when a motion is before the House or Senate. Thus the whips, together with the floor leaders, are responsible for reducing transaction costs for members of their party.

Organizations Within Congress

Finally, there are a number of formal and informal congressional groups that have been created to coordinate the parties in Congress, as well as groups of representatives with broader or more narrow common interests. The House Democratic Study Group (DSG) was formed in 1959 by primarily liberal, junior Democrats who were opposed to their conservative southern brethren. Today, about two-thirds of House Democrats belong to the DSG, which has its own staff, dues, and fund-raising office. Its staff performs research on legislative proposals, and it played a central role in the reforms of the 1970s that weakened the seniority system and strengthened the Democratic party caucus.

The House Democratic caucus has become much more important in recent years, with increased influence over committee chairmanships, the jurisdiction and number of subcommittees, and the membership of the powerful Rules Committee. The net effect of the changes has been to increase the power of the Speaker and other party leaders. The nearest Republican counterpart in the House to the Democratic caucus is its Committee on Committees, which approves committee assignments for Republicans but has been far less powerful than the Democratic organization.

In the Senate, the informal norms of behavior have made the roles of the Democratic and Republican organizations less essential. In addition, because senators serve broader constituencies, they are less likely to promote single issues; thus, senators may face lower transaction costs as compromises are arranged. Hence, the Senate Democratic organizations, like their Republican counterparts, tend to be less important than the House party organizations.

Congress also has additional groups and personnel to aid the legislative process. Several of these are permanent institutions. For example:

1. The *General Accounting Office,* created in 1921 to review the expenditure of funds by the executive, now also assesses the effectiveness of proposed and existing legislation.
2. The *Library of Congress* and its Congressional Research Service are responsible for legislative bookkeeping and research on public issues.
3. The *Office of Technology Assessment* was formed in 1972 to provide congressional committees with analyses of the impacts of congressional activities relating to science and technology policies.
4. The *Congressional Budget Office* was created in 1974 to analyze the president's economic forecasts and proposed congressional responses to the executive's budget requests.

In addition, legislators have overcome many ideological and partisan differences in response to constituent pressure and crises (e.g., New York City's fiscal problems in the 1970s) by creating informal groups that focus on particular issues. Before 1969, there were only three informal caucuses in Congress; however, by the early 1980s, there were more than sixty groups such as the Congressional Black Caucus, the Congresswomen's Caucus, the Steel Caucus (including more than one hundred and seventy members from thirty-seven states), the Congressional Mushroom Caucus, and the Congressional Roller and Ballbearing Coalition. Many of these groups have their own staff, usually financed by fund-raising dinners, which circulates information and performs legislative research. The growth of these groups is an indicator of the legislators' increasing need to compete with the information-gathering hordes of the executive branch.

Similarly, the personal and committee staffs of Congress grew from less than ten thousand people in 1972 to nearly twice that number in 1980. Congressional staffers, who tend to be young and well-educated, assist in legislative and constituency service chores. However, the growth in the number of staffers has been criticized because of what some see as their increasing influence over public policy. In fact, some senators and representatives have complained that an abundance of energetic, bright staffers has actually exacerbated their workload problems, because more issues are unearthed for which hearings and meetings must be held. This experience serves the staffers well: in 1980, about sixty members of Congress had at one time been someone else's staff assistant.

The committee and party systems of the United States Congress are closely intertwined; one cannot be understood without the other. The House and Senate are organized by a set of interlocking relationships among party leaders that makes it impossible to always locate legislative sources of power. Nevertheless, a system has developed in Congress that reduces the problems of organization, information, and transaction costs, while allowing members of Congress to pursue their incentives. As we will see, much of the legislative process takes place in committees.

HOW A BILL BECOMES LAW

The first step in the passage of legislation in Congress is the introduction of a bill in the House or the Senate. A bill can begin in the executive branch, with an interest group, an individual citizen, or with a member of Congress; whatever the source, however, it must be introduced by a senator or representative. In the House of Representatives, bills are introduced by being dropped in the *hopper* (i.e., a box at the front of the chamber) or by being handed to a clerk, after which they are numbered, with an "HR" prefix, and printed. In the Senate, the process begins by presenting a bill to a clerk of the presiding officer or by a senator introducing a bill on the floor, after which it is also

Tuesday, February 28, 1984

Daily Digest

HIGHLIGHTS

Senate passed Credit Card legislation.

Senate

Chamber Action

Routine Proceedings, pages S1825–S1915

Measures Introduced: Eleven bills and one resolution were introduced, as follows: S. 2355–2365, and S.J. Res. 248.   **Page S1890**

Measures Passed:

Price Differences for Credit Cards: Senate passed S. 2336, permitting price differences with respect to credit card sales transactions, after taking action on amendments proposed thereto, as follows: **Page S1876**

Adopted:

D'Amato Amendment No. 2752, providing that, within three years of the effective date of the Act, any State may enact a prohibition of or additional limitation upon any transaction involving a difference in price which is otherwise subject to the provisions of section 167 or section 171 of the Act.   **Page S1886**

Rejected:

By 22 yeas to 66 nays (Vote No. 19), D'Amato Amendment No. 2751, to make permanent the moratorium prohibiting credit card surcharges.   **Page S1880**

Price Differences for Credit Cards: Senate passed H.R. 4278, permitting the price differences with respect to credit card sales transactions, after striking all after the enacting clause and inserting in lieu thereof the text of S. 2336, Senate companion measure, as amended and passed earlier.   **Page S1886**

Temporary Extension of Credit Card Surcharge Prohibition: By unanimous vote of 84 yeas (Vote No. 20), Senate passed S. 2335, providing a temporary extension of the credit card surcharge prohibition.   **Page S1887**

Export Administration Act Amendments: Senate continued consideration of S. 979, to amend and reauthorize the Export Administration Act, with a committee amendment in the nature of a substitute, taking action on further amendments proposed thereto, as follows: **Page S1850**

Adopted:

Humphrey modified Amendment No. 2747, restricting further the export or retransfer of certain nuclear components and the export of nuclear technology.   **Page S1850**

Rejected:

By 38 yeas to 55 nays (Vote No. 18), McClure Amendment No. 2749 (to Humphrey modified Amendment No. 2747), in the nature of a substitute.   **Page S1861**

Senate will continue consideration of the bill and amendments proposed thereto on Wednesday, February 29.

Appointments by the Vice President: The Presiding Officer, on behalf of the Vice President, pursuant to 22 U.S.C. 276(d)–276(g), as amended, appointed Senator Grassley as a member of the Senate Delegation to the Canada-United States Interparliamentary Group during the 2nd Session of the 98th Congress, to be held in Puerto Rico, on March 8–12, 1984.   **Page S1888**

Message From the President: Senate received a message from the President transmitting the annual report relating to developments during 1982 in the administration of the Automotive Products Trade Act, which was referred to the Committee on Finance. (PM-120)   **Page S1888**

Nominations Received: Senate received routine lists of Army, Navy, Air Force, and Coast Guard nominations.   **Page S1915**

Messages From the President:	**Page S1888**
Messages From the House:	**Page S1888**
Communications:	**Page S1888**
Statements on Introduced Bills:	**Page S1890**
Amendments Submitted:	**Page S1904**
Notices of Hearings:	**Page S1905**
Additional Statements:	**Page S1905**

Record Votes: Three record votes were taken today. (Total—20)   **Pages S1874, S1886, S1887**

Recess: Senate convened at 11 a.m., and recessed at 7:26 p.m., until 11 a.m., on Wednesday, February 29, 1984. (For Senate's program, see the remarks of Senator Baker in today's Record on page S1914.)

259

origination clause:
Constitutional clause requiring that all revenue-raising (i.e., taxation) bills originate in the House of Representatives.

numbered, with an "S" prefix, and printed. The only limitation on the introduction of bills in Congress is found in Article I, Section 7: "All Bills for raising Revenue shall originate in the House of Representatives: but the Senate may propose or concur with Amendments as on other Bills." In other words, the **origination clause** requires that tax bills be considered first by the House, then by the Senate, although amendments to revenue laws already enacted may be introduced first in either chamber.

The Committee System

After a bill is introduced, it is referred to one of the committees of the chamber in which it was introduced. The House and the Senate each have rules that govern the referral of bills to committees. In the House, there are about two hundred and twenty classifications of measures that are used to determine which committee considers what bill. For example, the House Judiciary Committee has jurisdiction over about twenty categories of bills, including constitutional amendments, antitrust, civil liberties, patents, and so on. The Senate has about two hundred classifications. In the House, most referrals are handled routinely by the Speaker with the aid of the *parliamentarian,* who is consulted on formal rules of the House; in the Senate, by the president of the Senate, who is also vice president of the United States, or its presiding officer. However, when bills overlap jurisdiction, the assignment to a committee becomes more important. The decision in the Senate to send the 1964 Civil Rights Bill to the Commerce Committee (then chaired by a senator from the state of Washington) rather than the Judiciary Committee (then chaired by a Mississippian) was crucial to its passage. Another example of overlapping jurisdiction is the question of the sale of grain to the Soviet Union, which can be referred to the Agriculture Committee, to the Foreign Relations Committee, or to both.

After its referral, a bill enters the most important stage of the entire congressional process. Unlike the national legislatures in most countries, in the United States Congress, most of the life-or-death decisions about legislation occur in committees rather than on the floor of the legislature. As Woodrow Wilson wrote in *Congressional Government* in 1885, "Congress in session is Congress on public exhibition, whilst Congress in its committee-rooms is Congress at work."

The primary function of the congressional committee system is *specialization.* Given the enormous range of subjects that Congress must consider, its division into small, specialized units and the resulting reduction of information costs are essential. Even if all one hundred senators or the four hundred and thirty-five members of the House could somehow manage to hear debate on the many thousands of bills proposed on the floor of their chambers, they do not have the expertise to judge each bill accurately. Therefore, in the House and the Senate, proposed legislation is delegated to specialized committees.

THE PROBLEM OF JURISDICTION

The system of classification which the House of Representatives and the Senate use to assign bills to committees for initial consideration is based on the substance of each bill. The classification procedures usually work fairly well, but when a novel policy problem comes along, Congress may be ill prepared.

One important example is water policy. Since 1950, the nation's water use doubled to 450 billion gallons per day. The total waterflow in America's rivers and aquifers (underground water) is estimated to be approximately 1,400 billion gallons per day. But President Carter's Water Resource Council estimated that by the year 2000, one-fifth of the nation could be facing water shortages. Groundwater is rapidly being polluted by pesticides and other toxic substances that percolate down through the soil, and the removal of fresh water from coastal aquifers is allowing salty ocean water to invade the nation's usable water supply. The council also found that about 80 percent of all water currently used is devoted to farm irrigation. By 2020, they estimated, as much as 63 percent of the land that was being irrigated in 1975 may have to be removed from crop production because of water shortages. In other words, the problem is much more serious than most Americans realize.

Can we expect Congress to take the lead in devising effective water-resource policies? Probably not. As the following list indicates, there are so many committees and subcommittees in the House and the Senate with jurisdiction over water-resource issues that it would be difficult for a policy entrepreneur to lay claim to the topic and get the ball rolling.

House Committees and Subcommittees

Agriculture
    Conservation, Credit, and Rural Development
Appropriations
    Energy and Water Development
    Interior and Related Agencies

Energy and Commerce
    Energy Conservation and Power
    Health and the Environment
Government Operations
    Environment, Energy and Natural Resources
Interior and Insular Affairs
    Commerce, Transportation and Tourism
    Public Lands and National Parks
    Water and Power Resources
Merchant Marine and Fisheries
    Fishers and Wildlife Conservation and the
      Environment
    Oceanography
Public Works and Transportation
    Water Resources
Science and Technology
    Natural Resources, Agriculture Research and
      Environment

Senate Committees and Subcommittees

Agriculture, Nutrition and Forestry
    Soil and Water Conservation, Forestry and
      Environment
Appropriations
    Energy and Water Development
    HUD-Independent Agencies
Energy and Natural Resources
    Energy Conservation and Supply
    Public Lands and Reserved Water
    Water and Power
Environment and Public Works
    Environmental Pollution
    Water Resources
    Toxic Substances and Environmental Oversight
    Regional and Community Development

Sources: Lawrence Mosher, "Localities Begin to Challenge Government's Water Policy 'Vacuum,'" *National Journal*, January 28, 1984, pp. 164–168; "The Well Runs Dry," *The Economist*, May 14, 1983, pp. 41–50; list from *National Journal*, January 28, 1984, p. 167.

The division of the House and Senate into committees works because there are many incentives for representatives to respect the system. After all, members of Congress are likely to be interested in some bills that are not reported to their committees; not all senators and representatives from farming areas can be on the agriculture committees. Cooperation is assured by the exercise of *sanctions* and *reciprocity.* Congressional leaders can refuse to support the requests of uncooperative representatives, and the member who fails to respect the system of divided jurisdiction and the orderly advance of bills will find his or her favorite proposals being sidetracked or killed. Thus, members of Congress bow to the expertise of members of specialized committees, and they expect those members to reciprocate.

The first congressional committee was established in the House on the second day of its existence in 1789. In each chamber, the committee systems have grown and contracted in response to the strains that the changing legislative workload has imposed on Congress. Most of the current system of committees was established by the Legislative Reorganization Act of 1946, which reduced the number of committees in the House and Senate (although the number of subcommittees has since proliferated), reduced overlapping jurisdictions, and spread the work more evenly among members of Congress. In 1973, the House and the Senate adopted several reforms of the committee system, including:

1. "sunshine laws," which require almost all committee action to be open to the public
2. a weakening of the House Ways and Means Committee's power to dictate the provisions of new tax laws
3. a significant increase in the independence of subcommittees in the House of Representatives
4. a weakening of the seniority system in the House

Types of Committees   There are four basic types of congressional committee: standing, select (or special), joint, and conference. The most important are the **standing committees.** They are permanent, organized by policy area, and powerful because nearly all proposed bills must clear the appropriate committee before being considered by the entire House or Senate. In Table 8-2, the twenty-two standing committees of the House and the sixteen standing committees of the Senate are listed. Of course, all of these committees have jurisdiction over a broad range of issues, so they are further subdivided into **subcommittees.** For example, the Senate Armed Services Committee includes such subcommittees as Manpower and Personnel, Arms Control, and Tactical Aircraft. Although subcommittees are not new, they have acquired more power in the last decade as the Congress has tried to increase the specialization of members and the influence of its newer members. However, the proliferation of subcommittees has threatened the carefully arranged organization of jurisdiction and has made the coordination of legislative efforts more difficult.

standing committees: Permanent committees of the Senate and the House of Representatives.

subcommittee: A division of a congressional committee, similar in structure and function to a full committee but with narrower jurisdiction.

TABLE 8-2
STANDING COMMITTEES OF THE NINETY-SEVENTH CONGRESS, 1981–1982

House of Representatives	No. Subcommittees	Senate	No. Subcommittees
Agriculture	8	Agriculture, Nutrition, and Forestry	8
Appropriations	13	Appropriations	13
Armed Services	7	Armed Services	6
Banking, Finance, and Urban Affairs	8	Banking, Housing, and Urban Affairs	7
Budget	9	Budget	–
District of Columbia	3	Commerce, Science, and Transportation	8
Education and Labor	8	Energy and Natural Resources	6
Energy and Commerce	6	Environment and Public Works	6
Foreign Affairs	8	Finance	9
Government Operations	7	Foreign Relations	7
House Administration	5	Governmental Affairs	8
Interior and Insular Affairs	6	Judiciary	9
Judiciary	7	Labor and Human Resources	7
Merchant Marine and Fisheries	5	Rules and Administration	–
Post Office and Civil Service	7	Small Business	8
Public Works and Transportation	6	Veterans' Affairs	–
Rules	2		
Science and Technology	7		
Small Business	6		
Standards of Official Conduct	–		
Veterans' Affairs	5		
Ways and Means	6		

There are also special or **select committees** in the House and the Senate that are intended to study particular problems. For example, the House of Representatives has select committees on Aging, Intelligence (as in Central Intelligence Agency), and Narcotics Abuse and Control; the Senate has special, or select committees on Aging, Ethics, Intelligence, and Small Business. Because select committees cannot report new legislation to the floor of their parent chambers, they have relatively little direct influence on policy, although they often generate publicity for certain issues.

Congress also has **joint committees** composed of both senators and representatives. The Ninety-Seventh Congress (1981–1982) included four joint committees: Economic, Library, Printing, and Taxation. Because of the desire of each chamber to guard its prerogatives, joint committees generally do not generate much cooperation on important issues. One important exception was the Joint Committee on Atomic Energy (1946–1974), which largely determined the course of the United States civilian nuclear energy program for much of the post-World War II era.

select committee: A legislative committee, created to study a particular, often temporary, problem, but which is unable to report new legislation for consideration.

joint committee: A permanent congressional committee comprised of members of both the Senate and the House of Representatives.

conference committee: An ad hoc joint committee in Congress set up to resolve the differences between House and Senate versions of a bill.

The fourth major type of congressional committee is **conference committees.** These are temporary committees created to resolve the differences between the House and Senate versions of similar legislation. The function of these committees will be examined after a discussion of how the committee system works.

How Committees Work   To understand the operation of this most crucial part of the congressional system, it is necessary to consider (1) the membership and leadership of committees, (2) the responsibilities and operations of committees, and (3) what happens when a committee completes work on a bill.

As in any organization, the congressional committee requires a leader who can assure the generally smooth operation of the organization. Chairpersons of committees can usually decide whether, when, and for how long to hold hearings on bills that have been referred to their committees. They may also preside over meetings, decide on the number and organization of subcommittees, hire staff, recommend members of conference committees, and often manage bills on the floor of the parent chamber. Committee chairpersons are chosen from among the committee members belonging to the party holding a majority of seats in the appropriate chambers. Thus, if the Republicans outnumber the Democrats in the Senate, then all Senate committees will be chaired by Republicans; all committees in the House will be chaired by Democrats if that party controls the House. Subcommittees are also chaired by members of the majority party. The spokesperson for the minority party in each committee is called the *ranking member* and is usually the most senior minority committee member.

With these responsibilities, the committee chairperson has often had great power over committee affairs. Some have used that power to kill other committee members' legislation, with which they personally disagreed, by refusing to allow the committee to consider, debate, vote, or report on it to the parent chamber. Most, however, have respected the collegiality that unifies and strengthens a committee when it presents recommendations to the House or Senate. This is especially true in the Senate, where members tend to treat one another as more equal than in the House.

Not surprisingly, committee chairmanships are usually strongly coveted. But not all legislators have the opportunity to lead a committee. Beginning early in the twentieth century, the traditional method for selecting chairpersons has been **seniority:** the member of a committee with the most consecutive years on that committee was designated to chair. A tenacious practice rather than a formal rule, the seniority system gave leadership responsibilities to members with lengthy experience, if not great wisdom, by automatically allocating power and thereby avoiding untidy scrambles for it.

For most of this century, the seniority system was suspended only when members were stripped of the privileges of lengthy tenure for having supported the other party's presidential candidate or for unethical behavior. A member who represented a safe district or state could become a committee chairperson

seniority: A traditional congressional procedure of awarding benefits, such as committee chairmanships, on the basis of duration of uninterrupted service in Congress or on the committee.

and remain in that position for decades. During most of this century, southern Democrats held a disproportionate share of committee chairs in Congress because the South was a one-party (Democratic) region. The strongest criticism of the seniority system was that it introduced a systematic ideological bias into the legislative process, since most southern committee chairpersons were conservative.

During the 1970s, however, the effect of the seniority system changed. First, many southern states and districts ceased to be "safe" as Republicans became effective challengers in the region. Even more significant were reforms in the committee system agreed upon by congressional Democrats and Republicans. In 1971, both parties in the House agreed that seniority would not be the only criterion in naming committee leaders. While the seniority system is still an important guiding principle, the congressional parties are now more responsive to the wishes of the membership.

The membership of committees is also a major aspect of the legislative process and is of great concern to legislators. Members strive to be placed on the committees that are the most influential or of greatest relevance to their constituents. Some committees are so powerful that they are exclusive: in the House, members of the committees on Appropriations, Rules, and Ways and Means are not allowed to serve on any other committees, and it is a privilege that they gladly yield. Other legislators find benefits from serving on other committees. Members from rural districts or states usually seek service on the agriculture committees, while members with urban, and therefore strongly unionized, districts often request assignment to the House Education and Labor Committee or the Senate Human Resources (formerly Labor and Public Welfare) Committee. Committee assignments can strongly affect the ability of a member to pursue and achieve policymaking, status, and reelection goals. Thus, in the 1980s, seats on the House Energy and Commerce Committee are coveted because of its wide jurisdiction (e.g., over energy, pollution, telecommunctions, and health costs) and the resulting desire of lobbyists to contribute to its members.

At the beginning of each new Congress, new members must be assigned to committees, and previous members can request transfers. Assignments are based on several factors. Most important is party, because each committee has precise numbers of Republican and Democratic slots, roughly based on the percentage of seats held in the parent chamber by each party. Assignments are also affected by the seniority of the member, and because some balance of interests is sought on each committee, members are also appointed partly on the basis of geographic region, state, ideology, personal preference, and experience or expertise in the committee's policy areas.

The actual work of the committee consists of two major phases: hearings and votes. In our discussion of oversight, we indicated the importance of hearings for informing legislators and for transmitting congressional concerns to bureaucrats. In legislative matters, the primary purposes of a hearing are the investigation of problems, education of legislators, pacification of con-

Witnesses are sworn in before testifying at a 1982 hearing of the House Government Operations Committee's Subcommittee on the Environment on a proposal to allow an increase in the toxic-lead level in gasoline. From left are a mother and her son, who has lead poisoning; the coordinator for Lead Elimination Action in Washington, D.C.; and a professor of pediatrics. (© Art Stein, 1982/Photo Researchers, Inc.)

cerned individuals and interest groups, and grandstanding or propagandizing by legislators. Visitors can attend "open" meetings of committees and sub-committees; the Washington newspapers list the daily activities of Congress (see accompanying box). Although much useful information is presented by committee witnesses, the hearing procedure also serves as a safety valve for groups whose opposition can be blunted by granting them a chance to be heard. This may be costly and time-consuming, but it nevertheless serves to allow the legislative process to produce controversial bills. Similarly, the self-ish use of public hearings, especially those that are televised, by legislators seeking recognition is probably an unavoidable side effect of the American electoral and legislative systems.

Soon after the completion of hearings, which may continue for days and sometimes months, subcommittee members will consider the proposal. At this stage, the lobbying of Congress is usually the heaviest, because the transaction costs for interest-group representatives are lower when they can focus on a relatively small number of legislators. At a **markup session,** the subcommit-tee will consider the proposed bill, discuss changes in its wording or content, and then vote on it. The subcommittee may decide to report the bill to the full committee with a favorable recommendation, with or without amendments, or it may report the bill unfavorably and recommend that the bill not be passed. The subcommittee also may suggest that the committee *table* the bill (i.e., "lay the bill on the table"); this has the effect of postponing action indefinitely (i.e., killing the bill). If the bill has not been tabled, the full committee will

markup session: A session of a congressional committee or subcommittee at which the actual wording of a proposed bill is agreed upon.

discuss the subcommittee report. Once again, hearings may be held and the bill may be amended. The committee members then vote on the bill; they may recommend it to the parent chamber favorably (or, rarely, unfavorably or without recommendation), or they may table it. The formal reports of the subcommittee or full committee explain the purpose of the bill. They serve as resources for other legislators and, if the bill becomes law, for courts, agencies, and others who may need to decipher the legislative intent behind vague phrases in the law.

With the reporting of the bill to the House or the Senate, most of the work of the committee is completed. At this point, only about 10 percent of all proposed legislation will have survived. Thus, the committees serve the critical function of filtering out much of the legislation that might otherwise overload the capacity of the Senate or the House. For example, in the Ninety-fourth Congress (1974–1975), a total of 16,982 bills were introduced in the House of Representatives; only 985 or 5.8 percent, were reported. Because the hearings and votes in subcommittee and committee offer numerous access points for those opposed to or in favor of proposed legislation, the bill escapes to the floor only when a reasonable chance of final passage exists. By this time, the bill has acquired considerable legitimacy, an aroused constituency, and a number of congressional backers. Bills generally enter the floor with momentum.

Floor Action

In most cases, the committee phase of the legislative process ends with the reporting of the bill to the full chamber. The proportion of committee recommendations that are adopted by the parent chamber is striking. On the average, if at least 60 percent of a committee's members vote to support a bill, it has over a 90 percent chance of success on the floor; if over 80 percent of a committee's members support the bill, it is virtually certain to pass on the floor.

Congressional committees, however, do not always get their way. On particularly important or controversial legislation, Congress has a procedure for preventing defeat by an obstructive committee that refuses to report it to the floor. If a committee has not reported a bill within thirty days of its referral for committee consideration, a majority (i.e., 218) of the members of the House can sign a "discharge" petition; this forces the bill onto the floor of the House so that all of the members can vote on it. Similarly, in the Senate, a member can move to discharge a bill from committee after a "reasonable" time has passed since its referral.

Discharge petitions are seldom attempted, and a bill that is pried out of committee in this way rarely becomes law. However, the threat of a discharge may be effective, although it is impossible to know how often this tactic has worked.

"TODAY IN CONGRESS": A CALENDAR OF COMMITTEE MEETINGS, APRIL 23, 1983

Senate

Meets at 2 P.M.
Committees:

Appropriations—9:30 A.M. Open. Commerce, justice, state, judiciary sub. FY '84 budget hearings for the SBA. S-146 Capitol

Appropriations—2 P.M. Open. D.C. sub. FY '84 budget hearings for the Dept. of Human Services; housing and community devl.; corp. counsel, and Family Division of D.C. Courts. 192 Dirksen Office Building.

Appropriations—2 P.M. Open. Interior subc. FY '84 budget hearings for the ofc. of the secy. of the interior and ofc. of the solicitor. 138 DOB.

Appropriations—10 A.M. Open. Transportation sub. FY '84 budget hearings for programs under comte's jurisdiction. 124 DOB.

Armed Services—2 P.M. Open and Closed. Preparedness sub. Air Force readiness, operation, and maintenance. 222 Russell Office Building.

Armed Services—8 A.M. and 2 P.M. Open and closed. Strategic and theater nuclear forces sub. To hold open hearings on the MX. 2 P.M. To hold open-closed hearings on space defense. 253 ROB.

Banking, Housing, and Urban Affairs—9:30 A.M. Open. Oversight hearings on the competitive structure and other conditions within the domestic financial services industry. 538 DOB.

Energy and Natural Resources—10 A.M. Open. Mark-up pending calendar business (to include natural gas legislation). 366 DOB.

Foreign Relations—9:45 A.M. and 3:30 P.M. Open. Mark-up pending calendar business. 3:30 P.M. To hold hearings on the nomination of Helene A. Von Damm, of N.J., to be Ambassador to Austria. 419 DOB.

Governmental Affairs—10 A.M. Open. Trade reorganization legislation. 342 DOB.

Judiciary—10:30 A.M. Open. Pending comte. business. 226 DOB.

Labor and Human Resources—9:30 A.M. Open. S.771, the Health Promotion and Disease Prevention Amendments of 1983. 430 DOB.

Democratic Policy—Noon. Closed. Regular luncheon meeting. S-211 Cap.

Republican Policy—12:30 P.M. Closed. Regular luncheon meeting. S-207 Cap.

House

Meets at noon.
Committees:

Agriculture—10 A.M. Open. Conserv., credit & rural develop. sub. on misc. Texas & La. watershed projects. 1302 Longworth House Office Building.

Appropriations—9:30 A.M. Open (may close). Defense sub. On FY '83 supplemental. Defense Sec. Weinberger. H-140 Capitol.

Appropriations—2 P.M. Open. Foreign operations subc. On El Salvador. 2362 Rayburn House Office Building.

Appropriations—9:30 A.M. Open. Interior sub. on instit. and museum services; Natl. Endowment for the Arts. B-308 RHOB.

Appropriations—10 A.M. Open. Labor-HHS & edu. sub. On Natl. instit. on Aging; Natl. Instit. on Dental Res.; John Fogarty Intl. Center. 2358 RHOB.

Appropriations—9:45 A.M. Open. Legis. sub. on FY '83 suppl. (including W. Front of Capitol). H-302 Cap.

Appropriations—10 A.M. Open. Transportation sub. 2358 RHOB.

Appropriations—2 P.M. Open. Treas., postal serv. sub. On adv. comte. on federal pay. H-164 Cap.

Armed Services—9:30 A.M. Closed. Classified intelligence briefing. 2118 RHOB.

Armed Services—10:30 A.M. Open (may close). Military install. & facilities sub. Cont. on military construction auth. 1310 LHOB.

Armed Services—10:30 A.M. Open. Military personnel & comp. sub. Cont. on defense auth.: compensation issues. 2216 RHOB.

Armed Services—10:30 A.M. Closed. Procure. & military nuclear systems sub. Cont. on defense auth.: NATO conventional capability improvement initiatives. 2118 RHOB.

Armed Services—10:30 A.M. Open (may close). Readiness sub. On defense stock funds & readiness. 2337 RHOB.

Armed Services—10:30 A.M. Closed. Seapower sub. Mark-up shipbuilding portions of defense auth. 2212 RHOB.

Banking, Finance & Urban Affairs—9 A.M. Open. Housing & community develop. sub. Cont. mark-up housing auth. 2128 RHOB.

Banking, Finance & Urban Affairs—9:30 A.M. Open. Intl. trade, invest. & monetary policy sub. Cont. hrngs. on Intl. Monetary Fund. 2220 RHOB.

Banking, Finance & Urban Affairs—10 A.M. Open. Domestic monetary policy sub. HR1569, Amend Fed. Res. Act to implement a monetary policy which will achieve balanced full growth in the economy. 2222 RHOB.

Education & Labor—9:30 A.M. Open. Health & safety sub. Oversight hrngs. on OSHA. 2261 RHOB.

Education & Labor—2 P.M. Open. Postsecondary edu. sub. Hrng. on Instit. of Museum Services Tech. Amends. 2261 RHOB.

Education & Labor—11 A.M. Open. Sel. edu. sub. Mark-up session on Domestic Volunteer Service Amends. 2257 RHOB.

Energy & Commerce—10 A.M. Open. Mark-up resolution to cite Rita Lavelle for contempt of Congress; Energy Conserv. Daylight Savings Act; Health Res. Extension Act; HJ Res. 219, Declaring support of U.S. Govt. to bring soccer World Cup to U.S.; Congressional Adv. Comm. on Boxing Act. 2123 RHOB.

Energy & Commerce—2 P.M. Open. Telecommunications, consumer protection & finance sub. Mark-up legis. to amend the Securities Exchange Act. 2322 RHOB.

Energy & Commerce—2 P.M. Open fossil & synthetic fuels sub. Mark-up rate of fill for strategic petrol. res.; Increase aid for low income home energy assistance. 2123 RHOB.

Energy & Commerce—3 P.M. Open. Commerce, transport. & tourism sub. Mark-up Service Industries Commerce Develop. Act. 2218 RHOB.

Foreign Affairs—9:30 A.M. Open. Mark-up foreign aid & Peace Corps auth. 2172 RHOB.

Government Operations—9:30 A.M. Open. Intergovl. rel. & human res. sub. Hrng. on FDA regulation of the drug Zomax. 2154 RHOB.

Intelligence—9:30 A.M. Closed. Program & budget auth. sub. Cont. on natl. foreign intelligence program budget. (4 P.M.) Mark-up intelligence auth. H-405 Cap.

Interior & Insular Affairs—9:45 A.M. Open. Water & power res. sub. Mark-up pending legis. 2203 RHOB.

Interior & Insular Affairs—9:45 A.M. Open. Energy & environ. sub. Hrng. on status of Three Mile Island. 1324 LHOB.

Interior & Insular Affairs—9:45 A.M. Open. Public lands & natl. parks sub. Mark-up Natl. Park System Protect. & Res. Manage. Act. 340. Cannon House Office Building.

Judiciary—11 A.M. Open. Mark-up Fed. Anti-Tampering Act; Contract services for drug dependent offenders, extend auth. for Ofc. of Govt. Ethics. 2141 RHOB.

Merchant Marine & Fisheries—9:30 A.M. Open Panama Canal-OCS sub. Mark-up Panama Canal auth.; oversight hrng on OSC. 1334 LHOB.

Public Works & Transportation—10 A.M. Open. Economic develop. sub. Cont. hrngs. on short-term job creation proposals. 2253 RHOB.

Science & Technology—9:30 A.M. Open. Mark-up Energy Dept. auth. (civilian res. & develop.). 2318 RHOB.

Veterans' Affairs—9 A.M. Open. Comp., pension & insurance sub. Comp. benefits to vets exposed to herbicides. 334 CHOB.

Ways & Means—9:30 A.M. Open. Trade sub. Cont. on U.S.-Japan relations. B-318 RHOB.

Source: *Washington Post,* April 23, 1983, p. A4.

If a discharge petition is successful (or if it was unnecessary), the bill can be considered by the Senate or the House of Representatives. Not surprisingly, both chambers have developed procedures to bring some order into the way that bills are brought to the attention of all members and voted upon. Some of these devices are called *calendars*. The Senate has two such lists from which the presiding officer, in cooperation with the floor leaders and committee chairmen, calls bills for consideration by the Senate. The procedure in the House of Representatives is similar but much more complicated; the House uses a total of five calendars to arrange the schedule of various types of bills. These calendars in the House and the Senate do not remove all of the guesswork from the scheduling of debates and votes in each chamber; they do, however, provide some order, because on certain days of each month the various calendars are "privileged" orders of business with priority over other matters on the House and Senate floors. Nevertheless, the congressional leadership still has considerable discretion over the flow of legislation. For example, on the first and third Mondays of each month, the House can suspend the rules to permit any bill to be considered, regardless of its status in the legislative process.

There are other ways to avoid the "normal" legislative process in the House of Representatives. Certain committees may report some types of bills to the floor immediately, without waiting for the calendar or for rules from the Rules Committee. Examples of "privileged" reports are revenue bills from the House Ways and Means Committee and bills affecting the rules and procedures of the House. Most other bills of major consequence in the House are filtered through the Rules Committee, commonly called the "powerful Rules Committee," which, unlike other congressional committees, has a fixed ratio of members: two to one in favor of the majority party. The Rules Committee sets the terms of debate on the House floor by determining the number of hours of floor debate allocated to the bill, whether amendments may be offered (if the bill is given a "closed" rule, it cannot be amended), and whether certain parliamentary maneuvers (e.g., points of order) will be allowed. The Rules Committee is in a powerful position to determine the fate and shape of a major legislation. It acts as both an organizing body and a mechanism of control for the House leadership.

Because of its smaller size, the Senate does not need a strong Rules Committee. The legislative process in the Senate is managed not by its Rules Committee but by the majority leader. An agenda usually is decided upon by the floor leader for the majority party, often in consultation with the majority party's policy committee, the minority leader, and other senators. On routine legislation, the Senate operates under a "unanimous consent" rule, which, if no one objects, can be used to limit debate and to designate when a vote will be held.

There are three important characteristics of rules and procedures on the floor of the Senate. First, the Senate rules are generally much simpler and less rigidly enforced than those rules of the House. For example, unless a senator demands the "regular order," no one will enforce Senate rules (remember, the presiding officer of the Senate does not play an active role in its proceedings). Second, there is no rule that a proposed amendment to the bill on the floor be germane to the bill's subject matter, unless it is a general appropriation bill; **riders** to appropriate bills are prohibited unless two-thirds of the senators waive this rule. Thus, some bills become "Christmas tree" bills, containing many unrelated amendments that senators have added at the request of interest groups or constituents. In this way, important legislation that was never considered by committees can be passed by the Senate. For example, the 1964 Civil Rights Bill was an amendment to a bill that provided funds to a school district in Missouri.

The third major characteristic of Senate procedure is the **filibuster,** an attempt to defeat a bill by prolonging the debate. Under the rules of the Senate, a member can speak for an unlimited period of time unless three-fifths of his or her colleagues vote **cloture** to cut off the speech. Many senators have used filibusters to delay or prevent Senate action on bills they opposed; for example, in the 1960s, conservative southern senators used it to thwart civil-rights legislation. The cloture rule, first imposed on the Senate by itself in 1917, originally stipulated that the support of two-thirds of the senators present and voting was required to end a filibuster. The rule was strengthened in 1975, when the Senate lowered the requirement to three-fifths of the entire membership, or sixty senators. From 1960 to 1969, only four of twenty-three cloture votes were successful; in contrast, from 1970 to 1978, cloture was successful in thirty-three of ninety-five votes.

The floor procedures in the House of Representatives are much more rigid than those in the Senate. Filibusters are not allowed, and other attempts to slow down the business of the House are generally not tolerated. The House Rules Committee, the Speaker, and party leaders usually share an interest in keeping the legislative process moving, so the House has developed a number of ways to expedite debates and votes. One way is to vote itself into the Committee of the Whole House on the State of the Union. The Speaker cannot chair the Committee of the Whole, so a chairman is named. Because the members are sitting as a committee rather than as the House of Representatives, the rules for a **quorum** (i.e., a required number of members that must be present to conduct business) are much less burdensome: in the Committee of the Whole, a quorum is 100 instead of 218 when members are sitting as the House. If no quorum is present, a member may object to the continuation of House proceedings. Unless a sufficient number of members, summoned by bells throughout Capitol Hill buildings, returns to the chamber or the House sergeant at arms collects enough members from the hallways and rooms of the Capitol, the House must adjourn.

When the House meets as the Committee of the Whole, the length of debate is determined by the Rules Committee. Time is usually divided evenly between

rider: An amendment to a Senate bill that need not be germane to the subject of the original bill.

filibuster: An attempt to defeat a bill in the Senate by prolonging debate.

cloture: A vote of three-fifths of all senators to stop a filibuster.

quorum: The number of members of a legislature whose presence is required for the transaction of business; usually a majority of the membership.

the chairman and the ranking minority member of the committee that reported the bill under consideration; each may yield time to other members who wish to speak or ask questions. After the time for general debate is exhausted, amendments may be offered with five-minute explanations and five minutes for opposition. This five-minute rule is usually effective in preventing filibusters in the House. House floor procedures are also expedited when the Rules Committee issues a "gag rule," which requires that amendments can be offered only by members of the committee that reported the bill, and only when a majority of the committee members agree. Although there are parliamentary tricks in the House that opponents of a bill can use to delay action, floor procedures are generally much less amenable to obstructionist tactics (except those of the leadership) than in the Senate.

When the Committee of the Whole has considered a bill and its amendments, it reports the bill to the House, and the Speaker once again takes the reins. A House member then "moves the previous question," which, if a majority approves, cuts off debate; otherwise, debate may continue for one more hour. The bill is then voted on by the entire House. First to be voted on are the amendments that were reported by the Committee of the Whole, in the order in which they were reported. Then the members vote on the bill *with amendments;* the members never vote on a successfully amended bill without its amendments. If the bill passes, someone will move to reconsider it, since a House vote is never final until there has been an opportunity to reconsider it; the motion to reconsider, however, is nearly always automatically tabled, thereby postponing reconsideration indefinitely.

There are four methods by which the House of Representatives votes; three of these methods are also used by the Senate. The most common is a *voice vote:* members simply call out "aye" or "nay" in response to a prompt from the presiding officer. The chair then announces which side won. In each chamber, most noncontroversial bills are passed in this way. Both chambers also use the *division vote,* in which members stand to be counted as for or against a bill.

The Senate and the House may also vote by *roll call.* In recent years, roll-call votes have become increasingly common, especially in the Senate, where there are fewer members and roll calls can be scheduled in advance (no senator wants to miss too many recorded votes). The House uses a sophisticated electronic system for roll-call votes: each member places a personalized vote card (somewhat like an automatic bank-teller card) into a "vote station," and then presses a button to indicate "yea," "nay," or "present." The results are shown immediately on an electronic scoreboard on the wall over the Speaker's podium.

Finally, the House, but not the Senate, may vote by *teller.* To be counted, members walk down the center aisle, first those in favor of a bill, then those opposed to it.

At first, in view of the enormous range of issues and interests with which

Congress must wrestle, it may seem puzzling that any bill successfully achieves this stage in the congressional process. As we have seen, many do not. Yet, several aspects of the legislative process help to explain the passage of many bills, and they all involve the incentives that lead legislators to cooperate. One way that a bill can succeed is by attracting numerous amendments, each of which has a squad of congressional supporters who will vote for the entire bill to which the amendments are attached. Some of these bills are pork-barrel projects that provide public-works money (e.g., for dams and waterway projects) for various states or congressional districts. Another important incentive to form coalitions results from the fragmented nature of Congress: because legislators have so many bills to vote on, it is efficient for them to form majorities by *vote trading*. For example, one representative may tell another, "I need your vote on this education bill I sponsored"; "I owe you a vote on one of your favorite bills" will be implied by the request. This process, known as **logrolling,** is an important part of the legislative process, because it simultaneously reduces both information and transaction costs.

There is no guarantee that the Senate and the House will pass identical versions of the same bill. If fact, they are likely to disagree about how much money should be authorized or appropriated for a program, or about particular provisions or amendments. These differences must be resolved if the bill is to become a law. If the disagreements are minor, the chairman of the committee in the chamber originally responsible for the bill can ask his or her chamber to agree to the other chamber's version. If the differences are substantial, however, the Speaker and the president of the Senate appoint "managers," or conference committee members—usually those persons who handled the legislation in their respective chambers—to work out a compromise. Although the conferees may enter the bargaining with instructions from the Senate or the House to insist on certain provisions, they often have considerable flexibility in negotiating a compromise. Of course, they sometimes fail, causing the bill to die. However, in most cases, the conference committee members decide upon a bill that they think both chambers will accept. Because these versions cannot be amended by the House or the Senate, conferees often have considerable power in shaping legislation. For example, a 1966 water-pollution bill was crippled in conference committee when Congressman James Wright (D-Texas) added a one-word amendment: only "*grossly* negligent or willful" spilling of oil from vessels could be prosecuted—and *gross* negligence ("*total* neglect for the rights of others") is difficult to prove.[11]

At this stage, congressional action is nearly complete. The Speaker of the House and the president of the Senate each sign the bill, after which it is sent to the White House. If the president approves the bill, he signs it and the bill becomes law. If the president neither signs it nor returns it to Congress with his objections within ten days, the bill also becomes law. However, if Congress adjourns during that ten-day period, thereby preventing the bill's return, the bill does not become law; this is known as a **pocket veto**, and it cannot be

logrolling: The trading of votes in a legislature in order to secure the passage of legislation of particular importance to different members.

pocket veto: A special type of executive veto of legislative actions, not eligible for legislative override.

overridden by Congress. If the president returns the bill to Congress with his reasons for disapproval, the vote of two-thirds of the members present in *both* houses is needed to override the veto, or the bill is dead.

The veto power is rarely used by the president. Most bills that Congress passes are noncontroversial, and there is little for the president to gain by antagonizing its members. Presidents veto no more than 2 or 3 percent of the legislation presented to them. Most of those vetoes are upheld; legislators—especially of the president's party—are often reluctant to deny the chief executive the chance to implement his electoral "mandate." Presidents Kennedy and Johnson, both Democrats, vetoed few bills and had none overridden, largely because they had a Democratic House and Senate to send them the kind of legislation they wanted. Yet even Richard Nixon, who faced a Democratic Congress, had only seven of forty-three vetoes overridden.

If there is a single lesson to be drawn from this discussion of the legislative process, it is that because of the high cost of getting legislation passed, there is an enormous number of opportunities for a bill to be killed. Because legislation nearly always imposes a cost on someone by reallocating rights or wealth, most bills have bitter enemies. Thus, most bills never leave the subcommittee or committee room; those that do face potential obstruction or infinite delay on the floors of the House and the Senate, in conference committee, and perhaps in the White House. Some may think the primary job of Congress is to produce legislation; yet, Congress serves the equally important function of *not* producing much of the legislation that it considers, thereby favoring the status quo. At the same time, Congress has evolved a structure and procedures that reduce some of its internal costs. Whether it responds appropriately to demands and complaints depends largely on who is doing the evaluating—and whether that person or group benefited from congressional action.

Only in matters of great or continuing controversy do the structure and procedures of Congress change dramatically. We have seen how representatives and senators redesigned many of their procedures during the 1970s by weakening the seniority system and by strengthening the party caucuses and subcommittees. In the next section, we will describe another major change in the way Congress works: the transformation in the congressional budget process.

THE CONGRESSIONAL BUDGET PROCESS

For about one hundred and seventy years, the constitutional scheme for allocating authority over federal expenditures between the executive and legislative branches was relatively successful. Especially during the early days of the republic, presidents and legislators were careful not to spend more than the government received in revenues, except during major wars.

During the 1960s, the traditional caution about government spending began to disappear. Two major factors in contributing to this change were the war in Vietnam and the "Great Society" package of social programs proposed by Lyndon Johnson and largely accepted by Congress. Both were expensive. The deliberate decision to pursue both the war and the social programs without a sufficient tax increase meant that the federal government began to run consistent, increasingly large deficits. Between 1956 and 1974, federal expenditures in constant dollars more than doubled, and since 1961, only two federal budgets have not been in deficit.

During the administration of Richard Nixon (1969–1974), the federal budget became a matter of increasing concern. Not only was the size of the government increasing, but the failure to adequately pay for this increase was affecting the entire economy; as we will see in Chapter 12, government deficits contribute to inflation and higher interest rates. Congress could not avoid the blame, because it was becoming notoriously inefficient at controlling its budgetmaking process. From 1972 to 1974, Congress did not pass one appropriation bill on time (i.e., by the beginning of the fiscal year), and it had no mechanism by which it could assess the overall cost to society of the many separate appropriation bills that it passed each year.

Nixon responded with the increasing usage of **impoundment,** originally authorized by Congress in the 1880s, which allowed presidents to impound funds (i.e., to refuse to spend money that Congress had appropriated) if the expenditure of those funds would cause a federal deficit. Thus, like earlier presidents, Nixon in effect refused to carry out laws that Congress had passed. What was particularly irksome to many Democrats in Congress was that many

impoundment: The refusal of a president to spend money appropriated by Congress.

An interstate highway bridge under construction in Hartford, Connecticut. Since 1956, Congress has appropriated tens of billions of dollars to finance 90 percent of the costs of the 42,500 mile interstate highway system. (© David Plowden, 1977/Photo Researchers, Inc.)

of the impounded programs were in the areas of social and environmental policy. In response to the inadequacy of congressional budgetary procedures and the growth of presidential impoundments—and perhaps in response to the presidential weakness resulting from the Watergate scandal—Congress passed the Budget and Impoundment Control Act on July 19, 1974.

Considering the large scope of the Budget Act, the two-year period that Congress spent shaping it was relatively short. The major challenge to the reformers was to change both the structure and the processes of congressional budgetmaking without threatening the authority of existing leaders. Budgetary controls needed to be centralized and, it was hoped, thereby rationalized, but any alteration of the congressional system that took power away from influential committee chairmen was certain to be defeated. The solution was to overlay the new budgetary process on Congress without changing its basic structure.

The Budget Act included both structural and procedural changes. The major procedural innovation was the introduction of a *timetable* for the consideration of the president's proposed budget and for the setting of congressional budgetary goals. There were two important structural changes as well. The first was the creation of two *budget committees,* one in the House and one in the Senate, to coordinate the appropriations decisions of each chamber and to enforce discipline. The other was the establishment of the *Congressional Budget Office (CBO),* which was designed to give Congress improved information about the costs and benefits of its actions.

The Budget Committees

Before passage of the Budget Act, there were four "money" committees of Congress: the House Appropriations Committee, the Senate Appropriations Committee, the House Ways and Means Committee, and the Senate Finance Committee. The first two were primarily responsible for clearing the requests of the many substantive congressional committees for the funding of various programs; the latter two were the revenue-raising (i.e., taxing) committees. Needless to say, these were four of the most powerful committees in Congress; they still are. The Budget Act did not remove any of the most important powers of these committees, but it created two new budget committees to coordinate their actions.

The budgetary process is initiated long before Congress begins its considerations. As early as eighteen months before a new **fiscal year (FY)** begins, the many executive and independent agencies start compiling their plans for future expenditures with guidance from the Office of Management and Budget (OMB) in the Executive Office of the President. Almost a year before the fiscal year starts on October 1, the OMB and the president prepare their budget recommendations, and on January 18 of each year (or fifteen days after Congress convenes), the president submits the budget to Congress.

Guided by the timetable introduced by the Budget Act, the budget commit-

fiscal year (FY): The accounting period of the federal government, which runs from October 1 through September 30 of the following year.

tees of the House and Senate analyze (1) the effects of the president's budget requests on government programs and the economy and (2) the recommendations of the many committees of each chamber. With the assistance of the Congressional Budget Office (CBO), the budget committees report at least two concurrent resolutions that set targets for total federal spending in the coming fiscal year; these resolutions are to be passed by both chambers but are not subject to presidential approval. In other words, the budget committees were created so that they could forge a compromise among all congressional committees and between the two chambers as a clear and definitive response to a president's budget requests.

Although it may seem that the budget committees are very powerful, several factors have weakened their influence. First, the House Budget Committee was created as a temporary committee whose members could not serve more than four years in a ten-year period. Second, the other money committees in the House were given direct influence over the House Budget Committee: ten of its twenty-five members are drawn from the Appropriations and Ways and Means committees. Similar constraints were not imposed on the Senate Budget Committee, but its authority has also been undermined by the noncooperation of some influential Senate committee chairmen. Finally, it must be remembered that budget committee members, like all congressional representatives, are subject to the powerful effects of the electoral process. A primary incentive of any representative or senator must be reelection, so constituent and interest-group pressures will tend to inflate, not reduce, the budget committees' recommendations for government spending.

Congressional Budget Office

The Congressional Budget Office (CBO) was created as a resource for Congress in its considerations of the federal budget. It was intended to compensate for the analytical and informational imbalance created by the Office of Management and Budget in the executive branch. The CBO projects the cost of current and proposed programs, forecasts the effects of presidential and congressional budgets on the economy (particularly on inflation and unemployment), and estimates the impact of the economy on the budget.

This last task is particularly delicate, because it requires the CBO to forecast the performance of the American economy up to five years in advance and to estimate what its impact will be on the federal budget, which is itself of unknown size. If the economy plunges into a recession, unemployment will increase, thus (1) reducing the amount of taxable income that the government takes in while (2) increasing the amount of benefits paid to the unemployed, thereby increasing expenditures. Obviously, the assumptions and models that the CBO uses in its fiscal budget analysis can be important as well as controversial—but only if Congress takes the CBO seriously. During its first decade, the CBO became a significant policy institution because of its reputation as having "the best numbers in town."

The Congressional Budget Timetable

Recognizing that it takes at least nine months from the time Congress convenes for it to take care of its budgetary business, the Budget Act shifted the beginning of the fiscal year from July 1 of each year to October 1. More importantly, the act set deadlines for various stages of the congressional budgetary process as an incentive to members to make decisions and find compromises before the beginning of the fiscal year. If the October 1 deadline is not met, Congress must pass temporary laws, or **continuing resolutions,** which allow the federal government to continue to spend money at the level of the last fiscal year until the new appropriations bills finally pass.

The congressional budget timetable is shown in Table 8-3. There are four general phases of the process. In the first phase (from the fifteenth day after Congress convenes to April 15), the president submits both the current services budget (i.e., the dollar amounts that would be required next year to support the same services in this year's budget) and budget proposals for the next year. The CBO uses these figures to project the fiscal, economic, and budgetary effects of the president's proposals, and the budget committees begin compiling the wishes of the various congressional authorizing committees. On April 15, the budget committees report the *first concurrent budget resolution,* which sets proposed target figures for taxes and spending that the other committees will then use to limit their new authorizing legislation; this first budget resolution is only advisory.

During the second phase of the congressional budgetary process, the authorizing committees develop their legislative proposals for the upcoming year. Although the details of the spending and revenue targets in the proposed first concurrent budget resolution are somewhat flexible, the overall ceilings on nineteen functional categories of the budget are fixed. Thus, the committees have some slack with which to work, but they are expected to keep an eye on the category limits. By May 15, all committees are required to have reported all bills authorizing new budget authority, and Congress adopts its first joint concurrent budget resolution.

In the third phase, the appropriations committees of the House and Senate enact the spending bills. These committees must establish the budget authority for about eleven hundred different accounts in the federal budget (e.g., payroll, benefits, transportation, and supplies for every agency and department of the federal branch). By the seventh day after Labor Day (the first Monday in September), Congress should have completed action on all spending bills.

In the fourth and final stage, the appropriations bills of both chambers are compiled under the direction of the budget committees, which must report a *second concurrent budget resolution* by September 15. This second resolution reflects the deliberations of all the committees during the spring and summer, and provides a reassessment of Congress's spending, taxation, and debt requirements for the fiscal year that is about to start. If the second resolution sets a spending limit lower than the sum of the appropriations bills, the Senate

continuing resolution: A temporary law passed by Congress to appropriate money when formal appropriations bills have not been passed by the beginning of the new fiscal year.

TABLE 8-3
CONGRESSIONAL BUDGETARY TIMETABLE

Time	Action
October–December	Congressional Budget Office submits 5-year spending plan.
Phase I	
January	President submits current services budget.
Late January (within 15 days after Congress convenes)	President submits proposed budget.
Late January–March	Budget committees hold hearings and begin work on first budget resolution.
March 15	All legislative committees submit estimates and reviews to budget committees.
April 15	Budget committees report first concurrent budget resolutions to the House and Senate.
Phase II	
May 15	Committees report all bills with new budget authority. Congress adopts first concurrent resolution on the budget.
Phase III	
May 15 through the seventh day after Labor Day	Committees report all spending and budget authority bills; Congressional Budget Office issues reports on congressional compliance with first budget resolution; appropriations committees complete all action on spending bills.
Phase IV	
September 15	Congress adopts second concurrent resolution on the budget; no bills or amendments in excess of budget authority figures can be considered after this date.
September 25	All Senate-House differences are reconciled; if necessary, a reconciliation bill or resolution is passed.
October 1	New fiscal year begins.

and House must reconcile the differences so that the budget-resolution target can be met. The reconciliation process must be completed by September 25. Six days later, on October 1, the new fiscal year begins.

In 1976, the first full year of the Budget Act's implementation, all target dates in this schedule were met. The committees were generally cooperative, although the first chairmen of the budget committees, Robert Giaimo in the House and Edmund Muskie in the Senate, were occasionally forced to remind their colleagues of the dangers in ignoring these attempts at self-reform. By

1979, however, there were signs that the process was breaking down. Economists were particularly hard-pressed to make forecasts, since the economy was suffering from simultaneous inflation and unemployment (i.e., "stagflation"), which their models were not equipped to handle. The Democratic president, Jimmy Carter, was finding it difficult to get the Democrats on Capitol Hill to see national priorities his way, particularly since the Congressional Budget Office was now able to dispute the chief executive's budget and economic forecasts. In 1980, none of the congressional budgetary deadlines were met, and the FY 1981 budget was never completed. With Congress unable to discipline itself, "the reformed budget process appeared to provide the worst of both worlds: a firm roadblock against the President's power, and no improved Congressional alternative."[12]

It is ironic that Ronald Reagan was able to exploit the reformed congressional budget process in 1981 and 1982 to achieve his desired budget cuts. Under the new rules, Congress could require the authorizing and appropriating committees to produce a single omnibus bill reflecting the constraints imposed by the budget resolutions; Reagan, along with congressional Republicans (and many conservative Democrats), made sure that the budget cuts required by the resolutions occurred primarily in social rather than in defense programs.

As is so often the case, the congressional attempt at self-improvement could not succeed unless the legislators wanted it to. It may have been that the task was underestimated. For example, the Budget Act required that Congress state precisely what is to be done, but Congress would have to depend on forecasts that are extremely imprecise. Adding another institution (or two or three) could only complicate the process, not simplify and rationalize it. And perhaps the biggest oversight of the budget reformers was their failure to recognize that, above all else, a budget is *policy*. It is unrealistic to expect legislators to permanently yield the power that is both their reason for being in Congress and their tool for staying there. The same fate may await other simple solutions to the problems of the budgetary process.

THE ROLE OF CONGRESS

This examination of how Congress makes budgets and how it has tried to reform itself serves to illustrate the constraints and incentives that shape most aspects of the congressional process in the United States. It is a complex process, with numerous individual participants, many subdivisions of labor into subinstitutions, and significant information and transaction costs. Therefore, the control of a body such as Congress should be expected to be at least occasionally deficient. In some areas, however, it may be desirable that Congress be somewhat inefficient, because the exercise of its constitutional powers is thereby limited and its dependence on other branches of government and on the public are increased. If, as the late justice Felix Frankfurter wrote, "the history of liberty . . . cannot be dissociated from the history of procedural observances," then students of American government should pay close attention to the processes of Congress.[13] As we turn in the next chapter to the executive functions of American government, the assets and problems of Congress should be remembered, for it should be clear by now that the branches of government take many of their strengths and weaknesses from one another.

NOTES

[1] Woodrow Wilson, *Congressional Government* (Boston: Houghton Mifflin, 1885), p. 58.

[2] Hammer v. Dagenhart, 247 U.S. 251 (1918); NLRB v. Jones & Laughlin Steel, 301 U.S. 1 (1937).

[3] McCulloch v. Maryland, 17 U.S. (4 Wheat.) 316 (1819).

[4] U.S. v. Nixon, 417 U.S. 683 (1974).

[5] Panama Refining Co. v. Ryan, 293 U.S. 388 (1935); Schechter Poultry Co. v. U.S., 295 U.S. 495 (1935).

[6] See Morris S. Ogul, *Congress Oversees the Bureaucracy* (Pittsburgh: University of Pittsburgh Press, 1976).

[7] Richard F. Fenno, Jr., *Home Style: House Members in Their Districts* (Boston: Little, Brown, 1978).

[8] Morris P. Fiorina, *Congress: Keystone of the Washington Establishment* (New Haven: Yale University Press, 1977).

[9] Richard F. Fenno, Jr., *Congressmen in Committees* (Boston: Little, Brown, 1973).

[10] David R. Mayhew, *Congress: The Electoral Connection* (New Haven: Yale University Press, 1974).

[11] Bruce I. Oppenheimer, *Oil and the Congressional Process* (Lexington, Massachusetts: Lexington Books, 1974), p. 45.

[12] Norman J. Ornstein, "The Breakdown of the Budget Process," *Wall Street Journal,* November 24, 1981, p. 22.

[13] Archibald MacLeish and E. F. Prichard, Jr. eds. *Law and Politics* (New York: Harcourt Brace, 1939), p. 192.

BIBLIOGRAPHY

Davidson, Roger H., and Walter J. Oleszek. *Congress and Its Members.* Washington, D.C.: Congressional Quarterly Press, 1981. An analysis of Congress with emphasis on the forces that shape its organization and behavior.

Dodd, Lawrence C., and Bruce I. Oppenheimer, eds. *Congress Reconsidered,* 2nd ed. Washington: Congressional Quarterly Press, 1981. A collection of studies, focusing on the reforms of the 1970s and their effects.

Fenno, Richard F., Jr. *Congressmen in Committees,* Boston: Little, Brown, 1973. An important study of the behavior of members of the House of Representatives and the functions of committees.

————. *Home Style: House Members in Their Districts.* Boston: Little, Brown, 1978. A firsthand (and entertaining) examination of the links between congressional representatives and their constituents.

Fiorina, Morris P. *Congress: Keystone of the Washington Establishment.* New Haven: Yale University Press, 1977. A provocative, well-documented analysis of the role of Congress in the growth of the federal bureaucracy.

Kingdon, John W. *Congressmen's Voting Decisions.* 2nd ed. New York: Harper & Row, 1981. An examination, based upon numerous interviews, of factors that affect the way congressional representatives vote.

Mayhew, David R. *Congress: The Electoral Connection.* New Haven: Yale University Press, 1974. A short but useful book on the importance of the goal of reelection to members of Congress.

Oleszek, Walter J. *Congressional Procedures and the Policy Process.* Washington, D.C.: Congressional Quarterly Press, 1978. A detailed but readable discussion of the complex procedures by which bills become laws.

Ripley, Randall B. *Congress: Process and Policy.* 3rd ed. New York: Norton, 1983. A good standard text on congressional structure, procedures, and policymaking.

Schick, Allen. *Congress and Money: Budgeting, Spending, and Taxing.* Washington, D.C.: Urban Institute, 1980. By far the most useful book on the congressional budgetary process, with useful discussions of appropriations and finance procedures.

The President and The Executive Function

On March 4, 1933, Franklin Roosevelt took the presidential oath of office and became the most powerful public official in the United States. Armed with a commanding 17.7 percent lead in popular votes over his Republican rival, Herbert Hoover, Roosevelt quickly went to work on the nation's economy, which was in the depth of the Great Depression. Within five days of taking office, Roosevelt had suspended the export of gold and its convertibility from dollars by American citizens, temporarily closed all the banks in order to determine which ones were strong enough to stay open, and obtained emergency congressional legislation to expand the lending powers of the Federal Reserve System.

On November 8, 1960, John Kennedy was elected to the White House by a margin of only 0.3 percent—about a hundred thousand votes—over Richard Nixon. When inaugurated the following January, Kennedy was confronted with a mild recession (unemployment was at 7.7 percent); a fledgling civil-rights movement; a recently escalated cold war with the Soviet Union, which was exacerbated by worries about a "missile gap"; Cuba, which had recently turned Communist; and other problems. In marked contrast to Roosevelt, Kennedy acted slowly.[1] Because his support in Congress was weak, Kennedy was often reluctant to fight for his legislative programs. He focused more on international affairs, including relations with the Soviet Union and the direction of United States defense policy.

Why did the styles of Kennedy and Roosevelt differ so? Was the difference attributable to the presence of television in the 1960s, instead of radio, which Roosevelt had skillfully used? Or was it due to the absence of a devastating depression? Was Kennedy's smaller electoral mandate and the poor showing of congressional Democrats in 1960 responsible for Congress's refusal to implement his proposals for federal school aid or medical care for the aged? We cannot hope to single out specific factors in these two administrations, but there are some common institutional and political features in the operation of every president's term. In this chapter, as we examine the executive functions of the president, both as prescribed by the Constitution and as shaped by events of the last two hundred years, we will see that the executive can be understood only if viewed as part of a system of other institutions, traditions, and political forces.

In particular, we will focus on three important concepts that are fundamental to understanding the presidency. First, the president is threatened with having too much information while not being able to use it; no human being could absorb and understand all the facts and opinions that characterize the many policies over which the president has jurisdiction. Second, as a result of this dilemma, the president must organize his administration in such a way as to divide the labors of overseeing a bureaucracy of nearly three million employees. Third, in attempting to carry out constitutional duties and implement policies, the president must retain control not only of this bureaucracy but also, to some degree, of the other branches of government.

284

We will begin by discussing what the Constitution's framers thought they were creating, and then we will turn to the powers and functions of the president. Next, we will examine the organization of the presidency: the White House Office, the Executive Office of the President, the vice presidency, and the cabinet. In the final section, we will discuss the strategies and tools that presidents use in performing their duties, and the relationship of the American executive to the public, Congress, the courts, and the bureaucracy.

THE FUNCTIONS OF THE PRESIDENCY

In Chapter 2, we discussed the difficulty that the creation of the executive branch caused the nation's Founders. Unlike the judicial and legislative branches, the executive could not be closely modeled on the English system of monarchy. The writers of the Constitution also rejected an executive composed of a committee, for fear that it could be divided and therefore too weak to counter what they anticipated as the greater tendency of the legislature to abuse its power. The Founders also carefully considered the length of the president's term and the electoral mechanism for selecting the chief executive because they believed that these processes would affect the strength and behavior of the person in the office. The power of the presidency was to be derived from the provisions of the Constitution and the organizational unity of the office, and it was to be kept in check by the other branches of government.

Yet, as with other institutions in American government, that which is in the Constitution is only a part of the modern presidency. We will first examine the

President Franklin Roosevelt relaxes during a Democratic party fund-raising dinner in 1938, at which he spoke against a "handful" of selfish businessmen who were trying to undermine his administration's policies. (Thomas McAvoy/Time-Life Picture Agency © Time, Inc.)

constitutional functions of the president—executive, internal affairs, and external affairs—and then turn to other duties presidents have acquired as the nation and the world have changed.

Executive Power

Article II of the Constitution begins with the deceptively simple sentence, "The executive Power shall be vested in a President of the United States of America." The phrase *executive power* is not defined, so we do not know whether the Founders intended to limit the president to simply executing the laws of Congress and administering the executive departments of State, Treasury, and so on. From the outset, this general grant of authority gave rise to different interpretations. According to Alexander Hamilton, executive power included all of the powers traditionally assigned to chief executives (e.g., eighteenth-century English kings), subject only to the exceptions and qualifications expressed in the Constitution. James Madison, in contrast, argued for a more restrictive approach. To him, the phrase was a general statement that gave the president little power above that explicitly granted or clearly implied by the Constitution.[2]

The executive power of the president is further complicated by the charge in Article II, Section 3, that the president "shall take Care that the Laws be faithfully executed." Naturally, presidents have been inclined to interpret this to mean that they have the right to take any necessary and proper actions not forbidden by statute in order to protect the interests of the nation. For example, in 1890, Benjamin Harrison ordered marshals to defend a threatened Supreme Court justice, and Harry Truman ordered the seizure of the nation's railroads in 1947 in an attempt to deter a crippling strike by railroad workers. More commonly, presidents have taken unilateral action, without congressional approval, to make plans or policy, to interpret statutes, and to establish new agencies—all in pursuit of the execution of the laws. Yet, some people—often those in Congress—believe that the word *faithfully* limits presidential power and hold that the Constitution mandates the president to do precisely what Congress requires through statutes, and little more.

If we look at additional executive powers, we can see why such disputes have not been resolved in more than two hundred years. Article II, Section 2, says that the president "shall nominate, and by and with the Advice and Consent of the Senate, shall appoint Ambassadors, and other public Ministers and Consuls, Judges of the supreme Court, and all other Officers of the United States, whose Appointments are not herein otherwise provided for, and which shall be established by Law; but the Congress may by Law vest the Appointment of such inferior Officers, as they think proper, in the President alone, in the Courts of Law, or in the Heads of Departments." This provision implies that the Founders expected all officials in the United States to be (1) appointive and (2) either "presidential" officers or "inferior" officers.[3] (How could they have foreseen today's federal civilian bureaucracy of three million employees, with 98.2 percent of them in the executive branch?) In 1879, the Supreme Court ruled that any officials not appointed by this constitutional process were not, strictly speaking, "Officers of the United States."

PARTIAL GUEST LIST FOR A WHITE HOUSE DINNER HONORING PRESIDENT FERDINAND MARCOS OF THE PHILIPPINES, SEPTEMBER 1982

President Ferdinand Marcos and Imelda Marcos

Ferdinand R. Marcos, Jr., vice governor, Ilocos Norte

Irene R. Marcos

Cesar A. Virata, prime minister and minister of finance, and Mrs. Virata

Carlos P. Romulo, minister of foreign affairs, and Mrs. Romulo

Eduardo Z. Romualdez, ambassador to the United States, and Concepcion Romualdez

Juan Ponce Enrile, minister of national defense

Roberto V. Ongpin, minister of industry, trade and investment

Arturo Tanco, minister of agriculture

Geronimo Z. Velasco, minister of energy

Juan C. Tuvera, presidential executive assistant

Roberto Benedicto, chairman, Philippine Sugar Commission

George and Janice Abbott of New York City

Michael H. Armacost, U.S. ambassador to the Philippines, and Mrs. Armacost

James A. Baker III, chief of staff and assistant to the president, and Susan Baker

Robert A. Beck, chairman, Prudential Insurance Co. of America, and Mrs. Beck

Frances Bergen of Los Angeles

Vice President Bush and Barbara Bush

Sen. Harry F. Byrd, Jr. (Ind.-Va.)

Anna C. Chennault, president, TAC International Inc., and Gen. John Alison

Van Cliburn, pianist, and Riddle Bee Cliburn

Bob Colacello of *Interview Magazine*

Arlene Dahl, actress, and Marc Rosen, vice president, Elizabeth Arden

Donald Davis of United Press International

Michael K. Deaver, deputy chief of staff and assistant to the president, and Carolyn Deaver

Oscar de la Renta, fashion designer

Sen. Jeremiah Denton (R-Ala.) and Jane Denton

Richard Ferris, chairman, United Airlines Inc., and Kelsey Ferris

Rep. Thomas S. Foley (D-Wash.) and Heather Foley

Margot Fonteyn, ballerina, and Robert Arias, former Panamanian ambassador to Great Britain

Ted Graber, interior decorator

Gordon Hanna, editorial manager, Scripps-Howard Newspapers, and Annie Lou Hanna

Fred Hartley, chairman, Union Oil Co., and Margaret Hartley

Sen. S. I. Hayakawa (R-Calif.) and Marge Hayakawa

Marta Istomin, artistic director, Kennedy Center, and Eugene Istomin, pianist

Robert Trent Jones, Jr., golf course designer, and Claiborne Jones

John W. Kluge, of Metromedia Inc., and Patricia Kluge

Harding Lawrence, former chairman, Braniff International, and Mary Lawrence

Jody Jacobs, *Los Angeles Times*, and Bernard Leason

Robert McFarlane, deputy assistant to the president for national security affairs, and Jonda McFarlane

Edwin Meese III, counselor to the president, and Ursula Meese

Capt. John J. O'Donnell, president, Airline Pilots Association, and Frances O'Donnell

Yue-Kong Pao of World Wide Shipping Group, Hong Kong, and Doreen Cheng

Supreme Court Justice Lewis F. Powell, Jr., and Josephine Powell

David M. Roderick, chairman, U.S. Steel Corp., and Bettie Roderick

Selwa Roosevelt, chief of protocol, and Archibald Roosevelt

Dr. Frank Royal, president, National Medical Association, and Mrs. Royal

Dianne Sawyer of CBS

Secretary of State George P. Shultz and Helena Shultz

Attorney General William French Smith and Jean Smith

Liz (Mary) Smith, *New York Post*, and St. Clair Pugh

Rep. J. William Stanton (R-Ohio) and Peggy Stanton

Roger Staubach, sports personality, and Mrs. Staubach

John E. Swearingen, chairman, Standard Oil Co. of Indiana, and Bonnie Swearingen

C. William Verity, Jr., chairman, Armco Inc., and Peggy Verity

Andy Warhol, artist

William B. Webber, president, New York Banking Association, and Jacqueline Webber

Secretary of Defense Caspar W. Weinberger and Jane Weinberger

Charles Z. Wick, director, USIA, and Mary Jane Wick

Source: *Washington Post,* September 17, 1982, p. D4.

The importance of the appointive power lies at the highest levels of public office. In principle, when a president appoints top administrators to an agency, he carefully screens them for both competence and sympathy to his ideas. In turn, they might be expected to carefully control their subordinates to assure that the president's programs are carried out. In fact, this scheme frequently does not work as neatly in practice as it does in theory; as we will see in Chapter 10, even top-level appointees are often unwilling or unable to carry out the president's wishes, and it is impossible for the president to know precisely what his appointees will do. Furthermore, the Constitution clearly states that the president shares some of the appointive power with Congress. Executive-level officers must be approved by the Senate, and it is up to Congress to decide which positions fall into that category. For example, in 1974, Congress passed a law stating that the director and deputy director of the Office of Management and Budget, who are important presidential advisers, would henceforth require Senate confirmation. Because the president is given considerable leeway in choosing compatible appointees, Senate confirmation usually depends more on the fitness of the nominee than on his or her views on policy. On some occasions, however, the confirmation process is used to urge a change in presidential policy; for this reason, both Jimmy Carter and Ronald Reagan saw their top arms-control negotiators face delays in the Senate.

The appointive power of the president is clearly constitutional. But what about the power of the president to remove appointees? Is the power to fire the natural complement of the power to hire? The importance of the issue is clear: Andrew Johnson, the only American president who was successfully impeached, although not convicted, was charged with violating the congressional right to limit the removal power of presidents. The Constitution is silent on this matter, and not until 1926 did the Supreme Court take a clear and firm stand. In *Myers* v. *U.S.*, the Court ruled that "purely executive" appointees could be removed by the president without congressional interference, even if the appointment had required the "advice and consent" of the Senate.[4] In 1935, however, the issue resurfaced. The Supreme Court ruled that officers of agencies created by congressional statute, where the statute specified the terms of office and the causes for removal, could be removed by the president only for the reasons that Congress gave—an example of the potential for conflict between the president's executive power and his responsibility to execute the laws.[5] In practice, presidents usually remove their appointees only because of strong public-policy disputes or publicized misconduct. After all, the information costs to the president of monitoring the behavior of the thousands of appointees would be enormous. As we will see later in this chapter, there are other devices by which a president can control appointees.

Another executive power granted to the president by the Constitution is the power to "require the Opinion, in writing, of the principal Officer in each of the executive Departments, upon any Subject relating to the Duties of their respective Offices." In other words, the president can demand formal reports from the members of the cabinet. As Hamilton observed in *The Federalist*, no.

74, this is "a mere redundancy in the plan, as the right for which it provides would result of itself from the office."

Power over Internal Affairs

Pardons   Article II, Section 2, gives the president the power "to grant Reprieves and Pardons for Offences against the United States, except in Case of Impeachment." Technically, a *reprieve* suspends the penalties of the law without changing the legal guilt or innocence of an offender. A *pardon* forgives the offense and removes the threat of punishment, but stops short of conferring total innocence; a pardoned offender cannot hold a position of public trust, which the law denies to those convicted of crimes. The president alone grants pardons; the courts and Congress have no role. However, the president can pardon only offenses "against the United States"—that is, violations of national, not state, laws. (In some states, the courts can suspend the sentence of someone who has violated state laws.)

Presidents receive thousands of petitions for reprieves and pardons each year. They are screened first by attorneys in the Department of Justice, then by the prosecuting attorneys and judges in each case, and finally by the attorney general. The most notable presidential pardons have been Gerald Ford's pardon of Richard Nixon in 1974; Andrew Johnson's 1868 amnesty, which obliterated all legal record of guilt of those who had supported the secession movement; and the blanket pardon, initiated by President Ford and completed by President Carter, of Vietnam draft evaders.

Legislative Power   As we saw in Chapter 2, the doctrine of separation of powers was based largely on the importance of separating legislative power from the executive branch. At the same time, however, in order for legislative power to be checked, the other branches of government needed to have some influence over it. Thus, the courts can review legislative action (i.e., judicial review), and the Constitution explicitly grants the president several legislative duties. (Later in this chapter, we will examine many of the informal ways presidents affect domestic policymaking, in addition to their constitutional roles.)

The State of the Union Message   Under Article II, Section 3, the president "shall from time to time give to the Congress Information of the State of the Union." The ritual of the president marching grandly into a joint session of Congress, televised live by the three major networks, to deliver his agenda for the coming year—and to claim credit for the successes of the past one—is a recent tradition. The Constitution says nothing about how the message should be transmitted; in fact, Woodrow Wilson (1913–1921) was the first president since John Adams to address Congress in person. Regardless of the means of delivery, the State of the Union message is an important mechanism by which presidents inform the legislature, and the public, about the programs and policies that will be proposed in the coming year.

Legislative Proposals   Article II, Section 3, also states that the president shall "recommend to [Congress] such Measures as he shall judge necessary and expedient." The logic of this provision is clear: the president is in a unique position to speak with authority about problems facing the nation at home and abroad. He can claim to represent the entire nation, and he sits at the apex of an enormous bureaucracy with access to far more information than Congress can digest and analyze. The employees of the executive branch can detect emerging trends that require legislative attention, as well as be aware of the flaws in the design and implementation of past laws.

During most of the nineteenth century, presidents were reluctant to propose legislation. The major exception was Thomas Jefferson, who drafted legislation, organized his party's congressional representatives, and selected congressional party leaders. Woodrow Wilson tried to resurrect this active legislative role; in 1913, he wrote that the president must be "as much concerned with the guidance of legislation as with the just and orderly execution of law."[6] He also took advantage of the constitutional provision that the president can "on extraordinary Occasions, convene both Houses, or either of them." Wilson called Congress into a special session in 1913 to call for a reduction in trade tariffs.

Today, Congress expects a president to initiate hundreds of bills in each session. Although many of these proposals are routine modifications or extensions of previous statutes, many are fundamental. As political scientist Richard Pious observed, "Many legislators prefer to concentrate on constituent services, private bills, and oversight of agencies; for them the investment of time necessary to innovate may be greater than the anticipated return. By requiring the president to present a program, Congress avoids 'start-up' costs."[7] Of course, as we shall see, the president does not personally create most of these proposals. The various parts of the executive branch may devise ideas for new legislation, but they are expected to subject their proposals to legislative clearance—usually performed by the Office of Management and Budget— to ensure that they are in accord with the president's overall objectives.

The Veto Power   The presidential responsibility to sign bills into law or **veto** bills passed by Congress is provided by Article I, Section 7, of the Constitution. To Hamilton, the veto power was necessary lest the president "be stripped of his authorities by successive resolutions, or annihilated by a single vote," and in order to "guard the community against the effects of faction, precipitancy, or of any impulse unfriendly to the public good, which may happen to influence a majority of [Congress]."[8] The veto power applies to "Every Order, Resolution, or Vote to which the Concurrence of the Senate and House of Representatives may be necessary." Thus, the Constitution provided a guarantee that Congress would not be able to circumvent the veto power by calling a bill by another name. In practice, however, several types of congressional action have been exempted from the threat of a veto; these are (1) joint resolutions by which constitutional amendments are proposed, (2) measures dealing with the internal organization or rules of Congress, and (3) concurrent resolutions passed by both houses of Congress. These resolutions technically

veto: The president's withholding of approval of a bill or joint resolution passed by the House and the Senate, other than one proposing a constitutional amendment.

do not carry the force of law, but they express congressional opinions on issues and often have a real effect on policy.

The importance of the veto power lies as much in its nonuse as in its application. Often, the threat of a veto can affect the fate of a bill, but only if it is used early in the legislative process, while there is still time for compromise with the White House, or if the president can convince Congress that he will find enough support to prevent an override. Less than 5 percent of all presidential vetoes have been overridden, and these have often been controversial measures on which presidents have taken firm stands and therefore have risked a loss of prestige. The causes of vetoes and overrides are complex and sometimes idiosyncratic, and often have much to do with the party of the White House and the Congress. For example, Democrat Franklin Roosevelt, with a Democratic Congress, vetoed 635 bills during his twelve years in office, with only nine overrides, whereas Republican Gerald Ford, with a Democratic Congress, vetoed 72 bills in twenty-nine months, with twelve overrides.

Military Matters   A president can also affect internal affairs through the use of military powers. Defense, foreign policy, and war-making do not always occur outside national boundaries; to preserve the security of the nation, the president, acting as commander-in-chief, can take drastic steps. For example, when the Civil War began, Abraham Lincoln mobilized the state militias, increased the size of the army and navy in excess of congressional ceilings, bypassed the constitutional appropriations process, censored telegraph lines, and suspended many constitutional rights. Most of his actions, taken under the assertion that presidents have **prerogative powers** to defend the nation, even if constitutional limitations must be temporarily ignored, were later ratified by Congress and the courts.[9]

Other presidents have claimed similar prerogative powers, but they have sometimes been rebuffed. During World War II, Franklin Roosevelt's administration managed relations between workers and employers in order to avert strikes that could damage the war effort. When agreements could not be reached, the president referred to several congressional statutes that he claimed gave him authority to draft stubborn workers into the military or to withhold war contracts and raw materials from stubborn employers. Presidential authority to seize private property was upheld when Harry Truman took over coal mines in order to avert a nationwide strike that would have hurt the American effort in the Korean conflict, but it was denied when Truman tried to seize steel mills. In the latter case, the Supreme Court found evidence that Congress had rejected giving the president such powers. Hence, they could not be assumed to be implied by the Constitution's commander-in-chief clause.[10]

prerogative powers: Powers not mentioned in the Constitution that are claimed by presidents as being necessary to the execution of executive powers.

Power over External Affairs

In Chapter 8, we saw that Article I, Section 8, gives Congress the power to regulate commerce with foreign nations, to declare war, to raise and support armies, and to provide and maintain a navy. Article II, Section 2, gives the president the powers to command the armed forces, to participate in treaty-making, and to receive and appoint ambassadors. Power over external affairs may appear to be evenly split between the two branches, but in fact the president clearly dominates military matters and the making of foreign policy. In practice, it is almost always the president who conducts foreign relations for the United States.

The Head of State It is useful for a nation to have a single individual who can be a national symbol. Some countries, such as Great Britain, still have monarchs, who have few formal powers but who participate in official cere-monies and are the focus of allegiance. Other nations have prime ministers who actually perform executive functions, while their presidents are only fig-ureheads. In the United States, the role of head of state is combined with real executive power in the person of the president. He represents the entire nation when receiving ambassadors to the United States, when traveling abroad, and when negotiating foreign policy with representatives of other countries. In addition to the explicit constitutional basis for this role, the president and the vice president are the only individuals who can claim it, because they are the only nationally elected officials.

Commander-in-Chief In external affairs, of course, the president plays much more than a symbolic role. The Constitution names him "Commander in Chief of the Army and Navy of the United States, and of the Militia of the several States, when called into the actual service of the United States." Explaining this function in *The Federalist*, no. 74, Hamilton stated, "of all the cares or concerns of government, the direction of war most peculiarly demands those qualities which distinguish the exercise of power by a single hand." Yet, the phrase, "the direction of war," leaves open the question of what *commander-in-chief* means. Does it simply indicate that the president is the ultimate gen-eral and admiral of the armed forces? Or does it imply that the president has powers to do whatever he claims is necessary to protect the nation?

As mentioned previously, Abraham Lincoln took a broad view of his powers during the Civil War. The Supreme Court upheld him, ruling that in the event of insurrection or invasion, the president can deploy the military forces against any enemy, foreign or domestic, without waiting for a congressional declara-tion of war.[11] Since then, the courts have been reluctant to offer opinions on commander-in-chief matters (e.g., Nixon's mining of the harbors and ports of North Vietnam), unless there was a clear question about the constitutional role of Congress (e.g., Truman's attempted seizure of the steel mills). In fact, much of the expansion of the president's power as commander-in-chief has resulted from congressional delegations of power, either explicitly (i.e., by statute or joint resolution) or by congressional acquiescence.

Congressional action has also restricted the president's military powers. In 1973, for example, Congress overrode President Nixon's veto and passed the

George Washington reviewing the Western Army at Fort Cumberland, Maryland. Presidents have used their power as commander-in-chief not only to inspect the armed forces but also to engage in hostilities without a congressional declaration of war. (Painting by Frederick Kemmelmeyer/The Metropolitan Museum of Art/Gift of Col. and Mrs. Edgar William Garbisch, 1963)

War Powers Resolution. By this action, Congress attempted to limit the president's use of the armed forces by requiring the president:

1. to consult with Congress "in every possible instance" before committing American forces.
2. to remove forces from military action outside the United States, unless Congress declares war, authorizes the use of American forces by statute, or passes a concurrent resolution of support within sixty days of the beginning of American involvement (the president then would have had thirty days to safely remove American troops).

However, this attempt by Congress to "ensure that the collective judgment of both Congress and the President will apply to the introduction of United States Armed Forces into hostilities" was partially overturned by the Supreme Court in 1983, not because Congress exceeded its power by trying to limit the president but because the legislative veto mechanism was unconstitutional (see Chapter 8).

Treaty-making   The Constitution provides that the president "shall have Power, by and with the Advice and Consent of the Senate, to make Treaties, provided two thirds of the Senators present concur." On the question of whether treaty-making was a legislative function (under the constitutional requirement that Congress prescribe "rules for the regulation of the society") or an executive function, Hamilton wrote in *The Federalist,* no. 75, that "the power of making treaties is, plainly, neither the one nor the other. It relates neither to the execution of the subsisting laws, nor to the enaction of new ones; and still less to an exertion of the common strength." Yet since the term of George Washington, the process has not been so cooperative. In 1789, Washington tried to involve the Senate in the negotiation of an Indian treaty, but when the Senate balked he began the tradition of presenting senators with a package for them to accept or reject.

In practice, presidents clearly dominate the treaty-making process, although they are likely to consult with members of the Senate Foreign Relations Committee, whose recommendations usually determine the fate of a treaty in the entire chamber. The president also initiates, conducts, and concludes negotiations with foreign countries. The role of the Senate is usually to approve the president's package (1) unconditionally; (2) with "reservations," which limit the obligations of only the United States; or (3) with amendments, which change the treaty for all parties, and thus may cause it to be rejected by the president or the other nation. One study of more than a thousand treaties from 1789 to 1971 found that the Senate amended about 14 percent and rejected or modified another 12 percent so strongly that presidents or other nations dropped them completely.[12] A more recent example was President Carter's 1978 treaty to grant sovereignty over the Panama Canal to the Panamanians. Carter's failure to consult with key senators on the wording of the controversial treaty, which even sparked organized public opposition, led to several amendments that Carter had to persuade the Panamanians to accept.

Many treaties, once passed, contain general language that someone must interpret. Many foreign events occur too quickly and routinely or are too complex for congressional involvement. Also there are areas of foreign affairs that overlap the president's commander-in-chief and chief-executive powers. These are the major reasons that a president often bypasses the treaty-making process and negotiates an **executive agreement** with another nation. Sometimes, Congress authorizes the president to act without senatorial consent; for example, the Lend-Lease Act of 1941 gave Franklin Roosevelt the power to form many crucial agreements with the United States's World War II allies and authorized him to commit more than $40 billion in war supplies to other nations. Presidents have also used executive agreements to form what were in fact treaties with other nations without congressional involvement. Some of these have been routine (e.g., fishing-rights agreements with Canada), but many have been extremely important. Examples of executive agreements for which Congress gave no explicit approval are the 1898 protocol by which Spain gave up its claim to Cuba and ceded Puerto Rico to the United States; the Yalta and Potsdam agreements by which the Western allies and the Soviets divided postwar Europe; and some of Richard Nixon's commitments to the South Vietnamese regime. This executive function has been endorsed by the Supreme

executive agreement: An international agreement made between a president and a foreign nation that, unlike a treaty, is not ratified by the Senate.

Court, which has ruled that such agreements have a status and dignity "similar" to treaties.[13]

THE ORGANIZATION OF THE PRESIDENCY

Up to this point, we have referred to the president as an individual because the Constitution makes no provision for a White House bureaucracy; it only refers to "executive Departments." It is important to distinguish between the *president* and the *presidency;* the *presidency* refers to the institution, or the office, apart from the individual who happens to hold the title. Thus, presidents often speak of protecting the powers of the presidency, and, in fact, because the powers of presidents are based largely on the precedents and traditions established by their predecessors, the presidency remains even when an administration ends.

In addition, the *presidency* refers to an apparatus consisting of the president, his advisers, and his staff. Any one of the presidential functions discussed in the last section would be an enormous task for an individual working alone. No one person could read, hear, digest, or understand all of the information necessary for making decisions on foreign policy, domestic policy, and the execution of the law. Therefore, presidents allocate tasks to employees of the executive branch. However, under the necessary-and-proper clause, Article I gives the power to organize the executive branch to Congress; thus, presidents must receive statutory approval for changes. In most cases, Congress grants the president broad discretion in organizing the White House Office and the Executive Office of the President, but some presidential agencies are specifically mandated by Congress.

Of course, division of labor is useful only if the subdivisions of the organization are controlled and managed. Therefore, in the assortment of presidential offices and agencies, a hierarchy is necessary to maintain order, to assure the smooth flow of information to the top, and to make sure that the authority of the president is felt throughout the organization. How the presidency is managed varies a great deal from one president to another. For example, Jimmy Carter managed his administration personally and informally, becoming immersed in large amounts of facts and details. Ronald Reagan, on the other hand, took the role of chairman of the board, delegating authority to make particular decisions to White House advisers and the cabinet.[14]

The White House Office

The president brings to the White House a select group of personal assistants, many of them top campaign aides in whom he has special trust. Their loyalty is assumed, and they are expected to be thoroughly familiar with the basics of the president's program for the nation. Not only do they have unique access to the president, but they are able—and expected—to determine most of whom and what the president sees. Thus, top White House assistants organize, control, and reduce the president's information load. Not surprisingly, in most White House offices, squabbles occur among high-ranking aides for the president's attention and approval.

Many recent presidents have appointed a *chief of staff* to be responsible for managing the White House Office and to act as the ultimate filter of information and people that get to the president. Paperwork, briefings, and appointments are commonly routed through this office. Richard Nixon's chief of staff, H. R. Haldeman, characterized himself in this way: "Every President needs a son of a bitch, and I'm Nixon's. I'm his buffer and I'm his bastard. I get done what he wants done and I take the heat instead of him."[15] Other presidents rely heavily on a White House *counselor*; Ronald Reagan designated this important role to Edwin Meese, who oversaw cabinet activities and policy development. The position of *assistant for national security affairs,* or national security adviser, has become much more important since Henry Kissinger filled it during the early Nixon years and exerted more influence over foreign policy than the secretary of state. Finally, the White House staff includes other aides and deputies, a press secretary and staff, speechwriters, a personal lawyer for the president, and even a special staff for the First Lady.

The White House Office—which consisted of only 6 aides in 1939, peaked at about 640 in 1974, and declined to 435 in 1981—has been described as a government within a government. The benefits of a competent, vigorous White House Office are obvious, yet an overprotective top echelon, or one wracked by internal jealousies, can impose serious costs upon the president and the nation. Top staff members can insulate the president and, as experience has shown, can be more interested in protecting or promoting the president than the national interest. In addition, if a president is unable or unwilling to cope with the demands of the office, much of his decisionmaking authority may be delegated to his top aides. For example, when Richard Nixon was preoccupied with the Watergate scandal during the later stages of his presidency, he deferred to his staff during meetings and eventually cloistered himself in his White House quarters, allowing Henry Kissinger to make the important foreign-policy decisions. Nevertheless, given the size of the modern executive branch, there is a clear need for a White House Office to assist the president in the performance of his duties.

The Executive Office of the President

In a formal sense, the White House Office is a part of the Executive Office of the President, which was created by the 1939 Reorganization Act and subsequently reorganized many times. In another sense, however, each of these offices is distinct. The White House Office exists to serve the president's individual needs, whereas the Executive Office performs certain obligatory functions for the president, such as the preparation of the budget that he submits each year to Congress. In general, the principal functions of the Executive

Office are (1) to monitor and control the executive branch, (2) to engage in short- and long-range planning, and (3) to coordinate the fragmented and discrete activities of the many executive agencies into a coherent, or at least consistent, pattern, in compliance with the president's goals and objectives.

The Executive Office of the president contains many agencies (see Figure 9-1), three of which are particularly important. The Bureau of the Budget, formed in 1921 to assist the president in coordinating the overall budget needs of the administration, was given expanded powers and renamed the *Office of Management and Budget (OMB)* in 1970. Its primary duty is to compile the president's budget requests. Departments and agencies submit their anticipated budgetary needs, as well as proposals for new spending programs, to the OMB, which examines them in terms of their efficiency and compatibility with the president's policies. The overall budget is also assessed in terms of its fiscal impact on the economy (as we will see in Chapter 12). With this mandate, the OMB cannot avoid making policy decisions. Because the presi-

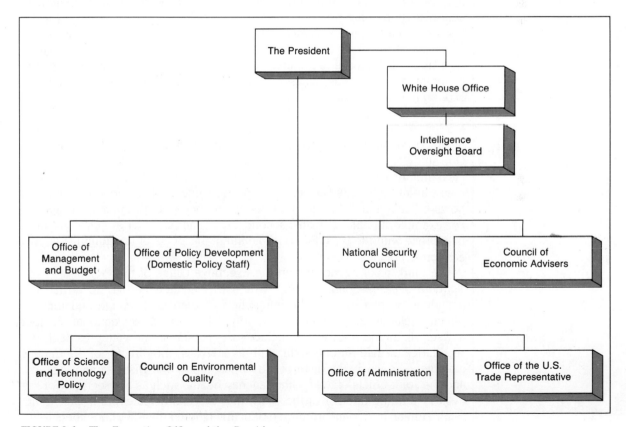

FIGURE 9-1   The Executive Office of the President

Source: *U.S. Government Manual, 1982–83* (Washington, D.C.: Government Printing Office, 1982), p. 798.

dent's budget requests to Congress are fundamental to overall policy goals, since the Nixon administration, the directors of the OMB have been principal presidential advisers on public policy.

In addition, the OMB performs other inherently political management functions. Like the budget requests, the legislative proposals of executive-branch agencies and departments are filtered through the OMB. This process of **legislative clearance** is intended to prevent contradictory programs from being presented to Congress; it is a principal mechanism by which presidents can control the future behavior of the executive branch. A related function was begun by Ronald Reagan's Executive Order 12291, which required agency heads to submit to the OMB their cost-benefit analyses of all proposed rules or regulations with an annual projected cost to the economy of $100 million or more. The OMB cannot formally block a proposed regulation, but because agency heads serve by the grace of the president, they are receptive to OMB criticisms. Finally, the OMB also periodically evaluates agency programs and performance to assess the implementation of policies. Whether or not the OMB performs all of these functions well, it is able to exert great influence on administration policies.

Another part of the Executive Office of the President shares some of the functions of the OMB (e.g., preparing policy programs) but has primary responsibility for informing the president about the overall performance of the economy and the steps that should be taken to improve it. The *Council of Economic Advisers (CEA),* formed in 1946, consists of three economists who prepare the annual *Economic Report of the President,* in which future trends are forecast and policies are recommended to attain the goals of high employment, relatively stable price levels, and a high rate of economic growth. One study of the CEA concluded that it gives the president knowledge, rationales, and advice that can be translated into power over the executive departments and Congress.[16] The academic prominence of the chairman of the CEA, however, may translate into more independence than the president desires. For example, Ronald Reagan's second CEA chairman, Martin Feldstein, publicly broke with the president on fundamental aspects of the administration's economic policies.

The third major agency within the Executive Office of the President is the *National Security Council (NSC)*, which was created in 1947 to advise the president "with respect to the integration of domestic, foreign and military policies relating to the national security." The president's national security adviser chairs the NSC, which includes the president and vice president, the secretaries of defense and state, and, as advisers, the director of the Central Intelligence Agency, the head of the Arms Control and Disarmament Agency, and the Joint Chiefs of Staff. Other agency heads, such as the secretary of the treasury and the director of the OMB, may also participate. Some presidents (e.g., Truman and Johnson) have practically ignored the NSC, and others (e.g., Eisenhower and Nixon) have relied heavily on it. The role of the NSC is constantly changing because it depends on the degree to which the president

legislative clearance: Practice that requires the president's Office of Management and Budget to decide whether legislative proposals devised by executive-branch employees are compatible with the president's programs.

relies on the secretary of state, the national security adviser, or ad hoc task forces.

The Executive Office of the President also includes agencies that cover domestic policy, foreign trade, environmental problems, and science and technology (Figure 9-1). These combine the three principal functions of the other agencies within the Executive Office: supervision, planning, and coordination. Like the other agencies, their importance to the president varies according to personalities and the importance of their subject matter; for example, science advisers were consulted frequently during the early days of the nuclear arms race and the nation's missile programs.

The Vice Presidency

The Constitution says little about the vice president. Vice presidents may succeed to the presidency, and they preside over the Senate in their role as president of that body. On a daily basis, however, the vice president has virtually no constitutional responsibilities. Most vice presidents are chosen for political purposes, being selected more on the basis of geographical roots or appeal to a different wing of the presidential candidate's party than on the basis of competence or closeness to the president.

Vice presidents are accorded some of the dignity—and staff (e.g., press secretary and legal counsel)—of the presidency. By statute, the vice president is a member of the National Security Council, but there is no guarantee that he or she will have an effect. Some presidents have relied heavily on their understudies to perform important policy roles in both the domestic and foreign policy areas; Walter Mondale was very active in the Carter administration, for example, and George Bush assisted Ronald Reagan in the areas of regulation-cutting, refugees, and cracking down on drug smuggling. But other presidents have done little more than send their vice presidents to represent them at the funerals of foreign dignitaries. Probably the most important function of vice presidents is to learn as much as they can so that they can fill the office of the presidency if need be. About one in three vice presidents have eventually occupied the White House—eight upon the death of a president, one upon a president's resignation, and four by obtaining their party's nomination and the public's vote.

The Cabinet

There is no mention of a cabinet in the Constitution; the Founders considered but rejected proposals to establish councils to assist the president. Yet, George Washington occasionally brought together the heads of the executive departments for conferences, and by 1793, the term *cabinet* was applied to the heads of these departments. Today, the cabinet is comprised of the heads of the thirteen executive departments and the ambassador to the United Nations, all of whom are appointed by the president, with the (usually *pro forma*) advice and consent of the Senate. (See Table 9-1.)

TABLE 9-1
THE EXECUTIVE DEPARTMENTS

Department	Created	Approximate Employment (September 1982)
State	1789	24,120
Treasury	1789	118,648
Defense[a]	1789	989,633
Justice[b]	1870	57,094
Interior	1849	78,869
Agriculture[c]	1889	121,175
Commerce[d]	1913	34,451
Labor[d]	1913	19,248
Health and Human Services[e]	1979	147,791
Housing and Urban Development	1965	14,279
Transportation	1966	62,392
Energy	1977	17,945
Education[e]	1979	5,692

[a]This was called the War Department until 1949. Employment figures are for civilians only.
[b]The position of attorney general was created in 1789. The Justice Department was formed in 1870.
[c]Created in 1862, the Department of Agriculture became a cabinet department in 1889.
[d]The Department of Commerce and Labor was created in 1903. It became two separate departments in 1913.
[e]In 1979, the Department of Health, Education, and Welfare (HEW), which had been created in 1953, was replaced by the Department of Health and Human Services and the Department of Education.

Source: *Statistical Abstract of the United States, 1984* (Washington, D.C.: Government Printing Office, 1984), p. 336.

In most other nations, the executive cabinet is a collective body that shares responsibility for the successes and failures of the head of government. The American cabinet, in contrast, often offers only a facade of unity. Individual cabinet members may be important confidantes of the president, but the cabinet as a whole is generally not. Although each president holds cabinet meetings, their relative unimportance as advisory bodies is illustrated by a remark made by President Lincoln after a particularly bitter meeting in which every cabinet member opposed him: "Seven nays, one aye, the ayes have it." In recent times, few of the matters most important to the president have been discussed or resolved in cabinet meetings; Dwight Eisenhower and Jimmy Carter both abandoned their efforts to give real policymaking significance to the cabinets, and other recent presidents have not even tried. John Kennedy, in fact, held only six cabinet meetings in nearly three years.

The cabinet as a whole plays a small role in the affairs with which the president is directly concerned, but the individual cabinet departments are important in the organization of the executive branch. The departments employ most of the executive branch's civilian employees and virtually all of its military employees; the only noncabinet departments employing large numbers of people are the Postal Service and the Veterans Administration. At the head of the cabinet departments are secretaries—or, in the case of the Department of Justice, the attorney general—who act as links between the president and the bureaucracies under them. Their tasks are to control their departments and to assure that the decisions made by their subordinates are compatible with (1) the president's goals and objectives, (2) the statutes governing their departments, (3) sound public policy, and (4) legal precedent. Sometimes, these objectives may be mutually contradictory.

Although cabinet secretaries are formally charged with controlling their employees, they are often unsuccessful at this task because the information costs required are staggering. We shall see in Chapter 10 that each cabinet department is itself a complicated organization, making and implementing wide ranges of policies on complex subjects. Despite the assistance cabinet secretaries may receive from undersecretaries, deputy undersecretaries, and so on, there is a wide information gap between them and the day-to-day activities of the civil servants in their departments. The problems of management, coupled with the fact that most cabinet secretaries leave lucrative private-sector jobs to join the president's team, are major factors in the short tenure of the average cabinet member; from 1960 to 1972, about 60 percent of all cabinet secretaries stayed in their jobs less than two years.[17]

As we have seen, the president's problems in performing the duties of the office fall into three basic categories. First, how can the enormous amount of information—which naturally flows into the Oval Office as the president tries to execute the laws, command the armed forces, balance the legislative power of Congress, and negotiate with foreign nations—be reduced? Second, how can the executive branch be organized so that one individual can redirect the momentum of previous presidents' programs while overcoming the inertia of the vast executive bureaucracy? Finally, how can the president control the apparatus that has been created in the executive branch so that the constitutional locus of the executive function remains where the Founders placed it? In the next section we will look at presidential policymaking in more detail. The importance of information, organization, and control will be illustrated as we examine the tools that presidents can use and the constraints that restrict them in the areas of domestic and foreign policy.

PRESIDENTIAL POLICYMAKING

Because the president's constitutional and informal duties combine to make him the nation's chief policymaker, it is important to understand his role in governmental decisions. Earlier in this chapter, we examined the president's function as chief legislator, but presidential policymaking includes much more than participating in the passage of laws; almost everything the president does has some policy significance, so he is continually "shaping the directions of governmental activity."[18] But exactly what does he do, and how does he do it?

To answer these questions, let us look at the ways in which presidents influence policy and the obstacles they face. It is rare for any president to directly formulate and implement a policy; even the Joint Chiefs of Staff, who are usually rigidly loyal to their commander-in-chief, may oppose a president on defense issues when they are called to testify before Congress. Instead, the president must enlist the support of Congress, the American public, and the executive bureaucracy. For each of these tasks, the president needs a different set of strategies and faces a different set of problems.

The President and Congress

The Constitution requires that the president occasionally interact with Congress. Thus, the chief executive advises legislators on problems facing the nation, asks for their advice and consent on appointments and treaties, and may veto the final results of their efforts. The process of obtaining policies is hardly this dainty, however. Every president has had to learn to deal with Congress in ways that are sometimes innovative, sometimes surreptitious, and sometimes less than dignified.

In his relationship with Congress, the president has a distinct and powerful advantage. As we have discussed, he has access to the information and ideas of millions of bureaucrats. In contrast, Congress has fewer than forty thousand employees, many of whom are hired primarily to find out what is happening in the executive branch; except for particularly controversial matters, the opportunity costs are too high for legislators to mount their own investigations of policy questions. Despite congressional efforts to reduce the disparity between the branches in information and analysis (e.g., the creation of the Congressional Budget Office and the Office of Technology Assessment), the president continues to have the edge.

We have also seen that the president sets the basic agenda for Congress. Through the State of the Union Message, the annual *Economic Report,* and other messages, the president establishes priorities that guide congressional action. In addition, the president dominates the choice of topics in policy debates by initiating the appointment- and treaty-approval processes in the Senate. Although individual legislators sometimes take the initiative—especially on domestic policy matters—the president's program provides Congress with "a handy and official guide to the wants of its biggest customer; an advance formulation of the main issues in each session; a work load ready to hand to every legislative committee."[19]

After the president has presented a policy proposal to Congress, he must convince a majority of legislators that it should be passed into law. Although he may have a cadre of die-hard supporters (usually members of his party), they will be too few to ensure the easy passage of his program. So, because almost all political issues are too complex and too value-laden for an objective, scientific computation of the correct course of action, the president and his advisers must be prepared to fight. Presidents have devised many tools and strategies, which can be roughly divided into three categories:

1. convincing members of Congress of the objective costs and benefits of various approaches
2. providing legislators with incentives to cooperate
3. using direct methods of control

These categories are not necessarily distinct; in fact, presidents often use all three simultaneously.

The Merits of a Policy

A president's first form of action—convincing legislators of the superiority of a policy—is easier to prescribe than to practice. The president may recruit a task force or a presidential commission composed of a wide range of experts (e.g., academics, community leaders, labor or business officials, and members of the other party), with the aim of persuading Congress and the public that the best policy has been proposed. Members of Congress often assume that presidential commissions are created in order to help presidents duck controversial issues or that they are merely political ploys, and sometimes such suspicions are correct. For example, the President's Committee on Civil Rights gave Harry Truman recommendations that had little chance of passage, but enabled him to propose policies that probably helped him win the 1948 election. On the other hand, some presidential commissions allow both the president and Congress to diffuse the responsibility for unpleasant choices. In the 1980s, President Reagan's Commission on Social Security Reform played such a role in the case of social security tax increases and benefit reductions.

The creation of special temporary study groups may sometimes add legitimacy and objectivity to a president's proposals, but presidents more commonly use members of the executive branch to deal with Congress. In many congressional hearings, cabinet secretaries or agency directors testify, often assisted by well-informed aides and mountains of data, thus trying to exploit their informational advantage. Nevertheless, presidential policymaking remains inherently political, so presidents must usually find additional ways to enlist support.

The Use of Incentives

In understanding incentives, the second major category of tools and strategies that presidents use in policymaking, it is important to note that because the Constitution mandates the sharing of legislative power by the executive and

Congress, the two share some common interests. One goal on which they generally agree is the formation of good public policy; they usually also share the goal of reelection. So, in order to gain congressional cooperation, the president exploits these common interests. His status places him in a unique position to provide legislators with incentives that will persuade them to join his efforts.

One form of incentive is direct. The president may dangle rewards in front of potential congressional supporters, or he may threaten retribution or the withholding of rewards from uncooperative representatives and senators. For example, the president can nominate or appoint friends or supporters of legislators to be federal district judges, United States attorneys and marshals, and executive-branch officials; the success in the House of Representatives of Jimmy Carter's energy program was partly attributed to his appointing several of House Speaker Thomas P. "Tip" O'Neill's acquaintances to the management of the General Services Administration. In addition, the president can promise to support the pet project of a member of Congress—perhaps a new post office or a federal construction project in the home district or state. Or, if the reluctant legislator is a member of the president's party, he or she may appreciate a prestige-boosting visit from the chief executive during a reelection campaign. On the other hand, the president can retaliate against members of Congress who criticize or attack him.[20] These measures can include the cancellation of projects in legislators' home states, the withholding of national campaign funds, and leaked allegations of wrongdoing. Presidents are reluctant to play rough, however, because such tactics often backfire.

More frequently, presidents use incentives to enlist congressional support by persuading members of Congress to bargain or compromise. In his book, *Presidential Power*, Richard Neustadt observed: "The separateness of institutions and the sharing of authority prescribe the terms on which a president persuades. When one man shares authority with another, but does not gain or lose his job upon the other's whim, his willingness to act upon the urging of the other turns on whether he conceives the action right for him. The essence of a President's persuasive task is to convince such men that what the White House wants of them is what they ought to do for their own sake and on their authority.[21] Neustadt quotes Harry Truman as saying, "I sit here all day trying to persuade people to do the things they ought to have sense enough to do without my persuading them. . . . That's all the powers of the President amount to."[22] As we have seen, the president can do more than this, but the effectiveness of making people believe that their self-interest is best served by cooperation cannot be overestimated. Altruism is sometimes in short supply, but self-interest seems to be a common commodity.

Each president has an individual style based on his personality, his electoral strength and public popularity, the nature of the issues he is addressing, and the strength of his party and supporters in Congress. For example, Lyndon Johnson was famous for "the treatment" he gave lawmakers: flattery, bullying, and friendly backslapping. Although other presidents may have been more diffident, they have all found it useful to invite congressional leaders to a White House breakfast or a weekend at the presidential retreat at Camp David. The presidential election campaign is good training, for once in office, a president must be able to offer an agenda to which people will rally, he must adapt to political forces that he cannot change, and he must present himself as a person of resolve and reason.

Most presidents are well-equipped to handle the task of persuading legislators. Communications with Congress are far from new, but only since World War II have they become institutionalized. Beginning with the Eisenhower administration, the White House Office has included an office for legislative liaison (now called the Office of Congressional Relations), which lobbies, recruits, and informs members of Congress, as well as keeps the president and his advisers up-to-date on useful strategies, pliable legislators, and the mood of Congress. Although White House tacticians may focus on members of the president's party, they usually direct their efforts at lawmakers of either party who are undecided about their support for an upcoming bill. These tacticians will stress the electoral mandate and popularity of the president, the interests and opinions of the legislators' constituents, and perhaps some of the direct rewards and sanctions discussed above. To show that the president is willing to compromise, they will solicit legislators' feelings on an issue and offer to bargain. It is an inescapably political task, and presidents who disdain these tactics lose support and respect.

Presidential Control of Congress

Finally, if the president cannot convince congressional representatives of the merits of a program or their personal stake in his policies, he may resort to the use of direct controls over lawmaking. Many presidents have occasionally wished they could send Congress home, and the Constitution gives them this power under certain circumstances; according to Article II, Section 3, the president can "on extraordinary Occasions, convene both Houses, or either of them, and in Case of Disagreement between them, with Respect to the Time of Adjournment, he may adjourn them to such Time as he shall think proper." However, no president has ever exercised this power. As we have seen, a president may also veto Congress's efforts, implement policies through executive orders or agreements, or remove certain obstructive officers. Moreover, he can delay the implementation of unwanted legislative policies by exploiting the bureaucratic maze. Finally, in some cases, presidents have refused to spend funds appropriated by Congress.

During the 1960s, some people believed that the powers of the president relative to Congress had become too unconstrained. According to historian Arthur Schlesinger, Jr., the office had developed into an "imperial presidency," largely because of the abuse of the president's power to wage war without congressional consent and his ability to keep information from Congress and the public. Yet, events in the 1970s graphically demonstrated that the constitutional scheme of checks and balances was not dead. As mentioned previously, the War Powers Resolution of 1973 was designed to restrain presidents who might wish to send American troops into battle without formal congressional approval. In the mid-1970s, the Senate and the House each established a permanent Select Committee on Intelligence to review the previously secret activities and budgets of the Central Intelligence Agency and other intelligence agencies. In 1976, Congress broke new ground by banning the expenditure of funds for American covert operations in Angola. Although Congress had already tightened the "purse strings" to control presidential foreign policymaking, the use of the appropriations process became more common during and after the Vietnam war.[23]

Concern about the growth in presidential power relative to Congress also extended to domestic policymaking. Since the term of Thomas Jefferson, who delayed spending a $50,000 congressional appropriation for gunboats until more advanced ships were available, presidents have occasionally impounded funds that were appropriated by Congress. Statutes have given the president authority to set money aside for contingencies and to spend less money than appropriated when the will of Congress could be realized at a lower cost. However, many presidents have treated impoundment as an executive power that allowed them to treat appropriations as permissions rather than requirements. The issue reached a climax during Richard Nixon's administration, when Nixon impounded funds intended for low-income housing subsidies, highways, school aid, pollution control, and other policies dear to the Democrats, who controlled both houses of Congress. The Supreme Court ruled that when Congress intends the president to spend funds, he cannot claim statutory authority to impound them.[24] In 1974, Congress passed the Budget and Impoundment Control Act, which, among other things, required a president to get congressional consent before lawfully deferring or rescinding expenditures. Nevertheless, subsequent presidents have continued to find ways to avoid spending money.

It is tempting to try to quantify each president's ability to move Congress in the direction of his policies. Observers of national politics often calculate presidential support scores or box scores, which purportedly indicate the success of a president's legislative program. These figures must be viewed cautiously, however, because they suggest a kind of simplicity in policymaking that does not exist. Presidents do not accord equal importance to every measure that the executive branch forwards to Congress for action. The substance of a president's bill may be radically changed by Congress, although the name of the legislation remains the same. The basic rules of competition differ according to policy area (e.g., between foreign and domestic policy), so good scores should differ according to the content of the legislation. Sometimes, presidents merely endorse the inevitable, thereby protecting their prestige but actually undermining their power. The interaction of presidential-congressional relations is complex and always changing, so convenient measures may mislead more than inform.

In its effort to constrain the executive branch, Congress has another important tool, which it shares with the president. By appealing directly to the public, to local electorates, or to special constituencies such as interest groups, members of Congress can sometimes get the White House to change its policies. As we will see in the next section, however, as the national leader, the president has a unique advantage in the battle for the attention and support of the American people.

The President and the Public

Every president claims that election or reelection is a mandate from the people to implement the policies he has proposed during his campaign. Although the size of electoral victories and therefore the strength of mandates vary widely, the president is usually elected with more than forty million votes, and he therefore has a right to such a claim. Thus, a president begins each term with a honeymoon period during which the mandate is still fresh. This period typically lasts only a few months, but it is a time when, as the man of the hour and leader of the people, the president can take advantage of his clean slate to push hard for his programs. The public, the press, and Congress are usually willing to give the president some benefit of the doubt during the honeymoon.

However, the president soon enters the arena of politics-as-usual, in which his pronouncements are dissected and analyzed, the new Congress organizes and spawns coalitions to oppose him, and dissension within the White House begins to emerge. All of these factors can have a devastating effect on the president's image and influence. While his early decisions may please some individuals and groups, they are certain to make others unhappy. Thus, once he occupies the Oval Office, the president must constantly convey to the American people that he is competent and in charge.

It is often necessary for presidents to narrow their focus from the general public to work on particular relevant political groups. One need not believe that elites run the United States to accept that the opinions and support of some people are more important than those of others. Once opinion leaders are recruited, for example, they can help organize grass-roots support for a president's programs and can press Congress to adopt his policies. Close advisers or high-ranking government officials often meet with business, labor, and interest-group leaders, and the president may invite well-placed individuals to the White House for a personal meeting. Of course, at the same time, these nongovernmental leaders try to shape the president's policies by communicating their own points of view to the executive branch. Again, the political art of bargaining and compromise is vital to a successful presidential program.

The Polls   In their attempts to persuade the mass media and the mass electorate, presidents must be attentive to what the nation wants. In the same way that a sales organization may undertake a marketing survey to study the type of product consumers are willing to buy, the White House organization uses press secretaries, media advisers, assistants to the president for public liaison, and even pollsters. The pollsters not only shape the president's messages for public consumption, but they also help the administration respond to changes in public opinion. Presidents seem to use polls more to avoid controversial topics or positions than to determine their policies. For example, Ronald Reagan's avoidance of the social issues of abortion, busing, and school prayer during his first year in office, when he was fighting hard for his economic policies, was not an indication that he had changed his positions on these issues; rather, it was part of a strategy not to give his opponents more to attack than necessary.

A president's popularity generally rises after he takes strong action in the international arena, even when the deed is disastrous, such as the 1961 Bay of Pigs invasion of Cuba. Even so, there is no evidence that presidents are adventurous merely to raise their standings in the polls. Sometimes, however, the polls offer a picture of the public mood that presidents cannot ignore. When Lyndon Johnson's popularity dropped to its lowest level ever following the 1968 Tet Offensive in South Vietnam, he announced that he would not run for reelection. Although other factors probably influenced the decision, such as Johnson's primary election victory over Senator Eugene McCarthy in New Hampshire by only 6 percent, the perception of impending disaster, which turned out to be premature, hastened the demise of his presidency.

The Media   More than forty years ago, a British political scientist wrote: "Every president has an incomparable audience waiting for the pronouncement he may choose to make; to whomever else the Americans may not listen . . . they will listen to *him*. In any crisis, in the discussion of any big problem, they expect him to speak; in a very real sense, when he has spoken, they feel that the nation has spoken. . . . No one else has the power that he has to mobilize public opinion; no one else can reach it so profoundly; no one else's judgement is, so decisively, 'front page' news."[25] Sweeping as this statement is, it is hardly an exaggeration. Theodore Roosevelt referred to the presidency as a "bully pulpit," from which presidents could exhort and educate their fellow citizens. Since the days of Franklin Roosevelt's fireside chats on the radio ("My friends, I want to tell you what has been done in the last few days, why it was done, and what the next steps are going to be . . . "), presidents who have been boxed in by a recalcitrant Congress have taken to the airwaves. John Kennedy boosted his popularity with his understanding of the political power of television; five days after his inauguration, he permitted the first live television coverage of a presidential press conference. Lyndon Johnson moved the time of his televised speeches, including the State of the Union Message, to prime-time evening hours. Since Kennedy, presidents have occasionally requested airtime for major addresses. Rebuttals by Congress or the other party need not be provided, although they often are, but they are never as widely viewed.

President John Kennedy responds to a question during a 1963 news conference. Kennedy was the first chief executive to permit—and exploit—live television coverage of these traditional meetings with the press. (AP/Wide World Photos)

Press conferences and major addresses are usually well-managed by the president and his staff. Speeches are carefully written and rehearsed, and presidents are briefed on questions likely to be asked at press conferences. A televised address or news conference is too short to allow a detailed examination of issues, so presidents are able to oversimplify complex problems (e.g., by declaring a war on poverty, drugs, or cancer) or to propose somewhat transparent symbols for their policies in order to enlist public support (e.g., naming the MX missile the "Peacekeeper"). The White House can try to manage the news in other indirect ways as well. "Highly placed officials in the White House" commonly leak information to reporters about the president's actions and policies. The president can then test the wind to see if the suggestion of a policy, which he can personally disavow, arouses too much controversy. In addition, many employees of the executive branch can be used to spread information favorable to the president or his programs. In 1970, the Office of Management and Budget estimated that 6,144 people in the executive branch held jobs primarily related to public relations. Of course, the higher the rank of the source, the more newsworthy the information may seem, so cabinet secretaries are often given the job of helping the president's press relations.

With all of these tools at the disposal of presidents, however, every one of them finds ample cause to complain about media treatment. A president simply cannot control what the press says about him. Members of Congress may not have the visibility of the president, but they can conduct investigations, leak information, and publicly excoriate him—all of which may be deemed newsworthy by the television networks, the major newspapers, and newsmagazines. Every White House develops its own leaks as conflicts and factions among the president's close advisers are made public. Events within the United States or abroad can dictate the agenda for the evening news, regardless of the president's attempts to orchestrate media coverage.

Some observers, both in the White House and the press, believe that during the 1970s, a subtle yet important change occurred in the relationship between the president and the news media. Recent critics have charged that because of the importance of entrepreneurial reporters in uncovering the numerous illegal White House activities covered by the name *Watergate,* the press has become too eager to uncover and magnify problems within the administrations of subsequent presidents. This alleged "wolfpack" journalism, in which the White House press corps seizes upon and overdramatizes a small misdeed or a loose word, has been accused of undermining the confidence of Americans in their leaders and weakening the ability of presidents to govern. Yet, it is not clear whether the decline in Americans' trust of the institutions of government is a result or a cause of reporters' post-Watergate zeal. Similarly, no one can be sure exactly how much skepticism concerning a president and his staff is healthy for democracy and how much is too much. Some individuals find it particularly worrisome that the control of the presidency—constitutionally, a function of the courts and Congress and, traditionally, a function of political parties—has perhaps shifted somewhat to television and newspaper organizations. Despite their importance to democracy, the media are not subject to democratic controls.

The President and the Courts

At the Constitutional Convention, James Madison pointed out that similarities existed between the executive function and the judicial function. They were both to be responsible for executing and expounding the laws, although in different circumstances: the executive would pursue the collective interest and would have greater discretion than the judiciary in its protection of individual interests.[26] Thus, there were basic grounds for both cooperation and conflict between the two branches of government. In *The Federalist,* no. 78, Hamilton also observed that "the judiciary is beyond comparison the weakest of the three departments of power." But we have already seen (e.g., when Truman attempted to seize the steel mills during World War II) that the courts are capable of restraining the president.

How do the executive and judicial branches interact? The president's greatest power over the judiciary is his appointive power. Presidents realize that their appointees, especially to the Supreme Court, will continue to affect policy long after the presidential term has ended. Therefore, they try to find nominees who reflect their general perception of government, who have outstanding records and qualifications, and who will be acceptable to the Senate when it considers their confirmation. Presidents screen candidates with the help of the attorney general, senators, the American Bar Association, and others. According to one study of Supreme Court nominations, however, "one justice in four has turned out to be quite different from what his appointer wanted."[27] One of the more notable surprises in recent years was Chief Justice Earl Warren. Appointed by President Dwight Eisenhower, Warren became known as much more of an activist on desegration and civil liberties issues than Eisenhower had expected.

Presidents have had more success with the qualifications of their Supreme Court nominees. Only one, Samuel Chase, has been impeached, and he was acquitted by the Senate in 1805. The Senate has rejected 26 of 136 Supreme Court nominees (4 in this century); such nominations are more likely to fail when the Senate is controlled by the opposite party or when the nomination is made in the last year of a presidential term. The political philosophy and personal characteristics of candidates have also affected a president's chances for pushing the Court in the direction he prefers. Franklin Roosevelt's attempt in 1937 to pack the Supreme Court with justices sympathetic to his New Deal policies by exceeding the traditional number of nine seats never received congressional approval. As a result, subsequent presidents have been able to fill vacancies on the Court only when a justice dies or resigns. Thus, some presidents, including Jimmy Carter, never had the opportunity to appoint a justice to the Court.

After the appointment stage, the president's relationship with the courts is usually rather distant, although some judges continue to informally and confidentially advise him on political or policy questions. To represent him in matters before the court, the president appoints a **solicitor general** with the consent of the Senate. The solicitor general usually selects and represents the executive branch in cases appealed from lower courts. The Supreme Court occasionally orders the president to perform some task, and, of course, he usually complies. Only one president (Andrew Johnson) has threatened to disobey the Court; only two (Abraham Lincoln and Martin Van Buren) have claimed the right to disobey it; and only one (Andrew Jackson) indirectly failed to enforce a Court decision. For a short while in 1974, there was some doubt whether Richard Nixon would obey a Court order to turn over tapes of White House conversations to the Watergate special prosecutor, but he did comply.

The Watergate case illustrates another point of occasional confrontation between the president and the courts, and in many cases, Congress. As we have seen, the president's control of information gives him a marked advantage over Congress; until recently, however, the practice of claiming **executive privilege**—that is, the right of a president or his advisers to withhold information—was relatively rare. On the few dozen occasions when it was invoked before 1968, presidents often claimed that the requested information was important to national security. However, Richard Nixon used executive privilege

solicitor general:
An official of the Department of Justice who represents the executive branch in legal proceedings.

executive privilege:
The argument that certain conversations and documents within the executive branch are protected from congressional scrutiny.

to obstruct congressional investigations of bombing raids in North Vietnam; foreign aid; the overthrow of the government of Chile; grain sales to the Soviet Union; and by designating his cabinet secretaries "White House assistants," the affairs of executive departments.

The issue of executive privilege became most controversial during the Watergate investigation. Nixon claimed that White House tapes and documents, subpoenaed by Special Prosecutor Leon Jaworski, were privileged through the president's "inherent and absolute" power to maintain the separation of powers by preventing one branch of government from demanding information about the internal deliberations or ongoing investigations of another. Allowing access to presidential materials, it was argued, would threaten the confidentiality and candidness of presidential advising. Ten years later, the Reagan administration argued that congressional subpoenas were threatening the Environmental Protection Agency's investigation of problems with its enforcement of a toxic-waste cleanup program. In 1974, the Supreme Court ruled that an executive privilege can exist, but that it is not absolute. The Court held that the power of the courts to conduct criminal investigations cannot be obstructed by claims of executive privilege, but left the door open to such claims if necessary "to protect military, diplomatic, or sensitive national security secrets."[28] Thus, some claimed that the Court's decision was a defeat for President Nixon, as it hastened his resignation, but a victory for the presidency.

After a nationwide television address, President Richard Nixon displays transcripts of White House tape recordings of Watergate conversations. Backing down from his earlier claim of executive privilege, Nixon announced that these selected transcripts would be delivered to the Watergate Special Prosecutor. (UPI/Bettmann Archive)

The President and the Bureaucracy

Regardless of whether the president has gained the cooperation of Congress, the support of the press and the public, and the endorsement of the Supreme Court, it remains his constitutional duty to "take Care that the Laws be faithfully executed." As the chief executive and the head of the executive branch, the president's authority to carry out this task *seems* clear. But his ability to guarantee that his policies will be carried out is far from certain. After Dwight Eisenhower was elected president in 1952, Harry Truman commented: "He'll sit here . . . and he'll say, 'Do this! Do that!' *And nothing will happen.* Poor Ike—it won't be a bit like the Army. He'll find it very frustrating."[29]

What sorts of tools does the president have with which to shape bureaucratic behavior? First, the president has *appointive power* and, to a lesser extent, *removal power* over many bureaucratic officials. Presidents have thousands of positions to fill in three general categories:

1. cabinet and subcabinet positions and bureau chiefs who can actually make policy
2. "schedule C" appointees, who are subordinate to those in the first category but whose jobs have a "confidential or policy-determining character"
3. "noncareer executive assignments," or professional and technical positions that are usually given to senior civil servants

Yet the degree to which a president's appointees are really *his* people depends on many factors. Congress, interest groups, and other high-ranking executive officials will affect those whom the president has chosen—and their behavior once they are in office. The information and organization costs of screening thousands of prospective employees, usually within the first few months after an election, are enormous. Similarly, the removal of an official who has not been a team player can create dissension or the appearance of poor management.

Another tool the president can use in his relations with the bureaucracy is the power to create departments and agencies, to reorganize them, or to put them out of existence. By creating new cabinet positions, presidents can at least appear to be emphasizing particular policy areas—although they often claim to be increasing the efficiency of government. When a president shifts responsibility for certain policies into new bureaucratic environments, he can weaken or strengthen his programs by changing the roster of his supporters and opponents who have access or jurisdiction. Yet, Congress must approve proposed reorganizations of the executive branch, and it has the power to define the duties of executive departments and agencies. It commonly accepts minor changes in bureaucratic organization, but has resisted major shifts. Congressional committees, relevant interest groups, and existing executive departments often form coalitions, which are sometimes called *subgovernments* or *iron triangles*. These coalitions can effectively resist presidential reorganization initiatives. Similarly, Congress and interest groups may resist presidential attempts to sway bureaucratic policymaking by changing their budgets. The president, working through the Office of Management and Budget, can recommend increases or cuts in agency budgets, but Congress often thwarts his efforts by appropriating more or less then he requests.

Finally, the president can push for his programs by asserting his constitutional role as the national leader. Armed with an electoral mandate, the president can insist that he has a more legitimate claim to speak for the nation as a whole than do bureaucrats, interest groups, or members of Congress. Of course, it is hard to measure the effectiveness of this ploy; for example, since 1976, the willingness of many regulatory agencies to reduce their intervention in private markets was accompanied by proclamations from Presidents Ford, Carter, and Reagan of a new era in deregulation, as well as congressional and private-group support.

Certainly, presidents face huge obstacles in trying to overcome bureaucratic inertia or momentum. A president's appointees are too new to the specific policymaking arenas to be able to grasp the information loads and organizational complexities that characterize all large bureaucracies. Similarly, the multiple layers of policymaking and the division of labor within and across agencies and levels of government complicate the president's job of managing and directing the course of government. As we will see in the next chapter, the inefficiencies and delays that most Americans, including presidents, complain about are companions of the bureaucratic task. Even the most powerful individual in American government must adjust to the fragmentation of policymaking.

NOTES

[1]See Jim F. Heath, *John F. Kennedy and the Business Community* (Chicago: University of Chicago Press, 1969), p. 26.

[2]See Charles C. Thach, Jr., *The Creation of the Presidency* (Baltimore: Johns Hopkins University Press, 1923).

[3]Harold W. Chase and Craig R. Ducat, eds., *Edward S. Corwin's "The Constitution and What It Means Today,"* 14th ed. (Princeton, New Jersey: Princeton University Press, 1978), p. 177.

[4]Myers v. U.S., 272 U.S. 52 (1926).

[5]Humphrey's Executor v. U.S., 295 U.S. 602 (1935).

[6]Arthur S. Link, *Wilson: The New Freedom* (Princeton, New Jersey: Princeton University Press, 1956), p. 147.

[7]Richard M. Pious, *The American Presidency* (New York: Basic Books, 1979), p. 148.

[8]*The Federalist*, no. 73.

[9]Pious, *The American Presidency*, chapter 2. For the extent of such prerogative powers, see, for example, U.S. v. Curtiss-Wright Export Corp., 299 U.S. 304 (1936).

[10]U.S. v. Pewee Coal Co., 341 U.S. ll4 (1951); Youngstown Sheet & Tube v. Sawyer, 343 U.S. 579 (1952).

[11]Prize Cases, 67 U.S. (2 Black) 635 (1863).

[12]Chase and Ducat, *Edward S. Corwin's "The Constitution and What It Means Today,"* p. 169.

[13]For example, U.S. v. Pink, 315 U.S. 203 (1942).

[14]See Paul J. Quirk, "What Must a President Know?" *Society,* January/February 1983, pp. 55–62.

[15]Jeb Stuart Magruder, *An American Life* (New York: Atheneum, 1974), p. 58.

[16]Edward S. Flash, Jr., *Economic Advice and Presidential Leadership* (New York: Columbia University Press, 1961), p. 309.

[17]Hugh Heclo, *A Government of Strangers* (Washington, D.C.: Brookings Institution, 1977), pp. 103–105.

[18]Laurence E. Lynn, Jr., and David deF. Whitman, *The President as Policymaker: Jimmy Carter and Welfare Reform* (Philadelphia: Temple University Press, 1981), p. 4.

[19]Richard E. Neustadt, "The Presidency and Legislation: Planning the President's Program," *American Political Science Review* 49 (December 1955): 1014.

[20]For examples from the administrations of Kennedy through Carter, see Pious, *The American Presidency,* p. 193. For a more recent example, see Dennis Farney, Leonard M. Apcar, and Rich Jaroslovsky, "How Reaganites Push Reluctant Republicans to Back Tax-Rise Bill," *Wall Street Journal,* August 18, 1982, p. 1.

[21]Richard E. Neustadt, *Presidential Power: The Politics of Leadership from FDR to Carter* (New York: Wiley, 1980), p. 27.

[22]Ibid., p. 9.

[23]For a list of statutory restrictions on the president's foreign-policy options, see Thomas E. Cronin, *The State of the Presidency.* 2nd ed. (Boston: Little, Brown, 1980), pp. 206–209.

[24]Train v. City of New York, 420 U.S. 35 (1973). However, the Court avoided the question of the president's constitutional authority to impound funds.

[25]Harold J. Laski, *The American Presidency* (New York: Harper, 1940), pp. 146–147.

[26]Max Farrand, ed., *The Records of the Federal Convention of 1787,* vol. II (New Haven: Yale University Press, 1937), p. 34.

[27]Robert Scigliano, *The Supreme Court and the Presidency* (New York: Free Press, 1971), p. 157.

[28]United States v. Nixon (418 U.S. 683).

[29]Neustadt, *Presidential Power,* p. 9. Emphasis in original.

BIBLIOGRAPHY

Cronin, Thomas E. *The State of the Presidency.* 2nd ed. Boston: Little, Brown, 1980. An examination of the politics of the presidency, with special attention to myths about the office and the constraints imposed on the president.

Fenno, Richard F., Jr. *The President's Cabinet.* Cambridge: Harvard University Press, 1959. A dated but still useful analysis of the functions and relations of the American cabinet in the twentieth century.

Fisher, Louis. *Presidential Spending Power.* Princeton: Princeton University Press, 1975. An analysis of what the president can and cannot do to affect the federal budget and the expenditure of funds.

Laski, Harold J. *The American Presidency.* New York: Harper, 1940. A study by a British political scientist that illustrates how little some things about the presidency change.

Light, Paul C. *Vice-Presidential Power.* Chicago: University of Chicago Press, 1982. Focusing on the vice-presidential careers of Nelson Rockefeller, Walter Mondale, and George Bush, Light argues that the office is becoming less superfluous.

Marcus, Maeva. *Truman and the Steel Seizure Case.* New York: Columbia University Press, 1977. An in-depth examination of the limits of presidential power.

Mueller, John E. *Presidents and Public Opinion.* New York: Wiley, 1973. How presidents can affect and are affected by public opinion, with emphasis on presidential popularity from Truman to Nixon.

Neustadt, Richard E. *Presidential Power: The Politics of Leadership from FDR to Carter.* New York: Wiley, 1980. A classic on the acquisition and application of power by presidents.

Pious, Richard M. *The American Presidency.* New York: Basic Books, 1979. A thorough, well-documented text on the presidency.

Schlesinger, Arthur M., Jr. *The Imperial Presidency.* Boston: Houghton-Mifflin, 1973. A critique of the growth of presidential power, especially in foreign policy.

Bureaucracy
and
The Policy Process

During the energy crisis of the 1970s, some manufacturers of home insulation advertised that their products could reduce home heating bills by 50 to 75 percent. Because there was no industry standard for measuring the effectiveness of insulation, consumers had little independent information about the validity of the manufacturers' claims or the relative quality of various types of insulation. As a result, in May 1977, the Federal Trade Commission (FTC) established a task force to protect consumers from fraudulent or misleading claims about these products.

The FTC's first step was to propose a rule calling for a standard measure—an "R-value"—of insulation effectiveness. After allowing time for comments from interested parties, the FTC began public hearings on the proposed rule in February 1978. For four weeks, FTC staff members heard the statements of various organizations and allowed representatives of nine different interest groups (e.g., environmental groups, consumer groups, government agencies, and manufacturers of mineral wool, cellulose, cellular plastic, and urea formaldehyde foam) to question witnesses. The FTC then allotted thirty days for written rebuttals of the evidence presented at the hearings. In July 1978, the FTC published its final staff report. Next, an FTC hearing officer issued a separate report, after which the nine interest groups were once again permitted to submit arguments. Finally, FTC commissioners examined the evidence and approved a rule calling for standardized R-value tests, labels, and explanations in insulation advertisements. This rule was scheduled to go into effect on November 30, 1979. However, the story was not yet over.

On August 31, four insulation manufacturers charged in federal court that the R-value testing methods and the explanations required in television advertisements were unjustified. The FTC delayed implementation of the rule until December 31. At the same time, Congress, which was reacting to other FTC regulations, barred the establishment of any new regulations until May 31, 1980. On June 3, 1980, the FTC proposed that, with the exception of the challenged segments, the R-value rule go into effect, and after the required comment period, the regulation became law on September 29, 1980. During this period, National Bureau of Standards testing indicated that increasingly thick layers of insulation did not reduce heating bills as much as industry had claimed, and in February 1982, the FTC proposed that the original rule—thus modified, and minus the section on advertising—go into effect. After almost five years, the final sections of the R-value regulation were approved. The bureaucracy had created a new policy, but only after making adjustments required by the courts, Congress, industry groups, consumer groups, and administrative law. Why the bureaucratic delay? Why were so many political actors able to influence the making of this policy? In this chapter, we will answer these and other questions about the nature of the American federal bureaucracy and the policy process.

In the preceding chapters, we examined the basic constitutional system of politics and government in the United States. We saw how the framers of the Constitution envisioned a political structure of individual and group partici-pation in public decisionmaking, how the fundamental tenets of law and jus-tice have constrained and ordered our behavior toward one another, and how the three basic institutions of government were designed. We also discussed the evolution of the Founders' creation as the nation has responded to the social and economic changes of two centuries. Yet, the basic structure as laid out in the Constitution has changed. Entirely new institutions have been created to cope with the increased complexity of government and society—institutions that are not mentioned in the Constitution and that are difficult to place within its framework.

In the first part of this chapter, we will examine the American bureaucracy, its roots, growth and organization, behavior, and effects on the American gov-ernment. In the second part, we will look at the intended output of bureaucracy and other governmental institutions. Like the constitutional branches of gov-ernment, the bureaucracy exists in order to make decisions and allocate re-sources—that is, to devise and implement policies by which the government affects the wealth, welfare, and rights of individuals and organizations. As we shall see in Chapters 11 through 13, the history and content of public policies

Alexander Graham Bell inaugurates the New York–Chicago telephone line in 1892. The growing role of federal regulators in business practices was largely a result of im-provements in transportation and communication that made interstate commerce much easier. (The Bettmann Archive, Inc.)

are varied and often complicated; nevertheless, there are some common threads to the policymaking process that make it easier to understand the substantive areas of economic, foreign, and social policy.

THE FEDERAL BUREAUCRACY

Congress passes laws, the president signs them into law (or issues his own executive orders independent of the legislature), and the courts assure compliance with congressional statutes and the Constitution. This is roughly the ideal by which the American government was designed to operate. However, the 545 men and women who comprise both houses of Congress (535), the presidency (1), and the Supreme Court (9) can actually do little more than make decisions. They must rely on agents of the federal government to implement and enforce their decisions.

Even in a small society, it would be unrealistic to expect a perfect fusion of the roles of decisionmaker and decision-implementor. As we have seen, the division of labor in American government serves many useful political and economic functions. First, because the policymaking and policy-implementing tasks are separate, political power is fragmented in a way that is congruent with the constitutional scheme of federalism and the separation of powers; groups or interests that are frustrated in their attempts to change the formal decisions of lawmakers can try to affect the ways in which laws are actually implemented. Second, as we have discussed previously, the courts, Congress, and the president reduce the costs of performing their functions by delegating some of their responsibilities to subordinate or special courts, to committees and staffs, and to White House and executive offices, respectively. By dividing the labor and organizing new institutions within each branch, national leaders have responded to new demands and increased workloads within the Constitution's guidelines. Thus, in each branch of government, the notion of organization has been used to reduce the costs of information and opportunity, to preserve and improve expertise, and to maintain the hierarchy of control that the Constitution dictates.

bureaucracy: An organization characterized by division of labor, hierarchies of authority, and formal rules for decisionmaking.

The term **bureaucracy** is usually interpreted to mean something functionally distinct from the staffs and support agencies of Congress, the president, or the courts. It generally refers to the mass of unelected employees of the federal government who are responsible for the implementation of public policies—those who process the forms, collect the taxes, mail the checks, analyze the results, and so on. In the next section, we will examine bureaucracies in detail.

What Is a Bureaucracy?

What is a bureaucracy? To answer this, we cannot turn to the Constitution. Unlike the other aspects of American government we have already discussed,

RULES AND REGULATIONS OF A FEDERAL AGENCY

Rules and Regulations

Federal Register

Vol. 49, No. 105

Wednesday, May 30, 1984

This section of the FEDERAL REGISTER contains regulatory documents having general applicability and legal effect, most of which are keyed to and codified in the Code of Federal Regulations, which is published under 50 titles pursuant to 44 U.S.C. 1510.
The Code of Federal Regulations is sold by the Superintendent of Documents. Prices of new books are listed in the first FEDERAL REGISTER issue of each week.

DEPARTMENT OF AGRICULTURE

Agricultural Marketing Service

7 CFR Part 908

[Valencia Orange Regulation 327, Amdt. 1; Valencia Orange Regulation 328]

Valencia Orange Grown in Arizona and Designated Part of California; Limitation of Handling

AGENCY: Agricultural Marketing Service, USDA.

ACTION: Final rule.

SUMMARY: Amendment 1 of Regulation 327 increases the quantity of fresh California-Arizona Valencia oranges that may be shipped to market during the period May 25–31, 1984. Regulation 328 establishes the quantity of Valencia oranges that may be shipped during the period June 1–7, 1984. These regulations are needed to provide for orderly marketing of fresh Valencia oranges for the periods specified due to the marketing situation confronting the orange industry.

DATES: Amended Regulation 327 (§ 908.627) becomes effective for the period May 25–31, 1984. Regulation 328 (§ 908.628) becomes effective June 1–7, 1984.

FOR FURTHER INFORMATION CONTACT: William J. Doyle, 202–447–5975.

SUPPLEMENTARY INFORMATION:

Findings

This rule has been reviewed under USDA procedures and Executive Order 12291 and has been designated a "non-major" rule. William T. Manley, Deputy Administrator, Agricultural Marketing Service, has certified that this action will not have a significant economic impact on a substantial number of small entities.

These actions are issued under the marketing agreement, as amended, and Order No. 908, as amended (7 CFR Part 908), regulating the handling of Valencia oranges grown in Arizona and designated part of California. The agreement and order are effective under the Agricultural Marketing Agreement Act of 1937, as amended (7 U.S.C. 601–674). The amendment and regulation are based upon the recommendation of and information submitted by the Valencia Orange Administrative Committee and upon other available information. It is hereby found that this action will tend to effectuate the declared policy of the Act.

The amendment and regulation are consistent with the marketing policy for 1983–84. The marketing policy was recommended by the committee following discussion at a public meeting on February 14, 1984, at Ventura, California. The committee met again publicly on May 22, 1984, to consider the current and prospective conditions of supply and demand for California-Arizona Valencia oranges. The committee reports the demand for Valencia oranges is very good. Since there are Valencia oranges available to meet this demand, it is in the interest of producers and consumers to increase the allotment for the period May 25–31, 1984. However, it is not expected that this level of demand will be maintained for the period June 1–7, 1984. Therefore, a lower allotment is established for that period.

It is further found that it is impracticable and contrary to the public interest to give preliminary notice, engage in public rulemaking, and postpone the effective date until 30 days after publication in the Federal Register (5 U.S.C. 553), because of insufficient time between the date when information became available upon which this amendment is based and the effective date necessary to effectuate the declared policy of the Act. Interested persons were given an opportunity to submit information and views on the regulations at an open meeting. To effectuate the declared purposes of the Act, it is necessary to make these provisions effective as specified, and handlers have been notified of these actions and their effective dates.

List of Subjects in 7 CFR Part 908

Marketing agreements and orders, California, Arizona, Oranges (Valencia).

1. Section 908.627 Valencia Orange Regulation 327 is hereby amended as follows:

§ 908.627 Valencia Orange Regulation 327.

The quantities of Valencia oranges grown in California and Arizona which may be handled during the period May 25–31, 1984, are established as follows:
(a) District 1: 324,000 cartons;
(b) District 2: 371,000 cartons;
(c) District 3: Unlimited cartons.
2. Section 908.628 is added as follows:

§ 908.628 Valencia Orange Regulation 328.

The quantities of Valencia oranges grown in California and Arizona which may be handled during the period June 1–7, 1984, are established as follows:
(a) District 1: 282,000 cartons;
(b) District 2: 318,000 cartons;
(c) District 3: Unlimited cartons.

(Secs. 1–19, 48 Stat. 31, as amended; 7 U.S.C. 601–674)

Dated: May 23, 1984.

Thomas R. Clark,
Deputy Director, Fruit and Vegetable Division, Agricultural Marketing Service.
[FR Doc. 84–14366 Filed 5–29–84; 8:45 am]
BILLING CODE 3410–02–M

---

7 CFR Parts 916 and 917

[Nectarine Regulation 14, Amdt. 5, Peach Regulation 14, Amdt. 5, Plum Regulation 19, Amdt. 5]

Nectarines, Pears, Plums and Peaches Grown in California; Amendment of Size and Grade Requirements

AGENCY: Agricultural Marketing Service, USDA.

ACTION: Interim rule with request for comments.

SUMMARY: This interim rule amends size and grade requirements for shipments of fresh nectarines, peaches and plums grown in California. These requirements are designed to promote marketing of suitable quality and sizes of fresh fruit in the interest of producers and consumers.

DATES: The interim rule is effective on May 30, 1984. Comments are due by June 29, 1984.

---

the purpose, function, and proper role of bureaucracy were not of major concern to the framers. After all, in the eighteenth century, there was no reason to be concerned with the topic, because the forces that led to the creation of the massive United States bureaucracy did not exist. However, bureaucracy is not a recent invention; elements of it can be found in the administration of public tasks in ancient Egypt and in most large governments since then.

The German sociologist Max Weber (1864–1920) summarized the characteristics of modern bureaucracies.[1]

1. There are "fixed and official jurisdictional areas." These include (a) clear rules for the division of labor,[2] (b) clear lines of authority (and strict limits on the methods that officials can use), and (c) clear, consistently applied standards for the employment of those who work for the bureaucracy.
2. There is "a firmly ordered system of super- and subordination in which there is a supervision of the lower offices by the higher ones."
3. Management is based upon "written documents," thus requiring a staff of clerks, whom Weber called "scribes," to maintain the files.
4. Effective management "presupposes thorough and expert training."
5. Bureaucratic activity is a full-time job for officials.
6. The bureaucracy "follows general rules, which are more or less stable, more or less exhaustive, and which can be learned."

Weber did not limit these characteristics to governmental organizations, but observed that they are also fundamental to modern businesses because the same advantages of bureaucracy are produced in both the public and the private sector. Bureaucracy, as Weber described it, performs several useful function. First, information costs are reduced by the division of labor because (1) all members of the organization need not be informed about all of its activities, and (2) the clear lines of authority and explicit rules of behavior will require consistency, which means that the bureaucracy can establish standard operating procedures. Similarly, opportunity costs are reduced because bureaucrats will be doing what they were hired to do and will not have the option of pursuing other activities. Third, transaction costs will be reduced because only officials with authority will be able to bargain with individuals or organizations outside the bureaucracy. Thus, to Weber, bureaucracies were efficient.

Furthermore, Weber argued that bureaucracies are beneficial for modern societies because they make decisions "without regard for persons." To Weber, this was a virtue, because "a consistent execution of bureaucratic domination means the leveling of status." Administrative specialization would produce decisions according to objective standards, so citizens would be equal before the law. Thus, "the more the bureaucracy is 'dehumanized,' the more completely it succeeds in eliminating from official business love, hatred, and all purely personal, irrational, and emotional elements which escape calculation. This is the specific nature of bureaucracy and it is appraised as its special virtue."[3]

It is ironic that Weber identified as virtues those aspects of modern bureaucracy that most people today consider to be its worst vices. To many modern critics, the Weberian bureaucracy is far from perfect: it ignores the skills and goals of individual employees, it raises the principle of merit in hiring and job advancement above the principles of equality and need, and it treats people as though they were cogs in a machine. Similarly, although Weber argued that democracy and bureaucracy go hand in hand, equalizing the treatment of nobles and the masses, many have pointed out that large bureaucracies can become powerful arms of government that are far more removed from democratic controls, such as elections, than are the constitutional branches of government.

Myths about Bureaucracies

Recent presidents—most notably, Gerald Ford, Jimmy Carter, and Ronald Reagan—have voiced the opinions of many Americans toward bureaucracy: it is inefficient, too costly, and immortal. To what degree are these criticisms accurate? Is the commonly held view of bureaucracy—that it is a wasteful monster with a life of its own—a myth?

First, Americans are not unanimous in their dislike of government bureaucracies. For example, about 80 percent of the respondents to a 1973 survey spoke favorably of bureaucrats with whom they had had contact, whereas only about 40 percent approved of bureaucrats "in general."[4] Apparently, many people dislike the idea of bureaucracy rather than their actual experience with it. A January 1982 poll showed that 57 percent of the respondents approved of President Reagan's proposal to remove many governmental regulations. Yet, when asked about specific regulations, only a small minority complained of too much government regulation. For example, only 19 percent were in favor of less regulation of automobile safety, and 62 percent approved of more stringent regulation of advertising claims.[5] Thus, we might conclude that Americans find bureaucracy distasteful but appreciate many of its functions.

The most common complaint about bureaucracy is that it burdens individuals and businesses with huge amounts of **red tape,** imposing unreasonable costs by requiring excessive paperwork and cumbersome procedures. In other words, contrary to Weber's expectation that bureaucracy would be an efficient administrative tool, bureaucracy is criticized for increasing the information and transaction costs paid by society.

red tape: Excessive government paperwork and cumbersome procedures.

But is bureaucratic waste limited to governmental bureaucracies? Many consumers who try to correct a faulty report from a credit bureau or who seek satisfaction from a large company that sold a defective product find a similar amount of red tape. It may be that all large bureaucratic organizations, whether in the private or public sector, impose such costs.

Second, a strong case can be made for the advantages of red tape. In our discussion of the legal and judicial processes we showed that cumbersome procedures, although far from speedy or economical, have evolved that survived largely because they help to protect rights. If people are to be treated

AN ORDER FROM A FEDERAL AGENCY

Title 16—Commercial Practices

CHAPTER I—FEDERAL TRADE COMMISSION

[Docket No. 8891–o]

PART 13—PROHIBITED TRADE PRACTICES, AND AFFIRMATIVE CORRECTIVE ACTIONS

Warner-Lambert Co.

Subpart—Advertising falsely or misleadingly: § 13.10 Advertising falsely or misleadingly; § 13.170 Qualities or properties of product or service; 13.170–10 Antiseptic, germicidal; 13.170–52 Medicinal, therapeutic, healthful, etc.; 13.170–70 Preventive or protective; § 13.190 Results; § 13.205 Scientific or other relevant facts. Subpart—Corrective actions and/or requirements: § 13.-533 Corrective actions and/or requirements; 13.533–10 Corrective advertising. Subpart—Misrepresenting oneself and goods—Goods: § 13.1710 Qualities or properties; § 13.1730 Results; § 13.-1740 Scientific or other relevant facts. Subpart—Offering unfair, improper and deceptive inducements to purchase or deal: § 13.2063 Scientific or other relevant facts.

(Sec. 6, 38 Stat. 721; 15 U.S.C. 46. Interprets or applies sec. 5, 38 Stat. 719, as amended; 15 U.S.C. 45)

In the Matter of Warner-Lambert Company a Corporation

Order requiring a Morris Plains, N.J., manufacturer and distributor of "Listerine" mouthwash preparation, among other things to cease misrepresenting the medicinal, therapeutic qualities, beneficial effects, and germicidal nature of its product. Respondent if further required to include a corrective advertising disclosure in its advertisements. The order dismisses the complaint allegation regarding the effects of "Listerine" on children who gargle with it twice a day. The final order, including further order requiring report of compliance therewith, is as follows: [1]

FINAL ORDER

This matter having been heard by the Commission upon respondent's appeal from the Initial Decision; and

The Commission having considered the oral arguments of counsel, their briefs, and the whole record; and

The Commission, for reasons stated in the accompanying Opinion, having denied the appeal; accordingly

It is ordered, That, except to the extent that it is inconsistent with the Commis-

[1] Copies of the Complaint, Initial Decision, Opinion and Final Order filed with the original document.

sion's Opinion, the Initial Decison of the Administrative Law Judge be, and it hereby is, adopted together with the Opinion accompanying this Order as the Commission's final findings of fact and conclusions of law in this matter;

It is further ordered, That the following order be, and it hereby is, entered:

PART I

It is ordered, That respondent Warner-Lambert Company, a corporation, its successors and assigns and respondent's officers, agents, representatives and employees, directly or through any corporation, subsidiary, division or other device, in connection with the labeling, advertising, offering for sale, sale or distribution of Listerine or any other non-prescription drug product in or affecting commerce, as "commerce" is defined in the Federal Trade Commission Act, do forthwith cease and desist from:

1. Representing, directly or by implication, that any such product will cure colds or sore throats;

2. Representing, directly or by implication, that any such product will prevent colds or sore throats;

3. Representing, directly or by implication, that users of any such product will have fewer colds than non-users.

PART II

It is further ordered, That respondent Warner-Lambert Company, a corporation, its successors and assigns and respondent's officers, agents, representatives and employees, directly or through any corporation, subsidiary, division or other device, in connection with the labeling, advertising, offering for sale, sale, or distribution of Listerine or any other mouthwash product in or affecting commerce, as "commerce" is defined in the Federal Trade Commission Act, do forthwith cease and desist from:

1. Representing, directly or by implication, that any such product is a treatment for, or will lessen the severity of, colds or sore throats;

2. Representing that any such product will have any significant beneficial effect on the symptoms of sore throats or any beneficial effect on symptoms of colds;

3. Representing that the ability of any such product to kill germs in of medical significance in the treatment of colds or sore throats or the symptoms of colds or sore throats.

PART III

It is further ordered, That respondent Warner-Lambert Company, a corporation, its successors and assigns, and respondent's officers, agents, representatives and employees, directly or through any corporation, subsidiary, division or other device, do forthwith cease and desist from disseminating or causing the

dissemination of any advertisements for the product Listerine Antiseptic unless it is clearly and conspicuously disclosed in each such advertisement in the exact language below that:

Contrary to prior advertising, Listerine will not help prevent colds or sore throats or lessen their severity.

In print advertisements, the disclosure shall be displayed in type size which is at least the same size as that in which the principal portion of the text of the advertisement appears and shall be separated from the text so that it can be readily noticed. In television advertisements, the disclosure shall be presented simultaneously in both the audio and visual portions. During the audio portion of the disclosure in television and radio advertisements, no other sounds, including music, shall occur. Each such disclosure shall be presented in the language, e.g., English, Spanish, principally employed in the advertisement.

The aforesaid duty to disclose the corrective statement shall continue until respondent has expended on Listerine advertising a sum equal to the average annual Listerine advertising budget for the period of April 1962 to March 1972.

PART IV

It is further ordered, That the allegations of Paragraphs Nine and Ten of the complaint be, and they hereby are, dismissed.

PART V

It is further ordered, That respondent shall forthwith distribute a copy of this order to each of its operating divisions.

It is further ordered, That respondent notify the Commission at least thirty (30) days prior to any proposed change in its structure such as dissolution, assignment or sale resulting in the emergence of a successor corporation, the creation or dissolution of subsidiaries or any other change in the corporation which may affect compliance obligations arising out of this order.

It is further ordered, That respondent shall, within sixty (60) days after the effective date of this order, file with the Commission a written report, setting forth in detail the manner and form of its compliance with this order.

Opinion of the Commission by Commissioner Engman.

The Initial Decision Order was issued Nov. 25, 1974.

The Final Order was issued by the Commission Dec. 9, 1975.

VIRGINIA M. HARDING,
Acting Secretary.

[FR Doc.76–1367 Filed 1–15–76;8:45 am]

Source: *Federal Register,* January 16, 1976, pp. 2381–2382.

impartially, Weber argued, procedures must be "dehumanized" and codified; in other words, a bureaucracy must develop procedures to ensure that all cases will be treated consistently. (Of course, standard operating procedures also reduce the decision costs for the bureaucracy, because such procedures remove the need to decide how to decide each case.) Abundant examples of excessive governmental red tape can indeed be found, but it is not clear that red tape is always to be avoided.[6]

Third, to many people, red tape is just one aspect of bureaucratic inefficiency. Because of lengthy procedures, overlapping jurisdictions, and confusion about the ultimate goals of the public policies they are intended to implement, bureaucracies are accused of being incapable of improving things—and sometimes of making things worse. To some degree, this criticism is accurate. But the concept of inefficiency suggests that a comparison is being made to a better process. What is it? Any efficient organization would need (1) clear authority to act, (2) precisely defined goals, and (3) organizational unity to prevent parts of the process from working against each other. In public bureaucracy, the clear authority is often missing in the legislative mandates to agencies, or the authority to act is unstably split between street-level bureaucrats (i.e., those who deal with the problems of the public on an individual basis) and top-level administrators. In addition, as we shall see later in this chapter, public policies are often stated in vague terms, which bureaucrats must interpret and implement—subject, of course, to review by the legislature, the courts, and the affected public. Inefficiency also arises because (1) many agencies either are not intended to be efficient (e.g., the Postal Service is not expected to make a profit on the delivery of every letter to remote rural households) or (2) they must work at cross-purposes with other agencies (e.g., the Department of Health and Human Services administers programs to provide low-cost food to poor families, while the Department of Agriculture carries out policies to support higher prices for many farm products). These inefficiencies are not the fault of bureaucracy.

Fourth, the American political system is sometimes criticized for its reliance on a network of bureaucracies that seem far from democratic. Bureaucracies are inherently *nondemocratic*. As Weber described them, they rely on a hierarchical authority structure in which officials can instruct subordinates without asking their opinions or taking votes. Early in this century, the Swiss sociologist Robert Michels found innate tendencies in large organizations such as bureaucracies and political parties to become oligarchic: that is, "ruled by the few."[7] Although it is not clear that Michels's "iron law of oligarchy" applies to all large organizations, bureaucracies do contain "elites" who supervise the activities of their "masses."

Are bureaucracies also *antidemocratic?* That is, do they tend to stifle democracy in the political system to which they belong? Critics have argued that the formation and implementation of public policy by small groups of non-elected specialists tend to create a *meritocracy*—a system of technocrats who hold positions of power solely on the basis of their abilities and training, thereby excluding the participation of social groups with fewer skills. In addition, these critics believe that we should strive for a bureaucracy that is representative of the general population. Although it may be possible to avoid such a meritocracy by actively recruiting and training minorities, the goals of bureaucracy are not the same as the goals of democracy. Therefore, we should not be surprised if one sometimes thwarts the other.

Finally, is it true that bureaucracies are immortal? One study of the tenacity of government agencies found that of 175 federal agencies existing in 1923, a

TABLE 10-1
FEDERAL CIVILIAN EMPLOYMENT, 1816–1982

Year	Total Federal Civilian Employees	Executive Branch	Legislative Branch	Judicial Branch
1816	4,837	4,479	243	115
1821	6,914	6,526	252	136
1831	11,491	11,067	289	135
1841	18,038	17,550	332	156
1851	26,274	25,713	384	177
1861	36,672	36,106	393	173
1871	51,020	50,155	618	247
1881	100,020	94,679	2,579	2,762
1891	157,442	150,844	3,867	2,731
1901	239,476	231,056	5,690	2,730
1911	395,905	387,673	5,902	2,330
1921	561,142	550,020	9,202	1,920
1931	609,746	596,745	11,192	1,809
1941	1,437,682	1,416,444	18,712	2,526
1942	2,296,384	2,272,082	21,657	2,645
1943	3,299,414	3,273,887	22,903	2,624
1944	3,332,356	3,304,379	25,314	2,663
1945	3,816,310	3,786,645	26,959	2,706
1946	2,696,529	2,665,520	27,946	3,063
1947	2,111,001	2,082,258	25,669	3,074
1951	2,482,666	2,455,901	22,835	3,930
1961	2,435,804	2,407,025	23,621	5,158
1971	2,847,276	2,809,665	30,362	7,249
1981	2,860,392	2,800,949	38,616	15,651
1982	2,824,768	2,769,985	38,791	15,992

Sources: U.S. Bureau of the Census, *Historical Statistics, Colonial Times to 1970* (Washington, D.C.: Government Printing Office, 1976), p. 1102; U.S. Bureau of the Census, *Statistical Abstract of the United States, 1972* (Washington, D.C.: Government Printing Office, 1972), p. 266; U.S. Bureau of the Census, *Statistical Abstract of the United States, 1982–83* (Washington, D.C.: Government Printing Office, 1982), p. 389.

TABLE 10-2 STATE AND LOCAL GOVERNMENT EMPLOYMENT, 1930–1980			
Year	Total Employed	Year	Total Employed
1930	2,622,000	1960	6,083,000
1935	2,728,000	1965	7,696,000
1940	3,206,000	1970	9,830,000
1945	3,137,000	1975	12,084,000
1950	4,098,000	1980	13,315,000
1955	4,727,000		

Sources: U.S. Bureau of the Census, *Historical Statistics, Colonial Times to 1970* (Washington, D.C.: Government Printing Office, 1976), p. 1104; *Statistical Abstract of the United States, 1982–83* (Washington, D.C.: Government Printing Office, 1982), p. 303.

total of 148 were still in existence fifty years later, and 246 new agencies had been formed in the same policy areas.[8] Parts of the bureaucracy may disappear when the need for their functions declines, when the organization becomes too inefficient, or when other agencies perform the same functions better. In the latter case, the bureaucracy does not really die; it has merely been swallowed by another agency.[9] Thus, statistics on the immortality of government agencies can be misleading.

What about the widely perceived explosion in the size of bureaucracy in American government? Table 10-1 traces the growth in the number of federal employees. With the exception of the Depression–World War II era, the federal bureaucracy has grown steadily until the last three decades, when the number of federal employees as a percentage of the total population actually shrank by about 25 percent. However, the number of state and local government employees increased enormously, due largely to shifts in administrative responsibilities from the federal to state and local government (see Table 10-2). The American bureaucracy has grown quickly, with the total number of government employees at all levels doubling in the past twenty-five years.

American bureaucracy is a complex phenomenon, with complex duties, and it operates within a complex political environment. In the next section, as we examine the actual institutions of the national bureaucracy, it should be remembered that these departments and agencies have been created and maintained in response to demands upon the political system. Therefore, we can expect the tensions and contradictions discussed so far to exist in all types of public bureaucracies.

Organization of the Federal Bureaucracy

The federal bureaucracy is an enormous organization composed of hundreds of smaller organizations—departments, agencies, commissions, offices, and so on. It has millions of employees pursuing a huge variety of tasks. The federal bureaucracy has evolved over the last two hundred years largely as the result of small incremental changes in the scope of governmental activities, not as the result of any grand design for an efficient, orderly division of labor. As we examine the largest federal bureaucracies, remember that what we see today is to some degree an "unorganization" of many individual organizations.

Civil Service   During the first hundred years of the United States, those who worked for the federal government were chosen, not according to Max Weber's standards of merit and skill, but rather on the basis of a spoils system by which victorious politicians filled government offices with their loyal supporters. During the 1870s, however, many European nations began to reform their administrative systems by instituting merit rules. These rules offered job security, anonymous—and therefore nonpolitical—competitive examinations for hiring and promotions, and standards for competency. American reformers pressed for similar improvements in civil administration. The first civil service commission was formed in 1871 but was abolished in 1875; party leaders in Congress joined President Ulysses Grant in clinging to the benefits of patronage. However, the reform movement continued, and when some unseemly struggles for spoils culminated in the assassination of President James Garfield in 1881 by a disappointed officeseeker, Congress and President Chester Arthur responded by passing the Pendleton Act in 1883. This act established the Civil Service Commission (CSC), which, "with the merit system as its instrument . . . set out on a task that amounted to nothing less than recasting the foundations of national institutional power."[10]

In 1978, the CSC was split into the Office of Personnel Management (OPM) and the Merit Systems Protection Board (MSPB). The OPM recruits and examines applicants for positions in the federal civil service; the MSPB hears and resolves disputes involving firings, demotions, pay increases and so on. There are two different merit systems at the federal level. The largest is the

A small part of the army of "faceless bureaucrats," these employees of the Internal Revenue Service process income tax returns at the IRS district office in Philadelphia. (Dennis Brack/Black Star)

General Schedule (GS) system for clerical, administrative, and professional personnel. It includes eighteen grades, ranging from GS1 for unskilled personnel to GS18 for top-level policymakers; within each grade, there are steps based on seniority, time in grade, and scarcity of skill. In addition, about 30 percent of federal employees work in agencies with separate merit systems. Such agencies usually require specially trained personnel, such as foreign service officers, scientists, doctors, FBI agents, and nuclear engineers.

There is also an "excepted service" category of federal employment that is exempt from competitive entry procedures and merit-system rules. It includes attorneys, because the OPM is prohibited from examining and rating lawyers; employees with specialized skills, such as Treasury Department bank examiners; and top-level executives. The Senior Executive Service, created in 1978, provides performance incentives in the form of year-end cash bonuses to about 8,500 governmental managers, but it also makes it easier for presidents to demote or remove top civil servants.

The federal civil service is often criticized for being overly generous to its employees. In fact, the salaries of top-level managers in government are less than those of their business counterparts and the average annual compensation of all government employees (in 1982, $22,464) is only slightly higher than the average compensation for workers in all domestic industries ($22,018).[11] Comparisons of private- and public-sector retirement benefits are somewhat more complicated because there are many government retirement programs (e.g., for the military, air-traffic controllers, and law enforcement officials). In general, however, the differences between public and private pension systems are not significant.[12] Finally, many people believe that it is almost impossible for a federal employee to lose his or her job. The merit system does provide lengthy procedural delays for federal workers threatened with dismissal, but many people leave government service involuntarily. In 1979, a total of 19,300 were "discharged," and another 50,300 lost their jobs through "reductions in force" (i.e., their jobs ceased to exist).[13]

Executive Departments In Chapter 9, we discussed the problems of the members of the president's cabinet. We saw that the heads of the executive departments face enormous information costs because each department combines a large number of programs dealing with a broad, but usually related, group of subjects. In addition, executive departments contain many other smaller organizations. For example, the Agriculture Department includes, among many other units, an Agricultural Marketing Service (AMS) and a Food Safety and Quality Service (FSQS). The AMS, charged with regulating the marketing of agricultural goods, consists of eight divisions, including the Dairy Division and the Fruit and Vegetable Division. In turn, the latter division includes the Fruit Branch, Regulatory Branch, Specialty Crops Branch, and Vegetable Branch. Similarly, the FSQS, which inspects goods at processing plants and regulates labels for truthfulness, includes five smaller units, one of which, Commodity Services, in turn, includes a Meat Quality Division, a Fruit and Vegetable Quality Division, and so on.

The AMS and the FSQS are only a small part of the vast Department of Agriculture, which, of course, is only one of thirteen executive departments, each of which is a similar labyrinth. In most instances, the departments administer programs with complex subject matters. Each program generates a large amount of information that is used in making specific decisions. Each cabinet secretary has a staff of close advisers to assist him or her in the same way that the president has the White House Office and the Executive Office of the President to help with his information and control problems. Each department typically has an undersecretary or a deputy secretary, assistants to the secretary, assistant secretaries, deputy undersecretaries, deputy assistant secretaries, and so on—each with their own staffs. Despite such assistance, the heads of the executive departments are unable to exercise complete control because of the gaps in information, experience, and proximity between policymakers and the civil servants who administer legislative programs.

In 1789, the nation began with three cabinet departments—State, War, and Treasury—plus an attorney general. (The Justice Department was not created until 1870.) Table 9-1 listed the executive departments as they exist today, along with their dates of creation and approximate employment. Each of these departments makes and administers policies in broad categories (e.g., public finance in the Department of Treasury or foreign affairs in the Department of State).

To a large degree, the creation and evolution of these departments reflects large-scale changes in American government. For example, by the beginning of the twentieth century, the Industrial Revolution had affected American society and business to such an extent that a catchall executive department was needed to oversee and administer the many federal policies that were emerging. As a result, the Department of Commerce and Labor came into being in 1903. Ten years later, Commerce and Labor became two separate departments. The Department of Commerce has acquired the Bureau of Foreign Commerce from the State Department; the Patent Office from the Department of the Interior; the Weather Bureau (now the National Weather Service, which is part of the National Oceanic and Atmospheric Administration); and the Maritime Administration. Lyndon Johnson tried to recombine Commerce and Labor in 1967; Richard Nixon proposed combining six departments, including Commerce, into four; and Jimmy Carter tried to move NOAA into a new Department of Natural Resources. All were unsuccessful. Ronald Reagan proposed removing all nonbusiness activities from the jurisdiction of the Commerce Department and renaming it the Department of International Trade and Industry. Such proposals must be approved by Congress, and there are usually interest groups that strongly oppose them because programs may be eliminated in the shuffle or because familiarity with the system may be lost.

Executive Agencies   In many ways, executive agencies are similar to executive departments. Like the secretaries and top officials of cabinet departments, the men and women who manage the executive agencies are appointed by the president with the approval of the Senate. Although executive agencies deal with matters of narrower scope than do the executive departments, they are important enough to be independent from them. The top officials of certain executive agencies participate in some of the important agencies within the Executive Office of the President (e.g., the head of the Central Intelligence Agency, who is a member of the National Security Council), but they usually do not sit in on cabinet meetings.

Like the cabinet departments, the executive agencies are expected to be responsive to the president's goals and objectives, their statutory mandates, legal precedent, and the top administrators' views of sound public policy—a difficult balancing act, as we have seen. In general, the president can exert less control over the executive agencies than over cabinet departments but more control than over the independent agencies for two primary reasons. First, the president can remove the top administrators of executive agencies at will, whereas the members of independent commissions serve for fixed and staggered terms; the president cannot fire independent commissioners, nor can he usually appoint all of the members of a commission. Second, each executive agency is headed by one administrator who is directly answerable to the president. An independent commission, on the other hand, is headed by a group of people—usually five—whose chairman is generally less powerful than the head of an executive agency.

Several executive agencies stand out as particularly important in policy-making. The Central Intelligence Agency (CIA) collects and evaluates intelligence relating to national security affairs and conducts counterintelligence and covert activities in foreign countries. The National Aeronautics and Space Administration (NASA) performs research on flights within and outside of the earth's atmosphere, and conducts space-exploration activities. The United States Arms Control and Disarmament Agency (ACDA) conducts research and engages in negotiations with foreign nations in the arms-control and disarmament field. The Environmental Protection Agency (EPA) regulates air, water, noise, radiation, and solid-waste pollution, and the Nuclear Regulatory Commission (NRC) oversees the safe construction and operation of nuclear power plants and nuclear materials. The Veterans Administration (VA) administers the system of benefits for veterans and their dependents and runs about four hundred hospitals and outpatient clinics. Finally, the General Services Administration (GSA) acts as a purchasing agent and distributor for most other agencies in the executive branch, providing paper clips, vehicles, telephone service, office space, and so on. The GSA's massive purchases of goods and services allow it to impose standards upon suppliers much as a regulatory agency does.

Independent Regulatory Commissions   The independent regulatory commissions constitute a uniquely American contribution to the form of government organizations. These agencies are headed by five or more members, each of whom is appointed by the president with the consent of the Senate at staggered intervals for a fixed term of years. One commissioner is designated by the president as the chairperson. Commissioners may be removed only for cause (e.g., dishonesty in office) and not because of a disagreement with the president's program. In contrast, an EPA administrator, for example, may be removed at the president's displeasure.

The peculiar nature of independent regulatory commissions is attributable to Congress's decision to maintain their relative independence from the president. The first independent regulatory commission, the Civil Service Commission (CSC), created in 1883 to reduce political influence over federal employees, was designed to be impartial: no more than a simple majority of its commissioners could be affiliated with any political party. Since then, each new independent regulatory commission has been required to have no more than half of its commissioners plus one (e.g., four out of seven) associated with a single political party.

Four years after the creation of the CSC, Congress created a second independent regulatory commission, the Interstate Commerce Commission (ICC). During a period in which the business world was being influenced by the idea that enterprise could be managed according to rational, technical principles, many legislators believed that similar principles could be applied to government. Thus, when it created the multimember ICC, Congress combined the call for technical expertise regarding railroad shipping rates with the need for political impartiality. In 1914, during the Progressive Era, the Federal Trade Commission (FTC) was created to regulate unfair methods of competition. It was deliberately patterned after the ICC. Subsequently, other such independent regulatory commissions were established, either as spin-offs from existing ones or modeled after them. The Securities and Exchange Commission (SEC) was spun off from the FTC in 1934 to regulate stock-exchange and stock-market practices, and the Commodity Futures Trading Commission (CFTC), patterned after the SEC, was created in 1974 to regulate the practices of the futures exchanges and futures market.

One of the principal reasons that these commissions are shielded from the president is that some of them behave much like legislatures (when they make rules or regulations that have the force of law) or like courts (when they adjudicate disputes between individuals or companies). Therefore, many of these agencies have been called "quasi-legislative" or "quasi-judicial." Insofar as they act like courts, they should operate without the interference of the president and his staff, just as ordinary courts do under the separation-of-powers doctrine. Each independent regulatory commission is assigned a number of *administrative law judges*, depending on the volume and nature of its business. Like a court, an independent regulatory commission conducts a trial before an administrative law judge. After presiding over the trial, the administrative law judge enters a proposed order and the justifications for it. Any side adversely affected—in regulatory matters, there can be many sides—can appeal to the full commission, which acts like an appeals court. Appeals of the commission's decision are made to the various courts of appeals, which review questions of law and determine whether sufficient evidence exists in the record to support the agency's findings. Finally, as in all other cases, there is the possibility of an appeal to the Supreme Court. If the commission has lost and wants to appeal, the solicitor general of the Department of Justice must decide whether to appeal on behalf of the commission.

Because independent regulatory commissions sometimes act as legislature, court, prosecutor, *and* jury, some critics have argued that special courts should be created to deal with the commissions' work. In addition, critics have stated that, because these commissions significantly affect the president's overall plans and objectives, they should thus be subject to closer presidential control. As a result, these commissions have been brought under the influence of the Office of Management and Budget (OMB), which reviews the budgetary requests and legislative proposals of most of the commissions on both policy and accounting grounds. Congress, too, has sought to exercise control over the commissions through the appropriations and oversight processes. There is widespread belief that even agencies such as the FTC and the Consumer Product Safety Commission, which are intended to protect consumers, can impose high costs upon major industries and major sectors of the economy. Presidents and Congress have thus sought to impose tighter control over independent regulatory commissions.

Subgovernments   Those responsible for making public-policy decisions are likely to have contact with individuals who have a stake in the outcome of these decisions. Workers in the Department of Interior's Bureau of Land Management (BLM), which oversees the protection and development of more than five hundred million acres of publicly owned land, should be expected to have more personal contact with officers of coal-mining companies than, for example, should workers in the Office of Civil Rights of the Department of Justice. Similarly, coal-mine operators and BLM bureaucrats will also have many occasions to talk with members and staff of the House Interior and Insular Affairs Committee and the Senate Energy and Natural Resources Committee. Such a cluster of individuals is sometimes labeled **subgovernment** (or "iron triangle" or "cozy little triangle")—that is, an interrelationship among bureaucrats, congressional personnel, and private-sector individuals and groups that together have primary responsibility for the formation of public policy in a specific area. Because of their special interest and expertise in an area, a subgovernment is granted authority, and sometimes autonomy, more or less by default. Organizations and persons with other responsibilities, including most private citizens, simply do not have the information, opportunity, resources, or incentives to become involved in such policymaking.

Of course, this description implies that something not entirely proper may occur when 99 percent of the government and populace defer to the 1 percent with a personal interest in a particular policy area. The existence of a subgovernment means that the transaction costs for an interest group seeking favorable policies are relatively low, because relatively few bureaucrats or members of Congress need to be influenced. Second, because members of Congress

subgovernments: Postulated cooperative arrangements among bureaucrats, congressional personnel, and private-sector individuals and groups that together have primary responsibility for the formation of public policy in specific areas.

often join subcommittees with jurisdiction over policy areas affecting their constituencies, the subgovernment phenomenon suggests that there is an inherent bias in the policymaking process that favors narrow interests over the public interest. In addition, bureaucrats need the support of both congressional representatives and organized interests if they are to successfully promote their policies—and perhaps even if they are to survive. Thus, some observers claim that bureaucrats, especially those in the independent regulatory commissions, tend to be captured by the economic interests under their jurisdiction. Finally, because of their shared interests and experiences, subgovernments make it easier for congressional and bureaucratic personnel to leave their jobs for lucrative positions in areas of the private sector with which they have worked, a phenomenon often referred to as the "revolving door."

It is not clear whether subgovernments exist in all policy areas, whether they are of constant and uniform strength, or whether the symbiotic parts of a subgovernment are always able to dominate policy. Nevertheless, because there is no incentive for anyone to make general, far-reaching policies, the concept is useful in explaining the incoherence of many individual public policies. It also suggests another reason for the abundance of interest groups in American politics: the fragmentation of policymaking makes it cheaper for interests to participate.

Controls on the Bureaucracy

So far, we have discussed various mechanisms by which the institutions of government interact and thereby check one another. Even though the federal bureaucracy is somewhat outside the constitutional scheme—a "fourth branch" of government—it is nevertheless subject to constraints. There are some things that bureaucrats, like everyone else, are prohibited or dissuaded from doing, regardless of their individual personalities or motivations. We can safely assume, for example, that most bureaucrats do not wish to go to jail, lose their jobs, or forgo future salary increases. Using such assumptions, when we observe patterns of behavior, we can infer that individuals are constrained to behave in particular ways.

What are the checks on bureaucratic behavior? Bureaucrats are constrained by the law in four major ways. First, like all citizens, they must obey the constitutional and legal restrictions against depriving other citizens of their life, property, or other rights. Second, as employees of organizations with legal mandates, they are subject to particular constraints on their behavior; they must not take actions that are in conflict with or unauthorized by the statutes covering their agencies. Recall that when Congress became convinced that the Federal Trade Commission (FTC) was exceeding the limits of its congressional mandate (i.e., the law that created the agency), they took the unusual step of allowing the agency's budget to disappear for one day, then statutorily ordered the FTC to suspend the issuance of any new rules or regulations for a few months. Third, there are laws restricting the personal behavior only of federal employees. For example, the 1978 Ethics in Government Act and other federal laws require a small percentage of federal employees to disclose their financial holdings. As a result, in 1982, the General Accounting Office found that ninety-two employees of the Interior Department's Bureau of Land Management owned stock in companies that held leases to develop mineral resources on federal lands; such a potential conflict of interest can be forbidden by Congress or the courts. Fourth, we have seen that the legal system includes numerous procedural safeguards designed to protect citizens' rights. Thus, if bureaucrats try to improperly cut some of the red tape required by administrative law, the courts are apt to uphold complaints against their actions.

There are also organizational constraints that prevent bureaucrats from behaving too independently. Although Max Weber's prescriptions for well-defined hierarchies of authority may not be observed in all federal agencies and departments, bureaucrats still have incentives to be cautious in expanding their own roles or trying to deflect more of the organization's resources toward themselves. It may be difficult to fire civil servants, but their superiors usually have the capability, if not always the will, to make wayward individuals regret their deviance. In addition, bureaucracies typically develop standard operating procedures—routine ways of handling routine problems—that not only reduce information and transaction costs but also impel bureaucrats to behave consistently. It has also been noted that some bureaucracies develop internal laws of administration that reduce the possibility of individual error. A study of how the Social Security Administration processes claims for disability payments found that (1) the agency was guided by "unpublished written instructions and interpretations combined with standard bureaucratic routines and with developmental and decisional practices" and (2) the result was something akin to justice.[14]

Finally, an enormous number of political constraints restrict the behavior of bureaucrats. Many of these have already been discussed. For example, Congress, often under pressure from interest groups, can check the activities of a federal agency by threatening to reduce its appropriations, by changing the laws that created the agency or defined its tasks, or by publicizing the agency's misbehavior in oversight hearings. Congress has tightened the eligibility requirements for food stamps, loosened the regulatory requirements on air-emission standards for automobile manufacturers, and gradually abolished the Civil Aeronautics Board. In addition, when representatives and senators perform casework services for constituents who have been frustrated by the bureaucracy, they can correct administrative errors as well as point out to the administrators where their procedures are conspicuously sloppy.

Similarly, the president has a variety of tools for constraining the executive-branch bureaucracy. In Chapter 9 we discussed the president's control over the appointment and removal of agency officials, the role of the Office of Management and Budget (OMB) in shaping agency budgets, and the OMB's legislative clearance function. We have also seen that the president can try to reorganize the executive branch. There have been twelve attempts at doing so in this century, and the Reorganization Act of 1939 gave the president the power to recommend such changes to Congress. However, either chamber can disapprove a reorganization within sixty days, and the creation or abolition of a cabinet department requires explicit statutory approval. One study concluded that administrative reorganizations "do not seem to have had a major impact on administrative costs, efficiency, or control."[15]

We can safely make several broad statements about the degree to which the federal bureaucracy is controlled by the constitutional institutions of government. First, the bureaucracy exists because of the complexity of governmental activity. Powers are delegated to agencies because they can specialize in particular policy areas and thereby reduce information and opportunity costs for elected officials. Therefore, any attempt to interfere with the operation of agencies will invoke costs for Congress, the president, or the courts, all of which lack the information and the time to routinely oversee the bureaucracy. Second, the bureaucracy exists in order to allocate resources, such as tax dollars, opportunities, and services. Some people or groups benefit from bureaucratic activity, and any attempt to change the procedures will invoke political costs. Third, the direction of influence between the bureaucracy and the other institutions of government is not entirely one-way. Not only are many statutes drafted within federal agencies, but, in their day-to-day activities, bureaucrats often have the chance to enlist support for their attempts to change the behavior of Congress or the president. Finally, it is not certain whether the bureaucracy needs stricter controls. The standardized procedures and administrative safeguards that have evolved over the past century work reasonably well, and the bureaucracy may be in no more need of improvement or control than Congress, the courts, or the president.

THE POLICY PROCESS

Nowhere in the Constitution did the Founders refer to a *policy process,* and neither James Madison, Alexander Hamilton, nor John Jay discussed it in *The Federalist Papers.* Few early American-government textbooks devoted separate sections to the topic. Yet, today, the study of the process by which American public policy is made constitutes a major portion of political science research and publications. Why wasn't policy of concern to the Founders of the republic?

The framers of the Constitution intended to create a limited national government consisting of three branches—executive, legislative, and judicial— each of which would exercise some control over the others by sharing their powers. The decisions of the national government would be an amalgamation of the actions of these three branches. Questions about the neutrality of the administrative system (i.e., those officials who would assist the president in executing the laws) were not considered important, because Hamilton and others assumed that administrators would only be carrying out the orders of the legislature.

Yet, we have seen that as government has grown in scope, producing more and more policies over a wider range of issues, there have been incentives for the three constitutional branches of government to defer much of their policymaking power to the bureaucracy. Thus, the policy process became more important as the importance and complexity of public policies grew. Implementing the decisions of Congress, the president, and the courts began to involve the exercise of bureaucratic discretion. At the same time, as the stakes in policy decisions grew larger both to private interests and to the entire public, the need for policy evaluation also grew. That is, it became more important to have procedures by which the policy actors could know whether their ideas were working well.

Thus far, we have described the most important policy actors—individuals, groups, the courts, Congress, the president, and the bureaucracy—and how each participates in the making of public decisions. We will now turn to a short case study in order to illustrate how the pieces of the policy process fit together. It must be stressed at the outset that there is no typical public policy. On the contrary, few policies share the same set of political actors and influences, legal constraints, legislative mandates, or economic, social, and technological characteristics. Yet, scholars have found some common patterns in policymaking that help us make sense of the negotiations, maneuverings, and decisions that comprise the policy process.

What Is a Public Policy?

The term *public policy* is commonly used as a synonym for governmental action—something that the government does in order to change things. Policies involve allocations. But we need to be more precise. For example, are policies the same as decisions? No. Why not? Mere intentions or verbal statements may be vague and inexpensive and have no real effects; the mere announcement of a war on crime does not constitute a policy. Then is the term *policy* to be limited to the impacts of decisions? Again, the answer is no. We would not want to characterize a set of governmental actions (e.g., the deregulation of air fares) as a policy to drive some air carriers into bankruptcy simply because that was one of the spin-off effects of deregulation. Furthermore, on some occasions, a decision *not* to act has intentional allocative effects—for example, if the federal government were to cease enforcing its regulations regarding disposal of toxic chemical wastes. For most purposes, it is sufficient to think of a public policy as "a goal-directed or purposive course of action followed by an actor or a set of actors in an attempt to deal with a public problem."[16] This definition allows both poorly designed courses of action, as well as courses of inaction, to be labeled "policies."

The Stages of the Policy Process

Since World War II—and particularly since the early 1960s—most Americans have enjoyed a fairly constant increase in their standard of living.[17] As consumers began to spend more money on more products, manufacturers became

Storefront in Greensboro, Alabama, 1936. Before the era of mass-produced, -preserved, and -packaged foods and other consumer products, there was no demand or justification for a large governmental role in the marketing of such items. (Library of Congress)

more reliant on advertising claims and improvements in product quality in their attempts to capture more consumer dollars. At the same time, the use of consumer credit has grown quickly as lenders devised new and often complex variations of charge accounts, installment accounts, and so on (e.g., total outstanding consumer credit grew by about 60 percent between 1960 and 1965). Along with these changes came increasing consumer dissatisfaction resulting from occasional false or misleading advertisements of products, services, and credit arrangements. As we saw previously, the costs to consumers of obtaining information about products can be high, and the problems in forming organizations to represent consumer interests are much greater than the costs to manufacturers of providing false or misleading advertising. In the late 1960s, the federal government took major steps to protect consumers, including the 1966 Fair Packaging and Labeling Act and the 1968 truth-in-lending act.

Agenda-Setting   The first step in the creation of public policy is the attraction of someone's attention to a problem or opportunity for government action. Consumers had long been faced with the imbalance in product information between suppliers and buyers. Legislation had been passed in 1939, 1951, and 1958 to require manufacturers to provide accurate information on the content of wool products, furs, and textile fiber products. The Federal Trade Commission (FTC) was empowered to prevent deceptive "slack-filling"—that is, the marketing of a box or can that is deliberately larger than its contents require. Similarly, bewildered borrowers were not a new phenomenon. How did fair packaging and truth in lending reach the national agenda?

An important study of agendas in American government distinguished between *systemic agendas*—all issues within the potential scope of government authority—and *institutional agendas*—"that set of items explicitly up for active and serious consideration of authoritative decision-makers."[18] Several factors can account for the movement of an issue from the systemic agenda to the institutional agenda. First, the world may change. Sometimes, a topic becomes important because of a crisis and not an individual's political plans. For example, the launching of Sputnik, the first man-made satellite, by the Soviet Union in 1957 immediately moved science and technology policy to the forefront of American policy priorities. And the swine flu scare of 1976 moved public-health issues temporarily into the public eye and therefore temporarily onto the agendas of governmental institutions.

Second, an entrepreneur can publicize an issue and thereby pay most of the information costs for unorganized latent groups (e.g., all consumers). Many such entrepreneurs have become involved in consumer issues, most notably Ralph Nader, but also members of the Senate (Estes Kefauver, Phillip Hart, and Warren Magnuson), congressional staff members, a few consumer groups (e.g., the Consumer Federation of America), and even journalists (e.g., columnists Drew Pearson and Jack Anderson). Sometimes, government agencies themselves act as entrepreneurs by investigating issues that can be brought to the attention of executive branch or legislative officials. In 1968, the FTC's Bureau of Economics performed a study that supported the conclusions of the National Advisory Commission on Civil Disorders, or the Kerner Commission, established by President Lyndon Johnson to investigate the causes of the urban riots of the mid-1960s. The commission found that the ghetto poor had some justification for feeling that they had been unfairly exploited by local white merchants and finance companies.

Political entrepreneurs had been investigating the fair-packaging issue at least since the late 1940s, but to little avail. Why did the fair-packaging issue succeed in 1966? Two reasons were President Lyndon Johnson and Senator Warren Magnuson (D-Wash.), chairman of the Senate Commerce Committee, which had jurisdiction over such legislation. It has been suggested that Johnson embraced consumer issues at that time in order to increase his popularity, which was slipping among liberals as a result of the Vietnam war. Consumerism had the added advantage of requiring small new appropriations from the federal budget.[19] Magnuson, who had served in the Senate since 1946, had been startled by his near-loss in 1962. Because he was also searching for a fresh issue with popular appeal, he quickly became a valuable ally of Michigan Democrat Phillip Hart, who had been pushing consumer issues in the Senate for years. (According to one story, Hart vowed to take action after opening a box of cereal one morning and finding it half empty.[20]) Michael Pertschuk, a young lawyer who was hired as "consumer counsel" to the Senate Commerce Committee and who later became chairman of the FTC, recalled that his assignment was "to help build a consumer record for Magnuson, to identify opportunities, develop strategies, shepherd bills and make certain that Magnuson received appropriate acknowledgement for his achievements."[21] The president's backing of the fair-packaging issue was matched by his endorsement of the truth-in-lending legislation, which had been unsuccessfully introduced in every congressional session since 1960.

The policy process for these two pieces of consumer legislation began long before the formal congressional introduction of the bills that eventually became law. Although the support of key entrepreneurial politicians was vital, the passage of these bills was built upon a foundation of years of unsuccessful efforts and increasing attention from public and consumer groups. The agenda-setting stage of the policy process is often at least this complex.

Formulation and Adoption Overcoming the political and institutional obstacles to placement on the national agenda may appear difficult, but it is only the prelude. The next step in the policy process is the formulation of a course of action and its adoption by the appropriate institution. Complaints about problems must be converted into suggestions for improvements, and coalitions of potential supporters must be consulted and mobilized. Not surprisingly, the formulation and adoption stage is usually when the most intense disputes occur, because the policymakers must agree on what the problem is and what the public goals are. Some problem definitions are deceptively easy (e.g., illegal drug trafficking), and some goals can be simply stated (e.g., "end the importation and sale of illegal drugs"), but it is obviously more difficult to devise a plan of action to achieve those goals. In other cases, such as fair packaging and labeling, policy formulation is inherently complicated because of the difficulty in defining the problem and the goals. *Some* manufacturers enclose their products in *somewhat* misleading containers, and *many* consumers are unjustly fooled, so *some* type of standards should be developed regarding packaging and labeling.

Of course, there are many other reasons why the policy-formulation stage is complicated. In most cases, the president and the executive branch play a major role in promulgating precise plans (again, because of the advantage that the bureaucracy has in expertise and information), but policy formulation is also strongly influenced by Congress and, in many cases, other groups. The latter includes interest groups and "think tanks" such as the Rand Corporation, the Brookings Institution, or the American Enterprise Institute. And because the location of a policy within the government (i.e., which agency will administer it) can be as important as the substance of its prescriptions, policy formulators are buffeted by interests as they try to decide both what should be done and who should do it.

In a world where information is free, resources are infinite, and people are geniuses with identical values, policy formulation could possibly be scientific and objective. One could define a problem, specify what would constitute a solution, devise hypothetical policies, test them, and select the best course of action. However, none of these conditions is found in the United States, so policy formulation cannot be perfectly scientific. Resources are to be allocated, and thus politics intrudes. We should often expect no more than approximate solutions, especially if the issue is new and creative proposals must be devised. The involvement of multiple actors implies that bargaining and negotiation are likely. The necessity of negotiation means that it is usually impossible to draw distinct boundaries between the formulation stage and the adoption stage, because policymakers design their proposals with a strategic eye on the likelihood of adoption.

What does the case of fair packaging and labeling tell us about the formulation and adoption stage? The process of formulating a fair-packaging-and-labeling bill was strongly shaped by the process of getting it onto the congressional agenda. Those who fought the hardest for it in the Senate were able to make the opening bid for a law that would give the federal government the power to establish standard package sizes and shapes. Not surprisingly, this proposal was vehemently opposed by manufacturers. They argued in favor of voluntary standards by which industry would regulate itself, and they pointed out that small manufacturers would suffer most from the costs of retooling their plants and from limits on creative packaging. Pertschuk reports that Magnuson ordered him to leak information—such as one senator's remark that "Any woman who feeds her children potato chips isn't worth protecting"—to Drew Pearson, whose column appeared in 1,100 newspapers.[22] Thus, when a compromise was offered by congressional staffers and employees of the White House and the Department of Commerce, industry officials were willing to accept an altered version of a fair-packaging-and-labeling bill. Under this compromise, mandatory standards would be imposed by the Commerce Department only if voluntary standards could not be agreed upon by industry. With this change, and with growing support from labor leaders and the White House, the bill was able to pass the first hurdle—the Senate Commerce Committee—by a 14–4 vote. This compromise made it possible for Senate Republicans to denounce the earlier extreme version of the bill and support the new version, which passed the entire Senate by a lopsided margin of 72 to 9.

The bill faced a tougher challenge in the House, which had not yet held any hearings on fair-packaging-and-labeling legislation. The Senate version reached the House Interstate and Foreign Commerce Committee, which was less liberal than its Senate counterpart, late in the session, when not much time remained for consideration and passage. The White House and Commerce Department sent top-level representatives to the House committee hearings and lobbied hard for the bill. At this stage, industry leaders were much more willing to discuss the bill, because they were now less likely to kill it completely, and again the bill was weakened. The final version, which passed the House by a 300–8 vote, had removed all provisions for mandatory standards; such standards could only be requested from Congress. Fair packaging and labeling would be primarily voluntary.

Implementation   Political scientist Eugene Bardach described the implementation stage of policymaking as, in part, an "assembly process."

> It is as if the original mandate, whether legislative or bureaucratic or judicial, that set the policy or program in motion were a blueprint for a large machine that was to turn out rehabilitated psychotics or healthier old people or better-educated children or more effective airplanes or safer streets. This machine must sometimes be assembled from scratch. It can sometimes be created by over-hauling and reconstituting an older, or preexisting machine. Putting the machine together and making it run is, at one level, what we mean by the "implementation process."[23]

In other words, laws do not implement themselves. Some person or agency must devise procedures for doing that. Employees must be reassigned or hired; for example, one-third of the FTC's requested budget increase for 1968 was earmarked for twenty-six new employees to enforce the FTC's responsibilities in implementing the Fair Packaging and Labeling Act. Yet, at this stage, because the mandate provided to the bureaucratic implementors is usually less than precise, confusion and conflict are common.

One aspect of this confusion and conflict can be illustrated by Jeffrey Pressman and Aaron Wildavsky's study of a program announced in 1966 in which the Economic Development Administration (EDA) planned to spend $23 million in Oakland, California, to build transportation facilities. It was proclaimed that the program would create 3,000 new jobs, primarily for unemployed inner-city minorities. Four years later, only $4 million had been spent and only 63 jobs had been created. Pressman and Wildavsky found that implementation of the projects had been stymied by two major problems. First, responsibility for the program had been split across many organizations at the federal, state, and local levels, and no mechanism existed to coordinate the plans. Second, various groups envisioned the accomplishment of different goals. For example, the EDA had strict guidelines for minority hiring, other groups were less interested in racial proportions than in the actual construction projects, and environmentalists objected to possible damage to marine and shore life.[24]

Implementation problems often arise when the administrators are laboring under a vague mandate. The necessary interpretations of what Congress really intended can be disputed, of course, and procedural disputes can add years or large expenses to programs. In fact, as Charles Jones observed,

> It may well be that the program was approved at all only because certain conflicts were avoided in the formulation and legitimation phases—conflicts bound to reappear in the implementation stage. How can this happen? Perhaps there is public pressure to do something, anything, about a problem (as with the devel-

opment of environmental control programs in the early 1970s), or the time may be right to get a program enacted even though the problems are not well understood (as with many of the Great Society programs in the mid-1960s).[25]

In the case of the Fair Packaging and Labeling Act, the implementation stage was complicated by two major features of the law. First, it had been passed at the expense of weakening it. Congress had forbidden federal agencies to issue mandatory packaging standards, so the responsible agencies could do relatively little to enforce the spirit of the law. Second, Congress had divided responsibility for fair packaging and labeling among the Commerce Department, the Food and Drug Administration (FDA), and the FTC. The Department of Commerce was told to encourage industry to avoid confusing packaging, either by helping industry groups to establish voluntary package standards (thus, the number of sizes of toothpaste tubes was reduced from fifty-seven to five) or by requesting mandatory standards from Congress if industry groups were unable to devise voluntary standards. The FDA was to require that labels on packages of food, drugs, cosmetics, and medical devices be uniform and accurate. The FTC could not limit the size, shape, weight, or dimensions of packages, but it could standardize the terms used to describe the size of packages (e.g., *giant* or *economy size*), regulate the use of promotional phrases such as *cents off*, require the listing of ingredients, and issue rules regarding slack-fill.

Evaluation The policy process "ends" with the assessment of the effectiveness of a governmental program. Policymakers want to know whether their ideas have worked, how they can be improved, and if past policies have had unintended side effects. Of course, the policy process does not really have an end. It is an ongoing process, and evaluation occurs throughout the stages already discussed. A problem might reach the political agenda because evaluations of past policies have revealed their shortcomings. Similarly, the formulation, adoption, and implementation of policies are likely to be shaped by assessments of previous experiences.

Much policy evaluation is performed by interested observers ranging from newspaper reporters to members of Congress. These seat-of-the-pants evaluations may be crucial in shaping the public's perception of policies, but they are usually less than perfect. The scandal-seeking bias of an investigative reporter or the ideological leanings of an unsympathetic congressional or White House official may cause a casual evaluation to be one-sided. In addition, these evaluations are often superficial. Nevertheless, they can carry great weight as the problems with programs are selectively advertised to the public and to lawmakers.

Some evaluations are much more systematic, however. Professional policy analysts are employed throughout the federal government to find the flaws, and possible corrections, in public programs. They may attempt cost-benefit analyses, converting all of the costs and benefits of programs to the single

	CEREAL	WITH MILK
CALORIES	110	180
PROTEIN	2 g	6 g
CARBOHYDRATE	25 g	30 g
FAT	0 g	4 g
SODIUM	285 mg	345 mg
POTASSIUM	30 mg	215 mg

PERCENTAGE OF U.S. RECOMMENDED DAILY ALLOWANCES (U.S. RDA)

	CEREAL	WITH MILK
PROTEIN	2	10
VITAMIN A	25	30
VITAMIN C	25	25
THIAMIN	25	30
RIBOFLAVIN	25	35
NIACIN	25	25
CALCIUM	*	15
IRON	10	10
VITAMIN D	10	25
VITAMIN B_6	25	30
FOLIC ACID	25	25
PHOSPHORUS	4	15
MAGNESIUM	2	8
ZINC	2	6
COPPER	4	4

*CONTAINS LESS THAN 2% OF THE U.S. RDA OF THIS NUTRIENT.

INGREDIENTS: RICE, SUGAR, SALT, CORN SYRUP, MALT FLAVORING,

VITAMINS AND IRON: VITAMIN C (SODIUM ASCORBATE AND ASCORBIC ACID), VITAMIN B_3 (NIACINAMIDE), IRON, VITAMIN A (PALMITATE), VITAMIN B_6 (PYRIDOXINE HYDROCHLORIDE), VITAMIN B_2 (RIBOFLAVIN), VITAMIN B_1 (THIAMIN HYDROCHLORIDE), FOLIC ACID, AND VITAMIN D.

TO KEEP THIS CEREAL FRESH, BHT HAS BEEN ADDED TO THE PACKAGING.

Fair-packaging legislation and other consumer-protection regulations are reflected in this panel from a box of cereal.

dimension of money and then calculating whether programs have yielded positive net benefits or costs. Another approach is the planning, programming, and budgeting system (PPBS), in which analysts focus on the interactions among policy areas (e.g., between rural industrialization programs and the cost of federal subsidies to railroads serving those areas). The PPBS was begun during Lyndon Johnson's administration, but was largely abandoned in 1971 because of (1) its threat to decentralized decisionmaking, (2) its exposure of irreconcilable conflicts among the goals of programs, and (3) the cost and complexity of examining all of the impacts of policies. For largely the same reasons, Jimmy Carter's zero-based budgeting (ZBB) system, which required continual reviews of entire agency budgets (rather than a review of only the requested changes in their budgets), ran into difficulty.

The problems of cost-benefit analysis, the PPBS, and the ZBB system illustrate the basic challenges facing policy analysts as they evaluate programs. They must overcome the inertia of past practices, they risk arousing the political constituencies of existing programs, and they must grapple with the same complexity that policy formulators and implementors face. To objectively evaluate a program, they must be aware of its goals. They must avoid oversimplifying the policy, and they must find accurate and valid measures of both problems and solutions. They must make assumptions both about the program's changing effectiveness over time—perhaps many years—and the uniformity of its effects across varying groups of people in different places. Finally, they must attempt to eliminate their own personal biases, as well as the values of powerful political individuals or groups who may have hired them to do the work. As a leading scholar on the subject wrote, "Evaluation has always had explicitly political overtones. It is designed to yield conclusions about the worth of programs and, in doing so, is intended to affect the allocation of resources."[26] Even the choice of what to evaluate and what to ignore can have sweeping effects on public policies.

The Fair Packaging and Labeling Act probably had a negligible impact on consumer welfare. The FTC introduced some regulations on labeling (e.g., limiting a manufacturer's use of the term *economy size* to one size of a package with a unit price "considerably less" than the unit price of other sizes), but took few steps on slack-filling.[27] In general, the actions of the FTC and the Commerce Department under the fair-packaging legislation had less impact than was desired by those who supported the original version of the bill in Congress.

More rigorous evaluations have been made of another law passed as part of the same consumer-protection movement: that is, the 1968 Consumer Credit Protection Act, or the truth-in-lending act. This law was intended to protect borrowers of money by requiring lenders to disclose the total finance charge, total payments, and annual interest rate on all loans. The Federal Reserve Board was to administer this law for banks, and the FTC was to regulate consumer loans by retail establishments. During the years immediately following passage of the truth-in-lending act, it was attacked for being almost useless. A 1971 survey showed that few consumers had any interest in the law, and studies showed that most poor people, who were intended to be the main beneficiaries of truth in lending, could not understand the detailed disclosures in retail credit agreements. In the late 1970s, it was reported that less than 20 percent of banks were in full compliance with the law.

Because analyses of the truth-in-lending law indicated that complex regulations were at least partially at fault for the poor results, Congress passed the Truth-in-Lending Simplification and Reform Act, which took effect in October 1982. A congressionally required evaluation of the effects of the reforms indicated that the cost of compliance actually jumped by 45 percent after the new rules took effect. However, it was acknowledged that the benefits from streamlined credit-disclosure regulations take longer to appear than the costs of changing to a new system. Furthermore, a survey indicated that about half of all mortgage lenders would stop routinely disclosing finance charges, total payments, and annual percentage rates if the truth-in-lending legislation were to disappear.[28] Clearly, the benefits of this policy are more difficult to define and measure than the policy's costs.

BUREAUCRACY AND POLICY: NO SIMPLE ANSWERS

The American political system relies heavily on a set of institutions that have no clear constitutional role. The bureaus, agencies, and departments known as the bureaucracy nevertheless fulfill functions that are necessary to the policy process. By providing information to elected leaders and accepting delegations of power for writing regulations and implementing laws, the bureaucracy has become a vital part of the political and economic system of the United States. Ironically, some of the virtues of American bureaucracy are also some of its faults. In particular, the often complicated procedures summarized by the term *red tape* confer both benefits and costs on society.

We have also examined the policy process in the federal government. Five major, but not always distinct, stages of the policy process were discussed and illustrated by consumer legislation. The portrait presented of the making of American policy should have conveyed some sense of the enormous problems—political pressures, lack of information, and inadequate understanding of the way the world works—faced by those who make, implement, and evaluate the actions of government. As we turn to the substance of three major policy areas in the next three chapters, these problems should be remembered, not to excuse the failures of public policies, but to help provide a realistic perspective. Perhaps the marvel is that the system works at all.

NOTES

[1]See Chapter 8 in H. H. Gerth and C. Wright Mills, *From Max Weber: Essays in Sociology* (New York: Oxford University Press, 1946).

[2]See Emile Durkheim, *The Division of Labor in Society* (Glencoe, Illinois: Free Press, 1952).

[3] Gerth and Mills, *From Max Weber,* p. 215.

[4]Daniel Katz, Barbara A. Gutek, Robert L. Kahn, and Eugenia Barton, *Bureaucratic Encounters* (Ann Arbor: Survey Research Center of the University of Michigan, 1975).

[5]Surveys by the *Los Angeles Times* and the Roper Organization, reported in *Public Opinion,* October/November, 1982, p. 23.

[6]Herbert Kaufman, *Red Tape: Its Uses and Abuses* (Washington, D.C.: Brookings Institution, 1977).

[7]Robert Michels, *Political Parties* (Glencoe, Ill.: Free Press, 1949).

[8]Herbert Kaufman, *Are Government Organizations Immortal?* (Washington, D.C.: Brookings Institution, 1976).

[9]Anthony Downs, *Inside Bureaucracy* (Boston: Little, Brown, 1967), p. 22.

[10]Stephen Skowronek, *Building a New American State: The Expansion of National Administrative Capacities 1877–1920* (New York: Cambridge University Press, 1982), p. 67.

[11]U.S. Bureau of the Census, *Statistical Abstract of the United States, 1984* (Washington, D.C.: Government Printing Office, 1984), p. 431.

[12]*Summary Report: The Future of Federal Retirement* (Washington, D.C.: National Association of Retired Federal Employees, 1978).

[13]U.S. Bureau of the Census, *Statistical Abstract of the United States, 1981* (Washington, D.C.: Government Printing Office, 1981), p. 266.

[14]Jerry L. Mashaw, *Bureaucratic Justice: Managing Social Security Disability Claims* (New Haven: Yale University Press, 1983), p. 213.

[15]James G. March and Johan P. Olson, "Organizing Political Life: What Administrative Reorganization Tells Us about Government," *American Political Science Review* 77 (June 1983): 281–296.

[16]James E. Anderson, *Public Policy-Making: Decisions and Their Implementation* (New York: Praeger, 1975), p. 3

[17]Much of the following discussion is based on Alan Stone, *Economic Regulation and the Public Interest: The Federal Trade Commission in Theory and Practice* (Ithaca, N.Y.: Cornell University Press, 1977), chapter 10. Also see David Price, *Who Makes the Laws?* (Cambridge: Schenkman, 1972), chapter 2, and Michael Pertschuk, *Revolt Against Regulation* (Berkeley: University of California Press, 1982).

[18]Roger W. Cobb and Charles D. Elder, *Participation in American Politics: The Dynamics of Agenda-Building* (Baltimore: Johns Hopkins University Press, 1972), p. 86.

[19]Mark V. Nadel, *The Politics of Consumer Protection* (Indianapolis: Bobbs-Merrill, 1971), p. 40.

[20]Price, *Who Makes the Laws?* p. 25.

[21]Pertschuk, *Revolt Against Regulation,* p. 24.

[22]Ibid., pp. 34–35.

[23]Eugene Bardach, *The Implementation Game* (Cambridge: MIT Press, 1977), p. 36.

[24]Jeffrey L. Pressman and Aaron Wildavsky, *Implementation* (Berkeley: University of California Press, 1973).

[25]Charles O. Jones, *An Introduction to the Study of Public Policy,* 2nd ed. (North Scituate, Massachusetts: Duxbury Press, 1977), pp. 151–152.

[26]Carol H. Weiss, "The Politicization of Evaluation Research," *Journal of Social Issues* 26 (Autumn 1970): 58. See also Weiss's *Evaluation Research* (Englewood Cliffs, New Jersey: Prentice Hall, 1972).

[27]Stone, *Economic Regulation and the Public Interest,* p. 240.

[28]The study was performed for the Federal Trade Commission by Louis Harris and Associates, "A Survey of the Mortgage Banking Industry Concerning Costs and Benefits," September 1982. The research is described in *Regulation* (July/August 1983): 54–55.

BIBLIOGRAPHY

Anderson, James E., David W. Brady, and Charles Bullock III. *Public Policy and Politics in America.* 2nd ed. Monterey, California: Brooks/Cole, 1984. A textbook with excellent chapters on such various public policy areas as energy, welfare, education, labor, and agriculture.

Bardach, Eugene. *The Implementation Game.* Cambridge: MIT Press, 1977. An examination of the implementation process, with special attention to bureaucratic techniques of blocking policies after they have been passed into law.

Dodd, Lawrence C., and Richard L. Schott. *Congress and the Administrative State.* New York: Wiley, 1979. How Congress and the bureaucracy do and do not get along.

Downs, Anthony. *Inside Bureaucracy.* Boston: Little, Brown, 1967. A thoroughly theoretical discussion of the behavior of bureaucrats in the context of institutional politics.

Gerth, H. H., and C. Wright Mills. *From Max Weber: Essays in Sociology.* New York:

Oxford University Press, 1946. The definitive collection of Max Weber's ideas on bureaucracy, politics, science, and other topics.

Jones, Charles O. *An Introduction to the Study of Public Policy.* 2nd ed. North Scituate, Massachusetts: Duxbury, 1977. An excellent textbook on the policy process, with chapters on each stage from agenda-setting to evaluation.

Meltsner, Arnold J. *Policy Analysts in the Bureaucracy.* Berkeley: University of California Press, 1976. A readable account of the problems facing professional policy advisers, with many interesting anecdotes and examples.

National Journal. A weekly magazine that is notably objective in its reporting of politics and public policy; useful for both current events and background information.

Rourke, Francis E. *Bureaucracy, Politics, and Public Policy.* 2nd ed. Boston: Little, Brown, 1976. This study emphasizes the role of bureaucracies in the policy process, with special attention to the sources of agency power.

Weiss, Carol H. *Evaluation Research.* Englewood Cliffs, New Jersey: Prentice-Hall, 1972. An excellent, straightforward discussion of the difficulties in evaluating public policies.

Wildavsky, Aaron. *The Politics of the Budgetary Process.* 3rd ed. Boston: Little, Brown, 1979. Bureaucratic and political strategies and responsibilities for making budgets.

PART IV

POLICIES: MEANS AND ENDS

Foreign-Defense Policy

I n 1954, Vietnam was divided into two temporary zones, pending elections, which never took place. In 1959, guerrillas associated with the Communist regime in the north launched a war against the anti-Communist regime in the south. The United States gradually increased its commitment to the Republic of South Vietnam, yet by 1964, victory remained elusive and the war was going badly for the American-supported forces.

What to do about the situation was a topic of intense, sometimes bitter debate in Washington. On August 2, 1964, a Washington communiqué announced that three North Vietnamese torpedo boats had fired at the American destroyer *Maddox* in the Gulf of Tonkin, international waters thirty miles from the North Vietnamese mainland. Another destroyer, the *Turner Joy,* was attacked two days later, and there was a new assault on the *Maddox.* That evening, President Lyndon Johnson announced in a nationwide television broadcast that the United States had taken retaliatory air action against North Vietnam. The next day, Johnson sent a message to Congress requesting a joint resolution supporting "the determination of the President . . . to take all necessary measures to repel any armed attack against the forces of the United States and to prevent further aggression." The Tonkin Gulf Resolution, which was passed almost immediately by the House (416–0) and Senate (88–2), obligated the United States, "as the President determines," to use armed force to aid its allies in Southeast Asia pursuant to the Southeast Asia Collective Defense Treaty. As a result, the document became the basis for the vast expansion of American military efforts in Indochina. By the time a cease-fire was announced in January 1973, the United States had sustained more than 47,000 deaths and 213,000 casualties in battle.

Shortly after the passage of the Tonkin Gulf Resolution, several investigators began to look into the circumstances of the original North Vietnamese action. Considerable doubt was raised as to whether the second attack actually took place. Furthermore, although the first attack clearly did occur, the South Vietnamese, to whom the United States had given torpedo boats, had been raiding North Vietnamese islands for some time. Accordingly, some critics of the Tonkin Gulf Resolution argued that the North Vietnamese had reason to believe that America destroyers in the area were aiding the South Vietnamese. In any event, the critics claimed that this information, which the president did not reveal, was a mitigating circumstance showing that the resolution and the United States armed forces commitment under it were out of proportion to the incidents.[1]

WHAT IS DIFFERENT ABOUT FOREIGN-DEFENSE POLICY?

In retrospect, the Tonkin Gulf incident was one of the most important events in post–World War II American foreign-defense policy. In many respects, it illustrates how foreign policy differs from domestic policy.[2] The most obvious difference is that foreign policy is almost always directed toward providing a public good; for example, national security or survival or national economic

353

well-being. We are all supposed to benefit from foreign-defense policy moves, and the benefits are not divisible. Defense preparations or a new foreign-trade policy is generally expected to benefit the nation as a whole. This is also true of some domestic policies (most notably macroeconomic policies), but a greater number of these are expected to help particular groups (e.g., the aged and the poor) or contain divisions along interest-group lines. In short, the self-interest in most foreign-policy decisions is equated with the national interest.

When an appeal to the national interest is successful, divisions within the population frequently disappear. For example, virtually all Americans supported World War II, and most of them approved the United States' posture toward communism in the aftermath of the war; Democrats and Republicans alike largely supported President Harry Truman's bipartisan foreign policy. Moreover, there was almost universal support during the first phases of the Korean war (1949–1953), and as the lopsided congressional vote in favor of the Tonkin Gulf Resolution shows, the appeal for national unity was largely successful before the large-scale commitment of American troops in Vietnam. However, since then, although most Americans strongly dislike communism and view the Soviet Union as the United States' principal adversary, divisions have occurred in some important policy areas. The failure to achieve quick results—indeed, the sense that the United States cannot attain its goals at a reasonable cost—and distaste for the conduct of some of the country's allies have contributed to both a decline in public support and party division in American foreign policy.

The national-interest concept is related to another important difference between foreign and domestic policy. In foreign policy, there is usually an adversary—most often a nation but sometimes a foreign group, such as the Palestine Liberation Organization (PLO). An adversary is not necessarily an enemy, although sometimes, as in the case of the Soviet Union, it is. Sometimes, an adversary is a friendly nation (e.g., Japan) that competes with the United States in a peaceful arena, such as commerce. In the case of the Tonkin Gulf incident, the adversaries were North Vietnam and its presumed military and economic supporter, the Soviet Union. In domestic policy, the nation does not confront adversaries, but, rather, problems such as inflation, low productivity, and poverty.

One important consequence of the adversary nature of foreign-defense policy is that much of it is conducted in secret. Whereas open debate is the norm in domestic policy, secrecy is the norm in foreign policy. The United States action in the Gulf of Tonkin was planned and executed in secret; only *after* the event were the American people told of it. In contrast, domestic policy is made in the form of laws and regulations after debate, hearings, and so on. Obviously, an adversary would have a significant advantage if told in advance of American foreign-policy moves. This, in turn, raises the costs necessary both to obtain information about other nations' intentions and to devise security arrangements to counter their efforts to penetrate American secrecy. For these reasons, intelligence activities are especially important in foreign-defense policy. Foreign policy thus requires the formulation of strategy designed to counter an adversary's potential moves. Although domestic policies sometimes require the use of strategy, they more commonly involve problems (e.g., unemployment or inflation) than adversaries.

There is another underlying characteristic of foreign-defense policy: the basic lawlessness of international relations. Persons and firms in the domestic area are constrained by the force of law: a person who defrauds another—or a corporation that violates antitrust laws—can be punished. In contrast, although there is a facade of lawfulness in the international arena as well as many international organizations and agreements, ultimately a nation will not be bound unless it believes that it is in its national interest to be so. For example, the Soviet Union's occupation of Afghanistan was not reversed, even after President Jimmy Carter's decision not to allow American participation in the 1980 summer Olympic games in Moscow. Both North Vietnam's subversion of South Vietnam, as well as the American actions in the Tonkin Gulf, were undertaken on the basis of perceived national interest. Although diplomats often legally justify actions after they are taken, such justifications are secondary. Nations do enter into agreements when they believe that net benefits outweigh net costs, but the basic anarchy of international relations can also lead to war—often conducted under a different name, such as *conflict* or *police action*—something that is not a factor in domestic policy. The vast expansion of American participation in Vietnam that followed the Gulf of Tonkin Resolution typifies something that could not have occurred in the domestic-policy arena.

When we combine the characteristics of foreign-defense policy with the risks, including national survival, and the greater role given to the chief executive in foreign policy by the Constitution, it is clear why our primary focus in this area is the president. Congress, of course, plays a role in foreign policy—the Senate must approve treaties, and both houses must appropriate money for foreign affairs. More than in the domestic arena, however, we look toward the president and a close set of executive-branch institutions—notably, the State and Defense departments, the National Security Council, and the Central Intelligence Agency—for foreign-defense policymaking. It was President Lyndon Johnson and officials from these agencies, not Congress, who were responsible for the American response in the Tonkin Gulf. Congress can react, investigate, protest, and impose restrictions on executive-branch actions, but it is almost always the executive branch that initiates foreign policy.

We began this chapter by focusing on a particular incident—the Tonkin Gulf attacks. But American foreign-defense policy cannot be understood by studying a single incident frozen in time. Rather, that incident, like so many others must be understood in a broader historical context.

The Cold War

In order to understand foreign-defense policy events that occur today, we must go back at least to World War II. The war, which cost between thirty-five and forty million lives, led to a great outpouring of idealism dedicated to building a world in which such a conflict could never occur again. Even before the war's conclusion, however, major disputes between the United States and the Soviet Union had broken out, although these were temporarily submerged for the sake of Allied unity. To the United States, the two principal issues at stake were (1) Soviet intentions toward other nations and (2) the extent to which the Soviet Union would control the activities of Communist parties throughout the world. Before the war, the Soviet Union had dominated the policies and activities of all Communist parties through an organization known as the Comintern. It allowed no deviation from Comintern policies, which, in turn, closely reflected the foreign-policy aims of the Soviet leaders. Would the same structure prevail in the postwar era?

From the perspective of the West, the Soviet Union had behaved like an expansionist power before it joined with the Allies in mid-1941. It had incorporated virtually the entire territory of the Old Russian empire, in the process absorbing large numbers of non-Russian people without offering them an opportunity to form independent nations. In 1940, it absorbed the previously independent republics of Latvia, Lithuania, and Estonia, and in 1939, it had attacked Finland and Poland, the latter in conjunction with Nazi Germany.

British Prime Minister Winston Churchill, President Franklin Roosevelt, and Russian Premier Joseph Stalin, in the patio at the palace in Yalta where they met in February 1945. (AP/Wide World Photos)

After the Nazis invaded the Soviet Union and the Japanese attacked Pearl Harbor, however, the United States and the Soviet Union were drawn into alliance. The Soviet subscription to the principles of a United Nations organization in 1942, the dissolution of the Comintern in 1943, and the acceptance of the Bretton Woods economic principles in 1944 cemented the alliance and temporarily allayed American suspicions of Soviet intentions.

Yet even during the wartime alliance, unity was being eroded by Soviet actions. As Soviet troops pushed the German army back during the later stages of the war, they entered the nations of eastern Europe. In Poland, Soviet troops treated the Polish anti-Nazi resistance movement as an enemy force, slaughtering many Polish patriots in the process. By 1948, the Soviets had set up puppet governments in Bulgaria, Hungary, Rumania, Czechoslovakia, and Poland.

In Greece, native Communists, supplied with arms and equipment from Communist countries on the Greek border, reinstituted a civil war against the government that had been elected to power in March 1946. During the same period, the Soviet Union demanded that Turkey, which had been neutral during World War II, cede to it considerable territory and permit the installation of military and naval bases in Turkish territory. Finally, several Western European countries, notably France and Italy, emerged from the war with powerful Communist parties that followed the Soviet Union's foreign-policy position.

Some analysts (known as "revisionists") interpreted Soviet actions as a response to American hostility and aggressiveness. According to their view, American behavior in the cold war threatened the Soviet Union's legitimate security interests by promoting anti-Soviet governments in Europe and by refusing any accommodation with the Soviets, as well as economic aid. The Soviet Union, according to the revisionists, was therefore compelled to set up friendly states nearby in order to assure its legitimate security interests. Finally, according to this view, the Soviets were interested, not in world conquest, but only in protecting their borders.[3]

Most observers—and, more importantly, most American policymakers—did not interpret Soviet actions in a revisionist manner. Instead, they saw (1) that American forces quickly demobilized after World War II while the Soviet army remained large, and (2) that the Soviets had absorbed a long list of nations into their orbit and were threatening still others.[4] Accordingly, under the leadership of President Truman, the United States undertook a series of moves designed to meet the Soviet threat. The underlying theory behind Truman's policy is termed **containment;** it was devised by George Kennan, then a State Department official. Spelled out in a 1947 article in the journal *Foreign Affairs,* containment is as important to understand today as it was then.[5]

Containment

The Soviet Union is ruled by a small group of ideologues who, employing a perverted conception of Marxism, operate on two fundamental propositions. The first is that there is an implacable hostility between the socialist world

containment: American foreign policy, devised by George Kennan in 1947, which is aimed at thwarting Soviet expansion into other nations.

THE TRUMAN DOCTRINE: SPEECH BEFORE CONGRESS (1947)

The gravity of the situation which confronts the world today necessitates my appearance before a joint session of the Congress. The foreign policy and the national security of this country are involved.

One aspect of the present situation, which I wish to present to you at this time for your consideration and decisions, concerns Greece and Turkey.

The United States has received from the Greek Government an urgent appeal for financial and economic assistance. Preliminary reports from the American Economic Mission now in Greece and reports from the American Ambassador in Greece corroborate the statement of the Greek Government that assistance is imperative if Greece is to survive as a free nation.

I do not believe that the American people and the Congress wish to turn a deaf ear to the appeal of the Greek Government.

The very existence of the Greek state is today threatened by the terrorist activities of several thousand armed men, led by Communists, who defy the Government's authority at a number of points, particularly along the northern boundaries. . . .

One of the primary objectives of the foreign policy of the United States is the creation of conditions in which we and other nations will be able to work out a way of life free from coercion. This was a fundamental issue in the war with Germany and Japan. Our victory was won over the countries which sought to impose their will, and their way of life, upon other nations.

. . . . We shall not realize our objectives, however, unless we are willing to help free people to maintain their free institutions and their national integrity against aggressive movements that seek to impose on them totalitarian regimes. This is no more than a frank recognition that totalitarian regimes imposed on free peoples, by direct or indirect aggression, undermine the foundations of international peace and hence the security of the United States.

The peoples of a number of countries of the world have recently had totalitarian regimes forced upon them against their will. The Government of the United States has made frequent protests against coercion and intimidation, in violation of the Yalta Agreement, in Poland, Rumania and Bulgaria. I must also state that in a number of other countries there have been similar developments.

At the present moment in world history nearly every nation must choose between alternative ways of life. The choice is too often not a free one.

One way of life is based upon the will of the majority, and is distinguished by free institutions, representative government, free elections, guarantees of individual liberty, freedom of speech and religion, and freedom from political oppression.

The second way of life is based upon the will of the minority forcibly imposed upon the majority. It relies upon terror and oppression, a controlled press and radio, fixed elections, and the suppression of personal freedoms.

I believe that it must be the policy of the United States to support free peoples who are resisting attempted subjugation by armed minorities or by outside pressures.

I believe that we must assist free peoples to work out their own destinies in their own way.

I believe that our help should be primarily through

(i.e., the Soviet Union and its allies) and the capitalist world, and that the victory of world socialism is inevitable. This does not mean that the Soviet leaders have a hard and fast timetable for the end of capitalism. To the contrary, they can be flexible and even retreat periodically. But ultimately, what they term *socialism* will prevail, especially if they seize the opportunities for socialist advance and capitalist retreat. In this undertaking, they can afford to be flexible and creative; diplomacy, internal disruption of capitalist economic life, guerrilla warfare, support of terrorism, or any other tactic may be appropriate if the opportunity to weaken capitalism is presented.

economic and financial aid which is essential to economic stability and orderly political processes.

The world is not static, and thus the status quo is not sacred. But we cannot allow changes in the status quo in violation of the charter of the United Nations by such methods as coercion, or by such subterfuges as political infiltration. In helping free and independent nations to maintain their freedom, the United States will be giving effect to the principles of the charter of the United Nations.

It is necessary only to glance at a map to realize that the survival and integrity of the Greek nation are of grave importance in a much wider situation. If Greece should fall under the control of an armed minority, the effect upon its neighbor, Turkey, would be immediate and serious. Confusion and disorder might well spread throughout the entire Middle East.

Moreover, the disappearance of Greece as an independent state would have a profound effect upon those countries in Europe whose peoples are struggling against great difficulties to maintain their freedoms and their independence while they repair the damages of war.

It would be an unspeakable tragedy if these countries, which have struggled so long against overwhelming odds, should lose that victory for which they sacrificed so much. Collapse of free institutions and loss of independence would be disastrous not only for them but for the world. Discouragement and possibly failure would quickly be the lot of neighboring peoples striving to maintain their freedom and independence.

Should we fail to aid Greece and Turkey in this fateful hour, the effect will be far reaching to the west as well as the the east. We must take immediate and resolute action.

I therefore ask the Congress to provide authority for assistance to Greece and Turkey in the amount of $44 million for the period ending June 30, 1948.

In addition to funds, I ask the Congress to authorize the detail of American civilian and military personnel to Greece and Turkey, at the request of those countries, to assist in the task of reconstruction, and for the purpose of supervising the use of such financial and material assistance as may be furnished. I recommend that authority also be provided for the instruction and training of selected Greek and Turkish personnel.

Finally, I ask that the Congress provide authority which will permit the speediest and most effective use, in terms of needed commodities, supplies, and equipment, of such funds as may be authorized. . . .

The seeds of totalitarian regimes are nurtured by misery and want. They spread and grow in the evil soil of poverty and strife. They reach their full growth when the hope of a people for a better life has died. We must keep that hope alive. The free peoples of the world look to us for support in maintaining their freedoms.

If we falter in our leadership, we may endanger the peace of the world—and we shall surely endanger the welfare of this nation.

Great responsibilities have been placed upon us by the swift movement of events. I am confident that the Congress will face these responsibilities squarely.

Source: *Documents of American History,* 7th ed. (New York: Appleton-Century-Crofts, 1963).

The second deeply ingrained foundation of Soviet foreign policy is that the Soviet leadership, guided by "scientific socialism," has a monopoly on political truth. Any ideas that deviate from the pronouncements of scientific socialism can only aid the capitalist world and, therefore, cannot be tolerated. Thus, the Soviets have ruthlessly crushed all internal dissension in the nations under their control; even alternative roads to socialism, such as those attempted in Czechoslovakia in 1968 and in Poland in 1980–1981, have been shattered. Communists in countries that subscribe to Soviet views must pursue policies that advance the goals set by the "infallible" Soviet leadership. The rigid structure of the Communist party was designed to assure this obedience; party members must obey the party line or face the threat of expulsion. Thus, Kennan concluded, Soviet "infallibility" and discipline reinforce the goal of world socialist victory.

George Kennan's containment policy called for a "long-term, patient but firm and vigilant containment of Russian expansive tendencies." The Western world, according to Kennan, should adopt a united stance that would meet the Soviet threat, "at a series of constantly shifting geographical and political points, corresponding to the shifts and maneuvers of Soviet policy." The United States could not roll back Soviet communism from the areas to which it had spread; realistically, Soviet power was simply too great for this to occur. The United States could, however, adopt diplomatic, military, and economic strategies to prevent the further spread of Soviet influence, and it could act at every point in the world where the Soviets might exploit instability. Most important, Kennan asserted, the United States must have a clear understanding of the threat, have the will to act resolutely, and be unified. Otherwise, the Communist world would be encouraged to take advantage of the signs of disunity, vacillation, or a retreat to inaction.

The containment theory was not a prediction of how the United States *would* react to the postwar world, but a prescription of how it *should* react. It did not foresee the splits that occurred within the Soviet bloc—the sharp break between the Soviet Union and Yugoslavia and, later, the split with China. On the other hand, nothing in containment theory is inconsistent with two or more centers of Communist power, each with its own structures and interests. Nor does it reveal precisely how the United States should meet Communist threats of conquest or other situations in which stability and peace are jeopardized. Rather, it remains as the ideal to which many American leaders have aspired, and it has been the basis for many American foreign-policy decisions and doctrines. In 1947, for example, the Truman administration, motivated by the concept of containment, implemented the **Truman Doctrine,** which included economic and military aid to threatened Greece and Turkey; in 1948, economic aid was provided to Western European economies through the *Marshall Plan.* The president supported lowered trade barriers to further strengthen the world economy and authorized a worldwide radio network, the Voice of America, to counteract Communist propaganda. The United States greatly aided in the rebuilding of West Germany and Japan, thus assisting the growth of industrial firms in those countries that would later prove to be the most intensive competitors American industry had ever faced.

In these endeavors, which did much to shape the postwar world and the United States' place and strategy in it, President Truman was attentive to two of the cardinal principles of containment: Allied unity and internal American unity. Together with Republican senator Arthur Vandenberg, Truman promoted consensus in American foreign policy, using the slogan "bipartisan foreign policy." Most Republicans and Democrats supported the president's foreign-policy proposals. To support American allies, Truman formally committed the

Truman Doctrine: A declaration made by President Harry Truman in 1947 that the United States would provide military and economic assistance to nations threatened by the Soviet Union or internal communist insurrection.

United States to defend Western Europe against a Soviet attack, sponsored American rearmament, and moved toward the creation of mutual security arrangements. The most important of these was the North Atlantic Treaty, signed in April 1949, under which the United States, Canada, and thirteen European nations created the North Atlantic Treaty Organization (NATO) and agreed to "unite their efforts for collective defense and for the preservation of peace and security." The central principle of the treaty is the *tripwire doctrine*, under which the United States views an attack upon any treaty signatory as an attack on itself.

As we have seen, containment is based on the ideas of monolithic communism under the leadership of an aggressive Soviet Union. Events in the postwar world, however, began to erode this premise. Yugoslavia, a Communist state, broke with the Soviet bloc in 1948, and since then, it has conducted a foreign policy independent of both the United States and the Soviet Union. More important, China, the most populous Communist state, not only broke with the Soviet Union in the 1960s, but also became one of its most fervid opponents. Futhermore, some Western European Communist parties developed foreign-policy positions that were at odds with the Soviet's. But the most difficult tests for containment concerned revolutions in less developed countries that were led by Communists. A corollary to containment known as the *domino theory* was devised during President Dwight Eisenhower's administration to deal with such revolutions.

The Domino Theory

The domino theory simply states that, like a line of dominoes standing on their edges, if one nation is pushed over into communism, the adjacent ones will soon topple. Three reasons account for this view. First, as George Kennan observed, any weakness or vacillation in the face of Communist aggression only encourages the Soviets and their associates to become more aggressive elsewhere at the time and place of their choosing; they interpret such weakness as a sign of capitalist decay and dispiritedness. Second, any such conquest provides a base area from which they can supply and support their allies in adjacent countries. Thus, China became a principal source of supply and support to the Communist forces in North Korea and North Vietnam. The final, and most subtle, reason advanced in support of the domino theory is that if Communist takeovers are unchecked by American resistance, the will of other nations to resist the spread of communism would be gradually sapped in the face of what they perceive to be the inevitable flow of history. They would become neutral and then, perhaps, would lean toward the Communist side. Eventually, the United States would find itself surrounded by a world of hostile, or at best indifferent, powers, and it, too, would ultimately succumb to the Soviets. Thus, the domino theory compelled the United States to meet Communist aggression every place the prospect for successful resistance was reasonably high.

The most serious test of the domino theory was the bloody Vietnam conflict, which lasted from 1961 through 1973. Despite the presence of more than 500,000 American troops in Indochina, the Communist guerrilla movement and the North Vietnamese army stalemated the United States, ultimately emerging victorious in 1973. Thus, the important proviso for American action under the containment theory—that Soviet-aligned forces can be constrained at *reasonable* cost—seemed to many observers to have been violated. Furthermore, many critics believed that the regime the United States was supporting was no better than the Communist regime. Some argued that the premise of Soviet control over Communist movements in less developed countries was highly questionable. In the early 1980s, as the focus shifted from Southeast Asia to Central America, many observers still considered containment applicable to less developed countries. Other observers, however, pointing to Vietnam, rejected containment and the domino theory, arguing that the United States should not become involved in such conflicts. In the early 1980s, opponents of President Reagan's Central American policies feared gradual and increasing American troop involvement in the region on behalf of such states as El Salvador and Guatemala, both of which had brutalized segments of their own population.

Containment Today

The world today is a very different place than it was when containment was announced. Containment has recently been criticized in connection with Communist-led revolutionary movements in less developed countries because it is believed that these movements stem from desperate conditions, not orders from Moscow. Also, the Soviet Union has lost control over much of world communism. It has shown some willingness to enter into arms control and other agreements with the United States and the NATO powers. To be sure, the Soviet Union, apparently willing to aid disorder and instability, remains the United States' principal enemy. Because so much else has changed, however, containment is now a much less sure guide to action, and the United States has not found a substitute guiding theory that is neatly applicable to the present world. As we have seen, the high information costs necessary to ascertain Soviet intentions and events in such diverse countries as Vietnam, Nicaragua, and Chad, coupled with the general lack of law in international relations, have eroded the predictability of the containment theory.

Consequently, much in American foreign policy appears to be vacillation, an inability to anticipate events or act clearly and consistently when they occur. American foreign policy, then, is to some extent improvised. Yet, in the diplomatic, military, and economic realms, the goals of national survival, opposition to Soviet expansionism, and international stability—the goals of containment—still remain the fundamental precepts of American foreign policy. We turn now to the three components of that policy: diplomacy, military policy, and foreign economic policy.

AMERICAN DIPLOMACY

The United Nations

As World War II drew to a close, an almost unanimous public sentiment arose in the Allied nations for creating a system to preserve international peace and security. An international organization that could peaceably settle disputes among sovereign nations was a necessity. It was natural for the leaders of the major Allied nations to take as their initial model the institution that was created to serve this purpose following World War I—the League of Nations. But the League had failed to stem the drift toward a second world war that began in the mid-1930s. Accordingly, the American, British, French, and Soviet leaders, seeking to create a better international organization after World War II, scrutinized the League of Nations for its failures in hope of learning from past mistakes.

The Allied leaders agreed upon several reasons for the League of Nations' failure to keep peace. First, the United States never belonged to the League, and Germany and the Soviet Union were not members for long periods. Second, the League's structure did not provide for the fact that all states are not equal in power and importance. Accordingly, the few large, powerful states could be easily outvoted by the more numerous smaller ones. Yet, realistically, peace and security could not be maintained without the large nations' active support, which they were unlikely to provide unless they concurred with a decision. Third, the League of Nations had no mechanism for enforcing its decisions. International conferences were the primary mechanism employed by the League to settle international disputes. If the parties agreed upon a solution to their dispute, the League was successful, but when a nation would not accept a proposed solution, it followed the dictates of its national policy without fear of League reprisal.

When the Allied powers began to plan the contours of the new international organization, the United Nations (U.N.), they intended to create structures that would correct the errors of the League of Nations. Thus, every nation claiming to subscribe to U.N. principles, including the United States and the Soviet

---

HIDDEN DIPLOMACY

In January 1984, the Soviet foreign minister, Andrei Gromyko, made a public speech denouncing the Reagan administration as "pathological" and "criminal." A few hours later, Gromyko was chatting pleasantly with the American secretary of state about the weather as the two officials prepared to discuss important matters concerning Soviet-American relations. Such private discussions between representatives of the major powers are frequent and often lead to important agreements, even when public relations between them are highly antagonistic.

A general view of the United Nations Security Council in session. (UN Photo 150,099 by Milton Grant)

Union, would be included. Second, because some nations are far more important than others in the world balance of power, two chambers were created in the U.N. policymaking structure: (1) the General Assembly, which includes every member state and gives them equal votes, and (2) the Security Council, consisting of fifteen nations, of which five (i.e., the United States, Soviet Union, United Kingdom, France, and China) are designated permanent members and ten are considered nonpermanent members. Most important, any permanent member can single-handedly veto a substantive decision by the Security Council. The word *veto* does not appear in the U.N. charter, but this document does require affirmative votes of all five permanent members on substantive matters in order for a proposal to take effect.

The reason for the veto provision was the likelihood that the international organization could not effectively carry out at an acceptable cost a decision that one of the permanent members resisted. Accordingly, the sponsoring members held that the high transaction costs necessary to gain the concurrence of the permanent members in a compromise solution would usually be lower than the costs imposed by a procedure that could leave one of the large powers dissatisfied. For, regardless of the flowery rhetoric associated with the founding of the U.N., each major state valued its own sovereignty and national interests above those of the U.N. And although the Security Council may investigate any dispute that threatens the peace, it can only recommend means for a peaceful settlement; it can require members to apply sanctions against a member that has been found guilty of a breach of the peace, but it ultimately has no way to force major (or even minor) members to comply with the requirement. In short, the U.N. has not solved the most glaring deficiency of the international system—anarchy. Each state pursues policies that it believes to be in its national interest and is constrained only when it believes that the costs of contemplated action will outweigh the benefits.

As the number of member nations expanded from 51 in 1945 to 158 in 1984, the United States and its Western allies frequently found themselves in the minority, swamped by the votes of Communist and Third World nations. The U.N. was thus a less valuable forum for discussion and negotiation than was intended, even though representatives from most of the world are present at its headquarters in New York City. High levels of inflammatory rhetoric that tend to heighten conflict, the lack of expertise among representatives to the organization on such major controversies as disarmament and trade among nations, and the presence of other forums for the discussion of major issues have combined to make the U.N. of limited usefulness in solving most international controversies.

If the U.N. provides a minimal security function and has not been a very useful forum for discussing or negotiating foreign-policy issues, what role does it play in the conduct of American foreign policy? The first role of the U.N., that of a symbol of humanity's unity, must not be downgraded, even though its benefits cannot be measured. The second role is considerably more concrete. The U.N. became the umbrella organization for many international cooperative enterprises in the areas of health, education, maritime matters, economic affairs, and so on. These specialized agencies include (1) the World Health Organization (WHO), which disseminates public-health information to nations and conducts campaigns designed to wipe out communicable diseases; (2) the Universal Postal Union (UPU), which aids the delivery of mail across international boundaries; and (3) The International Telecommunications Union (ITU), which allocates radio frequencies and promulgates rules for telecommunications, including communications satellites. In addition, the United States has participated in a series of U.N.-sponsored international conferences on such topics as the environment, women's rights, and maritime law.

Because of both the symbolic value of the U.N. and its umbrella function, each American president appoints a person of considerable stature to head the United States mission to the U.N. This representative also is provided with a sizable staff. Because the U.N. is a relatively unimportant forum for the conduct of international negotiations, however, the representative is usually not an important decisionmaker in American foreign policy. The representative is usually brought into the councils of top decisionmakers before they take action only when it will be necessary for him or her to forcefully defend American action before the Security Council or the General Assembly. In brief, the U.N. is accorded respect, but it does not play a major role in American diplomacy. The United States prefers to carry out its diplomatic initiatives through either bilateral programs or those involving just a few nations.

Bilateral Assistance

As we noted earlier, Western Europe was in ruins at the end of World War II. In response, the United States, through the Marshall Plan, provided $13.6 billion in economic aid to Western Europe. The Economic Cooperation Administration (ECA) administered the funding, as well as provided the services of businesspeople, economists, and skilled technicians to assist the Western Europeans in their reconstruction efforts. The program exemplified both American generosity and a sound commitment to American national-security interests through the building of stable, friendly societies in Western Europe. The Marshall Plan was not operated in a paternalistic manner; rather, decisions about specific programs were made jointly by Europeans and Americans. By 1952, which marked the formal termination of the Marshall Plan, industrial production in Western Europe was 35 percent higher than the prewar peak, and agriculture production was 10 percent above the prewar level. The great Western European economic boom had begun, and in no small part was it attributable to the Marshall Plan.

The success of the Marshall Plan in Western Europe colored American thinking about economic aid when programs to assist less developed countries began during the 1950s. After all, if economic aid to Western Europe could be translated into economic development and alliance in that region, why couldn't the same result occur in other regions? Such assistance, it was hoped, would create stability in the recipient country as a result of better living standards and would cement support for the United States in its struggle with the Soviet Union. Accordingly, in the 1950s and 1960s, less developed countries such as India, Pakistan, Egypt, Morocco, Tunisia, the Philippines, Bolivia, Brazil, and Mexico became major recipients of direct American economic aid. The results were far different, however, from those which occurred in Western Europe. There was no significant improvement in living standards. Much of the money was at best, expended foolishly or at worst, found its way into the pockets of corrupt officials and bureaucrats. Even farm commodities, given to poor countries under Public Law 480, were often sold by corrupt officials or stored in inadequate warehouses instead of distributed to the needy. And the direct transfer of aid did not solidify alliances or even goodwill between most less developed countries and the United States.

By the late 1970s, Americans of many different political persuasions, had concluded that most direct aid programs had failed in both their diplomatic and economic objectives. Even before then, however, it was clear that aid was not effective as a policy instrument. In 1949, economic aid constituted 2.8 percent of the United States' GNP; in 1960, this figure had declined to 0.5 percent, and in the late 1970s, it was 0.2 percent. By the 1980s, most American foreign policymakers believed that direct economic assistance had largely failed as a policy instrument.[6] Even such innovative forms of aid as President John Kennedy's Peace Corps, which sent young American volunteers to less developed countries to perform such tasks as constructing buildings or teaching school, did not achieve significant diplomatic or economic objectives.

Propaganda

When the cold war began, the United States, in contrast to the Soviet Union, was unable to convey information about its policies because the American media are largely privately owned. Accordingly, in the years just following

World War II, Congress gradually converted the government's wartime information service—the Office of War Information—into permanent peacetime service for international communication. In 1953, various information programs were consolidated into a new United States Information Service, which, in turn, was reorganized into the International Communication Agency (ICA) in 1978. Throughout these transformations, the goals of information policy have remained the same: "to tell the world about U.S. society and policies, in particular to U.S. commitment to cultural diversity and individual liberty."[7] In other words, the ICA's principal function is to contrast American life to Soviet life. The ICA performs this function by operating the Voice of America, and overseas libraries and by arranging cultural exchanges with other nations.

Bilateral and Multilateral Diplomacy

As we observed earlier, the U.N. has not been an effective forum in which to negotiate or conclude diplomatic agreements. Beginning in the Eisenhower administration, bilateral and multilateral meetings became the principal means by which the United States negotiated agreements with the Soviet Union and other powers. Reversing the trend that occurred during the Truman administration, Eisenhower reopened communication with the Soviet Union outside the framework of the U.N. In 1955, the United States, other Western powers, and the Soviet Union successfully negotiated a treaty reestablishing Austria as a sovereign independent nation and held a summit conference consisting of heads of state who discussed major foreign-policy differences between the Soviet Union and the Western powers. Although little was settled at the 1955 summit, the conference paved the way for many other meetings among the major powers and a substantial reopening of communication between the United States and the Soviet Union. In addition, in 1963, a "hot line" telephone connection between the president of the United States and the Soviet premier was set up so that both top officials could clearly explain a policy action that had been or would be taken, and thus help to avoid dangerous misunderstandings. Later conferences have occurred not only at the head-of-state level, but at lower levels as well; they have dealt with a variety of topics including arms control, foreign trade, and cultural relations. A parallel set of developments took place in 1972 when President Nixon visited the People's Republic of China, meeting the Communist-party chairman and reversing the trend established in 1949 of limiting American contact with that nation. Since then, the United States and China have participated in many bilateral and multilateral meetings.

During the Nixon administration, the United States' policy of establishing better relations with the Soviet Union was termed **détente.** Détente did not entail any trust in Soviet intentions toward the world. Rather, it was simply an American commitment to talk to the Soviets in an effort to reduce tensions.

In addition to bilateral and multilateral diplomacy with the Soviet Union and China, the United States has also engaged in **crisis management.** As explained earlier, the maintenance of world stability has been an important goal

détente: A lessening of hostility or tensions between nations, such as that which occurred in American-Soviet relations during the 1970s.

crisis management: The American foreign-policy doctrine of attempting to settle serious international disputes in which the United States is not directly involved.

of American foreign policy because the Soviet Union, as its leaders have openly acknowledged, intends to reap the benefits of instability and disorder. Accordingly, the United States has frequently tried to settle disputes in which it has not been directly involved, but which could lead to Soviet-American confrontation. For example, in 1982, the United States attempted to settle conflicts between the Arab nations and Israel over the latter's incursion into Lebanon, and between the United Kingdom and Argentina over the latter's occupation of the Falkland Islands. Crisis diplomacy usually consists of an American official attempting to negotiate an acceptable agreement between parties to a dispute. Such efforts have occasionally been successful.

AMERICAN MILITARY POLICY

The Cost of Defense

Government is the appropriate institution to provide a collective good such as national defense. But what is the appropriate level of cost of defense? What is the desired level of benefit? What policies can government pursue to achieve a given level of benefit? How can it best economize to attain a given level of national security? These are subjects of intensive debate. Clearly, the American level of expenditure is determined to some extent by the Soviet Union's level, its weapons, and its probable technological advances in weaponry. Although these considerations place an expenditure range on the military budget, this range is so large that considerable debate takes place on the budget's precise size. This is reflected in the significant changes shown in Table 11-1.

TABLE 11-1
NATIONAL DEFENSE OUTLAYS

Selected Fiscal Years	Total (in billion dollars)	% of Federal Outlays	% of GNP	Annual % Change (in 1972 dollars)
1950	12.4	29.1	4.7	−35.0
1955	39.8	58.1	10.4	21.0
1960	45.2	49.0	9.0	− 0.9
1965	47.5	40.1	7.2	−10.0
1970	78.6	40.0	8.1	− 8.0
1975	85.6	26.2	5.8	0.4
1980	135.9	23.4	5.3	3.6

Source: U.S. Bureau of Census, *Statistical Abstract of the United States, 1981* (Washington, D.C.: Government Printing Office, 1981), table no. 580.

THE RISING COST OF WEAPONS

In 1983, the United States Army spent about $2 billion on new tanks. Adjusted for inflation, this is approximately the same amount that it spent on tanks in 1953. But in 1953, this sum bought 6,735 new tanks, and in 1983, it bought only 701—a drop of 90 percent for the same money.

In 1951, the military paid $7 billion (in 1983 dollars) for 6,300 fighter planes. In 1983, the military paid $11 billion for only 322 fighters.

Source: *Time,* March 7, 1983, p. 12.

As these data show, defense expenditures as percentages of both GNP and federal government outlays declined sharply from 1955 through 1980. However, they have increased since then. The declines occurred when weapons systems were becoming more technologically complex and costly and military pay scales were rising. The data in Table 11-1 disprove the widely held but incorrect impression that defense expenditures as percentages of federal outlays or GNP, or in constant dollars (corrected for inflation), have almost continually risen in the post–World War II era; they clearly have not.

On the other hand, there is no reason why defense expenditures should necessarily grow either in constant dollars or as percentages of GNP or federal outlays. Even the fact that Soviet annual defense outlays rose in constant 1983 dollars from approximately $125 billion in 1958 to about $250 billion in 1981 (comparable American figures were $175 billion and approximately $170 billion, respectively) does not prove that the United States should spend more on defense. The most important factor determining the amount of military spending should be an overall strategy. When that strategy has been formulated, sums should be appropriated that most efficiently carry it out, without waste and without excess.

Nuclear Strategy

As we observed earlier, the United States has operated on the assumption that the Soviet Union is bent upon world conquest but is patient and flexible in attaining that goal. The Soviet government does not rely on military methods alone to carry out this goal, but instead employs political and economic strategies as well. Accordingly, the containment theory calls for American flexibility in countering Soviet objectives; within this framework, it is necessary to parry each Soviet move in some way, unless such a counteraction cannot reasonably succeed. A sequence of events that some foreign-policy observers term *appeasement* strongly influenced the theory of containment held by most American postwar presidents and their major foreign-policy advisers. In essence, they point to prewar Europe, in which Nazi Germany grabbed more and more European territory in a series of events beginning in the mid-1930s. Instead of standing firm, the democratic powers sought to appease the Nazis, hoping that each conquest would satisfy Germany and not lead to further aggression. Instead, as events clearly demonstrated, each unopposed conquest simply further whetted the Nazi leaders' appetite. Appeasement ended with the September 1939 Nazi invasion of Poland and the outbreak of World War II. The postwar American foreign-policy leaders were strongly influenced by prewar appeasement; they were determined not to make the same mistake with respect to the Soviet Union, which, like Nazi Germany, was seen as an expansionist, aggressive power.

As George Kennan observed in expounding the containment doctrine, the Soviets are capable of employing a variety of strategies, including different types of warfare. Therefore, American military doctrine must be prepared to respond to each type and, where possible, deter the Soviets from taking action by posing a credible threat. As American doctrine developed, warfare was divided into four categories.

1. *Nuclear warfare* involves the use of powerful strategic nuclear weapons.[8] Fortunately, there are no examples yet of this category.
2. *Conventional warfare* involves the confrontation of armies fighting for territory and includes the use of weapons such as chemical-biological weapons. The Korean war is an example.
3. In *guerrilla warfare,* at least one side uses forces that engage in raids upon the enemy, not to take territory but rather to gradually erode the enemy by defeating it in skirmishes, or through terrorist attacks, and then retreating. The Vietnam war is an example.
4. Finally, in *sublimited warfare,* a major power provides money or other assistance short of substantial military support to one side in a struggle. (Sublimited warfare might also be termed *proxy warfare.*) American assistance to the invasion force that unsuccessfully sought to overthrow the Castro regime at the Bay of Pigs in Cuba in 1961 is an example.

These are theoretically distinct types of warfare, but because they are practically connected, if for no other reason than that one type could conceivably escalate upward through the other types and into a nuclear war, the problem of American strategy is compounded. Obviously, the type of warfare that poses the most serious and potentially destructive threat to the United States is nuclear warfare.

The Soviet Union, which possessed almost fourteen hundred intercontinental ballistic missile launchers in early 1982, has the capacity to annihilate the United States. Conversely, the United States has the capacity to wreak incomprehensible destruction on the Soviet Union. American policymakers have thus given detailed thought, as have their Soviet counterparts, to the correct offensive weapons mix, defensive weapons, and to such questions as how to deter an enemy threat. The outline of United States nuclear warfare theory—termed **mutual assured destruction (MAD)**—will be traced below.[9] In considering

mutual assured destruction (MAD): A strategic nuclear policy in which one side can absorb a nuclear attack by another and have enough weapons and delivery systems left to impose enormous damage on the other side.

The tiled fireplace was all that remained to mark the spot in Hiroshima, Japan, where a house once stood. Beyond is complete ruin, the result of the force of the atom bomb dropped by the United States on August 6, 1945. (Stanley Troutman/Bettmann Archive)

the MAD doctrine, it is important to remember that under the NATO treaty, the United States is obligated to defend not only North America but also that of its NATO allies in Western Europe. We will see that this obligation greatly complicates the MAD theory.

The fundamental tenet of American strategic policy is that the United States have the ability to deter a Soviet attack on itself and/or its allies. The United States can accomplish this goal even after a surprise nuclear attack, by maintaining enough nuclear weapons to impose an unacceptable amount of destruction on the Soviet Union. In effect, the United States force must be sufficiently flexible and mobile so that the Soviet Union would not have the capacity to destroy so much American weaponry in a first strike that it would eliminate the American capacity to engage in a second strike that would impose unacceptable costs on the Soviet Union. To take a hypothetical example, if each side had 1,000 missiles and the Soviet Union could reasonably destroy all American missiles in a first strike, the United States would not have a credible deterrent. On the other hand, if the Soviets could destroy 500 American missiles, and the remaining 500 could, in a second strike, impose unacceptable damage upon the Soviet Union, the United States would have a sufficient assured destruction capability.

This point is important, for one of the principal errors that is made in determining the adequacy of America's nuclear arsenal is simply to count and compare American and Soviet missiles and delivery systems. As the last paragraph infers, a nation's ability to deter war (or, conversely, to start one) depends upon far more than a weapons count. Two nations may have precisely the same number of missile launchers, but one may have a first-strike capability due to greater technological sophistication and the other may not. Indeed, one nation may have a greater megatonnage of explosive power than the other but still have a lesser assured destruction capability. As a result, both the Soviet Union and the United States have taken steps to assure a second-strike capability.

Because of the information-cost problem that we have encountered in many other contexts, an arms race between the two powers began. Each side does not know precisely the capabilities of the other or the technological innovations that may soon be deployed. Of course, each side engages in intelligence activities (e.g., flights over Soviet territory) in order to obtain better information. At the same time, each side attempts to prevent the other from obtaining information by maximizing secrecy, concealing missiles, moving weapons, and other security measures. As a result, each side can only estimate, within a range, the other's capabilities. Given the costs to the society that would result from guessing wrong, however, each side must assume the worst reasonable case and make provisions to cope with it. Thus, to take a simple example, if the United States assumes that the Soviets have between five hundred and six hundred missile launchers, American leaders must assume the higher number in making plans. Similarly, the United States must assume that Soviet technological breakthroughs will occur sooner rather than later within the plausible range, and plan accordingly. This, in turn, impels the United States to greater efforts in the arms race than if better information were available about the Soviet arsenal and developments; the Soviets, in turn, are driven by the same dynamic. Thus, the arms race is fueled by imperfect information.

This still tells us nothing about the precise levels of weaponry or the desirable weapons mix. Many people believe that the United States has a sufficient number of accurate nuclear weapons to deter the Soviet Union; thus, they have called for an American nuclear freeze. Others are sure that the Soviet arsenal is superior to that of the United States. This disagreement has led to considerable congressional debate over both defense expenditures and the desirable mix of weapons. Nevertheless, the general contour of American nuclear policy is clear: the United States must have a number of weapons sufficient to constitute a second-strike capability either in constant motion or in hardened silos in order to withstand a Soviet first strike. For this reason, a significant part of the American nuclear force is located in submarines or airplanes, which cannot easily be targeted in a Soviet first strike. It also accounts for the desire of recent American presidents to further harden the silos of land-based intercontinental ballistic missiles (ICBM) and/or to develop a mobile system in which some land-based missiles can be kept in motion (i.e., the MX missile system).

Obviously, the United States has a strong incentive to increase the accuracy and penetration probability of its weapons, although some individuals argue that such programs can lead to greater instability because they increase the likelihood of an American first-strike capability, to which the Soviets would inevitably respond. The problems of nuclear strategy and deterrence also are made more complex when we consider their connections with conventional warfare and American treaty obligations, particularly those associated with the defense of Western Europe.

NATO and Conventional Warfare

As we have seen, there was little breathing space between the end of World War II and the beginning of the cold war. Because the Soviet Union had not demobilized its troops after the war, a military strategy was necessary in order to deter the Soviets from attacking Western Europe.

The American response to the Soviet threat was to enter into a series of defense pacts. By 1955, the United States had defense pacts with twenty Latin American nations (the Rio Treaty), Australia and New Zealand (the Anzus Treaty), thirteen European powers and Canada (the North Atlantic Treaty), and seven nations with interests in Asia (the Southeast Asia Treaty), as well as bilateral agreements with the Philippines, Japan, South Korea, and the Nationalist Chinese government in Taiwan. The most important of these was the 1949 North Atlantic Treaty, which created the North Atlantic Treaty Organization (NATO). At first, the NATO members agreed to rearm, and European troops as well as American air and naval units were stationed in the European theater pursuant to the obligation of the signatories "to unite their efforts for collective defense and for the preservation of peace and security." Neither this language nor the pledge of each NATO member to take "such action as it deems necessary, including the use of armed force" spelled out precisely what the United States—the organization's strongest member—would do in the case of a Soviet attack on a NATO member. Would the United States employ only conventional weapons to repulse a Soviet attack? Or would it also employ nuclear weapons to offset Soviet numerical superiority in such conventional weapons as troops and tanks?

The attack by North Korea on South Korea in 1950 had a major impact upon NATO strategy. The attack, which was probably instigated by the Soviet Union, made the United States and its NATO allies aware of the Soviet potential to institute conventional warfare not just in Europe but in other regions of the world as well. Strategically, it became necessary to build up NATO's conventional-warfare capability so that the Western powers would have the option of effectually responding to a Soviet conventional attack in Europe, and hence deterring it. Accordingly, the NATO allies agreed to station American troops in Europe, press for West German rearmament, and integrate NATO forces. The new strategy, known as the *shield and sword,* was intended to deter the far superior Soviet ground forces by an increase in NATO ground forces, including American forces (the "shield") backed up by the American atomic— later, the thermonuclear—"sword." In 1954, NATO began to rely on tactical nuclear weapons, such as atomic cannons, to further deter the superior Soviet land forces.

Virtually from NATO's creation, conventional and nuclear wars were closely related. Clear Soviet superiority in conventional-war capability in Europe has persisted to the present day; for example, in 1982, the Warsaw Pact powers (the Soviet Union and its Eastern European satellites) enjoyed approximately a three-to-one advantage in tanks. Accordingly, the United States had held to the doctrine of *flexible response*, reserving the right to respond with tactical or strategic nuclear weapons to a Soviet conventional attack on Western Europe. The United States also has refused to pledge never to be the first power to use nuclear weapons; according to the flexible response doctrine, such a pledge would actually encourage the Soviets to start a conventional war in Europe because to a large extent the American deterrent would have been eroded.

The doctrine of flexible response has tended to erode the NATO alliance, however. The French withdrew their military forces from the unified NATO command in 1967 because they believed that the United States would not risk the obliteration of its territory by the Soviets in order to save France, West Germany, or any other Western European nation. Given the Soviet capability of destroying much of the United States, would the United States launch a nuclear attack on the Soviet Union if the Soviets launched a conventional war against a Western European nation? To the French and many other Western Europeans, as well as to many Americans, the answer was clearly no. The French position on this question imposed strains on NATO that have been increased by other policy differences between the United States and its Western European allies.

The disputes within the Western alliance engendered by the flexible response doctrine and the credibility of an American nuclear response to a Soviet conventional, or even nuclear, attack on Western Europe triggered several different policy proposals. On the one hand, France has attempted to build up its own nuclear deterrent while in many ways remaining an American ally. Some strategists have called for a much stronger Western European strategic nuclear capability, and others have called for strengthening the tactical nuclear or conventional capability. Still other strategists have called for Western Europe's disassociation from the United States and neutrality in the cold war; finally, another group has called for an even greater American military presence in Western Europe. In brief, the unified Western belief about the role of NATO and the nature of conventional warfare that existed in 1949 has shattered into many disparate opinions. These divisions are, however, mild in comparison to opinions concerning American policy in guerrilla and sublimited warfare.

Guerrilla and Sublimited Warfare

Few events in American history have so divided the nation as the Vietnam war. The United States had engaged in many low-level military actions prior to the Vietnam war, and in most instances, its efforts proved militarily successful. For example, during the first twenty years of the twentieth century, American troops (usually the Marines) intervened in Mexico, Cuba, Haiti, Nicaragua, and the Dominican Republic.

In the post–World War II era, the United States, largely through the Central

Intelligence Agency (CIA), has in several instances intervened in the internal affairs of other nations. Many Americans have objected to this on the ground that such conduct constitutes a gross breach of international morality. Moreover, these critics argue that the regimes or forces the United States supported were often no better than the leftist regimes it opposed. Such criticism was confined to a relatively small number of people during the Eisenhower administration, when the United States helped a conservative revolt against a pro-Communist regime in Guatemala that had accepted arms from the Soviet bloc. Similarly, the assistance of the CIA in the 1953 overthrow of a fanatically anti-Western regime by pro-American Iranians drew little criticism. Even the ill-fated 1961 Bay of Pigs invasion, an attempt to overthrow the Communist regime in Cuba by Cuban exiles trained and assisted by the CIA, was not severely criticized, although it marked the first major American defeat in guerrilla and sublimited war; the event was, after all, concluded quickly.

It was the Vietnam war, which resulted in an American defeat after many years of warfare, that brought United States' efforts in sublimited and guerrilla warfare into substantial disrepute among large numbers of citizens. Notwithstanding the intellectual efforts of many military and civilian experts in what has been called *counterinsurgency warfare,* the United States was unable to devise a successful strategy that would defeat the Communist guerrillas at an acceptable cost. President John Kennedy recognized the fundamental quandary. Without imposing enormous costs upon innocent civilians, how does one defeat a guerrilla force that melts into the civilian population? As the media graphically covered American efforts to solve the problem, including forcibly moving civilians and defoliating the landscape, the guerrillas continued to function as a fighting force despite the vast destruction. Meanwhile, more and more Americans came to believe that the costs of counterinsurgency warfare grossly exceeded the benefits. When the Vietnamese Communists triumphed in May 1975, the American counterinsurgency strategy was in shambles. Notwithstanding the horrifying nature of the Communist regimes in Indochina, few Americans are now prepared to support any future counterinsurgency venture involving more than a handful of American advisers. For this reason, some Americans in the 1980s objected to President Ronald Reagan's support for anti-Communist guerrillas in Nicaragua and for the anti-Communist government fighting leftist guerrillas in El Salvador. Many Americans who are attentive to foreign-policy issues now believe that the principal military policy should be focused on arms control.

Arms Control

In the international arena, both the United States and the Soviet Union would be better off spending less money on their military budgets than more. Most people hope that military goods, unlike virtually every other good and service, will not be used. Regardless of whether defense costs as a percentage of GNP are rising or declining, both the Soviet Union and the United States could more profitably use the resources expended on defense in other areas. This is probably most true of the Warsaw Pact nations, which in 1980 spent approximately 10.59 percent of their collective GNP on defense; the comparable NATO percentage was only 4.34. Regardless of this asymmetry, both sides have a clear incentive to negotiate arms-control agreements.

As we will see, some progress has been made in arms control and the forbidding of certain weapons in warfare, although the problem of information cost—how to determine whether the other side is upholding the agreement—has limited the amount of progress that might have been made. Arms-control agreements have a long history, and more progress has been made in the area than many people realize. As early as 1817, the United States and England entered into an agreement limiting to a few vessels their naval forces on the Great Lakes. In the late nineteenth century, as weapons technology advanced rapidly, the urgency for arms-control agreements increased. In 1899 and 1907, two International Peace Conferences at The Hague, the Netherlands, outlawed such devices as dumdum bullets, asphyxiating gases, and poisoned weapons. Nevertheless, in World War I, both sides employed poison gas. During the period between the two world wars, a series of international arms-control conferences took place; they resulted in a number of agreements, including one signed by sixty-three nations that renounced war as an instrument of national policy. Several nations, however, notably Germany and Japan, blithely ignored the agreements. Imperfect information and the lack of an international enforcement mechanism rendered the pacts ineffectual.

When World War II ended, statesmen tried once again to reach arms-control agreements. Again, international anarchy and inadequate information limited progress. With the enormous technological advances in weaponry—especially the development of atomic and thermonuclear weapons, rocketry, and electronics—the potential for destruction took a quantum leap. Nevertheless, the earliest postwar attempt of the United States to bring about arms-control agreement was rebuffed by the Soviet Union. In 1946, the United States, then the only nation with atomic weapons, called for placing all atomic resources under the ownership and control of an independent international authority. All nations would be subject to inspection by the international authority. Although most U.N. members endorsed the plan, the Soviet Union rejected it, instead proposing that control over atomic activities remain in national hands, and that the ability of the international authority to conduct inspections be sharply curtailed. The Soviet's refusal to allow inspections in their territory, which was stated early in the postwar era, created a major stumbling block to international agreements.[10]

In the early 1950s, both major powers exploded thermonuclear devices (hydrogen, or fusion bombs, which are much more powerful than atomic, or fission, bombs) and began improving their delivery systems. The stakes had risen considerably. The General Assembly of the United Nations began discussions on general and complete disarmament in 1959. Proposals were advanced for the reduction and eventual elimination of weapons and armed forces in gradual stages that would not leave any nation's security weakened relative to its adversaries or potential adversaries. The differences in applying these general principles and the obstacle of verifying the steps that would be taken prevented agreements from being signed. In 1962, the Eighteen Nation Disarmament Committee (ENDC) began meeting, and its work eventually contributed to the signing of several arms-control agreements.[11]

The more important set of negotiations, however, were the bilateral and multilateral ones between the world's two superpowers. Given the distrust between the Soviet Union and the United States, it was inevitable that the first step would be modest. The Cuban Missile Crisis of 1962, in which the Soviets installed in Cuba missiles aimed at the United States, drew the two nations to the brink of war. The crisis ended when the United States navy "quarantined" the island of Cuba and the Soviet Union agreed to promptly withdraw its missiles. This situation underscored the need for close and direct communication between the two powers in order to reduce the risks of war through miscalculation or accident. On June 20, 1963, the United States and the Soviet Union signed the historic "hot line" agreement, establishing direct telephone communication between the top officials in each country. The hot line has proved extremely useful in settling disputes not only among the major powers but among other countries as well, most notably during the Arab-Israeli wars of 1967 and 1973.

The next major breakthrough concerned the testing of nuclear weapons. The critical problems were (1) securing information about tests and (2) enforcing the agreement that would be reached. The first test-ban treaty of 1963, which banned the testing of nuclear weapons in the atmosphere, outer space, and under water, was the fruit of eight years of arduous negotiations. There already existed verification systems for detecting radiation emanating from tests under the water or in the atmosphere, but the treaty did not cover underground testing, for which verification systems were inadequate. The treaty has been enforced because the Soviets realized that future negotiations and East-West agreements on virtually every other topic, including trade, would be impossible if they violated it. This incentive to comply was a powerful one, and on August 5, 1963, the two superpowers and the United Kingdom signed the Nuclear Test Ban Treaty. As verification technology developed, later treaties permitted the extension of the test ban to certain kinds of underground testing.

Technological development allowed the superpowers to verify compliance of testing from outside the territory of the great powers. Because the Soviet Union persisted in resisting the stationing of inspectors within its borders, however, verification methods could not detect the production, quantity, or quality of weapons. Further complicating the difficulties of producing an arms-control agreement were the greatly enhanced transaction costs required in order to negotiate; these costs were a result of France (which was increasingly pursuing independent foreign policies), China, and other nations developing atomic or nuclear arsenals of their own. Disarmament would require the concurrence of too many parties, some of which obstinately refused to consider the prospect. Consequently, in the 1960s, the goal of the superpowers shifted from disarmament to arms control: to reduce their nuclear weaponry and delivery systems, but not so much that they would be in a weakened position relative to the other significant nuclear powers. The first step, an agreement by the United States, the Soviet Union, and as many other nations as would sign to prevent the spread of nuclear weapons, was the Non-Proliferation Treaty. It was signed by the two superpowers and sixty other nations in 1968, but was not ratified by the United States Senate until 1970.

Clearly, both superpowers had a strong incentive to prevent the spread of nuclear weapons to possible competitors. The more difficult problem of arms control carried conflicting incentives. On the one hand, both sides could profit economically and reduce the risk of war if arms were reduced or even frozen. On the other hand, the logic of the arms race, as we have seen, calls for continuing qualitative improvement, and often an increase in quantity, so as to deprive the other side of a possible first-strike advantage. Not until 1969 did bilateral strategic-arms limitation talks between the Soviet Union and the United States begin. These talks, known as **SALT (Strategic Arms Limitation Treaty) talks,** lasted two and a half years. Both sides failed to achieve a comprehensive arms-control agreement, but the talks did lead to two narrower agreements.

SALT (Strategic Arms Limitations Treaty) talks: A series of negotiations between the United States and the Soviet Union designed to limit nuclear arms and delivery systems. One agreement (SALT I) was signed and ratified in 1972, but the second SALT treaty, although signed, was never ratified by the Senate.

In the first of these, the Anti-Ballistic Missile (ABM) Systems Treaty signed in May 1972, both sides agreed to limit themselves to two ABM deployment areas in their respective countries (later, the number of deployment areas was reduced to one). The enormous costs and questionable effectiveness of ABM systems provided an incentive to both sides to sign the treaty. It is also relatively easy to obtain information about a possible violation early in the erection of an ABM system.

The second agreement, covering offensive weapons, was limited to a five-year span and generally froze the existing levels of strategic ballistic missile launchers, including those under construction. The highly complex agreement that concluded the SALT I talks was subject to exceptions and limitations; one of the most important was that there was no limitation on the number of warheads. Nevertheless, both sides viewed the SALT I interim agreement as both a limited agreement and a prelude to a more comprehensive one. The SALT II talks, which began in November 1972, led to this more comprehensive agreement, limiting offensive nuclear arms, but it was not ratified by the Senate. The same difficulties—verification, distrust of Soviet motives and incentives, and enforcement—have continued to impede progress in arms control. In 1984, two separate arms-control negotiations begun in 1983—the strategic arms reduction talks (START) and the intermediate-range nuclear forces talks (INF)—were stalled.

In many ways, as we will see, arms-control problems parallel those of the international economic order. There are clear incentives to cooperate, but there are also incentives to compete.

FOREIGN ECONOMIC POLICY

The Pre–World War II Background

The current foreign economic policy of the United States can best be understood within the context of its historical background. Indeed, one must go back to 1776 to understand the central conflict that has shaped its most basic contradiction. The United States has favored free trade among nations in the abstract, and often in concrete policies as well, but it has occasionally adopted policies that protect native industries. Sometimes, these latter policies are undertaken in response to the protectionist moves of other countries; for example, if a nation restricts American exports to it of product A, the United States may respond by allowing less of that nation's product B to be brought into the country. At other times, the United States has initiated protectionist policies, usually in response to intense domestic political pressures, and has not simply responded in a defensive way. There have been periods in which the pendulum has swung toward free trade and other periods in which it has swung toward protectionism. Clearly, however, in the era following World War II, the swing has been toward free trade, albeit not without many policies leaning toward protectionism.

The system of free trade, unrestricted by tariffs (i.e., taxes on imported goods), import quotas, or other impediments to free and open competition between domestic and imported goods, was forcefully advocated by Adam Smith in his 1776 book, *The Wealth of Nations*. Smith favored free trade in the international arena for the same reasons he favored free and open competition in the national arena. In both cases, the forces of competition will allocate resources (land, labor, and capital) most efficiently. The magnet of profitability attracts the resources of business firms from less profitable uses to more profitable ones. In a profitable enterprise, the benefits to buyers necessarily exceed the costs of production and distribution. Consequently, if profitability is greater in making one product (A) than another (B), fewer resources are used in making A than B; that is, the costs of making A are lower than the costs of making B. Society has squandered fewer resources when making more productive use of them and, therefore, operates more efficiently. It has resources for further investment that would otherwise not be available.

Precisely the same principle operates in international trade. Resources should not be wastefully employed in producing things that can be more efficiently produced elsewhere.[12] Rather, they should be used in enterprises that can operate more efficiently in one's own country. A nation should specialize in the production of goods and services that are better suited to its unique combination of natural resources, climate, and human skills. It should trade the surplus of those goods and services for the specialties of other nations. In this way, each nation can also diversify its consumption. Finally, the proponents of free trade claim that their system tends to promote world peace. Because nations that freely trade with each other will prosper (both sides gain in a trade, or else they would not trade), there is a clear incentive to continue the system rather than risk war, which often destroys productive resources.

Unquestionably, there is considerable merit in the arguments for free trade, but most nations have usually erected barriers to it. At one level, the pro–free-trade argument ignores political reality. Even if a nation as a whole benefits from free trade, the shifting patterns of world development can cause specific industries and groups to suffer. These industries and groups will use whatever political influence they can muster to protect themselves, whatever the theoretical merits of free trade might be. Thus, the American automobile industry and the United Auto Workers (UAW) union, confronted with the deep inroads made by Japanese automobiles in the American market, saw profitability plummet and unemployment rise. Their response was to use the political arena to promote protectionist policies that would impede the domestic sale of Japanese cars. Many American industries faced with intensive foreign competition have adopted similar strategies, sometimes successfully.

The system of free trade has been criticized on the ground that tariffs can often protect infant native industries until they develop to the point that they can effectively compete on the world market. This argument guided much American foreign economic policy in the nineteenth and early twentieth centuries. Some tariffs (and subsidies as well) also have been justified on the ground that the industries protected are vital to the national security and defense.

The end result of these competing claims is that historically, American foreign economic policy has often been an inconsistent blend of free trade and protectionism.[13] Nevertheless, the tide began to turn sharply against protectionism after World War II. American thinking on reforming the international economic system had begun early in the war. The general thrust of the new approach was to promote a world system of relatively free trade and stable

Americans in recent years have become increasingly aware of international interdependence and trade. (Roger Malloch/© Magnum Photos, Inc.)

currencies that would presumably lead to greater prosperity for the nations of the world, including the United States. This system also would encourage freer investment, because capital could readily flow from country to country. The new proposed international economic order was also viewed as a necessary concomitant to world peace, because economic warfare by means of protectionism was thought to be a prelude and instigator of military warfare. Finally, since living standards would rise with free trade, the American policymakers believed that the jealousy and economic dissatisfaction that often led to war would disappear.

Bretton Woods and the World's New Economic Order

By 1943, two significant plans for reforming the international economic system had been proposed.[14] Both the British plan and the American plan (known as the "White Plan" after its main architect, Assistant Secretary of the Treasury Harry D. White) had similar objectives. Both favored free trade, stable currency relationships, sound but liberal credit arrangements, and a medium of exchange that would be stable yet sufficiently flexible and expansive to facilitate the hoped-for boom in world trade. The two plans formed the basis for a conference, held at Bretton Woods, New Hampshire, in 1944, that largely shaped the postwar international economic order and created some of its most important institutions—that is, the International Monetary Fund (IMF) and the International Bank for Reconstruction and Development (World Bank).

The agreements reached at Bretton Woods virtually assured that the dollar would be the most important means of exchange in international transactions. The participants did this, first, by requiring the forty-four countries in attendance to fix the value of their currencies in terms of gold, the traditional payment mechanism. However, nations were not required to exchange their currencies for gold upon the demand of a foreign creditor, because the quantity of gold in circulation was insufficient to support the expected postwar volume of international transactions. Instead, the agreements called for the free exchange of dollars into gold at thirty-five dollars an ounce, and for each nation to fix its currency at the desired dollar-exchange rate. Each country agreed to fluctuate its currency (i.e., to increase or decrease its value relative to other currencies) not more than 1 percent from the fixed dollar equivalent, which it would do by buying or selling foreign exchange or gold. Thus, no country could revert to the prewar practice of devaluating its currency (i.e., reducing currency values relative to other currencies) in order to gain a foreign trade advantage by reducing the price of exports. However, if a currency became too weak for a country's central bank to defend by buying or selling foreign currency or gold, it could be devalued up to 10 percent without IMF approval.

The IMF thus emerged as the central institution in the new international economic system.[15] The agency was originally funded by the subscribing members on quota amounts based on each member's expected postwar volume of trade. Thus, the United States quota was—and still is—the largest. Over the years, the total amount required has expanded considerably, and each nation's quota is periodically revised in approximate proportion to its foreign trade volume. Voting on policy matters within the IMF is in proportion to the quota amount contributed. Consequently, the United States has been able to exert a dominant influence in the IMF on such questions as changes in exchange rates and conditions attached to loans. At first, the principal task of the IMF was to advance credit to member nations that were facing temporary, not chronic, difficulties supporting their currencies. The system worked reasonably well until 1971, when, as we shall see, it was modified.

The other major institution to which Bretton Woods gave birth is the World Bank, which in 1981 was owned by its 139 member countries. Its original function was to aid the economic reconstruction of Europe through long-term loans at rates of interest sufficient to yield a profit to the bank. However, the Marshall Plan made loans at terms far more advantageous to borrowers, so the World Bank assumed a new function of making loans to governments of less developed countries and to organizations that have a government guarantee to pay their debts. Subscription quotas are, again, based on a country's wealth; therefore, as in the case of the IMF, the Western nations—especially the United States—and Japan dominate the World Bank's policies. Two other affiliates of the World Bank came into existence later. These are the International Finance Corporation (IFC), created in 1956, which makes loans to private enterprises in member countries, and the International Development Association (IDA), established in 1960, which makes loans to governments on highly generous, no-interest or low-interest terms. Thus, the IDA makes loans to the very poorest countries, which cannot borrow on prevailing market terms because of their inability to afford high interest rates and the risk that they cannot pay back the loans.

While discussions were proceeding on international monetary issues, talks were being held on international trade and commercial matters. The conflict between those nations favoring freer trade (led by the United States) and those committed to protectionism delayed the formation of an international trade authority. Significant progress was not made until 1947, when twenty-three countries took part in a trade conference in Geneva, Switzerland. This conference resulted in 123 agreements accounting for what was then approximately half the value of world trade. The United States cut tariffs on a large number of items, thus aiding European economic recovery. During the same period, the United States, as part of the Marshall Plan, spurred the nations of Western Europe to lower trade barriers to one another's products and to take steps toward economic integration. Thus, the United States was largely responsible for creating a principal economic competitor, the European Economic Community, or Common Market. Another significant step was taken in 1946, when several nations signed an American-drafted document calling for liberalized trade, giving birth to the central international organization concerned with world trade, the General Agreement on Tariffs and Trade (GATT). GATT has sponsored several meetings, attended by the United States trade representative and officials of other member nations, at which reciprocal reductions in tariffs and other barriers to free trade have been negotiated.

The most important breakthrough pursuant to GATT has been the most-favored-nation principle, under which any bilateral tariff reductions must be offered to all GATT members. Thus, if the United States reduced its tariff on French perfumes in exchange for a French tariff reduction on American automobiles, both countries would have to make similar reductions on these products to all GATT members. Yet, although substantial progress toward free trade has been made in comparison to the pre-World War II period, much protectionism still remains, and the political pressures for increased protectionism tend to grow when economic conditions worsen.

American Policy and Strains in the World Economic Order

Many changes have occurred in international economic relations since the late 1940s. Nevertheless, the institutional structure created at Bretton Woods and in other meetings during the same period has remained basically intact, but not without a struggle.

Let us recall that the centerpiece of the Bretton Woods system is the dollar. It alone was convertible to gold at thirty-five dollars an ounce and became the principal medium of international exchange. Thus, when the Soviet Union traded with a Western European nation, it made and accepted payments in dollars, often depositing dollars in European banks and thereby creating what is called the *Eurodollar market.* The dollar, in short, became the principal means of exchange, not only for transactions involving American firms but for those in which Americans were in no way involved. Of course, other capitalist nations developed tradable currencies as their economies became stronger. But the United States, whose share of world industrial production was about 35 percent in 1980 (compared to about 40 percent in 1963 and approximately 60 percent in 1950), still has the most important tradable currency. Consequently, a loss of confidence in the dollar or American domestic financial policies can have worldwide repercussions on international commerce.

Ironically, the international economic crisis that erupted in 1971 was partly attributable to the growing prosperity of Western Europe and Japan. The year 1959 marked the beginning of large deficits in the United States **balance of payments;** that is, more tradable currency and gold were leaving the country than were coming in.

A balance of payments is the accounting system used to measure transactions among nations. Items included on the positive side of the ledger are (1) the value of exports and (2) inflows of capital in the country through investment by foreign investors. On the negative side of the ledger are (1) the value of imports and (2) capital flows from a country through investment in other countries. It is evident that a country's balance of payments worsens when it has a negative **balance of trade** (i.e., when imports exceed exports) or when more investment capital flows from the country than enters it. Thus,

balance of payments: The difference in the value of tradable currency and gold leaving the country and that entering it.

balance of trade: The difference in value between a country's exports and imports.

a country seeking to cure negative balance of payments—one in deficit—may adopt policies pertaining to foreign trade and/or foreign investment.

As the American balance of payments continued to worsen, the major members of the IMF sought in 1967 to head off a crisis by creating new credit instruments termed *special drawing rights* (SDRs)—in the amount necessary to meet the needs of world trade. Each IMF member received SDRs in proportion to its IMF quota. The SDRs could be converted into exchangeable currency, but not into gold. Despite this innovation, crisis struck the international financial system in 1971.

In that year, the American balance-of-payments deficit reached an all-time high. In the summer of 1971, President Nixon ordered the Treasury Department to suspend convertibility of the dollar into gold and imposed a 10 percent surcharge on imports. These moves not only marked a shift toward protectionism; they also undermined the system developed at Bretton Woods. The important foreign currencies rose sharply against the dollar, thus effectively devaluating it (i.e., making the dollar worth less). The ten major trading countries met in Washington, D.C., in December 1971 and concluded the *Smithsonian Agreement.* Under it, the United States agreed to revalue its currencies upward. The hope was to improve the American balance-of-payments deficit by making American goods cheaper, thus improving the balance of trade (i.e., exports minus imports).

Dollar devaluation helped the American balance of payments sufficiently so that the United States removed all controls on the flow of capital in January 1974. However, the country then had another major complaint that it was attempting to deal with in GATT: economic protectionism through nontariff barriers. Although GATT negotiations had succeeded in lowering tariff barriers, some nations were imposing other impediments on imported goods. These included burdensome licensing and excessive paperwork requirements, artificial quality standards that were really intended to discourage imports, entry fees that were really tariffs in disguise, packaging and labeling standards designed to discourage imported goods, and antidumping laws. (Dumping involves the sale of imported goods to another country at prices lower than those in the exporter's domestic market.)

Negotiating the reduction or elimination of such nontariff trade barriers is difficult enough under the best of circumstances, and the period that began in October 1973 was not the best of circumstances. When an economic downturn occurs (i.e., when industries slow down and workers lose jobs), the cries for protection mount, putting almost insurmountable pressure on national governments. In October 1973, oil prices began a dramatic rise; by 1974, they had quadrupled. Under the impact of the "first oil shock," the developed world, including the United States, went into a recession from which it did not begin to recover until 1975. The extent of the blow is shown in Table 11-2.

The enormous price increases had a debilitating effect on the developed world, as well as on less developed countries. The high costs of imported oil caused America's balance-of-payments situation to again worsen, inflation rates

TABLE 11-2
PERCENTAGE GROWTH OF ANNUAL REAL GROSS
DOMESTIC PRODUCT

	1960–1973	*1973–1975*	*1975–1979*
Developed countries	5.0	0.3	4.0
United States	4.1	−0.8	4.5
Europe	4.8	0.8	3.4
Japan	9.9	0.6	5.2

Source: *World Economic Outlook,* Wharton Econometric Associates, 1982.

to accelerate, and wide fluctuations in currency exchange rates to increase. The international economic system was once again in disarray. Although economic recovery occurred from 1975 to 1979, the "second oil shock," caused by the members of the Organization of Petroleum Exporting Countries (OPEC), helped throw the world into another economic decline from which it did not begin to recover until 1983. The "second oil shock" aggravated the already weak state of the international economic system and at the same time dramatically revealed the world's economic interdependence.

The oil shocks clearly had an adverse effect upon the developed economies, but their effect on less developed countries was devastating. The less industrialized nations had been driven so deeply into debt in order to pay their oil bills that they were becoming increasingly unable to repay loans made to them by major international banks in the developed countries. This situation exerted great financial pressure on the banks and the currencies in which they do business. In turn, these effects and declining bank earnings (sometimes even bankruptcy) had an impact on the domestic economies of the major capitalist powers.

By the mid-1980s, the developed countries, notably the United States, had rebounded and at the same time had instituted significant energy-conservation measures. Yet, although the international oil crisis had been solved, at least temporarily, many problems remained in the international economic order, including trade barriers, precarious international bank lending positions, and, most important, the continuing stagnation of most LDCs. These and other problems raise enormous challenges for American foreign-defense policy in the foreseeable future.

CONFLICT, COOPERATION, AND CONTRADICTION

As our journey through the various components of American foreign-defense policy illustrates, the problems in this area are extraordinarily vexing. Starting from such consistent principles as containment, deterrence, the promotion of stability, and free trade, the intruding facts of international and domestic politics have led to inconsistencies and a frequent lack of clear-sightedness. George Kennan's containment arguments have been eroded by the development of Communist forces such as China and Yugoslavia, which are hostile toward or suspicious of the Soviet Union, as well as Communist revolutions in less developed countries that might have been triggered more by domestic discontent than Soviet instigation. Deterrence has been questioned by some—especially many clergy members. Others, not questioning deterrence, demand a nuclear freeze and arms-reduction agreements, claiming that the United States nuclear arsenal is excessive. Stability has been eroded by the observation of many that in its name, the United States has entered into alliances with regimes as abhorrent as those dominated by Communists. Free trade has been hampered by the many examples of protectionism in conflict with free-trade principles (e.g., the voluntary Japanese automobile export quota to the United States).

An almost universal consensus on American foreign-defense policy no longer exists. Yet, while there will be contradictions in goals and conflicts in policies, certain broad policy contours remain. Paramount among these is a commitment to deter the Soviet Union because of its expansionist tendencies. The precise level and mix of armaments, the strategies to undertake, and the role and importance of arms-control negotiations and agreements will remain in dispute. In this context, the United States will continue to operate on the principle that alliances of convenience with the enemies of the Soviet Union are both possible and desirable. For this reason, the United States will attempt to enjoy good working relationships with China, Yugoslavia, and non-Communist regimes with less than satisfactory records in civil liberties and democratic rights.

Second, the United States will maintain its firm commitments to those few nations in the world that do maintain high standards of civil liberties and democratic rights; these include Japan, Australia, New Zealand, Canada, several Caribbean nations, Israel, and the nations of Western Europe. Nevertheless, the days of America's hegemonic leadership over these nations are over, and disputes are likely to develop over specific international economic, military, and diplomatic policies. The disputes that arose over America's 1982 opposition to the Soviet–Western European gas-pipeline agreement and its 1983 liberation of Grenada from a Cuban-Soviet puppet regime typify the conflicts that will continue to erupt among the democratic nations. These conflicts, however, have occurred within a context of cooperation.

Third, the United States has maintained its general commitment to international stability, especially in the face of Soviet and Cuban attempts to promote instability. Nevertheless, good intentions sometimes do not lead to the intended results, as President Reagan's commitment of American Marines to Lebanon in September 1982 illustrated; the continued presence of American forces in that land did not lead to a stable government. Furthermore, it is often unclear which is the best policy to achieve stability, and bitter disputes have erupted among American policymakers over appropriate means. For example, what should be the appropriate mix of foreign and economic aid in achieving stability in Central America? Which forces should the United States aid or encourage in the Middle East? How should the United States deal with terrorist groups? To what extent should friendly authoritarian regimes be pushed to enlarge the scope of civil liberties and democratic rights in their lands? These and a host of other problems will continue to vex and divide American policymakers in their quest for stability.

Finally, the United States has been drawn into matters that are not directly concerned with national security, communism, or its relationships with other prosperous nations. Sometimes, these issues are moral questions, such as the United States' attitude toward the Union of South Africa, which denies blacks and persons of mixed color virtually all rights. At other times, these matters stem from the enormous income gulf that separates rich and poor nations. Many of these nations demand a new international economic order involving substantial transfer of resources from rich to poor nations, programs for stabilizing prices of commodities they produce, and the sharing of profits in such new areas of exploitation as the seas. These issues, and many others that will erupt in obscure corners of the world, will certainly tax American foreign-policymakers in the years ahead.

NOTES

[1]A history of the incident is Joseph C. Goulden, *Truth Is the First Casualty* (Chicago: Rand McNally, 1969).

[2]The best short analysis of these differences is George H. Quester, "Foreign Policy," in Theodore J. Lowi and Alan Stone, eds., *Nationalizing Government* (Beverly Hills, California: Sage Publications, 1978), pp. 393–395.

[3]The revisionist literature interpreting the cold war is immense. Among the best works of this school are William Appleman Williams, *The Tragedy of American Diplomacy* (New York: Dell, 1962) and D. F. Fleming, *The Cold War and Its Origins*, 2 vols. (Garden City: Doubleday, 1961). A devastating critique of revisionism is Robert James Maddox, *The New Left and the Origins of the Cold War* (Princeton: Princeton University Press, 1973).

[4]Among the leading conventional studies of the cold war are Desmond Donnelly, *Struggle for the World* (New York: St. Martin's, 1965) and John Spanier, *American Foreign Policy Since World War Two*, 10th ed. (New York: Holt, Rinehart & Winston, 1984).

[5]X (George F. Kennan), "The Sources of Soviet Conduct," *Foreign Affairs* 25 (July 1947): 566–582.

[6]See the discussion in Joan Edelman Spero, *The Politics of International Economic Relations*, 2nd ed. (New York: St. Martin's, 1981), Chapter 6.

[7]Office of the Federal Register, *The United States Government Manual 1981–1982* (Washington, D.C.: Government Printing Office, 1981), p. 555.

[8]"Strategic" weapons are designed to strike targets within the interior of the enemy's homeland; "tactical" weapons are intended for use within the battlefield area or against combatant forces.

[9]The clearest exposition is Robert S. MacNamara, *The Essence of Security* (New York: Harper & Row, 1968).

[10]An excellent recounting of the early postwar politics of arms control is John W. Spanier and Joseph L. Nogee, *The Politics of Disarmament* (New York: Praeger, 1962).

[11]Texts and explanations of arms-control agreements are collected in United States Arms Control and Disarmament Agency, *Arms Control and Disarmament Agreements* (Washington, D.C.: Government Printing Office, 1980).

[12]See Richard Caves and Ronald Jones, *World Trade and Payments* (Boston: Little, Brown, 1973).

[13]The classic history is F. W. Taussig, *The Tariff History of the United States*, 8th rev. ed. (New York: Putnam, 1931).

[14]On the creation of the postwar international economic order, see Richard N. Gardner, *Sterling-Dollar Diplomacy in Current Perspective*, new exp. ed. (New York: Columbia University Press, 1980).

[15]The best short study of international economic institutions and their functions is A. L. MacBean and P. N. Snowden, *International Institutions in Trade and Finance* (London: George Allen & Unwin, 1981).

BIBLIOGRAPHY

Caves, Richard and Ronald Jones. *World Trade and Payments.* Boston: Little, Brown, 1973. A clear exposition of the economic aspects of international transactions.

Donnelly, Desmond. *Struggle for the World.* New York: St. Martin's, 1965. An excellent history of the cold war that accepts the thesis of Soviet expansionism.

Fallows, James. *National Defense.* New York: Random House, 1981. A critical examination of America's defense posture.

Gardner, Richard N. *Sterling-Dollar Diplomacy in Current Perspective,* new exp. ed. New York: Columbia University Press, 1980. An insightful history of the major post–World War II international economic institutions.

MacBean, A. L., and P. N. Snowden. *International Institutions in Trade and Finance.* London: George Allen & Unwin, 1981. A lucid account of the major international economic institutions and their functions.

MacNamara, Robert S. *The Essence of Security.* New York: Harper & Row, 1968. Still the clearest exposition of America's nuclear doctrines.

Spanier, John. *American Foreign Policy Since World War Two,* 10th ed. New York: Holt, Rinehart & Winston, 1984. An excellent text on the institutions and substance of American foreign policy.

Spanier, John, and Joseph L. Nogee. *The Politics of Disarmament.* New York: Praeger, 1962. An early study of post–World War II disarmament politics that sheds considerable light on today's difficulties in the area.

Spero, Joan Edelman. *The Politics of International Economic Relations,* 2nd ed. New York: St. Martin's, 1981. A splendid text on international economic affairs.

Taussig, F. W. *The Tariff History of the United States,* 8th rev. ed. New York: Putnam, 1931. A classic history of American tariff policy.

Tew, Brian. *The Evolution of the International Monetary System, 1945–77.* London: Hutchinson, 1977. A classic text on the development of the International Monetary Fund and international financial problems.

Williams, William Appleman. *The Tragedy of American Diplomacy.* New York: Dell, 1962. A highly critical revisionist account of American foreign policy.

X (George F. Kennan). "The Sources of Soviet Conduct." *Foreign Affairs* 25 (July 1947): 566–582. The influential article that announced the doctrine of containment.

CHAPTER

12

Economic Policy

W e saw in Chapter 1 that in terms of aggregate statistics, the American economic system has been mostly successful. Although serious questions can be raised about how equitably the wealth of the United States has been distributed, the nation's net social welfare has generally improved. Of course, this development has not been continuous throughout American history. There have been economic booms and depressions; some periods have seen much faster growth than others, and some depressions have been deeper and longer than others.

The ordinary course of a business cycle (i.e., a period of growth followed by a period of contraction) has accounted for some of this economic behavior. Other important factors have also affected the economy, including changing climatic conditions that affect agriculture; the discovery of new natural resources; war or peace; world economic conditions, and technological development. Yet, without denying the importance of these factors, it is clear that political arrangements and policies have played critical roles in America's economic progress. A brief historical comparative digression will illustrate the reason for this view.

In the sixteenth and seventeenth centuries, Spain had conquered major portions of Central and South America. Major silver-mining strikes in Mexico and Peru, and the subjugation of native populations, had enriched Spain immensely. Yet, it was England, not Spain, that ultimately benefited from the new-found Spanish wealth. Britain, then a much poorer nation, manufactured woolen goods and other items, which it sold to the Spanish, and while England saved and invested the proceeds of its sales in the early stages of its capitalist development, Spain dissipated its treasure in consumption. England's institutions and policies were the keys to its growth, whereas those of Spain were the keys to its stagnation. There are parallels today. Japan, with few natural resources, has a much higher per-capita income than the African nation of Zaire, which is blessed with abundant mineral resources. There is no grand theory to explain these differences; the world is too complicated. But in each case, political arrangements and policies have played important roles in leading to economic growth or stagnation.

At the simplest level, policies and arrangements that have encouraged investment and trade have tended to help economic growth and development as long as financial incentives (i.e., profits) are available to those who make an effort or take a risk. This is a simple maxim that has long been part of American economic culture and folklore; for example, in the late nineteenth century, a writer named Horatio Alger was popular for his stories of hard work and clean living—which always ended with economic success. As we will see, however, these simple principles are just the starting point for constructing economic policy; life is usually more complicated. At times, one may have the will and desire to accept risks and hard work, but the opportunities might not be available—for example, during a depression when large numbers of people are unemployed and markets have shrunk. For the same reason, opportunities

391

Textile printing machines, circa 1836. Early in its history, the United States adopted the industrial path pioneered in England. (New York Public Library Picture Collection)

for trade might be slight and little capital might be available for investment. Large numbers of citizens may be denied the chance to succeed because of discrimination, lack of needed skills, or other reasons. The history of American economic policy is filled with attempts to solve such problems as they arise within the context of a system that has tried, not always consistently or successfully, to encourage trade, investment, hard work, risk-taking, and their rewards.

Of course, economic policy does not exist in a vacuum; it is embedded in a complex society with a variety of problems, some of which demand governmental action that is aimed at justice, not growth. Thus, the economic policies that we will examine have often been designed with more than one purpose in mind. Historian Arthur Schlesinger, Jr., wrote, "Capitalism has survived because of the continuing and remarkably successful effort to humanize the industrial order, to cushion the operations of the economic system, to combine pecuniary opportunity with social cohesion."[1] The American consensus on an economic system is definitely linked to that effort. Other historians have pointed out the contrast between the way Americans responded to the Great Depression's unemployment, hunger, and despair (e.g., no riots, no widespread loss of confidence in government) and the way they reacted to the problems of the 1960s and 1970s. During the past twenty years, the proportion of Americans who believe that "the government is pretty much run by a few big interests looking out for themselves" has quadrupled,[2] and more Americans have become suspicious of the role of profit in economy.[3]

The reasons for the change in public trust and acceptance of the economic system are complex and easily debatable, but we can suggest at least a few.

First, in the last twenty years, the traditional optimism in future economic growth has been seriously weakened. One major cause is the recognition of the ultimate scarcity of natural resources that was pointed out to Americans by the environmental movement of the 1960s and 1970s. Second, while the Vietnam war was sparking a counterculture of disenchanted young people, the government's "Great Society" social reforms were stumbling because of limited financial resources, occasional mismanagement and poor planning, and the inherent complexity of the task. In addition, the energy crisis of the 1970s seemed to indicate to many Americans that the system was out of control, or at least in the control of foreigners. Although surveys show that an overwhelming majority of American citizens still support the private business system, free enterprise, and the right to the rewards of hard labor and risk-taking, the legitimacy of the country's economic system has been weakened.

No crystal ball can tell us whether these trends will continue through the 1980s. Much depends on whether the nation's attempts to deal with economic and social problems are as effective, or at least as widely supported, as attempts to deal with earlier problems. As we will see, the United States has devised new economic policies to deal with occasional crises or changes, and these policies, once in place, have persisted and formed the substance of the American political economic system.

CAPITALISM AND PRIVATE LAW

In Chapter 6, we saw that a common law tradition has been supplemented by statutes formed by legislatures to facilitate the economic transactions on which the capitalist system depends. The fundamental common-law notions of property and contract have spawned a vast number of specific rules as Americans have devised new forms of buying and selling (e.g., installment sales, which require payment over time) and new forms of property (e.g., stock certificates). In this section, we will look briefly at some of the important changes in private law pertaining to contract, property, and an American economic innovation in business organization—the corporation.

Contract

As we discussed in Chapter 6, the idea of contract applies to many different kinds of agreements, including the sale of goods and property, commercial arrangements, and labor contracts. Although certain general principles cover all of these types of agreements, each kind of contract inevitably has unique problems. Thus, separate bodies of law concerning sales, negotiable instruments (e.g., checks drawn on bank accounts), and so on, have developed. In addition, states and the federal government have intervened more and more in the terms of the contract through regulation and other public-policy techniques.

For example, in 1887, Congress created the Interstate Commerce Commission and gave it the power to regulate the terms of rate agreements between railroads and shippers, partly because stability in the railroad industry and the offering of "reasonable" shipping rates were seen as a public concern. Another example is the Statute of Frauds, which is intended to prevent a party from making oral fraudulent claims about the terms of a contract by requiring certain contracts to be in writing. The Statute of Frauds helps to reduce risks and uncertainties in the contractual process, and thereby encourages people to enter into economic transactions. The vast array of laws (especially at the state level) and judicial decisions on contract and its subcategories plays a critical role in the millions of particular transactions that constitute the American economic system.

Property

Just as governments must devise rules pertaining to contracts, so they must make rules for property. Consider the disposition of America's most valuable preindustrial resource: land. During the preconstitutional period, Congress began to dispose of the vast western lands under the Land Ordinance of 1785 and the 1787 Northwest Ordinance, by dividing most western land into tracts and lots and selling them to private owners. The new owners received a piece of paper called a *title*, which described the property and declared the named person to be the owner of it. The basic system of granting title to private landowners continued through a succession of statutes culminating in the Homestead Act of 1862, which granted title free of charge on much of the remaining public land to those who would work it. In this way, much of the land in the United States came to be private property—although much public land was still reserved for government use, especially in the western states. Many of the original private owners sold their land to other persons or companies, who in turn resold in a process that continues to the present day. In each case, the new owner received title, just as in 1785. States protect title in various ways under statutes and the common law.

Property rights, as we observed in Chapter 6, came to apply not only to land but also to objects (e.g., cars and houses) and intangibles (e.g., stock certificates) that are not inherently usable but that represent ownership of something. Other innovations in property rights met new business needs. One of the most important new devices was the **license.** In the case of a patent, which is an inventor's exclusive right to make, use, or sell his or her invention for a given period of time, the inventor may permit another person or company—the licensee—to make and/or sell products based upon the patent. More recently, the **franchise** has become a valuable property right: for a fee, the franchisor permits the franchisee to use the former's trade name (e.g., McDonald's or Burger King), pursuant to certain conditions such as product quality or sanitation standards. The widespread use of the *mortgage,* under which a lender—usually a savings-and-loan association—advances a sum of

license: An agreement that allows a person or company to make or sell products based upon a patent held by another person or company.

franchise: In elections, the right to vote; in economic policy, a contract under which a trade name can be used by another firm or individual.

money to a borrower who has insufficient cash to buy a home outright, triggered the staggering increase in homeownership that followed World War II. The protections these sorts of legal devices afforded both sides in a transaction have encouraged the expansion of commerce.

Business Organization

Much has been written about the roles of individual entrepreneurs, such as Andrew Carnegie in the steel industry and John D. Rockefeller in the oil industry. Although such people played an important role in the development of American capitalism, they usually were at the tops of large business organizations, such as partnerships or corporations. Today, the most important form of business organization is the **corporation.** From the giant American Telephone and Telegraph Company (AT&T) to the small local store, most companies with which Americans do business are corporations. Yet only 125 years ago, almost all American business property was owned by individuals and partnerships. These simpler forms of business organizations are still important today, but the corporation has become the dominant form of business organization. An examination of the corporation's structure will reveal why.

The fundamental reason for the growth of the corporation is the ease with which it may raise capital funds in comparison to the partnership or individual enterprise. As the size of businesses grew during the latter part of the nineteenth century, the ability of one person or even a few in partnership to raise sufficient capital to sustain a company's activities declined considerably; the opportunities for investment greatly exceed the wealth of even the richest individuals. A corporation, however, can raise capital by selling numerous shares of stock to many investors, each share representing a portion of ownership in the corporation. In 1979, for example, AT&T had more than 710 million shares of outstanding common stock, each carrying one vote in the company's affairs. The largest single stockholder—a teachers' retirement fund—held less than 0.9 percent of the common stock; the other shares were held by millions of individuals and organizations. This pattern of stock ownership is characteristic of most other major corporations. In short, the corporation is an excellent institution to tap dispersed funds for investment and growth.

The corporation has other advantages as well. Foremost among these is its legal unity. Under the law, a corporation is treated as if it were a person for many reasons. Thus, it may sue and be sued, it may own property and enter into contracts with others; but, unlike a person, it is unaffected by the death or withdrawal of its shareholders or officers. From the shareholder's perspective, another principal advantage of the corporation is limited liability, under which debtors must look to the corporation for payment, whereas the corporation largely insulates individual shareholders from any obligation to pay corporate debts.

Despite these advantages, the transition to the corporate form in the United States during the latter nineteenth century was not smooth. Historically, in

corporation: A legal (usually business) entity with the rights, privileges, and liabilities of an individual that are distinct from those of the individuals making up the group.

England, the corporation had been associated with the grant of monopoly privileges by the government through charters, so in an era characterized by a belief in free competition, state legislators were fearful of chartering corporations. Also, many early corporations were guilty of fraudulent dealing and stock manipulation, which further reinforced legislative reluctance to permit general incorporation. In addition, as we have seen, a persistent theme in American history has been the opposition of many interest groups, especially agricultural groups, to big institutions, particularly large-scale business enterprises. Finally, many businesses feared that the widespread use of the corporate form would transfer control in business enterprise to bankers, speculators, and other groups not directly involved in the production and distribution of goods and services.

Thus, while pressure grew for the widespread use of the corporate form, other forces resisted it. However, in two breakthrough statutes in 1875 and 1888, New Jersey (1) permitted the formation of corporations in virtually any kind of business activity, and (2) allowed corporations to hold stock in other corporations. New Jersey enacted these laws in order to attract industry from New York, its principal rival, and to increase state revenue through corporate chartering fees and annual corporate income taxes. The New Jersey statutes had a widespread effect for two reasons. First, because these laws permitted corporations to transact business out of state, their impact was felt far beyond New Jersey. Second, the success of New Jersey's laws in attracting industry and raising revenues encouraged imitation by other states.

By 1900, the corporation had become the dominant form of business enterprise in the United States, and the body of statutory and judicial law pertaining to it had grown enormously. The market for stocks, bonds, and other corporate securities became highly developed, centering in the New York Stock Exchange and other securities exchanges. A large industry consisting of investment bankers and stock brokerage houses sprang up for the purposes of marketing new securities that corporations wished to sell in order to raise new capital and of trading securities already on the market. Since 1900, the law concerning corporations and securities has continued to develop rapidly, as has the sophistication and complexity of the securities market. The law on corporations began at the state level but gradually expanded to include national statutes and case law, reflecting the national, and international, scope of the modern corporation. At the same time, the number of people holding shares in corporations expanded (to about 30 million in 1980); it included many investors whose information about corporations and securities was minimal and who, therefore, required special protection.

The increasing complexity of securities markets during the boom years of the 1920s, followed by the stock-market crash in the fall of 1929, created a loud demand for national regulation. In 1933, the first major national securities statute—the Securities Act of 1933—was passed. It required those offering new issues of stock for sale to the public to provide certain information to investors, as well as the filing of a registration statement about the corporation with the

Securities and Exchange Commission (SEC), formed in 1934. It also forbade the sale of new securities that did not comply with these requirements. In 1934, Congress enacted the Securities Exchange Act, which completed the basic structure of securities regulation by extending coverage to securities already on the market, stockbrokers, and securities exchanges. Essentially, the statute sought to prevent and punish various forms of stock-market manipulation and authorized the SEC to prepare rules and regulations directed toward that end.

Thus, public policy toward business organization is now a compound of private law and public law. There are many reasons for the remarkable growth of the public-law component in the last half-century, but one basic reason stands out. Along with citizen and interest groups, many policymakers have concluded that the economic results of free markets and private law can be improved through government intervention. This reasoning underlies the growth of the four most important techniques of government intervention: subsidy, public enterprise, regulation, and macroeconomic policy.

THE TOOLS AND TECHNIQUES OF ECONOMIC POLICY

Through its legal system, the American government provides much of the raw material necessary for the operation of capitalism and free enterprise in the country. The basic rules governing economic transactions are laid out—although not always clearly—and protection is offered for those who might otherwise hesitate to trade. Of course, the role of government in the American economy goes much further. In the remainder of this chapter, we will see that economic policy has evolved into a complex set of policy tools and techniques. Some of these directly affect economics (which can be defined as "making choices about scarce resources"), and others have only indirect, but no less important, economic impacts. We will also see that these tools and techniques are not always well-coordinated. Indeed, they often work at cross-purposes, largely because (1) there are many different economic goals (e.g., growth, efficiency, stability) that may sometimes conflict with one another, (2) economic policies often have social impacts (e.g., on unemployment, income distribution, opportunity), and (3) Americans are far from unanimous on the details of social goals.

We will discuss four broad categories of economic tools and techniques: subsidy, public enterprise, regulation, and macroeconomic policy. There is one general point that must be remembered in order to understand economic policy. Since public policies always impose costs, which *may* outweigh the benefits they produce, an economic policy should be analyzed in two ways. First, does it increase the welfare of society in the aggregate (i.e., does it provide net social benefits)? Second, are the benefits and costs of the policy allocated among the members and groups of society in a fair and equitable way?

Subsidy Policy

What Is a Subsidy?   Economists divide economic policy into two categories: *demand management* and *supply management.* Demand management policies are designed to affect the demand for goods and services in the economy. For example, raising the overall level of taxes that individuals and corporations must pay to government reduces the amount of disposable income that may be used to buy goods and services. In other words, tax increases reduce the overall demand for goods and services; conversely, general tax decreases theoretically will have the effect of increasing the overall level of demand. Supply management policies, of which subsidy is one type, are designed to affect the production and supply of goods and services. For example, if government selectively reduces taxes on business firms that invest in new production facilities, theoretically the supply of such facilities will increase and the costs of production will decrease because the newer facilities will be more efficient (i.e., less wasteful of resources).

Why does government "subsidize" an activity? One reason may be to affect the production and supply of goods and services. For example, Japan, which has one of the most extensive subsidy policies in the industrial world, provides payments to companies to perform research on new or improved products. The Japanese government also provides tax concessions to encourage companies to install computers and advanced telecommunications devices, which make production and office management more efficient. Generally, the Japanese have used such policies, not to confer benefits on particular industries, but rather to attain broad supply objectives, such as strengthening Japanese industry in the international marketplace.

Although business subsidies have been successfully employed in Japan, in the United States the word *subsidy* is often equated with *giveaway.* In part, this stems from the American political tradition, in which many candidates for public office claim to be friends of the poor and enemies of big business. In addition, although the United States has employed subsidies, it has no general policy to help it decide when subsidies are justified and when they are not. The lack of guiding principles has led to the enactment of many poorly justified subsidy policies, which usually are described by other names.

Let us look at the "maritime construction differential," which historically has been one of the largest American subsidies. Under it, the Maritime Administration, an agency within the Department of Commerce, subsidized the difference between the costs of constructing ships in American shipyards and in foreign shipyards. It also guarantees the financing of such ships by offering to repay bank loans that the maritime firms cannot repay. While this subsidy may seem to be a gift to commercial interests, it has been justified on the grounds that an American merchant-marine service produces public goods by conferring benefits on the whole economy. For instance, it aids both our national defense (i.e., the fleet can be mobilized in wartime) and our balance of payments (i.e., by reducing the flow of American dollars to foreign shipyards). Whether the evidence supports this claim is, for the moment, unimportant.

In general, a **subsidy** is a benefit provided by government to a private company or person in exchange for which the recipient undertakes an activity that provides a social benefit. The recipient often remits no payment, service, or good directly to the government; sometimes, it provides the government with payment, services, or goods whose value is less than the amount of the subsidy. For example, if the government pays farmers for not growing crops on part of their land, a benefit has been conferred on the farmers, who remit nothing directly to the government. The justification for this subsidy is that without it, large numbers of farmers would change jobs because of the low prices that would otherwise occur due to the increased supply of agricultural products, eventually causing sharp disruptions in the supply of farm goods, which would be bad for consumers. In the case of the maritime construction subsidy, the purposes, as we saw, were to aid national defense and the balance of payments. Similarly, when the government guarantees the bank loans of private companies (e.g., Chrysler), it provides a valuable financial service to the company, which benefits by getting loans from banks at lower rates of interest than it would pay under normal market conditions. The public also is intended to benefit; in the case of Chrysler, assisting that company also assisted auto workers in such already distressed areas as Detroit.

Because subsidies are economic programs through which the recipients are paid or encouraged to perform activities that are believed to be beneficial to the public, the relevant public-policy questions for evaluating subsidies are (1) whether the private party would have undertaken the activity without a government subsidy or with a less costly one, (2) whether the policy goal sought from the private party is an appropriate one, and (3) whether the benefit expected from the private party is worth the government's outlay. With these criteria in mind, let us now look at some of the uses and types of subsidies.

Subsidies and American Economic Growth   In 1825, the Englishman George Stephenson began the first public passenger-carrying steam railroad. Less than five years later, American pioneers were testing and improving the new technology. Even before the beginning of practical commercial railroading, state and local governments were providing generous subsidies to aid the development of this new industry. Under an 1824 federal law, surveys for the purpose of constructing railways were made by government engineers at public expense. Beginning in 1850, free land grants were made to railroads; with these, railroad companies received not only land for rights-of-way but also sometimes land as far away as fifteen miles from where the track would be laid. In return for federal aid, which accounted for about 10 percent of all current railroad mileage, the railroads agreed to handle government traffic at reduced rates; it is estimated that this benefit eventually amounted to more than nine times the original value of the grants. However, the immediate effect of government subsidies was to spur the growth of the railroad industry. Mileage of railways in the United States rose from 73 miles in 1830, to 30,636 miles in 1860, and to 163,597 miles in 1890. In 1869, thanks again to subsidies, the

subsidy: A form of government support for private individuals or business firms.

first transcontinental rail link was completed at Promontory Point, Utah. The development of the railroad industry, in turn, triggered the vast growth of the American iron and steel industry, and spurred the development of technology such as the air brake and electric signals. Most importantly, the railroad substantially reduced the costs of transporting agricultural and industrial commodities throughout the country and to ports for export, thereby widening markets, lowering the costs of goods, and expanding trade.

Like other subsidies, subsidies to railroads have been viewed in two ways. One view condemns the government for transferring wealth to interests that were often already wealthy; the other focuses on the role subsidies played in developing the young nation. Railroads certainly would have been built without such subsidies, but at a much slower pace. The noted British political economist Arthur C. Pigou (1877–1959) argued that subsidies aiding the development of transportation and communications networks ultimately benefit the whole nation by assisting the development of local industries and their ability to move goods to distant markets, increasing competition, lowering unit production costs due to enlarged markets, and so on. All these benefits, Pigou noted, may ultimately outweigh the costs of the subsidy.

Types of Subsidy Policies   One of the major forms of government subsidies is the price support program administered by the Agricultural Department's Commodity Credit Corporation. Table 12-1 shows how the size of these programs has grown in recent years. The Agriculture Department also administers food-assistance programs for the needy. Changes in these programs are also shown in the table.

Agriculture is probably the largest current recipient of subsidies in the American economy, but it is hardly the only one. Airlines, for example, benefit from government construction and maintenance of airports and air-traffic control systems for which air carriers pay less than their proportion of the full costs. Homeowners receive tax subsidies in the form of mortgage interest deductions, and business firms receive large amounts of free information, such as market data from the Department of Commerce. Students attending state universities usually pay fees far below the actual costs required to educate them. Similarly, vacationers in national and state parks pay far less than their proportionate share of maintaining those parks. In short, we must not think that only a few industries or groups share in the general subsidy pie. Virtually every group in the country receives some direct or indirect subsidy, and the justification for each particular subsidy is often based more on the political efforts of a group to obtain the subsidy than on achieving a public benefit.

The most obvious form of subsidy is a *direct cash payment.* The maritime construction differential is an example of this type of subsidy. Because of the political risks in supporting such direct and obvious transfers, however, the variations used in other programs are more subtle. *Target prices,* used in connection with cotton and other farm products, require the government to pay farmers the difference between a set target price and the actual market

TABLE 12-1
RECENT CHANGES IN AGRICULTURAL PROGRAMS

	Dollars (in millions)				% Increase (1980–1983)
	1980	1981	1982	1983	
Feed grains[a]	$1,286	$ − 533[b]	$5,397	$6,815	430%
Wheat	879	1,543	2,238	3,419	289%
Rice	− 76	24	164	664	−[c]
Cotton	64	336	1,110	1,363	2,030%
Tobacco	− 87	− 51	103	880	−
Dairy	1,011	1,894	2,182	2,528	150%
Soybeans	116	87	169	288	148%
Total, all price support programs[d]	2,752	4,036	11,652	18,850	585%
Food assistance total[e]	13,890	16,186	15,719	17,997	30%
Agriculture Department total	52,701	60,046	58,119	71,900	36%

[a]Includes payments for corn, sorghum, oats, and barley.
[b]Negative expenditures on price support programs indicate that farmers were paying back old loans from the Commodity Credit Corporation.
[c]Not available.
[d]Sum of all listed programs, plus price supports for vegetable oils, sugar, and peanuts, export assistance, storage costs, and other administrative expenses.
[e]Includes food stamps, child nutrition programs, and the Special Supplement Program for Women, Infants, and Children (WIC).

Source: *National Journal,* February 11, 1984, p. 272.

price. Under *set-aside* programs, the Department of Agriculture makes direct payments to wheat and other feed-grain farmers, who agree to remove a specific amount of their farms from production. When the payment is made in exchange for farmers voluntarily agreeing to limit the acreage they have set aside for a particular crop, as has been the case in rice production, the subsidy is known as an *acreage allotment.* When the production restrictions are mandatory and the farmer may not allot more acreage to a crop than is legally permissible, the program is called a *marketing quota.*

The most subtle of these programs is the *price support,* which is used in connection with milk, wheat, and other agricultural products. Under this system, if a farmer cannot sell his crop at a designated price, he may obtain a government loan using his crop as collateral. If the market price later rises, he can sell the crop; if it fails to rise, he may keep the loan amount and the government keeps the crop. In fiscal year 1983, the cost of milk price supports was over $2 billion, and government inventories of dairy products exceeded eighteen billion pounds—costing taxpayers about $127,000 a day for storage. There are also other agricultural programs, such as marketing orders and agreements, which allow producers to collectively adopt quality standards, uniform prices, and so on.

A second form of subsidy is the provision of goods and services free or below the market value. These are called *in-kind subsidies.* We have noted that public education facilities and students are principal recipients of these subsidies, which raise the value of what economists term *human capital* (i.e., the value of productive skills and abilities), which in turn benefits the economy as a whole. The provision of airports for the use of airline companies and low waterway user charges paid by large companies are examples of in-kind transportation subsidies that are expected to make industries and services more efficient, thus benefiting the whole economy. Agriculture, too, is a recipient of in-kind subsidies. A large proportion of the water used for irrigation in western states is supplied at heavily subsidized prices.

Loan guarantees constitute the third form of subsidy. A loan guarantee is a governmental guarantee of a private bank loan to a business or person. If the loan is repaid, the government's cost is limited to only administrative costs. But if the borrower is unable to repay, the government must. Because the risk of default is an important factor in the interest rates a bank charges for a loan, guarantees constitute a valuable subsidy. Several major corporations, notably Lockheed and Chrysler, have been recipients of loan guarantees (of $250 million and $1.5 billion, respectively). In addition to these special cases, there have been important loan guarantee programs conducted on a regular basis, including those for (1) exporters by the Export-Import Bank, (2) aircraft purchases by local air services and small airlines, (3) railroad operation and maintenance, (4) defense contractors and subcontractors, and (5) real estate of many varieties. Although loan guarantees cost the government virtually nothing, except in the case of a default, there is a hidden drawback: because loan guarantees increase the demand for loans without increasing the supply of loanable funds, they may cause interest rates to rise so that a sufficient amount of capital may not be available to other potential borrowers, especially firms seeking capital for high-risk advanced technologies. Accordingly, critics of loan guarantee programs argue, this form of subsidy usually has an adverse impact on the economy.

Government has also engaged in making *direct loans* at reduced interest rates, the fourth form of subsidy. In contrast to loan guarantees, direct loans are financed from the federal budget. Many of these loans have been made to subsidize rural areas that otherwise might deteriorate or to promote small business. The Rural Electrification Administration (REA) of the Department of Agriculture makes loans to provide electric power and telephone services to farmers, and the Department of Commerce has provided loans for industrial and commercial development in areas attempting to redevelop. The Small

Business Administration (SBA) provides small businesses with two types of loans: loans for plant construction and the purchase of land, materials, and capital equipment; and disaster loans to small firms that suffer losses as a result of floods, hurricanes, and other natural calamities.

At first glance these programs may not appear to be beneficial to the public, but the underlying theory supporting them does point to such an effect. Without loans to encourage economic activity in rural areas, it is argued, urban areas will become even more crowded and ultimately intolerable. Advocates of loans to small businesses and blighted urban areas argue that American society ultimately benefits from an economy whose benefits are shared by all regions, and from a business system characterized by diversity and small firms supplying goods and services that the larger ones will not supply. Furthermore, the argument proceeds, the future economic benefits spawned by these subsidies will eventually exceed the costs.

Another indirect form of subsidy is provided to businesses and individuals in the form of *insurance*. These programs have assisted economic enterprises that took risks private insurance companies found excessive; without government insurance, some of these enterprises never would have gotten started or would have moved very slowly. The best example of subsidy by government insurance is in the nuclear power industry. During the early days of commercial nuclear power, not only were private companies unwilling to insure the power plants but even nearby homeowners were unable to obtain insurance that covered nuclear accidents. Without insurance, the industry was unwilling to build new plants, and homeowners had still another incentive to object to their construction. Thus, in 1957, Congress passed the Price-Anderson Act, under which the federal government provides insurance for nuclear power plants up to $500 million, provided that the utility companies obtained as much private insurance as they could—about $65 million. The Price-Anderson Act also limited the liability of utilities and manufacturers of reactors by declaring that they could not be sued for amounts exceeding a total of about $560 million.

Americans are usually more aware of some other forms of government insurance. These include housing insurance, agricultural programs such as the Federal Crop Insurance Corporation, and student loan insurance. Two of the most familiar federal insurance agencies are the Federal Deposit Insurance Corporation (FDIC), established by the Federal Reserve Act of 1933 in order to preserve public confidence in banks by insuring bank deposits, and the Federal Savings and Loan Insurance Corporation (FSLIC), which since 1934 has performed basically the same function for savings-and-loan associations. Ideally, the only costs to the taxpayer of such programs are administrative, because it is hoped that few banks or savings-and-loan associations will need federal help; in fact, however, most federal insurance programs involve at least small amounts of government subsidies.

The *tax incentive* (sometimes called tax expenditure or tax subsidy), the final type of subsidy we will describe, constitutes not the provision of something valuable from government to private groups but rather relief from a tax liability that would otherwise be owed under the tax laws. For example, home-owners may deduct their mortgage interest and real estate taxes in computing their federal income taxes, and owners of municipal bonds may usually deduct the interest they earn. The income tax laws and their accompanying regulations are rife with such deductions and exclusions from income, the purposes of which are to provide persons and firms with incentives to engage in certain economic behavior. When the government grants business firms tax credits for investing in new plant and equipment, the purpose is obviously to spur such investment and, thus, economic growth. In this sense, tax incentives are used as a public-policy instrument in the same way as direct subsidies, loans, and loan guarantees: to alter economic behavior "in the public interest."

There has always been controversy about American subsidy policy in general, and about the various forms of subsidy and particular programs. There are so many such programs whose effects are hard to calculate accurately in terms of costs and benefits that we must be careful not to make sweeping generalizations attacking or favoring subsidy policy. The same caution should be applied to the equally controversial category of public enterprise.

Public Enterprise

From the earliest days of the republic, private ownership has implied many of the rights that shape American politics. Indeed, one of the distinguishing characteristics of the American political economy is the reluctance, relative to other Western democracies such as France or Great Britain, of the public sector to expand its ownership and operation of factories, transportation and communications systems, and basic natural resources. Thus, the American system is still very much a capitalist one, because private individuals are intended to be the principal beneficiaries of most economic activities. Nevertheless, **public enterprise** is not necessarily the exact opposite of private ownership: most enterprises in the United States are at least partially public, because there is extensive control of business through regulation and subsidies. Similarly, public ownership need not be total: the government's share in an enterprise can range from 0.0 to 100 percent. Therefore, we must recognize that public enterprise can occur in different forms and in varying degrees.

public enterprise: Governmental or public ownership of productive resources that are used to provide goods for the public.

Several factors account for public enterprise in the United States. In some areas, a socially desirable activity (e.g., development of new resources or technologies) may be too costly or too risky for private firms to pursue, so the public sector may assume the risk and the expense. One example is the American manned space program, which despite its military applications, was promoted in part by a belief that the advances in science and technology that would spin off from space research should not wait for private industries to finance the huge sums the space program required. Another impetus for public enterprise is the bankruptcy of firms that provide what are considered to be vital services. When the northeastern railroad system failed in the late 1960s, the Consolidated Rail Corporation ("Conrail") was established to absorb the

Rationing-board line during World War II. Only in wartime has American government attempted to control virtually every aspect of production, distribution, and consumption. (John Vachon/Library of Congress)

bankrupt rail lines. Although the creation of Conrail was not without controversy, it was founded on the belief that the overall costs of maintaining a public railroad corporation would be lower than the costs to society of the collapse of a vital part of the American transportation system.

There are three major areas in which public enterprise is particularly significant in the United States: (1) public involvement in finance and industry, (2) public utilities, and (3) various other social and economic enterprises. In the first of these areas, the federal government has assumed a *financial* function. There are several public investment banks that make long-term loans and provide financial support for businesses. The largest of these was the Reconstruction Finance Corporation (RFC), begun by President Herbert Hoover in 1932 in order to supply credit to firms endangered by the Great Depression. Until it was dissolved in 1953, the RFC made 20,000 loans and distributed more than $48 billion in credit (and suffered a default rate of only 1 percent). Today, the Export-Import Bank assists in the financing of exports and imports between the United States and other countries. The Small Business Administration, as we already mentioned, also makes business loans.

natural monopoly:
An industry in which production is most efficient when performed by a single firm; in natural monopolies, such as electrical or water transmission, the government regulates the prices charged to consumers.

A second major form of public enterprise is the *publicly owned utility.* The rationale for public ownership of water systems or electric utilities is very important: a utility is usually considered to be a **natural monopoly.** A natural monopoly is said to exist when an industry cannot efficiently support more than one firm. Because the overall costs are much lower when only one local electric company, for example, must string wires all over a region, a natural monopoly is generally considered preferable to allowing or forcing competition in the provision of electric service. Thus, one alternative for policymakers is to allow the existence of a monopoly—either publicly or privately owned—subject to regulations that will prevent it from exploiting its control of a market.

There are hundreds of small municipal publicly owned electric systems in the United States (accounting for about 25 percent of the national supply) and hundreds of Rural Electrical Cooperative systems. Recently, the number of publicly owned electric utilities has grown; along with soaring electric rates in the early 1980s came movements in many areas (e.g., New Orleans and Long Island's populous Suffolk County) for municipalities to take over local power companies. The large publicly owned electric systems are in the states of Nebraska and New York and in the city of Los Angeles, and the federally owned Tennessee Valley Authority (TVA). The TVA was created in 1933 partly to control floods and cushion the impact of the depression on much of the Southeast, but its most significant aspect has been its production and distribution of electric power from hydroelectric dams. It is a semiautonomous agency, not subject to Civil Service rules but deriving its capital from the national treasury. Its facilities yield electricity that has been sold to residential customers in six states for about one-half the average United States price, largely because of its initial mandate to assist in the development of the Tennessee Valley region. During the 1970s, however, the TVA ran into strong criticism for raising rates in order to finance new construction of coal-fired and nuclear power plants.

The third major form of public enterprise is one that has been generally endorsed (even by Adam Smith): the post office.[4] Because it serves both an economic and a social service (by aiding commerce and social communication), and shows some of the characteristics of a natural monopoly (it would be more costly to have more than one national postal service), postal distribution is acknowledged to be a governmental function; in addition, the Constitution established an American postal system, and state-operated postal service is universally accepted in other nations. Despite the fact that since 1971 the Postal Service has been a public corporation, its mandate is complicated by a widespread belief that not all postal users should pay their proportionate share of the costs of postal services; nonprofit institutions and educational publications (including magazines and newspapers) have been partially subsidized by lower postal rates because their function was viewed as beneficial to society. The system faces a severe challenge in the near future, however, because the justification for a natural monopoly in postal service (i.e., the local delivery and pickup system) is being threatened by electronic mail and other communications systems.

Natural monopoly has been used as a rationale for still other public enterprises, although with varying degrees of validity. Local water and sewage systems, for example, are almost always public enterprises that usually do not lose much money but often exhibit some peculiar pricing schemes. In some places, water users are charged a flat fee for their water service (and apartment dwellers usually never even see their fee), thereby encouraging waste. In addition, new suburbs or office complexes are often supplied with water and sewage service at current rates even though the added customers may greatly increase the cost of the system because new purification and treatment plants must be built. Garbage disposal is another municipal service for which heavy users often do not pay their true share of the costs.

There are many other public enterprises in the United States, from the local to the federal level. Some states operate liquor stores or public lotteries as public corporations for the dual purpose of controlling illicit alcohol sales or gambling and generating tax revenues. Many levels of government participate in public radio and television broadcasting, such as the Public Broadcasting System and National Public Radio; these systems initially had strictly educational purposes, but they now contain more diverse forms of entertainment and information. We will conclude this section on public enterprise with a brief mention of one other fundamental economic and social goal pursued by the public sector.

In fiscal year 1983, the federal government was authorized to spend more than $7.5 billion on general science and space flight research and technology, and nearly $4 billion on health research. In addition, billions more dollars were allocated to the advance of science and technology through many other departments of government (e.g., the Department of Defense and the Agriculture Department). Some of these expenditures are pure subsidies, others take the form of public enterprises, and still others are hybrids of the two forms. An example of the latter is the Synthetic Fuels Corporation, created in 1980 to provide aid to the private sector; through price and loan guarantees and direct loans, the private sector was to operate commercial plants to produce synthetic substitutes—from biomass, oil shale, or coal tars—for imported oil. Furthermore, there are more than five hundred research laboratories receiving at least some federal aid; some of them, such as the Fermi National Accelerator Laboratory near Chicago, which investigates high-energy physics, superconductivity, and cryogenics, are actually public facilities. In fact, the Stevenson-Wydler Technology Innovation Act of 1980 requires all of these research agencies to make their scientific discoveries and innovations available to industry.

The most visible of the science-related public enterprises is the National Aeronautics and Space Administration (NASA). The many technological spin-offs of the space program (e.g., miniaturized medical monitoring devices, microcomputers, new ceramics and plastics) have spawned entire new industries in the United States, thereby making NASA, at least to some degree, a public research enterprise. NASA is a research agency and is therefore restricted by the law that created it from operating commercial systems (e.g., resource-sensing satellites or weightless factories carried into orbit by the space shuttle). Nevertheless, NASA, like many other federal research programs, has underwritten much of the risk and development costs of innovations that have benefited industries, workers, and citizens. Much of this work was not performed by NASA itself but was contracted out to hundreds of private companies.

The principal justifications for public enterprise are the underwriting of risk and the manipulation of competition. A particularly strong factor in the creation of public enterprises in the United States has been the existence of natural monopolies. As we will see in the next section, however, there is at least one alternative to public ownership or operation. The public sector may intrude on the private sector by imposing regulations on the activities of individuals or corporations.

Regulation

It is difficult to exaggerate the importance of competition to the American system. The democratic process relies on competition between candidates for the people's vote. Businesses and individuals are expected to compete for economic advancement, and, as we shall see in Chapter 13, even the basic concepts of social justice and equity in the United States rely on the idea of a fair contest. Competition is seen as a dynamic economic and social force encouraging hard work and its rewards.

Yet, monopoly also plays a role in the economic system. The Constitution includes a clause establishing a patent and copyright system that provides incentives to creativity in the form of monopoly grants, and thereby invites improvements in products and services.

The Justifications for Regulation   Today, many people equate Adam Smith's support of free markets in *The Wealth of Nations* with a strident call for excluding the government from all private-sector activities. In fact, Smith was more pro-competition than he was anti-anything, and he believed self-interest to be the fire that drove an individual's efforts to compete.

> Every individual necessarily labours to render the annual revenue of the society as great as he can. He generally, indeed, neither intends to promote the public interest, nor knows how much he is promoting it. . . . By directing that industry in such a manner as its produce may be of the greatest value, he intends only his own gain, and he is in this, as in many other cases, led by an invisible hand to promote an end which was no part of his intention. Nor is it always the worse for the society that it was no part of it. By pursuing his own interest he frequently promotes that of the society more effectively than when he really intends to promote it.[5]

Smith added that in order for competition and the "invisible hand" of self-interest to maximize the welfare of individuals, their economic relations had to be guided by a few basic principles: freedom from violence, the protection of life, liberty, and property, and the maintenance of a genuinely free competition. Thus, government had a role in prosecuting criminals, enforcing contracts, and providing "public works" (e.g., bridges and roads) where private enterprise was not likely to act. Most important, government, according to Smith, was obliged to take steps to protect the operation of the free market.

To understand the role of such government intervention, it is necessary to look at two very basic facts. First, monopoly, which can definitely arise in a free market, is a violation of the principles of competition. Second, some entirely private decisions cannot be allowed because they have external effects that can threaten the life or property of others. In our discussion of public enterprise, we described a natural monopoly—an industry in which a single supplier is the most efficient economic structure—but monopolies are usually bad. Put simply, a monopolist lacks one important incentive to produce as much as consumers demand or to restrain price increases on products that only he or she sells: if consumers do not like the monopolist's actions, they cannot turn elsewhere because there is no competitor. If there were only one supplier of heating fuel for northeastern states in the winter, and that company was completely free from any laws, regulations, or moral constraints, consumers could be forced to pay ten times the current charge or else freeze. An economy that includes monopolies cannot be free. In the words of Adam Smith, "monopolies derange more or less the natural distribution of the stock of the society."[6]

There is also the problem of external effects. If you decide to convert your house into a fireworks factory, your next-door neighbors will (probably unwillingly) share the risk of becoming part of your pyrotechnics. You do have the right to pursue your own self-interest, but you would have violated your neighbors' even more basic rights of physical safety and property protection. Although Adam Smith preferred state intervention in cases of **externalities** to be restricted to threats to society in general (and not just damage to other individuals), the problem is really one of degree, and many modern economists have recognized that external effects can often justify action by the state.

In the later years of the nineteenth century, the Industrial Revolution was transforming the society and the economy and creating problems that had never existed before. As we have described, the corporation emerged as a legal entity, and new forms of business competition began to raise questions about the obligations of businesses to be fair and honest. The spread of railroads, with their demand for long strips of land that often cut through people's property, and of networks of electrical and telephone wires forced policymakers to begin thinking about such matters as eminent domain (the power of government to acquire property) and natural monopoly. Similarly, industrial society brought with it increased population, urban crowding, poorly manufactured foods, and other problems for which individual action or private law

externalities: Side effects of actions that influence the well-being of persons who did not consent to the actions; these side effects may be benefits or costs.

seemed inadequate; thus, social equity also became a spur to government regulation (as we will see in Chapter 13). It was in response to new business practices that the first federal regulatory agencies emerged, so it is not surprising that as businesses and their techniques evolved, new regulatory mechanisms were devised. That evolutionary process has continued into the 1980s. As we shall see, regulation aimed at external effects has been a much more recent phenomenon.

The Beginning of Federal Regulation   In earlier parts of this book, we discussed the relationship between the public and private sectors during the early years of the nation, particularly the intermixture of the two realms of economic activity as far back as the founding of the republic. Yet the question of the constitutionality of regulation was not specifically addressed in the United States until 1877. The narrow issue in a major Supreme Court case (*Munn* v. *Illinois*) was whether the state of Illinois could pass a law establishing maximum fees for the storage of grain in Chicago. According to warehouseman Munn, the law had the effect of confiscating private property because it controlled his firm's income. The Supreme Court's ruling opened the door to business regulation in the United States: "Property does become clothed with a public interest when used in a manner to make it of public consequence, and affect the community at large. When, therefore, one devotes his property to a use in which the public has an interest, he, in effect, grants to the public an interest in that use, and must submit to be controlled by the public for the common good, to the extent of the interest he has thus created."[7] This "public interest" standard is extremely vague because most activities can conceivably have some impact on others in the "community at large." It is also extremely important, therefore, because it has been used many times since 1877 to justify the extension of public control over what could be considered private activities.

At about the same time as the *Munn* decision, another fledgling regulatory device (and justification) was emerging in Massachusetts. Because it made no sense to have many competing railroads laying tracks all over the densely populated state, Massachusetts began to enter into contracts with such companies. These contracts, called **certificates of public convenience and necessity,** bestowed on particular companies monopoly grants to operate railroads between certain towns, in exchange for which the companies would agree to perform stipulated tasks. These tasks included asking for state approval of freight rates, maintaining clean restrooms, providing unobstructive road crossings, and seeking prior approval from the state to cease rail service along any part of the companies' tracks.

By the beginning of the 1880s, many states had instituted a variety of policies designed to impose some type of public control over railroads. Because of their essential role in the industrial and agricultural development of America, railroad companies were under close scrutiny. Railroad companies also were emerging as extremely visible examples of the new corporate form of enter-

certificates of public convenience and necessity: Governmental contracts that grant a monopoly to a company in return for an agreement to abide by government regulations.

prise, and it was their experiments in new business practices that particularly caught the attention of public officials. Some carriers took advantage of their monopoly over freight traffic along certain routes by discriminating in the rates they charged different shippers. In order to attract business on those routes for which there was competition, railroad carriers would offer sizable rebates to some shippers in the hope of driving their weaker competitors bankrupt. In some regions, the railroad companies even collectively agreed to set rates and divide traffic among themselves. These "rate bureaus," or **cartels,** were attempts to exert monopoly power over the transportation market, but they almost always failed when one member of the cartel would cheat the others by making deals with shippers at the expense of the other members. The result of these business practices was general chaos in service and rates, overbuilding of unnecessary duplicate rail lines, and frequent bankruptcies of smaller rail companies.

cartel: An association of business firms, national governments, and so on, for establishing control or a monopoly by price fixing, limiting supplies, and so on.

The states had attempted to handle some of these problems through their certificates of public convenience and necessity, or by passing laws that forbade certain business practices. The railroads, however, were able to avoid the less agile legislative restrictions, and state governments usually lacked the power or the expertise to investigate transportation problems. The situation was complicated even further because many railroads were interstate, and thus would be subject to one set of state regulations on one section of track, and a different, often conflicting, set of regulations on another section of track in another state.

Then, in 1886, the Supreme Court ruled in *Wabash, St. Louis & Pacific Railway Co.* v. *Illinois* that any enterprise involving interstate commerce could not be regulated by the states in which it was located; only the federal government was given the power to regulate interstate commerce by the commerce clause of the Constitution.[8] Largely in response to this decision, Congress passed the Interstate Commerce Act in 1887. This law established the Interstate Commerce Commission (ICC), outlawed rate discrimination, and required interstate railroads to charge "reasonable and just" rates to shippers. There has been much controversy over which interests supported the formation of the first American regulatory agency; the railroads certainly had a stake in ending the confusion over business practices and state regulations, and the historical record suggests that they believed they would be able to live with the ICC, or even control it.

Partly because it was given limited enforcement powers, and partly because the Supreme Court took away its authority to set maximum railroad rates, the ICC had to wait until Congress strengthened it (in 1906 and 1910) to become a modern regulatory agency. By the beginning of World War I, the ICC had authority to prevent proposed rate increases (rather than passively wait until someone protested) and to investigate the records of railroad companies and hold their officers liable for legal violations, to name a few examples. Soon after the war, the ICC was given the power to establish minimum, as well as maximum, rates and to plan for massive railroad mergers that would strengthen

America's transportation system. In short, business regulation moved from its early period of "negative" regulation, when agencies could only tell companies what not to do, to the modern era of "positive" regulation, in which regulators also take an active role in promoting and preserving the industries they oversee.

The story of the early years of the ICC is important because this was the first of the federal regulatory agencies, and its behavior and difficulties were typical of other agencies that followed. Before briefly discussing the many regulatory agencies that now exist, however, it is necessary to explore another significant area of regulation that emerged soon after the ICC. Like that agency, this new type of regulation was a response to a change in business practices that violated widely held principles of fairness.

trust: A legal doctrine by which property is controlled by one group or person for the benefit of others; useful in the formation of industrial monopolies in the late 1800s.

The Regulation of Monopolies   In 1879, a lawyer who worked for John D. Rockefeller devised a way for one man or company to control all the firms in an industry. This technique, called a **trust,** involved the transfer of control of two or more companies to a legal entity (the trust), which could then manipulate the market and eliminate competition among what appeared to be separate companies. Rockefeller came to dominate the production, refining, and distribution of petroleum products in the late 1800s through the Standard Oil Trust, and the device was soon adopted by the gunpowder, sugar, tobacco, salt, paper bag, whiskey, and many other industries. Farmers formed organizations to oppose the "industrial giants" who allegedly paid them low prices and charged them high transportation rates, and other Americans blamed the trusts for poverty and intrusions on individual liberty. Monopoly, which had always been suspect in America, became a political issue.

In response to the outcry against trusts, in 1890 Congress passed the Sherman Anti-Trust Act. Its Section 1 made unlawful and criminal "every contract, combination . . . or conspiracy in restraint of trade"; Section 2 prohibited monopolizing, attempts to monopolize, and combinations or conspiracies to monopolize any part of interstate or foreign commerce. With little uniform common law against monopoly to draw upon, Congress created a new body of law—antitrust—that was, in effect, experimental. However, it is crucial to recognize that the Sherman Act did not outlaw monopoly itself, only monopolizing behavior. In other words, bigness was not necessarily badness. Yet in practice, the issue has not been so clear. In several cases (e.g., the 1927 *U.S.* v. *International Harvester*), the Supreme Court ruled that the law "does not make the mere size of a corporation, however impressive, or the existence of unexerted power on its part, an offense, when unaccompanied by unlawful conduct in the exercise of its power." By 1945, that doctrine had been modified; in *U.S.* v. *Aluminum Company of America* (Alcoa), an appeals court held that a firm that lawfully attained monopoly status could violate the law by using its great power to hold on to that status.[9] A firm held "monopoly power" when it had the power to control prices or exclude competition.

Clearly, this is a very complex area of the law. It is further complicated by

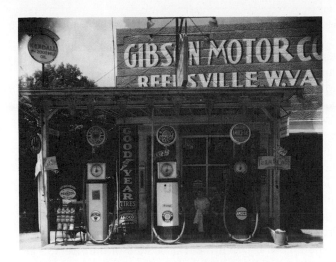

Filling station, West Virginia. Historically, petroleum is one of the industries most subject to regulation and antitrust suits. (Walker Evans/Library of Congress)

the inability of economists and lawyers to precisely define in all situations exactly what constitutes a monopoly. Yet this is not an abstract exercise. Antitrust law determines the bounds of the prices we must pay for many commodities, and even types of products and services we can hope to receive from companies. For example, the 1956 settlement of an antitrust suit filed against AT&T had the effect of excluding the telephone company from the emerging computer market, and (whatever the antimonopoly justification for the action) may have delayed innovations in both the computer and telecommunications industries.

Confusion arose because some early judicial interpretations of the Sherman Act appeared to restrict its application to existing trusts while preventing the government from taking actions against the creation of new ones. Thus, when the oil trust was "busted" in the landmark *Standard Oil Co. of N.J.* v. *United States* (1911), the Supreme Court ruled that only unreasonably anticompetitive trade restraints were prohibited by the Sherman Act.[10] Businesses needed information about what practices the law allowed, but, as in the case of early railroad regulation, any specific standards could have been circumvented. The answer was to supplement the Sherman Act with laws that prohibited certain types of business practices and created a new regulatory agency that could flexibly apply those guidelines. The Clayton Act of 1914 served the first purpose, and the Federal Trade Commission Act of 1914 created the new agency.

The Clayton Act declared that under certain circumstances, four restrictive or monopolistic acts were illegal but not criminal. Section 2 restricted price discrimination (the sale of a product at different prices to similar buyers); Section 3 outlawed exclusive dealing contracts, which required buyers to stop dealing with the seller's competitors; Section 7 prohibited mergers or acquisitions of competing companies; and Section 8 banned interlocking directorates (when a person might be on the board of directors of two or more competing firms). The first three of these provisions were qualified by the statement that such practices were illegal only "where the effect . . . may be substantially to lessen competition" or "tend to create a monopoly in any line of commerce." The Clayton Act also exempted labor unions and agricultural organizations from the antitrust laws, and many other areas have been exempted by subsequent legislation. Thus the act created a great task of clarification for its enforcers.

The Federal Trade Commission (FTC) was created in 1914 to enforce the Clayton Act, although it shares that responsibility with the Department of Justice. The major substantive provision in the FTC act was to prohibit "unfair or deceptive acts or practices" in business. The Sherman and Clayton acts also allowed individuals, corporations, and other governments to sue under the antitrust laws; private plaintiffs may receive treble damages (three times the damages that resulted from the antitrust violation) plus attorney's fees and court costs. In fact, private plaintiffs filed far more antitrust suits in the years between 1890 and 1969 than did the Department of Justice or the FTC (9,728, 1,551, and 1,064, respectively). Among the other remedies available under the law are divestiture (the breakup of a company into smaller ones) and consent decrees (under which a company promises not to behave in a certain way in the future). Considering what is usually at stake in antitrust actions, it is obvious that this form of government activity is controversial. Similarly, FTC prosecutions of companies or industries for "unfair or deceptive" practices are usually subject to dispute, because the agency's mandate is vague and not always consistently applied.

The Growth of Regulation   By World War I, much of the structure of federal regulation in the United States was in place. Economic regulation of particular industrial sectors had begun with the creation of the Interstate Commerce Commission; antitrust and trade-practice regulation had been initiated under the Sherman, Clayton, and FTC acts. The Federal Reserve Board (which will be discussed in the next section) was created by Congress in 1913 to regulate the nation's monetary policy. Most of these laws were aimed at competition, by either preserving or enhancing it. In addition, many states had established public utility (or "public service") commissions to regulate the activity and rates of the natural monopoly sectors of the communications, gas, and electric industries. Yet the evolution of regulation in America was far from complete.

The next major wave of regulatory innovation in the United States occurred during the New Deal years of the 1930s. For the most part, these advances were in the area of "economic" regulation (i.e., the intrusion of the public sector into market economy features such as supply, demand, price, and entry of new competitors). As we will discuss further in Chapter 13, the Food and Drug Administration (FDA) was given enlarged powers to administer the laws controlling the marketing of potentially dangerous foods and drugs. In 1934, two regulatory agencies were formed: the Federal Communications Commission (FCC) was given authority to regulate all interstate and foreign communications by radio or wire (and eventually also by television, cable, and satellite); the Securities and Exchange Commission (SEC) was intended to regulate trading of securities and the related activities of companies and brokers. In 1935, the Federal Power Commission, formed in 1920, was given greatly expanded powers to regulate interstate transmission of electricity and gas. In 1938, the Civil Aeronautics Authority (renamed in 1940 the Civil Aeronautics Board, or CAB) was established to regulate the economic, routing, and pricing practices of interstate and foreign airline companies. For several decades after the New Deal era, only one major new regulatory agency was formed. This was the Atomic Energy Commission (AEC), which in 1954 was given the somewhat contradictory tasks of simultaneously promoting and regulating the safety of the nuclear power industry (the AEC was reorganized into the Nuclear Regulatory Commission in 1974).

The newest wave of regulation, beginning in the 1960s, has been a diversion from the traditional pattern of public-sector interference in economic decisions (see Table 12-2). Unlike economic regulation, which focuses on questions of competition (e.g., how to increase it, how to compensate for its absence, and so on), "social" regulation is concerned with counteracting the effects of various types of market failure and other side effects of the American economic system (as we will see in Chapter 13). In brief, social regulations usually set industry standards, which hopefully will prod businesses to reduce the external effects of their actions or provide more information to consumers. During the 1970s, many such controls were imposed, and although the cost-benefit trade-offs were not always predictable, the political conflict over particular rules was.

Partly in response to the efforts of political entrepreneur Ralph Nader, the National Highway Traffic Safety Administration (NHTSA) was formed in 1966 to develop minimum safety standards for American motor vehicles. The Environmental Protection Agency (EPA) was established in 1970 to reduce pollution in the air and water and to control solid wastes, noise, radiation, and toxic substances. The EPA was given authority to issue and enforce standards for the emission of pollutants from automobiles, factories, and other sources in cooperation with state and local governments. It also administers the "Superfund," a $1.6 billion emergency fund created in 1980 to pay for the cleanup of toxic waste dumps; even the relatively new area of noise pollution is subject to regulation. In 1970, Congress also created the Occupational Safety and Health Administration (OSHA), which develops and administers standards for reducing the frequency of workplace diseases and injuries. In 1973, the Consumer Product Safety Commission (CPSC) was formed; it is charged with protecting the public against unreasonable risks of injury from consumer products.

Although economic regulation has also expanded since the 1960s, the significant change thus has been the rapid spread of social regulation. Largely prompted by the rise in consumerism and the environmental protection move-

TABLE 12-2
MAJOR FEDERAL REGULATORY LEGISLATION, 1970–1980

Year Enacted	Title of Statute	Year Enacted	Title of Statute
1970	Clean Air Amendments Occupational Safety and Health Act Egg Products Inspection Act Poison Prevention Packaging Act Securities Investor Protection Act Economic Stabilization Act Fair Credit Reporting Act	1974	Equal Credit Opportunity Act National Mobile Home Construction and Safety Standards Act
1971	Economic Stabilization Act Amendments Federal Boat Safety Act Lead-Based Paint Poisoning Prevention Act Wholesome Fish and Fisheries Products Act	1975	Energy Policy Conservation Act Securities Act Amendments
		1976	Railroad Revitalization and Regulatory Reform Act Consumer Leasing Act Medical Devices Act Antitrust Improvements Act Consumer Product Safety Commission Improvement Act U.S. Grain Standards Act Toxic Substances Control Act
1972	Consumer Product Safety Act Motor Vehicle Information and Cost Savings Act Noise Control Act Equal Employment Opportunity Act Federal Environmental Pesticide Control Act Federal Water Pollution Control Act Amendments Ports and Waterways Safety Act	1977	Surface Mining Control and Reclamation Act Clean Air Act Amendments Food and Agriculture Act Clean Water Act Fair Labor Standards Act Amendments
1973	Agriculture and Consumer Protection Act Emergency Petroleum Allocation Act Flood Disaster Protection Act	1978	Petroleum Marketing Practices Act Federal Pesticide Act Airline Deregulation Act Public Utility Regulatory Policies Act Futures Trading Act Natural Gas Policy Act
1974	Atomic Energy Act Commodity Futures Trading Commission Act Magnuson-Moss Warranty/FTC Improvement Act Council on Wage and Price Stability Act Employee Retirement Income Security Act Federal Energy Administration Act Transportation Safety Act Fair Labor Standards Act Amendments Safe Drinking Water Act	1979	Aviation Safety and Noise Abatement Act Pipeline Safety Act Trade Agreements Act
		1980	Staggers Rail Act Regulatory Institutions Deregulation and Monetary Control Act Federal Trade Commission Improvement Act Motor Carrier Reform Act Solid Waste Disposal Act Amendments

Source: James E. Anderson, "Economic Regulation," in Stuart Nagel, ed., *Encyclopedia of Policy Studies* (New York: Marcel Dekker, Inc., 1983), pp. 425–426.

ment, these extensions of government policy have often had large impacts on industries; in some cases, they have required industries to spend huge sums of money on revising product design, performance, and production methods or on devising new ways of reducing the external effects of their activities. Although regulation had always had social effects, during the early 1970s it became a direct tool of social policy. (In Chapter 13, we will delve deeper into the questions of equity and fairness that social regulations are intended to address.)

Whereas the first wave of regulation (from 1887 to about 1930) was to a large extent a series of experiments in public involvement in private markets aimed at restricting anticompetitive business practices, and the second wave (during the New Deal) mostly hoped to stabilize markets and coordinate business enterprise, the third wave intruded much deeper into the affairs of individuals and businesses. This expansion, and the large regulatory bureaucracy that it required, spawned an intense cry for reforms or deregulation in the late 1970s. Many observers believed that regulations were largely responsible for inflation and reduced economic growth (because many social regulations increased business costs without improving their productivity), although they occasionally ignored the benefits of social regulations (which are usually less easily measured than their costs).

The current wave of regulation is one of retreat and reform. In 1978, passage of the Airline Deregulation Act diminished the Civil Aeronautics Board's authority over pricing and started a process that would abolish the CAB by 1985. Other laws passed at the end of the decade removed many of the regulations in the trucking and railroad industries. Still other deregulatory moves were aimed at controlling new drugs, requiring that mass-transit facilities be accessible to the handicapped, and environmental problems. Yet deregulation is not the only type of change that was proposed during the Carter and Reagan administrations. There were also calls for procedural reforms ensuring that future regulations take into account all of the costs, both direct and indirect, of governmental action. (Once again, critics of such reforms pointed out that the benefits of regulation are usually much harder to measure than the costs.) Other procedural reforms called for "sunset" legislation (discussed in Chapter 8) for regulatory agencies, or for increased public participation in regulatory rulemaking.

Both the expansions of regulation and the resulting outcry against the growth in government interference had as their basis the recognition that the public and private sectors interact with each other. Business actions *do* affect the general public welfare and the allocation of resources and burdens in society, and government in many cases certainly has the power to tell businesses what to do. The final major area of economic policy we will look at—macroeconomic policy—is also founded on the realization that although there is a role for government in the American mixed economy, there is no consensus on the proper extent of that role.

MACROECONOMIC POLICY

What Is Macroeconomics?

microeconomics:
The study of the economic behavior of firms, business sectors, groups, and individuals.

macroeconomics:
The study of the performance of the economy as a whole.

Economists divide their subject into macroeconomics and microeconomics. The words *macro* and *micro*, taken from Greek, mean *large* and *small*, respectively. **Microeconomics** is the part of economics that deals with firms, sectors (e.g., the automobile industry), groups, and individuals within the economy. It examines the conduct and structure of the units that compose the economy. **Macroeconomics** is the study of the economy as a whole. It is concerned, for example, with trends in total employment, increases in the GNP, and overall price levels. Whereas microeconomic policies (e.g., farm subsidies or regulation of the airline industry) concern units of the economy, macroeconomic policies affect the entire economy. Thus, a microeconomic policy might be designed to increase employment in the steel industry; a macroeconomic policy would be designed to affect the problem of unemployment generally. One type of policy is not superior to the other; they merely operate at different levels. Because both micro- and macroeconomic policies are usually in effect at the same time, they interact with each other. For example, a regulatory policy that emphasizes pollution control will tend to conflict with a macroeconomic growth policy.

Macroeconomic policies were in operation before the 1930s, but their importance and sophistication took a huge leap forward during the period of the New Deal (1933–1939), and they have been continuously refined and developed since then. It is no accident that macroeconomic policies accelerated during the New Deal, because it was then that the conjunction between woeful economic conditions and a new awareness of government's potential to affect the economy became undeniable. Although the English economist John Maynard Keynes (1883–1946) is commonly credited with the modern development of macroeconomic policy, he was only one of the many economists and policymakers who contributed to its development. Futhermore—and this is as important today as it was during the 1930s—Keynes realized that the different branches of macroeconomic policy would have to be coordinated for any one of them to work successfully. Otherwise, as he argued in the early 1930s, the costs of employing one set of policies while ignoring others would probably outweigh the benefits. For this reason, in 1931 he opposed deficit spending (government spending more in a budgetary period than it receives in taxes and other revenues) but favored it in the latter part of the decade, when coordination between macroeconomic policies had occurred. Throughout this discussion, it should be remembered that the three major macroeconomic policy instruments we will discuss—fiscal, monetary, and supply-side policies—are not mutually exclusive choices. They are all ingredients in the same stew, but their differing proportions can have important consequences on the economic behavior they induce.

The Goals of Macroeconomic Policy

Macroeconomic policy has two broad, major purposes. First, it seeks to promote economic stability in place of widely fluctuating economic conditions. The period from the boom year of 1929 to the deep depression year of 1932 will illustrate the kinds of fluctuations that macroeconomic periods are designed to prevent. In 1929, the GNP was $214.2 billion; in 1932, it dropped to $153.8 billion. Private domestic investment in new plant, facilities, and so on declined from $42.9 billion in 1929 to a paltry $5.3 billion in 1932. Automobile production in 1932 was one-quarter what it was in 1929. The American economy had suffered similar sharp fluctuations throughout its history, although the depression that began in 1929 was the most severe. Macroeconomic policies have been, in part, designed to prevent a recurrence of this pattern. Since the end of World War II, the American economy has experienced ups and downs, but none has been as abrupt as earlier business cycles. To that extent, postwar macroeconomic policies have been successful and deserve the synonym stabilization policies.

Of course, stabilization at very low levels of GNP and employment is not desirable economic performance. Macroeconomic policies are also directed toward economic improvement as well as economic stability. By the later stages of World War II, many policymakers had developed a sufficient amount of confidence in such policies to formulate new goals for the federal government. The results are embodied in the Employment Act of 1946. Institutionally, the act created the Council of Economic Advisers in the executive branch and the Joint Economic Committee, composed of eight senators and eight members of the House of Representatives, in Congress. Substantively, it greatly enlarged the macroeconomic responsibilities of the federal government by requiring it "to promote maximum employment, production, and purchasing power." The act did not, however, specify the means and policies that should be used to meet these goals. Nor did it specify which economic problems (other than unemployment) the federal government should try hardest to correct; for example, the act does not mention price inflation. Thus, the act's principal effect was not to define policy but rather to confirm the federal government's commitment to macroeconomic policymaking. In the postwar era, the three major types of macroeconomic policies were used jointly to attempt to achieve the goals of the Employment Act of 1946.

Fiscal Policy

The Theory of Fiscal Policy In order to understand the significance of fiscal policy, one must appreciate economic orthodoxy prior to the rise of fiscal policy that was introduced by John Maynard Keynes and others. Strange as it may seem today, most orthodox economists then believed in a concept known as **Say's law.** Jean Baptiste Say (1767–1832) argued (erroneously) that the aggregate (total) demand for goods and services in a society will grow fast

Say's law: The prediction that free-market economic systems will reach equilibrium as aggregate supply "creates" sufficient demand to absorb and encourage economic expansion.

enough to absorb the increase in supply resulting from the growth of resources and advances in industrial technology (because no one would produce without an intention to consume or invest the proceeds). At the risk of oversimplification, Say's law held that supply creates its own demand. If 10,000 units are produced, then 10,000 units will be consumed. In this view, the equilibrium mechanism that leads to adjustment is price. If units are not being sold, the price must be reduced to achieve sales. Precisely the same formula was applied to labor. If unemployment exists, the "price" of labor (wages and salaries) must be reduced to achieve equilibrium. Therefore, the orthodox economists opposed government meddling with the natural equilibrium of the economic world.

In a complex, brilliant new theory of economic equilibrium, John Maynard Keynes refuted the older theory. We will summarize several of Keynes's views and policy prescriptions that relate to modern fiscal policy. First, he noted that even if prices and wages were flexible in response to supply-demand conditions, unemployment and an economic depression could persist for a long period because unemployment and low wages would reduce aggregate demand, which was already too low, even further. This, in turn, would give producers a disincentive to produce more, which in turn would lead to futher joblessness, lower demand, and so on. The upturn would begin only when stocks of existing goods were sold and producers had an incentive to increase their production. Thus, unemployment can be long-term (as it indeed was during the Great Depression), and equilibrium can be achieved at very low levels of output. Say's law might bring the economy back into full-employment equilibrium only in the long run, and, as Keynes observed, "in the long run we are all dead."

From the foregoing, Keynes deduced that there are many points of equilibria (where demand equals supply) in an economy, and these are a reflection of total output. In one of his famous formulations, Keynes concluded that $Y = C + I$, where Y is total output, C is consumption expenditures, and I is investment expenditures (e.g., savings or purchases of securities). This formulation, in turn, leads to two questions. What determines consumption and investment, and what can be done to influence the level of consumption and investment? The first question is properly discussed within the field of economics, although Keynes's answers have important policy consequences. The second question is within the framework of our discussion, because the answers provided by Keynes and his followers are the basis of fiscal policy. If policies can be devised to affect total output, they will also affect the level of employment. One of the policy prescriptions designed to affect total output is **fiscal policy**—changes in aggregate government expenditures and/or taxes.

fiscal policy: A policy that attempts to manage the economy by manipulating government spending or taxation.

To understand fiscal policy, we must accept the basic Keynesian formulation: if total output is falling because of insufficient consumption or investment in the private sector, higher spending in the public sector can compensate for it. Thus, government spending can be used to compensate for weaknesses in consumer spending and business investment. In order to effect such policies, the Keynesians had to demonstrate the fallacy of composition (i.e., "What is true for a part is true for the whole"). A governmental budget should not be viewed in the same light as the budget of a household or a private business (see Table 12-3). Budgets in the private sector should not be in deficit. A business should not spend more than its income—at least not for very long, because its objective is profit. In contrast, fiscal policy does not recommend a balanced government budget every year. Rather, it calls for a government deficit during periods of economic slowdown. Government should spend more than it takes in during such periods because it is precisely then that public spending must compensate for the weakness in private-sector consumption and investment expenditures. During periods of economic expansion, the theory calls for a budget surplus. Thus, according to the theory, over the long run of the business cycle, the budget is balanced.

Table 12-3 shows the changes in how the federal government spent money from 1981 (the last year of President Carter's budget) through 1985 (as pro-

TABLE 12-3
FEDERAL SPENDING, 1981–1985

	Budget Outlays ($ billions)				
Category	1981	1982	1983	1984	1985
National defense	$159.7	$187.4	$210.5	$237.5	$270.0
International affairs	11.3	10.1	9.0	13.5	17.5
General science, space, technology	6.4	7.1	7.7	8.3	8.8
Energy	10.3	4.7	4.0	3.5	3.1
Natural resources, environment	13.6	13.0	12.7	12.3	11.3
Agriculture	5.5	14.9	22.2	10.7	14.3
Commerce, housing credit	4.0	3.9	4.4	3.8	1.1
Transportation	23.4	20.6	21.4	26.1	27.1
Community, regional development	9.4	7.2	6.9	7.6	7.6
Education, jobs, social services	31.4	26.3	26.6	28.7	27.9
Health	26.9	27.4	28.7	30.7	32.9
Social security, Medicare	178.7	202.5	223.3	240.2	260.3
Income security	85.5	92.1	106.2	96.0	114.4
Veterans' benefits, services	23.0	24.0	24.8	25.8	26.7
Administration of justice	4.8	4.7	5.1	6.0	6.1
General government	4.4	4.5	4.8	5.7	5.7
General-purpose fiscal assistance	6.9	6.4	6.5	6.7	6.7
Interest	68.7	85.0	89.8	108.2	116.1
Undistributed offsetting receipts	− 16.5	− 13.3	− 18.6	− 17.5	− 35.3
Total[a]	657.2	728.4	796.0	853.8	925.5

[a]Numbers may not sum due to rounding.

Source: *National Journal,* February 4, 1984, p. 217.

posed by the Reagan administration). These figures are for outlays, or money actually spent, and they reveal the large-scale effects of the "Reagan revolution" on spending programs.

The Methods of Fiscal Policy We will turn later to the political dimensions of fiscal policy, because it is clear that the prescription of a budgetary surplus during times of economic expansion has not been rigidly followed (Table 12-3). For now, let us continue the examination of the general outlines of fiscal policy. First, it is clear that two fiscal policy methods may affect the economy. Taxes may be raised or lowered, and aggregate government spending may be raised or lowered (or both). Three factors, each involving the application of values, generally determine whether taxes or expenditures should be the principal instrument at any particular time. First, increasing government expenditures rather than reducing taxes implies a choice in the composition of goods and services in a society. Increased expenditures favor public goods (parks, national defense, and so on), whereas reduced taxes favor private goods (because consumers will be left with more of their income). Second, tax cuts tend to favor income groups in the middle and upper tax brackets, whereas expenditures favor the groups and sectors that receive government benefits. Thus, expenditures for defense favor workers and firms in that industrial sector, and higher welfare payments aid the poor. Third, programs that increase expenditures are more reliable than tax cuts to increase demand, because the government controls the former and individuals and business firms can exercise a great deal of discretion (consuming, saving, or moving funds out of the country) in the latter case.

To some extent, fiscal policy operates independently of the specific policy choices discussed thus far because *automatic stabilizers* are important components of it. These are features that automatically tend to promote a budget deficit in periods of economic decline and a budget surplus in periods of

TYPICAL KEY ECONOMIC INDICATORS

Economic policymakers use data such as the following to measure the performance of the economy.

1. Automobile sales
2. Capacity utilization (the proportion of total industrial production capacity that is actually being used)
3. Consumer Price Index
4. Durable goods orders
5. Employment
6. Housing starts
7. Industrial production
8. Inventories
9. Money supply (e.g., total currency and checking deposits)
10. Personal income
11. Productivity
12. Real gross national product
13. Retail sales
14. Savings rate
15. Weekly unemployment claims

economic expansion. For example, during boom times, individual and family income tends to rise, placing more and more taxpayers in higher income brackets under the progressive tax system. Thus, government income tax receipts tend to rise more rapidly than incomes, aiding the formation of a budget surplus. Similarly, because corporate income tends to rise during expansionary periods and decline during periods of economic contraction, corporate profit taxes also act as an automatic stabilizer. Finally, the unemployment compensation system also operates as an automatic stabilizer because during expansionary periods, when employment is high, government receipts are high, but when a contraction occurs unemployment will rise, receipts will be lower, and payouts to the unemployed will increase. We must be careful to view these stabilizers as simply tendencies, not as mechanisms that automatically put the economic system in full adjustment. In fact, during the 1970s, they proved to be of limited significance in stabilizing the economy.

The Reality of Fiscal Policy   Full-scale fiscal policy has never been tried. The principal economic problem during most of the period following World War II has not been a sustained and deep contraction of the type that occurred from 1929 to 1939, when one-quarter of the work force was unemployed in some periods, but growth in total output, accompanied by relatively low levels of unemployment and price inflation. Yet in most of those years in which the theory of fiscal policy called for budget surpluses, the budget was, in fact, still in deficit. The continuing deficits into the 1980s stemmed from the political aspects of fiscal policy, which the original economic theorists sometimes ignored. Specifically, presidents and legislators tend to favor spending programs that will attract support for them by the groups rewarded. Similarly, candidates for office generally want to avoid increasing taxes. Furthermore, when groups have become the beneficiaries of an expenditure program, it is politically difficult to dismantle or reduce the program in the face of the affected groups' wrath. For these reasons, even though most elected officials pronounce their support of a balanced budget or reduced expenditures generally, there has been a tendency for the budget deficit to increase over time.

In brief, some commentators term actual fiscal policy *one-way fiscal policy* because government has made little or no attempt to create a budget surplus during expansionary periods. They point, for example, to the period of 1967–1978, when larger deficits were consistently produced during the two years preceding a presidential election than in the two years following it, as evidence of the primarily political motivation of fiscal policy. But what is wrong with the continual budget deficits? In order to answer this question, we must look at the ways in which government expenditures are met: through taxes, borrowing from private investors, and creating money.

Increasing taxes, as we have seen, is politically unpopular. Borrowing is undertaken by the Department of the Treasury through the sale of government securities. It offers these securities for sale to private investors in securities markets in much the same way that corporations offer their new issues of stocks and bonds. However, private corporations are constrained in the interest rates they can offer to private investors by their probable future earnings. Government is not so limited and can therefore offer its securities at rates sufficiently attractive to guarantee their sale. Accordingly, when this method is used to finance the budget deficit, there is a tendency to both bid up interest rates and to crowd out the sale of private-sector securities that would be used for productive investment and growth. In turn, the rise in interest rates tends to provide firms with an incentive to defer new investment and the crowding-out effect will simply prevent new investment, especially in high-risk activities frequently on the technological frontier. In any event, government borrowing tends to retard private-sector development, and as the deficits become larger the adverse impact becomes greater. This leads to money creation, the third method of paying for budget expenditures. This will more properly be discussed under the second macroeconomic policy category.

Monetary Policy

Credit is the lifeblood of a complex capitalist society. It is obvious that there would be few transactions in American society if barter—the direct exchange of goods and services for other goods and services—were the sole means of conducting them. Few people would be able to walk into a supermarket and exchange some product or service for what the supermarket sells. Accordingly, in our transactions we pay either through money (a medium of exchange that serves as a common accounting unit) or credit (a promise to pay in the future). At one level, the difference between money and credit is clear. When you

Many people consider the New York Stock Exchange to be the principal barometer of American economic life. (© Joel Gordon 1981)

purchase a car with cash, you have parted with money. When you sign a note promising to pay the seller in two years, you have entered into a credit arrangement. When you borrow money from a bank and pay the automobile seller with that amount, both money and credit are involved. However, in the modern world, with its proliferation of payment mechanisms, the distinction becomes increasingly fuzzy. A check is both an accepted means of payment and a promise to pay. A credit card is both an accepted means of payment and a promise to pay the issuing bank what you owe at some future time. In short, neither money nor credit is what it seems to be.

Monetary policy, at the simplest level, concerns government manipulation of the complex jumble of activities involving money and credit in order to achieve certain macroeconomic ends. The principal actors in monetary policy—the Federal Reserve Board, its subsidiary institutions, other financial agencies (including the Treasury Department), and the nation's banks—are quite different from the cast in fiscal policy—the executive branch (principally the OMB, Treasury Department, and Council of Economic Advisers) and Congress. In short, we elect some of the principal actors in fiscal policy, but those who make monetary policy are much less constrained by the electoral process.

monetary policy: Government policy that attempts to influence the economy by manipulating the money supply and the availability of credit.

The Role of Banks   The first step in understanding monetary policy involves looking at the practice and structure of banking, its governmental control, and the ways in which money is created. Contemporary banks perform a variety of functions (some even operate travel agencies), but their major economic function is to see that money and credit are not hoarded but rather used in investment and consumption—in order to make a profit, of course. In performing these tasks, banks undertake a number of central activities. First, they accept deposits from customers that are repayable, either on demand (e.g., a checking account) or at a designated time (a certificate of deposit). Second, banks extend credit to borrowers by lending them money or promising to extend them credit in the future. Third, they transfer payments on order of their client-depositors to others designated by these clients. A check, for example, is an order by its writer to his or her bank to pay a sum of money to another party. Since credit, money, saving, and borrowing play such a critical role in a modern economy, it is obvious that banks are extremely important institutions and that their actions can have a major impact on general economic behavior.

The watershed event in the history of banking policy was the establishment in 1694 of the Bank of England—the world's second national bank. The Bank of England was empowered not only to issue bank notes that could be used as money but also to issue notes in excess of the deposits it held. This made possible a large increase in the money supply and consequently a large increase in the amount of credit for economic activity. The mechanism for this vast expansion was the *reserve ratio,* under which banks need to have on hand only a proportion of the cash and other reserves that would be needed to pay all depositors simultaneously (a highly unlikely event). The Bank of England established the precedent that characterizes all modern banking while at the same time it provided government with an important instrument to control the supply of credit in the society by raising or lowering reserve requirements.

The Bank of England also instituted another important feature of the modern banking system: centralization and integration. Most other industries consist of units that compete with one another, but banking combines competition with a set of cooperative institutions and instruments in which a central bank sits at the apex. Thus, banks frequently borrow money from one another and maintain clearinghouses which settle accounts between themselves and their customers. A pays B with a check drawn on the X Bank. B deposits the check in the Y Bank, which transmits it to a clearinghouse for payment by the X Bank, which in turn debits A's account. At the top of the system in the United States is the Federal Reserve System. The significance of this structure is that the apex institution makes rules and regulations affecting the entire system. The general structure of government banking control is relatively simple in many countries, but for historical and political reasons, in the United States it is most complex. The Federal Reserve Board (FRB) is the most important part of the structure, but all the other parts have some impact on the practice of banking and monetary policy.

The Federal Reserve System   To explain the role of the Federal Reserve System, we begin with the fact that, in some respects, government control over banking mirrors the federal system of government. Every bank must be chartered in order to lawfully operate. Some banks are chartered by state banking agencies; others are chartered nationally by the Office of the Comptroller of the Currency, created in 1863 as a division of the Treasury Department. Banks will sometimes move from a state system to the national system, and vice versa. The reasons for these movements stem from the restrictions and opportunities that banks see in the respective systems. The Comptroller and each of the states have established different rules about bank examinations and reports, reserve requirements, the establishment of branches, mergers with other banks and other types of companies, and other matters.

At the national level, the Comptroller of the Currency was only the first of many banking agencies. Even after its establishment, banks continued to fail in large numbers, erasing the deposits of large numbers of people, and financial panics frequently gripped the nation. Things came to a head in the Panic of 1907, during which the banking and stock market systems were in crisis. In response, Congress created in 1914 the Federal Reserve System, consisting of the Board of Governors of the Federal Reserve System (or Federal Reserve Board, FRB), under which were twelve regional Federal Reserve banks, located in the major financial centers of the United States. All national banks were required to join the Federal Reserve bank in whose districts they were located, and many state banks were induced to join by a combination of mechanisms designed to provide rapid credit to banks and by liberal reserve and lending requirements. Although the prevention of bank failures through the rapid injection of federal reserve credit provided the initial impetus for the creation of the Federal Reserve System, during the 1920s the set of macroeconomic techniques known as monetary policy began to be devised. As the FRB seized more and more power from the Federal Reserve banks, and as experience sharpened its ability, devising monetary policy became its most important function. At this point, then, many bank practices were jointly controlled either by a state regulatory agency and the FRB or two national-level agencies, depending upon where the bank's charter was taken out. Furthermore, many banks (principally smaller ones) chose not to join the Federal Reserve System.

Other Banking Institutions and Monetary Policy Even though bank safety provided the impetus for the creation of the Federal Reserve System in 1914, bank failures—mostly of small banks—reached record highs during the 1920s. The number of bank failures that began to occur with the onset of the Great Depression in 1929 wiped out the savings of millions of depositors. This led to a series of new banking statutes during the early years of the New Deal and the establishment of a third federal banking agency: the Federal Deposit Insurance Corporation (FDIC), whose principal function was to insure deposits up to a certain amount per account. Member banks are assessed a levy, which is put into the insurance fund. If a member bank fails, depositors are paid up to the insured amount. All member banks of the Federal Reserve System were required to participate in the FDIC system, and nonmember state banks were invited to do so; more than 90 percent of all commercial banks are now included in the system. In exchange for membership, banks submit to FDIC supervision over such matters as reserves and mergers as well as a host of other regulations. Thus, since 1934, it has been possible for a bank to submit to simultaneous supervision by up to three federal agencies or one state and two federal agencies.

Futher complicating the picture is the presence of other financial institutions that perform some of the functions of commercial banks and must submit to other federal and state authorities. Foremost among them have been savings-and-loan associations and mutual savings banks, whose principal business is making loans for single-family homes. At the national level, the activities of these institutions are regulated by the Federal Home Loan Bank Board (FHLBB), an independent regulatory agency. Their deposit insurance, corresponding to the FDIC system, is provided by the Federal Savings and Loan Insurance Corporation (FSLIC). State regulatory bodies also make rules affecting state-chartered mutual saving banks and savings-and-loan associations. Finally, credit unions, which are financial cooperatives owned by their members, are also regulated and insured at the national level.

Although the functional division between these various types of financial institutions was sharp and clear during the 1930s, the lines between them blurred during the 1960s as each type of institution began to compete in the territory of the others. For example, savings-and-loan associations, which had been forbidden to offer checking accounts, began to offer them, although under a different name and with some minor legal differences. The uncertainty created by the new forms of competition led Congress to enact the 1980 Depository Institutions Deregulation and Monetary Control Act, which set up yet another federal agency—the Depository Institutions' Deregulation Committee, consisting of members of other federal financial agencies, whose function was to devise rules that would settle conflicts among the various types of banking institutions. The 1980 statute also strengthened the powers of the Federal Reserve Board to make monetary policy, for, in the maze of conflicts among agencies, institutions, and other interests, the ability to effectively make monetary policy is paramount.

The Methods of Monetary Policy   In order to understand how the FRB manipulates banks, it is first necessary to understand the process of money creation. Money, as we observed earlier, is more than the coins and dollar bills in circulation; checks and other financial instruments serve the same principal purpose as money. When you go to most stores, you may purchase the goods offered for sale by paying cash or by check. Again, you may take a check given to you and demand payment in cash for it. For these reasons, checks and similar financial instruments (called *demand deposits*) are included with cash within the money supply under one definition of money called *M1*. There are other definitions of money that include other financial instruments and types of accounts, but we will not be concerned with them here. When we combine the idea of M1 with the idea of reserve requirements, we will see how the money supply expands and contracts. For example, suppose you deposit $100 in your checking account at the Porkville National Bank. The bank, with a 20 percent reserve requirement, can lend $80 of that amount. You still have your $100, and someone else has $80. The money supply has been increased to $180. The generation of money, however, does not stop with a single transaction. Suppose the person who borrowed $80 buys a new lamp from the ABC Company. The company deposits the check in the Beeftown State Bank, which can, in turn, lend $64 based on that deposit. The money supply has been further increased. The process of money creation is principally limited by three factors: (1) someone in the chain might decide to hold money rather than deposit it in a bank, (2) banks might be unable to find borrowers for all that they are permitted to lend, and (3) government policy.

It is the last factor that is most pertinent to monetary policy, for the FRB (or other banking agencies) can increase or decrease the money supply by decreasing or increasing the reserve requirements. In our example in the last paragraph, a 10 percent reserve requirement, rather than 20 percent, would have permitted the Porkville National Bank to lend $90, not $80, based on your original $100 deposit. The increase in the money supply through all subsequent transactions would have been larger. Although the FRB has changed reserve requirements in an effort to control the money supply, in recent years, for technical reasons, reserve policy has not been an effective tool in precisely controlling and predicting the future money supply. Instead, the FRB has come to rely more on open market operations and interest rate manipulations.

Open market operations are conducted by the Federal Open Market Committee (FOMC), consisting of the seven FRB governors and five presidents of the Federal Reserve banks (always including the Federal Reserve Bank of New York). The FOMC meets at least once a month to make open market policy, which consists of FRB sales and purchases of federal government securities issued by the Treasury Department. When the FRB sells such securities to firms that trade in them, these firms will pay for them with checks drawn on commercial banks, whose reserves will correspondingly decline so that they will be less able to create money. When the FRB buys such securities, the opposite effect occurs as sellers deposit proceeds in commercial banks. In contrast to directly adjusting reserve requirements, which compels all member banks to abide by the new ratios, some of which might be severely strained by reserve adjustments, open-market operations accomplish the same monetary policy objectives through the mechanism of a free market.

The final set of policies available to the FRB is interest rate manipulation. It can adjust the "discount rate"—the interest rate that banks must pay for loans from the Federal Reserve System. However, these funds usually constitute less than 1 percent of the loanable funds of commercial banks. Consequently, changes in the discount rate may not have a significant impact on the interest rates banks charge their customers. The FRB is under no legal obligation to lend funds to member banks, and they, in turn, have alternative sources of loans—most importantly, the federal funds market. (If bank A requires funds and bank B has spare funds, A borrows from B in the federal funds market.) Although the FRB is empowered to regulate federal funds rates (and has occasionally done so), it is usually reluctant to tamper with this important market mechanism for the interbank transfer of funds. Furthermore, open-market operations have an impact on the interest rates banks charge by increasing or decreasing the supply of loanable funds.

Through these mechanisms, particularly open-market operations, the FRB makes monetary policy, one of the principal advantages of which, in comparison to fiscal policy, is the speed with which policy may be changed. A meeting of the FOMC, rather than the full-scale enactment of a new statute, is the principal way in which monetary policy is made. To many policymakers, it complements fiscal policy. In times of economic stagnation, expansionary monetary policy can increase the availability of loanable funds and thus stimulate business activity. In inflationary times, restrictive monetary policy can make money more scarce, thereby causing interest rates to rise. In turn, this will lead business firms to forgo less profitable investment opportunities. Consumers, too, will forgo certain purchases because of the higher interest rates. This reduces aggregate demand and, therefore, inflationary pressures.

Although in this view monetary policy is a complement to fiscal policy, some economists known as "monetarists" would place almost exclusive reliance on monetary policy. In their opinion, an excess supply of money generated by expansionary monetary policy provides people with an incentive to buy, because their dollars are continually losing value, whereas restrictive money policy raises the value of money and consequently leads to saving rather than spending. According to this view of some economists (led by Milton Friedman), monetary policy provides the dominant and most reliable tool to guide economic behavior.

Supply-Side Policy

Although fiscal-monetarists and strict monetarists had reason to be confident during the first twenty-five years of the post–World War II era, their confidence began to slide during the 1970s. Economic growth rates declined, and while inflation rates during some periods in the 1970s reached new postwar highs, so did unemployment rates. Capital investment rates in new plant and equipment declined. Productivity growth per man-hour began to drop precipitously after 1967, contributing to the increasing costs of producing goods and services. The confidence in economic growth and better living standards that had characterized much of the postwar era gave rise to despondency about the future of the economy and shook the forefront positions of fiscal and monetary policy in the government's macroeconomic tool chest. In the late 1970s, policymakers began to listen to theorists who argued that primary attention should be paid to problems of supply—that is, reducing the costs of goods and services and increasing their supply.

supply-side policy:
An economic program that is based on the assumption that tax cuts will generate savings, investment, and economic growth.

Supply-side policy is not a new weapon in the macroeconomic policy arsenal. During many American wars, for example, the federal government instituted rationing and production controls to assure the orderly supply of goods and services in the economy. But a primary emphasis on policies that will affect the aggregate supply and cost of goods and services as well as their composition is new in a peacetime American economy. As the name suggests, supply-side policies focus on the long-run relationship between governmental actions and the supply of goods and services (remember that Keynesian policies are intended to stimulate demand, primarily in the short run). In particular, supply-side policymakers emphasize the effects of government taxing policies on how people and firms produce, work, save, and invest.

One supply-side approach advocates the use of selective tax incentives to encourage investment in new plant and equipment, research and innovation, and to make the production and distribution of goods more efficient. For example, supply-siders point to the investment tax credit of 1962, under which business firms were granted a credit against their tax liabilities for amounts invested in plant and equipment that would improve productivity and create jobs. At about the same time, the Kennedy administration accelerated depreciation (the time period during which assets could be deducted from corporate taxes as a cost) in order to further encourage investment. These selective tax incentives did trigger a flurry of new activity, but contemporary critics of selective tax incentives claim that particular economic conditions existed during the Kennedy years. The budget deficit was much lower than it has been since; consequently, selective tax incentives in the form of increased budget deficits would exceed the benefits from new investment. Furthermore, these critics argue, interest rates were much lower in the years of the Kennedy administration. Since the 1970s, much higher interest rates have deterred the borrowing required for much capital investment, notwithstanding the tax incentives.

In the 1980s, the most important recommendations of supply-side economists have been general *across-the-board tax cuts.* According to proponents of "supply-side fiscalism," lower tax rates are successful not because they stimulate demand but because they stimulate individuals to work harder, invest and save more, and produce with greater efficiency. Because the personal payoff to each of us is greater when taxes are lowered, we have a stronger incentive to engage in income-producing activity, or to save and invest money. Conversely, we have a strong disincentive to engage in additional productive effort if the tax rate on the additional income earned (the "marginal tax rate") is very high. The supply-side fiscalists point to the Revenue Act of 1964, which cut taxes for all individuals, to support their views. The tax cut was followed by an investment boom and fuller employment. In all, the overall impact of the 1964 tax cut lasted through 1966 and is estimated to have resulted in a $36.2 billion gain in the GNP. But critics argued that the same impact would not recur for the same reasons that selective tax cuts would not be as effective as they were during the Kennedy years.

Supply-side fiscalists also believe that an important consequence of general tax cuts and the resulting increase in economic output would be an increase in government tax revenues. The concept is represented by a Laffer curve (Figure 12-1), named after economist Arthur Laffer who popularized it. (The

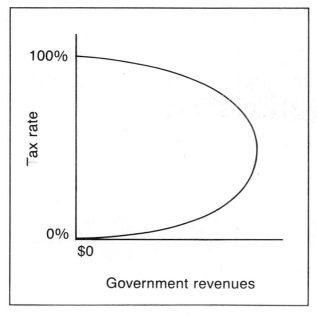

FIGURE 12-1
A Hypothetical
Laffer Curve

idea that a tax cut could increase tax revenues is not new, however; both Adam Smith and Alexander Hamilton discussed it.[11]) Clearly, when the tax rate is 0 percent, government tax revenues are nil. When the tax rate is 100 percent, people have no reason to work, and without production, the government has nothing to tax. Unfortunately, no one knows what the optimum tax rate is (i.e., where to find the rightmost point on the curve in Figure 12-1), or whether the United States is currently in a position where a reduction in tax rates will lead to an increase in revenues.

During the presidential campaign of 1980, candidate Ronald Reagan urged the voters to reject the traditional macroeconomic policies of Keynesian fiscalism and monetary controls in favor of the teachings of supply-side economists such as George Gilder and Arthur Laffer. In 1981, the new Reagan administration proposed a four-part economic plan (dubbed "Reaganomics") consisting of (1) regulatory reform, (2) a transfer of many social services from the federal government to state and local governments, (3) a reduction in the federal budget, especially in social benefit and entitlement programs, and (4) a three-year, 25 percent personal income tax cut, combined with more generous depreciation allowances and tax credits for businesses. Only the fourth element was based on supply-side economics. Many supply-siders recognized that the expected increase in government revenues would probably not appear immediately after reducing taxes, and the growth in federal deficits (Table 12-4) was definitely not part of the supply-side plan.

TABLE 12-4
THE FEDERAL BUDGET AND ECONOMIC GROWTH

Year	Deficit (−) or Surplus (+) (in $ billions)	% Change in GNP	Year	Deficit (−) or Surplus (+) (in $ billions)	% Change in GNP
1960	+ 0.3	+2.2	1972	− 23.4	+5.4
1961	− 3.4	+2.6	1973	− 14.9	+5.4
1962	− 7.1	+5.4	1974	− 6.1	−0.6
1963	− 4.8	+4.0	1975	− 53.2	−1.1
1964	− 5.9	+4.9	1976	− 73.7	+5.1
1965	− 1.6	+5.7	1977	− 53.6	+5.3
1966	− 3.8	+2.6	1978	− 59.2	+4.8
1967	− 8.7	+4.4	1979	− 40.2	+2.8
1968	−25.2	+4.4	1980	− 73.8	−0.3
1969	+ 3.2	+2.3	1981	− 78.9	+2.6
1970	− 2.8	−0.2	1982	−127.9	−2.0
1971	−23.0	+3.2	1983	−207.8	+3.3

Sources: *Budget of the U.S. Government, Fiscal Year 1985* (Washington, D.C.: Government Printing Office, 1984), pp. 9, 59–60; *Survey of Current Business* 60 (December 1980):17; *Economic Report of the President, 1984* (Washington, D.C.: Government Printing Office, 1984), p. 222.

AMERICAN MEDIOCRITY

Americans often complain about the quality of their products, adversely comparing American products to those made in other countries, especially Japan. Evidence indicates that the public is right. There is considerable debate about whether the poor American showing stems from poor workmanship, poor management, or government policies. The following table, comparing the assembly-line defect rates per 100 units of American and Japanese refrigerators, illustrates the point.

	American	Japanese
Leaks	3.1	0.12
Electrical defects	3.3	0.12
Total defects	63.5	0.95

Source: Table from *Financial Times*, October 17, 1983.

The example of the Reagan economic plan illustrates an absolutely vital aspect of economic policymaking, and of all public policy: a policy is rarely an only child. Most policies have twins, older siblings, and other more distant relatives. Policymakers usually have more than one tool at their disposal, so they use many or all of them; they pursue more than one goal, and often the goals conflict; and there is usually more than one set of policymakers. This combination of actors, goals, and tools makes economic policy difficult to perform as well as to analyze. Thus, as in so many other areas, the United States has found itself in a policy quandary in the 1980s in the area of economic policy. Many of the policy tools—subsidies, public enterprise, regulation, and macroeconomic policy—are blunt, and the interaction of the public and private sectors is so complicated that it is usually impossible to know the precise impacts of any particular government action. But the inexactness of the art of economic policymaking is only one part of the contemporary quandary. The other side, to which we have already alluded, is politics. Economic policies are intended to affect income and wealth, and there are always groups who benefit from the existing situation and others who benefit from changes.

We conclude this chapter with a brief discussion of a general economic policy topic that tries to integrate many of the tools we have discussed in this chapter. Like supply-side economics, "industrial policy" is not new, but it has received more attention in the early 1980s as public officials sought new solutions to old and new problems.

ECONOMIC POLICY IN THE 1980s

In this chapter, we have examined a variety of tools that American government uses to pursue the economic goals of growth and stability. The political system tries to finetune the economy with subsidies and regulations, while at the same

industrial policy:
Economic policy
intended to increase
the efficiency and
competitiveness of
American businesses.

reindustrialization:
The shift from
traditional
"smokestack"
industries to such
"high tech" industries
as computers and
telecommunications.

time it uses the blunt techniques of macroeconomic policy to provide coarse corrections to the overall economy. We have also pointed out that these efforts not only overlap but also interact, sometimes with contradictory effects. Finally, we have seen that economic policy does not stand alone but is shaped by political and social interests as they try to increase their personal welfare or their visions of social justice. All of these points are well-illustrated by the conflict over **industrial policy.** The term is not easily definable, because it means different things to different people. To some, it implies no more than a national dialogue on how to help American industries; to others, it entails an increasingly active role on the part of the national government in supporting specific industries.

In its general sense, industrial policy is intended to increase the competitiveness of American industries in the world market and to assist industrial sectors (e.g., transportation, manufacturing, services) in making the transition from one era to another. Thus, discussions of industrial policy in the 1980s usually involve **reindustrialization** (i.e., the shift from traditional "smokestack" industries to "high-tech" industries such as information processing and robotics). Yet the United States has always had some sort of industrial policy. In this chapter, we have seen how subsidies were used to assist the transition from horses and barges to railroads and to increase the productivity and stability of the agricultural sector. Public enterprise (e.g., the TVA) was used by government to provide needed services when the private sector could not or would not. Regulations have been used to protect and promote industries, and macroeconomic policies have been shaped by the need of American industries for an environment of stability and growth.

However, in recent years advocates of industrial policy—spurred largely by the apparent successes of industrial planning and support in Japan—have begun to press for more coordination of these various techniques. Critics of current business policy have pointed out that the United States is the only advanced industrial nation without a central statistical office for gathering information on economic and social trends. They have noted the decline of employment in traditional industries such as steel and automobiles, the increasing importance of the information, energy, finance, and health-care industries, and the lack of any American policy to help workers follow the demand for labor. In addition, critics have found contradictions in American policy, such as the attempts by the American government to increase the international competitiveness of its computer industry while simultaneously restraining the growth of IBM through antitrust lawsuits.

The wide range of solutions that have been proposed illustrates the complexity of the economic policy arena. Subsidy policies have been suggested to provide research and development assistance to businesses (either directly or through tax incentives), to provide tax investment credits on the purchase of new, more efficient equipment, and to provide loans from a new industrial development bank (perhaps resembling the New Deal era's Reconstruction

Finance Corporation). Public enterprise techniques have also been suggested, although there is a traditional American reluctance to massive shifts from private to public enterprise; the city of Chicago has proposed a for-profit municipal corporation to provide venture capital to help new companies, provided that they locate in Chicago. The emphasis on regulation has primarily been on reducing it in order to allow companies to increase their productivity and to allow more cooperative ventures (especially in research and development) without running afoul of antitrust laws.

In addition, macroeconomic tools have been suggested within the broad framework of industrial policy. For example, "indicative planning" (patterned largely on the French and Japanese economies) is based on the premise that firms can plan in the short run based on their individual market projections but not in the long run. Accordingly, a government agency charged with determining long-range trends in products, processes, and markets develops a program, which it proposes to industry. For the most part, the long-range forecasting has been formulated with the participation of industry. Japan's success in producing and selling electronic products, small automobiles, and many other advanced technological products has been attributed to the guidance provided by industrial policy. Government does not force companies to move in the directions it views favorably. Rather, it encourages cooperation by providing tax incentives or subsidies, by sharing the fruits of government-sponsored research, and in other ways induces the firm to move in the "correct" directions.

Critics of indicative planning claim that it will not work in the United States. American culture is unique; business and government in the United States are usually antagonists and not collaborators, as in Japan. Moreover, Japanese planners have made big mistakes, such as protecting agriculture and banking, and the British-French supersonic transport project lost billions of dollars for its government supporters. Clearly, the American process of picking the "winners" worthy of government support would also largely be political; declining industries would tend to be protected, not for competitive reasons but because of political pressures from business and labor interests.

The role of the political system in making economic policies is vital to both the successes and failures of any past or proposed industrial policies. After all, one of the major functions of politics is to reconcile the beliefs of disparate groups of Americans as they make private and collective decisions not only about increasing the net social welfare but also about improving their perceptions of social justice. Because industrial policy will affect the allocation of opportunities and wealth among citizens and groups, it is not "purely" economic policy. In the next chapter, we will examine more closely a variety of other governmental policies that are intended to distribute rights and resources, but it is important to remember the social policy implications of most government actions.

NOTES

[1]Arthur M. Schlesinger, Jr., "Neo-Conservatism and the Class Struggle," *Wall Street Journal,* June 2, 1981, p. 22.

[2]Everett Carl Ladd, "205 and Going Strong," *Public Opinion,* June/July 1981, pp. 7–12.

[3]See the discussion in Part II of Frederick D. Sturdivant and Larry M. Robinson, eds., *The Corporate Social Challenge,* rev. ed. (Homewood, Illinois: Irwin, 1981).

[4]Adam Smith, *The Wealth of Nations,* Book 5, Chapter 2, Part I.

[5]Ibid., Book 4, Chapter 2.

[6]Ibid., Book 4, Chapter 7, Part III.

[7]Munn v. Illinois, 94 U.S. 113 (1877).

[8]Wabash, St. Louis & Pacific Railway Co. v. Illinois, 118 U.S. 557 (1886).

[9]U.S. v. International Harvester, 274 U.S. 693 (1927); U.S. v. Aluminum Co. of America, 148 F. 2d 416 (1945).

[10]Standard Oil Co. of N.J. v. U.S., 221 U.S. 1 (1911).

[11]Smith, *The Wealth of Nations,* Book 5, Chapter 2, Part II; Alexander Hamilton, *The Federalist,* no. 21.

BIBLIOGRAPHY

Bartlett, Bruce. *Reaganomics.* Westport, Connecticut: Arlington House, 1981. A readable introduction to the Reagan administration's approach to supply-side macroeconomic policy.

Best, Michael H., and William E. Connolly. *The Political Economy,* 2nd ed. Lexington, Massachusetts: Heath, 1982. A radical leftist critique of American economic and social policy.

Carson, Robert B. *Economic Issues Today: Alternative Approaches,* 3rd ed. New York: St. Martin's, 1983. A collection of discussions of various macroeconomic and microeconomic problems, with conservative, liberal, and radical perspectives on each.

Lowi, Theodore J. *The End of Liberalism,* 2nd ed. New York: Norton, 1979. An explanation of the growth of the modern American state and the consequences of its expansion.

Mayer, Martin. *The Fate of the Dollar.* New York: Times Books, 1980. A rather conservative approach to the politics of international banking, Federal Reserve, and currency politics.

Reagan, Michael. *The Managed Economy.* New York: Oxford University Press, 1963. An excellent description of the growth of public intervention in the American economy.

Reich, Robert B. *The Next American Frontier.* New York: Times Books, 1983. A well-argued activist prescription for American industrial policy in the 1980s.

Schnitzer, Martin. *Contemporary Government and Business Relations,* 2nd ed. Chicago: Rand McNally, 1983. An excellent basic text on antitrust, social regulation, economic regulation, and other issues.

Stein, Herbert. *The Fiscal Revolution in America.* Chicago: University of Chicago Press, 1969. A history and analysis of the beginning and evolution of fiscal policy from Herbert Hoover to Lyndon Johnson.

Stone, Alan. *Regulation and Its Alternatives.* Washington, D.C.: Congressional Quarterly Press, 1982. An examination of critiques of markets and regulation, including economic, political, and legal perspectives.

Walsh, Annmarie Hauck. *The Public's Business.* Cambridge: MIT Press, 1978. A thorough study of government corporations such as the TVA and U.S. Postal Service.

Social Policy

D espite the far-reaching impact of foreign and economic policies, it is in the area of social policy that some of the most passionate political battles have been fought. We have seen that the American political system reflects a complex mixture of beliefs regarding justice, allocation, individual rights, and social obligations. When social problems arise, policymakers are forced to confront the conflicts and contradictions in the nation's basic rules and the desires of its citizens. It is in this arena that the economic goals of efficiency and net social welfare clash with the ethical goals of social justice and equity.

In this chapter, we will first examine some of the general problems that underlie the development of social policies, with particular attention to the concepts of cost, benefit, rights, and equity. Next, we will discuss the most important category of social policies: those that provide benefits to groups and individuals by (1) protecting their opportunities and choices, (2) directly transferring income or wealth to them, or (3) performing services for them. The chapter closes with a look at social regulations, which establish incentives for individuals and organizations to act in ways generally considered beneficial to all of society.

WHAT IS SOCIAL POLICY?

It is difficult to draw absolute distinctions between economic policy and social policy. Economic policy is primarily concerned with overall growth and stability, not with the distribution of resources among different groups within the population (although, of course, the impact of any economic policy will fall unevenly on different groups). For example, it is possible to adopt a tax policy that provides incentives for investment. However, because upper-income groups have more disposable income that may be used for investment purposes, they will benefit more from such a tax policy than lower-income groups, who must use their income primarily to buy food and housing, not stocks or real estate. Nevertheless, the primary purpose of such a tax policy is not to favor the rich over the poor but rather to stimulate overall economic growth.

In contrast, the immediate aim of social policy is to improve the well-being of citizens by providing every member of the community with a certain minimal standard of living and certain basic opportunities.[1] For example, the purpose of the Medicaid program is to provide a benefit in the form of medical services for lower-income persons. However, just as economic policies have social impact, social policies also have economic impact. During the 1970s, total state, local, and federal social welfare expenditures ranged from 15 to 20 percent of the GNP. The proportion of such expenditures to the total GNP is so large that a significant reduction or increase in social welfare programs can have a major impact on the economy. That is not the objective of social policy, however.

Like all governmental actions, social policies involve the allocation of costs

439

and benefits to different groups. These groups may vary from the entire population to relatively small classes of people, and some social policies are aimed at several groups or have multiple purposes. For example, environmental policies are intended to aid all air-breathers and water-drinkers—a group that includes all humans, but not business organizations such as corporations; at the same time, these policies have usually been constructed in such a way as to also protect the strength of industries. Civil-rights legislation is aimed at protecting groups of racial and other minorities, and unemployment insurance is intended to cover the relatively small class of unemployed persons. Groups need not be poor or of low social status in order to receive benefits, however. Homeowners and apartment dwellers, which include the wealthiest segments of our population, are also beneficiaries of some social policies. In short, the groups that receive benefits from social policies may be defined in almost any conceivable way.

The kinds of benefits a group receives also may be quite varied. As we saw in Chapter 1, benefits include anything that is of value to a person or organization. Some benefits are directly measurable in monetary terms—cash payments (e.g., social security), tax concessions (e.g., deductions for the blind), and services (e.g., the provision of disaster insurance)—whereas others are not. However, such benefits as the right to vote and many other civil rights cannot be translated into financial terms. Other social rights, such as the right of workers to bargain collectively through a trade union, can theoretically be translated into economic values (e.g., higher wages) but in practice are very difficult to measure.

We have also seen that the allocation of costs and benefits requires trade-offs. For example, if the government mandates stricter safety standards for automobiles, a benefit is conferred on car drivers and passengers. At the same time, however, a cost is imposed on automobile manufacturers and their customers, which is passed along in the form of higher prices. Similarly, if taxes are used to finance welfare payments to the poor, the beneficiaries will receive income that otherwise would have gone to the upper- and middle-income taxpayers who must finance the program. Again, in practice, it can be difficult to determine costs, benefits, and their balance. For example, when the 1935 National Labor Relations Act granted workers the right to determine whether or not they wanted to be represented by labor unions, the law clearly provided workers with a right or choice that did not previously exist. At one level, this provision took nothing away from management, but at another level, it reduced management's choices by reducing its opportunities to bargain with workers as individuals.

Choosing a Course of Action

Because social policies involve allocations, policymakers should try to tally the costs and benefits of any particular policy, and thereby determine whether there are cheaper alternatives by which the same or better results could be achieved. This is not an easy thing to do. In many health policies, for example, costs are measured in dollars and benefits are measured in lives saved; there is no common metric for assessing such policies. Yet sometimes there is a common metric. For example, some analysts have provided evidence that a 1962 drug law, which greatly stiffened the testing requirements for pharmaceutical manufacturers, has actually cost more lives than it has saved because it has discouraged manufacturers from the costly experiments required to test new and innovative drugs, and has greatly delayed the marketing of new drugs.[2]

The problems with cost-benefit analysis are symptomatic of the difficulties in selecting and assessing social policies. Frequently, there are alternative techniques to achieving similar results. In general, government is faced with four broad options when it seeks to address a social problem. It may (1) provide a direct benefit, (2) offer an indirect incentive to firms or persons in the private sector in order to induce them to provide others with benefits, (3) regulate firms and individuals in order to attain the benefit, or (4) do nothing and hope that the private sector will solve the problem through markets, private law, or private charity. Of course, government may devise strategies that combine these four general techniques. For example, in its effort to raise American health standards, the government (1) provides or pays for the services of physicians for the poor and aged, (2) grants tax deductions (an incentive) to individuals and firms that contribute to charities such as hospitals, (3) regulates drug companies at the national level and physicians at the state level, and yet (4) relies on private market incentives and private firms to discover and market new drugs.

The Guiding Principles of Social Policy

Equity   One of the most important concepts in the design of the American republic and its policies is **equity,** which, according to the dictionary, means "fairness, impartiality," and "evenhanded dealing" but is difficult to define precisely, and therefore difficult to apply in actual situations. Consider the following assertions. "Everyone should have an equal chance to succeed." "It is inequitable for some Americans to have huge amounts of inherited wealth while other Americans starve." Both claims include the notion of equity, but they suggest fundamentally different political choices. The first assertion prescribes **procedural equity:** fairness of opportunity. Under this principle, citizens would not be guaranteed success or security but would have a fair chance to use their skills and energies. Procedural equity implies that all parties entering a contract (e.g., a purchaser and a seller) must have access to adequate information in order to make rational choices free of coercion. It requires that restrictions be removed from those desiring employment, political office, housing, education, and so on—provided that they meet the appropriate, universally applied standards (e.g., past experience, a high-school diploma, certain reading and writing skills, or the money to pay for a home in a better neighborhood). In other words, procedural equity simply demands

equity: Fairness, justice, and impartiality.

procedural equity: Equal and fair treatment in a governmental proceeding.

Rich women, poor woman, 1943. By the mid-1980s, one percent of American families had incomes over $50,000, but had as much combined after-tax income as did most families in the bottom 20 percent. (Weegee: The Critic, 1943; David Schwartz Foundation, Inc. Purchase Fund)

substantive equity: In the formation of social policy, the requirement that some outcomes of even the fairest of procedures be prohibited if they entail unreasonable deprivation or disadvantage for some citizens.

that the game be fairly played, and public policy should go no further than to guarantee the consistent application of fair rules.

The second assertion is based on a demand for **substantive equity.** For example, some people feel that it is morally unjustifiable for the 1 percent of American families with incomes over $50,000 to have as much combined after-tax income as most families in the bottom 20 percent, regardless of how hard the rich may have worked. To insist that society prevent huge discrepancies in wealth or living standards is to demand a drastically different government role than procedural equity requires. Policies based on substantive equity would prohibit some outcomes of even the fairest contests. Examples of public policies that promote substantive equity at the expense of strict procedural fairness are the progressive income tax and affirmative action programs, which often require strict racial quotas in hiring or college placement as a means of counteracting past racial discrimination. Thus, substantive equity demands that government guarantee particular individuals or groups certain results.

It should be clear that it is exceedingly difficult to put either form of equity into practice. For example, in applying the principle of equality of opportunity, it is necessary to first decide what constitutes equality and what constitutes an opportunity. In the case of education, do we demand an equal chance for all to obtain a college education, and, if so, can we assume that all college educations are equal? Furthermore, should all high-school graduates be admitted to college, despite the fact that some have gone to inferior high schools (through no fault of their own) and are not adequately prepared? Or should we expect that college admission standards be impartially applied to all applicants, despite the fact that some (particularly those from wealthy families) went to private preparatory schools and received excellent educations?[3] Clearly, the pursuit of either procedural or substantive equity entails some very difficult choices for public officials. Thus, although debates about the goals and techniques of social policy are often phrased in terms of costs and benefits, the political aspects of policy questions are unavoidable because of the lack of consensus in the United States about the concept of equity.

Rights   Although equity is an important concept shaping social policies in the United States, it is more common to hear social policies attacked or defended on the basis of rights. This term is no easier to define than equity. There are several categories of rights. In Chapter 2, we discussed the concept of **natural rights**—those "inalienable" rights that, according to John Locke and the Declaration of Independence, are bestowed by the Creator and can never be violated justifiably. The key words in the doctrine of natural rights were *life, liberty, property,* and *the pursuit of happiness* (of course, one person's "liberty" may be another person's nuisance or trespass, and one person's "pursuit of happiness" may be another's lewdness). Fundamental to the principle of natural rights was the limited role of government, which was to be guided more by "shalt nots" than by "shalls."

Next, we can identify a group of **constitutional rights,** which can be abridged by the government only under the most unusual circumstances. These consist of the rights explicitly mentioned in the Constitution (especially the Bill of Rights) or clearly implied by the explicit rights (for example, the right to privacy and the right to travel). Again, this category of rights consists primarily of limitations on the exercise of governmental power. They are largely political rights, because they are exercised through the government.

Even from the first days of the American republic, not everyone was content with the list of natural and constitutional rights. To some dissidents, the best hope for human happiness lay in a positive role for government in promoting the welfare of citizens. Thomas Paine advocated the doctrine of **social rights** when, in 1792, he called for the establishment of a pension system, family allowances, subsidized education, and guaranteed employment. Paine's ideas were not quickly adopted. The American colonies had incorporated the English Poor Law—which sharply distinguished between the "worthy" poor (the disabled and children) and the "unworthy" (able-bodied)—and the influential Benjamin Franklin had written that ". . . if we provide encouragement for laziness, and supports for folly may we not be fighting against the order of God and Nature, which perhaps has appointed want and misery as the proper punishments for idleness and extravagance? . . ."

As we will see later in this chapter, during the nineteenth century some movement was made, especially at the state level, to provide public assistance; as the nation became more urban and the economic system more industrial, the poor began to be seen less as those from whom God's grace had been withheld and more as the victims of a harsh system.[4] Nevertheless, the idea that a citizen had a social right to some modicum of economic security grew slowly. Not until the Great Depression in the 1930s did the idea gain acceptance. Society's duty to care for the poor, even when they were "unworthy," began to imply a right of the poor to be cared for.[5]

natural rights: The doctrine that individuals have certain rights by virtue of the laws of nature, including life, liberty, and the right to hold and dispose of property.

constitutional rights: Rights mentioned or clearly implied by the Constitution.

social rights: The doctrine that people are entitled to certain minimal levels of income and security and that government is obligated to provide these benefits.

legal rights: Rights created and conferred on citizens by statutes.

Finally, in very recent years, the American political system has experienced the conversion of many social rights into **legal rights.** These are rights created and conferred on citizens by statute. Initially, government programs that provided benefits to individuals—social security, veterans' benefits, Medicare, Medicaid, food stamps, unemployment compensation, and so on—were treated as privileges that could be taken away by Congress, the courts, or administrative agencies. As early at 1931, however, the courts began to insist that recipients of such privileges could not be subjected to conditions (e.g., loss of free speech) that would otherwise be unconstitutional. In 1970, the Supreme Court ruled (in *Goldberg* v. *Kelly*) that benefits such as Aid to Families with Dependent Children (AFDC) were "entitlements . . . more like 'property' than a gratuity." Like other property (remember Locke's natural rights), benefits could not be denied without due process of law. The right to an education, a driver's license, and even a liquor license have been treated as legal rights that can be removed only by due process. Thus, in one sense, the American conception of "rights" has come full circle, with claims that the revolutionary doctrine of legal rights is rooted in the pre-American Revolution doctrine of natural rights.

In the remainder of this chapter, we will discuss social policies under the framework of two very broad categories of government action. First are social policies that are intended to provide benefits, whether directly or indirectly, to individuals and groups. These benefits can be in the form of enhanced opportunities, protection of choices, cash payments, in-kind payments, tax benefits, or a variety of services such as mass transit or education. The second category of social policies are those regulating behavior; the government requires the private sector to provide benefits through the regulatory devices of injunctions, standards, and requirements. Although these policies are also intended to create benefits, their targets are usually very large groups of people (e.g., air-breathers or consumers). Underlying all of these categories of social policies are varying and conflicting interpretations of what is equitable and what is a right. These disputes are the sources and the determinants of American social policy.

THE PROVISION OF OPPORTUNITIES AND CHOICES

The relationships among individuals in a society fall somewhere between slavery and anarchy. In a political system in which individuals have absolutely no rights, they are slaves; in a society in which all people have complete freedom from any restrictions on their choices, chaos exists. Thus, boundaries must be set, and if people are to form agreements—political or economic—everyone must understand and accept those boundaries. In the absence of a dictator, it becomes the people's collective task to determine where these boundaries are. In a large sense, that is what the Constitution does: it establishes certain basic limits and protections on rights and choices. However, it does not specify the precise rights and choices policymakers must balance as they make decisions about the complex trade-offs that social policies require.

Some of these policies are designed to protect what are commonly described as civil rights: basically, freedom from discrimination. These policies serve to prevent the restriction of choices. The concepts of liberty and procedural equity imply that individuals should be free to choose how to spend their time, money, and effort. Thus, a major category of social policy is the protection of individual choice. The state has a dual role under this mandate, however. It must avoid imposing governmental limitations on the behavior of individuals, yet it must also prevent individuals from restricting the choices of others. Clearly, this presents difficult trade-offs. To take a modern example, does an individual have the right to build a structure on his or her own property that has the side effect of blocking the sun from a neighbor's solar-power collector? In order to protect the rights of some, the government must sometimes restrict the choices of others.

Protection of the Right to Choose

The impossibility of compiling an exhaustive and precise list of the rights of Americans has shaped the development of social policies affecting the rights of citizens, and, therefore, it has influenced the ways in which we lead our lives. For example, until the Civil War, the distinction between the rights provided by the national government and those provided by state governments allowed the states to maintain slavery and impose some narrow restrictions on the freedoms of religion, press, and speech. The passage of the Thirteenth and the Fourteenth amendments to the Constitution radically changed this dual system, however. The Thirteenth Amendment prohibited slavery in all states, and the Fourteenth Amendment required that "No State shall make or enforce any law which shall abridge the privileges or immunities of citizens of the United States; nor shall any state deprive any person of life, liberty, or property, without *due process* of law; nor deny to any person within its jurisdiction the *equal protection* of the laws" (emphasis added). Although it took until the 1920s for the Supreme Court to begin exploring and applying all of the implications of the equal protection amendment, the United States now has (in law, if not always in practice) a unified, nationalized system of civil rights.

The interpretation and implementation of those rights have not been characterized by unanimity or cooperation. We saw in Chapter 5 that the right to vote was denied to many citizens—blacks, women, and young adults—for at least a hundred years after the Civil War. Americans have also witnessed other attempts to severely restrict civil rights: for example, the internment of American citizens of Japanese ancestry during World War II and continuing discrimination against blacks, Hispanics, and other groups. As early as 1909, the distinguished black leader, W. E. B. Du Bois, perceptively described such discrimination (see accompanying box). Thus, if social policies regarding the rights of citizens appear to change dramatically over the years, it is because, as the Supreme Court once said, the interpretation of those rights must be "a gradual process of judicial inclusion and exclusion" based on changing social attitudes.

W. E. B. DU BOIS: THE EVOLUTION OF THE RACE PROBLEM (1909)

Those who complain that the Negro problem is always with us and apparently insoluble must not forget that under this vague and general designation are gathered many social problems and many phases of the same problem; that these problems and phases have passed through a great evolutionary circle and that today especially one may clearly see a repetition, vaster but similar, of the great cycle of the past.

That problem of the past, so far as the black American was concerned, began with caste—a definite place preordained in custom, law, and religion where all men of black blood must be thrust. To be sure, this caste idea as applied to blacks was no sudden, full-grown conception, for the enslavement of the workers was an idea which America inherited from Europe and was not synonymous for many years with the enslavement of the blacks, although the blacks were the chief workers. Men came to the idea of exclusive black slavery by gradually enslaving the workers, as was the world's long custom, and then gradually conceiving certain sorts of work and certain colors of men as necessarily connected. It was, when once set up definitely in the southern slave system, a logically cohering whole which the simplest social philosopher could easily grasp and state. The difficulty was it was too simple to be either just or true. Human nature is not simple and any classification that roughly divides men into good and bad, superior and inferior, slave and free, is and must ever be ludicrously untrue and universally dangerous as a permanent exhaustive classification. So in the southern slave system the thing that from the first damned it was the free Negro—the Negro legally free, the Negro economically free and the Negro spiritually free.

How was the Negro to be treated and conceived of who was legally free? At first with perfect naturalness he was treated as a man—he voted in Massachusetts and in South Carolina, in New York and Virginia; he intermarried with black and white, he claimed and received his civil rights—all this until the caste of color was so turned as to correspond with the caste of work and enslave not only slaves but black men who were not slaves. Even this system, however, was unable to ensure complete economic dependence on the part of all black men; there were continually artisans, foremen and skilled servants who became economically too valuable to be slaves. In vain were laws hurled at Negro intelligence and responsibility; black men continued to hire their time and to steal some smattering of knowledge, and it was this fact that became the gravest menace to the slave system. But even legal and economic freedom was not so dangerous to slavery as the free spirit which continually cropped out among men fated to be slaves: they thought, they dreamed, they aspired, they resisted. In vain were they beaten, sold south and killed, the ranks were continually filled with others and they either led revolt at home or ran away to the North, and these by showing their human qualities continually gave the lie to the slave assumption. Thus it was the free Negro in these manifold phases of his appearance who hastened the economic crisis which killed slavery and who made it impossible to make the caste of work and the caste of color correspond, and who became at once the promise and excuse of those who forced the critical revolution.

Today in larger cycle and more intricate detail we are passing through certain phases of a similar evolution. Today we have the caste idea—again not a sudden full-grown conception but one being insidiously but consciously and persistently pressed upon the nation. The steps toward it which are being taken are: first, political disfranchisement, then vocational education with the distinct idea of narrowing to the uttermost of the vocations in view, and finally a curtailment of civil freedom of travel, association, and entertainment, in systematic effort to instill contempt and kill self-respect.

Here then is the new slavery of black men in America—a new attempt to make degradation of social condition correspond with certain physical characteristics—not to be sure fully realized as yet, and probably unable for reasons of social development ever to become as systematized as the economic and physical slavery of the past—and yet realized to an extent almost unbelievable by those who have not taken the pains to study the facts—to an extent which makes the lives of thinking black men in this land a perpetual martyrdom. . . .

Source: *Proceedings of the National Negro Conference,* New York, 1909.

Since the end of World War II, American leaders have tried to find a consensus on the limits of the rights of citizens—especially the prohibition of discrimination on the basis of race, color, sex, age, and so on. Although both the Republicans and the Democrats called for antidiscrimination measures in their 1944 party platforms, the first large-scale effort was made by President Harry Truman, who in 1948 called on Congress to establish "equal rights and equal opportunities" for all Americans. A Truman-appointed commission proposed fair employment practices, federal protection of the right to vote, the end of discrimination in interstate transportation, voting rights for the residents of the District of Columbia, and statehood for Hawaii and Alaska. The last two proposals were settled not quickly but without significant dispute; the remainder have provided part of the basic domestic policy agenda for the last thirty years. The second major wave of civil-rights legislation occurred during the 1960s, as black Americans pushed successfully for antidiscrimination measures in the areas of voting, housing, employment, and education (see Table 13-1).

Only a very lengthy book could describe all of the national efforts to protect the opportunities and choices available to citizens. We will briefly describe

TABLE 13-1
MAJOR ANTIDISCRIMINATION LEGISLATION

Year	Legislation	Major Provisions
1957	Civil Rights Act	Created Civil Rights Commission; established federal criminal penalties for attempting to prevent voting in federal elections
1960	Civil Rights Act	Allowed U.S. attorney general to investigate racial discrimination in voting
1964	Civil Rights Act	Impeded use of literacy tests; prohibited racial discrimination at restaurants, hotels, theaters, etc.; U.S. attorney general authorized to bring suit to desegregate schools; banned discrimination in employment; outlawed discrimination in any activity receiving federal assistance
1965	Voting Rights Act	Authorized federal examiners to oversee voter registration in all elections in many southern districts; banned literacy tests and other discriminatory measures
1968	Civil Rights Act	Outlawed discrimination in sale or rental of housing
1970	Voting Rights Act Amendments	Extended 1965 act and included some districts in northern states
1975	Voting Rights Act Amendments	Extended 1965 act and broadened antidiscrimination measures to include protection for language minorities (e.g., Hispanics, Native Americans)
1982	Voting Rights Act Amendments	Extended 1965 act and strengthened antidiscrimination measures by requiring only proof of *effect* of discrimination, not *intent* to discriminate

the policies that fall into two general substantive categories: education and employment.

Discrimination in the Schools

It should not be surprising that the schools have been a central arena for the fight for civil rights. It is to the public education system that parents entrust their children in order to acquire not only social skills and values but also the occupational talents needed for social and economic advancement. Given the importance of education to a child's attitudes and abilities, any general policy regarding the educational system will inevitably arouse controversy among parents.

In addition, federal attempts to introduce reforms into the public schools have run into jurisdictional obstacles. The immediate governing authority for nearly all elementary and secondary schools in the United States is the local school board, of which there were 14,851 in 1982. Counties and states also make policies affecting the schools. Thus, any effort to standardize the public schools across the nation (in terms of curriculum, policies for hiring teachers, or racial equality) is likely to flounder unless it (1) is based on clear (i.e., constitutional) authority, with (2) a well-defined set of goals and methods of implementing them, and (3) is accompanied by a believable enforcement mechanism to prevent states, counties, or school boards from blocking the policy.

We can judge the successes and failures of education-rights policies by how well those three requirements were met. The first step in the process was the establishment of the principle for desegregation. The Supreme Court provided that authority in its 1954 decision in *Brown* v. *Board of Education of Topeka, Kansas,* in which the Court ruled that separate (but "equal") educational facilities for the different races were inherently unequal because they gave black students a sense of inferiority.[6] In an earlier case (*Sweatt* v. *Painter*), the Court had based its call for desegregation on economic grounds: blacks must be admitted to predominantly white Texas law schools, because restricting them to predominantly black law schools would prevent them from establishing professional contacts that would later aid their careers.[7]

Of course, the mere establishment of the doctrine was not sufficient to produce results. Policies were also required that would precisely spell out who should do what in order to end racial discrimination in the schools. It was not the role of the Supreme Court alone to stipulate the exact goals or the policies to achieve them; the policy system also included the Senate, the House of Representatives, and the executive branch (especially the White House and the Justice Department). Because the political process in the United States often is sufficiently complicated for policies to be blocked at many stages, school desegregation policies were slowly devised and, in many cases, even more slowly executed. Implementation was further delayed by the Court's call in the *Brown* decision for desegregation "with all deliberate speed," which

Black students attempted to enter all-white Central High School in Little Rock, Arkansas, in September 1957. After mobs threatened the students, President Eisenhower ordered 1,000 paratroopers and 10,000 National Guardsmen to enforce a federal court's desegregation order. (AP/Wide World Photos)

allowed school districts to find delaying tactics; not until 1969 did the Supreme Court use the word *immediately* (*Alexander* v. *Board of Education*).[8]

Finally, the federal government did not have effective tools with which to force recalcitrant local school boards to carry out federal policies. The government can often exercise its will by attaching conditions to federal grant programs to states and communities. That technique was begun in education by the 1964 Civil Rights Act, which authorized the withholding of federal funds from institutions that practiced segregation and allowed the federal government to sue for the desegregation of schools. The effectiveness of the technique, however, was limited by the fact that school financing is primarily a local and state matter; less than 4 percent of all funds for elementary and secondary education in 1960 were provided by the federal government (the figure had climbed to only 8.7 percent in 1981). Policymakers needed a more effective tool.

Several other approaches to school desegregation have been tried. Some of these have been voluntary: for example, the "magnet school," which uses a specialized curriculum (e.g., in the performing arts or science) to draw students from many different neighborhoods. Courts and educators also have redrawn school attendance zones and constructed schools on the boundaries between black and white neighborhoods. However, the desegregation policy that has drawn the most attention—busing—has not been based on voluntary action; because children often live in segregated neighborhoods, courts have

TABLE 13-2
PUBLIC-SCHOOL DESEGREGATION, FALL 1968 to FALL 1971

Area	Year	% Black Pupils in 50%–99% White Schools	% Black Pupils in 80%–100% Black Schools
East, North, and West	1968	27.6%	57.4%
	1971	27.8%	57.1%
South	1968	18.4%	78.8%
	1971	43.9%	32.2%
Border[a] and Washington, D.C.	1968	28.4%	63.8%
	1971	30.5%	60.9%

[a]Oklahoma, Missouri, Kentucky, West Virginia, Maryland, Arkansas.

Source: U.S. Department of Health, Education, and Welfare, *HEW News*, January 13, 1972, p. 5.

required school districts to transport children, sometimes over long distances, in order to create appropriate balances of the races in schools. In 1971, the Supreme Court (in *Swann* v. *Charlotte-Mecklenburg Board of Education*) permitted busing that does not "risk the health of the children or significantly impinge on the educational process" to be used as a device to desegregate schools. [9] (The impact of these and other strategies in only a three-year period can be seen in Table 13-2.) Busing became a controversial topic, and in some cities attempts to bus white or black children were marked by violence. To some degree, the Supreme Court itself reflected ambivalence about the ultimate value of large-scale busing in 1974, when it sharply divided over the question of whether children in separate suburban school districts could be bused into inner cities across district lines. The majority ruled that metropolitanwide busing could be ordered only when district lines were deliberately intended to encourage segregation and when suburban schools were discriminating against minorities. The issue carried over into the 1980s as members of Congress sponsored antibusing amendments to the Constitution.

The problem of discrimination in schools has not been limited to racial segregation, however. Some social policies have been intended to protect the educational rights of the handicapped. Almost eight million mentally or physically handicapped children and teenagers were promised a "free appropriate public education" by a 1975 federal statute; by 1978, almost three million students were enrolled (at least part-time) in such programs, and by 1983 the cost of education for the handicapped had grown to $846 million. As always, however, there were questions about whether these policies produced benefits that matched or exceeded their costs. Because of the high cost of refitting schools with ramps, elevators, and other facilities, some have claimed that private-home tutors would have been a more cost-effective way of providing education to handicapped students.

Federal policymakers also have addressed the problem of sex discrimination. Title IX of the Education Amendments of 1972 prohibited discrimination by sex in any educational programs that directly or indirectly received federal financial assistance. In 1975, the Department of Health, Education, and Welfare issued regulations that covered 16,000 elementary and secondary schools and 2,700 colleges and universities (but not the military academies, or the Boy Scouts, Girl Scouts, and other private groups). These rules forbade discrimination in admissions policies, classes, housing, financial aid, employment, and athletics. The regulators avoided the problem of requiring female collegiate football teams by not forcing schools to form co-ed teams for contact sports, although schools were required to form separate teams for such sports if enough women wished to play.

The Rights of Workers and the Right to Work

In 1982, there were more than a dozen federal agencies, offices, and boards that had some responsibility for protecting opportunities and choices for people in the workplace. Some of these (e.g., the Equal Employment Opportunity Commission, the Civil Rights Division of the Department of Justice, and the Employment Standards Administration) carry out policies aimed at preventing racial or sexual discrimination in employment. Other federal offices focus on the relationship between employees and employers; they include the Labor-Management Services Administration, the National Labor Relations Board, and the Federal Labor Relations Authority. These and other efforts on behalf of workers are all relatively new; most are less than half a century old.

We need to look no further back than a hundred years to find a world in which there were few workers' rights. For example, many workers in the nineteenth century entered into labor contracts for specified periods (e.g., a year) in which wages were to be received at the end of the term. Because the courts were ruling that those workers who quit before the end of the contract were entitled to no pay for the time they had worked, employers had an incentive for making jobs unpleasant for workers near the end of the contract period. In fact, during the colonial and early American period, workers were often classified as "apprentices"; they had the same obligations to their employers ("masters") that sons had toward their fathers, and they were therefore unable to sue their employers for injury or negligence. The notion that workers had freely contracted to bear all risks when they took their jobs was finally challenged by the Employers' Liability Act of 1908.

The next major movement extending the rights of workers came during the New Deal years of the 1930s. The Norris-LaGuardia Act of 1932 prohibited workers' "yellow-dog" contracts—promises not to join trade unions—and affirmed workers' right to strike. In 1935, Congress passed the National Labor Relations ("Wagner") Act, which virtually guaranteed the rights of workers to organize and bargain collectively with employers; the National Labor Relations Board (NLRB) was created to administer the act. The last of the major New Deal labor laws was the Fair Labor Standards ("Wage and Hours") Act of 1938,

Child laborers in an American textile mill at the end of the nineteenth century. Until the 1930s, state and federal laws banning the employment of young children and limiting the hours of older children were either poorly enforced or ruled unconstitutional. (Lewis Hine/Library of Congress)

which established regulations on wages, hours, and child labor for almost all industries involved in interstate commerce.

Minimum-wage policies, originally proposed early in this century to protect the health and morals of women, were initially ruled unconstitutional by the Supreme Court, but once again the emergencies of the Great Depression allowed a new policy to take root in the American economy. The Fair Labor Standards Act of 1938 set a minimum wage of twenty-five cents per hour, justified on the basis of the need to protect the purchasing power of low-income groups. By 1981, the minimum wage had risen to $3.35 per hour, yet there was evidence that employers who were being forced to pay higher wages often would hire fewer people, thereby exacerbating the unemployment problem, or would reduce workers' fringe benefits.

After World War II, many public officials worried that the New Deal labor laws had gone too far in granting power to unions. The Taft-Hartley Act of 1947 banned "closed shops" (in which one must be a union member to be hired), limited "union shops" (in which workers must become union members), and absolutely prohibited strikes against the federal government. The antistrike injunction clause has been invoked several times when strikes threatened important sectors of the economy, such as steel, shipping, coal, and telephone service. Yet the fact that the controversy was about whether the rights of workers were appropriately balanced with the rights of employers, and not about whether workers *have* any rights, indicates how basic the concept of workers' rights has become.

The issue of workers' rights has not disappeared (the National Labor Relations Board considered about 45,000 unfair labor practice complaints in 1980), but most of the recent significant changes in social policies affecting employment have been in the areas of racial and sexual discrimination. Not until passage of the 1964 Civil Rights Act did Congress order "the removal of artificial, arbitrary, and unnecessary barriers to employment." In 1965, the Equal Employment Opportunity Commission (EEOC) was formed to implement this provision. Initially, the EEOC could only recommend that the Justice Department file suit to force compliance; not until 1972 could it file lawsuits against private employers, employment agencies, and unions (but not state or local governments).

The entrance of large numbers of women into the work force (twelve million in the 1970s and sixteen million in the 1980s) also has had a drastic effect on employment policies. The women's rights movement of the 1970s brought attention to the wage disparities between males and females and the failure of women to significantly penetrate many professions traditionally dominated by males (e.g., engineering, law, medicine, and politics). As is the case with most social phenomena, the causes of these disparities are complex, but by the end of the 1970s several factors were becoming clear. Increasing percentages of women in the labor force are heads of households (and therefore not merely supplementing their husbands' income), yet the wage differentials between the sexes—whatever their initial cause—actually increased during the 1970s.

The EEOC has the authority to prosecute employers who discriminate against women. Its biggest settlements (in 1973 and 1974) required American Telephone and Telegraph to award $15 million in back pay and up to $23 million in pay increases to women and minority males who had been denied equal pay and promotion opportunities in nonmanagement jobs; similar amounts were to be paid to women in management positions. Yet in the 1970s, many saw the need for a more fundamental guarantee of women's working rights than was provided by current statutes (which could, after all, be amended or rescinded by future legislators and presidents). Reflecting the growing political power of women, Congress submitted the Equal Rights Amendment to the states for ratification on March 22, 1972. Reading in full, "Equality of rights under the law shall not be denied or abridged by the United States or by any state on account of sex," the ERA aroused intense controversy, and many people of both sexes took opposing sides. Because the amendment was not ratified by enough states (three-fourths) during the seven-year period initially established by Congress, the national legislature resubmitted it, again without success. On the June 30, 1982, deadline it was officially pronounced that the Equal Rights Amendment had not been ratified by enough states. (It was revived in the House of Representatives in 1983, but its eventual passage is far from certain.)

Other policies have been designed to assure sexual and racial equality in employment. One of the most controversial is **affirmative action.** In a frontal assault on substantive inequity (or inequality of results), the government began

affirmative action:
The requirement that businesses, labor unions, government agencies, and schools actively recruit more minority-group members or females to compensate for alleged previous discrimination.

in the 1960s to promote policies that in effect transfer job opportunities from one group of people (usually white males) to other groups (primarily racial minorities and women). The idea behind affirmative action seems rather simple. Because procedural equity (i.e., equality of opportunity) has been denied to some social groups for so long, many people feel that these groups should be given compensation for past injustices. President Johnson stated the case in 1965: "You do not take a person who, for years, has been hobbled by chains and liberate him, bringing him up to the starting line of a race, and then say you are free to compete with all the others, and still just believe that you have been completely fair."[10] Today, affirmative action programs range from those that simply seek out and encourage minority and female job candidates to those with precise quotas for hiring victims of past discrimination (which some characterize as reverse discrimination).

In practice, affirmative action raises some difficult questions. In *Regents of the University of California* v. *Bakke,* a white applicant to the medical school at the University of California at Davis sued the school because a fixed number of places in the entering class had been reserved for minority students as an affirmative action program; Bakke claimed that he had been denied equal protection of the law because his credentials for admission were stronger than those of some of the "disadvantaged" students who were enrolled.[11] The Supreme Court decided the case on narrow grounds, finding that racial quotas were unconstitutional but that race could be one factor in school admissions. In the next year, in *Kaiser Aluminum Company* v. *Weber,* the Court found that an affirmative action job-training program operated voluntarily by a Louisiana factory did not discriminate against a white employee, even though a fixed number of positions in the program had been reserved for blacks, because the law did not prohibit "all private, voluntary, race-conscious affirmative action plans."[12] The Supreme Court avoided contradicting its decision in the *Bakke* case by relying on narrow technical reasoning, but its logic was not clear. Because the basic question underlying affirmative action is the meaning of *discrimination,* even a definitive Supreme Court ruling would not resolve the policy dispute over affirmative action: is it constitutional to discriminate against a member of the majority (in the case of hiring quotas) because it has, as a group, discriminated against a minority?

This discussion of social policies intended to protect citizens' rights has shown that there has been a pattern of change in the scope and techniques of social policy in the United States. As social circumstances have changed, new and extended forms of government intrusion into the private sphere have emerged. It should not be surprising, therefore, that the form of American social policy that today is by far the most extensive—and expensive—was a result of a major social upheaval that brought into question many basic concepts about the operations and interrelationships of the public and private spheres of action. The largest policy consequence of the Great Depression was the massive extension of government into the area of providing resources to citizens and the expansion of citizens' rights to include the legal right to receive government benefits.

THE PROVISION OF RESOURCES

As we have seen, social policies in the United States involve trade-offs. Some people receive benefits and others pay costs. When the intent of the policy is to transfer benefits from one group to another, the policy is said to involve **redistribution,** because the government is redistributing wealth, income, or other benefits. Such policies are often promoted on grounds of moral altruism and justice, but they also affect economic efficiency and the distribution of economic demand. The most massive programs of this sort involve income maintenance by *cash payments* or by the provision of *in-kind benefits.*[13]

As the terms imply, cash benefits and in-kind benefits differ in the form in which they are delivered to recipients. Although both types of payments involve the provision of benefits directly to individuals (who must individually apply and qualify), rather than to classes or groups of individuals (as is the case with many services, such as mass transit), the choice of providing cash or in-kind payments involves some basic concepts about the proper role of the government. When a cash benefit is given to an individual, that person has the ability to choose how to spend it; no bureaucrat or judge will follow someone who receives a government check to see whether the money is spent wisely. In contrast, this freedom is unavailable to the recipient of an in-kind benefit. When the government pays for a person's hospital care, school lunches, or college fellowship, the recipient has no discretion in the use of the funds. For example, school lunches that are provided by a government program cannot be used by students to buy magazines, and food stamps may not be used to purchase such items as liquor or pet food.

Most cash and in-kind payments are provided to individuals on the basis of need (either because of poverty or age) and are intended to provide support for the basic necessities of life—housing, food, medical care, and so on. Because there are many such programs, there are varying combinations of cash and in-kind benefits. Therefore, sharp boundaries between the two types of benefits are rare.

Cash Benefits

To many people, the government's role in redistributing income and wealth suggests socialism, with policy being guided by the maxim "from each according to his abilities, to each according to his needs." Although socialism does not necessarily entail a completely equal distribution of resources (e.g., Sweden, one of the most socialist of Western democracies, has allowed fifteen families to own two hundred corporations with 50 percent of the private industry work force), the fear of being labeled *socialist* has constrained the development of American policies intended to coerce the wealthy to share. Thus, when the American government was prompted by the Great Depression to follow the example of Germany (1889), Britain (1908), and France (1910) in establishing income maintenance policies, there was an attempt to scrupulously separate the two major forms of resource redistribution: **social insurance** and **public assistance.**

redistribution: The transfer of items of value from one group (e.g., the wealthy) to another group (e.g., the poor).

social insurance: A form of social policy characterized by workers making "contributions" (i.e., paying taxes) into a special governmental account, thereby earning the "right" to draw benefits from that account upon retirement, disability or illness, or survival of an eligible spouse or parent.

public assistance: A form a social policy intended to provide aid to those deemed needy (e.g., the aged, blind, and poor) and for which some evidence of need usually must be shown.

trust fund: A government financial account earmarked for a specific purpose, such as social security or highway construction, and therefore distinct from general revenues.

Social Insurance Social insurance began in the United States with the passage of the *Social Security Act of 1935.* Initially the program was promoted as a simple insurance plan, with workers making "contributions" (although in the form of special taxes, and therefore not voluntarily) into a **trust fund** (a specific government account for funds that can be used for only one purpose, and are therefore separate from "general revenues"), thereby earning pension "rights" in rough proportion to the contributions paid in. Similarly, unemployment insurance would be funded by "contributions" made by employers via a payroll tax and would be used to provide support for their workers if they were laid off. In fact, however, from the very start social security contained a welfare element, because the size of the benefits paid to some recipients would be based on tests of their need.

In 1939, the Social Security Act was amended to broaden coverage and extend its redistributive features even before the first benefits were paid (one Ida Mae Fuller received the first monthly check in 1940, for $22.54). Because many elderly people could not have participated in the program long enough to have paid in sufficient contributions to qualify for repayment, benefits were to be funded on a pay-as-you-go basis; current workers and their employers would pay for the current group of retirees and disabled workers. Benefits were also added for the dependents and survivors of retirees, and the payment scheme was further tilted toward the needy.

Further changes occurred in 1956, when disability benefits were added to the system, and in 1965, with the establishment of Medicare (an in-kind program in which cash is usually not paid directly to the beneficiary). Yet perhaps the largest expansion of the scope and cost of social insurance in the United States took place in 1972, when Congress passed a 20 percent across-the-board increase in benefits and created a system for automatically increasing future benefits based on the rate of inflation (indexing). Although indexing social security benefits may have been intended to protect the program from uncertainty and political manipulation, it has had the effect of greatly increasing the cost of the program. In the 1983 fiscal year, 35 million Americans received monthly social security checks (equal to 6 percent of the total income of all Americans), at a cost of $170 billion, and Medicare cost an additional $49 billion.

The social security program includes three trust funds: old-age and survivors insurance (OASI), disability insurance (DI), and hospital insurance (Medicare)—all nourished by social security payroll taxes. To cover doctor bills, there is also a voluntary, supplemental medical insurance program for the elderly (Medicare Part B), which is financed by premium payments (much like private insurance) and by general tax revenues. The fates of the three trust funds are closely intertwined. In 1982, the OASI fund spent $15 billion more than it received, thereby wiping out its surplus from previous years and requiring it to borrow $600 million from the disability fund.

The OASI problem shows that by the early 1980s, social security had become a serious financial—and political—problem. There were four related causes of the problem. First, the performance of the overall economy in the 1970s weakened the program in several ways: unemployment was higher than in the past (creating a drain on benefits while relatively fewer workers were contributing their tax dollars), and sustained inflation led to increases in the size of benefits. Second, some claimed that the inflation indicator to which increases in benefits were linked ("indexed") was an inaccurate and overly generous measure of the living costs of retirees. Third, medical care costs were increasing much faster than the overall inflation rate; total health costs accounted for 4.5 percent of the GNP in 1950, but climbed to nearly 10 percent in 1983. (If current trends hold, demands on the Medicare trust fund could exceed those on the social security trust fund by the year 2005.)

The fourth threat to the social security system was one over which policymakers had little control. As the elderly proportion of the American population increases, a huge strain is put on the pay-as-you-go scheme. In 1950, there were about sixteen workers contributing to the social security trust fund for each beneficiary, but by 1982 the ratio had dropped to about three and a half to one, and by 2020 the ratio may be only about two contributors for each beneficiary. The only feasible way to pay for the system in the future is to combine cuts in benefits (or at least slower growth) and a substantial increase in taxes. By 1985, individuals and their employers were each paying 7.05 percent of salaries in social security taxes. By 1988, the rate will be 7.51 percent. In 1983, a bipartisan presidential Commission on Social Security Reform (headed by Alan Greenspan) proposed to reduce the $200 billion trust fund deficit projected for 1989 by increasing taxes ($88 billion), reducing benefits ($40 billion) by delaying cost-of-living boosts from July to the following January, and by making other changes in coverage and accounting ($41 billion); these changes became law in mid-1983. Nevertheless, it was projected that over the next seventy-five years an additional $1.6 trillion would be needed.

The major redistributive element in the social security program has not been a shift in resources from the wealthy to the needy (although that has been one part of the package) but a redistribution across generations and across time. The younger generations of working-age people have contributed to the support of the older generation and, ideally, to their own support in the future as they join the ranks of retirees. As the average age of Americans continues to climb, perhaps the solution to the social security crisis will be found in redefining the term *aged;* if people are allowed or encouraged to work longer, until age seventy instead of sixty-five or sixty-six, the drain on benefits would be reduced, the salary pool from which they are paid would be increased, and, according to many psychologists and sociologists, older citizens would enjoy longer and more fulfilling lives.

Public Assistance Cash Benefits Although the social security system is by far the largest public policy for the distribution of cash to individuals, there are also programs that provide cash benefits to the needy. Public assistance programs date back to the pension programs for revolutionary war veterans in

1776, but until the Great Depression the federal government played no role in need-based income maintenance programs. Many states began assistance plans for the blind, poor mothers and children, and injured workmen during the early years of this century. It required the crisis of the Great Depression to push income maintenance onto the national agenda. We have already seen that the major federal effort began with the Social Security Act amendments of 1939; another major expansion of welfare programs occurred during President Lyndon Johnson's War on Poverty. In the years from 1964 to the early 1970s, the federal government extended the scope (and cost) of public assistance programs.

Some of the cash benefit programs to support the needy are connected with complementary in-kind benefit programs; for example, poor people can usually qualify for food stamps (an in-kind benefit) and, if unemployed, unemployment benefits (a cash benefit) at the same time, so when we evaluate an income maintenance program we should be careful not to consider it in isolation. The major cash benefit program today is Aid to Families with Dependent Children (AFDC), which provides cash payments to households with dependent children if one parent is missing or, in some states, if the head of the household is unemployed. AFDC is administered by the states, which set their own benefit levels and eligibility requirements (within some nationally mandated limits), but is funded jointly by the states and the federal government (see Table 13-3). AFDC has been criticized for encouraging the breakup of families (because benefits often are higher if the father is absent), for creating incentives for unwed mothers to have children, and for providing unequal benefits among different states.

Another major cash benefit program is unemployment insurance. The name *insurance* is based on the idea that employers will "contribute" to the cost of their employees' future unemployment benefits by paying federal and state payroll taxes; employees do not contribute to the program. Like AFDC payments, unemployment benefits are funded jointly by the federal and state governments and are administered by state agencies, which determine the size of payments and the number of weeks of eligibility (again, subject to some federal requirements). Because of the large variations among the states in workers' benefits, there have been calls for the nationalization of unemployment insurance. One method—intended primarily to replace AFDC but also claimed to rationalize unemployment insurance as well—would be a guaranteed annual income program in which all families would receive a minimum yearly income, regardless of their employment status. In 1969, President Richard Nixon actually endorsed such a plan (which he called the Family Assistance Plan, or FAP); although it passed in the House of Representatives, it was never passed by the Senate.

Another form of cash payment program is illustrated by an experiment that has been under way since 1972 in Green Bay, Wisconsin, and South Bend, Indiana. Rather than require families seeking government housing assistance to live in public housing or in designated private apartments (for which the

TABLE 13-3
MAJOR INCOME MAINTENANCE PROGRAMS, FY 1980

Program	Federal Outlays ($ millions)	State Outlays ($ millions)
Social Insurance and Retirement Programs		
	Cash Benefits	
OASI (old age and survivors) and railroad retirement	$117,118	$ 0
Unemployment compensation and disability insurance	4,632	15,298
Veterans' and survivors' compensation, medical and education programs, etc.	21,254	212
Worker's compensation and benefits	2,743	10,640
Public employee retirement	26,983	12,507
	In-Kind Benefits	
Medicare	34,992	0
Total	$207,722	$38,657
Public Assistance		
	Cash Benefits	
AFDC (Aid to Families with Dependent Children)	$ 6,964	$ 6,055
SSI (Supplemental Security Income)	6,440	1,787
Other	6,212	1,904
	In-Kind Benefits	
Food stamps	$ 9,083	$ 0
Child nutrition programs	4,209	1,080
Medicaid	14,550	12,844
Housing	6,608	601
Other	18,549	7,203
Total	$ 72,615	$31,474
Total Income Maintenance	$280,337	$70,131

Source: U.S. Bureau of the Census, *Statistical Abstract of the United States, 1984* (Washington, D.C.: Government Printing Office, 1984), pp. 368–369, 371.

government makes payments directly to landlords), about thirteen thousand low-income families received monthly checks of about one hundred dollars, with which they could supplement their own contributions to their rent, wherever they choose to live. This version of a **voucher** system is very popular with many political conservatives as well as some liberals. They see it as more efficient, because more of each dollar goes for actual rent; cheaper because

voucher: A subsidy or public assistance device that transfers benefits to individuals, but restricts their use of the benefits only within general categories (e.g., education or housing).

landlords cannot directly charge the government higher rents; and more respectful of the individual's freedom to choose where to live. The Reagan administration promoted extending the use of vouchers in the areas of employment, education, and medical care for the elderly.

In-Kind Benefits

The reasons American policymakers developed in-kind benefit schemes are not obvious. Some believe that in-kind benefits are the result of a sort of paternalism, with policymakers making sure that they, not the recipients, know best how a poor person's income should be spent. Yet others support in-kind payments because they provide at least some assurance that public funds will be spent by recipients for the purposes intended. It is clear that in-kind benefits form a greater proportion of public assistance (welfare) expenditures than of social insurance expenditures; for example, in 1977, about 58 percent of all benefits for which need had to be demonstrated were in-kind, whereas only about 16 percent of social insurance benefits were in-kind.

Social Insurance In-Kind Benefits   The only program that provides in-kind benefits to people without a specific test of need is Medicare. Although the idea had been around since the 1930s, Congress was not willing to enact a program until 1965. Medicare has become complex, but its basic provisions are simple: the Medicare system uses federal funds (collected with social security taxes, but kept in a separate trust fund) to reimburse hospitals and doctors for most of the expenses incurred by elderly people who are eligible for social security benefits. Unfortunately, the cost of the Medicare program has skyrocketed as medical costs have increased at a faster rate than overall inflation—in part, because the program removes incentives for patients or doctors to keep medical bills low (see Table 13-4). However, legislation was passed in 1983 that established fixed payments for specific hospital treatments and allowed hospitals to keep the difference if their actual costs were below the set levels.

Public Assistance In-Kind Benefits   The major public assistance in-kind benefit programs were shown in Table 13-3. Medicaid, established in 1965, provides payments to doctors and hospitals for expenses incurred by the needy, who are defined as those already receiving other public assistance. Medicaid also differs from Medicare in that it is funded by general state and federal revenues, not by a special fund, and is administered by the states, which decide how much assistance to provide within nationally set eligibility standards. Although the Medicaid program costs much less than Medicare, its cost has been rising at an equally steep rate: about $17 billion (in federal funds) in 1981, and an estimated $24 billion in 1985.

Food stamps were begun as an experiment in 1961, and the current program was established by the 1964 Food Stamp Act. Under this law, the federal

TABLE 13-4
HOW AMERICANS SPENT THEIR INCOME, 1947–1977

Item	% Shares of Total Consumer Spending	
	1947	1977
Food	34.7	21.8
Housing or rent	9.9	15.5
Household operation (utilities, appliances, etc.)	14.6	14.6
Clothing	14.1	8.0
Transportation	9.8	14.2
Recreation and entertainment	6.2	7.7
Personal services (insurance, legal, private education)	4.0	6.6
Medical care	4.5	9.6

Source: Alan S. Blinder, "The Level and Distribution of Economic Well-Being," in Martin Feldstein, ed., *The American Economy in Transition* (Chicago: University of Chicago Press, 1980), p. 427.

government sells stamps to the qualified poor for a fraction of the cost of what the stamps will buy. A person with no income receives free stamps; people with small incomes pay about 20 to 30 percent of the face value of the stamps. Food stamps are intended to be used only to buy food, and merchants are not allowed to accept food stamps for the purchase of other items. Like most social programs, food stamps have not been immune from abuse. Especially strong criticism has been directed at the use of food stamps by the "voluntary" poor, such as students, workers on strike, and those who prefer not to work; therefore, many reforms have been suggested to restrict the benefit to the most needy. For example, in 1981 Congress established a gross income eligibility limit at 130 percent of the national poverty level. The federal government also provides in-kind benefits for child nutrition by subsidizing meals for students in schools, child care centers, and other institutions. In 1983, almost 23.2 million children received free or reduced-price meals.

Most of the federal programs to provide benefits for education are services to groups, rather than in-kind payments. However, needy individual students have been the direct beneficiaries of several public policies that provide in-kind benefits. First, in 1944 Congress passed the Servicemen's Readjustment Act (or "GI Bill"), which provided financial assistance to more than eight million veterans who intended to return to school; these benefits later were extended to Korean and Vietnam war veterans. In 1958, largely in response to the perceived "technology gap" with the Soviet Union after the launch of Sputnik, the National Defense Education Act provided the first general financial aid to needy college students in the form of low-interest student loans. Today, the largest in-kind benefit program for needy students is the "Pell" grant, or Basic Educational Opportunity Grant, which was begun in 1972 to provide tuition support for college students.

Some in-kind payments also are intended to help the needy with their housing costs. During the late 1960s, rent-subsidy programs were developed in which the government paid a portion of a poor family's rent directly to a private landlord; at about the same time, a homeownership program began to provide in-kind assistance to lower-income families who wanted to buy their own homes. As we shall see, however, the largest housing assistance programs are more properly classified as services than benefits to individuals.

The final major type of in-kind benefit is public employment. In 1932, at the beginning of Franklin Roosevelt's first term in the White House, one-fourth of all American workers were without jobs. Within a short time of his inauguration, Roosevelt had begun several programs designed to quickly provide federally funded jobs for large numbers of the unemployed. Late in 1933, the Civil Works Administration was formed; within one month, 2.6 million people were working on projects ranging from school renovation to outhouse construction. Actors and writers were hired to give free shows and to record local histories; researchers were given such tasks as studying the history of the safety pin. Another program, the Public Works Administration, spent $6 billion in six years on such projects as construction of the Triborough Bridge in New York City, the Grand Coulee Dam in Washington, and the Chicago sewage system. Finally, the Works Progress Administration (WPA) was created in 1935 to provide about two million jobs per year; although the WPA has been criticized for inefficiency and occasional frivolity, it hired up to a third of all unemployed Americans.

The unprecedented scope of the New Deal job programs was a result of the emergency of the Depression; some Americans openly worried about the potential for revolution if the unemployed were not given jobs. The next big step in government policy on employment also was prompted by fear—in this case, fear that a serious decline in employment and production would follow the end of World War II. Although the Employment Act of 1946 carefully emphasized the preservation of "free competitive enterprise," it proclaimed that "it is the continuing policy and responsibility of the federal government . . . to promote maximum employment, production, and purchasing power." Putting the intent of the Employment Act into practice has not been simple, however, because unemployment is a complex problem.

Labor economists typically refer to three basic types of unemployment. First, there is always *frictional* unemployment; the entrance of four or five million workers into the work force each month due to people switching jobs or entering the job market for the first time (amounting to about a 4 percent unemployment rate) is generally considered unavoidable. Second, there is *structural* unemployment, which results when the characteristics of available unemployed workers do not match the needs of employers (e.g., as the American steel industry declines and the semiconductor industry expands) (see Table 13-5). Finally, there is *cyclical* unemployment, created when the economy does not generate enough demand for jobs because of recession and a lower demand for products and services. Federal employment policies that have provided in-kind benefits (e.g., temporary government work programs)

TABLE 13-5
THE CHANGING COMPOSITION OF WORK

Type of Work	Number of Employees		% Change
	1940	1980	
Agriculture	9,540,000	3,310,000	−65.3%
Nonagriculture	32,361,000	90,564,000	179.8
Construction	1,311,000	4,399,000	235.5
Financial[a]	1,485,000	5,168,000	248.0
Government			
Federal	996,000	2,866,000	187.7
State, local	3,206,000	13,383,000	317.4
Total	4,202,000	16,249,000	286.7
Manufacturing	10,985,000	20,300,000	84.8
Mining	925,000	1,020,000	10.3
Services[b]	3,665,000	17,901,000	388.4
Transportation, public utilities	3,038,000	5,143,000	69.3
Wholesale, retail trade	6,750,000	20,386,000	202

[a]Including insurance and real estate.
[b]Including personal and business.
Source: *New York Times*, November 15, 1981, p. 19.

have been aimed largely at cyclical unemployment, and job-training programs (services) have been aimed at structural unemployment.

THE PROVISION OF SOCIAL SERVICES

Another large class of social policies are **services,** which are intended to provide noncash benefits to general groups of people. Governmental services are generally intended to provide tools by which people can improve their own welfare. Although many service policies are aimed primarily at lower-income people, they are not income maintenance policies, because instead of providing cash or in-kind benefits directly to people, service policies tend to provide them with the skills or support to increase their income. We will examine several types of social services, but it should be remembered that this is only a partial listing of the efforts of government to support many of the basic functions of the economy—education, job training, housing, transportation, and so on.

Education We have already examined several aspects of educational policy in the United States. Public actions that require school attendance and forbid racial or sexual discrimination in education are based on a fundamental belief that learning can affect a person's future success. There is also a general

services: Social policies intended to provide noncash benefits to general groups of people.

perception that higher educational expenditures produce brighter students. Although social scientists have found the relationship between public school expenditures and student achievement surprisingly difficult to establish, for nearly twenty years federal policy toward education—particularly at the federal level—has been aimed largely at reducing the inequities between school finances in different places.[14] Table 13-6 shows that some states spend more than three times as much per pupil as other states. Since the total national bill for all public schools in the mid-1980s was about $110 billion, any effort to equalize school expenditures would be terribly expensive. In addition, such an effort would necessarily be a federal project because no state would willingly send its tax dollars to another state. The American educational system, however, is based on the idea of local control. Some states and communities choose to keep property tax rates low despite the effect on school expenditures; other states choose to raise taxes and provide higher teachers' salaries and better facilities.

Nevertheless, there have been a few efforts at the federal level to provide assistance to some school districts and to individual students. The Morrill Acts of 1862 and 1890 provided land grants and cash grants to the states for the purpose of aiding colleges with programs in agriculture and mechanics. The first federal educational policy based on some notion of financial need was the Lanham Act of 1940, which granted federal funds to school districts in "federally impacted areas" (e.g., areas with tax-exempt federal properties, usually military bases). The most dramatic federal attempt to provide comparable education to all students, regardless of their parents' income, was the Elementary and Secondary Education Act (ESEA) of 1965. As part of the Johnson

TABLE 13-6
PUBLIC-SCHOOL EXPENDITURES PER PUPIL IN SELECTED STATES, 1981

State	Expenditure	State	Expenditure
Alabama	$1,835	Nebraska	$2,445
Alaska	$5,369	New Jersey	$3,285
California	$2,427	New Mexico	$2,178
Connecticut	$2,683	New York	$3,769
Georgia	$1,721	Ohio	$2,321
Illinois	$2,720	Pennsylvania	$2,841
Indiana	$2,008	South Carolina	$1,916
Kansas	$2,251	Texas	$2,012
Kentucky	$1,835	Virginia	$2,193
Massachusetts	$2,964	Washington	$2,679
Michigan	$2,652	Wisconsin	$2,759
	U.S. Average = $2,473		

Source: U.S. Bureau of the Census, *Statistical Abstract of the United States, 1984* (Washington, D.C.: Government Printing Office, 1984), p. 153.

administration's War on Poverty, the ESEA was promoted as a way of increasing the ability of poor children to compete in the adult world. Yet the idea of general federal aid to public schools was controversial. Protestants had opposed any aid that benefited parochial schools, and Catholics objected to legislation that excluded private schools. The ESEA skirted that problem by allocating money without regard to type of school. It was also feared that federal aid to schools would be a tool by which the government could force desegregation, but that issue was rendered moot by passage of the 1964 Civil Rights Act, which prohibited the use of federal funds in any racially discriminatory program.

Manpower Training   There are two basic ways by which the government can deal directly with the problem of unemployment, apart from improving the conditions or incentives for businesses to create more jobs. The most direct way is through the creation of public jobs; these were described as in-kind public assistance policies. The other major way is by providing unemployed workers with the skills that will qualify them for existing jobs. As we saw, structural unemployment occurs when there is a poor match between the characteristics of the work force and the market for employees. In essence, the economy itself redistributes job opportunities as demands for old products and services drop and demands for new products and services increase; manpower programs attempt to help workers follow those jobs without putting them directly on the public payroll.

Federal efforts in this area began with the Manpower Development and Training Act of 1962, which was originally intended to retrain workers who had lost their jobs to automation but was modified when it was realized that young workers had the greatest need for job skills. The Economic Opportunity Act of 1964 established the Job Corps, which provided training to disadvantaged youths in neighborhood centers. These efforts were successful in increasing the earnings of trained workers, but they had little effect on the overall unemployment problem.

During the late 1960s, both inflation and unemployment began to increase, and by 1970 the federal government was under pressure to provide additional jobs for the unemployed. The largest of the job-training bills was passed in 1973, after intense conflict between the White House and Congress. The Comprehensive Employment and Training Act (CETA) was intended to provide on-the-job and classroom training, operate Job Corps and summer job programs for poor youths, and provide public service jobs. However, many cities used CETA employees to replace city workers, thereby substituting federal revenues for local taxes, and many workers hired under the program were neither disadvantaged nor unskilled. CETA was replaced in 1982 by the Job Training Partnership Act, which provided no public jobs; under this act, local businesses (chosen by local elected officials) replaced politicians in deciding how job training programs would operate based on the demands of the private sector for workers.

Cities Most Americans are familiar with many of the most troublesome characteristics of modern urban areas, and many agree that government has an obligation to try to overcome some of these problems, particularly where private or collective action is ineffective (e.g., in the areas of crime and transportation). Yet there are some aspects of city life that may not benefit from public action; for example, public policies that are intended to help the urban poor by limiting what their landlords can charge may actually increase the cost of urban housing in the long run by reducing its supply.

In addition, the question of what to do for the urban poor is complicated by several other characteristics of American cities. First, many cities are actually composed of many local governments, with fragmented towns and villages and overlapping city and county jurisdictions. This makes coherent local policy difficult and invites state or federal intervention in urban affairs. Second, in the years following World War II, many middle-income groups, especially whites, fled the cities and moved to the suburbs. This "white flight" had the effects of segregating inner-city areas and lowering the amount of taxes available in the cities to pay for government services for the poor. Third, during the 1970s, enormous numbers of people living in Frost Belt cities (e.g., Cleveland, Detroit, Philadelphia, and Baltimore) moved to the Sun Belt cities (e.g., Phoenix, Houston, and San Diego), thereby depriving entire metropolitan areas in the Midwest and Northeast of economic growth and stable tax bases. During the 1970s, the Frost Belt cities lost 0.2 percent of their population as the Sun Belt cities grew by 23.2 percent.

Although there are federal policies to help people buy homes by providing loan insurance and mortgage funds, these programs can actually make life more difficult for poor people if, for example, home buyers renovate an older urban neighborhood, which is good for the city's tax base, and thereby drive up rents and property values. Poor people living in cities were the deliberate targets of another set of federal housing policies, however.[15] These began with the Housing Act of 1937, which authorized federal slum-clearance and low-income housing projects. Few funds were devoted to these tasks until 1949, when a new Housing Act declared that "a decent home and a suitable living environment for every American family" was national policy. By the mid-1960s, the demand of some groups for increased public activity in improving urban housing was becoming louder, partly as a result of riots in racial ghettos during the years 1965 to 1968. The issue was elevated to cabinet level in 1965, when the Department of Housing and Urban Development (HUD) was created. Perhaps the most ambitious federal attempt to provide improvements for the residents of inner cities was the Model Cities program (1966), which was originally intended to demonstrate in a few cities that large infusions of federal funds and comprehensive planning could reshape the face of American cities. Opposition to the program by Republicans and conservative Democrats, who preferred private-sector solutions, kept the funding for Model Cities low, and some members of Congress blocked funding because their districts were not selected to participate in the program.

Other programs in the 1960s and 1970s were intended to divert large amounts of federal revenues into declining urban areas. The 1968 Housing and Urban Development Act covered a wide range of topics, including mass transit, flood insurance, and rental or mortgage-rate assistance to low-income families. To counteract the gradual transfer of political power from state and local governments to Washington through *categorical grants* (federal funds earmarked for specific purposes), the Nixon administration attempted to increase local control over the fate of cities by returning funds to state and local governments in *block grants* for them to use as they considered appropriate, although with a few restrictions. Yet a common criticism of many urban policies has been that they actually provide greater benefits to the middle-class suburban homeowner than to the poor ghetto resident. (One argument is that the housing construction industry is an important source of jobs, so single-family residence subsidies—like other public policies—serve more than one purpose.) In addition, some federal housing policies have been spectacular failures. Slum-clearance programs have often had the effect of forcing poor people out of their admittedly inadequate housing without providing any alternatives. Some urban renewal projects, involving the construction of huge subsidized public housing projects, have led to high concentrations of poor people in unsafe, poorly constructed, and commonly vandalized buildings.

Tax Benefits

Other than some social insurance programs, social policies—like most policies—are fueled by money taken from the United States Treasury. In turn, the Treasury (through its subsidiary, the Internal Revenue Service) takes money from people and businesses by taxation. That simple term disguises a great deal of complexity. Taxation is much more than simply a method for gathering government revenues. To a large degree, it is itself a redistributive policy. The American system of taxes imposes disproportionate costs on some people and confers special benefits on others.

For many years, taxation as a means of regulating commerce or causing social change was closely scrutinized by the courts, but during the 1930s the role of taxation was expanded to include the pursuit of social and economic ends. Franklin Roosevelt, echoing the sentiments of such earlier presidents as Theodore Roosevelt, Woodrow Wilson, and Herbert Hoover, spoke of using taxes to bring about a more equitable distribution of wealth in America, and the Supreme Court, in upholding the Social Security Act in 1937, stated that Congress was the ultimate judge of what aspects of the "general welfare" could be supported through taxation.[16] The difficulty for politicians in using taxes as a policy tool is clear: taxes are noticed because they usually involve taking cash out of people's pockets. Not surprisingly, then, there are a number of ways of performing that task.

One form of raising revenues, mainly at the local level, is by taxing property. *Property taxes* account for about one-half of all locally raised revenues. Another method, the state *sales tax,* was begun in the 1920s but became widespread during the depression. In recent years, the state and local sales tax has surpassed property taxes as the largest source of nonfederal government revenues. Sales taxes have come under attack because they tend to be regressive: poorer people tend to pay a larger percentage of their disposable income in sales taxes than do wealthier people because poorer people save and invest less, and spend a higher proportion of their income on necessary consumer items (e.g., clothing and food), which are usually subject to sales taxes. One possible way to compensate for the regressivity of the sales tax would be to selectively tax only those items the wealthy are likely to buy. At one time, *excise taxes* were promoted for that reason; they were to be applied primarily to "luxury" items. In fact, excise taxes do not discriminate against higher-income people, because the emergency excise taxes on liquor, tobacco, cosmetics, motor fuel, tires, and so on that were imposed during World War II for the most part have been continued, so today's excise taxes apply to many items that can hardly be called "luxury." In addition, *gift* or *estate taxes* may appear to be redistributive (because they usually are thought of as problems of the rich), but many gifts and estates escape the full tax burden through the clever use of complex tax laws.

The type of tax policy people are most acutely aware of is the *income tax.* Authorized in 1913 by the Sixteenth Amendment, the federal income tax has a number of characteristics that have made it attractive to government revenue-raisers. First, it is an accepted, if not loved, way of raising large amounts of revenues. Second, it provides policymakers with a flexible tool by which benefits can be selectively conferred on particular groups or for particular purposes. The primary mechanism by which this is done is the deduction. For example, because contributing to charities is viewed as a socially desirable goal, the tax system allows such contributions to be deducted from a person's income, thereby reducing the contributor's tax burden. Other deductions are provided for the blind, the aged, home mortgage interest payments (and interest on other items such as credit cards or automobile loans), medical costs over a certain amount (based on an individual's income), child care expenses, and business-related costs (because the conduct of business is considered to be good for society). All of the tax concessions provide benefits to selected people or groups—by not taking dollars from them—and thus clearly are forms of social policies.

Third, an income tax can be proportional (with all incomes taxed at the same percentage), or progressive (with higher tax rates for people with higher incomes). A progressive tax has been justified largely on the belief that the pain of paying, say, 10 percent of a $5,000 wage is greater than the pain of paying 10 percent of $50,000. The degree to which the American income tax system is truly progressive (and therefore redistributive) has been a matter of dispute for many years. On the one hand, we can see from statistics (Table 13-7) that families with higher incomes are charged progressively higher taxes. In 1979, the 5 percent of families with the highest income paid 37 percent of

TABLE 13-7
FEDERAL BUDGET RECEIPTS BY SOURCE, 1960–1980, AND AVERAGE
EFFECTIVE INCOME TAX RATE AT SELECTED INCOME LEVELS,
1960–1980.

	1960	1970	1975	1980
Sources of Federal Budget Receipts (%)				
Individual income tax	44.0	46.7	43.6	46.9
Social insurance tax	15.9	23.4	30.7	30.9
Corporate income tax	23.3	16.9	14.5	12.4
Excise taxes	12.6	8.2	5.9	4.7
Custom, estate, gift taxes	2.9	3.1	2.9	2.6
Other	1.3	1.8	2.4	2.4
Average Effective Income Tax Rate (%)[a]				
Single person, no dependents				
$ 5,000	12.0	7.5	4.0	5.0
10,000	15.5	13.8	11.4	11.8
20,000	19.3	17.0	16.7	19.2
35,000	24.4	21.1	23.2	26.3
50,000	29.6	24.8	27.7	32.1
70,000	36.7	30.2	34.4	39.1
Married couple, no dependents				
$ 5,000	6.1	1.9	0	0
10,000	12.0	10.2	7.0	7.0
20,000	15.5	13.8	13.0	13.7
35,000	18.3	17.1	18.2	20.9
50,000	21.0	19.9	22.3	26.0
70,000	25.3	24.7	28.3	32.6
Married couple, 2 dependents				
$ 5,000	0	− 10.0	− 10.0	− 10.0
10,000	6.1	5.8	1.2	3.7
20,000	12.2	11.4	10.2	11.3
35,000	16.1	15.3	16.1	14.0
50,000	19.0	18.3	20.5	24.2
70,000	23.6	23.3	26.8	31.2

[a]1980 dollars, adjusted gross income.

Source: U.S. Bureau of the Census, *Statistical Abstract of the United States, 1981* (Washington, D.C.: Government Printing Office, 1981), pp. 247, 160.

the total income tax bill. Yet there are many ways in which the relatively wealthy can deduct, shelter, or defer their taxes and thereby lower their contribution. There is also evidence that the progressivity of the federal income tax is partially offset by the regressivity of state and local sales and excise taxes, producing a net tax burden that is at best proportional and even slightly regressive overall. One way to use the tax system to assure that the poor bear a lighter burden is through a negative income tax, by which families with sufficiently low incomes would receive refunds from the Internal Revenue Service in excess of what they paid in; the Earned Income Tax Credit, begun in 1975, is a step in that direction, and some see such a system as a way to simplify and rationalize the complex federal welfare system.

The progressive income tax system has been accused of having several flaws. First, some believe it creates a disincentive for people to work harder, because their additional income is likely to be taxed at higher and higher rates. Second, it may encourage people to work in the "underground economy" of cash and barter, which creates unreported and untaxed income; as many as 30 percent of all American households fail to report all of their sources of income, and perhaps $400 billion in taxable income is hidden from the Internal Revenue Service each year. Finally, there has been a decline in support for the current tax system because it is widely perceived to be unfair; in a 1982 survey for *Business Week,* 86 percent of the public agreed with the statement that "while most lower- and middle-income people now pay their federal tax by taking standard deductions, most higher-income people get out of paying much of their taxes by hiring clever tax accountants and lawyers who show them how to use loopholes in the tax law."[17]

A commonly proposed remedy for these tax problems is the flat income tax, which, in its simplest form, would replace the current system of tax concessions—deductions, exemptions, credits, and so on—with a fixed and universal tax rate on all income, regardless of source. However, a simple, across-the-board flat tax rate would be proportional, and its effect would be regressive (see Table 13-8). Another option is a consumption tax, one that taxes only the portion of income that is devoted to consumption and does not tax savings or investment. A national sales tax or a value-added tax (VAT)—a tax on goods and services based on the value added at each stage of production—would simplify the tax system and, as some European nations have found, induce people to save more of their income. However, both types of consumption tax might threaten the social policy goal of progressivity.

Assessing Social Benefits Programs

There are several general conclusions to be drawn from this description of the social provision of rights and resources. The first is that public assistance ("welfare") programs are not the largest or most expensive of all income maintenance policies. As shown in Table 13-3, the largest of the public assistance programs accounts for less than one-sixth of all entitlement program expenditures, with retirement costs (social security, federal employee pensions, and military retirement) accounting for more than five times the cost of welfare. Second, it is very difficult to compare the cost of many other social policies. For example, the total cost to the federal government of tax benefits in 1981 could be estimated at about $230 billion (compared with about $600

TABLE 13-8
HOW A FLAT-RATE INCOME TAX WOULD AFFECT TAXPAYERS[a]

Income Class	% of All Federal Taxes Paid in 1979	% of All Taxes That Would Be Paid Under 14.5% Flat Rate
Less than $10,000	4.0%[b]	13.4%[b]
$10,000–$19,999	17.4%	25.6%
$20,000–$29,999	23.6%	25.5%
$30,000–$39,999	16.8%	15.0%
$40,000–$49,999	8.6%	6.2%
$50,000–$74,999	9.1%	5.8%
$75,000–$99,999	4.6%	2.7%
$100,000–$199,999	7.0%	3.1%
$200,000 and over	7.4%	2.4%

[a]The figures show that a 14.5 percent flat tax rate (with *all* taxpayers paying 14.5 percent of their income) would shift some burden from higher-income groups to lower-income groups.
[b]Numbers rounded.

Source: *Business Week,* July 19, 1982, p. 130.

billion in federal receipts), but this figure is based on many assumptions about what would happen to the economy (in terms of jobs, consumption, and so on) if such items as charitable contributions and mortgage interest were suddenly taxed instead of deducted. Similarly, the cost of many social programs is intertwined with other government expenditures. Therefore, policy anaylsts try to be careful when using numbers to describe various social policies.

In addition, we have seen that social policies usually have more than one effect. By increasing student aid, for example, not only is educational policy affected but (to take only one example) the work force also changes because college-age students find it easier to stay in school. If such policies have multiple effects, it follows that they are usually intended to serve multiple purposes. Among other things, this makes it difficult to analyze social policies. For a program with a variety of effects that cascade through society, what constitutes a "success"? Similarly, social policies are made by multiple actors within the federal government and often across state and local levels as well. As we have seen many times in this book, the fragmentation of American government serves to constrain not only the power of government but also its logic and efficiency.

Finally, it should be obvious by now that the system of social policies involves an enormous number of trade-offs. For example, we have seen that there are policies intended to provide assistance to the poor and unemployed, policies intended to encourage and enable people to work, and laws to assure that workers will receive reasonable wages. Consider, however, the following example. In 1982 the poverty line for a four-person family was drawn at $9,862, the income equivalent to that of a worker earning about $4.40 per hour after taxes. If the head of such a family were guaranteed a minimum income equal to the poverty line, there would be no incentive to take a job even if it paid considerably more than $4.40 per hour (which is itself above the minimum wage) because it costs money to work: there are expenses for transportation, work clothes, taxes, and so on. Using the same logic, a person earning $50,000 per year may pause before accepting additional tasks in return for a salary raise if half of that additional income would be lost to income taxes. Thus, almost any policy that provides benefits directly or indirectly to Americans must be carefully considered in terms of its costs, benefits, and effects on incentives. As we turn now to the other major form of social policies—regulation—this point should be remembered.

SOCIAL REGULATION

Social regulations are the group of government policies intended to confer benefits on a group of people—such as all air-breathers, buyers on credit, or users of medical services—by requiring or inducing individuals or firms to confer the benefit on themselves or on other people. Failure to do so can result in sanctions such as fines or imprisonment. For example, a federal law requires automobile manufacturers to install seat belts in each car they sell. The drivers and occupants of cars who gain from enhanced safety do not receive the benefit directly from the government, but the government provides an incentive for General Motors, Ford, and so on to provide added safety features: if they don't they are subject to fines.

Of course, social regulation is not always effective. The purpose of the safety-belt law is not to include extra equipment in cars but rather to enhance safety, and few people always use their seat belts. In addition, even if certain regulations are effective, sometimes their costs outweigh their benefits. Each regulation must be judged on its own merits and on opportunity-cost criteria: is there a less costly way to accomplish the same purpose? In addition, we should note that each social regulatory statute has its own peculiar political history in which conflicting interest groups attempt to influence its particular provisions. Some of these laws confirm the victory of one group and the loss of others, some are the embodiment of delicate compromises among interest groups, and still others are little more than special interest legislation under the guise of aiding the public interest. The Volstead Act, which outlawed alcoholic beverages during the 1920s, exemplifies the victory of one group (the prohibitionists); much environmental legislation represents compromise; and various state licensing statutes, such as those licensing taxicabs in the presumed interest of public safety, are little more than attempts to limit entry (i.e., competition) into an occupation.

Social regulation, then, can be very complex, so each statute must be individually evaluated. Even if it seems as if regulation is the best way to provide benefits to a target group, there is still the question of which regulatory technique is best. In general, there are three kinds of regulatory techniques in the social policy area: injunctions, standards, and requirements.

Injunctions

The biblical Ten Commandments are part of the moral foundation of the Western world. They prohibit such acts as murder, robbery, and adultery, and mandate observance of the Sabbath and obedience to parents. Societies have added (and deleted) somewhat from that list. Because standards and requirements also forbid or mandate certain types of behavior, distinguishing standards and requirements from injunctions may seem to be difficult, but often it is not. For example, the injunction against robbery is absolute; there is no category of legal robberies. However, nuclear power plants are not outlawed as a category; rather, they must meet certain construction and operating standards set by the Nuclear Regulatory Commission (NRC). Similarly, the advertising of products for sale is not generally outlawed, but a company must meet the requirement of truthful advertising in order to avoid having the Federal Trade Commission (FTC) step in.

Positive Injunctions   In effect, government sometimes tells us that we must perform particular acts "for our own good." This may be true, but those acts usually are considered beneficial to others as well. One example is the requirement that schoolchildren receive inoculations to prevent diseases such as smallpox, measles, and polio; not only are the recipients of the vaccines healthier but society is protected from the spread of disease (see Table 13-9). Other positive injunctions simply require people to help others. For example, many states have enacted laws requiring parents to support their children, and the Federal Office of Child Support Enforcement assists the states by helping to locate errant parents (if necessary, establishing paternity) and by obtaining child-support payments.

The most widespread positive injunction imposed on American citizens is school attendance. State laws mandate that every person in the nation spend about one-sixth of the average life span in the classroom, acquiring social values and intellectual skills that are purported to make each person "better" and, not incidentally, better equipped to participate in American society. In 1852, when the first compulsory school attendance law was passed, in Massachusetts, the average person attended school for only one year; in 1980, the average number of years of attendance was 12.5. The great burst in public education could not occur until the family farm declined, and agricultural productivity increased, and urban prosperity grew. Farm parents needed their children to help with planting and harvesting, and in the cities children were often put to work at early ages to help supplement their parents' income. For example, in 1910, New York City high schools graduated only 2,477 children (60 percent of them females) in a city of 4.7 million people.

TABLE 13-9
DEATH RATE BY SELECTED CAUSES, 1900–1980

Cause	No. Deaths per 100,000 Population			
	1900	1940	1970	1980
Tuberculosis	194.4	45.9	2.6	0.9
Syphilis	12.0	14.4	0.2	a
Typhoid	31.3	1.1	b	b
Scarlet fever	9.6	0.5	b	b
Diphtheria	40.3	1.1	b	b
Whooping cough	12.2	2.2	b	b
Measles	13.3	0.5	b	b
Cancer	64.0	120.3	162.8	183.9
Diabetes	11.0	26.6	18.9	15.4
Cardiovascular disease[c]	345.2	485.7	496.0	436.4
Influenza and pneumonia	202.2	70.3	30.9	24.1
Stomach/Intestinal diseases	142.7	10.3	0.6	a
Cirrhosis of liver	12.5	8.6	15.5	13.5
Motor-vehicle accidents	b	26.2	26.9	23.5
All other accidents	72.3	47.0	29.5	23.2
Suicide	10.2	14.4	11.6	11.9

[a]Not available.
[b]Less than 0.05 percent.
[c]Includes cerebrovascular, hypertensive, atherosclerosis, and other heart diseases.

Sources: U.S. Bureau of Census, *Historical Statistics of the United States, Colonial Times to 1970* (Washington, D.C.: Government Printing Office, 1976), Series B 149-166; U.S. Bureau of the Census, *Statistical Abstract of the United States, 1984* (Washington, D.C.: Government Printing Office, 1984), p. 78.

Some people in early America were opposed to compulsory education because it threatened to teach children to question their roles in life or in the general social order. Yet, in late nineteenth-century America, many people believed that compulsory public education was the only way to preserve social order as huge numbers of immigrants, with alien languages and foreign social values, arrived in the New World. Even today, the public schools are expected to supply children with at least a basic intellectual education, along with civic values and perhaps particular vocational skills. Thus, this positive injunction has almost unanimous support because children are expected to emerge from schools as "free" adults—able to earn an income, to make reasonable decisions, and to understand the society in which they live.

Negative Injunctions   Traditionally, negative injunctions have been associated with activities involving a strong moral taint. Many states, for example, still have laws that prohibit gambling or certain sexual practices. Perhaps the most dramatic example of negative injunction in American history was the prohibition of the sale of alcoholic beverages through the 1920s and into the early 1930s. As each of these examples shows, however, negative injunctions frequently backfire. Widespread gambling occurs everywhere it is outlawed, sexual tastes do not change in places where those tastes are outlawed, and the prohibition of the sale of alcoholic beverages caused many Americans to willingly break the law. In part, these policies have failed because of the enormous difficulty the state faces in obtaining sufficient information to secure legal convictions. They also fail because to many people it is none of the government's business whether they gamble, drink, smoke marijuana, or indulge their sexual preferences in ways they choose, and these people will feel justified in violating the law. Although most people would not object to a law forbidding driving while under the influence of alcohol, because doing so imposes a high risk of harm to others and is therefore not in the private sphere, they do resent being told that they cannot consume alcohol at all.

For these reasons, government in recent times has sharply reduced the number of activities covered by negative injunctions. Cigarette smoking is harmful to the health, but it is not outlawed. Instead, cigarette manufacturers are required to print a health warning, and cigarettes may not be smoked in certain places—an injunction designed to balance the preferences of smokers against the preferences of nonsmokers. Apart from certain negative injunctions carried over from the past, today's applications occur only when, in the judgment of Congress or administrators, the costs of an action outweigh the benefits under virtually all circumstances. Thus, the Delaney Amendment requires the Food and Drug Administration (FDA) to ban any food additive found to

A schoolroom in New York City, circa 1894. Despite overcrowded classrooms, the national illiteracy rate dropped from 20 percent in 1870 to 10 percent in 1900 as the demand for skilled workers and well socialized citizens prompted massive educational reforms. (Jacob A. Riis, Jacob A. Riis Collection, Museum of the City of New York)

cause cancer in animals or humans, and the Department of Agriculture has banned certain dangerous pesticides when other reasonable alternatives were available.

Standards

The idea of standards is an old one. A society with no common standards of measurement, such as inches, minutes, or pounds, or without common standards of money would be primitive. Standards serve many purposes. First, they provide an important source of information about things. Standards of meat products such as "prime," "choice," and so on tell us something about the relative quality of such products. Furthermore, common standards reduce transaction costs because buyers can rely on a description of standards rather than independent evaluations of products and services; for example, suppose you had to independently evaluate a stereo amplifier in order to determine its power output and other characteristics. In addition, standards imposed by the government can compel people and firms in the private sector to produce goods and services that attain a minimum quality. The standards the Nuclear Regulatory Commission (NRC) imposes on the operation of nuclear power plants and the maximum pollution levels the Environmental Protection Agency (EPA) imposes on industrial facilities are examples.

The oldest area in which standards have been employed is human health; in fact, health standards may be as old as agriculture. There are biblical references to the adulteration of food, and Pliny the Elder complained that "white earth" was added to bread in ancient Pompeii. The modern era of attempts to regulate health standards began in 1906 with the passage of the Pure Food and Drug Act. Although this legislation prohibited interstate commerce in adulterated or misbranded foods and drugs, it had weak enforcement provisions and was often disregarded. However, after at least seventy-three persons died in the autumn of 1937 from a patent medicine called "Elixir Sulfanilamide," Congress passed the Food, Drug, and Cosmetics Act of 1938; under this law, the Food and Drug Administration was required to prohibit the sale of unsanitary or dangerous foods, drugs, and cosmetics. The 1938 act was amended in 1954 (to establish regulations for pesticides), in 1958 (to regulate food additives), in 1960 (to regulate color additives), and in 1962 (to tighten the regulations on drugs). Major laws affecting safety and product performance standards are shown in Table 13-10.

Criticisms of the 1962 drug amendments, which required drug manufacturers to prove that their products were both safe and effective before they could be marketed, illustrate the difficulty in setting regulatory standards. This legislation was largely the result of the discovery that thalidomide —a drug that had caused severe birth defects in European children whose mothers had taken it—had been kept off the American market because an FDA chemist doubted its safety. The need for such caution has not been disputed, but FDA standards for the marketing of new drugs have been accused of being so complicated

TABLE 13-10
MAJOR CONSUMER SAFETY AND PRODUCT
PERFORMANCE LEGISLATION

Year	Legislation	Major Provisions
1906	Pure Food and Drug Act	Prohibited misbranded and adulterated food and drugs
1938	Food, Drug and Cosmetics Act	Required manufacturers to prove the safety of new drugs
1958	Food, Drug and Cosmetics Act Amendments	Required manufacturers to prove the safety of food additives; banned food additives that cause cancer in humans or animals
1962	Food, Drug and Cosmetics Act Amendments	Drug manufacturers required to prove effectiveness of new drugs in addition to safety
1966	Fair Packaging and Labelling Act	Prohibited unfair or deceptive packaging and labeling of some consumer products
1966	National Traffic and Motor Vehicle Safety Act	Authorized establishment of safety standards for tires and vehicles sold in U.S.
1968	Truth-in-Lending Act	Required lenders and merchants to inform consumers of total cost of loans and annual percentage rate; prohibited unsolicited distribution of credit cards
1972	Consumer Product Safety Act	Created Consumer Product Safety Commission; banned hazardous consumer products and required manufacturers to repair or replace hazardous products

that pharmaceutical companies cannot afford to introduce many useful new drugs.[18]

Few regulatory standards have generated more controversy than those of the Environmental Protection Agency (EPA) in water and air pollution. In order to understand environmental policy, we must understand the concept of **externalities.** Suppose A agrees to produce glue made from horse carcasses for B. In the process of transforming horses to glue, A imposes costs on C and others living in the neighborhood by emitting noxious odors and chemicals dangerous to the health. Economists call these costs "externalities" because they are imposed upon people external to the transaction—in this case, C and others. Thus, a mechanism is needed by which those external costs can be brought back to the responsible party, who can either compensate the innocent victims or avoid the costs by altering his or her behavior. In the area of the environment, there are abundant examples of externalities: the clear-cut logger who indirectly kills fish by increasing the silt in streams, the coal-burning electrical generating plant emitting sulfurous gases that may fall as acid rain thousands of miles away, and towns that dump raw sewage into streams. Yet,

externalities: Side effects of actions that influence the well-being of persons who did not consent to the actions; these side effects may be benefits or costs.

although we all may agree that pollution is a problem, there is also a problem in setting the appropriate level of government action. Individuals certainly have the right to drink clean water and breathe clean air, but how much air and water pollution is permissible? And what about the rights of producers to engage in their enterprises?

Today's environmental-quality standards have been devised by a wide variety of institutions at different levels of government:

1. both national and state legislatures, which establish basic standards and procedures
2. administrative agencies, most notably the EPA, which draw up the precise standards and attempt to implement them
3. the president's Council on Environmental Quality, which sets broad environmental policies and coordinates the environmental activities of federal agencies
4. the courts, which try to resolve disputes over the meaning of legal terms and the procedures of agencies

Not surprisingly, out of this process emerge no clear answers. State governments with particular economic interests (in automobiles, timber, agriculture, and so on) tend to reflect those interests, whereas the federal government tries to standardize the resulting policies. The more significant of those attempts are shown in Table 13-11.

One technique that has not been used in the United States is to tax pollution. If each polluter were required to pay a tax equal to the estimated costs imposed by the pollutant, there would be an incentive to install pollution-controlling equipment or to reduce pollution. This approach would differ from liability in that the polluters would not be required to reimburse the victims of their acts. A second technique is to establish a tolerable level of pollution emissions to which polluters would be restricted but to leave the choice of how to reduce pollution to the individual or firm. Thus, a firm might choose to retain a dirty technology but compensate by cleaning up another part of its operation, because the government would have set only a general standard for the quality of air in a "bubble" over all of the firm's plants.

There are many variations on these and other schemes for controlling pollution, but the dominant approach to environmental protection today is the imposition of narrow standards. Among the responsibilities of the EPA are (1) setting limits on the level of air pollutants that can be emitted from "stationary" sources (e.g., factories, incinerators, power plants) and from new motor vehicles; (2) issuing permits for the discharge of pollutants into many of the nation's rivers, lakes, and streams; (3) administering subsidies for the construction of sewage-treatment plants; and (4) keeping track of and occasionally assisting in the cleaning of hazardous waste dump sites. These tasks, along with many others, keep the EPA in a state of constant political tension because its decisions affect not only the profitability and growth potential of

TABLE 13-11
MAJOR ENVIRONMENTAL LEGISLATION

Year	Legislation	Major Provisions
1899	Refuse Act	Restricted dumping of hazardous wastes into navigable streams, lakes, rivers
1948	Water Pollution Control Act	Provided federal assistance to states in establishing water-quality programs
1955	Air Pollution Control Act	Provided federal assistance to states in establishing air-quality programs
1963	Clean Air Act	Authorized federal grants to develop and establish air pollution control programs
1970	National Environmental Protection Act	Established Environmental Protection Agency and required environmental impact statements for major federal projects
1970	Water Quality Improvement Act	Made oil companies liable (to $14 million) for damage caused by oil spills
1970	Clean Air Act Amendments	Authorized establishment of automobile pollution emission standards
1972	Federal Water Pollution Control Act Amendments	Required companies to obtain permits to discharge pollutants into rivers and lakes
1974	Safe Drinking Water Act	Authorized standards for safe public drinking water
1976	Toxic Substances Control Act	Banned PCBs (polychlorinated biphenyls) and authorized the EPA to require testing of toxic substances
1977	Federal Water Pollution Control Act Amendments	Authorized establishment of "best conventional technology" standards by 1984
1977	Clean Air Act Amendments	Delayed but strengthened automobile-emission and air-quality standards

nearly every type of productive enterprise in the United States, but also the health of current and future generations. In addition, the effects of environmental regulations are often difficult to predict. For example, when the EPA banned the pesticide DDT, farmers began using chemicals that were more toxic (and that, unlike the long-lasting DDT, had to be applied frequently), thus increasing the health risks to farm workers; but that was a problem under the jurisdiction of the Occupational Safety and Health Administration (OSHA). Regulators also are not equipped to predict the effects of their environmental standards on other questions such as the competitiveness of American goods abroad (because of higher costs resulting from pollution controls) and the productivity of American workers. Nevertheless, there are some strong indications that many environmental regulations have been, on balance, beneficial.

In addition to the many standards that apply to health, there are also many that apply to safety. Congress has given authority to promulgate standards for the safety and performance of products to several federal agencies and offices (see Table 13-10). The FDA sets standards for the safety and effectiveness of many consumable goods. Other agencies with responsibility for safety standards are the Consumer Product Safety Commission, which establishes mandatory safety standards for the design, construction, contents, performance, and labeling of consumer products; the National Highway Traffic Safety Administration, which sets performance standards for motor vehicles; and the Occupational Safety and Health Administration, which establishes workplace safety standards. There are many other agencies with some jurisdiction over aspects of safety and performance standards: for example, the Federal Aviation Administration, the Agriculture Department, the United States Coast Guard, the Federal Communications Commission, and the Department of Housing and Urban Development. None of these agencies has a simple task.

The experience of the FDA in trying to implement the 1958 and 1962 amendments clearly demonstrates that there is an enormous difference between risk and safety. Sometimes it is possible to estimate the likelihood that something will occur (e.g., the risk of an accident), but it is an entirely different problem to establish a measure of safety, because that depends on how much risk is acceptable. In the case of food additives, does a 20 percent chance that a rat will develop cancerous tumors from an equivalent daily dose of 100 artificially sweetened soft drinks indicate that saccharin is unsafe for humans? What about a 100 percent chance? Furthermore, regulators must often decide about the acceptable cost of a safety standard, assuming that it can be measured. For example, in 1972, the NHTSA estimated the social cost of a single death at $200,725: $173,000 in lost productivity, $1,125 in medical costs, $16,600 in funeral, legal, and various other costs, and $10,000 for the victim's "pain and suffering." The Ford Motor Company then used the NHTSA figure to calculate that proposed fuel-tank safety standards would yield a benefit of $49 million (multiplying $200,000 times the number of deaths and injuries that probably would be avoided) and cost consumers $137 million (or $11 per car); therefore, Ford argued, the proposed standards should be dropped. Some federal agencies have been criticized for not using such cost-benefit analyses to guide their regulatory standards. Yet the two agencies that have come under the strongest attack for their occasionally unreasonable product or safety standards—the CPSC and the OSHA—were reflecting the attitude of Congress when it established them: they were not allowed to apply cost-benefit analyses but were required to design regulations that would achieve the "maximum feasible" amount of safety.

Requirements

Although standards apply to quality, quantity, and production processes, requirements pertain to activities that are mandated in order to lawfully provide a product or service. Usually the regulation requires that information beneficial to purchasers or users of the good or service must be provided. For example, under several federal laws, the articles of clothing you purchase in stores must be truthfully labeled with respect to fiber content. If a shirt is composed of 50 percent cotton and 50 percent polyester, the label must indicate this. When we reflect upon this example, the reason for the regulation becomes apparent. A consumer cannot be expected to spend the large sums necessary to test the fiber content of all your clothing, especially when the cost of labeling is relatively low.

Content or performance information must be provided for many other articles of commerce. For example, every appliance must be accompanied by warranty information, and every loan or sale on credit is covered by the truth-in-lending law, discussed in Chapter 10. Like so many other social policies, however, good intentions and the enactment of a law are no guarantees that the information will be important to the intended beneficiaries, or even that they will be attentive to it.

Another set of information regulations is occupational licensing, which is usually regulated at the state or local level. Doctors, dentists, lawyers, architects, and many other occupations may not lawfully practice their trade unless licensed by a government agency. In order to be licensed, one must usually pass a series of qualifying examinations. The licensing certificate resulting from this process conveys a considerable amount of information to the consumer of the service about the licensee's competence. You would usually not be able to independently determine whether, for example, a person is competent to practice medicine without the licensing procedure. Yet licensing has its costs as well as its benefits. It obviously restricts the supply of a service and, therefore, will probably have an upward effect on its price. Because of this, some occupational groups have sought licensing even though there may be no justifications for it. For example, do dry cleaners, taxicab drivers, and real-estate brokers need to be licensed? Perhaps, but political considerations frequently enter here, as in every other social policy.

Requirements need not be positive in form; that is, they need not require someone to do something, such as label a container. They also may forbid certain forms of conduct. The Federal Trade Commission, for example, has a legal duty to prevent or order a stop to false and misleading advertising and labeling of many products. Accordingly, the FTC has entered thousands of orders and issued dozens of rules requiring advertisers to cease and desist from making certain claims. These have included claims that certain preparations can cure cancer, arthritis, the common cold, and other diseases; statements that goods are being sold at special prices when, in fact, these are the customary prices; and a host of other misleading claims that clever people have devised. Given the vast number of advertising messages generated in newspapers, magazines, radio, television, and direct mailings, it is not surprising that the FTC and state agencies with similar jurisdiction can cope with only a small percentage, and often not the most serious, of them. Thus, like the other types of social regulation, requirements have costs as well as benefits, failures as well as successes. Like all social legislation, we must avoid sweeping generalizations about requirements and evaluate each program and its alternatives separately.

POLICY GOALS AND OUTCOMES

If this chapter, and this book, has an underlying theme, it is that things are nearly always more complicated than they seem. Actions have effects, and those effects cause other effects, and so on. If we could assume that Congress intended only to eliminate the chances for a "bought" election when it passed a bill reforming political campaign financing, then evaluating the congressional action might seem to be straightforward: were candidates for office less likely to receive large amounts of cash from a few sources to whom they might be beholden? But one of the consequences of this law—the Federal Election Campaign Act—was to encourage the formation of political action committees, which in turn created a new set of campaign financing problems. Assessing this policy would not be simple, and, of course, the intent of Congress may have been as complicated as the effects of its action.

With multiple goals and complex consequences, governmental actions may appear to be beyond our capacity to decipher and analyze. In this book, however, we have examined many aspects of American government and politics using a small number of basic concepts. For example, in our attempts to understand and evaluate the performance of government and the results of its actions, we have used the ideas of incentives and constraints. If we ask both "Why should President Lyndon Johnson have wanted to pursue a War on Poverty during the 1960s?" (i.e., what were the benefits to him?) and "How were his actions constrained?" we have greatly simplified the problem. The answers still are not easy, of course. The intended benefits included both measurable payoffs (e.g., a reduction in urban riots, an increase in the standard of living for poor Americans, and so on) and those that are much harder to detect (e.g., the fulfillment of a presidential, congressional, and public need to be charitable and just). The constraints were both practical (e.g., budgetary and legal limits, and the costs of organizing and acquiring information about the problem of poverty) and political (how much reallocation of benefits would Americans tolerate, and with what trade-offs?). Yet because the concepts introduced in Chapter 1 encourage us to ask these sorts of questions, they suggest a kind of order to the governmental process.

We have seen that the American political and economic systems are far from perfect. Discrimination, injustice, and poverty persist, and probably always will. But an objective reading of the record of America's past and present will provide unmistakable evidence that great progress has been made. That progress is due in large part to the mixture of stability and flexibility that have characterized American political and economic history. As long as the nation continues to recognize and save its successes, while trying to understand and correct its failings, there is reason to be optimistic.

NOTES

[1]See the discussion in Richard M. Titmuss, *Social Policy* (New York: Pantheon, 1974), Chapter 2.

[2]Louis Lasagna, "Who Will Adopt the Orphan Drugs?", *Regulation,* November/December 1979, pp. 27–32; Sam Peltzman, "An Evaluation of Consumer Protection Legislation: The 1962 Drug Amendments," *Journal of Political Economy* (September/October 1973): pp. 1049–1091.

[3]See the articles in Frederick Mosteller and Daniel P. Moynihan, eds., *On Equality of Educational Opportunity* (New York: Vintage, 1972).

[4]See June Axinn and Herman Levin, *Social Welfare: A History of the American Response to Need,* 2nd ed. (New York: Harper & Row, 1982).

[5]T. H. Marshall, *The Right to Welfare and Other Essays* (New York: Free Press, 1981), p. 84.

[6]Brown v. Board of Education of Topeka, Kansas, 347 U.S. 483 (1954).

[7]Sweatt v. Painter, 399 U.S. 629 (1950).

[8]Alexander v. Holmes County Board of Education, 369 U.S. 19 (1969).

[9]Swann v. Charlotte-Mecklenburg Board of Education, 402 U.S. 1 (1971).

[10]Lyndon B. Johnson, *The Vantage Point* (New York: Holt, Rinehart and Winston, 1971), p. 166.

[11]Regents of the University of California v. Bakke, 438 U.S. 265 (1978).

[12]United Steelworkers of America v. Weber, and Kaiser Aluminum v. Weber, 443 U.S. 193 (1979).

[13]Not all income maintenance programs are intended to be redistributive. West Germany's pension system is state-subsidized, but it distinguishes between different categories of workers and pays benefits closely related to a worker's pre-retirement earnings. See Arnold J. Heidenheimer, Hugh Heclo, and Carolyn Teich Adams, *Comparative Public Policy,* 2nd ed. (New York: St. Martin's, 1983), pp. 215–216.

[14]Eric A. Hanushek, "Throwing Money at Schools," *Journal of Policy Analysis and Management* (Fall, 1981): pp. 19–41.

[15]As we noted earlier, sometimes policies cannot be easily categorized as in-kind benefits or service programs. Public housing could be either, depending on whether it was intended to help the poor (a redistributive goal) or improve the urban environment (a service to all), a largely semantic difference.

[16]Helvering v. Davis, 301 U.S. 619 (1937), decision on social security taxes.

[17]*Business Week,* August 16, 1982, p. 15.

[18]See note 2.

BIBLIOGRAPHY

Derthick, Martha, *Policymaking for Social Security.* Washington, D.C.: Brookings Institution, 1979. A review and analysis of the social security program.

Gordon, David M. *Problems in Political Economy: An Urban Perspective,* 2nd ed. Lexington, Massachusetts: Heath, 1977. An excellent collection of essays on a number of social problems.

Haveman, Robert H., and Julius Margolis. *Public Expenditure and Policy Analysis,* 3rd ed. Boston: Houghton Mifflin, 1983. Twenty-five articles that demonstrate the complexity of social issues and the difficulty of policy analysis.

Jencks, Christopher, et al. *Inequality: A Reassessment of the Effect of Family and Schooling in America.* New York: Basic, 1972. A thorough examination of the relationships among poverty, equality, and opportunity.

Kluger, Richard. *Simple Justice.* New York: Vintage, 1976. A detailed but very readable account of the development and implications of the *Brown* v. *Board of Education* desegregation case.

Moynihan, Daniel P. *The Politics of a Guaranteed Income.* New York: Random House, 1973. An examination by a participant (now a United States senator) of the development of Richard Nixon's ill-fated Family Assistance Plan.

Nadel, Mark V. *The Politics of Consumer Protection.* Indianapolis: Bobbs-Merrill, 1971. A case study of the actors (inside and outside of government) and other factors that have affected consumer protection regulation legislation.

Okun, Arthur M. *Equality and Efficiency: The Big Tradeoff.* Washington, D.C.: Brookings Institution, 1975. A short but extremely useful discussion of one of the most important unresolved disputes in American politics.

Sindler, Allan P. *Bakke, DeFuris, and Minority Admissions.* New York: Longman, 1978. An account of the rationale and implications of affirmative action.

Sowell, Thomas. *Race and Economics.* New York: McKay, 1975. A dissenting view by a black economist who argues that social programs—especially income-maintenance policies—hurt minorities.

APPENDIX A

The Declaration of Independence

When in the Course of human events, it becomes necessary for one people to dissolve the political bands which have connected them with another, and to assume among the Powers of the earth, the separate and equal station to which the Laws of Nature and of Nature's God entitle them, a decent respect to the opinions of mankind requires that they should declare the causes which impel them to the separation.

We hold these truths to be self-evident, that all men are created equal, that they are endowed by their Creator with certain unalienable Rights, that among these are Life, Liberty and the pursuit of Happiness. That to secure these rights, Governments are instituted among Men, deriving their just powers from the consent of the governed, That whenever any Form of Government becomes destructive of these ends, it is the Right of the People to alter or to abolish it, and to institute new Government, laying its foundation on such principles and organizing its powers in such form, as to them shall seem most likely to effect their Safety and Happiness. Prudence, indeed, will dictate that Governments long established should not be changed for light and transient causes; and accordingly all experience hath shown, that mankind are more disposed to suffer, while evils are sufferable, than to right themselves by abolishing the forms to which they are accustomed. But when a long train of abuses and usurpations, pursuing invariably the same Object evinces a design to reduce them under absolute Despotism, it is their right, it is their duty, to throw off such Government, and to provide new Guards for their future security. Such has been the patient sufferance of these Colonies; and such is now the necessity which constrains them to alter their former Systems of Government. The history of the present King of Great Britain is a history of repeated injuries and usurpations, all having in direct object the establishment of an absolute Tyranny over these States. To prove this, let Facts be submitted to a candid world.

He has refused his Assent to Laws, the most wholesome and necessary for the public good.

He has forbidden his Governors to pass Laws of immediate and pressing importance, unless suspended in their operation till his Assent should be obtained; and when so suspended, he has utterly neglected to attend to them.

He has refused to pass other Laws for the accommodation of large districts of people, unless those people would relinquish the right of Representation in the Legislature, a right inestimable to them and formidable to tyrants only.

He has called together legislative bodies at places unusual, uncomfortable, and distant from the depository of their public Records, for the sole purpose of fatiguing them into compliance with his measures.

He has dissolved Representative Houses repeatedly, for opposing with manly firmness his invasions on the rights of the people.

He has refused for a long time, after such dissolutions, to cause others to be elected; whereby the Legislative Powers, incapable of Annihilation, have returned to the People at large for their exercise; the State remaining in the mean time exposed to all the dangers of invasion from without, and convulsions within.

He has endeavoured to prevent the population of these States; for that purpose obstructing the Laws of Naturalization of Foreigners; refusing to pass others to

485

encourage their migration hither, and raising the conditions of new Appropriations of Lands.

He has obstructed the Administration of Justice, by refusing his Assent to Laws for establishing Judiciary powers.

He has made Judges dependent on his Will alone, for the tenure of their offices, and the amount and payment of their salaries.

He has erected a multitude of New Offices, and sent hither swarms of Officers to harass our People, and eat out their substance.

He has kept among us in times of peace, Standing Armies without the Consent of our legislature.

He has affected to render the Military independent of and superior to the Civil power.

He has combined with others to subject us to a jurisdiction foreign to our constitution, and unacknowledged by our laws; giving his Assent to their acts of pretended Legislation.

For quartering large bodies of armed troops among us:

For protecting them, by a mock Trial, from punishment for any Murders which they should commit on the Inhabitants of these States:

For cutting off our Trade with all parts of the world.

For imposing taxes on us without our Consent:

For depriving us in many cases, of the benefits of Trial by Jury:

For transporting us beyond Seas to be tried for pretended offences:

For abolishing the free System of English Laws in a neighbouring Province, establishing therein an Arbitrary government, and enlarging its Boundaries so as to render it at once an example and fit instrument for introducing the same absolute rule into these Colonies.

For taking away our Charters, abolishing our most valuable Laws, and altering fundamentally the Forms of our Governments:

For suspending our own Legislature, and declaring themselves invested with Power to legislate for us in all cases whatsoever.

He has abdicated Government here, by declaring us out of his Protection and waging War against us.

He has plundered our seas, ravaged our Coasts, burnt our towns, and destroyed the lives of our people.

He is at this time transporting large Armies of foreign Mercenaries to compleat the works of death, desolation and tyranny, already begun with circumstances of Cruelty & perfidy scarcely paralleled in the most barbarous ages, and totally unworthy the Head of a civilized nation.

He has constrained our fellow Citizens taken Captive on the high Seas to bear Arms against their Country, to become the executioners of their friends and Brethren, or to fall themselves by their Hands.

He has excited domestic insurrections amongst us, and has endeavoured to bring on the inhabitants of our frontiers, the merciless Indian Savages, whose known rule of warfare, is an undistinguished destruction of all ages, sexes and conditions.

In every stage of these Oppressions We have Petitioned for Redress in the most humble terms: Our repeated Petitions have been answered only by repeated injury. A Prince, whose character is thus marked by every act which may define a Tyrant, is unfit to be the ruler of a free People.

Nor have We been wanting in attention to our British brethren. We have warned them from time to time of attempts by their legislature to extend an unwarrantable jurisdiction over us. We have reminded them of the circumstances of our emigration and settlement here. We have appealed to their native justice and magnanimity, and we have conjured them by the ties of our common kindred to disavow these usurpations, which, would inevitably interrupt our connections and correspondence. They too have been deaf to the voice of justice and of consanguinity. We must, therefore, acquiesce in the necessity, which denounces our Separation, and hold them, as we hold the rest of mankind, Enemies in War, in Peace Friends.

We, therefore, the Representatives of the United States of America, in General Congress, Assembled, appealing to the Supreme Judge of the world for the rectitude of our intentions, do, in the Name, and by Authority of the good People of these Colonies, solemnly publish and declare, That these United Colonies are, and of Right ought to be Free and Independent States; that they are Absolved from all Allegiance to the British Crown, and that all political connection between them and the State of Great Britain, is and ought to be totally dissolved; and that as Free and Independent States, they have full Power to levy War, conclude Peace, contract Alliances, establish Commerce, and to do all other Acts and Things which Independent States may of right do. And for the support of this Declaration, with a firm reliance on the protection of divine Providence, we mutually pledge to each other our Lives, our Fortunes and our sacred Honor.

The Constitution of the United States of America

We the People of the United States, in Order to form a more perfect Union, establish Justice, insure domestic Tranquility, provide for the common defence, promote the general Welfare, and secure the Blessings of Liberty to ourselves and our Posterity, do ordain and establish this Constitution for the United States of America.

Article I

Section. 1. All legislative Powers herein granted shall be vested in a Congress of the United States, which shall consist of a Senate and House of Representatives.

Section. 2. The House of Representatives shall be composed of Members chosen every second Year by the People of the several States, and the Electors in each State shall have the Qualifications requisite for Electors of the most numerous Branch of the State Legislature.

No Person shall be a Representative who shall not have attained to the age of twenty-five Years, and been seven Years a Citizen of the United States, and who shall not, when elected, be an Inhabitant of that State in which he shall be chosen.

Representatives and direct Taxes shall be apportioned among the several States which may be included within this Union, according to their respective Numbers, *which shall be determined by adding to the whole Number of free Persons, including those bound to Service for a Term of Years,* and excluding Indians not taxed, *three fifths of all other persons* [1] The actual Enumeration shall be made within three Years after the first Meeting of the Congress of the United States, and within every subsequent Term of ten Years, in such Manner as they shall by Law direct. The Number of Representatives shall not exceed one for every thirty Thousand, but each State shall have at Least one Representative; and until such enumeration shall be made, the State of New Hampshire shall be entitled to chuse three, Massachusetts eight, Rhode-Island and Providence Plantations one, Connecticut five, New-York six, New Jersey four, Pennsylvania eight, Delaware one, Maryland six, Virginia ten, North Carolina five, South Carolina five, and Georgia three.

When vacancies happen in the Representation from any State, the Executive Authority thereof shall issue Writs of Election to fill such Vacancies.

The House of Representatives shall chuse their Speaker and other Officers; and shall have the sole Power of Impeachment.

Section. 3. The Senate of the United States shall be composed of two Senators from each State, *chosen by*

---

[1] Italics are used throughout to indicate passages that have been altered by subsequent amendments. In this case, see Amendment XIV.

the Legislature thereof,[2] for six Years; and each Senator shall have one Vote.

Immediately after they shall be assembled in Consequence of the first Election, they shall be divided as equally as may be into three Classes. The Seats of the Senators of the first Class shall be vacated at the Expiration of the second Year, of the second Class at the Expiration of the fourth Year, and of the third Class at the Expiration of the sixth Year, so that one third may be chosen every second Year; *and if Vacancies happen by Resignation, or otherwise, during the Recess of the Legislature of any State, the Executive thereof may make temporary Appointments until the next Meeting of the Legislature, which shall then fill such Vacancies.*[3]

No Person shall be a Senator who shall not have attained to the Age of thirty Years, and been nine Years a Citizen of the United States, and who shall not, when elected, be an Inhabitant of that State for which he shall be chosen.

The Vice President of the United States shall be President of the Senate, but shall have no Vote, unless they be equally divided.

The Senate shall choose their other Officers, and also a President pro tempore, in the Absence of the Vice President, or when he shall exercise the Office of President of the United States.

The Senate shall have the sole Power to try all Impeachments. When sitting for that Purpose, they shall be on Oath or Affirmation. When the President of the United States is tried, the Chief Justice shall preside: And no Person shall be convicted without the Concurrence of two thirds of the Members present.

Judgment in Cases of Impeachment shall not extend further than to removal from Office, and disqualification to hold and enjoy any Office of honor, Trust or Profit under the United States: but the Party convicted shall nevertheless be liable and subject to Indictment, Trial, Judgment and Punishment, according to Law.

Section. 4. The Times, Places and Manner of holding Elections for Senators and Representatives, shall be prescribed in each State by the Legislature thereof; but the Congress may at any time by Law make or alter such Regulations, except as to the Places of chusing Senators.

The Congress shall assemble at least once in a Year,

and such Meeting shall be on the first Monday in December, unless they shall by Law appoint a different Day.[4]

Section. 5. Each House shall be the Judge of the Elections, Returns and Qualifications of its own Members, and a Majority of each shall constitute a Quorum to do Business; but a smaller Number may adjourn from day to day, and may be authorized to compel the Attendance of absent Members, in such Manner, and under such Penalties as each House may provide.

Each House may determine the Rules of its Proceedings, punish its Members for disorderly Behavior, and, with the Concurrence of two thirds, expel a Member.

Each House shall keep a Journal of its Proceedings, and from time to time publish the same, excepting such Parts as may in their Judgment require Secrecy; and the Yeas and Nays of the Members of either House on any question shall, at the Desire of one fifth of those Present, be entered on the Journal.

Neither House, during the Session of Congress, shall, without the Consent of the other, adjourn for more than three days, nor to any other Place than that in which the two Houses shall be sitting.

Section. 6. The Senators and Representatives shall receive a Compensation for their Services, to be ascertained by Law, and paid out of the Treasury of the United States. They shall in all Cases, except Treason, Felony and Breach of the Peace, be privileged from Arrest during their Attendance at the Session of their respective Houses, and in going to and returning from the same; and for any Speech or Debate in either House, they shall not be questioned in any other Place.

No Senator or Representative shall, during the Time for which he was elected, be appointed to any civil Office under the Authority of the United States, which shall have been created, or the Emoluments whereof shall have been encreased during such time; and no Person holding any Office under the United States, shall be a Member of either House during his Continuance in Office.

Section. 7. All Bills for raising Revenue shall originate in the House of Representatives; but the Senate may propose or concur with Amendments as on other Bills.

Every Bill which shall have passed the House of

---

[2]See Amendment XVII.

[3]Ibid.

[4]See Amendment XX.

Representatives and the Senate, shall, before it become a Law, be presented to the President of the United States; if he approve he shall sign it, but if not he shall return it, with his Objections to that House in which it shall have originated, who shall enter the Objections at large on their Journal, and proceed to reconsider it. If after such Reconsideration two thirds of that House shall agree to pass the Bill, it shall be sent, together with the Objections, to the other House, by which it shall likewise be reconsidered, and if approved by two thirds of that House, it shall become a Law. But in all such Cases the Votes of both Houses shall be determined by Yeas and Nays, and the Names of the Persons voting for and against the Bill shall be entered on the Journal of each House respectively. If any Bill shall not be returned by the President within ten Days (Sundays excepted) after it shall have been presented to him, the Same shall be a Law, in like Manner as if he had signed it, unless Congress by their Adjournment prevent its Return, in which Case it shall not be a Law.

Every Order, Resolution, or Vote to which the Concurrence of the Senate and House of Representatives may be necessary (except on a question of Adjournment) shall be presented to the President of the United States; and before the Same shall take Effect, shall be approved by him, or being disapproved by him, shall be repassed by two thirds of the Senate and House of Representatives, according to the Rules and Limitations prescribed in the Case of a Bill.

Section. 8. The Congress shall have Power to lay and collect Taxes, Duties, Imposts and Excises, to pay the Debts and provide for the common Defence and general Welfare of the United States; but all Duties, Imposts and Excises shall be uniform throughout the United States;

To borrow Money on the credit of the United States;

To regulate Commerce with foreign Nations, and among the several States, and with the Indian Tribes;

To establish an uniform Rule of Naturalization, and uniform Laws on the subject of Bankruptcies throughout the United States;

To coin Money, regulate the Value thereof, and of foreign Coin, and fix the Standard of Weights and Measures;

To provide for the Punishment of counterfeiting the Securities and Current Coin of the United States;

To establish Post Offices and post Roads;

To promote the Progress of Science and useful Arts, by securing for limited Times to Authors and Inventors the exclusive Right to their respective Writings and Discoveries;

To constitute Tribunals inferior to the Supreme Court;

To define and punish Piracies and Felonies committed on the high Seas and Offences against the Law of Nations;

To declare War, grant Letters of Marque and Reprisal, and make Rules concerning Captures on Land and Water;

To raise and support Armies, but no Appropriation of Money to that Use shall be for a longer Term than two Years;

To provide and maintain a Navy;

To make Rules for the Government and Regulation of the land and naval Forces;

To provide for calling forth the Militia to execute the Laws of the Union, suppress Insurrections and repel Invasions;

To provide for organizing, arming, and disciplining, the Militia, and for governing such Part of them as may be employed in the Service of the United States, reserving to the States respectively, the Appointment of the Officers, and the Authority of training the Militia according to the discipline prescribed by Congress;

To exercise exclusive Legislation in all Cases whatsoever, over such District (not exceeding ten Miles square) as may, by Cession of particular States, and the Acceptance of Congress, become the Seat of the Government of the United States, and to exercise like Authority over all Places purchased by the Consent of the Legislature of the State in which the Same shall be, for the Erection of Forts, Magazines, Arsenals, dock-Yards, and other needful Buildings;—And

To make all Laws which shall be necessary and proper for carrying into Execution the foregoing Powers, and all other Powers vested by this Constitution in the Government of the United States, or in any Department or Officer thereof.

Section. 9. The Migration or Importation of such Persons as any of the States now existing shall think proper to admit, shall not be prohibited by the Congress prior to the Year one thousand eight hundred and eight, but a Tax or duty may be imposed on such Importation, not exceeding ten dollars for each Person.

The Privilege of the Writ of Habeas Corpus shall not be suspended, unless when in Cases of Rebellion or Invasion the public Safety may require it.

No Bill of Attainder or ex post facto Law shall be passed.

No Capitation, or other direct, Tax shall be laid, unless in Proportion to the Census or Enumeration herein before directed to be taken.

No Tax or Duty shall be laid on Articles exported from any State.

No Preference shall be given by any Regulation of Commerce or Revenue to the Ports of one State over those of another: nor shall Vessels bound to, or from, one State, be obliged to enter, clear, or pay Duties in another.

No Money shall be drawn from the Treasury, but in Consequence of Appropriations made by Law; and a regular Statement and Account of the Receipts and Expenditures of all public Money shall be published from time to time.

No title of Nobility shall be granted by the United States: And no Person holding any Office of Profit or Trust under them, shall, without the Consent of the Congress, accept of any present, Emolument, Office, or Title, of any kind whatever, from any King, Prince, or foreign State.

Section. 10. No State shall enter into any Treaty, Alliance, or Confederation; grant Letters of Marque and Reprisal; coin Money; emit Bills of Credit; make any Thing but gold and silver Coin a Tender in Payment of Debts; pass any Bill of Attainder, ex post facto Law, or Law impairing the Obligation of Contracts, or Grant any Title of Nobility.

No State shall, without the Consent of the Congress, lay any Imposts or Duties on Imports or Exports, except what may be absolutely necessary for executing its inspection Laws: and the net Produce of all Duties and Imposts, laid by any State on Imports or Exports, shall be for the Use of the Treasury of the United States; and all such Laws be subject to the Revision and Control of the Congress.

No State shall, without the Consent of Congress, lay any Duty of Tonnage, keep Troops, or Ships of War in time of Peace, enter into any Agreement or Compact with another State, or with a foreign Power, or engage in War, unless actually invaded, or in such imminent Danger as will not admit of delay.

Article II

Section. 1. The executive Power shall be vested in a President of the United States of America. He shall hold his Office during the Term of four Years, and, together with the Vice President, chosen for the same Term be elected as follows:

Each State shall appoint, in such Manner as the Legislature thereof may direct, a Number of Electors, equal to the whole Number of Senators and Representatives to which the State may be entitled in the Congress: but no Senator or Representative, or Person holding an Office of Trust or Profit under the United States, shall be appointed an Elector.

The Electors shall meet in their respective States, and vote by Ballot for two Persons, of whom one at least shall not be an Inhabitant of the same State with themselves. And they shall make a List of all the Persons voted for, and of the Number of Votes for each; which List they shall sign and certify, and transmit sealed to the Seat of the Government of the United States, directed to the President of the Senate. The President of the Senate shall, in the Presence of the Senate and House of Representatives, open all the Certificates, and the Votes shall then be counted. The Person having the greatest Number of Votes shall be the President, if such Number be a Majority of the whole Number of Electors appointed; and if there be more than one who have such Majority, and have an equal Number of Votes, then the House of Representatives shall immediately chuse by Ballot one of them for President; and if no Person have a Majority, then from the five highest on the List the said House shall in like Manner chuse the President. But in chusing the President, the votes shall be taken by States, the Representation from each State having one Vote; A quorum for this purpose shall consist of a Member or Members from two thirds of the States, and a majority of all the States shall be necessary to a Choice. In every Case, after the Choice of the President, the Person having the Greatest Number of Votes of the Electors shall be the Vice President. But if there should remain two or more who have equal Votes, the Senate shall chuse from them by Ballot the Vice President.[5]

The Congress may determine the Time of chusing the Electors, and the Day on which they shall give their Votes; which Day shall be the same throughout the United States.

No Person except a natural born Citizen, or a Citizen of the United States, at the time of the Adoption of this Constitution, shall be eligible to the Office of President; neither shall any Person be eligible to that Office who shall not have attained to the Age of thirty-five Years, and been fourteen Years a Resident within the United States.

[5]See Amendment XII.

The Case of the Removal of the President from Office, or of his Death, Resignation, or Inability to discharge the Powers and Duties of the said Office, the Same shall devolve on the Vice President, and the Congress may by Law provide for the Case of Removal, Death, Resignation or Inability, both of the President and Vice President, declaring what Officer shall then act as President, and such Officer shall act accordingly, until the Disability be removed, or a President shall be elected.

The President shall, at stated Times, receive for his Services, a Compensation which shall neither be encreased nor diminished during the Period for which he shall have been elected, and he shall not receive within that Period any other Emolument from the United States, or any of them.

Before he enter on the Execution of his Office, he shall take the following Oath or Affirmation:—"I do solemnly swear (or affirm) that I will faithfully execute the Office of President of the United States, and will to the best of my Ability, preserve, protect, and defend the Constitution of the United States."

Section. 2. The President shall be Commander in Chief of the Army and Navy of the United States, and of the Militia of the several States, when called into the actual service of the United States; he may require the Opinion, in writing, of the principal Officer in each of the executive Departments, upon any Subject relating to the Duties of their respective Offices, and he shall have Power to grant Reprieves and Pardons for Offences against the United States, except in Case of Impeachment.

He shall have Power, by and with the Advice and Consent of the Senate, to make Treaties, provided two thirds of the Senators present concur; and he shall nominate, and by and with the Advice and Consent of the Senate, shall appoint Ambassadors, and other public Ministers and Consuls, Judges of the supreme Court, and all other Officers of the United States, whose Appointments are not herein otherwise provided for, and which shall be established by Law; but the Congress may by Law vest the Appointment of such inferior Officers, as they think proper, in the President alone, in the Courts of Law, or in the Heads of Departments.

The President shall have Power to fill up all Vacancies that may happen during the Recess of the Senate, by granting Commissions which shall expire at the End of their next Session.

Section. 3. He shall from time to time give to the Congress Information of the State of the Union, and recommend to their Consideration such Measures as he shall judge necessary and expedient; he may, on extraordinary Occasions, convene both Houses, or either of them, and in Case of Disagreement between them, with Respect to the Time of Adjournment, he may adjourn them to such Time as he shall think proper; he shall receive Ambassadors and other public Ministers, he shall take Care that the Laws be faithfully executed, and shall Commission all the Officers of the United States.

Section. 4. The President, Vice President, and all civil Officers of the United States, shall be removed from Office on Impeachment for, and Conviction of, Treason, Bribery, or other High Crimes and Misdemeanors.

Article III

Section. 1. The judicial Power of the United States, shall be vested in one supreme Court and in such inferior Courts as the Congress may from time to time ordain and establish. The Judges, both of the supreme and inferior Courts, shall hold their Offices during good Behavior, and shall, at stated Times, receive for their Services, a Compensation, which shall not be diminished during their Continuance in Office.

Section. 2. The Judicial Power shall extend to all Cases, in Law and Equity, arising under this Constitution, the Laws of the United States, and Treaties made, or which shall be made, under their Authority;—to all Cases affecting Ambassadors, other public Ministers and Consuls;—to all Cases of admiralty and maritime Jurisdiction;—to Controversies to which the United States shall be a Party;—to Controversies between two or more States;—*between a State and Citizens of another State;*[6]—between Citizens of different States;—between Citizens of the same State claiming Lands under Grants of different states, *and between a State, or the Citizens thereof, and foreign States, Citizens, or Subjects.*[7]

In all cases affecting Ambassadors, other public Ministers and Consuls, and those in which a State shall be Party, the supreme Court shall have original Jurisdiction. In all the other Cases before mentioned, the supreme Court shall have appellate Jurisdiction, both as to Law and Fact, with such Exceptions, and under such Regulations as the Congress shall make.

[6]See Amendment XI.

[7]*Ibid.*

The Trial of all Crimes, except in Cases of Impeachment, shall be by Jury; and such Trial shall be held in the State where the said Crimes shall have been committed; but when not committed within any State, the Trial shall be at such Place or Places as the Congress may by Law have directed.

Section. 3. Treason against the United States, shall consist only in levying War against them, or in adhering to their Enemies, giving them Aid and Comfort. No person shall be convicted of Treason unless on the Testimony of two Witnesses to the same overt Act, or on Confession in open Court.

The Congress shall have Power to declare the Punishment of Treason, but no Attainder of Treason shall work Corruption of Blood, or Forfeiture except during the Life of the Person attainted.

Article IV

Section. 1. Full Faith and Credit shall be given in each State to the public Acts, Records, and judicial Proceedings of every other State. And the Congress may by general Laws prescribe the Manner in which such Acts, Records, and Proceedings shall be proved, and the Effect thereof.

Section. 2. The Citizens of each State shall be entitled to all Privileges and Immunities of Citizens in the several States.

A Person charged in any State with Treason, Felony, or other Crime, who shall flee from Justice, and be found in another State, shall on Demand of the executive Authority of the State from which he fled, be delivered up, to be removed to the State having Jurisdiction of the Crime.

No Person held to Service or Labour in one State, under the Laws thereof, escaping into another, shall, in Consequence of any Law or Regulation therein, be discharged from such Service or Labour, but shall be delivered up on Claim of the Party to whom such Service or Labour may be due.[8]

Section. 3. New States may be admitted by the Congress into this Union; but no new State shall be formed or erected within the Jurisdiction of any other State; nor any State be formed by the Junction of two or more States, or Parts of States, without the Consent of the Legislatures of the States concerned as well as of the Congress.

[8]See Amendment XIII.

The Congress shall have Power to dispose of and make all needful Rules and Regulations respecting the Territory or other Property belonging to the United States; and nothing in this Constitution shall be so construed as to Prejudice any claims of the United States, or of any particular State.

Section. 4. The United States shall guarantee to every State in this Union a Republican Form of Government, and shall protect each of them against Invasion; and on Application of the Legislature, or of the Executive (when the Legislature cannot be convened) against domestic Violence.

Article V

The Congress, whenever two thirds of both Houses shall deem it necessary, shall propose Amendments to this Constitution, or, on the Application of the Legislatures of two thirds of the several States, shall call a Convention for proposing Amendments, which, in either Case, shall be valid to all Intents and Purposes, as Part of this Constitution, when ratified by the Legislatures of three fourths of the several States, or by Conventions in three fourths thereof, as the one or the other Mode of Ratification may be proposed by the Congress; Provided that no Amendment which may be made prior to the Year One thousand eight hundred and eight shall in any Manner affect the first and fourth Clauses in the Ninth Section of the first Article; and that no State, without its Consent, shall be deprived of its equal Suffrage in the Senate.

Article VI

All Debts contracted and Engagements entered into, before the Adoption of this Constitution, shall be as valid against the United States under this Constitution, as under the Confederation.

This Constitution, and the Laws of the United States which shall be made in Pursuance thereof; and all Treaties made, or which shall be made, under the Authority of the United States, shall be the supreme Law of the Land; and the Judges in every State shall be bound thereby, any Thing in the Constitution or Laws of any State to the Contrary notwithstanding.

The Senators and Representatives before mentioned, and the Members of the several State Legislatures, and all executive and judicial Officers, both of the United States and of the several States, shall be bound by Oath or Affirmation, to support this Constitution; but no religious Test shall ever be required as a Qualification to any Office or public Trust under the United States.

Article VII

The Ratification of the Conventions of nine States, shall be sufficient for the Establishment of this Constitution between the States so ratifying the Same.

Done in Convention by the Unanimous Consent of the States present the Seventeenth Day of September in the Year of our Lord one thousand seven hundred and eighty seven and of the Independence of the United States of America the twelfth. In witness whereof We have hereunto subscribed our Names.

* * *

Articles in addition to, and amendment of, the Constitution of the United States of America, proposed by Congress, and ratified by the several States, pursuant to the Fifth Article of the original Constitution.

Amendment I[9]

Congress shall make no law respecting an establishment of religion, or prohibiting the free exercise thereof; or abridging the freedom of speech, or of the press; or the right of the people peaceably to assemble, and to petition the Government for a redress of grievances.

Amendment II

A well regulated Militia, being necessary to the security of a free State, the right of the people to keep and bear Arms, shall not be infringed.

Amendment III

No Soldier shall, in time of peace be quartered in any house, without the consent of the Owner, nor in time of war, but in a manner to be prescribed by law.

Amendment IV

The right of the people to be secure in their persons, houses, papers, and effects, against unreasonable searches and seizures, shall not be violated, and no Warrants shall issue, but upon probable cause, supported by Oath or affirmation, and particularly describ-

ing the place to be searched, and the persons or things to be seized.

Amendment V

No person shall be held to answer for a capital, or otherwise infamous crime, unless on a presentment or indictment of a Grand Jury, except in cases arising in the land or naval forces, or in the Militia, when an actual service in time of War or public danger; nor shall any person be subject for the same offence to be twice put in jeopardy of life or limb; nor shall be compelled in any criminal case to be a witness against himself, nor be deprived of life, liberty, or property, without due process of law; nor shall private property be taken for public use, without just compensation.

Amendment VI

In all criminal prosecutions, the accused shall enjoy the right to a speedy and public trial, by an impartial jury of the State and district wherein the crime shall have been committed, which district shall have been previously ascertained by law, and to be informed of the nature and cause of the accusation; to be confronted with the witness against him; to have compulsory process for obtaining witness in his favor, and to have the Assistance of Counsel for his defence.

Amendment VII

In Suits at common law, where the value in controversy shall exceed twenty dollars, the right of trial by jury shall be preserved, and no fact tried by a jury, shall be otherwise re-examined in any Court of the United States, than according to the rules of the common law.

Amendment VIII

Excessive bail shall not be required, nor excessive fines imposed, nor cruel and unusual punishments inflicted.

Amendment IX

The enumeration in the Constitution, of certain rights, shall not be construed to deny or disparage others retained by the people.

Amendment X

The powers not delegated to the United States by the Constitution, nor prohibited by it to the States, are reserved to the States respectively, or to the people.

[9]Ratification of the first ten amendments was completed December 15, 1791.

Amendment XI [*January 8, 1798*]

The Judicial power of the United States shall not be construed to extend to any suit in law or equity, commenced or prosecuted against one of the United States by Citizens of another State, or by Citizens or Subjects of any Foreign State.

Amendment XII [*September 25, 1804*]

The Electors shall meet in their respective states and vote by ballot for President and Vice President, one of whom, at least, shall not be an inhabitant of the same state with themselves; they shall name in their ballots the person voted for as President, and in distinct ballots the person voted for as Vice President, and they shall make distinct lists of all persons voted for as President, and of all persons voted for as Vice President, and of the number of votes for each, which lists they shall sign and certify, and transmit sealed to the seat of the government of the United States, directed to the President of the Senate:—The President of the Senate shall, in the presence of the Senate and House of Representatives, open all the certificates and the votes shall then be counted;—The person having the greatest number of votes for President, shall be the President, if such number be a majority of the whole number of Electors appointed; and if no person have such majority, then from the persons having the highest numbers not exceeding three on the list of those voted for as President, the House of Representatives shall choose immediately, by ballot, the President. But in choosing the President, the votes shall be taken by states, the representation from each state having one vote; a quorum for this purpose shall consist of a member or members from two thirds of the states, and a majority of all the states shall be necessary to a choice. And if the House of Representatives shall not choose a President whenever the right of choice shall devolve upon them, *before the fourth day of March next following,*[10] then the Vice President shall act as President as in the case of the death or other constitutional disability of the President.—The person having the greatest number of votes as Vice President, shall be the Vice President, if such number be a majority of the whole number of Electors appointed, and if no person have a majority, then from the two highest numbers on the list, the Senate shall choose the Vice President; a quorum for the purpose shall consist of two-thirds of

the whole number of Senators, and a majority of the whole number shall be necessary to a choice. But no person constitutionally ineligible to the office of President shall be eligible to that of Vice President of the United States.

Amendment XIII [*December 18, 1865*]

Section 1. Neither slavery nor involuntary servitude, except as a punishment for crime whereof the party shall have been duly convicted, shall exist within the United States, or any place subject to their jurisdiction.

Section 2. Congress shall have power to enforce this article by appropriate legislation.

Amendment XIV [*July 28, 1868*]

Section 1. All persons born or naturalized in the United States, and subject to the jurisdiction thereof, are citizens of the United States and of the State wherein they reside. No State shall make or enforce any law which shall abridge the privileges or immunities of citizens of the United States; nor shall any state deprive any person of life, liberty, or property, without due process of law; nor deny to any person within its jurisdiction the equal protection of the laws.

Section 2. Representatives shall be apportioned among the several States according to their respective numbers, counting the whole number of persons in each State, excluding Indians not taxed. But when the right to vote at any election for the choice of electors for President and Vice President of the United States, Representatives in Congress, the Executive and Judicial officers of a State, or the members of the Legislature thereof, is denied to any of the male inhabitants of such State, being twenty one years of age, and citizens of the United States, or in any way abridged, except for participation in rebellion, or other crime, the basis of representation therein shall be reduced in the proportion which the number of such male citizens shall bear to the whole number of male citizens twenty one years of age in such State.

Section 3. No person shall be a Senator or Representative in Congress, or elector of President and Vice President, or hold any office, civil or military, under the United States, or under any State who having previously taken an oath, as a member of Congress, or as an officer of the United States, or as a member of any State legislature, or as an executive or judicial officer of any State, to support the Constitution of the United States, shall have engaged in insurrection or rebellion

[10]See Amendment XX.

against the same, or given aid or comfort to the enemies thereof. But Congress may by a vote of two thirds of each House remove such disability.

Section 4. The validity of the public debt of the United States authorized by law, including debts incurred for payment of pensions and bounties for services in suppressing insurrection or rebellion shall not be questioned. But neither the United States nor any State shall assume or pay any debt or obligation incurred in aid of insurrection or rebellion against the United States, or any claim for the loss or emancipation of any slave; but all such debts, obligations, and claims shall be held illegal and void.

Section 5. The Congress shall have power to enforce, by appropriate legislation, the provisions of this article.

Amendment XV   [March 30, 1870]

Section 1. The right of citizens of the United States to vote shall not be denied or abridged by the United States or by any State on account of race, color, or previous condition of servitude.

Section 2. The Congress shall have power to enforce this article by appropriate legislation.

Amendment XVI   [February 25, 1913]

The Congress shall have power to lay and collect taxes on incomes, from whatever source derived, without apportionment among the several States, and without regard to any census or enumeration.

Amendment XVII   [May 31, 1913]

The Senate of the United States shall be composed of two Senators from each State, elected by the people thereof, for six years; and each Senator shall have one vote. The electors in each State shall have the qualifications requisite for electors of the most numerous branch of the State legislatures.

When vacancies happen in the representation of any State in the Senate, the executive authority of such State shall issue writs of election to fill such vacancies: *Provided,* That the legislature of any State may empower the executive thereof to make temporary appointments until the people fill the vacancies by election as the legislature may direct.

This amendment shall not be so construed as to affect the election or term of any Senator chosen before it becomes valid as part of the Constitution.

Amendment XVIII   [January 29, 1919]

Section 1. *After one year from the ratification of this article the manufacture, sale, or transportation of intoxicating liquors within, the importation thereof into, or the exportation thereof from the United States and all territory subject to the jurisdiction thereof for beverage purposes is hereby prohibited.*

Section 2. *The Congress and the several States shall have concurrent power to enforce this article by appropriate legislation.*

Section 3. *This article shall be inoperative unless it shall have been ratified as an amendment to the Constitution by the legislatures of the several States, as provided in the Constitution, within seven years from the date of submission hereof to the States by the Congress.*[11]

Amendment XIX   [August 26, 1920]

The right of citizens of the United States to vote shall not be denied or abridged by the United States or by any State on account of sex.

Congress shall have power to enforce this article by appropriate legislation.

Amendment XX   [February 6, 1933]

Section 1. The terms of the President and Vice President shall end at noon on the 20th day of January, and the terms of Senators and Representatives at noon on the 3rd day of January, of the years in which such terms would have ended if this article had not been ratified; and the terms of their successors shall then begin.

Section 2. The Congress shall assemble at least once in every year, and such meeting shall begin at noon on the 3rd day of January unless they shall by law appoint a different day.

Section 3. If, at the time fixed for the beginning of the term of the President, the President elect shall have died, the Vice President elect shall become President. If a President shall not have been chosen before the time fixed for the beginning of his term, or if the President elect shall have failed to qualify, then the Vice President elect shall act as President until a President shall have qualified; and the Congress may by law provide for the case wherein neither a President elect nor a Vice President elect shall have qualified, declaring who shall then act as President, or the manner in which one who is to act shall be selected, and such person

[11]Repealed by Amendment XXI.

shall act accordingly until a President or Vice President shall have qualified.

Section 4. The Congress may by law provide for the case of the death of any of the persons from whom the House of Representatives may choose a President whenever the right of choice shall have devolved upon them, and for the case of the death of any of the persons from whom the Senate may choose a Vice President whenever the right of choice shall have devolved upon them.

Section 5. Sections 1 and 2 shall take effect on the 15th day of October following the ratification of this article.

Section 6. This article shall be inoperative unless it shall have been ratified as an amendment to the Constitution by the legislatures of three fourths of the several States within seven years from the date of its submission.

Amendment XXI [*December 5, 1933*]

Section 1. The eighteenth article of amendment to the Constitution of the United States is hereby repealed.

Section 2. The transportation or importation into any State, Territory, or possession of the United States for delivery or use therein of intoxicating liquors, in violation of the laws thereof, is hereby prohibited.

Section 3. This article shall be inoperative unless it shall have been ratified as an amendment to the Constitution by conventions in the several States, as provided in the Constitution, within seven years from the date of the submission hereof to the States by the Congress.

Amendment XXII [*February 26, 1951*]

Section 1. No person shall be elected to the office of the President more than twice, and no person who has held the office of President, or acted as President, for more than two years of a term to which some other person was elected President shall be elected to the office of President more than once. But this Article shall not apply to any person holding the office of President when this Article was proposed by the Congress, and shall not prevent any person who may be holding the office of President, or acting as President, during the term within which this Article becomes operative from holding the office of President or acting as President during the remainder of such term.

Section 2. This article shall be inoperative unless it

shall have been ratified as an amendment to the Constitution by the legislatures of three fourths of the several States within seven years from the date of its submission to the States by the Congress.

Amendment XXIII [*March 29, 1961*]

Section 1. The District constituting the seat of Government of the United States shall appoint in such manner as the Congress may direct:

A number of electors of President and Vice President equal to the whole number of Senators and Representatives in Congress to which the District would be entitled if it were a State, but in no event more than the least populous State; they shall be in addition to those appointed by the States, but they shall be considered, for the purposes of the election of President and Vice President, to be electors appointed by a State; and they shall meet in the District and perform such duties as provided by the twelfth article of amendment.

Section 2. The Congress shall have power to enforce this article by appropriate legislation.

Amendment XXIV [*January 23, 1964*]

Section 1. The right of citizens of the United States to vote in any primary or other election for President or Vice President, for electors for President or Vice President, or for Senator or Representative in Congress, shall not be denied or abridged by the United States or any state by reason of failure to pay any poll tax or other tax.

Section 2. The Congress shall have power to enforce this article by appropriate legislation.

Amendment XXV [*February 10, 1967*]

Section 1. In case of the removal of the President from office or of his death or resignation, the Vice President shall become President.

Section 2. Whenever there is a vacancy in the office of the Vice President, the President shall nominate a Vice President who shall take office upon confirmation by a majority vote of both Houses of Congress.

Section 3. Whenever the President transmits to the President pro tempore of the Senate and the Speaker of the House of Representatives his written declaration that he is unable to discharge the powers and duties of his office, and until he transmits to them a written declaration to the contrary, such powers and duties shall be discharged by the Vice President as Acting President.

Section 4. Whenever the Vice President and a majority of either the principal officers of the executive departments or of such other body as Congress may by law provide, transmit to the President pro tempore of the Senate and the Speaker of the House of Representatives their written declaration that the President is unable to discharge the powers and duties of his office, the Vice President shall immediately assume the powers and duties of the office as Acting President.

Thereafter, when the President transmits to the President pro tempore of the Senate and the Speaker of the House of Representatives his written declaration that no inability exists, he shall resume the powers and duties of his office unless the Vice President and a majority of either the principal officers of the executive department[s] or of such other body as Congress may by law provide, transmit within four days to the President pro tempore of the Senate and the Speaker of the House of Representatives their written declaration that

the President is unable to discharge the powers and duties of his office. Thereupon Congress shall decide the issue, assembling within forty-eight hours for that purpose if not in session. If the Congress, within twenty-one days after receipt of the latter written declaration, or, if Congress is not in session, within twenty-one days after Congress is required to assemble, determines by two-thirds vote of both Houses that the President is unable to discharge the powers and duties of his office, the Vice President shall continue to discharge the same as Acting President; otherwise, the President shall resume the powers and duties of his office.

Amendment XXVI [June 30, 1971]

Section 1. The right of citizens of the United States, who are 18 years of age or older, to vote shall not be denied or abridged by the United States or by any state on account of age.

Section 2. The Congress shall have power to enforce this article by appropriate legislation.

Year	Candidates	Party	Popular Vote	Electoral Vote
1789	**George Washington**			69
	John Adams			34
	Others			35
1792	**George Washington**			132
	John Adams			77
	George Clinton			50
	Others			5
1796	**John Adams**	Federalist		71
	Thomas Jefferson	Democratic-Republican		68
	Thomas Pinckney	Federalist		59
	Aaron Burr	Democratic-Republican		30
	Others			48
1800	**Thomas Jefferson***	Democratic-Republican		73
	Aaron Burr	Democratic-Republican		73
	John Adams	Federalist		65
	Charles C. Pinckney	Federalist		64
1804	**Thomas Jefferson**	Democratic-Republican		162
	Charles C. Pinckney	Federalist		14
1808	**James Madison**	Democratic-Republican		122
	Charles C. Pinckney	Federalist		47
	George Clinton	Independent-Republican		6
1812	**James Madison**	Democratic-Republican		128
	DeWitt Clinton	Federalist		89
1816	**James Monroe**	Democratic-Republican		183
	Rufus King	Federalist		34
1820	**James Monroe**	Democratic-Republican		231
	John Quincy Adams	Independent-Republican		1

Year	Candidates	Party	Popular Vote	Electoral Vote
1824	**John Quincy Adams***	Democratic-Republican	108,740 (30.5%)	84
	Andrew Jackson	Democratic-Republican	153,544 (43.1%)	99
	Henry Clay	Democratic-Republican	47,136 (13.2%)	37
	William H. Crawford	Democratic-Republican	46,618 (13.1%)	41
1828	**Andrew Jackson**	Democratic	647,231 (56.0%)	178
	John Quincy Adams	National Republican	509,097 (44.0%)	83
1832	**Andrew Jackson**	Democratic	687,502 (55.0%)	219
	Henry Clay	National Republican	530,189 (42.4%)	49
	William Wirt	Anti-Masonic		7
	John Floyd	National Republican	33,108 (2.6%)	11
1836	**Martin Van Buren**	Democratic	761,549 (50.9%)	170
	William H. Harrison	Whig	549,567 (36.7%)	73
	Hugh L. White	Whig	145,396 (9.7%)	26
	Daniel Webster	Whig	41,287 (2.7%)	14
1840	**William H. Harrison†** **(John Tyler,** 1841)	Whig	1,275,017 (53.1%)	234
	Martin Van Buren	Democratic	1,128,702 (46.9%)	60
1844	**James K. Polk**	Democratic	1,337,243 (49.6%)	170
	Henry Clay	Whig	1,299,068 (48.1%)	105
	James G. Birney	Liberty	62,300 (2.3%)	
1848	**Zachary Taylor†** **(Millard Fillmore,** 1850)	Whig	1,360,101 (47.4%)	163
	Lewis Cass	Democratic	1,220,544 (42.5%)	127
	Martin Van Buren	Free Soil	291,263 (10.1%)	
1852	**Franklin Pierce**	Democratic	1,601,474 (50.9%)	254
	Winfield Scott	Whig	1,386,578 (44.1%)	42
1856	**James Buchanan**	Democratic	1,838,169 (45.4%)	174
	John C. Fremont	Republican	1,335,264 (33.0%)	114
	Millard Fillmore	American	874,534 (21.6%)	8
1860	**Abraham Lincoln**	Republican	1,865,593 (39.8%)	180
	Stephen A. Douglas	Democratic	1,382,713 (29.5%)	12
	John C. Breckinridge	Democratic	848,356 (18.1%)	72
	John Bell	Constitutional Union	592,906 (12.6%)	39
1864	**Abraham Lincoln†** **(Andrew Johnson,** 1865)	Republican	2,206,938 (55.0%)	212
	George B. McClellan	Democratic	1,803,787 (45.0%)	21
1868	**Ulysses S. Grant**	Republican	3,013,421 (52.7%)	214
	Horatio Seymour	Democratic	2,706,829 (47.3%)	80

Year	Candidates	Party	Popular Vote	Electoral Vote
1872	**Ulysses S. Grant**	Republican	3,596,745 (55.6%)	286
	Horace Greeley	Democratic	2,843,446 (43.9%)	66
1876	**Rutherford B. Hayes**	Republican	4,036,572 (48.0%)	185
	Samuel J. Tilden	Democratic	4,284,020 (51.0%)	184
1880	**James A. Garfield†**	Republican	4,449,053 (48.3%)	214
	(Chester A. Arthur, 1881)			
	Winfield S. Hancock	Democratic	4,442,035 (48.2%)	155
	James B. Weaver	Greenback-Labor	308,578 (3.4%)	
1884	**Grover Cleveland**	Democratic	4,874,986 (48.5%)	219
	James G. Blaine	Republican	4,851,981 (48.2%)	182
	Benjamin F. Butler	Greenback-Labor	175,370 (1.8%)	
1888	**Benjamin Harrison**	Republican	5,444,337 (47.8%)	233
	Grover Cleveland	Democratic	5,540,050 (48.6%)	168
1892	**Grover Cleveland**	Democratic	5,554,414 (46.0%)	277
	Benjamin Harrison	Republican	5,190,802 (43.0%)	145
	James B. Weaver	People's	1,027,329 (8.5%)	22
1896	**William McKinley**	Republican	7,035,638 (50.8%)	271
	William J. Bryan	Democratic; Populist	6,467,946 (46.7%)	176
1900	**William McKinley†**	Republican	7,219,530 (51.7%)	292
	(Theodore Roosevelt, 1901)			
	William J. Bryan	Democratic; Populist	6,356,734 (45.5%)	155
1904	**Theodore Roosevelt**	Republican	7,628,834 (56.4%)	336
	Alton B. Parker	Democratic	5,084,401 (37.6%)	140
	Eugene V. Debs	Socialist	402,460 (3.0%)	
1908	**William H. Taft**	Republican	7,679,006 (51.6%)	321
	William J. Bryan	Democratic	6,409,106 (43.1%)	162
	Eugene V. Debs	Socialist	420,820 (2.8%)	
1912	**Woodrow Wilson**	Democratic	6,286,820 (41.8%)	435
	Theodore Roosevelt	Progressive	4,126,020 (27.4%)	88
	William H. Taft	Republican	3,483,922 (23.2%)	8
	Eugene V. Debs	Socialist	897,011 (6.0%)	
1916	**Woodrow Wilson**	Democratic	9,129,606 (49.3%)	277
	Charles E. Hughes	Republican	8,538,221 (46.1%)	254
1920	**Warren G. Harding†**	Republican	16,152,200 (61.0%)	404
	(Calvin Coolidge, 1923)			
	James M. Cox	Democratic	9,147,353 (34.6%)	127
	Eugene V. Debs	Socialist	919,799 (3.5%)	

Year	Candidates	Party	Popular Vote	Electoral Vote
1924	**Calvin Coolidge**	Republican	15,725,016 (54.1%)	382
	John W. Davis	Democratic	8,385,586 (28.8%)	136
	Robert M. La Follette	Progressive	4,822,856 (16.6%)	13
1928	**Herbert C. Hoover**	Republican	21,392,190 (58.2%)	444
	Alfred E. Smith	Democratic	15,016,443 (40.8%)	87
1932	**Franklin D. Roosevelt**	Democratic	22,809,638 (57.3%)	472
	Herbert C. Hoover	Republican	15,758,901 (39.6%)	59
	Norman Thomas	Socialist	881,951 (2.2%)	
1936	**Franklin D. Roosevelt**	Democratic	27,751,612 (60.7%)	523
	Alfred M. Landon	Republican	16,681,913 (36.4%)	8
	William Lemke	Union	891,858 (1.9%)	
1940	**Franklin D. Roosevelt**	Democratic	27,243,466 (54.7%)	449
	Wendell L. Wilkie	Republican	22,304,755 (44.8%)	82
1944	**Franklin D. Roosevelt†** **(Harry S Truman,** 1945)	Democratic	25,602,505 (52.8%)	432
	Thomas E. Dewey	Republican	22,006,278 (44.5%)	99
1948	**Harry S Truman**	Democratic	24,105,587 (49.5%)	303
	Thomas E. Dewey	Republican	21,970,017 (45.1%)	189
	J. Strom Thurmond	States' Rights	1,169,063 (2.4%)	39
	Henry A. Wallace	Progressive	1,157,172 (2.4%)	
1952	**Dwight D. Eisenhower**	Republican	33,936,234 (55.2%)	442
	Adlai E. Stevenson	Democratic	27,314,992 (44.5%)	89
1956	**Dwight D. Eisenhower**	Republican	35,590,472 (57.4%)	457
	Adlai E. Stevenson	Democratic	26,022,752 (42.0%)	73
1960	**John F. Kennedy†** **(Lyndon B. Johnson,** 1963)	Democratic	34,227,096 (49.9%)	303
	Richard M. Nixon	Republican	34,108,546 (49.6%)	219
1964	**Lyndon B. Johnson**	Democratic	43,126,233 (61.1%)	486
	Barry M. Goldwater	Republican	27,174,989 (38.5%)	52
1968	**Richard M. Nixon**	Republican	31,785,148 (43.4%)	301
	Hubert H. Humphrey	Democratic	31,274,503 (42.7%)	191
	George C. Wallace	Amer. Independent	9,899,557 (13.5%)	46
1972	**Richard M. Nixon‡** **(Gerald R. Ford,** 1974)	Republican	45,767,218 (60.6%)	520
	George S. McGovern	Democratic	28,357,668 (37.5%)	17
1976	**Jimmy Carter**	Democratic	40,274,975 (50.6%)	297
	Gerald R. Ford	Republican	38,530,614 (48.4%)	240

Year	Candidates	Party	Popular Vote	Electoral Vote
1980	**Ronald Reagan**	Republican	43,899,248 (51.0%)	489
	Jimmy Carter	Democratic	36,481,435 (42.3%)	49
	John Anderson	Independent	5,719,437 (6.6%)	0
1984	**Ronald Reagan**	Republican	53,428,357 (59.1%)	525
	Walter Mondale	Democratic	36,930,923 (40.9%)	13

*Chosen by the House of Representatives.
†Died in office.
‡Resigned.
Note: Because only the leading candidates are listed, popular vote percentages do not always total 100%.

Glossary

activist: A person actively involved in a political activity, such as working for a political party during an election campaign.

administrative law: The general procedural guidelines developed by courts and legislative bodies concerning how administrative agencies should conduct themselves.

advice and consent: The power of the Senate to consider and approve presidential treaties and some presidential appointments.

affirmative action: The requirement that businesses, labor unions, government agencies, and schools actively recruit more minority-group members or females to compensate for alleged previous discrimination.

agenda-setting: The process of deciding which public-policy issues will be actively considered by policymakers.

allocation: The division of things into shares and portions.

amicus curiae ("friend of the court") brief: A written argument filed by interested individuals or groups to provide additional information or analysis of a case.

answer: A defendant's response to a plaintiff's complaint.

appeal: The complaint to a superior court that a lower court has committed an error that requires a reversal of its decision.

apportionment: The determination of how the seats in a legislative body will be distributed among the population of various geographical areas.

appropriation: The statutory release of governmental funds to finance particular programs; usually follows a legislative authorization.

arraignment: A criminal proceeding in which a prisoner is informed of the charges against him or her and is required to plead an answer to the charges.

Articles of Confederation: The basic document, ratified March 1, 1781, that governed the relations among the states before the ratification of the Constitution.

Australian ballot: A secret ballot for voting, begun in the United States in 1888.

authorization: A statute that permits the start or continuation of a government program, usually with spending ceilings, but does not actually make the money available.

balance of payments: The difference in the value of tradable currency and gold leaving the country and that entering it.

balance of trade: The difference in value between a country's exports and imports.

benefit: Anything for the good of a person, organization, or thing.

bicameralism: The division of a legislature into two houses or chambers.

bilateral assistance: The American policy of providing economic assistance directly to other nations, rather than through international organizations.

Bill of Rights: The first ten amendments to the Constitution.

bipartisan foreign policy: American foreign policy that has the support of both major political parties.

bureaucracy: An organization characterized by division of labor, hierarchies of authority, and formal rules for decisionmaking.

cabinet: In the United States, the heads of the executive departments and the vice-president.

capitalism: An economic system based on private ownership of property and of the means of production, in which resources are used to produce profits.

cartel: An association of business firms, national governments, and so on, for establishing control or a monopoly by price fixing, limiting supplies, and so on.

casework: Services that members of Congress perform for individual constituents, such as assisting them with bureaucratic procedures.

caucus: A closed meeting of like-minded people (such as political-party leaders) to discuss voting intentions, plot strategies, or choose candidates.

certificates of public convenience and necessity: Governmental contracts that grant a monopoly to a company in return for an agreement to abide by government regulations.

civil case: A noncriminal legal action that is instituted to compel payment, enforce a right, or prevent the violation of a right.

civil law: Law that applies to disputes between individuals, or between the government and individuals, over noncriminal matters.

civil liberties: The rights of citizens to fair trials, as well as the rights to speak, write, read, meet, and worship without government interference.

civil rights: The rights of citizens to receive governmental protection in the areas of voting, law, and the use of public facilities.

civil service: The nonmilitary government employee hiring system that is based upon a merit system of hiring and promoting.

closed primary: A primary election in which only registered party members can vote.

cloture: A vote of three-fifths of all senators to stop a filibuster.

coalition: A temporary alliance of individuals, groups, or parties for some specific purpose, such as passing a law or electing a candidate.

coattail effect: The phenomenon of candidates for less prestigious offices benefiting from being on the same ballot as a more popular candidate (usually a presidential candidate).

cold war: The rivalry that developed after World War II between the United States and the Soviet Union and their respective allies.

collective action: Efforts by individuals bound together by a common interest to obtain some benefit for all members of the group.

collective bargaining: Negotiation between organized workers and their employer for reaching an agreement on wages, hours, or working conditions.

collective benefit: A benefit that is distributed to all members of a group. Also called *collective good.* See **public good.**

commerce clause: The constitutional provision giving Congress authority to regulate commerce with foreign nations and among the states.

common law: Customary, judge-made law that relies on precedents and prevailing customs rather than on explicit statutes or constitutional authority.

complaint: A legal document giving a defendant basic information about the charge brought against him, her, or it.

concurrent powers: Powers shared by the states and the national government.

conference committee: An ad hoc joint committee in Congress set up to resolve the differences between House and Senate versions of a bill.

conservative: An ideological position that is generally opposed to government interference in the lives of citizens or the affairs of business.

conservative coalition: A coalition of ideologically compatible Republican and Democratic members of Congress.

constituency: The residents of a legislator's district.

constitutional law: Law based upon an interpretation of the Constitution.

constitutional rights: Rights mentioned or clearly implied by the Constitution.

constraints: Rules or forces that limit or shape the conduct of members of a group or organization.

containment: American foreign policy, devised by George Kennan in 1947, which is aimed at thwarting Soviet expansion into other nations.

continuing resolution: A temporary law passed by Congress to appropriate money when formal appropriations bills have not been passed by the beginning of the new fiscal year.

contract: A formal agreement between people, business firms, or the government to do something.

conventional warfare: Warfare carried out with armies fighting for territory without the use of nuclear arms.

corporation: A legal (usually business) entity with the rights, privileges, and liabilities of an individual that are distinct from those of the individuals making up the group.

cost: That which must be given up in order to buy, produce, accomplish, or maintain something.

crime: An act for which a person or organization can be legally punished, usually through fine or imprisonment.

crisis management: The American foreign-policy doctrine of attempting to settle serious international disputes in which the United States is not directly involved.

critical election: An election in which large numbers of voters make long-term changes in their party preference.

defendant: Organization or person against whom a lawsuit is brought.

deficit: In government finance, when a governmental body spends more than it receives in revenues.

democracy: Rule by the people.

desegregation: The removal of artificial, arbitrary, and unequal barriers to the mixing of the races in schools, workplaces, and so on.

détente: A lessening of hostility or tensions between nations, such as that which occurred in American-Soviet relations during the 1970s.

devaluation: A reduction of the value of a nation's currency relative to other currencies.

direct primary: A primary (i.e., preliminary) election in which voters determine the candidates who will run in a general election.

division of labor: The allocation of particular tasks to members of an organization in order to increase productivity or efficiency.

domino theory: The American foreign-policy doctrine that a communist takeover in a country hastens communist takeovers in adjacent countries and that, unless checked, the process will continue until the United States is directly threatened.

double jeopardy: A constitutional requirement that a person acquitted of a crime may not be tried again on the same charge or a lesser one related to it.

due process: Protection, mandated by the Fifth and Fourteenth Amendments, from arbitrary or unfair deprivation by the states of an individual's "life, liberty, or property."

electoral college: A group of electors who meet after each presidential election to officially elect the president and vice-president.

eminent domain: The power of government to seize property for public use if just compensation is awarded.

enabling powers: Governmental powers conferred by constitutional phrases such as "Congress shall have power to enforce this article by appropriate legislation."

enumerated powers: The powers of government explicitly granted by the Constitution.

equity: Fairness, justice, and impartiality.

European Economic Community (EEC) (Common Market): An organization of Western European nations established in 1957 to lower trade barriers and develop common commercial policies among the member nations.

executive agreement: An international agreement made between a president and a foreign nation that, unlike a treaty, is not ratified by the Senate.

executive order: An administrative decree issued by the president that usually has the effect of a law, but is not considered and passed into law by Congress.

executive privilege: The argument that certain conversations and documents within the executive branch are protected from congressional scrutiny.

externalities: Side effects of actions that influence the well-being of persons who did not consent to the actions; these side effects may be benefits or costs.

faction: An organization created to promote particular interests against competitors.

federalism: A system of government in which governing power is divided and shared among a central government and state governments.

Federalist Papers: A collection of articles, prepared in 1787 and 1788 by Alexander Hamilton, John Jay, and James Madison for New York newspapers, explaining and urging ratification of the Constitution.

filibuster: An attempt to defeat a bill in the Senate by prolonging debate. See **cloture.**

fiscal policy: A policy that attempts to manage the economy by manipulating government spending or taxation. See **monetary policy.**

fiscal year (FY): The accounting period of the federal government, which runs from October 1 through September 30 of the following year.

franchise: In elections, the right to vote; in economic policy, a contract under which a trade name can be used by another firm or individual.

franking privilege: Privilege that allows members of Congress to send material through the mail without paying postage costs.

free rider: A person who receives the benefits of group (i.e., collective) action without contributing to the costs of obtaining those benefits.

free trade: The system of imposing no taxes or restrictions designed to impede the importation of foreign goods.

gerrymander: To divide a territorial area into voting districts in such a way as to give an unfair advantage to one political party.

grandfather clause: Any legal provision intended to assure that persons having some right or benefit will not lose it as a result of changes in law. Originally used to allow whites to vote in the post–Civil War South while excluding blacks.

grand jury: A group of citizens convened to determine whether there is enough evidence in a legal case to justify the indictment of a person for a crime.

gross national product (GNP): The total value of all goods and services produced in a nation during a given year.

ideology: A comprehensive and coherent set of basic beliefs about political, economic, and social values. See **liberal** and **conservative.**

impeachment: A formal accusation against a government official, after which the official is tried and, if convicted, removed from office.

implementation: The process of interpreting and putting into effect a policy decision.

implied powers: The constitutional provision in Article I, Section 8, that grants Congress the power to "make all Laws which shall be necessary and proper for carrying into Execution" the enumerated powers. Also called the *elastic clause.*

impoundment: The refusal of a president to spend money appropriated by Congress.

incentive: That which encourages or incites desired behavior.

incumbent: A person currently holding a government office.

independent regulatory commission: A government agency that regulates some economic or social activity, and that is partially independent of the executive and legislative branches.

industrial policy: Economic policy intended to increase the efficiency and competitiveness of American businesses.

inflation: A general rise in prices.

information cost: The cost incurred in obtaining information about the prospective use of resources.

initiative: A procedure by which citizens or groups can propose new laws or constitutional amendments by obtaining sufficient signatures on a petition, after which the general public votes on the proposal.

injunction: A court order prohibiting a person or group from carrying out a given action or ordering a given action to be done.

in-kind payment: A government benefit provided in a form other than cash in order to control how that benefit is used.

interest group: An organization of people who share a common point of view and who attempt to influence government policies.

invisible hand: Adam Smith's concept of the tendency for the pursuit of individual self-interest to result in the efficient and automatic matching of consumer demand to economic production.

iron law of oligarchy: A postulated characteristic of organizations that tend to become oligopolies (i.e., organizations ruled by the few).

joint committee: A permanent congressional committee comprised of members of both the Senate and the House of Representatives.

judicial activism: The behavior of courts or individual judges who apply their own beliefs to the interpretation of public laws and thereby expand the power of the judicial system.

judicial review: The power of the courts to declare legislative and executive actions to be unconstitutional and therefore prohibited.

jurisdiction: The authority of a court or court system to consider or decide a case.

jury: A certain number of individuals, selected according to law, who decide questions of fact in a trial.

laissez-faire: The doctrine of governmental nonintervention in the economy.

law: Collection of rules that government establishes to supervise the relationship among individuals, groups, and governments.

legal rights: Rights created and conferred on citizens by statutes.

legislative clearance: Practice that requires the president's Office of Management and Budget to decide whether legislative proposals devised by executive-branch employees are compatible with the president's programs.

legislative veto: A provision in a bill that allowed one or both chambers of Congress to overturn an action by an executive or independent agency; it was ruled unconstitutional in 1983.

liberal: The ideological position that government has a proper and necessary role in intervening in social and economic affairs in order to improve people's lives.

liberty: Security under the rule of just laws.

license: An agreement that allows a person or company to make or sell products based upon a patent held by another person or company.

limited government: A government that is limited, by a constitution or other means, in what it may do and how it may exercise its powers.

lobbyist: A representative of an interest group or a special interest who tries to affect governmental action.

logrolling: The trading of votes in a legislature in

order to secure the passage of legislation of particular importance to different members.

macroeconomics: The study of the performance of the economy as a whole.

majority: More than fifty percent of the votes cast. See **plurality.**

majority leader: The leader and chief strategist of the majority party in a legislature; for example, the Senate and the House of Representatives each have a majority leader.

markup: A session of a congressional committee or subcommittee at which the actual wording of a proposed bill is agreed upon.

merit system: A method of hiring and promoting civil-service employees on the basis of competitive examinations rather than political connections.

microeconomics: The study of the economic behavior of firms, business sectors, groups, and individuals.

minimum winning coalition: The smallest number of members of a group needed for the group to continue winning.

minority leader: The leader of the minority party in a legislature.

monetary policy: Government policy that attempts to influence the economy by manipulating the money supply and the availability of credit.

monopoly: The control of a sector of the economy by one firm.

mutual assured destruction (MAD): A strategic nuclear policy in which one side can absorb a nuclear attack by another and have enough weapons and delivery systems left to impose enormous damage on the other side.

natural monopoly: An industry in which production is most efficient when performed by a single firm; in natural monopolies, such as electrical or water transmission, the government regulates the prices charged to consumers.

natural rights: The doctrine that individuals have certain rights by virtue of the laws of nature, including life, liberty, and the right to hold and dispose of property.

necessary-and-proper clause: Constitutional clause granting power to Congress to "make all Laws which shall be necessary and proper" for carrying out its enumerated powers.

net benefit: The result of subtracting the costs of a course of action from the benefits achieved.

net social welfare: A measure of the aggregate or average benefits received by members of a society, without implications about the fairness of distribution.

nonpartisan election: An election in which candidates do not run as members of political parties.

nonpartisan primary: A primary in which candidates do not run as members of political parties.

nontariff barriers: Methods of restricting the importation of foreign goods other than through taxes. These include burdensome licensing and paperwork requirements.

oligarchy: A system of government in which power is held by a small group of people such as an elite.

ombudsman: A person who serves as a link between private citizens and the government bureaucracy by answering questions and obtaining action.

omnibus bill: Piece of legislation to which many amendments on various subjects are attached.

open primary: A primary election in which voters can vote for members of any party regardless of their own party membership.

opportunity cost: The economic cost of one activity measured by the sacrifice of not employing the same resources, such as time or money, in another activity.

organization: A set of coordinated rules, structures, and processes established for a specific purpose.

origination clause: Constitutional clause requiring that all revenue-raising (i.e., taxation) bills originate in the House of Representatives.

oversight: The attempts of Congress to monitor the behavior of executive agencies to assure compliance with legislative mandates and intent.

party identification: A general feeling of preference and attachment for a political party.

patronage: The awarding of government jobs or contracts to friends or political supporters of officeholders.

per capita: Adjusted for population; an average for each individual in a group.

petit jury: A jury that decides on the facts of a case being tried in court.

plaintiff: The person or organization bringing a lawsuit.

platform: A statement of the positions and pledges of a candidate for office or a political party.

plurality: The number of votes received in an election by the leading candidate or proposal, but not necessarily the majority.

pocket veto: A special type of executive veto of legislative actions, not eligible for legislative override.

policy: A goal-directed or purposive course of action followed by an actor or a set of actors in an attempt to deal with a public problem.

political action committee (PAC): A committee established by a business or interest group for the purpose of influencing elections and policy actions, primarily through the distribution of campaign contributions.

political entrepreneur: Individual or group that bears the costs of actions that will benefit other people.

poll: A usually scientific survey of a sample of individuals with the purpose of determining what a larger population thinks.

pork barrel: Legislation that selectively provides benefits to the constituency of a particular member of Congress.

poverty line: A family income level deemed by government statisticians to provide a "minimum subsistance income."

precedent: An older court decision based on a factual situation similar to that currently before a court.

prerogative powers: Powers not mentioned in the Constitution that are claimed by presidents as being necessary to the execution of executive powers.

president pro tempore: The presiding officer of the Senate when the vice-president is absent.

private bill: A bill submitted to Congress or a state legislature to aid one individual rather than a class of citizens or all citizens.

private law: Legal action, brought by an individual or private association, which is intended to remedy a wrong against the individual or association.

privilege against self-incrimination: A rule contained in the Fifth Amendment (and by incorporation to the states through the Fourteenth Amendment) that a person may not be compelled to give testimony that might lead to his or her indictment or conviction for a crime.

procedural equity: Equal and fair treatment in a governmental proceeding.

progressive tax: A tax system in which higher-income people or firms pay a higher percentage of their income in taxes than poorer people.

property: A collection of rights over things that are guaranteed and protected by government.

protectionism: The practice of imposing high taxes or other nontariff restrictions on imported goods in order to make it difficult for those goods to enter a country.

public assistance: A form of social policy intended to provide aid to those deemed needy (e.g., the aged, blind, and poor) and for which some evidence of need usually must be shown.

public benefit: A benefit that is available to all members of a society, whether or not they are members of the group that was responsible for the production of the benefit; for example, military defense cannot be withheld from Americans who do not pay taxes.

public bill: A legislative proposal of general application.

public enterprise: Governmental or public ownership of productive resources that are used to provide goods for the public.

public good: A benefit that is available to all members of a society, whether or not they are members of the group that was responsible for the production of the benefit; for example, military defense cannot be withheld from Americans who do not pay taxes.

public interest: The interest of the entire population—or a majority of it—in contrast to a special interest.

public interest group: An organization of individuals who claim to seek a public, not just a collective, good.

public law: Legal action, usually brought by a government agency, intended to benefit the public.

public opinion: The attitudes and beliefs of the general public.

public utility: A company that needs government permission or cooperation to operate; these include natural monopolies and companies (e.g., gas pipeline or electric companies) that require access to continuous rights of way for their facilities.

quorum: The number of members of a legislature whose presence is required for the transaction of business; usually a majority of the membership.

real dollars: Dollars adjusted for inflation, which are therefore comparable over time.

realignment: An election in which enough voters switch their party allegiance to cause a reversal in the majority-minority status of the parties.

reapportionment: The alteration of the boundaries of electoral districts due to population growth and shifts.

recession: A period of relatively minor economic slowdown, characterized by a decline in the gross national product and an increase in unemployment.

redistribution: The transfer of items of value from one group (e.g., the wealthy) to another group (e.g., the poor).

red tape: Excessive government paperwork and cumbersome procedures.

referendum: An election in which citizens directly choose whether to approve a proposed public policy without the immediate intervention of their representatives.

regressive tax: A system of taxation in which poorer persons pay a share of their income equal to or greater than the rate of tax paid by wealthier persons.

regulation: Governmental intervention in economic or social affairs, usually for the purpose of correcting market failures (e.g., monopoly or externalities), providing information to consumers, or directly protecting certain groups.

reindustrialization: The shift from traditional "smokestack" industries to such "high tech" industries as computers and telecommunications.

remedy: The act of a court enforcing a right or preventing the violation of a right.

republic: A form of government in which supreme power rests with all the citizens entitled to vote, and in which power is exercised by representatives chosen by the electorate.

rider: An amendment to a Senate bill that need not be germane to the subject of the original bill.

roll-call vote: A legislative vote in which the choice of each member is recorded by name.

runoff election: An election following a general election in which the two candidates winning the largest shares of the vote face each other in a two-person race, thereby guaranteeing that one will win a majority, as opposed to a mere plurality.

runoff primary: An election following a primary, in which the two candidates winning the largest shares of the vote face each other in a two-person race, thereby guaranteeing that one will win a majority, as opposed to a mere plurality.

safe seat: An electoral position for which an incumbent is likely to face only a minimal challenge.

SALT (Strategic Arms Limitations Treaty) Talks: A series of negotiations between the United States and the Soviet Union designed to limit nuclear arms and delivery systems. One agreement (SALT I) was signed and ratified in 1972, but the second SALT treaty, although signed, was never ratified by the Senate.

Say's law: The prediction that free-market economic systems will reach equilibrium as aggregate supply "creates" sufficient demand to absorb and encourage economic expansion.

segregation: The separation of racial groups, whether by custom or enforced by law, in housing, education, and so on.

select committee: A legislative committee, created to study a particular, often temporary, problem, but which is unable to report new legislation for consideration.

selective incorporation: The theory that guides the Supreme Court in determining which of the protections of the Bill of Rights are applicable to the states through the Fourteenth Amendment.

seniority: A traditional congressional procedure of awarding benefits, such as committee chairmanships, on the basis of duration of uninterrupted service in Congress or on the committee.

separation of powers: The constitutional doctrine that individual liberty is best preserved by distributing the legislative, executive, and judicial powers of government among branches, each with some ability to check the others.

services: Social policies intended to provide non-cash benefits to general groups of people.

single-issue group: An interest group that tries to influence public policy in a single policy area.

single-member district (SMD): An electoral district in which voters may choose only one candidate for an office, with the common result that minority parties often win no seats despite significant electoral support.

social insurance: A form of social policy characterized by workers making "contributions" (i.e., paying taxes) into a special governmental account, thereby earning the "right" to draw benefits from that account upon retirement, disability or illness, or survival of an eligible spouse or parent.

social rights: The doctrine that people are entitled to certain minimal levels of income and security and that government is obligated to provide these benefits.

social services: A form of social policy that provides noncash benefits to general groups of people, such as education for children, subsidies for mass-transit riders, or crime prevention for all citizens.

socialization: The process of acquiring social values and political opinions through exposure to those of parents, teachers, peers, and so on.

solicitor general: An official of the Department of Justice who represents the executive branch in legal proceedings.

Speaker of the House: The presiding officer and usually the most powerful member of the House of Representatives.

split ticket: A vote for candidates of different parties in the same election.

spoils: Favoritism in the distribution of government contracts. See **patronage.**

standards: Governmental regulations that restrict certain aspects of economic activity, usually for the purpose of consumer protection, product interchangeability, or economic efficiency.

standing committees: Permanent committees of the Senate and the House of Representatives.

stare decisis: Legal doctrine under which a court's decision constitutes a precedent that should be followed by that court, and courts inferior to it, when resolving future disputes; literally, "let the decision stand."

statutory law: Law created by legislatures.

straight ticket: Voting for candidates of only one party in an election.

subcommittee: A division of a congressional committee, similar in structure and function to a full committee but with narrower jurisdiction.

subgovernments: Postulated cooperative arrangements among bureaucrats, congressional personnel, and private-sector individuals and groups that together have primary responsibility for the formation of public policy in specific areas.

subpoena: An order to appear before a court or Congress in order to present evidence or testimony.

subsidy: A form of government support for private individuals or business firms.

substantive equity: In the formation of social policy, the requirement that some outcomes of even the fairest of procedures be prohibited if they entail unreasonable deprivation or disadvantage for some citizens.

suffrage: The right to vote.

summons: A legal doctrine notifying a person or organization that a legal proceeding has been instituted against him, her, or it.

sunset laws: Legislation requiring government agencies to be periodically reviewed and reauthorized or face automatic abolition.

sunshine laws: Laws requiring governmental bodies such as legislative committees to hold meetings in public except in unusual circumstances.

supply-side policy: An economic program that is based on the assumption that tax cuts will generate savings, investment, and economic growth.

supremacy clause: Clause in Article VI of the Constitution that asserts that the Constitution, treaties, and national laws are the supreme laws of the land.

tariff: A tax on imports designed to protect domestic firms from foreign competition by making foreign products more expensive.

third party: A political party that attempts, usually unsuccessfully, to challenge the domination of the two major parties.

Three-Fifths Compromise: The agreement at the Constitutional Convention to consider five slaves equal to three voters for apportionment purposes.

tort: A private or civil wrong or injury, other than a breach of contract, for which a court will provide a remedy in the form of an action for damages.

trade-off: The incorporation and consideration of both costs and benefits in a course of action.

transaction costs: The costs incurred in reaching and enforcing an agreement.

Truman Doctrine: A declaration made by President Harry Truman in 1947 that the United States would provide military and economic assistance to nations threatened by the Soviet Union or internal communist insurrection.

trust: A legal doctrine by which property is controlled by one group or person for the benefit of others; useful in the formation of industrial monopolies in the late 1800s.

trust fund: A government financial account earmarked for a specific purpose, such as social security or highway construction, and therefore distinct from general revenues.

unit rule: A now-obsolete requirement of political parties that delegations at a party convention must vote as a bloc.

United Nations (UN): International organization of nations, established in 1945 to maintain international peace and security.

veto: The president's withholding of approval of a bill or joint resolution passed by the House and the Senate, other than one proposing a constitutional amendment.

voucher: A subsidy or public assistance device that transfers benefits to individuals, but restricts their use of the benefits only within general categories (e.g., education or housing).

warrant: A legal document, such as a search warrant, issued by a judge authorizing or directing a law officer to perform an act.

Watergate: General term encompassing a variety of misdeeds and crimes associated with the 1972 reelection campaign of President Richard Nixon, which led to his resignation in 1974.

wealth: A person's possessions (i.e., money, property, and so on) having economic value measurable in price.

whip: An assistant floor leader of the majority or minority party in the House or Senate who serves as a communications link between party leaders and party members.

white primary: A primary election in which black citizens were forbidden or strongly discouraged from participating.

writ of certiorari: An order from an appeals court to a lower court to send up the record of a case so that it can be reviewed.

writ of habeas corpus: A writ directed to a person (e.g., a government official) who is detaining another individual, requiring a justification for the confinement.

writ of mandamus: A court order that requires a person, corporation, or public official to perform duties required by law.

Index